connect

A Writer's Resource

A Handbook for Writing and Research

Sixth Edition MLA Update

©Anton Khrupin/Shutterstock

Elaine P. Maimon
Governors State University

Kathleen Blake Yancey
Florida State University

A WRITER'S RESOURCE: A HANDBOOK FOR WRITING AND RESEARCH,
SIXTH EDITION MLA UPDATE

1 2 3 4 5 6 7 8 9 LCR 21

ISBN 978-1-266-71775-8
MHID 1-266-71775-7

Portfolio Manager: *Penina Braffman Greenfield*
Product Developer: *Elizabeth Murphy*
Lead Content Project Managers: *Lisa Bruflodt, George Theofanopoulos*
Buyer: *Susan K. Culbertson*
Senior Design: *Jessica Cuevas*
Content Licensing Specialist: *Brianna Kirschbaum*
Cover Image: ©*Anton Khrupin/Shutterstock*
Compositor: *Lumina Datamatics*

All credits appearing on page or at the end of the book are considered to be an extension of the copyright page.

Library of Congress Cataloging-in-Publication Data
Names: Maimon, Elaine P., author. | Yancey, Kathleen Blake, 1950- author.
Title: A writer's resource: a handbook for writing and research / Elaine P.
 Maimon, Kathleen Blake Yancey Florida State University.
Description: Sixth edition. | New York, NY: McGraw-Hill Education, [2016]
Identifiers: LCCN 2018020896 (print) | LCCN 2018022431 (ebook) | ISBN
 9781260494365 (online) | ISBN 9781260087840 (softcover: acid-free paper) |
 ISBN 9780078036187 (acid-free paper) | ISBN 0078036186 (acid-free paper)
Subjects: LCSH: English language—Rhetoric—Handbooks, manuals, etc. |
 English language—Grammar—Handbooks, manuals, etc. | Report
 writing—Handbooks, manuals, etc.
Classification: LCC PE1408 (ebook) | LCC PE1408 .M3366 2016b (print) | DDC
 808/.042—dc23
LC record available at https://lccn.loc.gov/2018020896

The Internet addresses listed in the text were accurate at the time of publication. The inclusion of a website does not indicate an endorsement by the authors or McGraw-Hill Education, and McGraw-Hill Education does not guarantee the accuracy of the information presented at these sites.

mheducation.com/highered

About the Authors

Elaine P. Maimon is president of Governors State University (GSU), a public university in suburban Chicago, where she is also professor of English. At GSU she has presided over transformative change, reallocating resources to support full-time faculty members in freshman composition; infusion rather than proliferation of courses; and navigable pathways from community college to the university. Previously she was chancellor of the University of Alaska Anchorage, provost (chief campus officer) at Arizona State University West, and vice president of Arizona State University as a whole. In the mid-1970s, she initiated and then directed the Beaver College (now Arcadia University)  writing-across-the-curriculum program, one of the first WAC programs in the nation. A founding executive board member of the Council of Writing Program Administrators (CWPA), she has directed national institutes to improve the teaching of writing and to disseminate the principles of writing across the curriculum. With a PhD in English from the University of Pennsylvania, where she later helped to create the Writing Across the University (WATU) program, she has also taught and served as an academic administrator at Haverford College, Brown University, and Queens College (CUNY). In 2018, she published a book on higher education reform, *Leading Academic Change: Vision, Strategy, Transformation* (Stylus, 2018).

Kathleen Blake Yancey, Kellogg W. Hunt Professor of English and Distinguished Research Professor at Florida State University, has served as President of the National Council of Teachers of English; Chair of the Conference on College Composition and Communication; President of the Council of Writing Program Administrators; and President of the South Atlantic Modern Language Association. Co-founder of the journal *Assessing Writing*, she is immediate Past Editor of *College Composition and Communication*. Currently, she leads an 8-site "Transfer of Transfer" research project on students' transfer of writing knowledge and practice, funded by both CCCC  and CWPA, that includes faculty from community colleges and private and public four-year schools researching together. Author, editor, or co-editor of 14 scholarly books—among them the 2014 *Writing Across Contexts: Transfer, Composition, and Sites of Writing*; the 2016 *A Rhetoric of Reflection*; and the 2017 *Assembling Composition*—she has two additional edited collections in press: *Rhetoric, Composition, and Disciplinarity*; and *ePortfolio-as-Curriculum: Diverse Models and Practices*. Author or co-author of over 100 articles and book chapters, she is the recipient of several awards, including the CCCC Research Impact Award; the Purdue Distinguished Woman Scholar, the best book award from the Council of Writing Program Administrators; and the FSU Graduate Teaching and Mentor Awards.

A Resource

A Writer's Resource helps writers identify the fundamental elements of any writing situation—from academic assignments to blog and social media posts—and teaches innovative, transferable strategies that build confidence for composing across various genres, media, and the academic curriculum. With its numerous examples from a rich cross-section of disciplines, *A Writer's Resource* foregrounds the transfer of skills learned in the writing course to demonstrate that every major, every field of study, and every potential career path depends on written communication. Throughout the chapters, a comprehensive set of features supports this approach:

- **New coverage of transfer.** Transfer strategies are highlighted throughout, including an entirely new section in Chapter 1 that answers the question "Why study composition?" by describing the transferable skills students will learn in the writing course. Special emphasis is also given to writing situations beyond college, including writing for social media and drafting emails for professional purposes.

- **New and revised student sample assignments.** Three new sample papers on contemporary topics demonstrate successful informative and persuasive strategies, and two revised examples feature updated research and citations that students can learn from and model. An expanded and updated section on portfolio creation includes a new annotated sample ePortfolio geared toward outcomes.

- **Greater emphasis on multimodal assignments.** Six assignment chapters offer guidelines for writing that informs, analyzes, and argues in different settings, including expanded coverage of multimodal writing. *A Writer's Resource* now also provides instruction for repurposing material created for a formal assignment, including how to present the same material to multiple audiences.

- **Updated box features.** Throughout the sixth edition, the following practice boxes highlight the skills students gain in the composition course:

  - **The Evolving Situation** provides guidance on navigating a range of writing situations, such as those introduced by new media and technologies;

  - **Navigating through College and Beyond** supports the transfer of writing practices to situations across the disciplines and outside the classroom;

  - **Know the Situation** and **Consider Your Situation** provide opportunities for practice in identifying and responding to different writing situations;

  - **Checklists** on topics ranging from editing a paper to planning a Web site help students apply what they have learned to their own writing assignments.

for Transferring Skills to Any Writing Situation

CHECKLIST Reading Critically

☐ **Preview** the text before you read it.
☐ **Read** the text for its topic and point.
☐ **Analyze** the *who, what,* and *why* of the text by **annotating** it as you reread it and **summarizing** what you have read.
☐ **Synthesize** through making connections.
☐ **Evaluate** what you've read.

- **Opportunities for practice.** *Connect Composition* offers ample opportunities for students to practice the skills they learn in class.
  - *Power of Process* supports critical reading, thinking, and writing development through reading assignments that instructors can customize to their course needs.

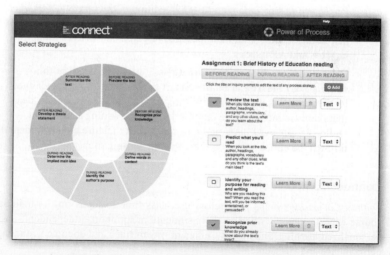

- Access to the *Connect Composition* eReader, enhanced with over 75 readings that are easily uploaded to *Power of Process*, allows students to engage with examples that demonstrate a variety of genres and purposes.
- *LearnSmart Achieve* assignments, including writing process coverage and grammar tests, helps students practice their skills with an adaptive tool that responds to their individual levels.

# A Resource

A Writer's Resource teaches students to read, write, and think critically. Numerous topical examples throughout the text engage student interest and demonstrate how such skills apply to all phases of the writing process.

- **Critical reading and writing instruction.** Using the writing situation as a framework, Chapter 4, Reading and Writing: The Critical Connection, introduces techniques of critical reading and thinking, while connecting students to resources for argument writing. This chapter shows students how to read actively, summarize texts, and respond to others' work as a precursor to creating their own.

- **Expanded research coverage.** The research chapters in Tab 5 provide up-to-date guidelines for critically evaluating and drawing on digital sources, including new instruction for identifying and eradicating fake news sources from research papers and social media posts. With readings uploaded to *Power of Process* students can put into practice the source evaluation strategies they've learned.

- **Updated documentation chapters.** Documentation chapters include coverage that aligns with the latest updates to the 9th edition of the *MLA Handbook*, the 7th edition of the *Publication Manual of the American Psychological Association*, and the 17th edition of the *Chicago Manual of Style*. *Connect Composition* offers interactive documentation guides that help students understand and practice research and writing standards in MLA and APA styles.

- **Enhanced coverage of writing situations.** Entirely updated for this edition, **Start Smart** and **Source Smart** guides demonstrate guidelines for working through common writing situations, reinforcing the idea that there are recognizable landmarks in every writing assignment. Online, in *Connect Composition*, this interactive feature guides students through the eBook based on their specific writing situations.

Connect Composition

Connect Composition helps instructors use class time to focus on the highest course expectations, by offering their students meaningful, independent, and personalized learning, and an easy, efficient way to track and document student performance and engagement.

Connect Composition offers adaptable assignments for instructors to choose from, including study modules in *LearnSmart Achieve*, Discussion Board activities, and *Power of Process* assignments that provide students with plenty of practice in critical reading and writing as well as style, grammar, and punctuation.

for Thinking Critically about Writing

Feature	Description	Instructional Value
Simple LMS Integration	■ Seamlessly integrates with every learning management system.	■ Students have automatic single sign-on. ■ *Connect* assignment results sync to LMS's gradebook.
LearnSmart Achieve	■ Continuously adapts to a student's strengths and weaknesses, to create a personalized learning environment. ■ Covers *The Writing Process, Critical Reading, The Research Process, Reasoning and Argument, Multilingual Writers, Grammar and Common Sentence Problems, Punctuation and Mechanics, and Style and Word Choice.* ■ Provides instructors with reports that include data on student and class performance.	■ Students independently study the fundamental topics across composition in an adaptive environment. ■ Metacognitive component supports knowledge transfer. ■ Students track their own understanding and mastery and discover where their gaps are.
A Writer's Resource eBook	■ Provides comprehensive course content, exceeding what is offered in print. ■ Supports annotation and bookmarking.	■ The eBook allows instructors and students to access their course materials anytime and anywhere, including four years of handbook access.
Connect eReader	■ Provides access to more than 60 readings that are assignable via *Connect Composition.*	■ Sample essays provide models for students as well as interesting topics to consider for discussion and writing. Can replace a costly stand-alone reader.
Power of Process	■ Guides students through the critical reading and writing processes step-by-step.	■ Students demonstrate understanding and develop critical thinking skills for reading, writing, and evaluating sources by responding to short answer and annotation questions. Students are also prompted to reflect on their own processes. ■ Instructors or students can choose from a preloaded set of readings or upload their own. ■ Students can use the guidelines to consider a potential source critically.
Writing Assignments with *Peer Review*	■ Allows instructors to assign and grade writing assignments online. ■ Gives instructors the option of easily and efficiently setting up and managing online peer review assignments for the entire class.	■ This online tool makes grading writing assignments more efficient, saving time for instructors. ■ Students import their Word document(s), and instructors can comment and annotate submissions. ■ Frequently used comments are automatically saved so instructors do not have to type the same feedback over and over.

Feature	Description	Instructional Value
Writing Assignments with *Outcomes-Based Assessment*	■ Allows instructors or course administrators to assess student writing around specific learning outcomes. ■ Generates easy-to-read reports around program-specific learning outcomes. ■ Includes the most up-to-date Writing Program Administrators learning outcomes, but also gives instructors the option of creating their own.	■ This tool provides assessment transparency to students. They can see why a "B" is a "B" and what it will take to improve to an "A." ■ Reports allow a program or instructor to demonstrate progress in attaining section, course, or program goals.
Insight	■ Provides a quick view of student and class performance and engagement with a series of visual data displays that answer the following questions: 1. How are my students doing? 2. How is this student doing? 3. How is my section doing? 4. How is this assignment working? 5. How are my assignments working?	■ Instructors can quickly check on and analyze student and class performance and engagement.
Instructor Reports	■ Allow instructors to review the performance of an individual student or an entire section. ■ Allow instructors or course administrators to review multiple sections to gauge progress in attaining course, department, or institutional goals.	■ Instructors can identify struggling students early and intervene to ensure retention. ■ Instructors can identify challenging topics and/or assignments and adjust instruction accordingly. ■ Reports can be generated for an accreditation process or a program evaluation.
Student Reports	■ Allow students to review their performance for specific assignments or the course.	■ Students can keep track of their performance and identify areas they are struggling with.
Pre- and Post-Tests	■ Precreated non-adaptive assessments for pre- and post-testing.	■ Pre-tests provide a static benchmark for student knowledge at the beginning of the program. Post-tests offer a concluding assessment of student progress.
Tegrity	■ Allows instructors to capture course material or lectures on video. ■ Allows students to watch videos recorded by their instructor and learn course material at their own pace.	■ Instructors can keep track of which students have watched the videos they post. ■ Students can watch and review lectures from their instructor. ■ Students can search each lecture for specific bits of information.

New to the Sixth Edition

The sixth edition of *A Writer's Resource* continues to focus on the most common writing assignments and situations students will encounter and uses the writing situation as its framework for instruction. This new edition also includes three new sample student papers (two research projects and a literary analysis) and two revised student papers that feature updated content, research, citations, and annotations. Here is a quick look at just a few of the other changes you will find within the chapters:

Chapter 1, Writing across the Curriculum and beyond College

- New section introduces students to the concept of transfer and explains how the skills they gain in the composition course can be applied to other disciplines and other areas of their lives

Chapter 2, Writing Situations

- Updated coverage of the core outcomes of successful writing
- Updated coverage of multimodal assignments in addition to a broader discussion of, and genres that benefit from, multimedia elements
- New guidelines for writing e-mail for academic and professional purposes
- Updated explanation of virtual classrooms and course management software

Chapter 5, Planning and Shaping

- Expanded coverage of assessing writing situations
- Additional practice for applying multimodal elements in professional scenarios

Chapter 6, Drafting Text and Visuals

- New examples of photos and illustrations and updated example of a visual that compares and contrasts

Chapter 8, Designing Academic Texts and Portfolios

- Updated instruction around portfolio creation emphasizes ePortfolios and the importance of the introductory reflective text
- New annotated student example of an ePortfolio geared toward outcomes

Chapter 9, Informative Reports

- New sample informative report on Olympic doping by a health and human performance major

Chapter 10, Interpretive Analyses and Writing about Literature

- New sample student interpretive analysis of Iranian poet Mohsen Emadi's poem "Losses"

Chapter 11, Arguments

- New example of an argument posed by a public-service image on the topic of violence against women
- Revised sample student proposal on the topic of cyberbullying includes updated research and citations

Chapter 12, Other Kinds of Assignments

- New examples demonstrate using a conversational tone in an essay and connecting your experience to a larger issue

Chapter 13, Oral Presentations

- New sample *PowerPoint* slides for a presentation on the topic of cyberbullying

Chapter 15, Service Learning and Community-Service Writing

- New example of a well-designed newsletter

Chapter 18, Understanding Research

- Updated coverage for researching using online sources

Chapter 19, Finding and Managing Print and Online Sources

- Updated discussion of exploring online communication

Chapter 20, Finding and Creating Effective Visuals, Audio Clips, and Videos

- Updated coverage of selecting the appropriate graphics for displaying data accurately, including new examples of effective and ineffective use of graphs and charts
- Searching from appropriate images in online and print sources

Chapter 21, Evaluating Sources

- Entirely new section on identifying and eradicating fake news from academic research and social media posts

Chapter 24, Working with Sources and Avoiding Plagiarism
- New sample bibliography notecards and annotated bibliography
- New sample annotated Web page printout
- New examples of taking notes on a research journal
- New section on paraphrasing for multiple audiences

- New examples of integrating quotations and summarizing information from sources

MLA Documentation Style

- Updated examples of in-text citations
- Brief introduction to the container concept as presented in the 9th edition of the *MLA Handbook*
- In keeping with the 9th edition, specific citation examples are reorganized by types of sources
- New student sample informative research paper on the topic of fake news

APA Documentation Style

- Completely revised to align with the 7th edition *Publication Manual of the American Psychological Association.*
- Reorganization of specific citation examples by source type
- New student sample research paper informs on the use of performance-enhancing drugs by Olympic athletes

Chicago and CSE Documentation Styles

- Updated examples of in-text citations
- Reorganization of specific citation examples by source type
- New excerpt from a research paper on the topic of fake news

Grammar

- Updated examples throughout, including updates to the Grammar Checker feature

WPA Outcomes Statement for First-Year Composition

Introduction

This Statement identifies outcomes for first-year composition programs in U.S. postsecondary education. It describes the writing knowledge, practices, and attitudes that undergraduate students develop in first-year composition, which at most schools is a required general education course or sequence of courses. This Statement therefore attempts to both represent and regularize writing programs' priorities for first-year composition, which often takes the form of one or more required general education courses. To this end it is not merely a compilation or summary of what currently takes place. Rather, this Statement articulates what composition teachers nationwide have learned from practice, research, and theory.[1] It intentionally defines only "outcomes," or types of results, and not "standards," or precise levels of achievement. The setting of standards to measure students' achievement of these Outcomes has deliberately been left to local writing programs and their institutions.

In this Statement "composing" refers broadly to complex writing processes that are increasingly reliant on the use of digital technologies. Writers also attend to elements of design, incorporating images and graphical elements into texts intended for screens as well as printed pages. Writers' composing activities have always been shaped by the technologies available to them, and digital technologies are changing writers' relationships to their texts and audiences in evolving ways.

These outcomes are supported by a large body of research demonstrating that the process of learning to write in any medium is complex: it is both individual and social and demands continued practice and informed guidance. Programmatic decisions about helping students demonstrate these outcomes should be informed by an understanding of this research.

As students move beyond first-year composition, their writing abilities do not merely improve. Rather, their abilities will diversify along disciplinary, professional, and civic lines as these writers move into new settings where expected outcomes expand, multiply, and diverge. Therefore, this document advises faculty in all disciplines about how to help students build on what they learn in introductory writing courses.

Rhetorical Knowledge

Rhetorical knowledge is the ability to analyze contexts and audiences and then to act on that analysis in comprehending and creating texts. Rhetorical knowledge is the basis of composing. Writers develop rhetorical knowledge by negotiating purpose, audience, context, and conventions as they compose a variety of texts for different situations.

---

[1] This Statement is aligned with the *Framework for Success in Postsecondary Writing*, an articulation of the skills and habits of mind essential for success in college, and is intended to help establish a continuum of valued practice from high school through to the college major.

By the end of first-year composition, students should
- Learn and use key rhetorical concepts through analyzing and composing a variety of texts
- Gain experience reading and composing in several genres to understand how genre conventions shape and are shaped by readers' and writers' practices and purposes
- Develop facility in responding to a variety of situations and contexts calling for purposeful shifts in voice, tone, level of formality, design, medium, and/or structure
- Understand and use a variety of technologies to address a range of audiences
- Match the capacities of different environments (e.g., print and electronic) to varying rhetorical situations

Faculty in all programs and departments can build on this preparation by helping students learn
- The expectations of readers in their fields
- The main features of genres in their fields
- The main purposes of composing in their fields

Critical Thinking, Reading, and Composing

Critical thinking is the ability to analyze, synthesize, interpret, and evaluate ideas, information, situations, and texts. When writers think critically about the materials they use—whether print texts, photographs, data sets, videos, or other materials—they separate assertion from evidence, evaluate sources and evidence, recognize and evaluate underlying assumptions, read across texts for connections and patterns, identify and evaluate chains of reasoning, and compose appropriately qualified and developed claims and generalizations. These practices are foundational for advanced academic writing.

By the end of first-year composition, students should
- Use composing and reading for inquiry, learning, critical thinking, and communicating in various rhetorical contexts
- Read a diverse range of texts, attending especially to relationships between assertion and evidence, to patterns of organization, to the interplay between verbal and nonverbal elements, and to how these features function for different audiences and situations
- Locate and evaluate (for credibility, sufficiency, accuracy, timeliness, bias and so on) primary and secondary research materials, including journal articles and essays, books, scholarly and professionally established and maintained databases or archives, and informal electronic networks and internet sources
- Use strategies—such as interpretation, synthesis, response, critique, and design/redesign—to compose texts that integrate the writer's ideas with those from appropriate sources
- Faculty in all programs and departments can build on this preparation by helping students learn
  - The kinds of critical thinking important in their disciplines

- The kinds of questions, problems, and evidence that define their disciplines
- Strategies for reading a range of texts in their fields

Processes

Writers use multiple strategies, or *composing processes*, to conceptualize, develop, and finalize projects. Composing processes are seldom linear: a writer may research a topic before drafting, then conduct additional research while revising or after consulting a colleague. Composing processes are also flexible: successful writers can adapt their composing processes to different contexts and occasions.

By the end of first-year composition, students should
- Develop a writing project through multiple drafts
- Develop flexible strategies for reading, drafting, reviewing, collaborating, revising, rewriting, rereading, and editing
- Use composing processes and tools as a means to discover and reconsider ideas
- Experience the collaborative and social aspects of writing processes
- Learn to give and to act on productive feedback to works in progress
- Adapt composing processes for a variety of technologies and modalities
- Reflect on the development of composing practices and how those practices influence their work

Faculty in all programs and departments can build on this preparation by helping students learn
- To employ the methods and technologies commonly used for research and communication within their fields
- To develop projects using the characteristic processes of their fields
- To review work-in-progress for the purpose of developing ideas before surface-level editing
- To participate effectively in collaborative processes typical of their field

Knowledge of Conventions

Conventions are the formal rules and informal guidelines that define genres, and in so doing, shape readers' and writers' perceptions of correctness or appropriateness. Most obviously, conventions govern such things as mechanics, usage, spelling, and citation practices. But they also influence content, style, organization, graphics, and document design.

Conventions arise from a history of use and facilitate reading by invoking common expectations between writers and readers. These expectations are not universal; they vary by genre (conventions for lab notebooks and discussion-board exchanges differ), by discipline (conventional moves in literature reviews in Psychology differ from those in English), and by occasion (meeting minutes and executive summaries use different registers). A writer's grasp of conventions in one context does not mean a firm grasp in another. Successful writers understand, analyze, and negotiate conventions for purpose, audience, and genre, understanding that genres evolve in response to changes in material conditions and composing technologies and attending carefully to emergent conventions.

By the end of first-year composition, students should
- Develop knowledge of linguistic structures, including grammar, punctuation, and spelling, through practice in composing and revising
- Understand why genre conventions for structure, paragraphing, tone, and mechanics vary
- Gain experience negotiating variations in genre conventions
- Learn common formats and/or design features for different kinds of texts
- Explore the concepts of intellectual property (such as fair use and copyright) that motivate documentation conventions
- Practice applying citation conventions systematically in their own work

Faculty in all programs and departments can build on this preparation by helping students learn
- The reasons behind conventions of usage, specialized vocabulary, format, and citation systems in their fields or disciplines
- Strategies for controlling conventions in their fields or disciplines
- Factors that influence the ways work is designed, documented, and disseminated in their fields
- Ways to make informed decisions about intellectual property issues connected to common genres and modalities in their fields.

Acknowledgments

A Writer's Resource is built on the premise that it takes a campus to teach a writer. It is also true that it takes a community to write a handbook. This text has been a major collaborative effort. And over the years, that ever-widening circle of collaboration has included reviewers, editors, librarians, faculty colleagues, and family members. We would like to give special thanks to Janice Peritz, one of the original authors, who created a foundation for the many subsequent revisions.

Mort Maimon brought to this project his years of insight and experience as a writer and as a secondary and post-secondary English teacher. Gillian Maimon, Ph.D., elementary school teacher, University of Pennsylvania part-time professor, and writing workshop leader is a constant motivation. She has miraculously applied principles inherent in this text successfully to the first-grade classroom. Alan Maimon, investigative researcher, journalist, and author, continues to be a source of encouragement. Elaine also drew inspiration from her granddaughters, Dasia and Madison Stewart, Annabelle Elaine Maimon, and Lisette Rose Maimon, who already show promise of becoming writers.

David Yancey, Genevieve Yancey, Sui Wong, Matthew Yancey, and Kelly Yancey—whose combined writing experience includes the fields of biology, psychology, medicine, computer engineering, mathematics, industrial engineering, information technology, graphic design, and user experience—helped with examples as well as with accounts of their writing practices as they completed many kinds of classroom assignments, as they applied to medical and graduate schools, as they wrote for internships and currently write on the job. And as the younger Yanceys delight in learning language and ways of communicating, they—Calder Yancey-Wong, Clara Yancey, and Amelie Yancey-Wong—have reminded us of the importance of communication of all kinds.

At Governors State University (GSU), Penny Perdue, who is herself an exemplary writer, provided research and expert editorial support. We also welcome the opportunity to thank Penny for her outstanding work in managing administrative operations in the Office of the GSU President, thereby freeing Elaine to pursue her career-long passion for helping students become independent writers and thinkers. Dr. Lydia Morrow Ruetten provided up-to-date information on the GSU library.

From Florida State University, we thank the Rhetoric and Composition program and the many good ideas that come from students and faculty alike. Specifically, we thank Liane Robertson—now at William Paterson University of New Jersey—and Kara Taczak—now at the University of Denver—who have brought their experiences as excellent teachers of writing to many pages of this book.

We are grateful to Harvey Wiener and the late Richard Marius for their permission to draw on their explanations of grammatical points in *A Writer's Resource*. We also appreciate the work of Maria Zlateva of Boston University; Karen Batchelor of City College of San Francisco; and Daria Ruzicka, who prepared the ESL materials. Thanks also go to librarians Debora Person, University of Wyoming, and Ronelle K. H. Thompson, Augustana College. Our colleague Don McQuade has inspired us, advised us, and encouraged us throughout the years of this project. We thank Lisa Moore and Christopher Bennem for orchestrating our work on early editions.

Within the McGraw-Hill Education organization, many wonderful people have been our true teammates on this sixth edition. We appreciate Kelly Villella-Canton's excellent work as director and Penina Braffman Greenfield's as portfolio manager for English. We are grateful to Kelly and Penina for helping us to concentrate on what only the authors could do, while they took care of so much else. Crucial support came from David Patterson, managing director for English and Mary Ellen Curley, product development manager. Thanks to Janet Smith, Andrea Pasquarelli, Paula Kepos, and Michael O'Loughlin, all of whom worked diligently on *Connect Composition*. Lisa Bruflodt, content project manager, monitored every detail of production; Debra Kubiak and Jessica Cuevas, designers, supervised every aspect of the striking text design and cover; and designer Robin Mouat was responsible for the stunning visuals that appear throughout the book. Thanks to Brianna Kirschbaum, DeAnna Dausener, and Mark Schaefer for their help in clearing text permissions for this edition.

This book has benefited enormously from three extraordinary product developers: David Chodoff, the remarkable Carla Samodulski, and the incredibly talented Elizabeth Murphy. Elizabeth joined the team to shepherd us through the fifth edition and it has been a pleasure working with her. Carla and Elizabeth worked together to strengthen and refine the digital tools available in Connect for *A Writer's Resource*.

Finally, many, many thanks go to the reviewers who read chapters from the new edition of one of our handbooks, generously offered their perceptions and reactions to our plans, and had confidence in us as we shaped our texts to address the needs of their students. We wish to thank the following instructors:

Content Consultants and Reviewers

Arizona Western College, Yuma
 Jennifer M. Hewerdine
 Stephen Moore

Baton Rouge Community College
 Shelisa Theus

Bridgewater State University
 Deborah Barshay

Cumberland County College
 Joshua Austin

Delaware Technical Community
College
 Rob Rector

Durham Technical Community College
 Jonathan Cook

Dyersburg State Community College
 Linda Weeks

East Central College
 Sue Henderson

 Leigh Kolb
 Patsy Watts

Eastern Illinois University
 Melissa Caldwell
 Dalva Markelis

Front Range Community
College
 Donna Craine

Glendale Community College
 Alisa Cooper

Hawaii Pacific University
 Robert Wilson

Howard University
 David Green

Husson University
 Maria Cahill

Idaho State University
 Harold Hellwig

Illinois Central College
Michael Boud
James Dekcer

Isothermal Community College
Jeremy Burris

Ivy Tech Community College, Columbus
John Roberts

Ivy Tech Community College,
Central Indiana
Judith LaFourest
Brenda Spencer

Jacksonville State University
Don Bennett
Christy Burns
Deborah Prickett

West Kentucky Community and
Technical College
Kimberly Russell

Lane College
Unoma Azuah

Lees-McRae College
Kathy H. Olson

Lincoln College
Judy Cortelloni

Lincoln Land Community College
Jason Dockter

McNeese State University
Corliss Badeaux
Rita D. Costello

Mercer University
Jonathan Glance

Michigan State University, East
Lansing
Nancy Dejoy

Northwest Arkansas Community College
Audley Hall
Megan Looney

Palm Beach State College, Lake Worth
Susan Aguila

Palm Beach State College
Patrick Tierney

Porterville College
Melissa Black

Quinnipiac University
Glenda Pritchett

St. Louis Community College,
Florissant Valley
Lonetta Oliver

Santa Fe College
Akilah Brown

Southern Illinois University
Tara Hembrough

Southwestern Assemblies of
God University
Diane Lewis

Southwestern Illinois College
Judi Quimby

Tarrant County College, Southeast
Campus
Elizabeth Joseph

Texas Christian University
Brad Lucas

Tidewater Community College,
Virginia Beach Campus
Doris Jellig

Tulsa Community College,
Metro Campus
Greg Stone
Jeanne Urie

Tulsa Community College
Ken Clane

The University of Arkansas at
Pine Bluff
Janice Brantley

Union University
David Malone

University of Alabama
Karen Gardiner
Jessica Kidd

University of Hartford
Susan M. Aliberti

The University of Missouri,
Kansas City
Daniel Mahala

University of Montana
Amy Ratto-Parks

The University of Toledo
  Anthony Edgington

The University of West Georgia
  Kevin Casper

University of Wisconsin-Stout
  Andrea Deacon

Wayne County Community College District
  Bakkah Rasheed-Shabazz
  Sharon Wallace

Western Technical College
  Pamela Solberg

William Paterson University
  Mark Arnowitz

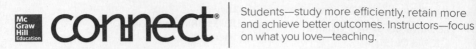

McGraw Hill Education

connect®

Students—study more efficiently, retain more and achieve better outcomes. Instructors—focus on what you love—teaching.

SUCCESSFUL SEMESTERS INCLUDE CONNECT

FOR INSTRUCTORS

You're in the driver's seat.

Want to build your own course? No problem. Prefer to use our turnkey, prebuilt course? Easy. Want to make changes throughout the semester? Sure. And you'll save time with Connect's auto-grading too.

65%

Less Time Grading

They'll thank you for it.

Adaptive study resources like SmartBook® help your students be better prepared in less time. You can transform your class time from dull definitions to dynamic debates. Hear from your peers about the benefits of Connect at **www.mheducation.com/highered/connect**

Make it simple, make it affordable.

Connect makes it easy with seamless integration using any of the major Learning Management Systems—Blackboard®, Canvas, and D2L, among others—to let you organize your course in one convenient location. Give your students access to digital materials at a discount with our inclusive access program. Ask your McGraw-Hill representative for more information.

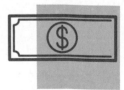

©Hill Street Studios/Tobin Rogers/Blend Images LLC

Solutions for your challenges.

A product isn't a solution. Real solutions are affordable, reliable, and come with training and ongoing support when you need it and how you want it. Our Customer Experience Group can also help you troubleshoot tech problems—although Connect's 99% uptime means you might not need to call them. See for yourself at **status.mheducation.com**

Effective, efficient studying.

Connect helps you be more productive with your study time and get better grades using tools like SmartBook, which highlights key concepts and creates a personalized study plan. Connect sets you up for success, so you walk into class with confidence and walk out with better grades.

©Shutterstock/wavebreakmedia

"I really liked this app—it made it easy to study when you don't have your textbook in front of you."

- Jordan Cunningham, Eastern Washington University

Study anytime, anywhere.

Download the free ReadAnywhere app and access your online eBook when it's convenient, even if you're offline. And since the app automatically syncs with your eBook in Connect, all of your notes are available every time you open it. Find out more at **www.mheducation.com/readanywhere**

No surprises.

The Connect Calendar and Reports tools keep you on track with the work you need to get done and your assignment scores. Life gets busy; Connect tools help you keep learning through it all.

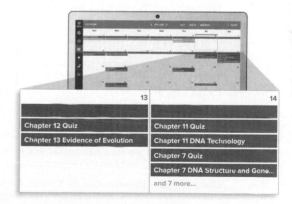

13	14
Chapter 12 Quiz	Chapter 11 Quiz
Chapter 13 Evidence of Evolution	Chapter 11 DNA Technology
	Chapter 7 Quiz
	Chapter 7 DNA Structure and Gene...
	and 7 more...

Learning for everyone.

McGraw-Hill works directly with Accessibility Services Departments and faculty to meet the learning needs of all students. Please contact your Accessibility Services office and ask them to email accessibility@mheducation.com, or visit **www.mheducation.com/about/accessibility.html** for more information.

How to Find the Help You need in *A Writer's Resource*

A Writer's Resource is a reference for all writers and researchers. When you are writing in any situation, you are bound to come across questions about writing and research. *A Writer's Resource* provides you with answers to your questions.

Begin with Start Smart.   If you are responding to an assignment, go to the Start Smart feature at the beginning of Tab 1 to determine the type of writing the assignment requires, along with the steps involved in constructing it and one or more examples. A brief Start Smart box opens each subsequent tab, posing questions aligned with the WPA outcomes; this feature will guide you to the sections of the text that answer these questions. These features give you an easy means of accessing the many resources available to you within *A Writer's Resource*, from help with finding a thesis to advice on documenting your sources.

Check the table of contents.   If you know the topic you are looking for, try scanning the complete contents on the last page and inside back cover, which includes the tab and chapter titles as well as each section number and title in the book. If you are looking for specific information within a general topic (how to correct an unclear pronoun reference, for example), scanning the table of contents will help you find the section you need.

Look up your topic in the index.   The comprehensive index at the end of *A Writer's Resource* (pp. I-1–I-43) includes all of the topics covered in the book. For example, if you are not sure whether to use *I* or *me* in a sentence, you can look up "*I vs. me*" in the index.

Check the documentation resources.   By looking at the examples of different types of sources and the documentation models displayed at the opening of each documentation tab, you can determine where to find the information you need to document a source. By answering the questions posed in the charts provided (for MLA style at the beginning of Tab 6 and for APA style at the beginning of Tab 7), you can usually find the model you are looking for.

Look in the grammar tab-opening pages for errors similar to the ones you typically make.   Tab 9 opens with a chart of the most common errors students make. Each error includes an example and a reference to the section and page number where you can find a more detailed explanation and examples. Flip through these pages to find a quick reference guide for multilingual writers.

Look up a word in the Glossary of Usage.   If you are not sure that you are using a particular word such as farther or further correctly, try looking it up in the Glossary of Usage, available in the ebook in Connect.

Refer to Tab 12 if you are a multilingual writer.   Chapters 69–72 provide tips on the use of articles, helping verbs, and other problem areas for multilingual writers.

Check the list of Discipline-Specific Resources.   Further Resources for Learning, available in the ebook in Connect, includes a comprehensive list of sources that have already been checked for relevance and reliability.

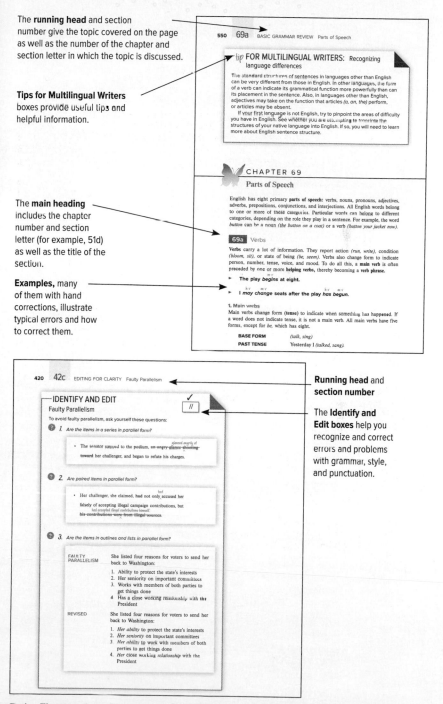

The **running head** and section number give the topic covered on the page as well as the number of the chapter and section letter in which the topic is discussed.

Tips for Multilingual Writers boxes provide useful tips and helpful information.

---

550   69a   BASIC GRAMMAR REVIEW   Parts of Speech

tip FOR MULTILINGUAL WRITERS: Recognizing language differences

The standard structures of sentences in languages other than English can be very different from those in English. In other languages, the form of a verb can indicate its grammatical function more powerfully than can its placement in the sentence. Also, in languages other than English, adjectives may take on the function that articles (a, an, the) perform, or articles may be absent.

If your first language is not English, try to pinpoint the areas of difficulty you have in English. See whether you are attempting to translate the structures of your native language into English. If so, you will need to learn more about English sentence structure.

CHAPTER 69
Parts of Speech

English has eight primary **parts of speech**: verbs, nouns, pronouns, adjectives, adverbs, prepositions, conjunctions, and interjections. All English words belong to one or more of these categories. Particular words can belong to different categories, depending on the role they play in a sentence. For example, the word button can be a noun (the button on a coat) or a verb (button your jacket now).

69a   Verbs

Verbs carry a lot of information. They report action (run, write), condition (bloom, sit), or state of being (be, seem). Verbs also change form to indicate person, number, tense, voice, and mood. To do all this, a **main verb** is often preceded by one or more **helping verbs**, thereby becoming a **verb phrase**.

▶ The play *begins* at eight.

▶ I *may change* seats after the play *has begun*.

1. Main verbs
Main verbs change form (tense) to indicate when something has happened. If a word does not indicate tense, it is not a main verb. All main verbs have five forms, except for be, which has eight.

BASE FORM   (talk, sing)

PAST TENSE   Yesterday I (talked, sang).

The **main heading** includes the chapter number and section letter (for example, 51d) as well as the title of the section.

Examples, many of them with hand corrections, illustrate typical errors and how to correct them.

---

420   42c   EDITING FOR CLARITY   Faulty Parallelism

IDENTIFY AND EDIT   ✓
Faulty Parallelism   //

To avoid faulty parallelism, ask yourself these questions:

1. Are the items in a series in parallel form?

• The senator stepped to the podium, ~~an angry glance shooting~~ *glanced angrily at* toward her challenger, and began to refute his charges.

2. Are paired items in parallel form?

• Her challenger, she claimed, had not only accused her *had* falsely of accepting illegal campaign contributions, but *had accepted illegal contributions himself.* ~~his contributions were from illegal sources.~~

3. Are the items in outlines and lists in parallel form?

FAULTY PARALLELISM	She listed four reasons for voters to send her back to Washington:
	1. Ability to protect the state's interests
	2. Her seniority on important committees
	3. Works with members of both parties to get things done
	4 Has a close working relationship with the President
REVISED	She listed four reasons for voters to send her back to Washington:
	1. *Her ability* to protect the state's interests
	2. *Her seniority* on important committees
	3. *Her ability* to work with members of both parties to get things done
	4. *Her close working relationship* with the President

Running head and section number

The **Identify and Edit boxes** help you recognize and correct errors and problems with grammar, style, and punctuation.

Design Elements: (butterfly/computer): ©Visual Generation/Shutterstock; (other design icons): ©McGraw-Hill Education

1

Writing Today

The adequate study of culture, our own and those on the opposite side of the globe, can press on to fulfillment only as we learn today from the humanities as well as from the scientists.

–Ruth Benedict

©Peerayot/Shutterstock

The compass has long been a tool for explorers and mapmakers. This book was designed to be a compass for writing in any discipline.

1 Writing Today

Section dealing with visual rhetoric. For a complete listing, see the Quick Guide to Key Resources in Connect.

START SMART Addressing the Writing Situation

Start Smart will help you understand your writing situation and find the advice you need to get your project off to a good start. It also provides an overview for any kind of writing project. If you get stuck, come back here to jump-start your work.

Step 1 What should your assignment or project do?

Look for these keywords

Inform: classify, define, describe, explore, illustrate, report, survey
Interpret or Analyze: analyze, compare, explain, inquire, reflect
Argue or Persuade: agree, defend, evaluate, justify, propose, refute

Step 2 Go to

A: Writing That Informs
B: Writing That Interprets and Analyzes
C: Writing That Argues/Persuades

A: Writing That Informs

Begin with the Writing Situation:

- What topic are you writing about? (Ch. 5, pp. 36–38)
- Who is going to read your writing? (Ch. 5, p. 36)
- How should you talk about this topic for your readers? (Ch. 5, p. 38)
- What is the required length, deadline, and format, as well as the background for your assignment? (Ch. 5, p. 38)
- What kind of text is it; how should you present it? (Ch. 5, pp. 38–39)
- What design conventions are appropriate for this type of writing? (Ch. 8, p. 84)

Compose Using Writing Processes:

- How can you find a worthwhile thesis or claim for your topic? (Ch. 5, pp. 43–45)
- What strategies can help you organize your writing? (Ch. 6, pp. 52–65)
- What strategies can help you revise? (Ch. 7, pp. 65–77)

Think Critically about Using Sources:

- Does your writing require research? (Ch. 18, pp. 191–97)
- If yes, how many and what kind of sources are needed? (Ch. 18, pp. 196–97)
- What resources are appropriate for your course and available? (See Further Resources for Learning in Connect)
- Should you use tables, graphs, or images? Audio or video? (Ch. 5, pp. 48–51)

Think Carefully about Your Final Steps:

- Did you cite all your sources correctly? (Ch. 25, pp. 257–59)
- Did you carefully edit and proofread your writing? (Ch. 7, p. 79–81)

Some Samples

- Informative report (pp. 87, 102, 351)
- Newsletter (p. 177)
- Brochure (p. 176)
- Annotated bibliography (p. 241)

connect For an interactive version of this Start Smart guide, along with more samples, go to connect.mheducation.com

Sample Informative Report

> **The thesis or claim summarizes the writer's knowledge of this topic.**

> **Tone is objective; writer does not express an opinion.**

> **Bar chart illustrates key point made in the text.**

> **Caption explains bar chart.**

> **Procedure illustrates key idea as a numbered list.**

The Caring Express Food Bank

The Caring Express Food Bank serves a varied population of clients, including chronically homeless people, temporarily homeless people, recent immigrants, elderly people on fixed incomes, and people in need of temporary services. As Figure 1 shows, while the number of homeless, both temporary and permanent, that Caring Express assisted in 2008 decreased during the summer months, the number of immigrant workers increased. The percentage of elderly people and people in need of temporary services remained fairly stable throughout the year.

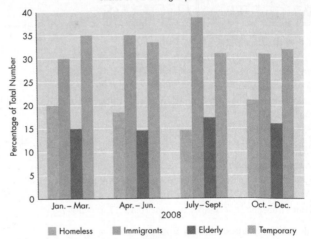

Figure 1. Percentage of clients in each group during 2008

How Caring Express Helps Clients

When new clients come to Caring Express, the volunteers follow this procedure:

1. The volunteer fills out a form with the client's address (if he or she has one), phone number, income, and employment situation.
2. Clients who do not live in Maple Valley are referred to a food bank or outreach program in their area.
3. Clients who qualify check off the food they need from a list.
4. The food is packed and distributed to them.

A successful informative report should

- have a thesis or claim that summarizes the writer's knowledge of the topic.
- have an objective tone.
- illustrate key ideas with examples from research.

Additional information about report design is available on pages 85–92.

B: Writing That
Interprets and Analyzes

Begin with the Writing Situation:

- What topic are you interpreting or analyzing? (Ch. 5, pp. 36–38)
- Who is going to read your writing? (Ch. 5, p. 36)
- How should you talk about this topic for your readers? (Ch. 5, p. 38)
- What is the required length, deadline, and format, as well as the background for your assignment? (Ch. 5, p. 38)
- What kind of text is it; how should you present it? (Ch. 5, pp. 38–39)
- What design conventions are appropriate for this type of writing? (Ch. 8, p. 84)

Compose Using Writing Processes:

- How can you find a worthwhile thesis or claim for your topic? (Ch. 5, pp. 43–45)
- What strategies can help you organize your writing? (Ch. 6, pp. 52–65)
- What strategies can help you revise? (Ch. 7, pp. 65–77)

Think Critically about Using Sources:

- Does your writing require research? (Ch. 18, pp. 191–97)
- If yes, how many and what kind of sources are needed? (Ch. 18, pp. 196–97)
- What resources are appropriate for your course and available? (See Further Resources for Learning in Connect)
- Should you use tables, graphs, or images? Audio or video? (Ch. 5, pp. 48–51)

Think Carefully about Your Final Steps:

- What citation style, if any, should you use? (Ch. 25, pp. 257–59)
- Did you cite all your sources correctly? (Ch. 24, pp. 250 and 257)
- Did you carefully edit and proofread your writing? (Ch. 7, pp. 79–81)

Some Samples

- Visual analysis (p. 82)
- Analysis of a poem (p. 117)

connect For an interactive version of this Start Smart guide, along with more samples, go to connect.mheducation.com

3

A Sample Visual Analysis

Diane Chen

Professor Defeo

Art 251: History of Photography

6 December 2017

Inspiring Empathy: Dorothea Lange's *Migrant Mother*

Topic is identified, followed by statement of a focused, powerful thesis.

American photographer Dorothea Lange is perhaps best known for her work commissioned by the Farm Services Administration photographing the social and economic effects of the Great Depression. Her arresting portraits of displaced farmers, migrant families, and the unemployed skillfully depict the dire consequences of the Depression for America's working classes. Artful though her photographs are, Lange's technique involved more than artistic skill. Lange considered herself primarily a photojournalist, whose goal was to encourage social action through her work. As a photojournalist who empathetically captured the struggles of her subjects on film, Lange was able to impart compassion to her audience and in turn inspire change.

Uses a thoughtful tone.

One of Lange's most famous photographs, *Migrant Mother*, (see fig. 1) is an example of her unique ability to document such struggles. *Migrant Mother* is not simply a portrait of one mother's hardship, but is a raw depiction of the plight of thousands of displaced families during the Depression. The mother in this photograph, Florence Owens Thompson, was a migrant worker in Nipomo, California, in 1936, whom Lange encountered sitting outside her tent in a migrant camp. Lange took several exposures of Thompson, moving closer to her subject with each shot. This technique helped her to capture an image that communicated to viewers what poverty looked like at a human level. But the power of Lange's image is not confined to history; even today, *Migrant Mother* remains an iconic reminder of the struggles of the poor.

A description of the image that illustrates the main point.

The photograph's composition reveals Lange's compassion for her subject. Although four figures make up the photograph, the mother, whose face we see in full, is its main subject. She gazes outward, worriedly, as her three children huddle around her. The children frame her figure, two of them with faces hidden behind her shoulders, either out of shyness or shared distress, while the third rests across the mother's lap. The mother's expression conveys a desperate concern, presumably for her children's wellbeing. Her children cling to her, but her own faraway gaze gives evidence that she is too distracted by her worries to give them comfort. Lange emphasizes the mother's expression by making it the focal point of the photograph. In doing so, she encourages viewers to identify with the mother and even to wonder what thoughts pass through her mind.

Fig. 1. Dorothea Lange,
Migrant Mother, 1936.

Source: Library of Congress Prints and
Photographs Division [LC-DIG-fsa-8b29516]

Caption gives the title of the photograph.

———————————— [New page] ————————————

Work Cited

Lange, Dorothea. *Migrant Mother*, 1936. Prints and Photographs Division,
  Library of Congress, https://lccn.loc.gov/2017762891.

A successful visual analysis should
- have a focused and purposeful thesis.
- have a thoughtful tone.
- include a description of the image illustrating the main point. If possible, include a copy of the image under discussion.

Full analysis is available (in draft form) on pages 82–84.

C: Writing That
Argues/Persuades

Begin with the Writing Situation:
- What topic are you writing about? (Ch. 5, pp. 36–38)
- Who is going to read your writing? (Ch. 5, p. 36)
- How should you talk about this topic for your readers? (Ch. 5, p. 38)
- What is the required length, deadline, and format, as well as the background for your assignment? (Ch. 5, p. 38)
- What kind of text is it; how should you present it? (Ch. 5, pp. 38–39)
- What design conventions are appropriate for this type of writing? (Ch. 8, p. 84)

Compose Using Writing Processes:
- How can you find a thesis or claim for your topic? (Ch. 5, pp. 43–45)
- What strategies can help you organize your writing? (Ch. 6, pp. 52–65)
- What strategies can help you revise? (Ch. 7, pp. 65–77)

Think Critically about Using Sources:
- Does your argument require research? (Ch. 18, pp. 191–97)
- If yes, how many and what kind of sources are needed? (Ch. 18, pp. 196–97)
- What resources are appropriate for your course and available? (See Further Resources for Learning in Connect.)
- Should you use tables, graphs, or images? Audio or video? (Ch. 5, pp. 48–51)

Think Carefully about Your Final Steps:
- What citation style, if any, should you use? (Ch. 25, pp. 257–59)
- Did you cite all your sources correctly? (Ch. 24, p. 250)
- Did you carefully edit and proofread your writing? (Ch. 7, pp. 79–81)

Some Samples
- Arguments (pp. 136, 306)
- Persuasive Web site (p. 8)
- Persuasive PowerPoint/Oral presentation (p. 160)

∎ connect For an interactive version of this Start Smart guide, along with more samples, go to connect.mheducation.com

A Sample Argument

Joseph Honrado

Professor Robertson

English 201

1 October 2017

Cyberbullying: An Alarming Trend for the Digital Age

Before the advent of social media and cell phones, bullies used to harass their

victims on the playground, on the school bus, and in the lunchroom. In response to

these confrontations, adults advised kids to stand up to bullies or simply to avoid them.

However, in today's digital society, bullying can take place anytime and anyplace. That

means standing up to a bully is much more difficult. According to a program run by

the Minnesota Parent Training and Information Center (PACER), definitions of

bullying differ by locality and even by school; however, most definitions have traits in

common, including repeated behavior that "hurts or harms another person physically

or emotionally" and targets individuals who are unable to defend themselves (National

Bullying Prevention Center). The Web site *Stopbullying.gov*, which is supported by the

United States Department of Health and Human Services, updates this definition to

include "bullying that takes place using electronic technology," also known as

cyberbullying ("Bullying Definition"). Cyberbullying is a significant, destructive problem

among young people. It is especially harmful because of its immediacy, scope, and

permanence: humiliation is easily inflicted online, where large audiences can continue

to witness it indefinitely. With new technologies affecting the ways kids interact, adults

must consider new ways to deal with the problem of bullying. If the problem of

cyberbullying is ever to be overcome, students, parents, educators, and the media must

work together to promote healthy guidelines for online behavior.

> Introduces the issue of cyberbullying using a reasonable tone.

> Presents definition of cyberbullying.

> Thesis or claim.

A successful argument should

- include a thesis or claim that clearly states the writer's position.
- identify key points that support and develop the thesis, with evidence for each point.
- use a structure that is appropriate for the content and context of the argument.
- have a reasonable tone.
- conclude by emphasizing the importance of the position and its implications and by answering the "So what?" question.

Full argument is available on pages 136–42.

A Sample Persuasive Web Site

Headline highlights key points of article.

Link to regional data climate change in the United States.

Text has a reasonable tone.

GlobalChange.gov
U.S. Global Change Research Program

ABOUT USGCRP   WHAT WE DO   AGENCIES

Understand
Climate Change

Explore
Regions & Topics

Browse & Find
Resources, Data, & Multimedia

Follow
News & Updates

Engage
Connect & Participate

CLIMATE CHANGE

Impacts on Society

Climate change is affecting the American people in far-reaching ways. Impacts related to climate change are evident across regions and in many sectors important to society—such as human health, agriculture and food security, water supply, transportation, energy, ecosystems, and others—and are expected to become increasingly disruptive throughout this century and beyond.

Climate change affects human health and wellbeing through more extreme weather events and wildfires, decreased air quality, and diseases transmitted by insects, food, and water. Climate disruptions to agriculture have been increasing and are projected to become more severe over this century, a trend that would diminish the security of America's food supply. Surface and groundwater supplies in some regions are already stressed, and water quality is diminishing in many areas, in part due to increasing sediment and contaminant concentrations after heavy downpours.

UNDERSTAND CLIMATE CHANGE

What's Happening & Why
Impacts on Society
Response Options

LEARN MORE

Findings of the National Climate Assessment
FAQs
Glossary

Source: US. Global Change Research Program, www.globalchange.gov

A successful Web site should
- include pages that capture and hold interest.
- be readable, with a unified visual appearance.
- be easy to access and navigate.

A successful persuasive Web site should
- have a reasonable tone.
- highlight key points so that readers can spot them quickly.
- include links to authoritative sources that support the writer's position.
- use visual cues to establish credibility. Avoid clip art or images/patterns that are cluttered or "cute."

PowerPoints for a
Persuasive Oral Presentation

P P Cyberbullying:
An Alarming Trend for the Digital Age

Joseph Honrado
October 4, 2017

A compelling opening, clearly presented on the slide.

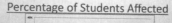

Percentage of Students Affected

7.4% have had a mean or hurtful video of them posted online
12.2% have been threatened online
20.1% have had rumors about them posted online
22.5% have had mean or hurtful comments about them posted online
33.8% have been cyberbullied

Nationally representative sample of 12–17 year olds, n=5,707
Hinduja and Patchin, "2016 Cyberbullying Data," 2016

Visual aid or source is used to support an important point.

Reasons Students
Don't Report Cyberbullying*

- Fear of being seen as weak or a tattletale
- Fear of retaliation by their bullies
- Belief that no one cares or could understand

A focused discussion. Text used sparingly.

* stopbullying.org

Dr. Sameer Hinduja and Dr. Justin W. Patchin. "Cyberbullying Victimization." *Cyberbullying Research Center*, July-Oct. 2016, cyberbullying.org.

A persuasive oral presentation should
- have a compelling opening.
- have a clear focus and organization.
- use visual aids and sources to support key points and highlight content (with text used sparingly).
- conclude memorably.
- be delivered extemporaneously (avoid reading the slides).

Tab 1: Learning across the Curriculum

This section will help you answer questions such as the following:

Rhetorical Knowledge

- What is a rhetorical situation, and how can understanding this term help me now and as a writer throughout college and life? (2a)
- How do I respond appropriately to different writing situations? (2a)
- How can belonging to more than one culture help my writing? (3)
- Why is it fine for me to use emoticons and abbreviations in text messages but not in a college assignment? (2e)

Critical Thinking, Reading, and Writing

- How can writing help me learn in all my college courses? (1c)
- How can I plan my time in college? (1d)
- How can writing help me develop fluency in English? (3)

Processes

- What do social media have to do with college writing? (2b)
- How can digital technology help me work with other students on writing projects? (2b)

Knowledge of Conventions

- What is a discipline? (1b)
- How can I tell what my instructors expect of me in college? (1d, 3a)
- What conventions should I follow when writing e-mail for professional purposes? (2e)

For a general introduction to writing outcomes, see 1e, pages 14–15.

CHAPTER 1

Writing across the Curriculum and beyond College

College is a place for exploration, opening new pathways for your life. You will travel through many courses, participating in numerous conversations—spoken and written—about nature, society, and culture. As you navigate your college experience, use this book as your map and guide.

- As a map, this text will help you understand different approaches to knowledge and see how your studies relate to the larger world.
- As a guide, this text will help you write in college—for classes and in exams and research reports—and in other areas of your life where you will write résumés, brochures, complaints, and business correspondence.

As a permanent part of your library, this text can help guide you through college and beyond.

1a   Learn to transfer composition skills to other contexts.

You may think that only those who aspire to write for a living should study composition. You may have already decided on a career that you assume will require little writing. However, that clear, effective writing is expected in just about every career. It's likely in any case that you will change careers, not once but several times. With that in mind, we encourage you to put mission before major. Think about what you want to accomplish in the world and seek guidance from professors and career counselors. You will find that many different majors will prepare you for a fulfilling life.

As a citizen, you will find knowing how to write gives you a voice to address issues in your community. As a family member and friend, you will write to your children's teachers, to distant relatives, and to people requesting recommendations. Whether you use e-mail, social media, or notepaper, writing is essential to relationships.

But writing is more than putting words together. Your study of composition will improve your powers of critical and innovative thinking. Writing is a way of learning and a way of knowing. The trick is to transfer what you learn in composition to contexts that look very different from the immediate assignment. For example, learning to argue against cyberbullying will help you to argue for improved funding for public schools. The topics are very different, but you can transfer your ability to keep a reasonable tone, include a thesis that states your position, use a structure that supports and develops the thesis, and concludes by responding to the question audiences of persuasive messages are likely to ask: "So what?" Learning to evaluate sources for an academic research paper will help you recognize questionable sources on a news feed or in a social media post. You will apply the skill of evaluating sources for credibility every time you use the Internet. As the phenomenon of "fake news" continues to spread and confuse our understanding of events in the world, source evaluation skills are becoming increasingly important to our ability to act as responsible citizens.

Learning to transfer skills from one situation to another is the essence of education. As you identify and pursue your mission in life, you will make many different kinds of transfers. In your composition course, start to reflect on how to make those transfers effectively.

1b   Study the world through a range of academic disciplines.

To some extent, each department in your college represents a specialized territory of academic study, or area of inquiry, called a **discipline**. A discipline has its own history, issues, vocabulary, and subgroups. The discipline of sociology, for example, is concerned with the conditions, patterns, and problems of people in groups and societies. Sociologists collect, analyze, and interpret data connected to that focus; sociologists also debate questions of reliability and interpretation. These debates occur in classrooms with students, in conferences with colleagues, in journals and books that reach national and international academic audiences, and in conversations, presentations, and publications addressing members of the public, including elected officials.

Most college students take courses across a range of disciplines. You may be asked to take one or two courses each in the humanities (the disciplines of literature, music, and philosophy, for example), the social sciences (sociology, economics, and psychology, for example), and the natural sciences (physics, biology, and chemistry, for example). When you write in each discipline—taking notes, writing projects, answering essay-exam questions—you will join the academic conversation, deepen your understanding of how knowledge is constructed, and learn to see and think about the world from different vantage points. You will also discover that courses and assignments overlap in interesting ways. Developing the ability to see and interpret experience from different perspectives goes beyond college to success in life. Every day—every hour—the context shifts. Sizing things up, figuring out what is required, and shaping your responses appropriately will help you to manage any situation. Both personally and professionally, empathizing with other points of view, while sustaining the integrity of your own principles, will take you far.

1c   Use writing as a tool for learning.

Writing is a great aid to learning. Think of the way a simple shopping list jogs your memory once you get to the store, or recall the last time you jotted down notes during a meeting. Because of your heightened attention, you undoubtedly knew more about what happened at that meeting than did anyone else in the room. Writing helps you remember, understand, and create.

- **Writing aids memory.** From taking class notes *(see Figure 1.1)* to jotting down ideas for later development, writing helps you to retrieve important information. Write down ideas inspired by your course work—in any form or order. These ideas can be the seeds for a research project or other types of critical inquiry, or you can apply them to your life outside the classroom.

- **Writing sharpens observations.** When you record what you see, hear, taste, smell, and feel, you increase the powers of your senses. Note the smells during a chemistry experiment, and you will more readily detect changes caused by reactions; record how the aroma of a new bar of soap makes you feel, and you will better understand your own moods.

- **Writing clarifies thought.** After composing a draft, carefully reading it helps you pinpoint what you really want to say. The last paragraph of a first draft can become the first paragraph of the next draft.

- **Writing uncovers connections.** Maybe a character in a short story reminds you of your neighbor, or an image in a poem makes you feel sad. Writing down the reasons you make these connections can help you learn more about the work and more about yourself.

- **Writing aids reflection.** Thinking and writing about something factual opens up possibilities for further consideration and interpretation. Writing about surveys of voter behavior, for example, invites evaluation of methodology and the application of findings.

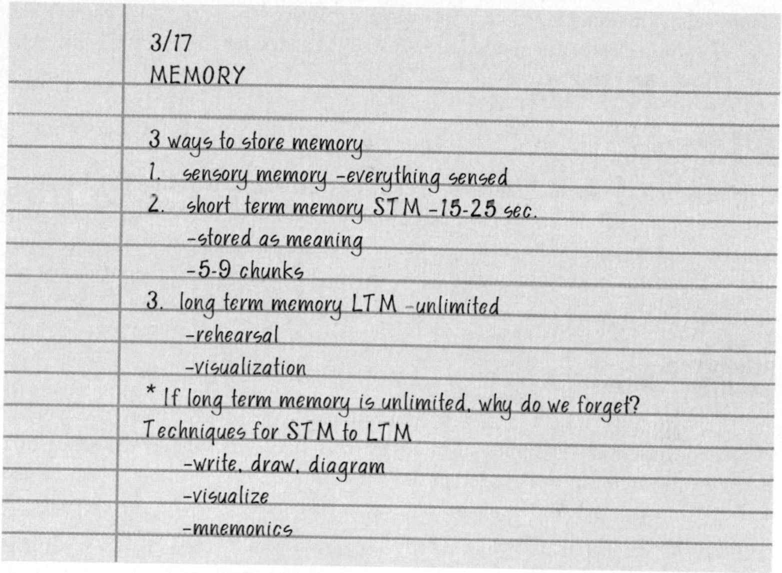

> 3/17
> MEMORY
>
> 3 ways to store memory
> 1. sensory memory -everything sensed
> 2. short term memory STM -15-25 sec.
>   -stored as meaning
>   -5-9 chunks
> 3. long term memory LTM -unlimited
>   -rehearsal
>   -visualization
> * If long term memory is unlimited, why do we forget?
> Techniques for STM to LTM
>   -write, draw, diagram
>   -visualize
>   -mnemonics

FIGURE 1.1 Lecture notes. Recording the main ideas of a lecture and the questions they raise helps you become a more active listener.

- **Writing improves reading.** When you read, annotating the text—or taking notes on the main ideas—and drafting a brief summary of the writer's points sharpen your reading skills and help you remember what you have read. Because memories are often tinged with emotion, writing a personal reaction to a reading can connect the material to your own life, thereby enhancing both your memory and your understanding. *(For a detailed discussion of critical reading and writing, see Chapter 4.)*

- **Writing strengthens argument.** In academic projects, an argument is not a fiery disagreement, but rather a path of reasoning to a position. When you write an argument supporting a claim, you work out *the connections among your ideas*—uncovering both flaws that force you to rethink your position and new connections that make your position stronger.
  Through writing, you also address your audience and the objections they might raise. Success in life often depends on understanding opposing points of view and arguing for your own ideas in ways that others can hear. *(For a detailed discussion of argument, see Chapter 11.)*

1d   Take responsibility for reading, writing, and research.

The academic community assumes that you are an independent learner, capable of managing your workload without supervision. For most courses, the syllabus will be the primary guide to what is expected, serving as a contract between you and your instructor. It will tell you what reading you must do in advance of each class, when tests are scheduled, and when formal assignments or stages of projects (for example, topic and research plan, draft, and final project) are due. Use the syllabus to map out your weekly schedule for reading, research, and writing. *(For tips on how to schedule a research project, see Chapter 18.)*

1e Recognize that writing improves with practice.

Composition courses are valuable in helping you learn to write at the college level, but your development as a writer only begins there. Writing in all your courses, and in your cocurricular experiences and personal situations, throughout your academic career will prepare you for a lifetime of confidence as a writer.

1f Achieve the core outcomes of successful writing.

As you write any project, you will communicate your ideas more effectively if you keep these four outcomes in mind. Although they are presented separately here, these outcomes work together as you compose. For example, you will use critical thinking (part of one outcome) as you revise your project (part of another outcome).

- **Rhetorical Knowledge** includes writing successfully for a given rhetorical situation, bringing together the appropriate context, purpose, audience, and conventions. It also means using the most appropriate genre and technologies to achieve that purpose, employing conventions necessary to the genre, and taking an appropriate rhetorical stance. *See Chapters 2 and 5a.*

- **Critical Thinking, Reading, and Writing** include reading, analyzing, interpreting, and evaluating verbal and visual texts. Writers identify the assumptions, claims, and kinds of support provided in other texts; they also read across these texts to find patterns of similarity and points of difference. Writers draw on these materials to create their own claims, to select sources, and to integrate such support—through summaries, paraphrases, and quotations—with their own ideas. *See Chapters 4, 11b, and 21.*

- **Processes** are flexible strategies for drafting and revising that can be adapted for different writing situations. Writers also work with others in practicing peer review and composing collaboratively with others. Through reflecting, writers understand and change their composing processes as needed. *See Chapters 5-7.*

- **Knowledge of Conventions** are formal and informal guidelines governing different genres (for example, a résumé or a literary analysis) and enacting those guidelines correctly—for syntax, punctuation, and spelling, for example—in every writing project. *See Chapter 8, Tab 4, and Tabs 9-11.*

Throughout this handbook, Start Smart boxes (like the one that appears at the beginning of this chapter) will help keep you focused on the concerns you are most likely to encounter at each moment in the writing process.

NAVIGATING THROUGH COLLEGE AND BEYOND

Study Skills and Dealing with Stress

Whether you are fresh out of high school or are returning to school after many years, college, like all new and challenging experiences, can be stressful. Here are some strategies for dealing with the stress of college and achieving success:

- **Make flexible schedules.** Schedules help you control your time and avoid procrastination by breaking big projects into manageable bits. Be sure to build some flexibility into your schedule, so that you can manage the unexpected.

- **Make the most of your time by setting clear priorities.** Deal with last-minute invitations by saying "no," getting away from it all, and taking control of phone, text, and e-mail interruptions.

- **Take good notes.** The central feature of good note taking, in college and in life, is listening and distilling the important information—not writing down everything that is said.

- **Build reading and listening skills.** When you read, identify and prioritize the main ideas, think critically about the arguments, and explain the writer's ideas to someone else. Listen actively: focus on what is being said, pay attention to nonverbal messages, listen for what is *not* being said, and take notes.

- **Improve your memory.** Rehearsal and making connections are key strategies in remembering important information. Repeat the information, summarize it, and associate it with other concepts or memories.

- **Evaluate the information you gather.** Consider how authoritative the source is, whether the author has potential biases, how recent the information is, and what facts or other evidence is missing from the research. In college, as in life, critical thinking is essential.

- **Take care of yourself.** Eating healthful food, exercising regularly, and getting plenty of sleep are well-known stress relievers. Some people find meditation to be effective. Stopping for a few seconds to take some deep breaths can do wonders.

- **Reach out for support.** If you find it difficult to cope with stress, seek professional help. Colleges have trained counselors on staff as well as twenty-four-hour crisis lines.

Based partly on Robert S. Feldman, *P.O.W.E.R. Learning: Strategies for Success In College and Life*, 2nd ed., McGraw Hill, 2003.

CHAPTER 2

Writing Situations

The **rhetorical situation**—also known as the **writing situation**—refers to the considerations that all writers take into account as they write. When writers think about their situation, they reflect on the following:

- The primary **purpose**
- The **audience(s)** to address
- The **context** in which they are writing
- The **stance**, or authorial tone
- The **genre** and **medium** most appropriate for the purpose, audience, and writing task

Martin Luther King Jr., for example, wrote "A Letter from Birmingham Jail" to achieve a specific purpose, persuading others to rethink their views about achieving racial justice in the South in the 1960s; for a specific audience, those who disagreed with his approach of nonviolent civil disobedience; in a given genre, an *open letter* addressed to a specific group but intended for publication. A student composing a review evaluating a recent film for a blog has a different purpose, to provide a recommendation about whether the film is worth seeing; to a given audience, the readers of the blog; in the form of a review, another genre. The context for Martin Luther King Jr. was very different from the context for the student writer, of course. A writer's context includes the means of communication, current events, and the environment in which the communication takes place. See an illustration of how these elements are related in Figure 2.1.

2a View the situation as the framework for approaching any writing task.

To manage a writing situation successfully, writers must consider its purpose, audience, and context, both before writing and as they compose. By keeping their rhetorical situation in mind, writers find the writing process easier to manage, and the project that results will be stronger and more effective.

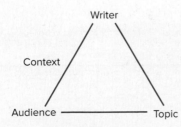

FIGURE 2.1 Elements of a writing situation.

1. Understanding your purpose

You write to achieve many different purposes. Sometimes, as when you create research notes, your purpose may seem important only to you: to compose notes allowing you to create a strong research project. At other times, you write for a more directly social purpose, such as when you compose a job application letter or send an e-mail or a text message to inform a family member that you have arrived at your destination safely. Whether your writing **informs** your readers by telling them what you know about a topic or issue, **interprets** and **analyzes** by exploring the meaning of your subject, **argues** or **persuades** by proving a point or supporting an opinion through logic and concrete evidence, or simply **expresses** your feelings, it is always keyed to achieving a given purpose.

2. Thinking about audience

A second, equally important feature of the writing situation is the audience, the readers you are writing to and for. Thinking of your potential readers can help you shape your writing. An exercise program, for example, would look very different if you were to write it as a journal entry for a health class, post it on *Facebook*, or craft it as a press release on a Web site for a business enterprise or community organization. Thinking about the needs of your audience can help you decide what to include in your writing project as you compose—and what medium you use.

3. Considering your context

Context, or the larger circumstances surrounding a text, exerts a major influence on the rhetorical situation. Consider how the meaning of a single word can change, depending on the context. For example, a *chair* can be a piece of furniture or someone who leads a committee or department. Likewise, because the contexts differ, writers discussing immigration patterns in an academic context know that their readers expect a balanced and informed discussion of this controversial issue, whereas writers in the context of the Internet or a personal letter may address the same issue in a more personal and impassioned way. Although it is impossible to know the full context of any situation, it is important to identify what you do know and keep that information in mind as you write.

4. Choosing an appropriate stance

A *rhetorical stance* is the attitude a writer takes in relation to a topic and the tone used in addressing the audience. A dignitary giving a commencement address tries to inspire the audience, for example, while a friend consoles another friend on a loss. When you are exploring an issue that could divide your audience, you might take the stance of someone who inquires rather than someone who argues. When creating a résumé, most people take the stance of a competent future employee. Considering your stance carefully is an important part of writing well.

2b   Decide on the best medium.

When you know your rhetorical situation, you can select an appropriate medium to support your purpose and communicate with your audience. A **medium** is a means of communication—you can communicate with your audience via print, screen, or network. Print can take various forms: a letter to the editor of a newspaper will probably be published in print and online, whereas a poster for a science presentation is in print, supersized, with images as well as text. A screen composition might consist of a set of Prezi slides detailing election results, or it might be a digital photo essay. A composition posted on a computer network could be a blog on athletes' salaries or a video on the issue of abandoned children. Increasingly, all disciplines require that students compose in each of these three media. In some cases, the medium will be determined by the rhetorical situation: a neighborhood improvement campaign would probably call for print posters and flyers. In other cases, you can decide which medium is best.

These questions can help you select the appropriate medium:

1. Does the rhetorical situation provide guidance for which medium to use? What will the audience expect?

2. Does your composition require or should it make use of electronic sources such as an animated graphic or streaming video? Consider a digital or networked medium such as a Web site.

3. What kind of distribution will your composition require? If you plan to send it to a small group, consider print or an e-mail attachment. For a larger distribution, consider a networked medium such as a Web page or social network site, such as *Facebook*.

4. How large is your audience, and where is it located? You can reach a small, local audience with a print text such as a flyer. If your audience is large and diversified, consider a networked medium such as a blog.

◉ 2c   Make effective use of multimodal elements and genres.

All writers write multimodally: modes are the various resources—from page layout to font style and size—writers use to make meaning. The word *multimodality* can also refer to the multimedia resources, such as photos, videos, and audio files, writers include in their composing. Multimodality can also refer the various ways writers share texts, especially through digital technologies. On Web sites and *blogs*, writers combine texts with photos, videos, and audio files, using all these options to achieve a variety of purposes. Social media sites such as *Facebook* and *YouTube* facilitate connections across time and space.

As you plan to compose for a specific writing situation, consider two possibilities for presenting, and sharing, your text:

1. Which *genre* best suits your purpose

2. Whether your text will include *electronically multimodal elements* (for example, graphs, hyperlinks, video or audio clips)

1. Choosing the best genre

When you know your rhetorical situation, you can select a genre, or kind of writing, that best fits that situation. Poems, stories, and plays are genres of literature, and audiences have different expectations for each. Most of the writing you will be asked to produce in college will be nonfiction, that is, writing about real events, people, and things for the purpose of information, interpretation, or argument. Within nonfiction, however, there are many additional genres of writing such as letters, brochures, case studies, lab reports, and literary analyses. Some types of writing, like the case study, are common in several fields, such as sociology and finance, though the conventions for each vary. Here are some typical genres for the three purposes you will be using most commonly in academic writing:

- **Informative:** research report, newsletter, lab report, design study, medical record

- **Interpretive:** literary analysis, case study, data analysis, feasibility study, film/music/restaurant review

- **Argument:** editorial, letter to the editor, proposal, position paper, undergraduate thesis

2. Incorporating multimodal elements

Digital technology allows you to include sound files, hyperlinks, and other **multimodal elements** in digital projects to convey ideas richly and powerfully. You can create these elements yourself or import them from other sources. Use multimodal resources to serve your overall purpose, placing a photo, sound file, or link strategically and always citing the source of any item you import into your work.

Posting your text online enables you to include an even greater variety of media. You could help your reader hear the music you analyzed by providing a link to an audio file. You could demonstrate the power of political speeches with a link to a video clip of a politician giving a speech.

Presentation software such as *PowerPoint* and Prezi allows you to integrate audio and visual features into your oral presentations or stand-alone presentations posted online on a site like *SlideShare*. Animation applications literally show certain effects (like the result of a faulty bridge design), but they should always serve a specific and appropriate purpose.

(For details on creating effective visuals and other multimodal elements, see Chapter 5: Planning and Shaping; Chapter 6: Drafting Text and Visuals; and Chapter 7: Revising and Editing. For information on creating oral and multimodal presentations, see Chapter 13: Oral Presentations and Chapter 14: Multimodal Writing. For help with finding appropriate visuals, see Chapter 20: Finding and Creating Effective Visuals, Audio Clips, and Video.)

👁 **2d** Become aware of the persuasive power of images.

For many rhetorical situations, carefully chosen visuals—photographs, diagrams, graphs, maps, and other visual types—can help to convey information, illustrate a point, or persuade an audience. If you are reviewing the causes of World War I, you may find it useful to include a map of contested territory. If you are showing how the number of ocean pirates has increased in the past ten years, you could demonstrate that growth with a diagram, and if it were an electronic text, you could connect it to *Google Maps*. When you are defining a rhetorical task, consider whether a photo, diagram, or chart might help to present evidence, illustrate a point, add details, or clarify relationships. In a project for a political science course, for example, a photograph like the one shown on page 21 *(Figure 2.2)* can illustrate at a glance how a new generation of protestors has changed the course of world events using social media.

A graph *(see Figure 2.3, p. 21)* can effectively portray important trends for a history assignment. A time line, like the one in *Connect*, can help your readers grasp the relationships among important events. To use images effectively, though, writers need to analyze them with care.

We live in a world of images—in advertising, in politics, in books, and in classrooms. Increasingly, images function together with words, and often without words, to persuade as well as to instruct. Like words, images, require careful, critical analysis. A misleading graph or an altered photograph can easily distort the way readers and viewers perceive a subject. The ability to understand visual information and evaluate its credibility is an essential tool for learning and writing. *(For details on evaluating visuals, see Chapter 4: Reading and Writing, pp. 29–35; for an example of a misleading graph and a revised version that corrects the problem, see Chapter 7: Revising and Editing, p. 76.)*

2e Take advantage of online and other electronic tools for writing and for learning.

Digital technology makes it possible to transcend the constraints of the clock and the calendar and engage in educational activities twenty-four hours a day, seven days a week. Different electronic tools work best for different purposes.

All the genres of electronic writing that follow allow you to communicate with friends next door, professors across campus, fellow researchers across the world, and prospective employers in another city. In each of these writing situations, you create an online persona. While writers often text each other using emoji and a kind of shorthand, you should always write formally and correctly in all academic and professional situations, especially in e-mails. In fact, e-mail is the preferred vehicle for business, professional, and academic correspondence. Most potential employers require letters of application and résumés as Word attachments. Be sure to compose these electronic documents with care and review them attentively. E-mail is also a useful way to communicate with your professors to ask questions or to make appointments. Write courteously and concisely, and do not expect an instant response.

FIGURE 2.2 **The impact of social media on world events.** As this photo vividly illustrates, when protests against the Egyptian government erupted in Cairo in spring 2011, social media such as *Facebook* played a major role in sustaining the rebellion in the face of attempts by officials to shut it down.

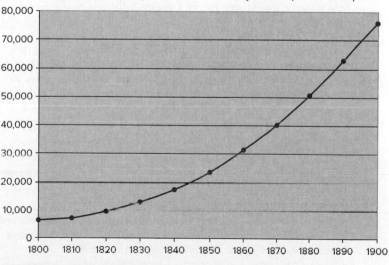

FIGURE 2.3 **A line graph showing trends over time.** To learn how to create a graph like this one, see Figure 20.1 on page 214.

- **E-mail.** **E-mail** is one of the most frequently used forms of written communication. In most classes, you will use e-mail to write to your professor and other students; you may also be able to e-mail a consultant in your school's writing center.

- **Instant messaging.** You can use **instant messaging (IM)** to further your learning in much the same way as e-mail. Some instructors may encourage you to contact them in this way. Otherwise, use IM to save time, and as a complementary tool in a Webinar or on *Facebook.*

- **Text messages.** **Texting** is especially useful for very short, timely messages. Its abbreviations can also make note taking faster.

- **Course Web sites.** Most courses have accompanying Web sites that teachers use to distribute course information: the class syllabus, class assignments, and readings. You may also be working on this site, posting comments on a discussion board or blog and turning in formal assignments. For more on course Web sites, see pages 22-24.

- **Virtual classrooms.** Computers and the Internet make it possible for students to engage in distance learning. Classes conducted entirely online in **virtual classrooms**, and in spoken discussions—sometimes via webcams—allow students to interact in writing, making it easier to save ideas and comments for future use in a first draft.

- **Blogs.** A **blog** is a continually updated site that features dated entries with commentary on a variety of topics and links to Web sites the author (or authors) find interesting, as well as those that permit visitors to upload various kinds of multimedia files, and (sometimes) a space for readers to add comments. These readers, as well as the blog's author, may or may not be experts on the topics. *(For information on assessing a blog's credibility, see Chapter 21, pp. 219-26.)* A class blog may allow students to respond to and analyze readings and comment on one another's drafts. Students may also create their own posts on the blog. Faculty also may use blogs as sites for sharing assignments, where students can access them at any time and ask for clarification. Students can also use a class blog as a site for compiling shared resources. *(See Chapter 14, pp. 169-71.)*

- **Podcasts.** Instructors may record their lectures as downloadable audio or video **podcasts**, making them available to the class for repeated listening or viewing. Popular radio shows, television shows, and newspapers frequently include podcasts; the *New York Times*, for example, has a print book review section and a podcast of reviews. Reputable podcasts such as these are important sources for research projects.

- **Videos.** Outside school and in some college classes, many students and instructors create short videos, which they may post on video sharing sites such as *YouTube*, or *Vimeo.* Although writing projects often address a designated audience, many Web sites intend to address anyone on the Web. Creating your own videos will prepare you to analyze informative and persuasive videos in your life outside school, as well as for course assignments.

─ *the* EVOLVING SITUATION

Netiquette

The term *netiquette* combines the words *Internet* and *etiquette* to form a new word that stands for good manners online. Here are some netiquette guidelines that hold across all electronic rhetorical situations:

- **When you are interacting with real humans**, not machines, practice kindness, patience, and good humor.

- **Limit e-mails to a single topic, and use accurate subject headers.** Include a sufficient portion of the previous text when responding to an e-mail, or use a dash to keep the conversation flowing and to provide context. **For official e-mails, include your name and contact information at the end of every e-mail you send.**

- **Remember that most forms of electronic communication can be reproduced.** Avoid saying anything you would not want attributed to you or forwarded to others. You should not forward another person's words without consent (although this practice is fairly common).

- **Always seek permission to use other people's ideas**, and acknowledge them properly.

- **Always quote and cite correctly the words of others: do not copy other people's words and present them as your own.** This practice, known as plagiarism, is always wrong. *(See Tabs 6–8 for help with citing Internet sources.)*

- **Bear in mind that without cues such as facial expressions, body language, and vocal intonation, your message can easily be misunderstood.** Be wary of including humor that could be misread as sarcasm. Misunderstandings can escalate quickly into *flaming*, the sending of angry, inflammatory posts characterized by heated language.

- **Avoid ALL CAPS.** Readers will think writers are SHOUTING in such messages.

- **When sending text messages, use abbreviations appropriately.** The standard for acceptable shorthand is determined by the level of familiarity between you and the recipient as well as the subject matter of the text.

- **Consider your tone.** Informality is appropriate when interacting with friends, but remember the need for greater formality in using digital communication for academic and professional purposes.

- **Always keep in mind that, although digital communication looks temporary, its traces can last forever.** When you burn a piece of paper, it's gone. Even if you delete something from cyberspace, it can almost always be recovered.

- **Use words economically** and edit carefully.

- **Social media sites.** Sometimes students use **social media sites**—including blogs, Facebook, Twitter, Snapchat, and Instagram—to discuss writing projects, conduct surveys, and locate experts. Postings may be private, from person to person; or public, from one person to many. As is the case with other social media sites (like your own blog), what you post on these sites is potentially public; is visible to colleagues, family, and prospective employers; and may follow you forever.

- **Wikis.** A **wiki** is a Web site that is created collaboratively, often with interlinking Web pages that, taken together, form databases of information. Because multiple people create and edit pages on a wiki site, college students and instructors often use wikis to create collaborative projects. The popular online encyclopedia *Wikipedia* can be accurate but is not always so because not all the people creating or editing it are experts; therefore, instructors tend to discourage its use as a source. The content of some other wikis is created and monitored by specialists and therefore may be more credible. In college, as in life, you must learn enough about a wiki to assess its credibility. *(See Chapter 21: Evaluating Sources, pp. 219-26).*

Most colleges offer course management systems (CMS) like Blackboard, Desire to Learn, Canvas, and Sakai. Although these sites vary, they typically include common features that students can access at any time via a password-protected course Web page.

Some CMS platforms include tools for **peer review**, in which students comment on one another's writing at specific points in the writing process. Specialized software, like the e-book that accompanies this text, makes peer review an efficient, helpful, and accessible writing tool. If your course has such a home page, take time at the beginning of the semester to become familiar with its features—as well as with any related course requirements. *(For more on chat rooms, see Chapter 5: Planning and Shaping, p. 42 and p. 43.)*

CHAPTER 3

Audience and Academic English

To some extent, all college students, indeed all people, must navigate multiple cultures and languages. To solve a problem with your computer software in Dallas, you may be speaking to a tech support person in India. As you stock shelves in a toy store in Omaha, you may be interacting with a supply chain that originates in Shanghai.

The college environment will introduce you to a wide range of cultural contexts that may be new to you. Each of these contexts presents a rhetorical situation that you must learn to navigate:

- **Social contexts:** Whether you are attending a full-time residential program, commuting to classes at a local community college, or taking classes online, college offers opportunities to join new social groups. These groups may be connected by social action within a community, a shared cultural heritage, a common interest, or simply the residence hall in which you live. They may be connected by social media as friends on *Facebook* or as followers on *Twitter*. Whatever context you find yourself in, you should be aware that colleges are generally gathering places for people from a wide range of cultures and backgrounds, with differences in language, communication practices, and social conventions. Learning to respect, accommodate, and enjoy these differences is an essential part of the college experience.

- **Workplace contexts:** Whether you are working as a barista at the local Starbucks, a home health aide for seniors, or an assistant in the campus library, your job will likely come with new demands and expectations, and you will have an advantage if you can communicate effectively. Chapter 17 will present suggestions for navigating the particular situations involved in trying to get or keep a job.

- **Academic contexts:** Disciplines have distinctive languages and cultural expectations. The language of statistics or anthropology, for example, probably sounds strange and new at first to most students who take those courses. Academic English in general involves conventions and forms that require familiarity for college success. This text presents these conventions, and, although it cannot cover the terminology of every academic discipline, it will prepare you for the vast majority of college courses.

In the ways just described, all students are language learners and cultural explorers. In college, however, students who know two or more languages and cultures may find that they have an advantage over those who know only one. Multilingual students can contribute insights about other cultures in a world that is interconnected in ever more complex and sophisticated ways.

This book uses the term *multilingual* to address students from varied cultural, national, and linguistic backgrounds. You may be an international student learning to speak and write English. You may have grown up speaking standard American English at school and another language or dialect at home. Perhaps your family has close ties to another part of the world. You may have moved between the United States and another country more than once. If you came to the United States when young, you may read and write English better than you do your parents' native language.

Because the way we talk influences the way we write, blended forms of English often appear in college students' writing. There is no single "correct" English, but Standard Written English is expected in academic and workplace contexts. Academic language is formal, with an expanded vocabulary as well as complex syntax and culturally specific usage patterns. In addition, disciplines have their own language features. Interacting with classmates as you explore together the specialized language of these academic subjects will provide many benefits. Monolingual and multilingual speakers have much to learn from one another.

3a Become aware of your audience.

If you are familiar with at least two languages and cultures, you already know about multiple ways to interact politely and effectively with other people. All students must carefully assess the classroom situation as a special culture. What does the instructor expect? What counts as evidence? What is polite, and what is not?

1. Joining the academic conversation

In some cultures, asking a question indicates that the student has not done the homework or has not been paying attention. In contrast, instructors in the United States generally encourage students to ask questions and participate in class discussion. The American philosopher Richard Rorty makes the point that the history of philosophy is all about sustaining a lively intellectual conversation, and U.S. classrooms often reflect that principle. Students are usually encouraged to approach the instructor or fellow students outside class to keep the conversation going.

2. Finding out what instructors expect

Just as students are not all the same, neither are instructors. Take advantage of your instructor's office hours—a time designated for further conversation on material discussed in class—to ask questions about assignments as well as other matters.

Instructors in the United States often ask students to form small groups to talk over an issue or solve a problem. All members of such groups are expected to contribute to the conversation and offer ideas. Students usually speak and interact much more informally in these groups than they do with the instructor in class. Peer study groups, whether assigned or formed spontaneously, can be excellent resources for interpreting assignments.

Instructors in different disciplines may use key words in different ways. When biology professors ask for a description of "significant" results, for example, that term may mean something different from what English professors mean when they compare two "significant" fictional characters. Pay attention especially to the terms *analyze, critique*, and *assess* that are used variously. Terms like these are discussed in this book *(see p. 37)*, and your instructor and peers can be helpful, too.

3. Determining what your audience expects

Colleges in the United States, and English-speaking culture more generally, emphasize openly exchanging views, clearly stating opinions, and explicitly supporting judgments with examples, observations, and reasons. In the United States, being direct is highly valued. Audiences in the United States expect speakers and writers to come to the point and will feel impatient without an identifiable thesis statement. *(See 5c on thesis statements.)* At the same time, to communicate successfully in a global context, you should be aware of differing expectations. If, for example, you are sending business correspondence to a Japanese company, you may accomplish your goals more successfully by spending time on courteous opening remarks. Everything depends on the context.

4. Choosing evidence with care

Different cultures, as well as different academic disciplines, expect varying forms of evidence. Most scientists and mathematicians, for example, are convinced by the application of the scientific method. In that sense, science and math are universal languages, but scientists from different fields rely on different kinds of methods and evidence. Some scientists compare the results from experimental groups and control groups, while others emphasize close observation and quantitative analysis. Likewise, different cultures assign varying degrees of importance to firsthand observations, expert opinion, and quotations from sacred or widely respected sources. Once again, it's essential to figure out the context, the writing situation, and what you are trying to achieve within it.

5. Considering the organization your audience expects

Some texts, such as a laboratory report, are organized according to expectations determined by the discipline. *(See 12b.)* But the organization of other texts can vary. In the classroom, careful study of the assignment and the advice provided in this book will assist you in organizing your project effectively. Practicing this kind of analysis should help in writing to multiple, international audiences as well. Seek guidance by studying effective communication in a particular culture. In addition, it never hurts to ask those familiar with the expectations of readers and listeners in a given situation how to communicate politely and successfully.

6. Choosing an appropriate tone

Writing to strangers is different from writing to friends. Whether you are communicating by e-mail or by formal letterhead stationery, you should use a level of formality when addressing professors, and others who are not your close friends, that you would not use in other writing situations. That attention to tone means typing "Dear Professor Maxell" even in an e-mail, using full paragraphs, and avoiding abbreviations. Texting, in contrast, is the ultimate shorthand used by people who know each other well and can literally finish each other's sentences. Once in a while, a professor may invite you to send a text on a simple matter—to confirm, for example, that you have received a message about a classroom relocation. When choosing an appropriate tone, let the writing situation guide you. *(See Chapter 47 for more on tone.)*

3b   Use reading, writing, and speaking to learn more about Academic English.

To develop your facility with Academic English, try using the following strategies:

- **Keep a reading and writing notebook.** Write down thoughts, comments, and questions about the reading assignments in your courses and class discussions. Try to put ideas from the readings into your own words (and note the source). Compare your understanding of a reading with those expressed by your classmates. Make a list of new words and phrases from your reading and from what you overhear. Be alert to idioms, words and phrases that have a special meaning not always included in a simple dictionary definition. Go over these lists with a tutor, a friend, or your writing group.

- **Write a personal journal or blog.** Using English to explore your thoughts, feelings, and questions about your studies and your life in college will help make you feel more at home in the language.

- **Join a study group.** Research shows that nearly all college students benefit from belonging to a study group. Discussing an assignment helps you understand it better. Study groups also provide opportunities to practice some of those new words on your list.

- **Write letters in English.** Letters are a good way to practice the informal style used in conversation. Write to out-of-town acquaintances who do not speak your first language. Write a letter to the college newspaper (though you'll need to be more formal in that situation). You can also write brief notes on paper or through e-mail to instructors, tutors, librarians, secretaries, and other proficient speakers of English.

3c Use learning tools that are available for multilingual students.

The following reference books can also help you as you complete writing tasks for your college courses. You can purchase them in your college's bookstore and find copies in the reference room of your college's library.

ESL dictionary A good dictionary designed especially for second-language students can be a useful source of information about word meanings. Ordinary dictionaries frequently define difficult words with other difficult words. An ESL dictionary defines words more simply.

Thesaurus Look up a word in a thesaurus to find other words with related meanings. The thesaurus can help you expand your vocabulary. However, always look up synonyms in a dictionary before using them because all synonyms differ slightly in meaning.

Dictionary of American idioms An idiom is an expression that is peculiar to a particular language and cannot be understood by looking at the individual words. "To catch a bus" is an idiom.

Desk encyclopedias In the reference room of your college's library and online, you will find brief encyclopedias on every subject from U.S. history to classical or biblical allusions. You may find it useful to look up people, places, and events that are new to you, especially if the person, place, or event is referred to often in U.S. culture.

Credit

Chapter 2: p. 16 From Elaine P. Maimon, et al., *McGraw-Hill Handbook*, 2nd ed. Copyright ©2010 The McGraw-Hill Companies, Inc.

Design Elements: (butterfly/computer): ©Visual Generation/Shutterstock; (other design icons): ©McGraw-Hill Education

2

Writing and Designing Texts

I like to do first drafts at night, when I'm tired, and then do the surgical work in the morning when I'm sharp.

–Alex Haley

©Historical Picture Archive /Corbis/Getty Images

Illuminated manuscripts from the Middle Ages often depict scribes and writers, such as this portrait of the Georgian poet Shota Rustaveli (c. 1160–c. 1220). Then as now, writers transform words and visuals into finished works through careful planning, drafting, revision, and design.

2 Writing and Designing Texts

 Section dealing with visual rhetoric. For a complete listing, see the Quick Guide to Key Resources in Connect.

Tab 2: Writing and Designing Texts

This section will help you answer questions such as these:

Rhetorical Knowledge

- What is a writing situation? (5a)
- When should I use visuals in my writing? What type of visuals fit my writing situation? (5e)
- What should I *not* put on my blog or social networking page? (14d)
- How can I use presentation software (like PowerPoint) effectively? (13d)

Critical Thinking, Reading, and Writing

- How can annotation and summary help me with reading assignments? (4a)
- How can I analyze photographs and other images? (4a)

Processes

- What are the components of the writing process? (5, 6, 7)
- What is a thesis statement? (5c)
- How should I give feedback on my classmates' work? (7a)
- What steps should I take in planning my Web site? (14c)

Knowledge of Conventions

- How can I make my paragraphs clear and effective? (6b)
- What features of document design can help convey my meaning? (8a)

For a general introduction to writing outcomes see 1e, pages 13–15.

CHAPTER 4

Reading and Writing: The Critical Connection

Like writing, critical reading is a process that involves moving back and forth, rather than in a straight line. Critical readers, thinkers, and writers get intellectually involved. They recognize that meanings and values are made, not found, so they pose pertinent questions, note significant features, and examine the credibility of various kinds of texts.

—CHECKLIST   Reading Critically

☐ **Preview** the text before you read it.
☐ **Read** the text for its topic and point.
☐ **Analyze** the *who, what,* and *why* of the text by **annotating** it as you reread it and **summarizing** what you have read.
☐ **Synthesize** through making connections.
☐ **Evaluate** what you've read.

In this context, the word *critical* means "thoughtful." When you read critically, you recognize the literal meaning of the text, make inferences about unstated meanings, and then make your own judgments in response.

Advances in technology have made it easier than ever to obtain information in a variety of ways. It is essential to "read" critically not just written texts but visuals, sounds, video, and other multimedia texts as well. We use the word *text* to refer to works that readers, viewers, or listeners invest with meaning and that can be critically analyzed.

👁 **4a**   Read critically.

1. Previewing
Critical reading begins with **previewing** a text—looking over the information about its author and publication and quickly scanning its contents to gain a sense of its context, purpose, and meaning.

Previewing written texts   As you preview a text, ask questions about its approach and claims, and assess the credibility of its evidence and arguments.

- **Author:** Who wrote this piece? What are the writer's credentials? Who is the writer's employer? What is the writer's occupation? Age? What are their interests and values?
- **Purpose:** What do the title and first and last paragraphs—which are often the points of greatest emphasis—tell you about the purpose of this piece? Do the headings and visuals provide clues to its purpose? What might have motivated the author to write it? Is the main purpose to inform, to interpret, to argue, to entertain, or is it to accomplish something else?
- **Audience:** Who is the target of the author's information or persuasion? Is the author addressing you or readers like you?

- **Content:** What does the title tell you about the piece? Does the first paragraph include the main point? What do the headings tell you about the gist of the text? Does the conclusion say what the author has focused on or show its significance?

- **Context:** Is the publication date current? Does the date matter? What kind of publication is it? Where and by whom was it published? Does the publisher have biases about the topic? If it was published electronically, was it posted by the author or by an organization with a special interest? What resources is the author drawing on and how current are they? Did it undergo a peer review process?

Previewing visuals   You can use most of the previewing questions for written texts to preview visuals. You should also ask some additional questions, however. For example, suppose you were asked to preview the public service advertisement shown in Figure 4.1.

Here are some preview questions and possible responses:

- **In what context does the visual appear?** Was it intended to be viewed on its own or as part of a larger work? Is it part of a series of images (for example, a graphic novel, a music video, or a film)? This public service advertisement appeared in several publications targeted to

Source: United States Peace Corps, www.peacecorps.gov

FIGURE 4.1 Peace Corps advertisement. The text superimposed on this photograph reads: "**What happens in Botswana doesn't stay in Botswana.** When you help make a better life for others abroad, you also develop skills and experience that will serve your community back home. Life is calling. How far will you go?"

college students. As the logo in the lower right-hand corner indicates, the ad was produced by the Peace Corps to recruit volunteers.

- **What does the visual depict? What is the first thing you notice in the visual?** The scene is a bare schoolroom in Botswana. *(Look at the world map in* Connect, *to find Botswana in Africa.)* As sun streams from a window, one young man in the foreground looks on as a younger boy erases a blackboard. On the blackboard, a handwritten poster appears with points of advice, for example, "Accept responsibility for your decision." The sunlight shining directly on the boy at the blackboard draws the viewer's attention to him. (Compare the light in this advertisement with that in Johannes Vermeer's painting *The Geographer* in Tab 13.)

- **Is the visual accompanied by audio or printed text?** Bold text appears in the center of the image, followed by smaller print directly addressed to the viewer. The phone number and Web address for the Peace Corps are printed in the lower left, and another appeal to the viewer, followed by the Peace Corps logo, is printed in the lower right.

─ the EVOLVING SITUATION

Evaluating Context in Different Kinds of Publications and Disciplines

Nothing can be understood in isolation. We evaluate meaning in terms of surrounding conditions including types of publications and academic disciplines.

- **For a book:** Are you looking at the original publication or a reprint? What is the publisher's reputation? University presses, for example, are selective and usually publish scholarly works. A vanity press—one that requires authors to pay to publish their work—is not selective at all.

- **For an article in a periodical:** Look at the list of editors and their affiliations. What do you know about the journal, magazine, or newspaper in which this article appears? Are the articles reviewed by experts in a particular field before they are published?

- **For a Web page:** Who created the page? A Web page named for a political candidate, for example, may actually have been put on the Web by opponents.

Whether you are studying a book, an article, or a Web page, consider how the same topic is handled from the perspective of different disciplines. A book on the fall of the Berlin Wall (1989) will differ, for example, depending on whether the author addresses the topic from a historical, a political, or an economic point of view.

2. Reading and recording initial impressions

Read the selection for its literal meaning. Identify the topic and the main point. Note difficult passages to come back to as well as interesting ideas. Look up unfamiliar terms. Record your initial impressions:

- If the text or image is an argument, what opinion is being expressed? Were you persuaded by the argument?
- Did you have an emotional response to the text or image? Were you surprised, amused, or angered by anything in it?
- What was your initial impression of the writer or speaker?
- What key ideas did you take away from the work?

3. Using annotation and summary to analyze a text

Once you understand the literal or surface meaning of a text, you can analyze and interpret it. To **analyze** a text is to break it down into significant parts and examine how those parts relate to each other. Critical readers analyze a text in order to **interpret** it and come to a better understanding of its meanings.

Annotation combines reading with analysis. To annotate a text, read through it slowly and carefully while asking yourself the *who, what, how,* and *why* questions. As you read, underline or make separate notes about words, phrases, and sentences that strike you as significant or puzzling—even if you don't know why at that point—and write down your questions and observations.

SAMPLE ANNOTATED PASSAGE

In July 2016, the lower portion of a valley glacier in the Aru Range of Tibet detached and barreled into a nearby valley, killing nine people and hundreds of animals. The huge avalanche, one of the largest scientists had ever seen, sent a tongue of debris spreading across 9 square kilometers (3 square miles). With debris reaching speeds of 140 kilometers (90 miles) per hour, the avalanche was remarkably fast for its size.

Researchers were initially baffled about how it had happened. The glacier was on a nearly flat slope that was too shallow to cause avalanches, especially fast-moving ones. What's more, the collapse happened at an elevation where permafrost was widespread; it should have securely anchored the glacier to the surface.

Two months later, it happened again—this time to a glacier just a few kilometers away. One gigantic avalanche was unusual; two in a row was unprecedented. The second collapse raised even more questions. Had an earthquake played a role in triggering them? Did climate change play a role? Should we expect more of these mega-avalanches?

—ADAM VOILAND, "What Caused Twin Mega-Avalanches in Tibet?"

Opens with a description of an event that inspired the curiosity of climate scientists.

The author converts kilometers to miles—helpful for readers unfamiliar with the metric system of measurement.

Should the author explain how widespread permafrost could prevent such an occurrence?

A **summary** conveys the basic content of a text. When you summarize an essay or article, your goal is to condense, without commentary, the text's main points into one paragraph. Even when you are writing a summary of a longer work, use the fewest words possible. A summary should be clear and brief, descriptive and not evaluative. A summary requires getting to the essence of the matter without oversimplification and misrepresentation. *(For specific instructions on how to write a summary, see Chapter 24: Working with Sources and Avoiding Plagiarism, pp. 237–54.)*

Questioning the text   Analysis and interpretation require a critical understanding of the *who, what, how,* and *why* of a text:

- **What is the writer's stance, or attitude toward the subject?** Does the writer appear to be objective, or does the writer seem to have personal feelings about the subject?

- **What is the writer's voice?** Is it like that of a reasonable judge, an enthusiastic preacher, or a reassuring friend?

- **What assumptions does the writer make about the audience?** Does the writer assume that readers agree, or does the writer try to build agreement? Does the writer choose examples and evidence with a certain audience in mind?

- **What is the writer's primary purpose?** Is it to present findings, offer an objective analysis, or argue for a particular action or opinion?

- **How does the writer develop ideas?** Does the writer define key terms? Include supporting facts? Tell relevant stories? Provide logical reasons?

- **Does the text appeal to emotions?** Does the writer use words, phrases, clichés, images, or examples that are emotionally charged?

- **Is the text fair?** Does the writer consider opposing ideas, arguments, or evidence fairly?

- **Is the evidence strong?** Does the writer provide sufficient and persuasive evidence?

- **Where is the argument strongest and weakest?**

- **Is the text effective?** Have your assumptions on this subject been changed by the text?

Visuals, too, can be subjected to critical analysis, as the comments a reader made on the Peace Corps ad indicate *(see Figure 4.2).*

4. Synthesizing your observations in a critical-response paper

To **synthesize** means to bring together, to make something out of different parts. In the last stage of critical reading, you pull together all your thinking—in your summary, analysis, and interpretation—into a coherent whole to support a claim. Whether you realize it or not, you synthesize material every day. When you hear contrasting accounts of a party from two different people, you

Composition of the photograph like Vermeer's paintings of sunlight illuminating an indoor scene. Subtle appeal to students of art history?

Reference to Las Vegas slogan, "What happens here stays here." Secrets of Las Vegas (superficial fun) stay there because of shame. Working with the Peace Corps (worthwhile life direction) in Botswana illuminates your life–and the world (Reference to sunlight?).

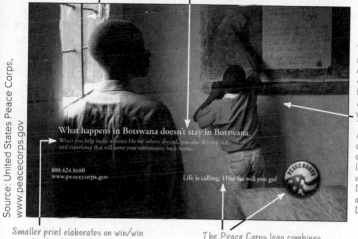

The boy is reaching up to erase or wash something from the blackboard. An older boy watches–also "reaching"? A poster covering part of the board lists principles valuable in Botswana and in the U.S.A.

Smaller print elaborates on win/win opportunity of the Peace Corps vs. odds of losing games in Las Vegas.

The Peace Corps logo combines the globe with the American flag–a global view of patriotism. How far will you go geographically and personally?

Source: United States Peace Corps, www.peacecorps.gov

FIGURE 4.2 Sample annotations on the Peace Corps ad.

assess the credibility of each source; you select the information that is most pertinent to you; you evaluate the story that each one tells; and, finally, you create a composite, or synthesis, of what you think really went on. When you synthesize information from two or more texts, you follow the same process.

4b   Write critically.

Sharpening your ability to think critically and to express your views effectively is one of the main purposes of undergraduate study. When you write critically, you gain a voice in the important discussions and decisions of our society. Writing can help you do this.

In college and beyond, you will apply critical-thinking skills to different writing purposes. Tab 3 of this book (*Common Assignments across the Curriculum*) focuses on writing to **inform** (*Chapter 9, pp. 97–110*), to **analyze** (*Chapter 10, pp. 110–119*), and to **argue** (*Chapter 11, pp. 119–42*). In each case, you will present evidence that supports a central point, or **thesis**. For your writing to be convincing and effective, you must consider your rhetorical situation: your purpose, audience, and the context of your assignment.

CHAPTER 5

Planning and Shaping

This chapter will help you determine the kind of writing a particular assignment requires and offer strategies for beginning a first draft. After reviewing an assignment, be sure to seek clarification from your instructor. It is far better to ask questions early on rather than to start over later or, even worse, to turn in an assignment that does not do the job.

5a Learn how to approach assignments.

As a first step toward the goal of completing an assignment successfully, gain a clear understanding of the writing situation, and then make choices based on that knowledge.

1. Understanding the writing situation

Writers respond to **writing situations.** When you write a lab report for a science class, create a flyer for a student government candidate, or send an e-mail inviting a friend for coffee, you shape the communication (**message**) to suit the purpose, audience, and context. The results for each situation will differ. All communication occurs because something is at stake, which the message addresses. **Exigence** refers to the issue or situation that prompts the occasion for the message. The **audience** receives the message. Audience members may be friendly or hostile to the writer's message, and their cultures and backgrounds will influence their reactions. Your **purpose** may be to inform them or to move them to action. Your **context** is the environment in which the communication takes place, including the means of communication available to you and the events that are occurring around you. *(For more on the writing situation, or rhetorical situation, see Chapter 2, pp. 16-17.)*

2. Writing about a question

Most of your academic writing will be in response to assignments that pose a question or ask you to formulate one. The particular course you are taking defines a range of questions that are appropriate within a given discipline. Here are examples of the way your course could help define the questions you might ask if, for example, you are writing about Thomas Jefferson:

> **U.S. history:** Did Jefferson's ownership of slaves affect his public stance on slavery, and, if so, how?

> **Political science:** To what extent did Jefferson's conflict with the courts redefine the balance of power among the three branches of government?

> **Education:** Given his beliefs about the relationship between democracy and public education, what might Jefferson think about contemporary proposals for a school voucher system?

3. Being clear about your purpose

What is the kind of assignment you are responding to? Think beyond the simple statement "I have to write an essay." Are you expected to inform, interpret, or argue?

- **Informing:** writing to transmit knowledge. Terms like *classify, illustrate, report,* and *survey* are often associated with the task of informing.

- **Interpreting:** writing to produce understanding. Terms like *analyze, compare, explain,* and *reflect* are more likely to appear when the purpose is interpreting.

- **Arguing:** writing to make a claim or negotiate matters of public debate. Terms like *agree, assess, defend,* and *refute* go with the task of arguing.

Some terms, such as *comment, consider,* and *discuss,* do not point to a particular purpose, but many others do. If you are not clear about the kind of work you are expected to do, ask your professor.

4. Selecting the appropriate genre and medium

Genre simply means kind of writing. Poems, stories, and plays are genres of literature; lab reports, essays, and case studies are genres of nonfiction.

Sometimes an assignment will specify the kind of work, or genre, you are being asked to produce. For example, you may be asked to write a report (an informative genre), a comparative analysis (an interpretive genre), or a critique (an argumentative genre).

Some genres, like the case study, are common in particular fields such as sociology and finance but not in other disciplines. Understanding the genre that is called for is important in completing an assignment successfully. If you are supposed to write a description of a snake for a field guide, you will not be successful if you write a poem—even a very good poem—about a snake. *(See Tab 3: Common Assignments across the Curriculum, pp. 97–172.)* Understanding genre also helps you make decisions about language. For a description of a snake in a field guide, you would use highly specific terms to differentiate one type of snake from another. A poem would incorporate striking images—vivid words and phrases that evoke the senses—and other forms of literary language.

Writers today have wide choices in **medium,** whether in print or online, and many instructors may encourage you to use the appropriate technology for your writing situation. You can ask yourself, for example, what might be the best medium to persuade your college administration to repave the parking lot with materials that protect the environment. Would the print or online medium available in your student newspaper be best, or would it be more effective to use presentation software at a student senate meeting? Or perhaps a Web page or *YouTube* video might make the point more emphatically? In 1964, when Marshall McLuhan coined the now famous aphorism "The medium is the message," he anticipated the possibilities for expression available today.

5. Asking questions about your audience

Who makes up your audience? In college, instructors—and sometimes classmates—are usually your primary readers, of course, but they may represent a larger group who have an interest or a stake in your topic. An education professor reads and evaluates a text as a representative of several possible groups—other students in the course, other professors in the program, experts in educational policy, school board members, public school principals, and parents of school-age children, among others.

6. Determining an appropriate rhetorical stance

Your **stance** is determined by the position you take in relationship to your audience and to the evidence. In other words, you might take one stance in your workplace writing as an employee and possibly shift to another stance when you assume leadership responsibilities. As a college student, your stance is seldom that of an expert, though you can take the stance of a novice who is becoming an expert, someone who is informed, reasonable, and fair.

7. Deciding on your tone

The identity, knowledge level, and needs of your audience will determine the tone of your writing. In speech, the sentence "I am surprised at you" can express anger, excitement, or disappointment depending on your tone of voice. In writing, your content, style, and word choice communicate **tone.** Consider the differences in tone in the following passages on the subject of a cafeteria makeover:

SARCASTIC	"I am special," the poster headline under the smirking face announces. Well, good for you. And I'm *especially* glad that cafeteria prices are up because so much money was spent on motivational signs and new paint colors.
SERIOUS	Although the new colors in the cafeteria are electric and clashing, color in general does brighten the space and distinguish it from the classrooms. But the motivational posters are not inspiring and should be removed.

The tone in the first passage is sarcastic and obviously intended for other students. An audience of school administrators probably would not appreciate the humor. The second passage is more serious and respectful—the appropriate tone for most college writing—while still offering a critique. *(For more on appropriate language, see Chapter 47.)*

8. Considering the context

The context, or surrounding circumstances, influences how an audience receives your communication. Your assignment goes a long way toward establishing the context in which you write. Your instructor probably has specified a length, due date, and genre. Context also involves broader conversations about your topic.

— CHECKLIST   Understanding the Writing Situation

Ask yourself these questions as you approach a writing assignment.

Topic *(See 5a.3.)*

☐ What are you being asked to write about?

☐ Have you narrowed your topic to a question that interests you?

☐ What kind of visuals, if any, would be appropriate for this topic?

☐ What types of sources will help you explore this topic? Where will you look for them?

Purpose *(See 5a.4.)*

☐ What do you want your writing to accomplish? Are you trying to inform, analyze, or argue? (Which key words in your assignment indicate the purpose?)

☐ Do you want to intensify, clarify, complicate, or change your audience's assumptions or opinions?

Genre and Medium *(See 5a.4.)*

☐ What genre would best support your purpose?

☐ What medium are you using (print text, video podcast, Web site, presentation software) and why?

Audience, Stance, and Tone *(See 5a.6, 5a.7, and 5a.8.)*

☐ What are your audience's demographics (education level, social status, gender, cultural background, and language)? How diverse is your audience?

☐ What does your audience know about the topic?

☐ What common assumptions and different opinions do these audience members bring to the issue? Are they likely to agree with you, or will you have to persuade them?

☐ What is your relationship to them? How does that relationship influence your rhetorical stance?

☐ What sort of tone would appeal to this audience: informal, entertaining, reasonable, or forceful? Why?

Context *(See 5a.8.)*

☐ Does your topic deal with issues of interest to the public or to members of an academic discipline?

☐ What have other writers said recently about this topic?

☐ How much time do you have to complete the assignment?

☐ What is the desired length (which may be expressed in a specific number of pages or words)?

Your course gives you background on what others in the discipline have said and what issues have been debated. Current events, on campus and in society as a whole, provide a context for public writing.

5b   Explore your ideas.

The following **invention techniques** or **prewriting activities** are designed to help you begin. Remember that what you write at this stage is for your eyes only—no one will be judging your work. You can explore ideas in either a print or digital **journal,** which is simply a place to record your thoughts on a regular basis. *(For more on journals, see p. 42.)* *(For more on journals, see p. 42.)* Your class notes constitute a type of academic journal, as do the notes you take on your reading and research.

As you explore, turn off your internal critic and generate as much material as possible.

1. Freewriting

To figure out what you are thinking, try **freewriting,** typically for a limited period of time (five minutes, for example). Just write whatever occurs to you about a topic. If nothing comes to mind, then write "nothing comes to mind" until you do think of something. The trick is to keep pushing forward without stopping or worrying about spelling, punctuation, or grammar. Usually, you will discover some implicit point in your seemingly random writing. You might then try doing some **focused freewriting,** beginning with a point or a specific question to jump-start your thinking. The following is a portion of Diane Chen's freewriting about Dorothea Lange's photograph *Migrant Mother* in response to an assignment to analyze an image.

> I want to talk about what it means to view photographs of poverty, but also to admire the artistic components of such photographs. I feel like those two things shouldn't go together—but my reaction to Dorothea Lange's work inspires me to consider both. In fact, her skill as a photographer makes it harder to look away from the sometimes difficult images she captured.

(You can read the second draft of Chen's essay in Chapter 7 on pp. 82–84.)

2. Listing or brainstorming

Another strategy is to **brainstorm** by starting with a topic and listing all the words, phrases, images, and ideas that come to mind; again, limiting the time to five minutes or so can "force" ideas. When you brainstorm in this way, don't worry about whether the individual thoughts or ideas are "right." Just get them down on paper or on screen.

Once you have completed your list, go through it looking for patterns and connections. Highlight or connect related ideas, or group related material together. Move apparently extraneous material or ideas to the end of the list or to a separate page. Now zero in on the areas of most interest, and add any new ideas that occur to you. Arrange the items into main points and subpoints if necessary. Later, this material may form the basis of an outline for your paper.

Here is part of a list that Diane Chen produced for her paper about a photograph:

> Documentary photography—photojournalism versus art photography
> Migrant workers—what is the story/history behind this photo?
> Composition communicates information about subject, and the mother's facial expression is significant

3. Clustering

Clustering, sometimes called **mapping,** is a brainstorming technique that generates categories and connections from the beginning. To make an idea cluster, do the following:

- Write your topic in the center of a piece of paper, and circle it.

- Surround the topic with subtopics that interest you. Circle each, and draw a line from it to the center circle. You may also connect the circles to each other.

- Brainstorm more ideas, connecting each one to a subtopic already on the sheet or making it into a new subtopic.

Web sites such as <https://bubbl.us> allow you to use this technique on the computer, alone or in groups. As she explored her ideas about the Dorothea Lange photograph, Diane Chen prepared the cluster that appears in Figure 5.1.

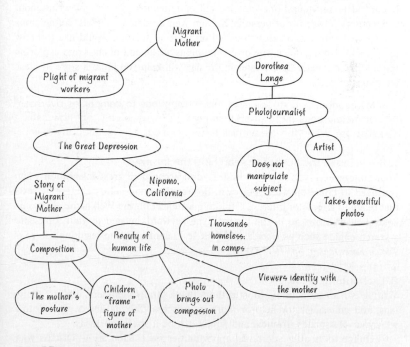

FIGURE 5.1 Diane Chen's cluster about Lange's photograph.

4. Questioning

The journalist's five *w*'s and an *h (who? what? where? when? why?* and *how?)* can help you find specific ideas and details. For example, here are some questions that would apply to the photograph:

- Who is the photographer, who are her subjects, and who is the audience?
- What is the photographer's attitude toward her subjects?
- Where was this picture shot and first exhibited?
- When did these events take place?
- Why are the people in this photograph living in a camp?
- How do I react to this image?

For other examples of what to question and how, you should take note of the problems or questions your professor poses in class discussions. If you are using a textbook in your course, check out the study questions.

5. Reviewing your notes and annotations

Review your notes and annotations on your reading or research. *(For details on annotating, see Chapter 4. For details on keeping a research journal, see Chapter 24.)* If you are writing about something you have observed, review your notes and sketches. These immediate comments and reactions are excellent sources for ideas.

6. Keeping a journal or notebook

Record ideas and questions in a journal or notebook. You might write about connections between your personal life and your academic subjects, connections among your subjects, or ideas touched on in class that you would like to know more about. Jotting down one or two thoughts at the end of class and exploring those ideas at greater length later in the day will help you build a store of ideas for future projects.

> My economics textbook says that moving jobs to companies overseas ultimately does more good than harm to the economy, but how can that be? When the electronics factory closed, it devastated my town.

7. Browsing in the library or searching the Internet

Your college library is filled with ideas—and it can be a great inspiration when you need to come up with your own. Browse the bookshelves containing texts that relate to a topic of interest. Exploring a subject on the Web is the electronic equivalent of browsing in the library. Type keywords related to your topic into a search engine such as *Google,* and visit several sites on the resulting list. *(See Tab 5: Researching, pp. 191–259.)*

8. Exchanging ideas

Writing is a social activity. Most authors thank family members, editors, librarians, and colleagues for help on work in progress. Talking about your writing with your classmates, friends, and family can be a source of ideas.

Online tools offer additional opportunities for collaboration. Discuss your assignments by exchanging e-mail. If your class has a Web site, you might exchange ideas using peer review software. Other options include instant messaging (IM), text messaging, social media, and blogs. *Facebook* and *Twitter* provide additional opportunities to discuss your work with friends. Keep a list of your interactions so that you can write a note or page of acknowledgment for the help and encouragement you receive.

Writing e-mail   When you work on papers with classmates, you can use e-mail in the following ways:

- To check your understanding of the assignment
- To try out various topics
- To ask each other questions
- To share freewriting, listing, and other exploratory writing
- To respond to each other's ideas

Chatting about ideas   You can use online chat rooms as well as other virtual spaces to share ideas. **Instant messaging (IM)** also permits real-time communication. Exchanging ideas with other writers via IM can help you clarify your thinking on a topic.

Exchanging text messages   **Text messaging** can be useful to writers in two ways. First, you can text your ideas for an assignment to a classmate (or—with permission—your instructor) for response. Second, you can use abbreviations commonly used in texting for speedier note taking both in class and for outside research. Such shorthand should *never* be used in submitted work.

5c   Develop a working thesis.

The **thesis** or **claim** is the central idea of your project. It should communicate a specific point about your topic and suit the purpose of the assignment. As you explore your topic, ideas for your thesis will begin to emerge. You can focus these ideas by drafting a preliminary or working **thesis statement,** which is typically one or two sentences long. As you draft and revise, you may change your thesis several times to make it stronger.

To develop a thesis, answer a question posed by your assignment. *(For more about questions, see p. 42.)* For example, an assignment in a political science class might ask you to defend or critique "The Limits of the Welfare State," an article by George Will on the conflict between limited government and unlimited human rights. The question your thesis must answer is, "Is George Will's position that government should not be responsible for the economic welfare of its citizens reasonable?"

To create a strong thesis, you will need to think critically, developing a point of view based on reading course materials and doing research. Not all theses can be stated in one sentence, but all strong theses are suitable, specific, and significant.

1. Making sure your thesis is suitable

All theses make an assertion about a topic, but these assertions differ. A thesis for an argument will take a clear position on an issue or recommend an action; a thesis for an informative or interpretive project will often preview the project's content or express the writer's insight into the topic. All the following theses are on the same topic, but each is for a project with a different purpose:

THESIS TO INFORM

James Madison and Woodrow Wilson had different views on the government's role in the economic well-being of its citizens.

THESIS TO INTERPRET

The economic ideas George Will expresses in "The Limits of the Welfare State" are more reactionary than politically conservative.

THESIS TO ARGUE

George Will's contention that government should not be responsible for the economic well-being of its citizens does not adequately take into account the economic complexities of twenty-first century society.

2. Making sure your thesis is specific

Vague theses usually lead to weak, unfocused texts. Avoid thesis statements that simply announce your topic, state an obvious fact about it, or offer a general observation:

ANNOUNCEMENT

I will discuss the article "The Limits of the Welfare State" by George Will. [*What is the writer's point about the article?*]

STATEMENT OF FACT

The article "The Limits of the Welfare State" by George Will is about the need for limited government. [*This thesis gives us information about the article, but it does not make a specific point about it.*]

GENERAL OBSERVATION

George Will's article "The Limits of the Welfare State" is interesting. [*While this thesis makes a point about the article, the point could apply to many articles. What makes this article worth reading?*]

In contrast, a specific thesis signals a focused, well-developed composition.

SPECIFIC

George Will, in his article "The Limits of the Welfare State," is wrong about the government's lack of responsibility for the economic welfare of its citizens. His interpretation of the Constitution is questionable, his reasoning about history is flawed, and, above all, his definitions of limits are too narrow.

In this example, the thesis expresses the writer's particular point—there are three reasons to reject Will's argument. It also forecasts the structure of the whole project.

Note: A thesis statement can be longer than one sentence (if necessary) to provide a framework for your main idea. All the sentences taken together, though, should build to one specific, significant point that fits the purpose of your assignment and of the rhetorical situation. (Some instructors may prefer that you limit your thesis statements to one sentence.)

---

3. Making sure your thesis is significant

A topic that makes a difference to you is much more likely to make a difference to your readers, though you should be sure to connect your interest to theirs. When you are looking for possible theses, be sure to challenge yourself to develop one that you care about.

5d   Plan a structure that suits your assignment.

Every writing project should have the following components:

- A beginning, or **introduction,** which hooks readers and usually states the thesis

- A middle, or **body,** which develops the main idea of the project in a series of paragraphs—each making a point supported by specific details

- An ending, or **conclusion,** which gives readers a sense of completion, often by offering a final comment on the thesis

Typically, you will state your thesis in the introduction. However, in personal, narrative, or descriptive writing, you may instead imply the thesis through the details and evidence you present. Or you may begin with background and contextual material leading up to your thesis. In other cases, the thesis may be most effective at the end. This tactic works well when you are arguing for a position that your audience is likely to oppose.

It is not essential to prepare an outline before you start drafting; indeed, some writers prefer to discover how to connect and develop their ideas as they compose. However, an outline of your first draft will help you spot organizational problems or places where the support for your thesis is weak.

—the EVOLVING SITUATION

Using Presentation Software as a Writing Process Tool

Presentation-software slides provide a useful tool for exploring and organizing your ideas before you start drafting. They can also prompt feedback from peer reviewers and others. Here is a way to begin:

- Far in advance of the due date, create a brief, three- to five-slide presentation—with visuals if appropriate—that previews the key points you intend to make in the paper.

- Present the preview to an audience of friends, classmates, or perhaps even your instructor. Ask for suggestions for improvement and advice for developing the presentation into a completed text.

1. Preparing an informal plan

A **scratch outline** is a simple list of points, without the levels of subordination found in more complex outlines. Scratch outlines are useful for briefer papers. Here is a scratch outline for an analysis of Dorothea Lange's photograph *Migrant Mother*:

- *Migrant Mother* raised awareness of the issue of poverty in America during the Great Depression, and called for social change.

- Lange felt for her subjects; her consideration of them allows her photographs to illustrate the need for social change.

- *Migrant Mother*—describe the subjects, framing, and overall composition, and the emotions it evokes.

- Support Lange's credibility by mentioning her Guggenheim Fellowship.

A **do/say plan** is a more detailed type of informal outline. To come up with such a plan, review your notes and other relevant material. Then write down your working thesis and list what you will say for each of the following "do" categories: introduce, support and develop, and conclude. Here is an example:

Thesis: George Will is wrong about the government's lack of responsibility for the economic welfare of its citizens.

1. **Introduce** the issue and my focus.

   - Use two examples to contrast rich and poor: during the period 2007–2009, the poverty rate increased to 14.3%, a 15-year high (Eckholm). During the same period, the income levels of the wealthiest Americans continued to increase; for example, the top 0.1% had 8% of the total income in the United States in 2008, up from 2% in 1973 (Noah). Say that the issue is how to evaluate increasing economic inequality and its consequences, and introduce Will's article "The Limits of the Welfare State." Summarize Will's argument.

- Give Will credit for raising issue, but then state thesis: he's wrong about limited government when it comes to citizens' economic well-being.

2. **Support and develop** thesis that Will's argument is wrong.

- Point out that Will relies on a strict construction of the Constitution in his defense of natural economic rights.

- Point out one thing that Madison and Wilson would agree on: government should be limited in the exercise of "untrammeled power" over its citizens.

- Show that government's actions for the well-being of its citizens are appropriate given the natural right of "the pursuit of happiness."

- Say that Will makes fun of those who see the Constitution as a living document in response to evolving times. Will's idea of limited government is too narrow. If government does not focus on economic well-being, then how will U.S. society thrive in times of economic hardship?

3. **Conclude** that Will doesn't ask or answer such key questions because he believes, quoting former British prime minister Margaret Thatcher, that government "always runs out of other people's money." Follow with quote from political analyst James Carvell, "It's the economy, stupid!"?

In outlining his plan, this student has already begun drafting because as he works on the outline, he gets a clearer sense of what he thinks is wrong with Will's argument. He starts writing sentences that he is likely to include in the first complete draft.

2. Preparing a formal outline

A **formal outline** classifies and divides the information you have gathered, showing main points, supporting ideas, and specific details by organizing them into levels of subordination.

A **topic outline** uses single words or phrases; a **sentence outline** states every idea in a sentence. Because the process of division always results in at least two parts, in a formal outline every I must have a II; every A, a B; and so on. Also, items placed at the same level must be of the same kind; for example, if I is London, then II can be New York City but not the Bronx or Wall Street. Items at the same level should also be grammatically parallel; if A is "Choosing screen icons," then B can be "Creating away messages" but not "Away messages."

Here is a formal sentence outline for an analysis of Dorothea Lange's photograph *Migrant Mother*:

Thesis Statement: As a photojournalist who empathetically captured the struggles of her subjects on film, Lange was able to impart compassion to her audience and in turn inspire change.

I. Lange was commissioned to photograph migrant workers and families in the Depression era, and her work in this area is well known.

II. Lange had empathy for her subjects and her consideration of them allows her photographs to illustrate the need for social change.

A. She showed the public the reality of life for migrant workers.
   1. She was not just an artist, but a photojournalist using documentary techniques.
   2. Lange's work was important in that it provided a perspective on poverty and inspired social change.
B. The photograph *Migrant Mother* is one of Lange's most famous.
   1. The photograph depicts harsh conditions faced by a migrant worker and her three children in Nipomo, California, in 1936.
   2. Lange's technique involved taking many shots, getting closer to the subject as she photographed.
   3. It captures the real-life struggle and allows viewers to see the despair suffered at this time in our history.
   4. The photo remains an iconic representation of poverty and injustice.
C. This photo reveals Lange's compassion for her subjects.
   1. Her three children are gathered around her, with the mother's face as the central focus of the photograph.
   2. The mother's expression looks to the distance and shows evidence of her distress and worry.
   3. Her children cling to her but look away, depicting their need and the mother's helplessness.
   4. The mother's expression tells the story of her despair.
   5. The mother's posture and the hand placed against her face with elbow in her lap suggest deep thought—and possibly depression.
   6. The physical posture of the mother also represents her family's social position.
   7. The ragged and dirty clothes of the children and mother help illustrate the extent of the hardships suffered by migrant workers.
   8. Lange communicates the dire circumstances through these details.
III. *Migrant Mother* and others in Lange's body of work raised awareness of the issue of poverty in America during this time, and called for social change.
   1. In 1941, Lange won a Guggenheim Fellowship for her work.
   2. Lange was recognized as one of the most iconic photographers of the twentieth century.
   3. Her legacy is the photographs like *Migrant Mother,* which opened Americans' eyes to social issues of the time and inspired change.

5e Consider using visuals and multimedia elements, depending on your purpose and audience.

Technology makes it easy to include other types of elements such as pictures, graphs, sounds, and videos—all with the goal of improving a specific project. Always ask, What do multimedia materials contribute to the project?

When you use graphs, images, audio files, or videos, always credit your source, and be aware that most visuals and other multimodal elements are protected by copyright. If you plan to use a photograph as part of a Web page, for example, you will usually need to obtain permission from the copyright holder. *(For information about finding visuals, audio, and video, see Tab 5: Researching, pp. 191–259.)*

1. Using visuals effectively

Visuals such as tables, charts, and graphs can clarify complex data or ideas. Effective visuals are used for specific purposes, and each type of visual illustrates some kinds of material better than others. For example, compare the table and the line graph on pages 49–50. Both present data that show changes over time, but does one strike you as clearer or more powerful than the other?

Caution: Because the use of visual elements is more acceptable in some fields than in others, you may want to ask your instructor for advice before planning to include visuals in your project.

---

2. Using audio and video effectively

You might use audio elements such as music, interviews, or speeches to present or illustrate your major points. Video elements—clips from films, TV, *YouTube, Vimeo,* or your personal archive—are likewise valuable for clear explanation or powerful argument. *Camtasia* is a useful tool for creating and editing your own demonstration videos by recording what you see on your screen. You might also consider using Prezi as a more dynamic alternative to PowerPoint as it can incorporate videos.

Types of Visuals and Their Uses

TABLES

Tables organize precise data for readers. Because the measurements in the example include decimals, it would be difficult to plot them on a graph without including very small cells.

Emissions from Waste (Tg CO_2 Eq.)

Gas/Source	1990	2005	2007	2008	2009	2010	2011
CH_4	**163.7**	**129**	**128.2**	**130.2**	**129.8**	**123.2**	**119.2**
Landfills	147.8	112.5	111.6	113.6	113.3	106.8	103.0
Wastewater treatment	15.9	16.5	16.6	16.6	16.5	16.4	16.2
N_2O	**0.5**	**0.4**	**0.4**	**0.4**	**0.4**	**0.4**	**0.4**
Incineration of waste	0.5	0.4	0.4	0.4	0.4	0.4	0.4
Total	**164.2**	**129.4**	**128.6**	**130.6**	**130.2**	**123.6**	**119.6**

Note: Totals may not sum due to independent rounding.
U.S. Environmental Protection Agency. "Inventory of U.S. Greenhouse Gas Emissions and Sinks: 1990–2011." *U.S. Environmental Protection Agency, Apr. 2013:27–29.* Web. Oct. 2013.

BAR GRAPHS

Bar graphs highlight comparisons between two or more variables, such as the percentage of men and women employed in various jobs in the nation's newsrooms. They allow readers to see relative sizes quickly.

Data from Table L, "2013: U.S. Newsroom Employment Declines," *ASNE Newsroom Census* (American Society of News Editors; 25 Jun. 2013; Web; 30 Nov. 2013).

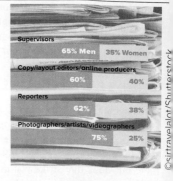

PIE CHARTS

Pie charts show the size of parts in relation to the whole. The segments must add up to 100 percent of something, differences in segment size must be noticeable, and there should not be too many segments, as shown in these pie charts illustrating changes in American households over time.

Data from Richard Schaefer. *Sociology in Modules*. McGraw-Hill. 2011, p. 353. Estimate for 2010 based on Bureau of the Census.

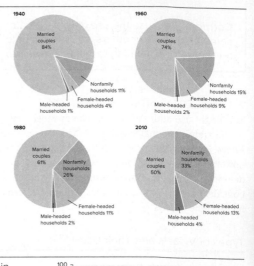

LINE GRAPHS

Line graphs show changes in one or more variables over time. The example shows how the life goals of U.S. college students have changed over a span of thirty-three years.

Data from Richard Schaefer. *Sociology in Modules*. McGraw-Hill. 2011, p. 78.

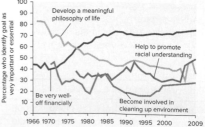

DIAGRAMS

Diagrams show processes or structures visually. Common in technical writing, they include timelines, organization charts, and decision trees. The example shows the factors involved in the decision to commit a burglary.

Data from Ronald V. Clarke and Derek B. Cornish. "Modeling Offenders' Decisions; A Framework for Research and Policy." *Crime and Justice,* vol. 6, 1985, pp. 147–185.

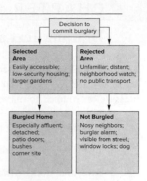

PHOTOS

Photos can reinforce your point by showing readers what your subject actually looks like or how it has been affected. This image could support a portrayal of The Deferred Action for Childhood Arrivals (DACA) as an immigration policy with significant support.

©Brendan Smialowski/ AFP/Getty Images

MAPS

Maps highlight locations and spatial relationships and show relationships between ideas. This one shows the routes followed by slaves escaping to freedom in the nineteenth century, prior to the Civil War.

Source: Harrison, Brigid and Jean Harris. *A More Perfect Union.* McGraw-Hill, 2011, p. 178.

ILLUSTRATIONS

Like photographs, illustrations make a point dramatically. (*A larger version of this image appears on p. 146.*)

Source: Library of Congress Prints & Photographs Division [LC-USZC2-1005]

CHAPTER 6

Drafting Text and Visuals

Think of drafting as an attempt to discover a beginning, a middle, and an end for what you have to say, but remember that a draft is preliminary. Avoid putting pressure on yourself to make it perfect, and leave ample time to revise and edit.

6a   Use electronic tools for drafting.

The following tips will make this process go smoothly:

- **Save your work.** Always protect your hard-won drafts from power surges and other electronic hiccups. Save often, and make backups. Consider using cloud-based tools, such as Google Drive and Dropbox to save your work to the Internet. This will ensure your work is saved should something happen to your computer or external hard drive.

- **Label revised drafts with different file names.** Use a different file name for each successive version of your manuscript. For example, you might save drafts of a project on work as Work1, Work2, Work3, and so on.

NAVIGATING THROUGH COLLEGE AND BEYOND

Avoiding Writer's Block

Use these tips to get an early start on a first draft:

- **Resist the temptation to be a perfectionist.** For your first draft, do not worry about getting the right word, the stylish phrase, or even the correct spelling.

- **Take it "bird by bird."** Writer Anne Lamott counsels students to break down writing assignments into manageable units and to finish each unit in one session. She passes along her father's advice to her brother, who had procrastinated on a report about birds and was paralyzed by the size of the project: "Bird by bird, buddy. Just take it bird by bird."

- **Start anywhere.** If you are stuck on the beginning, select another section where you know what you want to say. Writers often compose the introduction after drafting a complete text. You can go back later and work out the transitions.

- **Generate more ideas.** If you hit a section where you are drawing a blank, you may need to do more reading, research, or brainstorming. Be careful, though, not to use reading and research as stalling tactics.

- **Set aside time and work in a suitable place.** Many writers find that working undistracted for at least half an hour at a stretch is helpful. And some writers go to the same place for specific tasks, like brainstorming or drafting.

—the EVOLVING SITUATION

Using Internet Links as a Writing Process Tool

As you compose, add links to supplemental material that you may—or may not—decide to use in a later draft. For example, you might include a link to additional research, or to a source that refutes an argument, or to interesting information that is not directly relevant to the primary subject. Readers can be helpful in advising you on whether or not to include the linked material in the next draft. Before the final draft, be sure to remove all links.

6b   Develop ideas using patterns of organization and visuals.

The following strategies can help you develop the ideas that support your thesis into a complete draft. Depending on the purpose of your composition, you may use a few of these patterns throughout or a mix of all of them. For example, for a report about a local issue for your political science course, you might use narration to provide background and then compare two local officials' differing positions. In the process, you might define key terms that readers need to understand the issue.

Photographs, tables, graphs, and audio and video clips can also support your ideas, as long as they serve the overall purpose of the work and are not used just for fun or decoration. Regardless of the type of visual you use, be sure to discuss it in the body of your text. *(See pp. 49-51 for more on types of visuals and their purposes.)*

1. Illustration

To appeal to readers, showing is better than telling. Detailed examples and well-chosen visuals *(see Figure 6.1)* can make abstractions more concrete and generalizations more specific, as the following paragraph shows:

> As Rubin explains, "for much of the Accord era, the ideal-typical family . . . was composed of a 'stay-at-home-mom,' a working father, and dependent children. He earned wages; she cooked, cleaned, cared for the home, managed the family's social life, and nurtured the family members" (97). Just such an arrangement characterized my grandmother's married life. My grandmother, who had four children, stayed at home with them, while her husband went off to work as a safety engineer. Sadly, when he died, she was left with nothing. She needed to support herself, yet had no work experience, no credit, and little education. But even though society frowned on her for seeking employment, my grandmother eventually found a clerical position—a low-level job with few perks.
>
> —JENNIFER KOEHLER, "Women's Work in the United States: The 1950s and 1990s," student text

FIGURE 6.1 **Visuals that illustrate.** This advertisement shows an idealized version of the lives of many women in the 1950s and 1960s.

©Apic/Hulton Archive/Getty Images

Source: Library of Congress Prints and Photographs Division [LC-DIG-ppmsca-29087]

FIGURE 6.2 **Visuals that narrate.** Images that narrate can reinforce a message or portray events you discuss in your writing. This detail from a magazine illustration published in 1894 helps tell the story of the origins of "fake news."

2. Narration

When you narrate, you tell a story. *(See Figure 6.2 for an example of a narrative visual.)* The following paragraph comes from an essay on the phenomenon of fake news as it once played out in the newspapers of the nineteenth century.

Although these days his name is somewhat synonymous with journalism of the highest standards, through association with the Pulitzer Prize established by provisions in his will, Joseph Pulitzer had a very different reputation while alive. After purchasing *The New York World* in 1884 and rapidly increasing circulation through the publication of sensationalist stories he earned the dubious honour of being the pioneer of tabloid journalism. He soon had a competitor in the field when his rival William Randolph Hearst acquired the *The New York Journal* in 1885 (originally begun by Joseph's brother Albert). The rivalry was fierce, each trying to outdo the other with ever more sensational and salacious stories. At a meeting of prominent journalists in 1889 *Florida Daily Citizen* editor Lorettus Metcalf claimed that due to their competition "the evil grew until publishers all over the country began to think that perhaps at heart the public might really prefer vulgarity."

Notice that the author begins this story in the present, focusing on a detail that is familiar to contemporary readers. Then, using the past tense, the author recounts in chronological sequence some key events in the history of "fake news."

3. Description

To make an object, person, or activity vivid for your readers, describe it in concrete, specific words that appeal to the senses of sight, sound, taste, smell, and touch. *(See Figure 6.3 for an example of a descriptive visual.)* In the following paragraph, Diane Chen describes her impression of the photograph in Figure 6.3:

> The photograph's composition reveals Lange's compassion for her subject. Although four figures make up the photograph, the mother, whose face we see in full, is its main subject. She gazes outward, worriedly, as her three children huddle around her. The children frame her figure, two of them with faces hidden behind her shoulders, either out of shyness or shared distress, while the third rests across the mother's lap. The mother's expression conveys a desperate concern, presumably for her children's wellbeing. Her children cling to her, but her own faraway gaze gives evidence that she is too distracted by her worries to give them comfort. Lange emphasizes the mother's expression by making it the focal point of the photograph. In doing so, she encourages viewers to identify with the mother and even to wonder what thoughts pass through her mind.

> —DIANE CHEN, "Inspiring Empathy: Dorothea Lange's
> *Migrant Mother,*" student text

FIGURE 6.3 Visuals that describe.
Pay careful attention to the effect your selection will have on your project. This photograph by Dorothea Lange appeals to the viewer's emotions, evoking sympathy for the migrant workers' plight.

Source: Library of Congress Prints and Photographs Division [LC-DIG-fsa-8b29516]

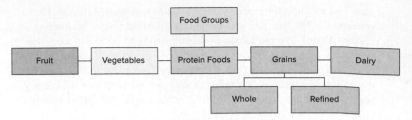

FIGURE 6.4 Visuals that classify or divide. An image can help you make the categories or parts of complex systems or organizations easier to understand.

4. Classification

Classification is a useful way of grouping individual entities into identifiable categories. *(See Figure 6.4.)* Classifying occurs in all academic disciplines and often appears with its complement—**division,** or breaking a whole entity into its parts.

In the following passage, the United States Department of Agriculture (USDA) classifies the elements of a healthy diet in terms of five major food groups: fruits, vegetables, protein foods, grains, and dairy. According to the USDA, oils also play an important role in healthy eating habits, but not enough so to make up their own group within this classification. Grains, on the other hand, can be divided into even more specific categories, namely whole grains and refined.

> The *2015-2020 Dietary Guidelines for Americans* emphasizes the importance of an overall healthy eating pattern with all five groups as key building blocks, plus oils. (While oils are not a food group, they are emphasized as part of a healthy eating pattern because they are a major source of essential fatty acids and vitamin E). Each food group includes a variety of foods that are similar in nutritional makeup, and each group plays an important role in an overall healthy eating pattern. Some of the food groups are broken down further into subgroups to emphasize foods that are particularly good sources of certain vitamins and minerals. For example, the subgroups within the Grains Group encourage whole grains, which provide more fiber, magnesium, and zinc than refined grains.

5. Definition

Define concepts that readers need in order to follow your discussion. *(See Figure 6.5 for an example of a visual that defines.)* Interpretations and arguments often depend on one or two key ideas that cannot be quickly and easily defined. In the following example, NASA's Web site defines black holes:

> Don't let the name fool you: a black hole is anything but empty space. Rather, it is a great amount of matter packed into a very small area—think of a star ten times more massive than the Sun squeezed into a sphere approximately the diameter of New York City. The result is a gravitational field so strong that nothing, not even light, can escape. In recent years, NASA instruments have painted a new picture of these strange objects that are, to many, the most fascinating objects in space.

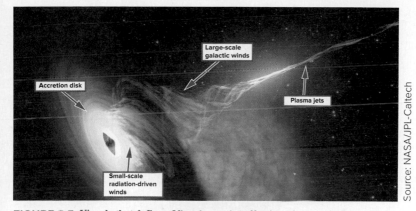

Source: NASA/JPL-Caltech

FIGURE 6.5 Visuals that define. Visuals can be effective when used to support a written definition or to identify parts of a whole. This image uses labels and leader lines to identify the parts of a black hole.

Although the term was not coined until 1967 by Princeton physicist John Wheeler, the idea of an object in space so massive and dense that light could not escape it has been around for centuries. Most famously, black holes were predicted by Einstein's theory of general relativity, which showed that when a massive star dies, it leaves behind a small, dense remnant core. If the core's mass is more than about three times the mass of the Sun, the equations showed, the force of gravity overwhelms all other forces and produces a black hole.

6. Comparison and contrast

When you *compare,* you explore the similarities and differences among various items. When the term *compare* is used along with the term *contrast, compare* has a narrower meaning: "to spell out key similarities." *Contrast* always means "to itemize important differences." *(See Figure 6.6.)*

In the following example, the student writer uses a **subject-by-subject** pattern to contrast the ideas of two social commentators, Jeremy Rifkin and George Will:

Rifkin and Will have different opinions about unemployment caused by downsizing and the widening income gap between rich and poor. Rifkin sees both the decrease in employment and the increase in income disparity as evils that must be immediately dealt with lest society fall apart: "If no measures are taken to provide financial opportunities for millions of Americans in an era of diminishing jobs, then . . . violent crime is going to increase" (3). Will, on the other hand, seems to believe that both unemployment and income differences are necessary to the health of American society. Will writes, "A society that chafes against stratification derived from disparities of talents will be a society that discourages individual talents" (92). Apparently, the society that Rifkin wants is just the kind of society that Will rejects.

—JACOB GROSSMAN, "Dark Comes before Dawn," student text

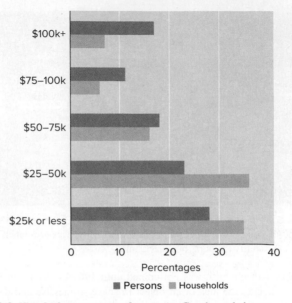

FIGURE 6.6 Visuals that compare and contrast. Graphs and charts are effective for comparing parallel sets of data. Using census figures from 2014, this bar chart compares the percentages of persons and households in various income groups.

Notice that Grossman comments on Rifkin first and then turns to his second subject, Will. To ensure paragraph unity, Rifkin begins with a topic sentence that mentions both subjects.

In the following paragraph, the student writer organizes her comparison **point by point,** rather than subject by subject. Instead of saying everything about Smith's picture before commenting on the AP photo, she moves back and forth between the two images as she makes and supports two points: (1) that the images differ in figure and scene and (2) that they are similar in theme:

> Divided by an ocean, two photographers took pictures that at first glance seem absolutely different. W. Eugene Smith's well-known *Tomoko in the Bath* and the less well-known AP photo *A Paratrooper Works to Save the Life of a Buddy* portray distinctively different settings and people. Smith brings us into a darkened room where a Japanese woman is lovingly bathing her malformed child, while the AP staff photographer captures two soldiers on the battlefield, one intently performing CPR on his wounded friend. But even though the two images seem as different as women and men, peace and war, or life and death, both pictures convey something similar: a time of suffering. It is the early 1970s—a time when the hopes and dreams that modernity promoted are being exposed as deadly to human beings. Perhaps that is why the bodies in both pictures seem humbled. Grief pulls you down onto your knees. Terror impels you to crawl along the ground.
>
> —ILONA BOUZOUKASHVILI, "On Reading Photographs," student text

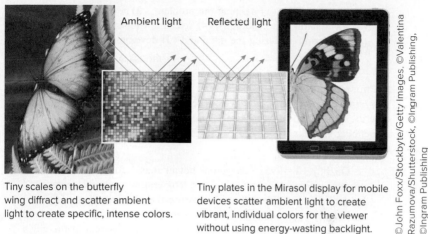

Tiny scales on the butterfly wing diffract and scatter ambient light to create specific, intense colors.

Tiny plates in the Mirasol display for mobile devices scatter ambient light to create vibrant, individual colors for the viewer without using energy-wasting backlight.

©John Foxx/Stockbyte/Getty Images. ©Valentina Razumova/Shutterstock. ©Ingram Publishing. ©Ingram Publishing

FIGURE 6.7 Visuals as analogies. Visual analogies operate in the same way as written analogies. This figure uses the image of a butterfly wing to illustrate how the display on a mobile device works.

7. Analogy

An **analogy** compares topics that at first glance seem quite different (*see Figure 6.7*). A well-chosen analogy can make new or technical information appear more commonplace and understandable:

> The brilliant iridescent blue of the various Morpho species, for example, comes not from pigment, but from "structural color." Those wings harbor a nanoscale assemblage of shingled plates, whose shape and distance from one another are arranged in a precise pattern that disrupts reflective light wavelengths to produce the brilliant blue. To create that same blue out of pigment would require much more energy— energy better used for flying, feeding and reproducing . . . Like the butterfly's wings, "the display is taking the white ambient light around us, white light or sunlight, and through interference is going to send us back a color image," [Brian] Gally says. Unlike conventional LCD screens, the Mirasol doesn't have to generate its own light. "The display brightness just automatically scales with ambient light."
>
> —TOM VANDERBILT, *Smithsonian* magazine

8. Process

When you explain how to do something or show readers how something is done, you use process analysis (*see Figure 6.8*), explaining each step in the process in chronological order, as in the following example:

> The scientific method requires precise preparation in developing useful research. Otherwise, the research data collected may not prove accurate. Sociologists and other researchers follow five basic steps in the

scientific method: (1) defining the problem, (2) reviewing the literature, (3) formulating the hypothesis, (4) selecting the research design and then collecting and analyzing the data, and (5) developing the conclusion.

—RICHARD T. SCHAEFER, *Sociology*

9. Cause and effect

This strategy can help you trace the causes of some event or situation, to describe its effects, or both *(see Figure 6.9)*. In the following example, Eric Klinenberg explains the possible reasons for the deaths of 739 Chicagoans in the 1995 heat wave:

> On July 12, 1995, a dangerous hot-air mass settled over Chicago, producing three consecutive days of temperatures over 99 degrees Fahrenheit, heat indices (which measure the heat experienced by a typical person) around 120, high humidity, and little evening cooling. The heat wave was not the most extreme weather system in the city's history, but it proved to be Chicago's most deadly environmental event. During the week of the most severe weather, 485 city residents, many of

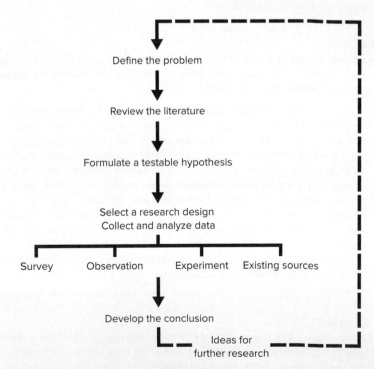

FIGURE 6.8 Visuals that show a process. Flow charts and diagrams are especially useful when illustrating a process. This one shows the scientific method used in disciplines throughout the sciences and social sciences. Note that the thesis/hypothesis is not discovered until well into the process.

whom were old, alone, and impoverished, died of causes that medical examiners attributed to the heat. Several hundred decedents were never autopsied, though, and after the event the Chicago Department of Public Health discovered that 739 Chicagoans in excess of the norm had perished while thousands more had been hospitalized for heat-related problems.

—ERIC KLINENBERG, "Heat Wave of 1995"

6c   Write focused, clearly organized paragraphs.

Paragraphs break the text into blocks for your readers, allowing them to see how your essay builds step by step and establishing a rhythm for their reading. Introductory and concluding paragraphs have special functions, but all paragraphs should have a single, sharp focus and a clear organization. (Paragraphs on the Web tend to be short, with links at the end so readers do not navigate away.)

1. Focusing on one main point or example
In a strong paragraph, the sentences form a unit that explores one main point or elaborates on one main example. When you are drafting, start a new paragraph when you introduce a new reason in support of your thesis, a new step in a process, or a new element in an analysis. New paragraphs also signal shifts

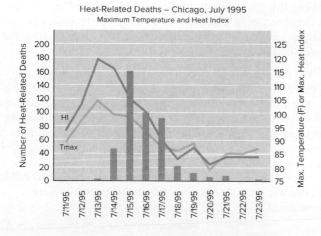

This graph tracks maximum temperature (Tmax), heat index (HI), and heat-related deaths in Chicago each day from July 11 to 23, 1995. The orange line shows maximum daily temperature, the green line shows the heat index, and the bars indicate number of deaths for the day.

FIGURE 6.9 Visuals that show cause and effect. Visuals can provide powerful evidence when you are writing about causes and effects. Although graphs like this one may seem self-explanatory, you still must analyze and interpret them for your readers.

in time and place, changing speakers in dialogue, contrasts with earlier material, and changes in level of emphasis. As you draft, bear in mind that each paragraph develops a main point or example.

In the following example, the paragraph focuses on a theory that the writer will refer to later in the essay. The main idea is highlighted:

The main idea is introduced in the highlighted sentences.

Details of attachment theory are developed in the rest of the paragraph.

Current thinking on the topic of loss and mourning rests on foundations constructed by the British psychiatrist John Bowlby. Using examples from animal and human behavior, Bowlby (1977) posited "attachment theory" as a means of understanding the powerful bonds between humans and the disruption that comes when the bonds are jeopardized or destroyed. The bonds are formed because of a need for security and safety, are developed early in life, are long enduring, and are directed toward a few special individuals. In normal maturation, the child becomes ever more independent, moving away from the figure of attachment, and returning periodically for safety and security. If the bonds are threatened, the individual will try to restore them through crying, clinging, or other types of coercion; if they are destroyed, withdrawal, apathy, and despair will follow.

—JONATHAN FAST, "After Columbine: How People Mourn Sudden Death"

2. Signaling the main idea of your paragraph with a topic sentence

A topic sentence can be a helpful starting point as you draft a paragraph. In the following paragraph, the topic sentence (highlighted) provides the writer with a launching point for a series of details:

The topic sentence announces that the paragraph will focus on a certain kind of evidence.

The excavation also revealed dramatic evidence for the commemorative rituals that took place after the burial. Four cattle had been decapitated and their skulls symbolically placed in a ditch enclosing the burial pit. In the soil above the skulls archaeologists found the butchered bones of at least 250 slaughtered cattle, evidence for a huge ceremonial feast. Clearly this was an expensive way to commemorate a leader. Indeed, the huge quantity of meat suggests that the entire tribe may have gathered at the grave to take part in a ritual feast. Perhaps this was one way the bonds between scattered communities were strengthened.

—DAMIAN ROBINSON, "Riding into the Afterlife"

Sometimes the sentences in a paragraph will lead to a unifying conclusion (highlighted), as in this example:

The nation's community colleges are receiving much deserved attention, from the Oval Office to the family living room. Community colleges in Indiana and Illinois offer great value: high quality at an affordable price. As the academic year moves forward and high school students complete college applications, I recommend that those who intend to continue their education close to home take a look at pathways that lead from the community college to university graduation.

—ELAINE MAIMON, "Students Must Focus
on Degree Completion"

If a topic sentence would simply state the obvious, it can be omitted. In the following example, it is not necessary to state that the paragraph is about Igor Stravinsky's preprofessional life:

Stravinsky was born in Russia, near St. Petersburg, grew up in a musical atmosphere, and studied with Nikolai Rimsky-Korsakov. He had his first important opportunity in 1909, when the great impresario Sergei Diaghilev heard his music.

—ROGER KAMIEN, *Music: An Appreciation*

3. Writing paragraphs that have a clear organization

The sentences in your final draft should be clearly related to one another. As you draft, make connections among your ideas and information to move your writing forward. The strategies covered in 6b are suggestions for developing your ideas. Another way to make your ideas work together is to use one of the common organizational schemes for paragraphs, which can also be used for essays as a whole. *(For advice on using repetition, pronouns, and transitions to relate sentences to one another, see Chapter 7, pp. 70-74.)*

- **Chronological organization:** The sentences in a paragraph with a chronological organization describe a series of events, steps, or observations as they occur in time: this happened, then that, and so on.

- **Spatial organization:** The sentences in a paragraph with a spatial organization present details as they appear to a viewer: from top to bottom, outside to inside, east to west, and so on.

- **General-to-specific organization:** As we have seen, paragraphs often start with a general topic sentence that states the main idea and then proceed with specifics that elaborate on that idea. The general topic sentence can include a question that the paragraph then answers or a problem that the paragraph goes on to solve.

- **Specific-to-general organization:** The general topic sentence can come at the end of the paragraph, with the specific details leading up to that general conclusion *(see the paragraph from "Students Must Focus on Degree Completion," pp. 62-63)*. This organization is especially effective when you are preparing readers for a revelation.

4. Drafting introductions and conclusions

As you begin your first draft, you may want to skip the introduction and focus on the body of your text. Later you can go back and sketch out the main ideas for your introduction.

To get readers' attention, show why the topic matters. The opening of your text should encourage readers to share your view of its importance. Except for essay exams, it's best not to refer directly to the assignment or to your intentions ("In this paper I will . . ."). Avoid vague general statements ("Jane Austen is a famous author"), and try instead to find a way to arouse readers' interest. Here are some opening strategies:

- Tell a brief story related to the issue your thesis raises.
- Begin with a relevant, attention-getting quotation.
- Begin with a paraphrase of a commonly held view that you immediately question.
- State a working hypothesis.
- Define a key term, but avoid the tired opener that begins, "According to the dictionary. . . ."
- Pose an important question.

For informative reports, arguments, and essays, your opening paragraph or paragraphs will include a claim, usually at the beginning but sometimes near the end of the introduction. If your purpose is interpretive, however, you may instead choose to build up to your thesis. For some types of writing, such as narratives, an explicitly stated claim may not be needed if the main idea is clear without it.

Just as the opening makes a first impression and motivates readers to continue reading, the closing makes a final impression and motivates readers to think further. While you should not merely repeat the main idea that you introduced at the beginning of the text, you should also avoid overgeneralizing or introducing a completely new topic. Your conclusion should remind readers of your text's significance and satisfy those who might be asking, "So what?" or "What's at stake?" Here are some strategies for concluding:

- Refer to the story or quotation you used in your introduction.
- Answer the question you posed in your introduction.
- Summarize your main point.
- Call for some action on your readers' part.
- Present a powerful image or forceful example.
- Suggest implications for the future.

6d   Integrate visuals and multimodal elements effectively.

If you decide to use a table, chart, diagram, photograph, or video or audio file, keep this general advice in mind:

- **Number tables and other figures** consecutively throughout your text: Table 1, Table 2, and so on. Do not abbreviate *Table. Figure* may be abbreviated as *Fig.*
- **Refer to the visual element in your text** before it appears, placing the visual as close as possible to the explanation of the reason for including it. If your project contains complex tables or many other

visuals, you may want to group them in an appendix. Always refer to a visual by its label—for example, "See Fig. 1."

- **Give each visual a title and caption** that explains what the visual shows. A visual with its caption should be clear without the discussion in the text, and the discussion of the visual in the text should be clear without the visual itself.

- **Include explanatory notes below the visuals.** If you want to explain a specific element within the visual, use a superscript letter (not a number) both after the specific element and before the note. The explanation should appear directly beneath the graphic, not at the foot of the page or at the end of your paper.

- **Credit sources for visuals and multimedia elements.** You must credit all visuals and multimedia elements that you have imported from other sources. Unless you have specific guidelines to follow, you can use the word *Source,* followed by a colon and complete documentation of the source, including the author, title, publication information, and page number if applicable.

Note: The Modern Language Association (MLA) and the American Psychological Association (APA) provide guidelines for figure captions and crediting sources of visuals that differ from the preceding guidelines. *(See Chapter 29: MLA Style: Paper Format, p. 303, and Chapter 33: APA Style: Paper Format, p. 349.)*

CHAPTER 7

Revising and Editing

To revise means to see something again. In the **revising** stage of the writing process, you review the entire composition, adding, deleting, and moving text as necessary. After you are satisfied with the substance of your draft, **editing** begins. When you edit, you both refine sentences so that you say what you want to say as effectively as possible and correct grammatical and mechanical errors.

This chapter focuses on revising. It also introduces the concepts and principles of editing, which are covered in greater detail in Tabs 9-12.

7a   Get comments from readers.

Asking actual readers to comment on your draft is the best way to get fresh perspectives. (Most professors encourage peer review, but it is wise to check.) Always acknowledge this help, in an endnote, a cover note, a preface, or an acknowledgments page.

─NAVIGATING THROUGH COLLEGE AND BEYOND

Re-Visioning Your Work

Revising is a process of "re-visioning"—of looking at your work through the eyes of your audience. Here are some tips for getting a fresh perspective:

- **Get feedback from other readers.** Candid, respectful feedback can help you discover strengths and weaknesses.
- **Let your draft cool.** Try to schedule a break between drafting and revising. A good night's sleep, a movie break, or some physical exercise will help you view your draft as a reader rather than as a writer.
- **Read your draft aloud.** Some find that reading aloud helps them "hear" their words the way their audience will.
- **Use revising and editing checklists.** The checklists in this chapter will assist you in evaluating your work systematically.
- Even better, create your own editing checklist based on the changes you make to final drafts.

1. Using peer review

Peer review involves reading and critiquing your classmates' work while they review yours. You can send your draft to your peer reviewers electronically (also print out a copy for yourself) or exchange drafts in person.

Help your readers help you by giving them information and asking them specific questions. When you share a draft with readers, provide answers to the following questions:

- **What is the assignment?** Readers need to understand the context for your project—especially your intended purpose and audience.
- **How close are you to being finished?** Your answer lets readers know where you are in the writing process and how best to assist you in taking the next step.
- **What steps do you plan to take to complete the project?** If readers know your plans, they can either question the direction you are taking or give you more specific help, such as the titles of additional sources you might consult.
- **What kind of feedback do you need?** Do you want readers to summarize your main points so you can determine if you have communicated them clearly? Do you want a response to the logic of your argument or the development of your thesis?

Reading other writers' drafts will help you view your own work more objectively, and comments from readers will help you see your own writing as others

— CHECKLIST   Guidelines for Giving and Receiving Feedback

Giving Feedback

☐ **Begin with strengths.** Let writers know what you think works well so that they can build on those parts and try similar approaches again.

☐ **Be specific.** Give examples to back up your general reactions.

☐ **Be constructive.** Instead of saying that an example is a bad choice, explain that you did not understand how the example was connected to the main point, and suggest a way to clarify the connection.

☐ **Ask questions.** Jot down any questions that occur to you while reading. Ask for clarification, or note an objection that readers of the final version might make.

(For help giving feedback, see Revising Your Draft for Content and Organization on p. 69.)

Receiving Feedback

☐ **Resist being defensive.** Keep in mind that readers are discussing your draft, not you, and their feedback offers a way for you to see your writing from another angle. Be respectful of their time and effort. Remember that you, not your readers, are in charge of decisions about your work.

☐ **Ask for more feedback if you need it.** Some readers may be hesitant to share all of their reactions, and you may need to do some coaxing.

see it. As you gain more objectivity, you will become more adept at revising your work. In addition, the approaches that you see your classmates taking to the assignment will give you ideas for new directions in your own writing.

2. Responding to readers

While you should consider your readers' suggestions, you are under no obligation to do what they say. Sometimes you will receive contradictory advice: one reader may like a particular sentence that a second reader suggests you eliminate. Is there common ground? Yes. Both readers stopped at that sentence. Ask yourself why—and whether you want readers to pause there.

7b   Use electronic tools for revising.

Even though word-processing programs can make a first draft look finished, it is still a first draft. Check below the surface for problems in content, structure, and style. Move paragraphs around, add details, and delete irrelevant sentences. You may find it easier to revise if you have a printed copy so that you can see the composition as a whole.

To work efficiently, become familiar with the revising and editing tools in your word-processing program:

- **Comments:** Many word-processing programs have a "Comments" feature allowing you to add notes to sections of text. This feature is useful for giving feedback on someone else's draft. Some writers also use it to make notes to themselves.

- **Track changes:** The Track Changes feature allows you to revise and edit a piece of writing while also maintaining the original text. Usually, marginal notes or strike-through marks show what you have deleted or replaced. Because you can still see the original text, you can judge whether a change has improved the draft. If you change your mind, you can restore the deleted text. When collaborating with another writer, save the Track Changes version as a separate file.

You can see the Track Changes and Comments features in the second draft of Diane Chen's analysis on pages 82–84. In addition, many Web-based tools such as *Google Docs* enable work to be shared, edited, and revised online.

7c   Focus on the writing situation (topic, purpose, audience, genre, and medium).

As you revise your draft within your selected rhetorical situation, think about your purpose, rhetorical stance, and audience. Is your primary purpose to inform, to interpret, to analyze, or to argue? *(For more on purpose, see Tab 2: Writing and Designing Texts, p. 37.)*

Clarity about your rhetorical situation and writing purpose is especially important when an assignment calls for interpretation, which differs significantly from a description. With this principle in mind, Diane Chen read over her first draft meant to interpret Lange's *Migrant Mother*. Here is a portion of that draft:

FIRST DRAFT

In addition to the mother's expression, her body language is also important to note. Lange's subject leans an elbow on her lap with a hand touching her face, a gesture of concern. Through her subject's physical position, Lange depicts the poverty in which the mother lives and seems to be reinforcing an important point about the mother's social position. The family's dirty and ragged clothes are proof of the hardships they face and the limited possibilities for escaping those conditions. By capturing this moment in a photograph, Lange shows us important truths about the social implications of poverty.

Keeping the writing situation in mind, Chen realized that she needed to discuss the significance of her observations—to interpret and analyze the details for readers who would see a copy of the photograph incorporated into her online text. Within the framework of a review, she revised to demonstrate how the formal elements of the photograph function.

CHECKLIST   Revising Your Draft for Content and Organization

- ☐ **Purpose:** What is the purpose of the text? If it is not clear, what changes would make it apparent?
- ☐ **Thesis:** What is the thesis? Is it clear and specific? What revisions would make it clearer?
- ☐ **Audience:** How does the approach—including evidence and tone—appeal to the intended readers?
- ☐ **Structure:** How does the order of the key points support the thesis? Would another order be more effective? How might overly long or short sections be revised?
- ☐ **Paragraphs:** How might the development, unity, and coherence of each paragraph be improved?
- ☐ **Visuals:** Do visuals communicate the intended meaning clearly, without unnecessary clutter? How might they be improved?

REVISION

The mother's posture is also telling of Lange's compassion for her subject. She leans an elbow on her lap with a hand touching her face, a gesture of concern. Through her subject's physical position, Lange seems to be reinforcing an important point about the mother's social position: the same hand that labors in the field also cares for and comforts a family. The family's dirty and ragged clothes are proof of the hardships they face and the limited possibilities for escaping those conditions. By capturing this moment in a photograph, Lange communicates important truths about the social implications of poverty and implores her audience to empathize.

7d   Make sure you have a strong thesis.

Remember that a thesis makes an assertion about a topic. It links the *what* and the *why*. Is your thesis evident on the first page of your draft? Before readers get very far along, they expect an answer to the question "What is the point of all this?" If you do not find the point on the first page, its absence is a signal to revise, unless you are deliberately waiting until the end to present your thesis. *(For more on strong theses, see Chapter 5, pp. 43-45.)*

Many writers start with a working thesis, which often evolves into a more specific, complex assertion as they develop their ideas. One of the key challenges of revising is to compose a clear statement of this revised thesis. When she drafted a paper on Germany's economic prospects, Jennifer Koehler stated her working thesis as follows:

WORKING THESIS

Germany is experiencing a great deal of change.

During the revision process, Koehler realized that her working thesis was weak. A weak thesis is predictable: readers read it, agree, and that's that. A strong thesis, on the other hand, stimulates thoughtful inquiry. Koehler's revised thesis provokes questions:

REVISED THESIS

With proper follow-through, Germany can become one of the world's primary sources of direct investment and maintain its status as one of the world's preeminent exporters.

Sometimes writers find that their ideas change altogether, and the working thesis needs to be completely revised.

Your thesis should evolve throughout the draft. Readers need to see a statement of the main idea on the first page, but they also expect a more complex general statement near the end. After presenting evidence to support her revised thesis, Koehler concludes by stating her thesis as a more complex generalization:

If the government efforts continue, the economy will strengthen over the next decade, and Germany will reinforce its position as an integral nation in the global economy.

7e Review the structure of your draft.

Does the draft have a beginning, a middle, and an end, with bridges between those parts? When you revise, you can refine and even change this structure so that it supports what you want to say more effectively.

One way to review your structure is by outlining your first draft. *(For help with outlining, see Chapter 5, pp. 45–48.)* Try listing the key points of the draft in sentence form; whenever possible, use sentences that actually appear in the draft. Ask yourself whether the key points are arranged effectively or if another arrangement would work better. The following structures are typical ways of organizing texts:

- **Informative:** Presents the key points of a topic.
- **Exploratory:** Begins with a question or problem and works step-by-step to discover an answer or a solution.
- **Argumentative:** Presents a set of linked reasons plus supporting evidence.
- **Analytic:** Shows how the parts come together to form a coherent whole and makes connections.

7f Revise for paragraph development, paragraph unity, and coherence.

As you revise, examine each paragraph, asking yourself what role it plays—or should play—in the work as a whole. Keeping this role in mind, check the paragraph for development and unity. You should also read each paragraph for coherence—and consider whether all of the paragraphs together contribute to the work as a whole. Does the length of sections reflect their relative importance? *(For more on paragraphs, see Chapter 6: Drafting Text and Visuals, pp. 61-65.)*

1. Paragraph development

Paragraphs in academic texts are usually about a hundred words long. Consider dividing any that exceed two hundred words or that are especially dense, and develop or combine paragraphs that seem very short. Would more information make the point clearer? Perhaps a term should be defined. Do generalizations need to be supported with examples? Make stylistic choices about paragraph length. In most cases, similar length sets a rhythm for the reader, although you may sometimes use a short paragraph for emphasis.

Note how this writer developed one of her draft paragraphs, adding details and examples to make her argument more effective:

FIRST DRAFT

> A 1913 advertisement for Shredded Wheat illustrates Kellner's claim that advertisements sell self-images. The ad suggests that serving Shredded Wheat will give women the same sense of accomplishment as gaining the right to vote.

REVISION

> According to Kellner, "advertising is as concerned with selling lifestyles and socially desirable identities . . . as with selling the products themselves" (193). A 1913 ad for Shredded Wheat shows how the selling of self-images works. At first glance, this ad seems to be promoting the women's suffrage movement. In big, bold letters, "Votes for Women" is emblazoned across the top of the ad. But a closer look reveals that the ad is for Shredded Wheat cereal. Holding a piece of the cereal in her hand, a woman stands behind a large bowlful of Shredded Wheat biscuits that is made to look like a voting box. The text claims that "every biscuit is a vote for health, happiness, and domestic freedom." Like the rest of the advertisement, this claim suggests that serving Shredded Wheat will give women the same sense of accomplishment as gaining the right to vote.

—HOLLY MUSETTI, "Targeting Women," student text

2. Paragraph unity

A unified paragraph has a single, clear focus. To check for **unity**, identify the paragraph's topic sentence *(see pp. 62-63),* and make sure everything in the paragraph is clearly and closely related to it. Ideas unrelated to the topic sentence should be deleted or developed into separate paragraphs. Another option is to revise the topic sentence.

Compare the first draft of the following paragraph with its revision, and note how the addition of a topic sentence (in bold in the revision) makes the paragraph more clearly focused and therefore easier for the writer to revise further. Note also that the writer the underlined ideas because they did not directly relate to the paragraph's main point:

FIRST DRAFT

Adelphi University, which has a main campus on Long Island and another in Manhattan, felt the effects of Hurricane Sandy. But perhaps more memorable than the storm's effects were the students' responses. Shortly after the storm, in the course of a single day, university students collected donations, including roughly $1,000 in cash, wrote thank-you cards for first responders, and participated in a blood drive (Peterkin, 2012). Volunteer work continued in many different ways. "Students on Facebook are posting things like 'It's a humbling experience,' and it's positive to see that reaction," said Michael J. Berthel, Senior Assistant Director of Adelphi's Center for Student Involvement (as cited in Peterkin, 2012). This is but one example of student engagement among countless others. There is little doubt that the current generation is doing its part to make the world a better place, in a wide variety of ways (see Figure 1).

REVISION

Historically, college students planning to enter service professions such as nursing or social work have volunteered their time as part of their professional development; however, today all students can make especially valuable contributions in disastrous circumstances, such as the aftermath of Hurricane Sandy. Adelphi University, which has a main campus on Long Island and another in Manhattan, felt the effects of Sandy. But perhaps more memorable than the storm's effects were the students' responses. Shortly after the storm, in a single day, university students collected donations, including roughly $1,000 in cash, wrote thank you cards for first responders, and participated in a blood drive (Peterkin, 2012). "Students on Facebook are posting things like 'It's a humbling experience,' and it's positive to see that reaction," said Michael J. Berthel, Senior Assistant Director of Adelphi's Center for Student Involvement (as cited in Peterkin, 2012). There is little doubt that the current generation is doing its part to make the world a better place, in a wide variety of ways (see Figure 1).

—PEGGY GIGLIO, "The New Volunteer: Civic Engagement through Social Media"

3. Coherence

A coherent paragraph flows smoothly, with an organization that is easy to follow and each sentence clearly related to the next. *(See Chapter 6, pp. 61-64, for tips on how to develop well-organized paragraphs.)* You can improve coherence both within and among the paragraphs in your draft by using repetition, pronouns, parallel structure, synonyms, and transitions:

- Repeat key words to emphasize the main idea and provide transition:

  A photograph displays a unique *moment.* To capture that *moment . . .*

- Use pronouns and antecedents to form connections between sentences and avoid unnecessary repetition. In the following example, *it* refers to *Germany* and connects the two sentences:

  Germany imports raw materials, energy sources, and food products. *It* exports a wide range of industrial products, including automobiles, aircraft, and machine tools.

- Repeat sentence structures to emphasize connections:

  Because the former West Germany lived through a generation of prosperity, its people developed high expectations of material comfort. *Because the former East Germany* lived through a generation of deprivation, its people developed disdain for material values.

- Use **synonyms**—words that are close in meaning to words or phrases that have preceded them:

  In the world of photography, critics *argue* for either a scientific or an artistic approach. This *controversy . . .*

- Use transitional words and phrases. One-word transitions and **transitional expressions** link one idea with another, helping readers see the relationship between them. Compare the following two paragraphs, the first version without transitions and the second with transitions (in bold type):

FIRST DRAFT

As the credibility of online sources has been called into question, the value of subject experts has increased. Amateur journalists do not guarantee fact checking and do not always have professional experience relevant to the topics they cover. Professional journalist Tony Rogers points out that "most bloggers don't produce news stories on their own. Bloggers comment on news stories already out there—stories produced by journalists." While this is often true, bloggers can also break, or at least advance, a news story. In their report "Post-Industrial Journalism: Adapting to the Present,"

C. W. Anderson, Emily Bell, and Shirky contend that the bike-racing blog *NYVelocity* covered the Lance Armstrong performance enhancement story better than the "professional" press (20). Today an event can become news before members of the press begin to cover it, and in fact they may cover it only after their audience has become aware of it another way (Shirky, *Here Comes Everybody* 64–65).

REVISION

As the credibility of online sources has been called into question, the value of subject experts has increased. Amateur journalists do not guarantee fact checking and do not always have professional experience relevant to the topics they cover. Professional journalist Tony Rogers points out that "most bloggers don't produce news stories on their own. **Instead** they comment on news stories already out there—stories produced by journalists." While this is often true, bloggers can also break, or at least advance, a news story. **For example,** in their report "Post-Industrial Journalism: Adapting to the Present," C. W. Anderson, Emily Bell, and Shirky contend that the bike-racing blog *NYVelocity* covered the Lance Armstrong performance enhancement story better than the "professional" press (20). **Furthermore,** today an event can become news before members of the press begin to cover it, and in fact they may cover it only after their audience has become aware of it another way (Shirky, *Here Comes Everybody* 64–65).

—KRIS WASHINGTON, "Breaking News:
Blogging's Impact on Traditional and New Media"

- Use **transitional sentences,** which refer to the previous paragraph and move your essay on to the next point, to show how paragraphs in an essay are related to one another:

    The mother in this photograph, Florence Owens Thompson, was a migrant worker in Nipomo, California, in 1936, whom Lange encountered sitting outside her tent in a migrant camp. Lange took several exposures of Thompson, moving closer to her subject with each shot. This technique helped her to capture an image that communicated to viewers what poverty looked like at a human level. But the power of Lange's image is not confined to history; even today, "The Migrant Mother" remains an iconic reminder of the struggles of the poor.
    The photograph's composition reveals Lange's compassion for her subject. Although four figures make up the photograph, the mother . . .

- Avoid confusing shifts between person and number of verbs and pronouns, as well as verb tenses. *(See Tab 9: Editing for Clarity, Chapter 41: Confusing Shifts, pp. 415-18.)*

—TRANSITIONAL EXPRESSIONS

- **To show relationships in space:** above, adjacent to, against, alongside, around, at a distance from, at the . . . , below, beside, beyond, encircling, far off, forward, from the . . . , in front of, in the rear, inside, near the end, nearby, next to, on, over, surrounding, there, through the . . . , to the left, up front

- **To show relationships in time:** afterward, at last, before, earlier, first, former, formerly, immediately, in the first place, in the meantime, in the next place, in the last place, later on, meanwhile, next, now, often, once, previously, second, simultaneously, sometime later, subsequently, suddenly, then, third, today, tomorrow, until now, when, years ago, yesterday

- **To show addition or to compare:** again, also, and, and then, besides, further, furthermore, in addition, last, likewise, moreover, next, too

- **To give examples that intensify points:** after all, as an example, certainly, clearly, for example, for instance, indeed, in fact, in truth, it is true, of course, specifically, that is

- **To show similarities:** alike, in the same way, like, likewise, resembling, similarly

- **To show contrasts:** after all, although, but, conversely, differ(s) from, difference, different, dissimilar, even though, granted, however, in contrast, in spite of, nevertheless, notwithstanding, on the contrary, on the other hand, otherwise, still, though, unlike, while this may be true, yet

- **To indicate cause and effect:** accordingly, as a result, because, consequently, hence, since, then, therefore, thus

- **To conclude or summarize:** finally, in brief, in conclusion, in other words, in short, in summary, that is, to summarize

▶ **7g**   Revise visuals and multimedia elements.

If you have used visuals to display data in your paper, return to them during the revision stage to eliminate what scholar Edward Tufte calls **chartjunk,** or distracting visual elements. The checklist on page 76 contains Tufte's suggestions for editing visuals so that your readers will focus on your data rather than your "data containers." Likewise, review multimedia elements—like presentation slides, audio files, and video—to be sure that you have included only what you need; to eliminate distractions, like unnecessary animations on presentation slides; and to provide sufficient context for the viewer.

┌───

— CHECKLIST   Revising Visuals

☐ **Are grid lines needed in tables?** Eliminate grid lines or, if the lines are needed for clarity, lighten them. Tables should not look like nets with every number enclosed. Vertical rules are needed only when space is extremely tight between columns.

☐ **Are there any unnecessary 3D renderings?** Cubes and shadows can distort the information in a visual. For most charts, including pie charts, a flat image makes it easier for readers to compare parts.

☐ **Are data labeled clearly,** avoiding abbreviations and legends if possible? Does each visual have an informative title?

☐ **Do bright colors focus attention on the key data?** For example, if you are including a map, use muted colors over large areas, and save strong colors for areas you want to emphasize.

☐ **Do pictures distract from the visual's purpose?** Clip art and other decorative elements seldom make data more interesting or substantial.

☐ **Are data distorted?** In the first graph in Figure 7.1 on page 76, each month gets its own point, except for January, February, March, and April, creating a misleading impression of hurricane activity by month. The revision corrects this problem.

└───

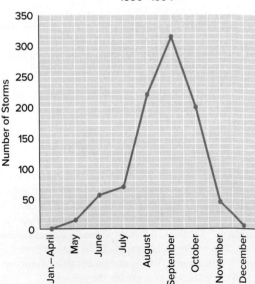

**Tropical Storms and Hurricanes
1886–1994**

FIGURE 7.1 Misleading (top) and revised graphs. In the graph at the top, the activity in the first part of the year is combined into one point on the axis, misrepresenting the data and misleading readers. The graph at the bottom has been revised to correct this problem.

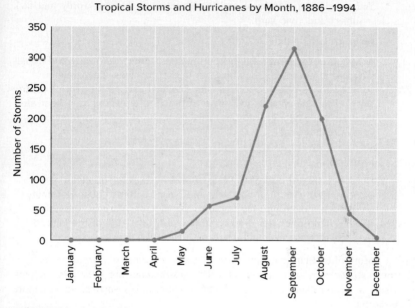

Tropical Storms and Hurricanes by Month, 1886–1994

FIGURE 7.1   (*continued*)

7h   Edit sentences.

Tabs 9 and 10 of this handbook address the many specific questions writers have when they are editing for clarity, word choice, and grammatical conventions.

1. Editing for clarity

As you edit, concentrate on sentence style, aiming for clearly focused and interestingly varied writing. A series of short, choppy sentences is like a bumpy ride: consider combining them. An unbroken stream of long, complicated sentences can put readers to sleep. For general audiences, you should strive to vary sentence openings and structure. In the example that follows, notice how the revised version connects ideas for readers and, consequently, is easier to read:

DRAFT

My father was a zealous fisherman. He took his fishing rod on every family outing. He often spent the whole outing staring at the water, waiting for a nibble. He went to the kitchen as soon as he got home. He usually cleaned and cooked the fish the same day he caught them.

REVISED

A zealous fisherman, my father took his fishing rod on every family outing. He would often spend the whole afternoon by the shore, waiting for a nibble, and then hurry straight to the kitchen to clean and cook his catch.

You should also condense and focus sentences that are wordy and lack a clear subject and vivid verb:

DRAFT

Although both vertebral and wrist fractures cause deformity and impair movement, hip fractures, which are one of the most devastating consequences of osteoporosis, significantly increase the risk of death, since 12%–30% of patients with a hip fracture die within one year after the fracture, while the mortality rate climbs to 40% for the first two years postfracture.

REVISED

Hip fractures are one of the most devastating consequences of osteoporosis. Although vertebral and wrist fractures cause deformity and impair movement, hip fractures significantly increase the risk of death. Within one year after a hip fracture, 12%–20% of the injured die. The mortality rate climbs to 40% after two years.

More often than not, sentences beginning with *it is* or *there is* or *there are* (or *it was* or *there was*)—called **expletive constructions**—are weak and indirect. Using a clear subject and a vivid verb usually makes such sentences more powerful:

DRAFT

There are stereotypes from the days of a divided Germany.

REVISED

Stereotypes formed in the days of a divided Germany persist.

2. Editing for word choice

Different disciplines and occupations have their own terminology. The word *significant,* for example, has a mathematical meaning for the statistician and a comparative meaning for the literary critic. When taking courses in a discipline, you should use its terminology accurately.

As you review your draft, look for general terms that should be more specific:

DRAFT

Foreign direct investment (FDI) in Germany will probably remain low because of several *factors*. [Factors *is a general word. To get specific, answer the question* "What *factors?*"]

REVISED

Foreign direct investment (FDI) in Germany will probably remain low because of *high labor costs, high taxation, and government regulation.*

—CHECKLIST   Editing for Style and Grammar

To create a personalized checklist, fill in the boxes next to your trouble spots, as determined by personal lists you have kept in the past, your instructor's comments, and diagnostic tests.

1. **Clarity** *(Tab 9, Chapters 38–46, pp. 408–32):* Does every sentence communicate the intended meaning in a clear, direct style? Does the text contain any of the following common causes of unclear sentences? Note sections that could be clarified.

   ☐ Wordiness
   ☐ Missing words
   ☐ Mixed constructions
   ☐ Confusing shifts
   ☐ Faulty parallelism
   ☐ Misplaced and dangling modifiers
   ☐ Problem with coordination and subordination
   ☐ Other: _____

2. **Word choice** *(Tab 9, Chapters 47–50, pp. 432–49):* How could the choice of words be more precise, especially given your rhetorical situation? Does the text include slang, biased language, clichés, or other inappropriate usages? Does it misuse any commonly confused words (for example, *advice* vs. *advise*) or use any nonstandard expressions (for example, *could of*)? Are any words at odds with your authorial stance?

3. **Grammatical conventions** *(Tab 10, pp. 451–95):* Does the draft contain any common errors that may confuse or distract readers?

   ☐ Sentence fragments
   ☐ Comma splices
   ☐ Run-on sentences
   ☐ Subject–verb agreement problems
   ☐ Incorrect verb forms
   ☐ Inconsistent verb tenses
   ☐ Pronoun–antecedent agreement problems
   ☐ Incorrect pronoun forms
   ☐ Problems with use of adjectives or adverbs
   ☐ Other: _____

If you are in the process of developing fluency in English, consult Tab 12: Basic Grammar Review for more editing advice.

Your search for more specific words can lead you to a dictionary and thesaurus. *(For more on using a dictionary and a thesaurus, see Chapter 49.)*

3. Editing for grammatical conventions

Sometimes, writers will construct a sentence or choose a word form that violates the rules of standard written English:

DRAFT

Photographs of undocumented immigrants being captured by the US border patrol, of emotional immigrants on the plane to their new country, and of villagers fleeing rebel gangs. [*This is a sentence fragment because it lacks a verb and omits the writer's point about these images.*]

EDITED SENTENCE

Photographs of undocumented immigrants being captured by the US border patrol, of emotional immigrants on the plane to their new country, and of villagers fleeing rebel gangs exemplify the range of migration stories.

A list of common abbreviations and symbols used to note errors in a manuscript can be found at the end of this text. Your instructor and other readers may use these.

7i   Proofread carefully.

Once you have revised your draft at the essay, paragraph, and sentence levels, it is time to give it one last check to make sure that it is free of typos and other mechanical errors.

Even if you are submitting an electronic version of your project, you may still prefer to proofread a printed version. Placing a ruler under each line can

the EVOLVING SITUATION

You Know More Than Grammar and Spell Checkers!

Grammar and spell checkers can help you spot some errors, but they miss many others and may even flag a correct sentence. Consider the following example:

Thee neighbors puts there cats' outsider.

Neither a spelling nor grammar checker detected the five errors in the sentence. (Correct version: *The neighbors put their cats outside.*)

As long as you are aware of the limitations of these checkers, you can use them as you edit your manuscript. Be sure, however, to review your writing carefully yourself.

—CHECKLIST Proofreading

☐ Have you included your name, the date, your professor's name, and the paper title? *(See Tabs 6–8 for the formats to use for MLA, APA, Chicago, or CSE style.)*

☐ Are all words spelled correctly? Be sure to check the spelling of titles and headings. *(See Chapter 68, pp. 543–48.)*

☐ Have you used the words you intended, or have you substituted words that sound like the ones you want but have a different spelling and meaning, such as *too* for *to, their* for *there,* or *it's* for *its? (See Chapter 50, pp. 441–49.)*

☐ Are all proper names capitalized? Have you capitalized titles of works correctly and either italicized them or put them in quotation marks as required? *(See Chapter 63, pp. 530–34, and Chapter 66, pp. 538–40.)*

☐ Have you punctuated your sentences correctly? *(See Tab 12.)*

☐ Are sources cited correctly? Is the works-cited or references list in the correct format? *(See Tabs 6–8.)*

☐ Have you checked anything you changed—for example, quotations and tables—against the original?

make it easier to focus. You can also start at the end and proofread your way backward to the beginning, sentence by sentence. Some students read their drafts aloud. Do not read for content but for form and correctness.

7j   Use campus, Internet, and community resources.

You can call on a number of resources outside the classroom for feedback on your paper.

1. Using the campus writing center

With your instructor's permission, you might ask tutors to read and comment on drafts of your work. They can also help you find and correct problems with grammar and punctuation.

2. Using online writing labs (OWLs)

Most OWLs offer information about writing, including lists of useful online resources that you can access anytime. (Always check with your instructor before accessing this help, and be sure to acknowledge the assistance.) OWLs with tutors can be useful in the following ways:

- You can submit a draft via e-mail, or another system the writing center uses, for feedback. OWL tutors will return your work, often within forty-eight hours.

- You can post your draft in a public access space, such as Google, where you will receive feedback from more than just one or two readers.
- You can read others' drafts online and learn how they are handling writing issues.

You can learn more about what OWLs have to offer by checking out Purdue University's Online Writing Lab: <http://owl.purdue.edu>.

3. Working with experts and instructors

In addition to sharing your work with classmates, through e-mail, or in online environments, you can consult electronically with your instructor or other experts. Your instructor's comments on an early draft are especially valuable. Be sure to think long and hard about the issues your instructor raises and revise your work accordingly.

👁 **7k**   Learn from one student's revisions.

In the second draft of Diane Chen's analysis of Dorothea Lange's photograph, you can see how she revised to tighten the focus of her descriptive paragraphs and edited to improve clarity, word choice, and grammar. The photograph Chen focuses on appears on p. 83.

Inspiring Empathy: Dorothea Lange's *Migrant Mother*

American photographer Dorothea Lange is ~~most known~~ perhaps best known for her work commissioned by the Farm Services Administration photographing the social and economic effects of the Great Depression. Her arresting portraits of displaced farmers, migrant families, and the unemployed ~~show us how they suffered in the~~ skillfully depict the dire consequences of the Depression for America's working classes. Artful though her photographs are, Lange's technique involved more than artistic skill. Lange considered herself primarily a photojournalist, whose goal was to encourage social action through her work. As a photojournalist who empathetically captured the struggles of her subjects on film, Lange was able to impart compassion to her audience and in turn inspire change.

> **Diane Chen 2/4/14**
> **11:38 AM**
> Comment: Reorganize to first discuss Lange as artist, then expand to her role as photojournalist who inspired change.

One of Lange's most famous photographs, *Migrant Mother* (Fig. 1), is an example of ~~the way she showed her audience~~ her unique ability to document such struggles. ~~While~~ *Migrant Mother* is not simply a portrait of one mother's hardship, but is ~~it depicts~~ a raw depiction of the ~~harsh reality for many~~ plight of thousands of displaced families during the Depression. The mother in this photograph, Florence Owens Thompson, was a migrant worker in Nipomo, California, in 1936, whom Lange encountered sitting outside her tent in a migrant camp. Lange took several exposures of Thompson, moving closer to her subject with each shot. This technique helped her to capture an image that communicated to viewers what poverty looked like ~~for real people~~ at a human level. But the power of Lange's image ~~goes beyond the time of the Depression~~ is not confined to history; even today, *Migrant Mother* remains an iconic reminder of the struggles of the poor.

The photograph's composition reveals Lange's compassion for her subject. Although ~~there are four people in~~ four figures make up the photograph, ~~we mostly see~~ the mother, whose face we see in full, is its main subject. ~~Her expression is worried.~~ She gazes outward, worriedly, as her three children huddle around her. The children frame her figure, two of them with faces hidden behind her shoulders, ~~hiding their shyness and despair~~ either out of shyness or shared distress, while the third rests across the mother's lap. The mother's expression ~~shows~~ conveys a desperate concern, ~~probably~~ presumably for her children's wellbeing. Her children cling to her, but ~~she is suffering her own despair.~~ her own faraway gaze gives evidence that she is too distracted by her worries to give them comfort. Lange ~~displays~~ emphasizes the mother's expression by making it the focal point of the photograph. In doing so, she encourages viewers to identify with the mother and even to wonder what thoughts pass through her mind.

> **Diane Chen 2/4/14 11:45 AM**
> Comment: Revise wording to objectively analyze the image and how it might be interpreted by all viewers, rather than conveying how you interpret the image.

~~In addition to the mother's expression, her body language is also important to note.~~ The mother's posture is also telling of Lange's compassion for her subject. She leans an elbow on her lap with a hand touching her face, a gesture of concern. Through her subject's physical position, Lange ~~depicts the poverty in which the mother lives~~ seems to be reinforcing an important point about the mother's social position: ~~her laborer's hand~~ the same hand that labors in the field also cares for and comforts a family. The family's dirty and ragged clothes are proof of the hardships they face and the limited possibilities for escaping those conditions. By capturing this moment in a photograph, Lange ~~shows us the truth~~ communicates important truths about the social implications of poverty and ~~asks~~ implores her audience to empathize.

As *Migrant Mother* powerfully demonstrates, Lange's work did a great deal to encourage awareness and understanding among her viewers, and in doing so, to inspire social change. Her ability to capture the realities of the Great Depression won Lange a Guggenheim Fellowship in 1941, and helped to solidify her as one of the most iconic photographers of the twentieth century. But perhaps Lange's greatest ~~achievement was~~ legacy is her impact on artists whose work has continued to open our eyes to social issues such as poverty and injustice with the goal of inspiring social change.

> **Diane Chen 2/4/14 12:05 PM**
> Comment: Add more about Lange's award to illustrate her credibility.

Fig. 1: Dorothea Lange, *Migrant Mother*, 1936.

----------------------[New page]----------------------
Work Cited

Lange, Dorothea. *Migrant Mother*. 1936. Prints and Photographs Division, Library of Congress, https://lccn.loc.gov/2017762891.

CHAPTER 8

Designing Academic Texts and Portfolios

A crucial writing task is to format your text so that readers can "see" your ideas clearly. In this chapter, we focus on designing responses to academic writing assignments. *(Multimodal presentations, posters, and Web sites can be found in Chapters 13 and 14 and brochures, newsletters, résumés, and other documents in Chapters 15 and 17.)*

In college and in your professional life, you may wish to showcase your writing and related work in a print or an online portfolio. This chapter offers guidelines for designing effective portfolios.

8a Consider audience and purpose.

As you plan your document, consider your purpose and the needs of your audience. If you are writing an informative project for a psychology class, your instructor—your primary audience—will probably prefer that you follow the guidelines provided by the American Psychological Association (APA). If you are writing a lab report for a biology or chemistry course, you will likely need to follow a well-established format and use the documentation style recommended by the Council of Science Editors (CSE) to cite sources. A history review might call for the use of the Chicago style. Interpretive analyses for language and literature courses usually use the style recommended by the Modern Language Association (MLA). *(For help with these documentation styles, see Tabs 6-8.)*

8b Use the tools available in your word-processing program.

Most word-processing programs provide a range of options for editing, sharing, and, especially, designing your document. For example, if you are using Microsoft Word 2016, you can access groups of commands by clicking on the various tabs at the top of the screen. Figure 8.1 shows the Home tab, which contains basic formatting and editing commands. You can choose different fonts and sizes; add bold, italic, or underlined type; insert numbered or bulleted lists; and so on. Other tabs allow you to add boxes and drawings, make comments, and change the page layout.

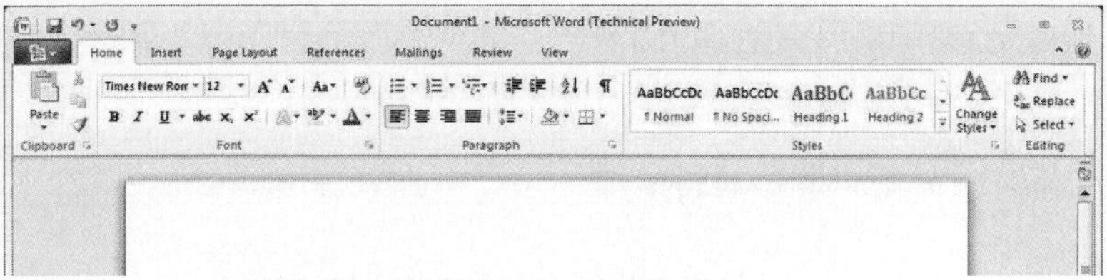

Source: Microsoft

FIGURE 8.1 The Home Tab in Microsoft Word 2016.

Word-processing programs vary in their arrangement of options. Some include menus of commands on toolbars instead of on tabs. Take some time to learn the different formatting options available in your program.

8c   Think intentionally about design.

For any document that you create in print or online, whether for an academic course or for a purpose and an audience beyond college, apply the same basic design principles:

- Organize information for readers.
- Choose fonts and use lists and other graphic options to make your text readable and to emphasize key material.
- Format related design elements consistently.
- Include headings to organize long texts.
- Use design elements intentionally.
- Meet the needs of all readers, including those with disabilities.

A sample page from a student's report on a local food bank, which includes information that she gathered while serving as a volunteer, illustrates these principles. The content in the sample shown in Figure 8.2 on page 86 is not presented effectively because the author deviated from these principles. By contrast, because of its design, the same material in Figure 8.3 on page 87 is clearer and easier for readers to understand.

1. Organizing information for readers

You can organize information visually and topically by grouping related items, using boxes, indents, headings, spacing, and lists. For example, in this book, headings help to group information for readers, and bulleted and numbered lists like the bulleted list in the Navigating through College and Beyond box on page 89 present related points. These variations in text appearance help readers scan material, locate important information, and dive in when they need to know more about a topic. If a color printer is available to you and your instructor allows you to use color, you have another tool for organizing information. For instance, in this text, headings are in red type and subheadings

The Caring Express Food Bank

The Caring Express Food Bank serves a varied population of clients, including chronically homeless people, temporarily homeless people, recent immigrants, elderly people on fixed incomes, and people in need of temporary services.

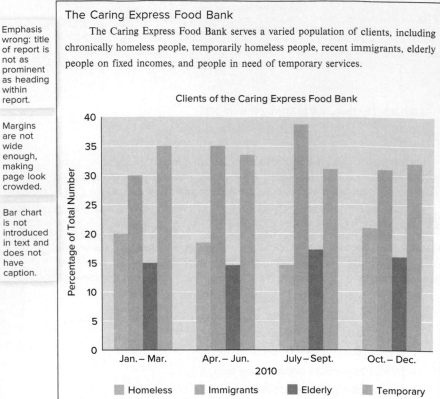

While the number of homeless, both temporary and permanent, that Caring Express assisted in 2010 decreased during the summer months, the number of immigrant workers increased. The percentage of elderly people and people in need of temporary services remained fairly stable throughout the year.

How Caring Express Helps Clients

When new clients come to Caring Express, a volunteer fills out a **form** with their **address** (if they have one), their **phone number,** their **income,** their **employment situation,** and the help they are receiving, if any, from the local department of human services. Clients who do not live in Maple Valley are referred to a food bank or outreach program in their area. Clients who qualify check off the food they need from a list, and then that food is packed and distributed to them.

FIGURE 8.2 **Example of a poorly designed report.**

The Caring Express Food Bank

The Caring Express Food Bank serves a varied population of clients, including chronically homeless people, temporarily homeless people, recent immigrants, elderly people on fixed incomes, and people in need of temporary services. As Figure 1 shows, while the number of homeless, both temporary and permanent, that Caring Express assisted in 2010 decreased during the summer months, the number of immigrant workers increased. The percentage of elderly people and people in need of temporary services remained fairly stable throughout the year.

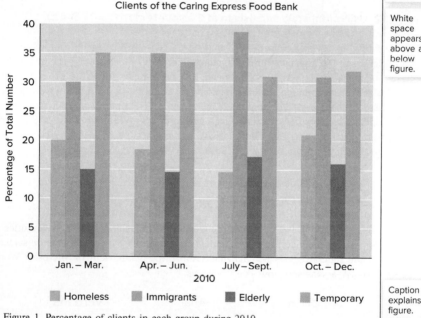

Figure 1. Percentage of clients in each group during 2010

How Caring Express Helps Clients

When new clients come to Caring Express, the volunteers follow this procedure:

1. The volunteer fills out a form with the client's address (if the client has one), phone number, income, and employment situation.
2. Clients who do not live in Maple Valley are referred to a food bank or outreach program in their area.
3. Clients who qualify check off the food they need from a list.
4. The food is packed and distributed to them.

Sidebar annotations:
- Title is centered and in larger type than text and heading.
- Bar chart is introduced and explained.
- White space appears above and below figure.
- Caption explains figure.
- Heading is subordinate to title.
- Procedure is explained in numbered list. Parallel structure used for list entries.

FIGURE 8.3   Example of a well-designed report.

are in blue type. Use color with restraint, and remember that colors may look different on screen and on paper. Choose colors that display well for all readers *(pp. 91–92).*

White space, areas of a document that do not contain type or graphics, can also help you organize information. Generous margins and plenty of white space above headings and around other elements make the text easier to read.

You should also introduce visuals within your text and position them so that they appear near—but never before—the text reference. Balance your visuals and other text elements; for example, don't try to cram too many visuals onto one page.

2. Using font style and lists to make your text readable and to emphasize key elements

Fonts, or *typefaces,* are designs that have been established by printers for the letters in the alphabet, numbers, punctuation marks, and special characters. For most academic texts, choose a standard, easy-to-read font and a 11- or 12-point size. You can manipulate fonts for effect: for example, 12-point Times New Roman can be **boldfaced,** *italicized,* and underlined. Serif fonts have tiny lines at the ends of letters such as *n* and *y;* sans serif fonts do not have these lines. Standard serif fonts such as the following have traditionally been used for basic printed text because they are easy to read:

Times New Roman   Courier

Bookman Old Style   Palatino

Sans serif fonts like the following are used for headings because they offer a contrast, or for electronic documents because they are more readable on screen. (Some standards may be changing. Calibri, the default font in Microsoft Word 2016, is a sans serif font.)

Calibri   Arial   Verdana

Usually, if the main text of a document is in a sans serif font, headings should be in a serif font, and vice versa. In general, you should not use more than two fonts in a single text.

Many fonts available on your computer are known as *display fonts,* for example:

Curlz   Old English

Lucida Sans   *Monotype Corsiva*

These should be used rarely, if ever, in academic texts, on the screen, or in presentations. They can be used effectively in other kinds of documents, however, such as brochures, flyers, and posters.

Numbered or bulleted lists help you cluster large amounts of information, making the information easier for readers to reference and understand. Because they stand out from your text visually, lists also help readers see that ideas are related. You can use a numbered list to display steps in a sequence, present checklists, or suggest recommendations for action.

Format text as a numbered or bulleted list by choosing the option you want from your word-processing program's formatting commands. Introduce the list with a complete sentence followed by a colon (:); use parallel structure in your list items; and put a period at the end of each item only if the entries are complete sentences.

Putting information in a box provides emphasis and makes it easy to locate for future reference. Most word-processing programs offer several ways to enclose text within a border or box.

3. Formatting related design elements

In design, the key practices are simplicity, contrast, and consistency. If you emphasize an item by putting it in italic or bold type or in color, or if you use a graphic element such as a box to set it off, consider repeating this effect for

— NAVIGATING THROUGH COLLEGE AND BEYOND
The Basics: Margins, Spacing, Fonts, and Page Numbers

Here are a few basic guidelines for formatting academic texts:

- **First page:** In an assignment under five pages, you can usually place a header with your name, your professor's name, your course and section number, and the date on the first page, above the text. *(See the first page of Joseph Honrado's project on p. 136.)* If your text exceeds five pages, page 1 is often a title page. *(See the first page of Rachel Anthony's project, on p. 351.)*

- **Font:** Select a common font and choose the 10- or 12-point size.

- **Margins:** Use one-inch margins on all four sides of the text. Adequate margins make your document easier to read and give your instructor room to write comments and suggestions.

- **Margin justification:** Line up, or justify, the lines of your document along the left margin but not along the right margin. Leaving a "ragged right"—or uneven—right margin, as in this box, enables you to avoid odd spacing between words.

- **Spacing:** Double-space unless you are instructed to do otherwise, and indent the first line of each paragraph five spaces. (Many business documents are single-spaced, with an extra line space between paragraphs, which are not indented.)

- **Page numbers:** Place page numbers in the upper or lower right-hand corner of the page. Some documentation styles require a header next to the page number. *(See Tabs 6–8.)*

similar items so that your document has a unified look. Even a simple horizontal line can be a purposeful element in a long document when used consistently for organization.

4. Using headings to organize long documents

In short texts, headings can be disruptive and unnecessary. In longer texts, though, they can help organize complex information. *(For headings in APA style, see Chapter 33.)*

Effective headings are brief, descriptive, and consistent in grammatical structure and formatting:

PHRASES BEGINNING WITH -*ING* WORDS

Fielding Inquiries

Handling Complaints

NOUNS AND NOUN PHRASES

Customer Inquiries

Complaints

QUESTIONS

How Do I Field Inquiries?

How Do I Handle Complaints?

IMPERATIVE SENTENCES

Field Inquiries Efficiently

Handle Complaints Calmly and Politely

Headings at different levels can be in different forms. For example, the first-level headings in a book might be imperative sentences, while the second-level headings might begin with -*ing* words.

Place and highlight headings consistently throughout the text. If you have not already done so, preparing a formal topic outline will help you decide what your main points and second-level points are and where headings should go. *(For help with topic outlines, see Chapter 5, pp. 45-48.)* You might center all first-level headings, which correspond to the main points in your outline. If you have second-level headings—your supporting points—you might align them at the left margin and underline them. Third-level headings, if you have them, could be aligned at the left margin and set in plain type:

First-Level Heading

Second-Level Heading

Third-Level Heading

If a heading falls at the very bottom of the page, move it to the top of the next page.

5. Using design elements sparingly and intentionally

If you use too many graphics, headings, bullets, boxes, or other elements in a document, you risk making it as "noisy" as a loud radio. Standard fonts have become standard because they are easy on the eye. Bold type, italic type, underlining, and other graphic effects should not continue for more than one sentence at a time.

6. Meeting the needs of readers with disabilities

If your potential audience might include the visually or hearing impaired, take these principles into account:

- **Use a large, easily readable font:** The font should be 14 point or larger; 18 is best, and bold the entire text. Use a sans serif font such as Arial, as readers with poor vision find these fonts easier to read. Make headings larger than the surrounding text (rather than relying on a change in font, bold, italics, or color to set them apart).

- **Use ample spacing between lines:** The American Council of the Blind recommends a line space of at least 1.5.

- **Use appropriate, high-contrast colors:** Black text on a white background is best. If you use color for text or visuals, put light material on a dark background and dark material on a light background. Use colors from different families (such as yellow on purple). Avoid red and green because colorblind readers may have trouble distinguishing them. Do not use glossy paper.

- **Include narrative descriptions of all visuals:** Describe each chart, map, photograph, or other visual in your text. Indicate the key information and the point the visual makes. (This is more important when writing for the Web because individuals may use screen-reader software [*p. 168*].)

NAVIGATING THROUGH COLLEGE AND BEYOND

Standard Headings and Templates

Some types of documents, such as lab reports and case studies, have standard headings, for example, "Introduction," "Abstract," and "Methods and Materials" for a lab report. *(See Chapter 12, pp. 145–48.)*

Word-processing programs allow you to create **templates,** preformatted styles that establish the structure and settings for a document and apply them automatically. If you make use of a specific format—such as a lab report—on a regular basis, consider creating a template for it.

- **If you include audio or video files in an electronic document, provide transcripts:** Also include a narrative description of what is happening in the video.

For further information, consult the American Council of the Blind (<http://acb.org/large-print-guidelines>), Lighthouse International (<http://li129-107.members.linode.com/accessibility/design/accessible-print-design/making-text-legible/>), and the American Printing House for the Blind (<www.aph.org/research/design-guidelines/>).

8d Compile an effective print or electronic portfolio.

Students, job candidates, and professionals are often asked to collect their writing in a portfolio. Although some portfolios consist of a collection of texts in print form, more often writers create electronic writing portfolios incorporating a variety of media.

Portfolios, regardless of medium, share at least three common features:

- They are a *collection* of work.
- They are a *selection—or* subset—of a larger body of work.
- They are introduced, narrated, or commented on by a text (for example, print or video) that offers *reflections* on the work.

Like all types of writing, portfolios serve a purpose and address an audience—to demonstrate your progress in a course for your instructor, for example, or to present your best work for a prospective employer. Portfolios allow writers to assess their work and set new writing goals.

1. Assembling a print portfolio

Course requirements vary, so always follow the guidelines your instructor provides. You will usually engage in the five activities mentioned below.

Gathering your writing Create a list, or inventory, of the items that you might include, such as early and final drafts. Make sure all material includes your name and that your final drafts are error free.

Reviewing written work and making appropriate selections Keep the purpose of the portfolio in mind as well as the criteria that will be used to evaluate it. If you are assembling a presentation portfolio, select your very best work. If you are demonstrating your improvement as a writer in a process portfolio, select work that shows your development.

Always consider the audience for the portfolio when deciding which selections will be most appropriate. Who will read it, and what qualities will they be looking for?

Arranging the selections deliberately If you have not been told how to organize your portfolio—for instance, in the order in which you wrote the pieces or according to the outcomes of the course—think of it as if it were a single text and decide on an arrangement that will serve your purpose, perhaps from weakest to strongest when showing development, for example.

Writing a reflective essay or letter   The reflective statement may take the form of an essay or a letter, depending on purpose and requirements. Sometimes the reflective essay will be the last one in a portfolio, so the reader can review all the work before reading the writer's interpretation. Alternatively, a reflective letter can open the portfolio. Regardless of its genre or placement, the reflective text gives you an opportunity to explain something about your writing and about yourself as a writer. Common topics in the reflective text include

- How you developed various assignments
- Which projects you believe are particularly strong and why
- What you learned as you worked on these assignments
- Who you are now as a writer

To write a successful reflective text, be sure to employ the writing process, including drafting, obtaining feedback, and revising. Once you have completed it, assemble all the components of your print portfolio in a folder or notebook.

Polishing your portfolio   In the process of writing the reflective letter or essay, you might discover a better way to arrange your work. Or as you arrange the portfolio, you might want to review all your work again. Do not be surprised if you find yourself repeating some of these tasks. As with any writing, peer review will help you revise your portfolio to be most effective.

Most students learn about themselves and their writing as they compile portfolios and write reflections on their work. The process makes them better writers and helps them learn how to demonstrate their strengths to others.

2. Preparing an electronic portfolio

For some courses or professional purposes, you will want to present your work in an electronic portfolio, or ePortfolio. An education student might be required to provide an ePortfolio of lesson plans, writing assignments, and other instructional materials, while a media studies student applying for graduate school might want to showcase videos and social media posts. Electronic portfolios are typically published on the Web.

The process of creating an ePortfolio differs somewhat from that of creating a print portfolio in three basic ways: (1) the kind of artifacts it includes; (2) the multiple opportunities for arrangements it offers; and (3) its use of the visual. See the Checklist box on page 94 for the essential steps.

Gathering your written work as well as your audio, video, and visual texts   Depending on your assignment and purpose, you should consider these four inventories:

- A verbal inventory, consisting of your written work (including any handwritten work, which you should scan)
- A visual inventory (examples: photographs, drawings, presentation slides)

- An audio inventory (examples: speeches, music, podcasts)
- A video inventory (examples: movie clips, videos you have created)

Because ePortfolios are posted on the Internet, and the Internet is a visual medium, selecting visuals defining the ePortfolio is a critical second step. Identifying font style and size, background colors, and appropriate visuals that can unify the various "pages" of your ePortfolio can help you think about how to describe your work. A student studying oceanography might use an ocean image, or variations of that image, across multiple pages. A student double majoring in business and international affairs might include images of countries visited to highlight interest in work around the globe.

Selecting appropriate texts and making connections among them   Choose works from your inventory based on your portfolio's purpose, audience, and criteria for evaluation. Consider two kinds of relationships. First, the connections across your external materials—those that you created—should reveal something about you and your writing. They will become the links that help the reader navigate your digital portfolio. *Internal links* connect items within the portfolio. For instance, you might link an earlier draft to a later one or link a PowerPoint presentation to a final draft on the same topic. *External links* connect the reader to related files external to the portfolio but relevant to it. If you collaborated with a colleague or a classmate on a project, you might link to that person's electronic portfolio. *(See Chapter 14: Multimodal Writing, pp. 161-72.)*

Deciding on an arrangement, navigation, and presentation   You have many possibilities for arrangement in an ePortfolio, and many ePortfolio composers provide two ways to navigate—through links between pages and tabs at the top, bottom, or sides of the main page. Possible arrangements include according to (1) project, (2) genre, (3) time, (4) outcomes, or (5) medium. Once you have decided on an arrangement, help your reader navigate the portfolio. Create a storyboard or chart that shows each item in your portfolio and how it is linked to others. *(See Chapter 14: Multimodal Writing, pp. 163-68.)* After you have planned your site's structure, add hyperlinks to the pages hosting the documents. The link text should be clearly descriptive (a link reading "Résumé," for example, should lead to your résumé).

CHECKLIST Creating an Electronic Portfolio

- ☐ Gather all your written work and audio, video, and visual texts.
- ☐ Make selections, and consider connections.
- ☐ Decide on arrangement, navigation, and presentation.
- ☐ Include a reflective essay or letter.
- ☐ Test your portfolio for usability.

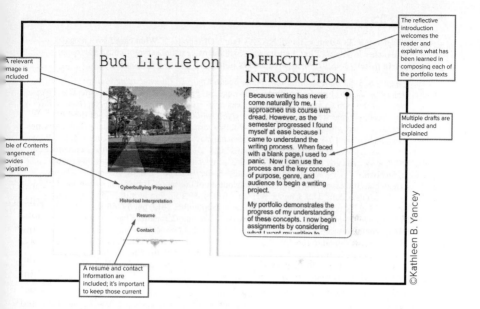

The reflective introduction welcomes the reader and explains what has been learned in composing each of the portfolio texts

A relevant image is included

Multiple drafts are included and explained

ble of Contents angement ovides vigation

A resume and contact information are included; it's important to keep those current

©Kathleen B. Yancey

FIGURE 8.4 A screen from a student's electronic portfolio. Note the many links for easy navigation.

The portfolio in Figure 8.4 on page 95 features a menu of links that appears on each page, as well as links in the reflective text. Consider how the opening screen will establish your purpose and appeal to your audience. Choose colors and images for the front page and successive pages, as well as fonts that visually present you as a writer and establish a tone appropriate for your purpose.

Writing or videotaping a reflective text   As in a print portfolio, the reflective text introduces readers to the ePortfolio. A digital environment, however, offers more possibilities for presenting this reflection. You can make it highly visual; for example, you might have it cascade across a series of screens. Another option would be to link to open the ePortfolio with an audio or video file in which you talk directly to the reader; if you choose this approach, be sure to plan what you will say before taping, and be sure to keep the introduction focused and concise. No one likes a talking head!

Testing your electronic portfolio   Make sure your portfolio works—both conceptually and structurally—before publishing it. Navigate through the portfolio yourself, and ask a friend to do so from a different computer. Sometimes links fail to work, or files stored on one machine do not open on another. Your friend will undoubtedly have constructive comments and suggestions about the portfolio's structure and content. You might acknowledge this help in a section of acknowledgments where you thank others who have supported your efforts.

Credits

Chapter 4: p. 33 Adam Voiland, NASA's Earth Observatory "What cased twin mega-avalanches in Tibet?" Blog, February 6, 2018. https://earthobservatory.nasa.gov/blogs/earthmatters/2018/02/06/what-caused-twin-mega-avalanches-in-tibet/.

Chapter 6: p. 53 Beth Rubin, *Shifts in the Social Contract: Understanding Change in American Society* (Pine Forge Press, 1996). **pp. 54–55** From "Yellow Journalism: The 'Fake News' of the 19th Century" This article was originally published in *The Public Domain Review*, http://publicdomainreview.org/collections/yellow-journalism-the-fake-news-of-the-19th-century/. Used with permission of The Public Domain Review. **p. 56** William Galle, *Business Communication: A Technology Based Approach.* (New York: McGraw-Hill, 2000). **p. 56** "Back to Basics: All About MyPlate Food Groups" U.S. Department of Agriculture, September 26, 2017. www.usda.gov/media/blog/2017/09/26/back-basics-all-about-myplate-food-groups. **p. 56** NASA, "What We Study: Black Holes" https://science.nasa.gov/astrophysics/focus-areas/black-holes. **p. 58** Data from "Distribution of household income in 2014 according to U.S. Census data" U.S. Census Bureau, 2014. **p. 59** Tom Vanderbilt, "How Biomimicry Is Inspiring Human Innovation" *Smithsonian*, September 2012. **pp. 59–60** Richard Schaefer, *Sociology in Modules* New York: McGraw-Hill, 2011. **p. 62** Jonathan Fast, "After Columbine: How People Mourn Sudden Death" *Social Work*, vol. 48 no. 4, October 2003. **p. 62** Damian Robinson, "Riding into the Afterlife" *Archaeology*, vol. 57 no. 2, March/April 2004. **pp. 62–63** Elaine Maimon, "Students Must Focus on Degree Completion" *The Times of Northwest Indiana*, November 7, 2010. **p. 63** Roger Kamien, *Music: An Appreciation* New York: McGraw-Hill Education, 2012.

Chapter 7: p. 71 Douglas Kellner, *Media Culture: Cultural Studies, Identity and Politics Between the Modern and the Post Modern* London: Routledge, 1995. p 252. **p. 72** Michael J. Berthel, Senior Assistant Director of Adelphi's Center for Student Involvement, quoted in Caitlin Peterkin, "A Week After Hurricane Sandy, Students Step Up Their Relief Work," *The Chronicle of Higher Education*, November 8, 2012. **p. 74** Tony Rogers, "Why Bloggers Can't Replace the Work of Professional Journalists," ThoughtCo, August 25, 2017, www.thoughtco.com/bloggers-professional-journalists-2074116. **p. 76** *Mathematics: Applications and Connections - Course 2* New York: McGraw-Hill Education, 1998.

Design Elements: (butterfly/computer): ©Visual Generation/Shutterstock; (other design icons): ©McGraw-Hill Education

3

Common Assignments across the Curriculum

Anybody who is involved in working across the disciplines is much more likely to have a lively mind and a lively life.

–Mary Field Belenky

© Joymsk140/Shutterstock

Auguste Rodin's sculpture *The Thinker* evokes the psychological complexity of human thought and suggests the spirit of critical inquiry common to all disciplines across the curriculum.

3 Common Assignments

◉ Section dealing with visual rhetoric. For a complete listing, see the Quick Guide to Key Resources in Connect.

Tab 3: Common Assignments across the Curriculum

This section will help you answer the following questions about your writing.

Rhetorical Knowledge

- How can I argue persuasively? (11b)
- How can I keep my audience interested in my oral presentation? (13b)
- What should I *not* put on my blog or social media page? (14d)

Critical Thinking, Reading, and Writing

- How do I analyze a literary work? (10b)
- How can I defend my thesis against counterarguments? (11b)

Processes

- What is the best way to prepare for essay exams? (12d)
- How can I use presentation software (such as PowerPoint) effectively? (13c, 14a)
- What steps should I take in planning my Web site? (14c)

Knowledge of Conventions

- What is a review of the literature, and where do such reviews appear? (9d, 12c)
- What disciplines use lab reports and case studies? (12b, c)

For a general introduction to writing outcomes, see 1e, pages 14–15.

Most college courses require writing—from the lab report in chemistry to the policy proposal in economics. This section gives you tips on writing the most common kinds of college assignments and explains the distinctive features of each kind.

CHAPTER 9

Informative Reports

Imagine what the world would be like without records of what others have learned. Fortunately, we have many sources of information to draw on, including informative reports.

9a   Understand the assignment.

An **informative report** shares what someone has learned about a topic or issue; it teaches. An informative report gives you a chance to do the following:

- Learn more about an issue that interests you
- Make sense of what you have read, heard, and seen
- Teach others what you have learned

9b   Approach writing an informative report as a process.

1. Selecting a topic that interests you

The major challenge in writing informative reports is engaging readers' interest. Selecting a topic that interests you makes it more likely that your report will interest others.

Connect what you are learning in one course with a topic you are studying in another course or with your personal experience. For example, student Rachel Anthony, a health and human performance major, aspired to a career in physical education. For her topic, she decided to investigate the impact of doping on Olympic athletes. *(Anthony's essay begins on p. 102.)*

2. Considering what your readers know about the topic

Assume that your readers have some familiarity with the topic but that most of them do not have clear, specific knowledge of it. In her report on Olympic doping, Anthony assumes that her readers are familiar with the consequences athletes face when caught using performance-enhancing drugs, but they may not know about some of the other impacts of cheating.

3. Developing an objective stance

A commitment to objectivity gives your report its authority. Present differing views fairly, and do not take sides in a debate. Your voice will sound unbiased if you carefully select words that are precise without being emotional.

KNOW THE SITUATION   Informative Reports

Purpose: To inform

Audience: Classmates and instructor, other readers on campus interested in the topic, and athletes who may be affected by it.

Stance: Reasonable, informed, objective

Genre: Informative report

Medium: Print, digital text, Web page, video, audio, poster

Commonly used: In most disciplines, the workplace, and public life

— the EVOLVING SITUATION

Informative Reports

Informative reports are published across print and new media formats and are commonly written by members of humanities, social sciences, and natural sciences disciplines, as these examples indicate:

- In a published article, an anthropologist surveys and summarizes a large body of material on indigenous warfare among the Pueblos before the arrival of the Spanish explorers.

- For an encyclopedia of British women writers, a professor of literature briefly recounts the life and work of Eliza Fenwick, a recently rediscovered eighteenth-century author.

- In an academic journal, two biochemists summarize the findings of more than two hundred recently published articles on defense mechanisms in plants.

- A researcher at the Pew Research Center's *Journalism Project*, a Web site that tracks trends in the news media, reports on the five indicators of sustainability in the nonprofit news sector.

4. Composing a thesis that summarizes your knowledge of the topic

An informative thesis typically reports the results of the writer's study. Before you commit to a thesis, review the information you have collected. Compose a thesis statement that presents the goal of your paper and forecasts its content. *(For more on thesis statements, see Tab 2: Writing and Designing Texts, pp. 43–45.)*

In the report on Olympic doping, Anthony develops a general thesis that she supports in the body of her report with information about why athletes cheat, how they cheat, and what the impacts of their actions are on their careers and on their fellow athletes.

Although cheating by Olympic athletes is nothing new, their reasons for cheating and the methods they use to do so have evolved over time. And the consequences that cheaters and their fellow athletes endure as a result are far-reaching and significant.

Notice how Anthony forecasts the body of her report. We expect to learn something about each of the subtopics she lists in her thesis.

5. Providing context in your introduction

Informative reports usually begin with a simple introduction to the topic and a straightforward statement of the thesis. Provide relevant context or background, but get to your specific topic as quickly as possible, and keep it in the foreground. *(For more on introductions, see Tab 2: Writing and Designing Texts, pp. 63-64.)*

6. Using classification and division as one way to organize your information

Develop ideas in an organized way by classifying and dividing information into categories, subtopics, or the stages of a process. *(See Tab 2: Writing and Designing Texts, pp. 56-57.)*

7. Illustrating key ideas with examples

Use specific examples to help readers understand your ideas. In her report on Olympic doping, Anthony provides specific examples, including statistical information on doping, quotations from athletes affected by cheating, and a discussion of the historic origins of cheating. Examples make her report interesting as well as educational. *(See Tab 2: Writing and Designing Texts, p. 53, for more advice on using examples.)*

8. Defining specialized terms and spelling out unfamiliar abbreviations

Specialized terms (such as foreign words or discipline-specific terminology) will probably not be familiar to most readers. Explain these terms with a synonym or a brief definition. For example, Anthony provides a definition of doping in the seventh paragraph of her informative report. *(For more on definition, see Tab 2: Writing and Designing Texts, pp. 56-57.)* Unfamiliar abbreviations like WADA (World Anti-Doping Agency) are spelled out the first time they are used, with the abbreviation in parentheses.

9. Concluding by answering "so what?"

Conclude by referring to a common idea or an example that speaks to the importance of the information. The conclusion reminds readers of the topic and thesis. It then answers the "so what?" question by giving readers a sense of why they should care about what they have just read.

At the end of her report on Olympic doping, for example, Anthony answers the "so what?" question by emphasizing the consequences of cheating, not only for the athletes who have resorted to cheating, but also for their fellow athletes.

> The cost of doping—financial and otherwise—is incalculable and affects all athletes, whether they are medalists or not. The decision to take away Jones's five medals may have affected the status of dozens of athletes ("Jones stripped"). Take away a gold medal and the silver medalist moves up; then the bronze winner; then suddenly, like Lowe, the sixth-place finisher is a medal winner—sometimes years later,

CONSIDER YOUR SITUATION

Author: Rachel Anthony, a health and human performance major interested in a career in physical education

Type of writing: Informative report

Purpose: To inform readers about cheating in the Olympic Games

Stance: Reasonable, informed, objective

Audience: Classmates and instructor standing in for general public

Medium: Print and digital text attached to an e-mail

Anthony writes: After writing this informative report, I know a great deal more about how and why some athletes resort to using performance-enhancing drugs, and I want to share that information with readers.

without the medal ceremony, the endorsements, and the additional competition opportunities. As Lowe explained, "It rewrites my story" (Williams, 2017).

(For more on conclusions, see Tab 2: Writing and Designing Texts, p. 64.)

9c   Student sample: Informative report

In the informative report that follows, Rachel Anthony synthesizes what she has learned about the impact of cheating on Olympic athletes. As you read her report, notice how Anthony provides a context for her topic, cites various sources (using APA documentation style), divides the information into subtopics, and illustrates her ideas with examples, all hallmarks of a clear, carefully developed report. The annotations in the margin point out specific features of the informative report.

Note: For details on the proper formatting of a text in APA style, see Chapter 33 and the student sample that begins on page 351.

SAMPLE STUDENT INFORMATIVE REPORT

Olympic Doping

Rachel Anthony

SOC 101

History and Sociology of Sport

Professor Filippo

April 29, 2020

--[new page]--

Olympic Doping

Following APA Style, Anthony includes a separate title page. Her abstract is given its own page, following the title page. See p. 351 for an example of proper formatting of an abstract in APA style.

Chaunté Lowe's story showcases both the best and the worst of the Olympic Games. A high jumper, Lowe competed in four games—in 2004, 2008, 2012, and 2016—without winning a medal. She did, however, become "a favorite of the track crowds, with her high bounding steps and leaps, slithering up, up and over that bar" (Powell, 2017, para. 26). Her appeal is evident: "She lands and bounds to her feet, clapping, smiling, doing a little boogie" (Powell, 2017, para. 26). Lowe has the backstory that Olympic announcers love to feature, according to Powell. She grew up with an unreliable mother and a father in jail, and she experienced a house foreclosure followed by a period of homelessness. In spite of these early difficulties, she eventually found a much-needed sense of stability in her grandmother, with whom she lived, and later in a supportive and committed coach at Georgia Tech (Powell, 2017).

The first use of a source in this paper includes reference to the author (Powell), date (2017), and location within the text. This source has no page numbers, so a paragraph number is included instead.

Topic introduced.

Doping plays a huge role in the current chapter of Lowe's life story. In November 2016, Lowe was notified that retroactive drug tests revealed that the third-, fourth-, and fifth-place finishers in the 2008 Olympics in Beijing had resorted to doping. This revelation effectively moved Lowe from sixth place to third, which meant that she earned a bronze medal (Powell, 2017). Telling her story on John Williams's WGN radio show (Williams, 2017), she sounds happy and wistful, not bitter. "Cheating was never an option for me," she told Williams. But still, she can understand the pressures on others to do so.

Although cheating by Olympic athletes is nothing new, their reasons for cheating and the methods they use to do so have evolved over time. And the consequences that cheaters and their fellow athletes endure as a result are far-reaching and significant.

Thesis stated.

Olympic Origins

Although the true origin of the Olympics is unknown, Phippen (2016), a journalist, related a story that might provide insight into why some athletes cheat. Pelops, a suitor for the hand of Greek King Oenomaus' daughter, began the games roughly 3,000 years ago to "commemorate his triumph" after besting King Oenomaus in a chariot race, thus becoming the king's son-in-law. To ensure a win, Pelops "bribed a man" to rig Oenomaus' chariot. In this version of the origins of the Olympics, the games were actually created because of cheating.

Context provided in introduction.

According to some sources, including Phippen, "plenty of athletes cheated" (2016, para. 10), despite swearing to Zeus to compete fairly. Cheaters were sometimes flogged or were excluded from the games. They also paid fines that were used to erect *Zanes*, or honorific statues in the likeness of Zeus (Cartwright, 2013). Each *Zane* included a "small plaque that chastised competitors accused of misconduct" (Phippen, 2016, para. 9). The *Zanes*, however, were not a deterrent (Spivey, 2004). "This warning, and the overt, long-standing disgrace of miscreants, did not deter further incidents of bribery and subterfuge: the number of *Zanes* multiplied" (p. 166).

Over the years since those first games, "the manner of cheating has evolved," wrote Phippen, but "the human desire to cheat has not" (2016, para. 4). The games that have come to be known as the Modern Olympics, the first games after A.D. 393, began in 1896 in Athens, when 241 participants from 14 nations competed in 43 events (International Olympic Committee, n.d.-a). For these games the marathon was created "as a tribute to the legend of Pheidippides, a courier who ran roughly twenty-five miles, from a great battle . . . and then collapsed and died from the effort" (Staton, 2012, para. 2). The third-place marathon winner of the 1896

The letter "a" helps distinguish between two sources by the same author (the IOC) with the same date (or, in this case, no date, "n.d.")

games was discovered to have used a carriage to complete a portion of the course. Eight years later, a car replaced the carriage in a similar incident (Staton, 2012, para. 5). So began the modern era of Olympic cheating.

Modern-Day Cheating

Today, an Olympic athlete jumping into a car for a few miles seems practically impossible; cameras capture competitors' every move on the course. However, there are other ways of cheating, such as doping—broadly defined by the World Anti-Doping Agency (WADA) as "the occurrence of one or more of the anti-doping rule violations," which include the use, attempted use, or "presence of a *Prohibited Substance* . . . in an *Athlete's Sample*" (2015, p. 18). Even though athletes are monitored and tested on a routine basis, many do not seem to be deterred from doping.

It is worth noting that some athletes cheat without knowing they are doing so. The East German women's swimming team is a famous example. Reporting from Berlin in 2000 for *The New York Times*, Alan Maimon covered the court case of Lothar Kipke. As the head doctor in charge of the drug program of the East German Swimming Federation from 1975 to 1985, Kipke was ultimately convicted "of doping and causing bodily harm to 58 swimmers" (Maimon, 2000, introduction, para. 4). The girls who were doped, some as young as 10 years old, were given "40 pills a day," which were "taken under strict supervision" (Maimon, 2000, "A Regimen of Pills," para. 3). Years later, many swimmers reported major medical issues, including pregnancies resulting in birth defects (Maimon, 2000).

Others cheat purposefully. Edwards quotes Dick Pound, the former WADA chairman, on five of the top reasons athletes choose to use performance-enhancing drugs:

1. A desire to win at all costs – even if that means lying.
2. For financial reasons – with professionals trying to extend a career.
3. National pressures – as exemplified by the old East German system.

Margin notes:

First use of unfamiliar abbreviation spelled out.

Quotation integrated into writer's sentence.

Example given for clarity and interest.

Source named in signal phrase.

Citation of a specific part of a source (its "introduction") with no page numbers.

Development by classification (see p. 53).

4.   Individual pressure from coaches – who get paid better if they coach winners, and that can apply for administrators, too.

5   Finally, they dope because they believe they will not get caught – they believe they are invincible. (2010, para. 10)

By all accounts, the pressures on Olympians are intense, and significant funds are required for training and competing even before an athlete reaches the Olympic Games. However, the temptation to cheat is great. "Once you start winning, sponsors will be attracted and then money will come," explained South African athlete Hezekiel Sepeng, who won a silver medal at the 1996 Olympic Games but lost his career when he later tested positive for an anabolic steroid (Edwards, 2012, "Leveling the Playing Field," para. 8). Another example is US sprinter Marion Jones, who in 2007 lost millions of dollars in sponsorship deals when stripped of her Olympic medals (Edwards, 2012). A December 12, 2007, ESPN.com story describes Jones, "once the world's biggest track and field star," as a "disgraced drug cheat" (2007, para. 2).

Citation of a specific part of an electronic source: Paragraph 8 in the section titled "Leveling the Playing Field."

The perspectives of athletes are important to this topic, so are quoted directly.

Money and medals aside, Edwards has noted that the "sad truth is that many [athletes] do successfully beat the drug testers" (2012, para. 16). Moreover, while many athletes dope in order to boost their already considerable talents, others say they dope not to gain advantage, but rather to avoid disadvantage. If other athletes are doping, then the competition is unfair (Edwards, 2012). On October 9, 2012, George Hincapie, an elite cyclist, posted a statement on his website that supports this theory:

Paraphrase with a source provided in parenthetical citation.

It is extremely difficult today to acknowledge that during a part of my career I used banned substances. . . . Early in my professional career, it became clear to me that, given the widespread use of performance enhancing drugs by cyclists at the top of the profession, it was not possible to compete at the highest level without them. (Hincapie, para. 3)

Source
given for
data.

Hincapie is not alone. Gifford (2016), writing for *Scientific American* online, cited an anonymous survey revealing that 29% of polled athletes confessed to resorting to performance-enhancing drugs. "Clearly, plenty of cheaters are getting away with it," Gifford (2016, para. 6) concluded.

The website of the International Olympic Committee does not provide a list of athletes who have been stripped of their medals. A search for medalists from the 2008 Beijing Games turns up this official statement: "Please note that because a number of anti-doping rules violations procedures are still in progress—including procedures involving . . . the samples collected in Beijing 2008 and London 2012—the information contained in the list is not final" (International Olympic Committee, n.d.-b). However, a 2015 report posted on the WADA website (World Anti-Doping Agency, 2017) offers some statistics on anti-doping rule violations (see Figure 1).

While many cheaters are never discovered, in the long run, the odds seem to be against athletes who dope: "In order to compete, athletes must give up their privacy, notifying officials of their whereabouts every single day of the year, so they can be located for on-the-spot, out-of-competition testing overseen by the World Anti-Doping Agency" (Gifford, 2016, introduction, para. 7). In her WGN interview, Chaunté Lowe supported Gifford's findings when she explained that drug tests happen randomly and frequently, several times a week. According to Lowe, samples are saved and retested for years to "allow the technology to catch up to the methods of cheating" (Williams, 2017).

The Cost of Doping

The cost of doping—financial and otherwise—is incalculable and affects all athletes, whether they are medalists or not. The decision to take away Jones's five medals may have affected the status of dozens of athletes ("Jones stripped"). Take away a gold medal and the silver medalist moves up; then the bronze winner; then suddenly, like Lowe, the sixth-place finisher is a medal winner—sometimes years later, without the medal ceremony, the endorsements, and the additional competition opportunities. As Lowe explained, "It rewrites my story" (Williams, 2017).

In the years since the summer 2007 Olympics, winners have had the potential to gain millions in endorsement and sponsorship deals. Nonmedalists often do not have that option, even when they receive their awards years later. In other words, winners who are later found to be cheaters nevertheless prosper, at least in the short term. On the other hand, competitors later found to be medal winners are cheated out of possibilities. For example, the pole-vaulter Derek Miles was belatedly awarded a bronze medal for his performance in the Beijing Olympic Games. Today, he is an assistant track coach at the University of South Dakota (Powell, 2017). Coaching track is not a bad job, but winning athletes should have the chance to benefit from their performance. If nothing else, Miles was denied his moment on the dais, standing below the US flag and accepting the congratulations of the 2008 Olympic crowd. Instead of receiving his medal in a cheering stadium, Miles accepted his belated honor on April 17, 2017, in what looks like a windowless classroom. Miles was emotional as he spoke to the small group—thankful, grateful, and appreciative. Like Lowe, he was not bitter. Instead, he spoke of being lucky and of the opportunities he has had to surround himself with great people ("Derek Miles," 2017).

Back in 773 B.C., athletes stood in front of the bronze icon "Zeus the Oath Giver" and "swore an oath to the god of thunder vowing they would follow the regulations of the Olympics and play fair" (Phippen, 2016, para. 1). Today, one Olympian from each host country takes the official Olympian oath for all those competing. One wonders how seriously some athletes treat this oath, as it seems doping is likely to continue for the foreseeable future. Still, other athletes, like Lowe and Miles, continue to take this oath to heart. In doing so, they commit to competing "clean," to benefiting not from drugs, but from skill, passion, and dedication. They are the true Olympians.

References list follows APA style and begins on a new page.

Source: Encyclopedia entry retrieved online.

Source: online video.

Source: Article from a news site.

No site name included because the author and site are the same.

Source: Public statement published on a Web site.

Source: Short article from a Web site.

Special report from an online news source.

------------------------------------[new page]------------------------------------

References

Cartwright, M. (2013, March 23). Olympic Games. In *Ancient History Encyclopedia*. http://www.ancient.eu/Olympic_Games/#related_articles

Derek Miles receives Olympic bronze medal [Video]. (2017, April 17). Argus Leader. http://www.argusleader.com/videos/sports/college/university-of-south-dakota/2017/04/17/video-derek-miles-receives-olympic-bronze-medal/100575290/

Edwards, P. (2012, December 11). The gain game: Why do sports stars cheat? *CNN*. http://www.cnn.com/2012/12/11/sport/sport-cheats-suarez-cazorla/index.html

Gifford, B. (2016, August 5). The *Scientific American* guide to cheating in the Olympics. *Scientific American* https://www.scientificamerican.com/article/the-scientific-american-guide-to-cheating-in-the-olympics/

Hincapie, G. (2012, October 9). [Statement from George Hincapie]. http://hincapie.com/ourstory

International Olympic Committee. (n.d.-a). Athens, 1896. https://www.olympic.org/athens-1896

International Olympic Committee. (n.d.-b). Athletics. https://www.olympic.org/beijing-2008/athletics

Jones stripped of five Olympic medals, banned from Beijing Games. (2007, December 12). ESPN. http://www.espn.com/olympics.trackandfield/news/story?id=3151367

Maimon, A. (2000, February 6). One tale of doping and birth defects [Special report]. *The New York Times*. http://www.nytimes.com/library/sports/other/020600swim-germany.html

Phippen, J. W. (2016, August 19). A brief history of cheating at the Olympics. *The Atlantic*. https://www.theatlantic.com/news/archive/2016/08/cheating-at-the-olympics/495938/

Powell, M. (2017, July 7). Olympic medal, earned; glory, denied; future, uncertain. *The New York Times*. https://www.nytimes.com/2017/07/07/sports/chaunte-lowe-olympics-doping-high-jump.html

Spivey, N. (2004). *Ancient Olympics: A history*. Oxford University Press.

Staton, S. (2012, August 3). Crossing the line. *The New Yorker*. http://newyorker.com/news/sporting-scene/crossing-the-line

Williams, J. (Host). (2017, July 12). "Donald Trump Jr. defends emails" [Audio podcast episode]. In *The John Williams Show*. http://wgnradio.com/2017/07/12/the-john-williams-show-full-podcast-07-12-17-human-chain-rip-tide-rescuer-donald-trump-jrdefends-e-mails-olympics-bronze-medalist-chaunte-lowe/

World Anti-Doping Agency. (2015, January 1). *World anti-doping code 2015*. https://www.wada-ama.org/sites/default/files/resources/files/wada-2015-world-antidoping-code.pdf

World Anti-Doping Agency. (2017, April 3). *2015 Anti-doping rule violations [ADRVs] report*. https://www.wada-ama.org/sites/default/files/resources/files/2015_adrvs_report_web_release_0.pdf

Print book with no assigned DOI.

Source: Audio Podcast.

Source: Report by an organization, retrieved online.

———————————— [New page] ————————————

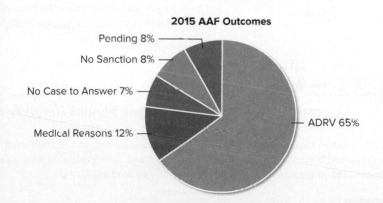

2015 AAF Outcomes

Pending 8%
No Sanction 8%
No Case to Answer 7%
Medical Reasons 12%
ADRV 65%

FIGURE 1. Sports that had the highest numbers of anti-doping rule violations (ADRVs) in 2015. Adapted from "Statistics on anti-doping rule violations (ADRVs)," by the World Anti-Doping Association, 2017, *2015 Anti-doping rule violations [ADRVs] report, p.6* (https://www.wada-ama.org/sites/default/files/resources/file/2015_adrvs_report_web_release_0.pdf). Copyright 2017 by WADA.

9d Write reviews of the literature to survey ideas.

In upper-division courses, instructors sometimes assign a special kind of informative report called a **review of the literature**. Here the term *literature* refers to published research reports—not to novels, poetry, or drama—and the term *review* means a survey of others' ideas, not an evaluation, argument, or opinion. A review presents an organized account of the current state of knowledge in a specific area, something that you and other researchers can use as context for a research question and as a basis for new projects and new directions for research. A review of the literature may also be a subsection within a research report.

The following paragraph is an excerpt from the review of the literature section in an article by psychologists investigating the motivations for suicide.

> One source of information about suicide motives is suicide notes. International studies of suicide notes suggest that women and men do not differ with regard to love versus achievement motives. For example, in a study of German suicide notes, Linn and Lester (1997) found that women and men did not differ with regard to relationship versus financial or work motives. In a study of Hong Kong suicide notes, Ho, Yip, Chiu, and Halliday (1998) reported no gender or age differences with regard to interpersonal problems or financial/job problems. Similarly, in a UK study, McClelland, Reicher, and Booth (2000) found that men's suicide notes did not differ from women's notes in terms of mentioning career failures. In fact, in the UK study, relationship losses were reported more often in men's than in women's suicide notes.
>
> —SILVIA SARA CANETTO AND DAVID LESTER,
> "Love and Achievement Motives in
> Women's and Men's Suicide Notes"

CHAPTER 10

Interpretive Analyses and Writing about Literature

Interpretation means working to understand a written document, literary work, cultural artifact, social situation, or natural event and then explaining what you understand in a meaningful and convincing way to readers.

10a Understand the assignment.

When an assignment asks you to compare, explain, analyze, or discuss something, you are expected to study that subject closely. An **interpretive analysis** moves beyond simple description and examines or compares particular items for a reason: to enhance your readers' understanding of people's conditions, actions, beliefs, or desires.

—KNOW THE SITUATION   Interpretive Analyses

Purpose: To enhance understanding
Audience: Classmates and Instructor, representing readers interested
in the topic and the arts
Stance: Thoughtful, inquisitive, open-minded
Genres: Review, critique, blog
Medium: Print, digital text, Web page, video, audio
Commonly used: In the arts, humanities, and many other disciplines

---

10b   Approach writing an interpretive analysis as a process.

Writing an interpretive analysis typically begins with critical reading. *(See Chapter 4: Reading and Writing: The Critical Connection.)*

1. Discovering an aspect of the subject that is meaningful to you
Think about your own feelings and experiences while you read, listen, or observe. Connecting your own thoughts and experiences to what you are studying can help you develop fresh interpretations.

2. Developing a thoughtful stance
Think of yourself as an explorer. Be thoughtful, curious, and open minded as you discover possible meanings. When you write your analysis, invite your readers to join you on an intellectual journey, saying, in effect, "Come, think this through with me."

3. Using an intellectual framework
To interpret your subject effectively, use a relevant perspective or an intellectual framework. For example, the elements of a work of fiction, such as plot, character, and setting, are often used to analyze stories.

In the student essay that begins on page 117, Isabella Jacobi does a close reading of Mohsen Emadi's poem "Losses." Jacobi bases her analysis on the conventions of love poetry. She began this assignment by closely reading the poem, as well as two secondary sources that helped inform her understanding of what it means to write from the perspective of a political exile. Jacobi then applied her own interpretive skills to write her analysis.

No matter what framework you use, analysis often entails taking your subject apart, figuring out how the parts make up a cohesive whole, and then putting it all back together. Because the goal of analysis is to create a meaningful interpretation, you need to treat the whole as more than the sum of its parts. Determining meaning is a complex problem with multiple solutions.

NAVIGATING THROUGH COLLEGE AND BEYOND

Interpretive Analyses

You can find interpretive analyses like the following in professional journals like *PMLA (Publications of the Modern Language Association)* as well as popular publications like the *New Yorker* and the *Atlantic Monthly.* For example, a cultural critic might contrast the way AIDS and cancer are talked about, imagined, and therefore treated, or a musicologist might compare the revised endings of two pieces by Beethoven to figure out what makes a work complete.

Students are often called on to write interpretive analyses such as the following:

- A student in an English course analyzes the poetic techniques in Mohsen Emadi's "Losses."
- A student majoring in music spells out the emotional implications of the tempo and harmonic progression in Schubert's *Der Atlas.*
- By applying an econometric model of nine variables, a student in an economics course explains that deregulation has not decreased the level of airline safety.

4. Listing, comparing, questioning, and classifying to discover your thesis

To figure out your thesis, it is often useful to explore separate features of your subject. If you are analyzing fiction, you might consider the plot, the characters, the setting, and the tone before deciding to focus your thesis on one character's personality.

Try one or more of the following strategies:

- Annotate the text as you read, or make notes as you experience a movie or concert, and if it helps, write a summary.
- Ask yourself questions about the subject you are analyzing, and write down any interesting answers. Imagine what kinds of questions your instructor or classmates might ask about the artifact, document, or performance you are considering. In answering these questions, try to figure out the thesis you will present and support.
- Name the class of things to which the item you are analyzing belongs (for example, memoirs), and then identify important features of that class (for example, scene, point of view, friends, and turning points).

5. Making your thesis focused and purposeful

To make a point about your subject, focus on one or two key questions. Resist the temptation to describe everything you see. Consider this example of a focused, purposeful thesis for an interpretive analysis of Mohsen Emadi's "Losses."

In an essay on Iranian poets writing in exile, poet and professor of comparative literature Persis Karim explains that "exile [is] a mixed blessing of losing and leaving behind but also acquiring new perspectives, languages, and experiences that enrich and texture their writing." Emadi's "Losses," written in exile, typifies the "mixed blessing" Karim describes. In it, the age-old themes of love and loss are indeed enriched by the poet's newly acquired perspective, language, and experience.

Text continues on page 115.

QUESTIONS FOR ANALYZING LITERATURE

Fiction

Plot and Structure

- What events take place over the course of the work?
- What did you think and feel at different places?
- How do the parts of the work relate to one another?

Characters

- What are the relationships among the people, and how are they portrayed?
- How do they change?
- What does dialogue reveal about their motivations?

Setting

- What is the significance of the time and place?
- What associations does the writer make with the location?

Point of View

- Is there a first-person narrator ("I"), or is the story told by a third-person narrator who reveals what one, all, or none of the characters is thinking?

Tone

- Is the work's tone stern or playful, melancholy, or something else?

Language

- Does the work conjure images that appeal to the senses?
- Does it use **simile** to compare two things directly using *like* or *as (his heart is sealed tight like a freezer door)*?
- Does it use **metaphor** to link two things implicitly *(his ice-hard heart)*?
- What feelings or ideas do individual words suggest?

Theme

- What is at issue in the work?
- What statement is the author making about the issue?

(continued)

QUESTIONS FOR ANALYZING LITERATURE *(Continued)*

Poetry

Speaker and Tone

- Who is speaking? Is it a parent, a lover, an adult or a child, a man or a woman?
- What is the speaker's tone—is it serious or lighthearted, sorrowful or elated, nostalgic or hopeful?

Connotations

- What feelings or ideas do individual words in the poem connote? Although both *trudge* and *saunter* mean "walk slowly," their connotations (associative meanings) are very different.

Imagery

- Does the poem evoke images that appeal to any of your senses—for example, the shocking feeling of a cold cloth on feverish skin or the sharp smell of a gas station?
- How do the images shape the mood of the poem? What ideas do they suggest?

Figurative Language

- Does the poem use **simile** to directly compare two things using *like* or *as?*
- Does it use **metaphor** to implicitly link one thing to another?
- How does the comparison enhance meaning?

Sound, Rhythm, and Meter

- What vowel and consonant sounds recur through the poem?
- Do the lines of the poem resemble the rhythms of ordinary speech, or do they have a more musical quality? Consider how the sounds of the poem create an effect.

Structure

- Notice how the poem is organized into parts or stanzas, considering spacing, punctuation, capitalization, and rhyme schemes. How do the parts relate to one another?

Theme

- What is the subject of the poem?
- What does the poet's choice of language and imagery suggest about their attitude toward that subject?

Although you want your point to be clear, you also want to make sure that your thesis anticipates the "so what?" question and sets up an interesting context for your interpretation. Unless you relate your specific thesis to some more general issue, idea, or problem, your interpretive analysis may seem pointless to readers. *(For more on developing your thesis, see Tab 2: Writing and Designing Texts, pp. 43–45.)*

6. Introducing the general issue, a clear thesis or question, and relevant context

In interpretive analyses, it often takes more than one paragraph to do what an introduction needs to do:

- Identify the general issue, concept, or problem at stake. You can also present the intellectual framework that you are applying.
- Provide relevant background information.
- Name the specific item or items you will focus on.
- State the thesis or pose the main question(s) your analysis will address.

NAVIGATING THROUGH COLLEGE AND BEYOND
Ideas and Practices for Writing in the Humanities

- **Base your analysis on the work itself.** Works of art affect each of us differently, and any interpretation has a subjective element. There are numerous critical theories about the significance of art. However, the possibility of different interpretations does not mean that any one interpretation is as valid as any other. Your reading of the work needs to be grounded in details from the work itself.

- **Consider how the concepts you are learning in your course apply to the work you are analyzing.** If your course focuses on the formal elements of art, for example, you might look at how those elements function in the painting you have chosen. If your course focuses on the social context of a work, you might look at how the poem or story shares or subverts the belief system and worldview that was common in its time.

- **Use the present tense when writing about the work and the past tense when writing about its history.** Use the present tense to talk about the events that happen within a work: "In Aristophanes' plays, characters frequently *step* out of the scene and *address* the audience directly." Use the past tense, however, to relate historical information about the work or its creator: "Kant *wrote* about science, history, criminal justice, and politics as well as philosophical ideas."

You need not do these things in the order listed. Sometimes it is a good idea to introduce the specific focus of your analysis before presenting either the issue or the background information. Even though you may begin with a provocative statement or a stimulating example, make sure that your introduction does the four things listed in the preceding section. *(For more on introductions, see Tab 2: Writing and Designing Texts, pp. 63-64.)*

7. Planning your analysis so that each point supports your thesis
After you pose a key question or state your thesis, you need to organize your points to answer the question or support your thesis. Readers must be able to follow your train of thought and see how each point you make is related to your thesis. *(For more on developing your ideas, see Tab 2: Writing and Designing Texts, pp. 52-61.)*

As you guide readers through your analysis, you will integrate source material, including important quotations, as Jacobi does in her analysis of Mohsen Emadi's "Losses" on pages 117-19. When you are writing about a painting or photograph, your pointed description of visual elements will enhance effective communication.

8. Concluding by answering "so what?"
The conclusion of an interpretive analysis needs to answer the "so what?" question by saying why your thesis—as well as the analysis that supports and develops it—is relevant to the larger issue identified in the introduction. What does your interpretation reveal about that issue? *(For information about conclusions, see Tab 2: Writing and Designing Texts, p. 64.)*

10c Student sample: Interpretive analysis

Although literary analysis can never tell us exactly what a poem is saying, it can help us think more deeply about possible meanings.

First read the complete poem without stopping, and then note your initial thoughts and feelings. Re-read the poem several times, paying close attention to the rhythms of the lines (reading aloud helps) and the poet's choice of words. Think about how the poem develops. Do the last lines represent a shift from or fulfillment of the poem's opening? Look for connections among the poem's details, and think about their significance. The questions in the box on page 114 may help guide your analysis.

Use the insights you gain from your close reading to develop a working thesis about the poem. In the student interpretation that begins on page 117, Isabella Jacobi focuses on the title, "Losses," and how losses in the poet's life correspond to those the poem traces.

—CONSIDER YOUR SITUATION

Author: Isabella Jacobi

Type of writing: Literary analysis/interpretation

Purpose: To analyze a poem and illuminate its themes

Stance: Reasonable, appreciative, clarifying

Audience: Classmates and instructor representing readers unfamiliar with Mohsen Emadi and interested in understanding poetry

Medium: Print, digital text, part of e-Portfolio

Jacobi writes: Writing an analysis of Mohsen Emadi's poem "Losses" has helped me understand the many forms loss can take.

Losses
MOHSEN EMADI

Losses,
not in our nature
but in our human intention,
happen.

However the body enjoys
kissing you or her,

the invention of the human being
might have been a mistake.

Snow falls without reason
and the poem written with a human intention
does not heal.

Kiss me!

- Translated by Lyn Coffin

> **Note:** For details on the proper formatting of a text in MLA style, see Chapter 29 and the student sample that begins on page 303.

SAMPLE STUDENT ANALYSIS OF A POEM

Writer connects with the reader by addressing the expected initial response to a poem that says, "Kiss me!"

Writer signals the use of biographical information as an interpretive frame.

Thesis of paper identified.

Writer uses a biographical lens to interpret the theme.

Examples provided to illustrate and interpret the theme.

Writer demonstrates that the poetic technique of metaphor communicates emotion and enhances the poem's theme.

Mohsen Emadi's "Losses"

At first glance, "Losses," by Iranian poet Mohsen Emadi, reads like a love poem. "Kiss me!" the speaker of the poem exclaims in a passionate expression of desire for a lost beloved. Love and loss are familiar themes throughout the poetic canon. However, in "Losses," Emadi does not merely echo those traditions but uses poetic techniques to explore a theme of timelier significance.

In an essay on Iranian poets writing in exile, poet and professor of comparative literature Persis Karim explains that, "exile [is] a mixed blessing of losing and leaving behind but also acquiring new perspectives, languages, and experiences that enrich and texture their writing." Emadi's "Losses," written in exile, typifies the "mixed blessing" Karim describes. In it, the age-old themes of love and loss are indeed enriched by the poet's newly acquired perspective, language, and experience.

Emadi's perspective on loss is informed by personal history. "Tehran exists in many of my poems," the poet explains in an interview with the online magazine *Words Without Borders*, in which he talks about the violence that erupted in 1999 during the student protests in Iran. As the title of his poem suggests, his subject is not one loss, but multiple "losses." In the interview, he describes losing many friends in the events that followed the protests; and, in 2009, he too was forced into political exile. The multiple losses he bore include not only loved ones, but also the loss of home and of strongly felt hopes and ideals.

The language of "Losses," translated into English by American poet Lyn Coffin, describes the intimate feelings and gestures one might bestow upon a loved one: "However the body enjoys / kissing you or her . . ." (lines 5-6). In the same breath the poet acknowledges that with love comes the potential for loss. Love may be in "our nature," as the poet assures us, but its loss is precipitated by "human intentions," such as those expressed in the violent and oppressive acts he experienced (2-3).

With the experience of loss comes longing and sadness. Emadi's poem expresses longing in the enjoyment of the memory of a kiss. But sadness quickly settles in, like "snow that falls without reason" (9). Human beings are responsible, through wars and acts of political and social injustice, for the world's losses. Therefore, the speaker of the poem believes that "the invention of the human being / might have been a mistake" (7-8). These words evoke the loneliness and resignation brought on by losses that even "the poem . . . / does not heal" (11-12).

In "Losses," Emadi applies new perspective, language, and experience to the themes of love and loss, creating a poem that helps readers better understand what it means to live in exile. The poet mourns many losses—of loved ones, of places, and of beliefs and ideals. But the final declarative line—"Kiss me!"—rings hopeful in a reader's ear. With it, perhaps, the poet takes a step toward retrieving some of what was lost, toward possessing it once again.

Writer reflects on the poem as a whole, and concludes with an interpretation of the poem's last line.

--------------------------------[new page]--------------------------------

Works Cited

Emadi, Mohsen. "Losses." Translated by Lyn Coffin. *Standing on Earth*, Phoneme Media, 2016.

Handal, Nathalie. "The City and the Writer: In Iran with Mohsen Emadi." *Words Without Borders Daily*, 7 Apr. 2015, www .wordswithoutborders.org/dispatches/article/the-city-and-the -writer-in-tehran-with-mohsen-emadi.

Persis, Karim. "Writing Beyond Iran: Reinvention and the Exilic Iranian Writer." *World Literature Today*, vol. 89, no. 2, Mar.-Apr. 2015.

CHAPTER 11

Arguments

An **argument** makes a reasoned assertion about a debatable issue. In this chapter, we look at how to evaluate arguments presented by others and then how to construct arguments on important issues.

11a   Understand the assignment.

In college, opinions based on personal feelings have less weight than reasoned positions expressed as written arguments. When you write an argument, your purpose is not to win but to take part in a discussion by stating and supporting your position on an issue. Written arguments appear in various forms:

- **Critiques:** Critiques address the question "What is true?" or "What is accurate?" A critique fairly summarizes someone's position before either refuting or defending it. *Refutations* expose the reasoning of the position as inadequate or present evidence that contradicts the position. *Defenses* clarify the author's key terms and reasoning, present new arguments to support the position, and show that criticisms of the position are unreasonable or unconvincing.

- **Reviews:** Reviews address the question "What is good?" In a review, the writer evaluates an event, an artifact, a practice, or an institution, judging by reasonable principles and criteria. Diane Chen's consideration of a photograph by Dorothea Lange in Chapter 7 *(pp. 82-84)* is an example of this genre.

- **Proposals, or policy papers:** Proposals, sometimes called policy papers, address the question "What should be done?" They are designed to cause change in the world. Readers are encouraged to see a situation in a specific way and to take action.

⊙   **11b**   Learn how to evaluate verbal and visual arguments.

Three common ways to analyze verbal and visual arguments are (1) to concentrate on the type of reasoning the writer is using; (2) to question the logical relation of a writer's claims, grounds, and warrants, using the Toulmin method; and (3) to examine the ways an argument appeals to its audience.

1. Recognizing types of reasoning

Writers of arguments may use either inductive or deductive reasoning. When writers use **inductive reasoning,** they do not prove that the statements that make up the argument are true; instead they convince reasonable people that the argument's assertion is probable by presenting **evidence** (facts and statistics, telling anecdotes, and expert opinions). When writers use **deductive reasoning,** they claim that a conclusion follows necessarily from a set of assertions, or **premises**—if the premises are true and the relationship between them is valid, the conclusion must be true.

Consider the following scenarios.

Inductive reasoning   A journalism student writing for the school newspaper makes the following claim:

> As Sunday's game shows, the Philadelphia Eagles are on their way to the playoffs.

Reasoning inductively, the student presents a number of facts—her evidence—that support her claim but do not prove it conclusively.

FACT 1   With three games remaining, the Eagles have a two-game lead over the second-place NY Giants.

FACT 2   The Eagles' final three opponents have a combined record of 15 wins and 24 losses.

FACT 3   The Giants lost their first-string quarterback to a season-ending injury last week.

FACT 4   The Eagles will play two of the last three games at home, where they are undefeated.

—NAVIGATING THROUGH COLLEGE AND BEYOND
Assessing Evidence in an Inductive Argument

- **Is it accurate?** Make sure that any facts presented as evidence are correct and not taken out of context.
- **Is it relevant?** Check to see if the evidence is clearly connected to the point being made.
- **Is it representative?** Make sure that the writer's conclusion is supported by evidence gathered from a sample that accurately reflects the larger population (for example, it has the same proportion of men and women, older and younger people, and so on). If the writer is using an example, make sure that the example is typical and not unique.
- **Is it sufficient?** Evaluate whether there is enough evidence to satisfy questioning readers.

A reader would evaluate this student's argument by judging the quality of her evidence, using the criteria listed in the box on page 121.

Inductive reasoning is a key feature of the **scientific method.** Scientists gather data from experiments, surveys, and careful observations to formulate **hypotheses**—statements that can be proved or disproved—that explain the data. They then test their hypotheses by collecting additional information.

Deductive reasoning The basic structure of a deductive argument is the **syllogism.** It contains a **major premise,** or general statement; **minor premise,** or specific case; and conclusion, which follows when the general statement is applied to the specific case. Suppose the journalism student were writing about historically great baseball teams and made the following argument.

MAJOR PREMISE	Any baseball team that wins the World Series more than 25 times in 100 years is one of the greatest teams in history.
MINOR PREMISE	The New York Yankees have won the World Series more than 25 times in the past 100 years.
CONCLUSION	The New York Yankees are one of the greatest baseball teams in history.

This is a deductive argument: if the relationship between its premises is valid and both premises are true, the conclusion must be true. The conclusion follows from the premises. For example, it is not accurate to say: "The train is late. Jane is late. Therefore, Jane must be on the train." Jane could be late because her car broke down. However, if the train is late and Jane is on the train, Jane must be late.

If the logical relationship between the premises is valid, a reader must evaluate the truth of the premises themselves. Do you think, for example, that the number of World Series wins is a proper measure of a team's greatness? Or the only measure? If not, you could claim that the major premise is false or suspect and does not support the conclusion.

Deductive reasoning predominates in mathematics and some humanities disciplines, including philosophy. However, you can use both types of reasoning in college courses and in life.

2. Using the Toulmin method to analyze arguments

Philosopher Stephen Toulmin's analysis of arguments is based on **claims** (assertions about a topic), **grounds** (reasons and evidence), and **warrants** (assumptions or principles that link the grounds to the claims).

Consider the following sentence from an argument by a student.

The death penalty should be abolished because if it is not abolished, innocent people could be executed.

This example, like all logical arguments, has three facets.

CLAIM	The death penalty should be abolished.
GROUNDS	Innocent people could be executed (related stories and statistics).
WARRANT	It is not possible to be completely sure of a person's guilt.

1. **The argument makes a claim.** Also known as a *point* or a *thesis,* a **claim** makes an assertion about a topic. A strong claim responds to an issue of real interest to its audience in clear and precise terms. It also allows for some uncertainty by including qualifying words such as *might* or *possibly,* or describes circumstances under which the claim is true. A weak claim is merely a statement of fact or a statement that few would argue with. Because personal feelings are not debatable, they are not an appropriate claim for an argument.

WEAK CLAIMS	The death penalty is highly controversial.
	The death penalty makes me sick.

2. **The argument presents grounds for the claim. Grounds** consist of the reasons and evidence (facts and statistics, anecdotes, and expert opinion) that support the claim. As grounds for the claim in the example, the student would present statistics and stories related to innocent people being executed. The box on page 124 should help you assess the evidence supporting a claim.

3. **The argument depends on assumptions that link the grounds to the claim.** When you analyze an argument, be aware of the unstated assumptions, or **warrants,** that underlie both the claim and the grounds that support it. The warrants underlying the example argument against the death penalty include two ideas: (1) it is wrong to execute innocent people; and (2) it is not possible to be completely sure of a person's guilt. Warrants differ from discipline

to discipline and from one school of thought to another. If you were studying the topic of bullfighting and its place in Spanish society in a sociology course, for example, you would probably make different arguments with different warrants than would the writer of a rhetorical analysis of Ernest Hemingway's book about bullfighting, *Death in the Afternoon* You might argue that bullfighting serves as a safe outlet for its fans' aggressive feelings. Your warrant would be that sports can have socially useful purposes. A more controversial warrant would be that it is acceptable to kill animals for entertainment.

As you read the writing of others and as you write yourself, look for **unstated assumptions.** What does the reader have to assume to accept the reason and evidence in support of the claim? Hidden assumptions sometimes show **bias,** positive or negative inclinations that can manipulate unwary readers. Assumptions also differ across cultures.

3. Analyzing appeals

Arguments support claims by way of three types of appeals to readers, categorized by the Greek words **logos** (logic), **pathos** (emotions), and **ethos** (character):

- **Logical appeals** offer facts, including statistics, as well as reasoning, such as the inductive and deductive arguments on pages 120–21.

- **Emotional appeals** engage an audience's feelings and invoke beliefs that the author and audience share.

- **Ethical appeals** present authors as fair, reasonable, and trustworthy, backed up with the testimony of experts.

Most arguments draw on all three appeals. A proposal for more nutritious school lunches might cite statistics about childhood obesity (a logical appeal). The argument might address the audience's emotions by describing overweight children feasting on junk food available in the cafeteria (an emotional appeal). It might quote a doctor explaining that healthful food aids concentration (a logical appeal) and that all children deserve to have nutritious food available at school (an ethical appeal). When writing an argument, tailor the type and content of appeals to the specific audience you are addressing. For example, school administrators, charged with making decisions about cafeteria food, might be persuaded by statistics demonstrating the relationship of the cost of food to its nutritional value (logical appeal) and the impact of good nutrition on learning (logical appeal).

4. Avoiding fallacies

In their enthusiasm to make a point, writers sometimes commit **fallacies,** or mistakes in reasoning. Fallacies also can be understood as misuses of the three appeals. Learn to identify fallacies when you read and to avoid them when you write.

⌐TYPES OF EVIDENCE FOR CLAIMS

- **Facts and statistics:** Relevant, current facts and statistics can persuasively support a claim. People on different sides of an issue can **interpret** the same facts and statistics differently, however, or can cite different facts and statistics to prove their point. Facts don't speak for themselves: they must be interpreted to support a claim.

- **Anecdotes:** An anecdote is a brief narrative used as an illustration to support a claim. Because stories appeal to the emotions as well as to the intellect, they can be very effective. Be especially careful to check anecdotes for logical fallacies *(see pp. 124–27)*. Though useful, anecdotes should be only one of the types of evidence you use.

- **Expert opinion:** The views of authorities in a given field can also be powerful support for a claim. Be sure that the expert cited has credentials related to the topic.

Logical fallacies   These fallacies involve errors in the inductive and deductive reasoning processes already discussed:

- **Non sequitur:** A conclusion that does not logically follow from the evidence or one that is based on irrelevant evidence.

   EXAMPLE   Students don't care about responsibility; they often default on their student loans. [*Students who default on loans could be faced with high medical bills or prolonged unemployment.*]

   Generalizing based on evidence is an important tactic of argument. However, the evidence must be relevant. Non sequiturs also stem from dubious assumptions.

- **False cause or post hoc:** An argument that falsely assumes that because one thing happens after another, the first event was a cause of the second event.

   EXAMPLE   I drank green tea and my headache went away; therefore, green tea makes headaches go away. [*How do we know that the headache did not go away for another reason?*]

   Although writers frequently describe causes and effects in argument, fallacies result when writers assume a cause without providing sufficient evidence.

- **Self-contradiction:** An argument that contradicts itself.

   EXAMPLE   No absolute statement can be true. [*The statement itself is an absolute.*]

- **Circular reasoning:** An argument that restates the point rather than supporting it with reasonable evidence.

  EXAMPLE   The wealthy should pay more taxes because taxes should be higher for people with higher incomes. [*The statement does not explain why the wealthy should pay more taxes; it just restates the position.*]

- **Begging the question:** A form of circular reasoning that assumes the truth of a questionable opinion.

  EXAMPLE   The President's poor relationship with the military has weakened the armed forces. [*Does the President really have a poor relationship with the military?*]

  Some claims contain assumptions that must be proven first.

- **Hasty generalization:** A conclusion based on inadequate evidence.

  EXAMPLE   It took me over an hour to find a parking spot downtown. Therefore, the city should build a new parking garage. [*Is this evidence enough to prove this very broad conclusion?*]

- **Sweeping generalization:** An overly broad statement made in absolute terms. When made about a group of people, a sweeping generalization is a **stereotype.**

  EXAMPLE   College students are carefree. [*What about students who work to put themselves through school?*]

  Legitimate generalizations must be based on evidence that is accurate, relevant, representative, and sufficient *(see the box on p. 121).*

- **Either/or fallacy:** The idea that a complicated issue can be resolved by resorting to one of only two options when in reality there are additional choices.

  EXAMPLE   Either the state legislature will raise taxes, or our state's economy will falter. [*Are these really the only two possibilities?*]

  Frequently, arguments consider different courses of action. Authors demonstrate their sense of fairness and their understanding of issues by considering a range of options.

Ethical fallacies These fallacies undermine a writer's credibility by showing lack of fairness to opposing views and lack of expertise on the subject of the argument.

- **Ad hominem:** A personal attack on someone who disagrees with you rather than on the person's argument.

  EXAMPLE   The district attorney is a lazy political hack, so naturally she opposes streamlining the court system. [*Even if the district attorney usually supports her party's position, does that make her wrong about this issue?*]

This fallacy stops debate by ignoring the real issue.

- **Guilt by association:** Discrediting a person because of problems with that person's associates, friends, or family.

  EXAMPLE   Smith's friend has been convicted of fraud, so Smith cannot be trusted. [*Is Smith responsible for his friend's actions?*]

This tactic undermines an opponent's credibility and is based on a dubious assumption: if a person's associates are untrustworthy, that person is also untrustworthy.

- **False authority:** Presenting the testimony of an unqualified person to support a claim.

  EXAMPLE   As the actor who plays Dr. Fine on *The Emergency Room,* I recommend this weight-loss drug because . . . [*Is an actor qualified to judge the benefits and dangers of a diet drug?*]

Expert testimony can strengthen an argument, as long as the person cited is an authority on the subject. This fallacy frequently underlies celebrity endorsements of products.

Emotional fallacies   These fallacies stir readers' sympathy at the expense of their reasoning.

- **False analogy:** A comparison in which a surface similarity masks a significant difference.

  EXAMPLE   Governments and businesses both work within a budget to accomplish their goals. Just as business must focus on the bottom line, so should government. [*Is the goal of government to make a profit? Does government instead have different goals?*]

Analogies can enliven an argument and deepen an audience's understanding of a subject, provided the things being compared actually are similar.

- **Bandwagon:** An argument that depends on going along with the crowd, on the false assumption that truth can be determined by a popularity contest.

EXAMPLE   Given the sales of that book, its claims must be true. [*Sales volume does not indicate the truth of the claim. How do we know that a popular book presents accurate information?*]

- **Red herring:** An argument that diverts attention from the true issue by concentrating on an irrelevant one.

EXAMPLE   Hemingway's book *Death in the Afternoon* is unsuccessful because it glorifies the brutal sport of bullfighting. [*Why can't a book about a brutal sport be successful? The statement is irrelevant.*]

5. Reading visual arguments

Like written arguments, visual arguments support claims with reasons and evidence, rely on assumptions, and may contain fallacies. They make logical appeals, such as a graph of experimental data; emotional appeals, such as a photograph of a hungry child; and ethical appeals, such as a corporate logo. Like written works, visual arguments are created by an author to achieve a purpose and to address an audience within a given context. *(See Chapter 2, pp. 16-17.)*

Toulmin's system, as we saw, analyzes arguments based on the claims they make, the grounds (evidence and reasons) for those claims, and the warrants (underlying assumptions) that connect the grounds with the claims. *(See the explanation of Toulmin analysis on pp. 122-23.)* While these elements function similarly in verbal and visual arguments, unstated assumptions play a larger role in visual arguments because we are not used to "reading" visuals and interpreting the implicitly stated claims and grounds.

For example, consider a photograph of a politician with her family members. The image makes a claim (she is a good public servant) and implicitly offers grounds (because she cares for her family). The warrant is that a person's

---

CHECKLIST Reading Visual Arguments Critically

Review the questions for previewing a visual from Chapter 4, pages 31–32, and add the following:

- ☐ What can you tell about the visual's creator or sponsor?
- ☐ What seems to be the visual's purpose? Does it promote a product or message?
- ☐ What features of the visual suggest the intended audience? How?
- ☐ How do aspects of design such as the size and position of the elements, the colors, and shapes of images affect the visual's message?
- ☐ What is the effect of any text, audio, or video that accompanies the visual?

family life indicates how she will perform in office. This assumption may be false.

Advertisements combine text and images to promote a product or message to an audience in a social context. They use the resources of visual design: type of image, position, color, light and shadows, typefaces or fonts, layout, and white space. *(See the questions on previewing a visual in Chapter 4, pp. 31-32 and the discussion of design in Chapter 8, pp. 85-92.)* The image in Figure 11.1 was developed by Getty Images—a resource that, for a fee, offers access to visual content like photographs, videos, and infographics—and could be used in a public-service ad to prevent violence against women.

The image is a word cloud in the shape of a human hand, which has multiple meanings. The hand is held up as a signal to stop—to cease and desist from violence. But the hand can also be an instrument of violence.

What claims do you think this image makes? One claim might be "violence against women has no place in a civilized society." The evidence is supplied by the reader's prior knowledge about domestic violence. The argument's assumptions include the viewer's familiarity with news accounts and personal experience on this crucial subject.

©paci77/DigitalVision Vectors/Getty Images

FIGURE 11.1 A public-service image calling for a stop to violence against women.

Fallacies frequently occur in visual arguments. For example, celebrity endorsements of products rely on our respect for the celebrity's character. However, a photo of an athlete driving a particular type of car demonstrates false authority, unless the athlete also happens to be an expert on cars. *(See p. 126.)*

> **11c**   Approach writing your own argument as a process.

Selecting a topic that you care about will give you the energy to think matters through and make cogent arguments. Of course, you will have to go beyond your personal emotions to make the most convincing case. You will also have to empathize with potential readers who may disagree with you about a subject that is important to you.

1. Figuring out what is at issue
Before you can take a position on a topic like noise pollution or population growth, you must figure out what is at issue. Ask questions about your topic. Do you see indications that all is not as it should be? Have things always been this way, or have they changed for the worse? From what different perspectives— economic, social, political, cultural, medical, geographic—can problems like world food shortages be understood? Do people interested in the topic disagree about what is true, what is good, or what should be done?

Based on your answers to such questions, identify the issues your topic raises, and decide what is most important, interesting, and appropriate to write about.

2. Developing a reasonable stance that negotiates differences
When writing arguments, you want your readers to respect your intelligence and trust your judgment. By influencing readers to trust your character, you build **ethos.** Conducting research on an issue can make you well informed; reading

—the EVOLVING SITUATION

Blogs

Weblogs, or *blogs* for short- the continually updated sites linking an author's comments to other sites on the Web- frequently function as vehicles for public debate. For example, online editions of many newspapers include blogs that invite readers to comment on the news of the day and to present dissenting opinions. While online debate can be freewheeling, it's important to search for common ground with your readers. *(For more on blogs, see Chapter 14, pp. 169–71.)*

Looking at blogs can help you learn about an issue or find counterarguments to your position. *(See Chapter 19, p. 210.)* However, evaluate blogs carefully before using them as support for an argument *(see Chapter 21, pp. 219–26).* Many blogs rely heavily on personal opinion, and some are not factually accurate.

— KNOW THE SITUATION Arguments

Purpose: To persuade

Audience: Audience members can be close to a writer (for example, classmates) or distant (for example, citizens of an unfamiliar country), but in either case, keying in on members of that audience is important because reasons, examples, and stories should speak to them.

Stance: Reasonable

Genres: Arguments appear as stand-alone genres and inside other genres like reviews, critiques, and proposals.

Medium: Print, digital, or networked depending on the audience and the topic. (A proposal for a new bridge might be more compelling in a visual medium, for example.)

Commonly used: In most disciplines, the workplace, and public life

other people's views can enhance your thoughtfulness. Pay attention to the places where you disagree with the opinions of others, but also note what you have in common—topical interests, key questions, or underlying values. *(For more on appeals to your audience, see p. 123.)*

Avoid language that may promote prejudice or fear. Misrepresentations of other people's ideas reduce your ethos and weaken your argument, as do personal attacks. Write arguments to expand thinking, your own and that of others. *(See the box on blogs on p. 129.)*

Trying out different perspectives can also help you figure out where you stand on an issue. *(Also see the next section on stating your position.)* Make a list of the arguments for and against a specific position; then compare the lists and decide where you stand, perhaps on one side or the other or somewhere in between. Does one set of arguments seem stronger than the other? Do you want to change or qualify your initial position?

3. Composing a thesis that states your position

A successful argument requires a strong, engaging, arguable thesis. As noted in the section on the Toulmin model of argument, personal feelings and accepted facts cannot serve as an argument's thesis because they are not debatable *(see pp. 122-23)*.

PERSONAL FEELING, NOT A DEBATABLE THESIS

I feel that developing nations should not suffer food shortages.

ACCEPTED FACT, NOT A DEBATABLE THESIS

Food shortages are a growing problem in many developing nations.

DEBATABLE THESIS

Current food shortages in developing nations are in large part caused by climate change and the use of food crops in biofuels.

In proposals and policy papers, the thesis presents a solution in terms of the writer's definition of the problem. The logic behind a thesis for a proposal can be stated like this:

Given these key variables and their underlying cause, one solution to the problem would be . . .

Because this kind of thesis is both complex and qualified, you will often need more than one sentence to state it clearly. Draw on numerous well-supported arguments to make it credible. Readers finally want to know that the proposed solution will not cause more problems than it solves.

4. Identifying key points to support and develop your thesis

A strong, debatable thesis should be supported and developed with sound reasoning and carefully documented evidence. You can think of an argument as a dialogue between writer and readers. The writer states a debatable thesis, and one reader wonders, "Why do you believe that?" Another reader wants to know, "But what about this factor?" Anticipate readers' questions, and answer them by presenting reasons that are substantiated with evidence and by refuting opposing views. Define any abstract terms, such as *freedom,* that figure importantly in your arguments. In his proposal for eliminating cyberbullying, Joseph Honrado defines cyberbullying and shows how it both compares to traditional bullying and differs from it *(pp. 136–43).*

Usually, a well-developed argument includes more than one type of claim and more than one kind of evidence. Employ generalizations based on empirical data or statistics, authoritative reasons based on the opinions of experts, and ethical reasons based on the application of principle. In his argument, Honrado provides data from the Cyberbullying Research Center showing the percentages of teens who have been victimized by acts of cyberbullying as well as anecdotal evidence on a school program that helped to raise awareness of the issue.

As you conduct research, note evidence—facts, examples or anecdotes, and expert testimony—that can support each argument for or against your position. Demonstrate your trustworthiness by properly quoting and documenting the information you have gathered from your sources. Joseph Honrado adds credibility to his argument by quoting experts on his topic, integrating the quotation seamlessly into his own sentence:

Dr. Deborah Hall, a psychology professor at Arizona State University's New College of Interdisciplinary Arts and Sciences, explains that the biggest difference between face-to-face bullying and cyberbullying is that the latter can take place anywhere, day or night: "with cyberbullying there is no safe time or space" (Arizona State University).

Also build your credibility by paying attention to **counterarguments,** substantiated claims that do not support your position. Consider whether a reader could reasonably draw different conclusions from your evidence or disagree with your assumptions. Use one of the following strategies to address potential counterarguments:

- Qualify your thesis in light of the counterargument by including a word such as *most, some, usually,* or *likely:* "Students with credit cards usually have trouble with debt" recognizes that some do not.

- Add to the thesis a statement of the conditions for or exceptions to your position: "Businesses *with over five hundred employees* saved money using the new process."

- Choose at least one or two counterarguments, and refute their truth or their importance.

Introduce a counterargument with a signal phrase like "Others might contend . . ." *(See Tab 5: Researching, p. 250, for a discussion of signal phrases.)* Refute a counterargument's claim by questioning the author's interpretation of the evidence or the author's assumptions. Honrado acknowledges that teens often don't report instances of cyberbullying, but he refutes the idea that adults can't help by pointing to resources—such as one site's list of warning signs—that can help adults identify bullying and take quick action to stop it.

5. Creating a linked set of reasons

Arguments are most effective when they present a chain—a linked set—of reasons. Honrado states his thesis in the introductory paragraph and then identifies two types of cyberbullying and ways to combat them. Although you can order an argument in many ways, include the following parts (arranged below following **classical structure**):

- An introduction to the topic and the debatable issue, establishing your credibility and seeking common ground with your readers

- A thesis stating your position on the issue

- A point-by-point account of the reasons for your position, including the evidence (facts, examples, authorities) you will use to substantiate each major reason

- A fair presentation and refutation of one or two key counterarguments

- A response to the "so what?" question. Why does your argument matter? If appropriate, include a call to action.

If you expect your audience to disagree with you, consider using a **Rogerian structure:**

- An introduction to the topic and the debatable issue

- An attempt to reach common ground by naming values you share and providing a sympathetic portrayal of your readers' (opposing) position

- A statement of your position and presentation of supporting evidence
- A conclusion that restates your view and suggests a compromise or synthesis

6. Appealing to your audience

You want your readers to see you as *reasonable, ethical,* and *empathetic*—qualities that promote communication among people who have differences. *(For more on appeals, see p. 123.)* When you read your argument, pay attention to the impression you are making. Ask yourself these questions:

- Would a reasonable person be able to follow my logic and acknowledge the evidence I offer in support of my thesis?
- Have I presented myself as ethical and fair? What would readers who have never met me think of me after reading what I have to say?
- Have I expressed my feelings about the issue? Have I been fair in seeking to arouse the reader's emotions?

7. Emphasizing your commitment to dialogue in the introduction

To promote dialogue with readers, look for common ground—beliefs, concerns, and values you share with those who disagree with you and those who are undecided. Sometimes called **Rogerian argument** after the psychologist Carl Rogers, the common-ground approach is particularly important in your introduction, where it builds bridges with readers who might otherwise become too defensive or annoyed to read further. Joseph Honrado includes in his discussion of cyberbullying an explanation of the shared responsibility among students, parents, educators, and the media to overcome the problem. Keep the dialogue open throughout your essay by maintaining a reasonable tone and acknowledging opposing views. If possible, return to that common ground at the end of your argument.

8. Concluding by restating your position and emphasizing its importance

After presenting your reasoning in detail, remind readers of your thesis. To encourage readers to appreciate your argument's importance, make the version of your thesis in your conclusion more complex and qualified than in your introduction. Readers may not agree with you, but they should know why the issue and your argument matter.

9. Using visuals in your argument

Consider including visuals that support your argument's purpose. Each should relate directly to your argument as a whole or to a point within it. Visuals also may provide evidence: a photograph can illustrate an example, and a graph can present statistics that support an argument.

Visual evidence makes emotional, logical, and ethical appeals. The public-service image on page 128 makes an ethical appeal by illustrating, in a word

─CHECKLIST Reviewing Your Own and Other Writers' Arguments

First identify what the text is doing well, and find ways to build on those strengths. Then identify parts in the text that are confusing, underdeveloped, or inaccurate, and share ways of addressing those problems:

☐ **What makes the thesis strong and arguable?**

☐ **Is the thesis supported with a sufficient number of reasons, or are more needed?**

☐ **Are the reasons and evidence appropriate for the purpose, audience, and context?**

☐ **Does the argument contain mistakes in logic?** Refer to pages 124–27 to check for logical fallacies.

☐ **How is each reason developed?** Is the reason clear? Where are its key terms defined? Is the supporting evidence sufficient?

☐ **Does the argument quote or paraphrase from sources accurately and document them properly?** *(For more on quoting, paraphrasing, and documenting sources, see Tab 5 Researching, and Tabs 6–8, which cover commonly used documentation styles.)*

☐ **Has at least one significant counterargument been addressed?** How have opposing views been treated?

☐ **In what way does each visual support the thesis?** How are the visuals tailored to the audience?

☐ **Are logical, ethical, and emotional appeals used consistently and effectively?**

cloud, the range of actions that constitute violence against women. The graph of types of cyberbullying in Joseph Honrado's argument *(p. 137)* makes a logical appeal by presenting evidence that supports his claim, demonstrating the depth of his research while at the same time building his ethos.

Consider how your audience is likely to react to your visuals. Non-specialists will need more explanation of charts, graphs, and other visuals. When possible, have members of your target audience review your argument and visuals. Provide specific captions that identify each visual, showing how it supports your argument. Mention each image in your text. Make sure charts and graphs are free of distortion or chartjunk *(see Chapter 7: Revising and Editing, p. 75)*. Also acknowledge data from other sources and obtain permission when needed. *(See pp. 212-19.)*

—CONSIDER YOUR SITUATION

Author: Joseph Honrado

Type of writing: Argument in the form of a proposal

Purpose: To show that (1) cyberbullying is a new form of bullying and (2) if it is to be stopped, students, parents, educators, and the media must work together to overcome the problem

Stance: Informed and reasonable

Audience: Students, parents, educators, and the media

Medium: This argument is developed in two media: print and slides.

Honrado writes: As I worked on this argument, I was at first worried that the wonders of technology have opened up new opportunities for emotional violence. But then I realized the importance of calling upon students, parents, educators, and the media to address the issue.

10. Reexamining your reasoning

After you have completed the first draft of your argument, take time to reexamine your reasoning for errors. Step outside yourself, and assess your argument objectively. Peer review can be especially helpful in testing your reasoning and persuasive powers.

11d   Student sample: Proposal

In an English course, Joseph Honrado conducted research on cyberbullying and then constructed a policy paper (sometimes called a proposal) to address the question, "What should be done?" In the humanities, as well as in other disciplines, arguments like Joseph Honrado's are designed to bring about change. Honrado documents the impact of cyberbullying, evaluates its negative consequences, and then argues that students, parents, educators, and the media must take action.

> *Note:* For details on the proper formatting of a text in MLA style, see Chapter 29 and the sample research report that begins on page 306.

SAMPLE STUDENT ARGUMENT

Joseph Honrado

Professor Robertson

English 201

1 October 2017

Cyberbullying: An Alarming Trend for the Digital Age

Before the advent of social media and cell phones, bullies used to harass their victims on the playground, on the school bus, and in the lunchroom. In response to these confrontations, adults advised kids to stand up to bullies or simply to avoid them. However, in today's digital society, bullying can take place anytime and anyplace. That means standing up to a bully is much more difficult. According to a program run by the Minnesota Parent Training and Information Center (PACER), definitions of *bullying* differ by locality and even by school; however, most definitions have traits in common, including repeated behavior that "hurts or harms another person physically or emotionally" and targets individuals who are unable to defend themselves (National Bullying Prevention Center). The website *Stopbullying.gov*, which is supported by the United States Department of Health and Human Services, updates this definition to include "bullying that takes place using electronic technology," also known as *cyberbullying* ("Bullying Definition"). Cyberbullying is a significant, destructive problem among young people. It is especially harmful because of its immediacy, scope, and permanence: humiliation is easily inflicted online, where large audiences can continue to witness it indefinitely. With new technologies affecting the ways kids interact, adults must consider new ways to deal with the problem of bullying. If the problem of cyberbullying is ever to be overcome, students, parents, educators, and the media must work together to promote healthy guidelines for online behavior.

Cyberbullying is commonly carried out through social networking sites like *Facebook* and *Twitter*, or through texting, instant messaging, and e-mail. While cyberbullying can take many

Introduces the issue of cyberbullying.

Presents definition of cyberbullying.

Thesis statement.

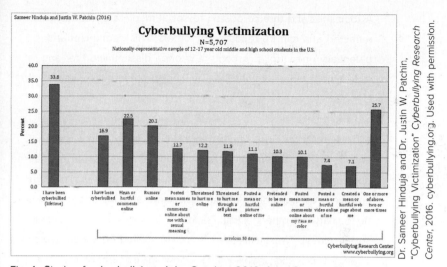

Fig. 1. Study of cyberbullying, July–October 2016, from Sameer Hinduja and Justin W. Patchin, "Cyberbullying Victimization." *Cyberbullying Research Center,* 2016, cyberbullying.org/2016-cyberbullying-data.

forms, most often it involves the posting of hurtful comments or rumors online. As Fig. 1 shows, in a study presented by the *Cyberbullying Research Center,* 22.5 percent of 5,707 twelve- to seventeen-year-olds surveyed between July and October 2016 reported that "mean or hurtful" comments were posted about them and just over 20 percent reported being the subject of rumors posted online. Moreover, 25.7 percent of the same group said they were the targets of two or more forms of cyberbullying on more than two occasions (Hinduja and Patchin).

Cyberbullying is especially dangerous because digital technologies, as well as the communication they support, are ubiquitous. Dr. Deborah Hall, a psychology professor at Arizona State University's New College of Interdisciplinary Arts and Sciences, explains that the biggest difference between face-to-face bullying and cyberbullying is that the latter can take place anywhere, day or night: "with cyberbullying there is no safe time or space" (Arizona State University). The hurtful messages can be targeted to one person privately or posted publicly for the target's peers to see.

Presents a detailed explanation of cyberbullying, and a visual that indicates the extent of the problem.

Also, insults and threats posted to social media are not easily retracted and can be reposted by others. This permanent and potentially uncontrollable content is often disseminated far and wide before the victim can do anything to prevent it (Arizona State University).

Who are these cyberbullies? The website *Stopbullying.org* explains that two types of children are more likely than others to engage in bullying. The first group includes those who are considered popular. They are "well connected to their peers, have social power, are overly concerned about their popularity, and like to dominate or be in charge of others" ("Risk Factors"). The second group is far less socially adept. These children are "more isolated from their peers and may be depressed or anxious, have low self-esteem, be less involved in school, be easily pressured by peers, or not identify with the emotions or feelings of others" ("Risk Factors"). Though cyberbullies and their victims range from young children to students in college, cyberbullying may be most destructive to younger teens because they lack the maturity to handle such situations and rarely seek help from adults. Teens also spend a large amount of time online. A recent Pew survey reported that almost three-quarters of thirteen- to seventeen-year-olds have access to a smartphone and roughly a quarter of teens "go online 'almost constantly'" (Lenhart). In addition, 71 percent of teens reported using more than one type of social media (Lenhart). Given this amount of opportunity, parents cannot oversee all of their children's electronic activity. When unsupervised, children and teens can become bullies or targets.

The serious consequences of cyberbullying are more and more evident. In November 2016, the American Psychological Association (APA) declared that preventing bullying is one of its top priorities ("Policy Brief"). Referencing a study published in *Social Psychology of Education*, the APA reports that "childhood bullying inflicts the same long-term psychological trauma on girls as severe physical or sexual abuse and that the behavior can undermine victims' mental health into adulthood" ("Policy Brief").

Provides factual support indicating who cyberbullies are; development by classification (see p. 53).

Summarizes research on the conditions of the problem of cyberbullying.

Establishes the nature of the problem and demonstrates its seriousness.

Understandably, bullying causes depression and anxiety in children. Even more chilling, bullied children can either externalize their feelings by turning violent, or internalize them, which can lead to other difficulties. Since cyberbullying is still relatively new, there are few long-term studies on victims. However, one such study, originally published in *JAMA Psychiatry in America*, associates cyberbullying with "an elevated risk of psychiatric problems that extends into adulthood" (qtd. in France 5). Scott Freeman, director of the Cybersmile Foundation, agrees. He believes that "we're going to have a delayed mental health issue with cyberbullying," predicting "long-term problems" (qtd. in France 5).

Presents a quotation from a person who is engaged with the problem.

One major obstacle to controlling cyberbullying is that many children struggle to talk about their experiences as victims. Louise France, reporting for *The Times*, cites age as one reason kids do not report abuse. Teenage years are a time when kids claim independence from their parents, when "one's peers mean more than anyone else" (3). To a teen in trouble, turning to parents or other adults for help may not feel like a viable option. The website *Stopbullying.gov* lists several other reasons, including (1) the fear of being seen as "weak" or as a "tattletale," (2) the fear of retaliation by their bullies, and (3) the belief that "no one cares or could understand" ("Warning Signs").

Establishes reasons the problem often goes unreported by victims.

Given this information, parents need to become aware of the culture and the dangers of cyberbullying. France notes that while parents tend to restrict the physical places their children can go—to the mall or the movies, for example—too often they are not paying attention to their children's activities on the Internet (8). *Stopbullying. gov* encourages parents to talk to their children ("Warning Signs"), especially to make sure their children understand bullying and feel comfortable bringing any issues to their attention. In addition, Barbara Trolley and Constance Hanel, authors of *Cyber Kids, Cyberbullying, Cyber Balance*, caution that beyond enforcing guidelines, adults need to teach young people to adopt a healthy balance of online and offline activities (82).

Establishes that students and educators are becoming more aware of the problem and they need to take action.

Even as educators continue to respond to specific incidents of cyberbullying, they must also become proactive in their efforts to prevent future incidents. Reporting for the *Daily Journal* in Kankakee, Illinois, Lori Krecioch writes about a group of teenagers from local high schools brought together by the Kankakee County Center Against Sexual Assault. These students act as an advisory committee as the center devises "new ways of reaching out to teens about heavy topics . . . such as cyberbullying . . . in ways that really will work." Another state that has taken preventative action is Texas, which recently passed legislation known as David's Law. This new law "encourages schools to invest in counseling and rehabilitation services for victims and aggressors of bullying" (Guzman). Meanwhile, schools in Alabama have instituted anti-bullying programs. Quoting Donna Clark, the Huntsville City Schools' coordinator of School Counseling Services, Stephanie Mills, a reporter for *WAFF 48 News* in Huntsville, Alabama, explains the wide-ranging scope of such programs: "Schools pick three activities they can do to promote anti-bullying and also tolerance and acceptance and diversity" (Mills). Communities need more programs like these.

Establishes that media corporations also need to be responsible for finding solutions to the problem.

Finally, mass media and social media outlets should become increasingly powerful advocates for cyberbullying prevention. In a June 29, 2017, blog post, *Instagram*'s CEO and cofounder Kevin Systrom announced "two new tools to help keep *Instagram* a safe place for self-expression"—a filter for offensive comments and another for spam. And *Facebook* engineers recently explained that *Instagram* will use an algorithm that "can understand with near-human accuracy the textual content of several thousand posts per second" (qtd. in Bayern). *Facebook* has also taken on the problem. In partnership with Yale University's Center for Emotional Intelligence, *Facebook* has created a cyberbullying prevention hub, "a resource for teens, parents and educators seeking support and help for issues related to bullying and other conflicts" ("Bullying Prevention Hub"). We need more such initiatives.

If cyberbullying is ever to be eliminated, students, parents, educators, and the media must work together to establish guidelines for proper online behavior. With increasing awareness of the impact of cyberbullying on its victims, families and schools can teach children how to balance technology use with common sense and prepare them to identify and report incidents of cyberbullying before those incidents result in significant harm. Trolley and Hanel suggest families adopt an approach to cyberbullying they call "Stop, Save, and Share." They offer simple tips, such as stopping to consider consequences before reacting to a cyberbully attack, saving the information as proof, and sharing that information with a trusted adult (79). Websites like *Stopbullying.gov* also offer a wide variety of resources for dealing with cyberbullies, including links to counseling services, community outreach organizations, workshops, and a helpline. Through solutions like these, the very technology that has allowed cyberbullying to exist can also play an important role in addressing it.

Conclusion sums up the issue and encourages readers to take action.

--[new page]--

Works Cited

Arizona State University. "Valley Youth Will Be Asked for Their Ideas and Solutions." *ASU Conference to Fight Adolescent Depression, Cyberbullying*, 24 Jan. 2017, asunow.asu.edu/20170124-solutions-asu-west-sponsors-largest-arizona-youth-conference-to-fight-adolescent-depression.

Bayern, Macy. "How AI Became Instagram's Weapon of Choice in the War on Cyberbullying." *TechRepublic*, 14 Aug. 2017, www.techrepublic.com/article/how-ai-became-instagrams-weapon-of-choice-in-the-war-on-cyberbullying/.

"Bullying Definition." *Stopbullying.gov*, www.stopbullying.gov/what-is-bullying/definition/index.html. Accessed 17 Aug. 2017.

"Bullying Prevention Hub." *Facebook*, www.facebook.com/safety/bullying. Accessed 15 Aug. 2017.

France, Louise. "Cyberbullying and Its Teenage Victims." *The Times* [London], 15 June 2013, pp. 22–28.

List of works cited begins on a new page and is formatted according to MLA style, ninth edition.

Guzman, Victor. "Cyberbullying the Topic of Central High School's Orientation." *Concho Valley KLST News,* 4 Aug. 2017, www .conchovalleyhomepage.com/news/local-news/cyberbullying-the -topic-of-central-high-schools-orientation/783377365.

Hinduja, Sameer, and Justin W. Patchin. "2016 Cyberbullying Research Data." *Cyberbullying Research Center*, 2016, cyberbullying.org/2016-cyberbullying-data.

Krecioch, Lori. "KC-CASA Finds New Ways to Get through to Teens." *Daily Journal* [Kankakee], 15 Aug. 2017, www.daily-journal.com /life/kc-casa-finds-new-ways-to-get-through-to-teens /article_81c02983-03db-56b9-8fba-1cc28ecf067e.html.

Lenhart, Amanda. "Teens, Social Media and Technology Overview 2015." *Pew Research Center*, 9 Apr. 2015, www.pewinternet .org/2015/04/09/teens-social-media-technology-2015/.

Mills, Stephanie. "School Officials Work to Prevent Bullying in TN Valley Schools." *WAFF 48 News,* 2 Aug. 2017, www.waff.com /story/36031536/school-officials-work-to-prevent-bullying-in -tn-valley-schools.

National Bullying Prevention Center. "What Parents Should Know about Bullying." *PACER*, www.pacer.org/bullying/resources /parents/definition-impact-roles.asp. Accessed 13 Aug. 2017.

"Policy Brief: Bullying Prevention Is a Top APA Priority." *Monitor on Psychology,* vol. 47, no. 10, Nov. 2016, p. 16.

"Risk Factors." *Stopbullying.gov*, www.stopbullying.gov/at-risk/factors /index.html. Accessed 17 Aug. 2017.

Systrom, Kevin. "Keeping *Instagram* a Safe Place for Self-Expression." *Instagram*, 29 June 2017, instagram-press.com/blog/2017/06/29 /keeping-instagram-a-safe-place-for-self-expression/.

Trolley, Barbara C., and Constance Hanel. *Cyber Kids, Cyber Bullying, Cyber Balance*. Corwin, 2010, pp. 79–82.

"Warning Signs." *Stopbullying.gov*, www.stopbullying.gov/at-risk/ warning-signs/index.html. Accessed 17 Aug. 2017.

CHAPTER 12

Other Kinds of Assignments

12a Personal essays

The personal essay is a literary form. Like a poem, a play, or a story, it should feel meaningful to readers and relevant to their lives. A personal essay should speak in a distinctive voice and be both compelling and memorable.

1. Making connections between your experiences and those of your readers

When you write a personal essay, you are exploring your experiences, clarifying your values, and composing a public self. Since the writing situation involves an audience of strangers who will be more interested in your topic than in you, it is important to make distinctions between the personal and the private. Whether you are writing a personal essay about a tree in autumn, a trip to Senegal, or an athletic event, your purpose is to engage readers in what is meaningful to you—and potentially to them—in these objects and experiences.

When we read a personal essay, we expect to learn more than the details of the writer's experience; we expect to see the connections between that experience and our own.

2. Turning your essay into a conversation

Personal essayists usually use the first person (*I* and *we*) to create a sense of open-ended conversation between writer and reader. Your rhetorical stance— whether you appear shy, thoughtful, or friendly in this conversation, for example—will be determined by the details you include in your essay as well as the connotations of the words you use. Consider how writer and professor Kerri Morris represents herself by using the second person (*you*) in the following excerpt from her blog *Cancer Is Not a Gift*:

> Just outside the back door, there is a giant blue umbrella. As far as outdoor umbrellas go, it's pretty high end. A few years ago, the wind destroyed the old green one, along with the roof. Remember that insurance replaced it all (after the deductible).
>
> You used the full amount that insurance allotted to buy an umbrella in a dazzling periwinkle blue. You've looked up into it and have relaxed and have been at peace.
>
> Remember that blue umbrella, because you tend to see the world in black and white, but the world isn't black and white. It's red and yellow and green and gray. And periwinkle blue. Even if you can't see these many colors, trust that they are there. Let the black and white go.

As part of her blog entry, Morris includes a visual element that illustrates how she came to see the world in "periwinkle blue" (see Figure 12.1).

FIGURE 12.1 The giant periwinkle-blue umbrella.

―*the* EVOLVING SITUATION

Personal Writing and Social Media Web Sites

In addition to writing personal essays for class, you may use social media sites like *Facebook* or *Twitter* for personal expression and autobiographical writing. Since these sites are networked, it's important to remember that strangers, including prospective employers, may have access to your profiles and comments.

3. Structuring your essay like a story

There are three common ways to narrate events and reflections:

- **Chronological sequence:** uses an order determined by clock time; what happened first is presented first, followed by what happened second, then third, and so on.
- **Emphatic sequence:** uses an order determined by the point you want to make; for emphasis, events and reflections are arranged from either least to most or most to least important.
- **Suspenseful sequence:** uses an order determined by the emotional effect the writer wants the essay to have on readers. To keep readers engaged,

the essay may begin in the middle with a puzzling event, then flash back or go forward. Some essays may even begin with the end and then flash back to recount how the writer came to that insight.

4. Letting details tell your story

It is through the details that the story takes shape. The details you emphasize, the words you choose, and the characters you create communicate the point of your essay.

Consider, for example, the following passage by Gloria Ladson-Billings:

> Mrs. Harris, my third-grade teacher, was quite a sharp dresser. She wore beautiful high-heeled shoes. Sometimes she switched to flats in the afternoon if her feet got tired, but every morning began with the click, click, click of her high heels as she greeted us up and down the rows. I wanted to dress the way Mrs. Harris did. I didn't want to wear old-lady comforters like Mrs. Benn's, and I certainly didn't want to wear worn-out loafers like those of my first-grade teacher, Miss Schwartz. I wanted to wear beautiful, shiny, high-heeled shoes like Mrs. Harris's. That was the way a teacher should look, I thought.
>
> —GLORIA LADSON-BILLINGS, *The Dreamkeepers: Successful Teachers of African-American Children*

Ladson-Billings uses details to make her idea of a good teacher come alive for the reader. At one level—the literal—the "click, click, click" refers to the sound of Mrs. Harris's shoes. At another level, it represents the glamorous teacher. And at the most figurative level, the "click, click, click" evokes the kind of feminine power that the narrator both longs for and admires.

5. Connecting your experience to a larger issue

To demonstrate the significance of a personal essay to readers, writers usually connect their individual experiences to a larger issue. For example, here Morris connects her experience as a woman and cancer survivor through posters from the 1930s (see Figure 12.2) to the larger history of cancer awareness and treatment:

> In addition to their sheer beauty, I wanted to share them because they reveal how our attitudes have shifted over the years about this disease and how they've remained the same. From the beginning, women have been instrumental in the cancer community, moving attitudes from fear to confrontation. It's quite a balancing act. In order to get people to be screened and tested, they need to be motivated but not overwhelmed by fear. We can see how artists helped to find this balance.

> **12b**   Lab reports in the experimental sciences.

Scientists form hypotheses (tentative answers to research questions that can be proved true or false) and plan new experiments as they observe, read, and write. When they work in the laboratory, they keep detailed notebooks. They also write and publish lab reports to share their discoveries with other scientists.

Source: Library of Congress Prints and Photographs Division

FIGURE 12.2 A poster from the 1930s created to raise awareness about cancer treatment.

Lab reports usually include the following sections: Abstract, Introduction, Methods and Materials, Results, Discussion, Acknowledgments, and References. Begin drafting the report, section by section, while your experiences in the lab are still fresh in your mind.

Follow the scientific conventions for abbreviations, symbols, and numbers (often listed in your textbook). Use numerals for dates, time, pages, figures, tables, and standard units of measurement. Spell out numbers between one and nine that are not part of a series of larger numbers.

1. Abstract

An **abstract** is a one-paragraph summary of your lab report. It answers these questions:

- What methods were used in the experiment?
- What variables were measured?
- What were the findings?
- What do the findings imply?

2. Introduction

In the introduction, state your topic, summarize prior research, and present your hypothesis.

Employ precise scientific terminology *(α-amylase)*, and spell out the terms that you will later abbreviate *(gibberellic acid [GA])*. Use the passive voice when describing objects of study, which are more important than the experimenter. *(For a discussion of active and passive voices, see Tab 9: Editing for Clarity, pp. 430–32.)* Use the present tense to state established knowledge ("the rye seed *produces*"); use the past tense to summarize the work of prior researchers ("Haberlandt *reported*"). The writer of the excerpt below cites sources using a superscript number system. *(For information about CSE style, see pp. 388–99.)*

> According to studies by Yomo[1], Paleg[2], and others[3,4], barley seed embryos produce a gibberellic acid (GA) which stimulates the release of hydrolytic enzymes, especially α-amylase. These enzymes break down the endosperm, thereby making stored energy sources available to the germinating plant. What is not evident is how GA actually works on the molecular level to stimulate the production of hydrolytic enzymes. As several experiments[5-8] have documented, GA has an RNA-enhancing effect. Is this general enhancement of RNA synthesis just a side effect of GA's action, or is it directly involved in the stimulation of α-amylase?

The first sentence names both a general topic, barley seed embryos, and a specific issue, GA's stimulation of hydrolytic enzymes. The last sentence poses a question that prepares readers for the hypothesis by focusing their attention on the role enhanced RNA synthesis plays in barley seed germination.

3. Methods and materials
Select the details that other scientists will need to replicate the experiment. Using the past tense, recount in chronological order what was done with specific materials.

4. Results
In this section, tell readers about the results that are relevant to your hypothesis, especially those that are statistically significant. Results may be relevant even if they are different from what you expected.

You might summarize results in a table or graph. For example, the graph in Figure 12.3, which plots the distance (in centimeters, *y*-axis) covered by a glider over a period of time (in seconds, *x*-axis), was used to summarize the results of an engineering assignment.

Every table and figure you include in a lab report must be referred to in the text. Point out relevant patterns the table or figure reveals. If you run statistical tests on your findings, do not make the tests themselves the focus of your writing. Reserve interpretations for the Discussion section.

Note: Like the terms *correlated* and *random,* the term *significant* has a specific statistical meaning for scientists and should therefore be used in a lab report only in relation to the appropriate statistical tests.

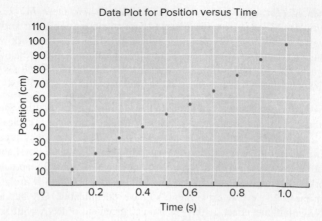

FIGURE 12.3 **A graph used to summarize the results of an engineering assignment.**

5. Discussion
In discussing your results, interpret your major findings by explaining how and why each finding does or does not confirm the original hypothesis. Connect your work with prior scientific research, and look ahead to potential future research.

6. Acknowledgments
In professional journals, most reports of experimental findings include a brief statement acknowledging those who assisted the author(s).

7. References
Include at the end of your report a listing of all manuals, books, and journal articles you consulted during the research and writing process. Use one of the citation formats developed by the Council of Science Editors (CSE style), unless your instructor prefers another format. *(See Tab 8: Chicago and CSE Documentation Styles.)*

12c Case studies in the social sciences.

Social scientists are trained observers and recorders of individual and group behavior. They write to see clearly and remember precisely what they observe and then to interpret its meaning.

1. Choosing a topic that raises a question
In writing or conducting a case study, your purpose is to connect what you observe with issues and concepts in the social sciences. Choose a topic, and turn it into a research question. Write down your hypothesis—a tentative answer

to your research question. Record types of behavior and other categories (for example, appearance) to guide your research in the field.

2. Collecting data

Make a detailed and accurate record of what you observe and when and how you observe it. Whenever you can, count or measure, and record word-for-word what is said. Use frequency counts—the number of occurrences of specific, narrowly defined instances of behavior. If you are observing a classroom, for example, you might count the number of teacher-directed questions asked by several children. Your research methodologies course will address many ways to quantify data.

3. Assuming an unbiased stance

In a case study, you are presenting empirical findings, based on careful observation. Avoid value-laden terms and unsupported generalizations.

4. Discovering meaning in your data

As you review your notes, try to uncover connections, identify inconsistencies, and draw inferences. For example, ask yourself why a subject behaved in a

—NAVIGATING THROUGH COLLEGE AND BEYOND

Case Studies

Social scientists publish their findings in such journals as the *American Sociological Review, Harvard Business Review,* and *Journal of Marriage and the Family.* For example, a developmental psychologist might study conflict resolution in children by observing a group of four-year-olds in a day care center and publish her findings in a journal. As a student, you will find case studies used in a number of social science disciplines:

- **In sociology:** You may be asked to analyze a small group to which you have belonged or belong now. Your study will address such issues as the group's norms and values, cultural characteristics, and stratification and roles. Your audience will be your professor, who wants to see how your observations reflect current theories on group norms.

- **In nursing:** For a nursing class, you may note details of patient care that corroborate or differ from the norm. Your audience is the supervising nurse, who is interested in the patient's progress and your interactions with the patient.

- **In education:** As a student teacher, you may closely observe and write about students in the context of their socioeconomic and family backgrounds. Your audience will be the cooperating teacher, who seeks greater insight into students' behavior.

specific way, and consider different explanations for the behavior. Draw on the techniques for quantitative analysis that you have learned in a statistics course.

5. Presenting your findings in an organized way

There are two basic ways to present your findings in the body of a case study: as stages of a process and in analytic categories. Using stages of a process, a student studying gang initiation organized her observations chronologically into appropriate stages. If you organize your study this way, be sure to transform the minute-by-minute history of your observations into a pattern with distinct stages. Using analytic categories, a student observing the behavior of a preschool child organized his findings according to three categories from his textbook: motor coordination, cognition, and socialization.

6. Including a review of the literature, a statement of your hypothesis, and a description of your methodology in your introduction

The introduction presents the framework, background, and rationale for your study. Begin with the topic, and review related research, working your way to the specific question that the study addresses. Follow that opening with a statement of your hypothesis, accompanied by a description of your **methodology—** how, when, and where you made your observations and how you recorded them.

> **Note:** *If possible, develop stages or categories while you are making your observations.* In your analysis, be sure to illustrate these stages or categories with material drawn from observations— with descriptions of people, places, and behavior, as well as with well-chosen quotations.

7. Discussing your findings in the conclusion

The conclusion of your case study should answer these three questions: (1) Did you find what you expected? (2) What do your findings show, or what is the bigger picture? and (3) What should researchers explore further?

12d Essay exams.

Spending time in advance thinking about writing essay exams will reduce stress and increase success.

1. Preparing with the course and your instructor in mind

Consider the specific course as your writing context and the course's instructor as your audience:

- What questions or problems did your instructor explicitly or implicitly address? What frameworks did your instructor use to analyze topics?

- What key terms did your instructor repeatedly use during lectures and discussions?

2. Understanding your assignment

Essay exams are designed to test your knowledge and understanding, not just your memory. Make up some essay questions that require you to do the following:

- **Explain** what you have learned in a clear, well-organized way.
- **Connect** what you know about one topic with what you know about another topic.
- **Apply** what you have learned to a new situation.
- **Interpret** the causes, effects, meanings, value, or potential of something.
- **Argue** for or against some controversial statement about what you have learned.

Almost all these directions require you to synthesize what you have learned from your reading, class notes, and projects.

3. Planning your time

Quickly look through the whole exam, and determine how much time you will spend on each part. You will want to move as quickly as possible through the questions with lower point values and spend the bulk of your time responding to those that are worth the greatest number of points.

4. Responding to short-answer questions by showing the significance of the information

The most common type of short-answer question is the identification question: Who or what is X? In answering questions of this sort, present just enough information to show that you understand X's significance within the context of the course. For example, if you are asked to identify "Federalists" on an American history exam, don't just write, "political party that opposed Thomas Jefferson." Instead, craft one or two sentences that identify the Federalists as a party that supported the Constitution over the Articles of Confederation but then evolved, under the influence of Alexander Hamilton, into support for an elite social establishment.

5. Responding to essay questions tactically

Keep in mind that essay questions usually ask you to do something specific with a topic. Begin by determining precisely what you are being asked to do. Before you write anything, read the question—all of it—and circle key words.

> (Explain)(two) ways in which Picasso's *Guernica* evokes(war)'s terrifying (destructiveness.)

To answer this question, you need to focus on two of the painting's features, such as color and composition, and their connection to war, not on Picasso's life.

6. Using the essay question to structure your response

Usually, you can transform the question itself into the thesis of your answer. If you are asked to agree or disagree with the Federalists' characterization of Thomas Jefferson in the election of 1800, you might begin with this thesis.

> In the election of 1800, the Federalists characterized Jefferson as a dangerous radical. Although Jefferson's ideas were radical for the times, they were not dangerous to the republic.

Take a minute or two to list evidence for each of your main points, and then write the essay.

7. Checking your work

Save a few minutes to read quickly through your completed answer, looking for words you might have omitted or key sentences that make no sense. Make corrections neatly.

SAMPLE ESSAY TEST RESPONSE

A student's response to an essay question in an art appreciation course appears below. Both the question and the student's notes are provided.

QUESTION

Both of these buildings (Figure 1 and Figure 2) feature dome construction. Identify the buildings, and discuss the differences in the visual effects created by the different dome styles.

STUDENT'S NOTES

Fig 1: Pantheon. Plain outside-concrete, can barely see dome. Dramatic inside-dome opens up huge interior space. Oculus to sky: light, air, rain. Coffered ceiling.

Fig 2: Taj Mahal. Dramatic exterior-dome set high, marble, reflecting pool, exterior lines go up. Inside not meant to be visited.

STUDENT'S ANSWER

The Pantheon (Figure 1) and the Taj Mahal (Figure 2) are famous for their dome construction. The styles of the domes are dramatically different, however, resulting in dramatically different visual effects.

The Pantheon, which was built by the Romans as a temple to the gods, looks very plain on the exterior. The dome is barely visible from the outside, and it is made of a dull grey concrete. Inside the building, however, the dome produces an amazing effect. It opens up a huge space within the building, unobstructed by interior supports. The sides of the dome are coffered, and those recessed rectangles both lessen the weight of the dome and add to its visual beauty. Most dramatically, the top of the dome is open to the sky, allowing sun or rain to pour into the building. This opening is called the oculus, meaning 'eye' (to or of Heaven).

The Taj Mahal, which was built by a Muslim emperor of India as a tomb for his wife, is the opposite of the Pantheon-dazzling on the outside and plain on the inside. The large central dome is set up high on the base so that it can be seen from far away. It is made of

FIGURE 1

FIGURE 2

white marble, which reflects light beautifully. The dome is surrounded by other structures that frame it and draw attention to its exterior—a long reflecting pond and four minarets. Arches and smaller domes on the outside of the building repeat the large dome's shape. Because the Taj Mahal's dome is tall and narrow, however, it does not produce the kind of vast interior space of the shorter, squatter Pantheon dome. Indeed, the inside of the Taj Mahal is not meant to be visited. Unlike the Pantheon, the dome of the Taj Mahal is intended to be admired from the outside.

12e   Coauthored projects.

A project is coauthored when more than one person is responsible for producing it. In many fields, working collaboratively is essential. Here are some suggestions to help you make the most of this challenge:

- Working with your partners, decide on some ground rules, including meeting times, deadlines, and ways of reconciling differences. Will the majority rule, or will some other principle prevail? Is there an interested and respected third party who can be consulted if the group's dynamics break down?

- Will the group meet primarily online or in person? See the box above for guidelines for online communication.

- Divide the work fairly so that everyone has a part to contribute to the project. Keep in mind that each group member should do some

—the EVOLVING SITUATION

Coauthoring Online

Computer networks make it easy for two or more writers to coauthor texts. Wikis, a type of writing environment that is supported by *cloud technology,* allow writers to contribute to a common structure and edit one another's work. Other cloud technologies like *Google Docs* may be available to make coauthoring easy. Most courseware (such as Canvas) includes chat and texting tools and discussion boards for posting and commenting on drafts, and communication services like *Skype*, *FaceTime*, and *Google Hangout* can host real-time meetings. Word-processing software also allows writers to make tracked changes in files.

If your group meets online, make sure a transcript of the discussion is saved. If you exchange ideas via e-mail, you automatically will have a record of how the project developed and how well the group worked together. Archive these transcripts and e-mails into designated folders. In all online communications, be especially careful with your tone. Without the benefit of facial expressions and other cues, which e-mails and text messages lack, writers can easily misinterpret even the most constructive criticism.

researching, drafting, revising, and editing. Responsibility for taking notes at meetings should rotate.

- In your personal journal, record, analyze, and evaluate the intellectual and interpersonal workings of the group as you see and experience them. If the group's dynamics begin to break down, seek the assistance of a third party.

- After all group members have completed their assigned part or subtopic, gather the whole group face to face or online to weave the parts together and create a focused piece of writing with a consistent voice. At this point group members usually need to negotiate with one another. Although healthy debate is good for a project, tact is essential.

CHAPTER 13

Oral Presentations

Preparing an oral presentation, like preparing any text, is a process. Consider your rhetorical situation—your audience, purpose, and context—as you determine focus and level of communication. Gather information, decide on the main idea, think through the organization, and choose visuals that support your points.

13a   Plan and shape your oral presentation.

Effective oral presentations seem informal, but that effect is the result of careful planning and strategic shaping of the material.

1. Considering the interests, background knowledge, and attitudes of your audience

Find out as much as you can about your listeners before you prepare the speech. What does the audience already think about your topic? Do you want to intensify your listeners' commitment to already existing views, provide new and clarifying information, provoke more analysis and understanding, or change listeners' beliefs?

If you are addressing an unfamiliar audience, ask the people who invited you to speak to fill you in on the audience's interests and expectations. You also can adjust your speech once you get in front of the actual audience, making your language more or less technical, for example, or offering additional examples to illustrate points.

2. Working within the time allotted to your presentation

Gauge how many words you speak per minute by reading a passage aloud at a conversational pace (about 120 to 150 words per minute is ideal). Be sure to time your presentation when you practice it.

13b Draft your presentation with the rhetorical situation in mind.

1. Making your opening interesting

A strong opening puts the speaker at ease and gains the audience's confidence and attention. During rehearsal, try out several approaches to your introduction to see what gets the best reactions. Stories, brief quotations, striking statistics, and surprising statements are good attention getters. Try crafting an introduction that lets your listeners know what they have to gain from your presentation—for example, new information or new perspectives on a subject of common interest.

2. Making the focus and organization of your presentation explicit

Select two or three ideas that you most want your audience to hear—and remember. Make these ideas the focus of your presentation, and let your audience know what to expect by previewing the content of your presentation—"I will make three points about fraternities on campus"—and then listing the three points.

The phrase "to make three points" signals a topical organization. Other common organizational patterns include chronological *(at first . . . later . . . in the end)*, causal *(because of that . . . then this follows)*, and problem-solution *(given the situation . . . then this set of proposals)*. A question-answer format also works well, either as an overall strategy or as part of another organizational pattern.

3. Being direct

What your audience hears and remembers has as much to do with how you speak as it does with what you say. Use a direct, simple style:

- Choose basic sentence structures.
- Repeat key terms.
- Pay attention to the pace and rhythm of your speech.
- Don't be afraid to use the pronouns *I, you,* and *we.*

Notice how applying these principles transforms the following written sentence into a group of sentences appropriate for oral presentation.

WRITTEN

Although the claim that the position of the stars can help people predict the future has yet to be substantiated by either an ample body or an exemplary piece of empirical research, advocates of astrology persist in pressing the claim.

ORAL

Your sign says a lot about you. So say advocates of astrology. But what evidence do we have that the position of the stars helps people predict the future? Do we have lots of empirical research or even one really good study? The answer is, "Not yet."

4. Using visual aids: Posters and presentation software

Slides, posters, objects, video clips, and music help make your focus explicit, but avoid oversimplifying your ideas to fit them on a slide. Make sure the images, videos, or music fit your purpose and audience. Presentation software such as PowerPoint and Prezi can help you stay focused while you are speaking. *(For more on using presentation software to incorporate multimedia elements into a presentation, see Section 13c.)*

When preparing a poster presentation, keep the poster simple with a clear title, bullets listing key points, and images that support your purpose. Be sure that text can be read from several feet away. *(For more on design principles, see Chapter 8: Designing Academic Texts and Portfolios, pp. 84–95.)*

5. Concluding memorably

Make your ending memorable: return to that surprising opener, play with the words of your opening quotation, look at the initial image from another angle, or reflect on the story you have told. Make sure your listeners are aware that you are about to end your presentation, using such signal phrases as "in conclusion" or "let me end by saying," if necessary. Keep your conclusion short to hold the audience's attention.

> **13c**   Use presentation software to create multimedia presentations.

Presentation software makes it possible to incorporate audio, video, and animation into a talk. This software can also be used to create multimodal compositions that viewers can review on their own.

1. Using presentation software for an oral presentation

Presentation slides that accompany a talk should identify major points and display information in a visually effective way.

Remember that slides support your talk; they do not replace it. Limit the amount of information on each slide to as few words as possible, and plan to show each slide for about one minute. Use bulleted lists and phrases keyed to your major points rather than full sentences. Make fonts large enough to be seen by the person in the last row of your audience: titles should be in 44-point type or larger, subheads in 32-point type or larger. High-contrast color schemes and sufficient blank space between slide elements will also increase the visibility of your presentation.

2. Using presentation software to create independent projects

With presentation software, you can also create projects that run on their own or at the prompting of the viewer. This capability is especially useful in distance learning settings, where students attend class and share information electronically.

3. Preparing a slide presentation

The following guidelines will help you prepare effective slides.

Decide on a slide format   Begin thinking about slides while you plan what you are going to say because the slides and the words will inform each other. As you decide on the words for your talk or independent project, you will think of visuals that support your points, and, as you work out the visuals, you are likely to see additional points you can make—and adjust your presentation as a result. Every feature of your slides—fonts, images, and animations—should support your purpose and appeal to your audience.

Before you create your slides, establish their basic appearance. What background color will they have? What font or fonts? What design elements, such as borders and icons? Will the templates provided by the software suit your talk, or should you modify a template to suit your needs? Since the format you establish will be the canvas for all your slides, avoid distractions and make sure that it complements the images and words you intend to display.

Incorporate images into your presentation   Include images when appropriate. To summarize quantitative information, you might use a chart or graph. To show geographical relationships, you would likely use a map. You can also add photographs that illustrate your points. In all cases, select appropriate, relevant images that support your purpose.

Incorporate relevant audio, video, and animation   Slides can also include audio files, which can provide background information for each slide in an independent composition project. For a presentation on music, you can insert audio files to show how a type of music has developed over time. Be sure the audio files are sufficiently loud.

Video files and animated drawings and diagrams can also be useful. An animated diagram of the process of cell division could help illustrate a presentation on cellular biology. If you are using audio, video, or animation files that belong to others, cite the source. If you plan to make your presentation publicly available online, provide citations or obtain permission to use these items from the copyright holder. *(For more on finding and citing multimodal elements, see Chapter 20, Finding and Creating Effective Visuals, pp. 212-18.)*

Incorporate hypertext links   You might use an internal link within a slide sequence to jump to another slide that illustrates or explains a particular point or issue or an external link to a site on the Internet. For instance, for a presentation on insects, you might include a hyperlink to a slide about insects specific to the part of the country in which you live, complete with an image of one of them. You can also create external links to resources about insects on the Web. Be careful not to rely too much on external links, however, because they can undermine the coherence of a presentation and can sometimes take a long time to load.

4. Reviewing a slide presentation

Once you have the text of your presentation in final form and the multimodal elements in place, you should carefully review your slides to make sure they work together coherently:

- **Check how slides in your software's slide sorter window move one to the next.** Do you have an introductory slide? Should you add transitional effects that reveal the content of a slide gradually or point by point? Use transitional effects to support your rhetorical situation. For example, would audio help make your point? Do you have a concluding slide?

- **Make sure that the slides are consistent with the script of the talk you plan to deliver.** If the slides are to function independently, do they include enough information in the introduction, an adequate explanation of each point, and a clear conclusion?
- **Check the arrangement of your slides.** Try printing them and spreading them out over a large surface, rearranging them if necessary, before implementing needed changes on the computer.
- **Be sure the slides have a unified look.** For example, do all the slides have the same background? Do they all use the same fonts in the same way? Are headers and bullets consistent?

For an example of a slide presentation created to accompany a talk about the issue of cyberbullying, see Figure 13.1 on page 160.

Caution: If you plan to make external links part of your presentation, make sure that you have a functioning Web browser on your computer and that a fast connection to the Internet is available where you will be giving the presentation. If possible, do a practice run of your presentation on site so you can be sure that your links work.

13d   Prepare for your presentation.

Your oral presentation will have the appropriate effect on an audience if you make certain crucial decisions in advance.

1. Deciding whether to use notes or a written script

When giving your talk, make eye contact with your listeners to monitor their responses and adjust your message accordingly. For most occasions, it is inappropriate to write out everything you want to say and then read it word for word, nor do you want to read from the slides. Instead, speak from an outline or bullet points, and write out only those parts of your presentation where precise wording counts, such as quotations.

In some scholarly or formal settings, precise wording may be necessary, especially if your oral presentation is to be published or if your remarks will be quoted by others. Sometimes the setting for your presentation may be so formal or the audience may be so large that a script feels necessary. In such instances, do the following:

- Triple-space the typescript of your text.
- Avoid carrying sentences over from one page to another.
- Mark your manuscript for pauses, emphasis, and the pronunciation of proper names.

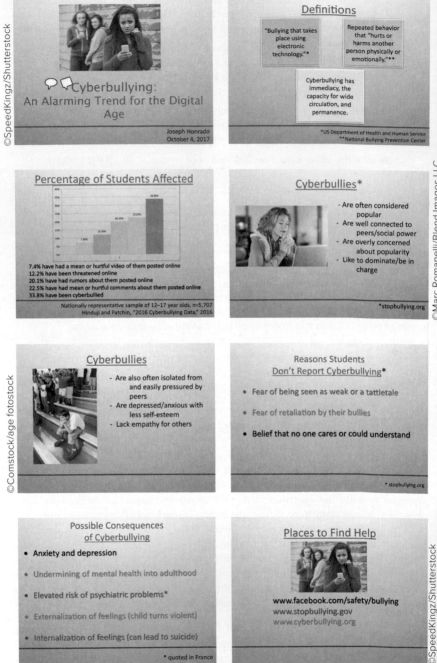

FIGURE 13.1 Sample PowerPoint slides for a presentation on the topic of cyberbullying.

2. Rehearsing, revising, and polishing

Whether you are using an outline or a script, practice your presentation aloud. Revise transitions that don't work, points that need further development, and sections that are too long. After you have settled on the content of your speech and can present it comfortably, polish delivery. Ask your friends to watch and listen to your rehearsal. Check that your body posture is straight but relaxed, that your voice is loud enough and clear, that you keep your hands away from your face, and that you make eye contact around the room. Time your final rehearsals, adding and cutting material as necessary.

3. Accepting nervousness as normal

The adrenaline surge you feel before a presentation can actually invest your talk with positive energy. Practice and revise your presentation until it flows smoothly, and make sure that you have a strong opener to get you through the first, most difficult moments. Remember that other people cannot always tell that you are nervous.

13e   Prepare a version of TED talks.

TED is a nonprofit organization, founded in 1984, devoted to "Ideas Worth Spreading." TED stands for Technology, Entertainment, Design—the original topics of the conference that gave TED its name. The TED talk—strictly limited to no more than eighteen minutes—has become a new genre for effective oral communication—delivered concisely and without notes. Take a look at the TED Web site for further information and sample talks: www.ted.com/pages/about/our-organization.

CHAPTER 14

Multimodal Writing

Multimodal writing combines words with images, video, or audio into a single composition. The most common form of multimodal writing—discussed in many chapters of this handbook—is a combination of words and still visuals such as photographs, maps, charts, or graphs; these texts can be composed for class assignments, for ePortfolios used to apply for jobs, and for personal writing to be shared with others. Another form is an oral presentation, as part of a class presentation or pitch for funding a community effort, with any kind of visual support from a diagram on a Smartboard to a Prezi slide show *(see Chapter 13, Oral Presentations)*. Digital technology also allows writers to combine written words with sound, video, and animation. On social media Web sites, such as *Facebook,* users integrate text, images, and other multimodal elements.

Like any form of composition, multimodal writing is governed by the rhetorical situation; you use multimodal resources to convey a message effectively to a particular audience for a particular purpose: to inform, to interpret, or to persuade. A video or audio segment—like a photograph, map, or recording—must support your purpose and be appropriate for the audience to whom you are writing.

14a Learn about tools for creating multimodal texts.

Multimodal writing can take a variety of forms and can be created with a variety of software tools. Here are a few options:

- Most word-processing programs permit you to insert still images into a word document, and many also make it possible to create a composition that links to various files—including audio, image, and video files *(see 14b and 14c).*

- Most presentation software allows you to include audio and video files in your presentation as well as still visuals *(see 13c, pp. 157-59).*

- A variety of programs and Web-based tools allow you to create your own **Web pages** and **Web sites,** which can include a wide range of multimodal features *(see 14c).*

- You can create a **blog** on which, in addition to your written entries, you can post multimodal files and links to files on other blogs and Web sites. You also can collaborate with other writers on a **wiki.** *(See 14d.)*

14b Combine text and image using a word-processing program to analyze images.

Two types of assignments you might be called on to write are an image analysis and a narrative that explains an image.

1. Composing an image analysis

You may be asked to analyze a single image such as a piece of art from a museum (possibly viewed online), as Diane Chen does in her analysis of the Dorothea Lange photograph in Chapter 7 *(see pp. 83-84).* In an image analysis, you have two tasks: (1) describe the picture as carefully as possible, using adjectives, comparisons, and words that help readers focus on the picture and the details that compose it; and (2) analyze the argument the image seems to be making.

2. The narrative behind the image

Sometimes a writer tries to imagine the story behind an evocative photograph. Often the story that results is as much an expression of the writer as it is a statement about the photograph.

Some photographs, like the one in Figure 14.1 by Pulitzer Prize–winning photojournalist Tyler Hicks, tell universal stories through immediate incidents. The photograph of the 2013 terrorist attack on a Kenyan shopping mall is literally pictured on a slant, conveying fear and disorientation. Hicks conveys the horror of destruction—the worst of humanity—in the context of the best—a

FIGURE 14.1 **A mother and her children hide during the 2013 terrorist attack on a Kenyan shopping mall.**

mother's protective love. But there is nothing sentimental about the photograph. Everyday objects—cups, toasters, all in disarray—surround the family as they hide from the evil thrust upon them.

14c   Create a Web site.

Thanks to Web editing software, it is now almost as easy to create a Web site and post it on the Internet as it is to write a print text using word-processing software. Many Web-based businesses like *Google, Weebly,* and *Wix* provide free server space for hosting sites and offer tools for creating Web pages. Many schools also make server space available for student Web sites.

To be effective, a Web site must be well designed and serve a well-defined purpose for its audience. In creating a Web site, plan the site, draft its content, and select its visuals; then revise and edit as you would for any other composition. *(See Tab 2: Writing and Designing Texts.)* The following sections offer guidelines for composing a Web site.

1. Planning a structure for your site

Like most print documents, a Web site can have a hierarchical, linear structure, where one page leads to the next. Because of the hyperlinked nature of this medium, however, a site can also be organized in a hub-and-spoke structure, with a central page leading to other pages. The diagrams in Figure 14.2 on page 164 illustrate these two structures. To choose the structure that will work best, consider how users will want to access information or opinion on the site. For example, visitors intrigued by the topic of Tyler County's historic buildings may want to explore the topic further. Caregivers visiting a site offering them professional resources will want to find specific information quickly.

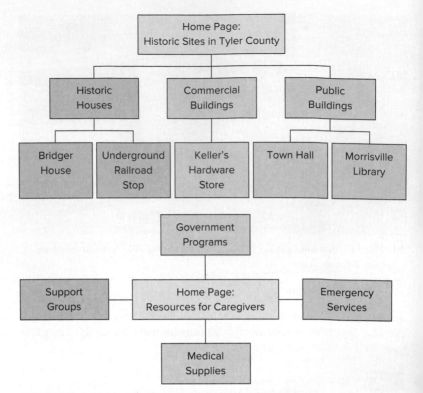

FIGURE 14.2 Hierarchical (top) and hub structure (bottom).

KNOW THE SITUATION Web Sites

Purpose: To inform or persuade

Audience: Audience members for the Web can be people who need information about your topic (and may be knowledgeable themselves) or those who are only mildly interested. Writing for the Web is often more complicated than other types of situations because of the wide range of audiences that may visit a site.

Stance: Knowledgeable

Genres: Web sites often host several genres, for instance, reports, reviews, and opinion pieces

Medium: Digital and networked

To determine your site's structure, try mapping the connections among its pages by arranging them in a storyboard. Represent each page with an index card, and rearrange the pages on a flat surface, experimenting with different possible arrangements. Alternatively, use Post-it notes on a whiteboard, and

─CHECKLIST   Planning a Web Site

When you begin your Web composition, consider these questions about this writing situation:

☐ What is your purpose?

☐ Who are your viewers, and what are their needs? Will the site be limited by password protection to a specific group of viewers, or should you plan for a broader audience?

☐ What type of content will you include on your site: images, audio files, video files?

☐ Will you need to get permission to use visuals or other files that you obtain from outside sources?

☐ What design elements will appeal to your audience and complement your purpose and content?

☐ Given your technical knowledge, amount of content, and deadline, how much time should you allot to each stage of building your site?

☐ Will the site be updated, and, if so, how frequently?

draw arrows connecting them. Also begin planning the visual design of your site. For consistency, establish a template page, including background color and fonts. Choose a uniform location (for example, at the top, in the middle) for material that will appear on each such as site title, page title, navigation links, a repeated visual or theme unifying all the pages, and your contact information. *(See pp. 166-67 on designing a site with a unified look.)*

2. Gathering content for your site

The content for a Web site will usually consist of written work along with links and graphics. Depending on the situation, you might also provide audio files, video files, and even animation.

Follow these special requirements for written content on a Web site:

- Usually readers do not want lengthy text explanations; they expect chunks of information—short paragraphs—delivered quickly.

- Chunks for each topic or point should fit on one screen. Avoid long passages that require readers to scroll.

- Use links to connect your interests with those of others and to provide extra sources of credible and relevant information. Integrate links into your text, and give them descriptive names, such as "Historic Houses" for one of the Web sites in Figure 14.2. Place links at the end of a paragraph so readers do not navigate away in the middle.

As you prepare your written text, gather the graphics, photographs, and audio and video files that you plan to include. Some sites allow you to download images, and some images, including many of the historical photographs available through the Library of Congress, are in the public domain. Another useful site for visual, audio, and video files is *Creative Commons* (search.creativecommons .org), which directs you to material licensed for specific types of use, and all the images on *Wikipedia* are *Creative Commons,* so approved for use as well. Check the license of the material to see what is permitted, and always provide acknowledgments.

Always cite any material that you do not generate yourself. If your Web text will be public, request permission for use of any material not in the public domain unless the site says permission is not needed. Check for a credit in the source, and if the contact information of the creator is not apparent, e-mail the sponsor of the site and ask for it. *(For citation formats see Tabs 6-8.)*

3. Designing Web pages to capture and hold interest

On reader-friendly Web sites, you will find such easy-to-follow links as "what you'll find here," FAQs (frequently asked questions), or "list of those involved." In planning the structure and content of your site, keep your readers' needs in mind.

4. Designing a readable site with a unified look

The design of your site should suit its writing situation, in the context of its purpose and intended audience: a government site to inform users about copyright law will present a basic, uncluttered design that focuses attention on the text. A university's **home page** might feature photographs of young people and sun-drenched lawns to entice prospective students. Readers generally appreciate a site with a unified look. "Sets" or "themes" are readily available at free graphics sites offering banners, navigation buttons, and other design elements. You also can create visuals with a graphics program, scan your own art, and scan or upload personal photographs. Design your home page to complement your other pages, or your readers may lose track of where they are in the site—and lose interest in staying:

- Use a design template—a preformatted style with structure and headings established—to keep elements of page layout consistent across the site.

- Align items such as text and images.

- Consider including a site map—a Web page that serves as a table of contents for your entire site.

- Select elements such as buttons, signs, and backgrounds with a consistent design suited to your purpose and audience. Use animations and sounds sparingly.

- Use colors that provide adequate contrast, white space, and sans serif fonts to make text easy to read. Pages that are too busy are not visually compelling, and too much white space makes the site feel empty. *(For more on design, see Tab 2: Writing and Designing Texts, pp. 85-92.)*

—*the* EVOLVING SITUATION

Understanding Web Jargon

- **Browser:** software that allows you to access and view material on the Web. When you identify a site you want to see on the Web by typing in a URL (see below), your browser (*Microsoft Internet Explorer, Google Chrome,* or *Safari,* for example) tells a distant computer—a **server**—to allow you to access it.

- **JPEG:** format for photographs and other visuals that is recognized by browsers. Photographs that appear on a Web site should be saved in JPEG format, which stands for Joint Photographic Experts Group. The file extension is .jpg or .jpeg.

- **HTML/XML:** hypertext markup language/extensible markup language. These languages tag or code text so that your browser can rebuild a document from the compressed files that travel through the Internet. It is not necessary to learn HTML or XML to publish on the Web. Programs such as *Publisher, Dreamweaver, Wix.com, Squarespace,* and *Mozilla* provide a WYSIWYG (What You See Is What You Get) interface for creating Web pages. Most word-processing programs have a "Save as HTML" option.

- **URL:** uniform resource locator or Web address. When you type or paste a URL into your Web browser, you are sending a request through your browser to another computer, asking it to allow you access.

- Limit the width of your text; readers find wide lines of text difficult to process.
- Leave time to find appropriate image, audio, and video files created by others and to obtain permission to use them.
- Always check your Web site to be sure all the pages and links load as planned.

The home page and interior page shown in Figure 14.3 on page 168 illustrate some of these design considerations.

5. Designing a Web site that is easy to access and navigate

Help readers find their way to the areas of the site they want to visit. Make it easy for them to take interesting side trips without wasting their time or losing their way:

- **Identify your Web site on each page, and provide a link to the home page.** Remember that readers will not always enter your Web site through the home page. Give the title of the site on each page, and provide an easy-to-spot link to your home page.

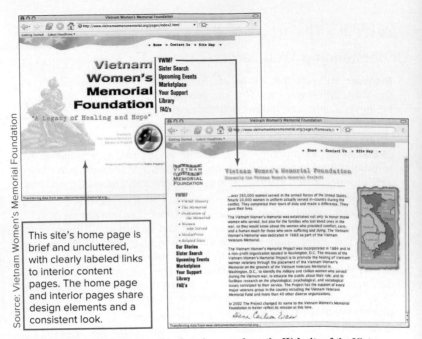

This site's home page is brief and uncluttered, with clearly labeled links to interior content pages. The home page and interior pages share design elements and a consistent look.

FIGURE 14.3 Home page and an interior page from the Web site of the Vietnam Women's Memorial Foundation.

- **Provide a navigation bar on each page.** A **navigation bar** can be a simple line of links that you copy and paste at the top or bottom of each page. A navigation bar on each page makes it easy for visitors to move from the site's home page to other pages and back again.

- **Use graphics that load quickly.** Limit the size of your images to no more than 40 kilobytes so that they will load faster.

- **Use graphics judiciously.** Your Web site should not depend on graphics alone to make its message clear and interesting. Graphics should reinforce your purpose. The designers of the Library of Congress Web site *(Figure 14.4)* use icons such as musical notation and a map to help visitors navigate the site. Avoid clip art, which often looks unprofessional.

- **Be aware of the needs of visitors with disabilities.** Provide alternate ways of accessing visual and auditory information. Include text descriptions of visuals, media files, and tables (for users of screen-reader software or text-only **browsers**). All audio files should have captions and full transcriptions. For more information, visit *Webmonkey* <www.webmonkey.com>. *(See Chapter 8, Designing Academic Texts and Portfolios, pp. 85–92.)*

FIGURE 14.4 The home page of the Web site of the Library of Congress.

Source: Library of Congress Prints and Photographs Division

6. Using peer feedback to revise your Web site

Before publishing your site, to be read by anyone in the world, proofread your text carefully, and ask friends to look at your site in different browsers and share their responses with you. Make sure your site reflects favorably on your abilities.

14d   Create and interact with blogs and wikis.

Blogs are Web sites that can be continually updated. They often invite readers to post comments on entries. Some blogs provide a space where a group of writers can discuss one another's work and ideas. In schools, students blog to discuss issues, organize work, develop sources, compile portfolios, and gather and store material and commentary.

Blogs are important as vehicles for public discussion and commentary. Most presidential campaigns maintain blogs on their Web sites, and nearly all conventional news sources, like the *New York Times,* link to their own blogs. Compared to other types of publications and academic writing, blogs have an informal tone that combines information, entertainment, and personal opinion. Courses often include a blog where students compose homework assignments; this blog often makes an excellent place for students to discuss class readings, plan a group project, or share a draft in process.

---CHECKLIST Setting up a Blog

When you begin your blog, consider these questions about your writing situation:

☐ What is your purpose? How will your blog's visual design reflect that purpose? What other multimedia elements can contribute to your purpose?

☐ To whom will you give access? Should the blog be public for all to see or be limited to a specific group of viewers?

☐ Do you want to allow others to post to your blog, comment on your posts, or both?

☐ Do you want to set up a schedule of postings or a series of reminders that will cue you to post?

☐ Do you know others with blogs? Do you want to link to their sites? Should they link to yours and comment on it?

A **wiki** is another kind of Web-interfaced database that can be updated easily. One well-known wiki is the online encyclopedia *Wikipedia (see Chapter 19, p. 202).* Many instructors do not consider Wikipedia a credible source for research because almost anyone can create or edit its content. Although changes are reviewed before appearing on the site, the reviewers may not have the requisite expertise. Verify that the information provided is correct by confirming it with another source that is credible. Some other wikis, such as Citizendium, rely on experts in a discipline to write and edit articles.

1. Creating your own blog

To begin blogging, set up a blog site with a server such as *Blogger* (blogger.com) or *WordPress* (wordpress.org). Be sure about your writing situation, especially regarding purpose, which may be very specifically focused on a single issue or, alternatively, provide space for opinions on a range of issues.

> *Caution:* Blogs and profiles on social media sites are more or less public depending on the level of access they allow. Do not post anything (including photographs and videos) that you would not want family members, teachers, and prospective employers to view.

2. Setting up a wiki

A wiki is an updateable Web site for sharing and coauthoring content. In addition to using wikis to conduct research together, students often use them simply to share their writing and various kinds of information—for instance relevant videos or Web sites related to a common research topic. Coauthors and peer reviewers find wikis useful because they provide a history of the revisions in any document. To create a wiki, begin by identifying the writing situation and

— CHECKLIST   Setting Up a Wiki

When you begin your wiki, consider these questions related to your writing situation:

☐ What is your purpose?

☐ Who is the audience, and to whom will you give access? Will the wiki have broad participation, or is it designed for a specific group of participants?

☐ Given the tasks that participants will work on, do you want to set up a schedule of deadlines or post reminders to the group?

☐ What design elements will appeal to the participants and to your audience?

☐ Do you have a preference for the specific content? Should participants contribute images? Audio files? Video files?

☐ Will you need to get permission to use any visuals or other files that you obtain from other sources?

☐ Given your technical knowledge, the amount of content you anticipate, and your deadline, how much time should you allot to each stage of building your site?

☐ Will the site be updated, and if so how frequently?

the platform you will use, probably one like *wikispaces.com* or *pbwiki,* which provides set-up tools and directions.

Like blogs, wikis can have a limited number of participants or be open to the world.

Credits

Chapter 9: p. 109 World Anti-Doping Agency, "The sports with the highest number of ADRVs," from *2015 Anti-Doping Rule Violations (ARRVs) Report*, page 6. Used with permission of the World Anti-Doping Agency. **p. 110** Silvia Sara Canetto and David Lester. "Love and Achievement Motives in Women's and Men's Suicide Notes." *The Journal of Psychology*, Vol. 136, Issue 5, 2002. pp 573–576

Chapter 10: p. 117 Mohsen Emadi, "Losses" from *Standing On Earth*, translated by Lyn Coffin. Phoneme Media, 2016. Used with permission.

Chapter 12: p. 143 Kerri K. Morris, "For My Future Self: Remember These Things for Tomorrow" *Cancer Is Not a Gift*, July 13, 2017. www.chicagonow.com/cancer-is-not-a-gift/2017/07/for-my-future-self-remember-these-things-for-tomorrow/ Used with permission. **p. 145** Excerpt from Gloria Ladson-Billings, *The Dreamkeepers: Successful Teachers of African American Children* Copyright © 2009 John Wiley & Sons, Inc. Reproduced by permission of John Wiley & Sons, Inc.

Design Elements: (butterfly/computer): ©Visual Generation/Shutterstock; (other design icons): ©McGraw-Hill Education

4

Writing Beyond College

The aim of education must be the training of independently acting and thinking individuals, who, however, see in the service of the community their highest life problem.

–Albert Einstein

©John Lamb/Getty Images

Health-care professionals write frequently to record their observations and update their colleagues. Writing is an integral part of the world of work as well as of our civic lives.

4 Writing Beyond College

 Section dealing with visual rhetoric. For a complete listing, see the Quick Guide to Key Resources in Connect.

Tab 4: Writing beyond College

This section will help you answer questions such as the following:

Rhetorical Knowledge

- How can I design brochures and newsletters to reach a particular community? (15b)

Critical Thinking, Reading, and Writing

- What is the best way to make my voice heard on an issue in the community? (16a)
- How can I write a letter of complaint that will help me as a consumer? (16b)

Processes

- How do I apply for a job? (17b, c, d)
- What are some online resources for job-hunting? (17e)

Knowledge of Conventions

- What should go on my résumé? (17b)
- How should I format my résumé and cover letter? (17b, c)
- How do I organize a business memo? (17e)
- What do I need to consider when writing professional e-mail? (17e)

For a general introduction to writing outcomes see 1e, pages 14–15.

Although college may be unfamiliar territory to the newcomer, it is part of the larger world. Writing represents an access road—a way of connecting classroom, workplace, and community.

CHAPTER 15

Service Learning and Community-Service Writing

Your ability to research and write can be of great value to organizations that serve the community. Courses at every level of the university, as well as co-curricular activities, offer opportunities to work with organizations such as homeless shelters, tutoring centers, and environmental groups.

15a   Address the community to effect change.

You may be assigned or volunteer to assist in a homeless shelter, tutoring center, hospice, or other not-for-profit with the goal of helping to communicate with various audiences. Your first task will be to understand the writing situation. Members of each organization have a particular way of talking about issues. As someone coming from the outside, you will have opportunities to converse with insiders and then assist the group in achieving its purposes by drafting newsletters, press releases, or funding proposals.

Writing on behalf of a community organization almost always involves negotiation and collaboration. A community organization may revise your draft to fit its needs, and you will have to live with those revisions. In these situations, having a cooperative attitude is as important as having strong writing skills.

Even if you are not writing on behalf of a group, you can write in your own name to raise an issue of concern in a public forum—for example, a newspaper editorial or a letter to a public official.

👁 **15b**   Design posters, brochures, and newsletters with an eye to purpose and audience.

If you are participating in a service learning program or an internship, you may design posters to create awareness and promote events and brochures and newsletters for wide distribution. To create an effective poster, brochure, or newsletter, you will need to integrate your skills in document design with what you have learned about purpose and audience. Here are a few tips:

- Consider how readers will access the pages of the brochure or newsletter. How will it be mailed or distributed? What are the implications for the overall design? For instance, can you create a newsletter with space on the back page for the organization's address?

- Sketch the design in pencil or on a whiteboard before using the computer.

- Make decisions about photographs, illustrations, type fonts, and design in general to create the sponsoring organization's overall image.

- If the organization has a logo, include it; if not, suggest designing one. A **logo** is a small visual symbol, like the Nike "swoosh" or the distinctive font used for Coca-Cola.

- Create a template for the poster, brochure, or newsletter so that you can easily produce future versions. In word-processing and document design programs, a **template** is a blank document that includes all the necessary formatting and codes. When you use a template, you add new copy and visuals since the format and design are already done.

Notice, for example, how the poster in Figure 15.1 directs the eye to the large mobile phone that dominates the space. The screen displays an important message about responding to cyberbullying, summarized in the acronym "REACT."

The brochure *(Figure 15.2 on p. 176)* carefully defines terms, reviews consequences, and suggests countermeasures. On the second page, a photo of a young woman standing alone in a hallway evokes isolation and victimhood; the red text in the top left corner encourages her to REACT, a response to bullying that is summarized in the panel to the right. The complementary image and text are elegant in their simplicity and impact.

The newsletter also has a simple, clear design *(Figure 15.3, p. 177)*. Shaded boxes grab readers' attention by highlighting important statistics. Within the text, bullet points help break down and organize information in list form, making it easier for readers to digest. *(For more information about document design, see Chapter 8, Designing Academic Texts and Portfolios, pp. 84–96.)*

FIGURE 15.1 Example of a well-designed poster.

(Laptop): ©Gregor Schuster/Photographer's Choice/Getty Images; (Hallway): ©Tetra Images/Vstock LLC/Getty Images

(Man): ©George Doyle & Ciaran Griffin/Stockbyte/

The purpose of the brochure is to be informative by providing a definition of cyberbullying and giving advice. The audience is high school students.

Don't fall victim to being cyberbullied:

Educate yourself

Take preventative measures

Have zero tolerance

REACT

For more information on how to educate and protect yourself from cyberbullying, visit the following Web sites:

http://www.stopbullying.gov/cyberbullying

http://www.cyberbullying.us

STOP CYBERBULLIES IN THEIR TRACKS:

Recognize and **REACT**

NO BULLY ZONE

Are You Being Bullied?

What Is a Bully?

A bully is someone who makes you feel uncomfortable, often in a threatening way. It is the person who won't leave you alone and says mean and nasty things to you.

What Is a Cyberbully?

A cyberbully uses digital technologies like text messaging and Internet communication to threaten or scare someone else. Cyberbullies can be more dangerous than a traditional bully because they can hide behind digital technology and because their threats or intimidations can be dispersed to a wider audience through social media.

Consequences of Being Bullied

Victims are more likely to feel anxious and depressed. They think that because one person is mean to them, lots of people will be mean to them. Even when the bullying stops, victims can be haunted by negative memories. Do not let yourself become a victim: REACT! Now.

A brochure is meant to inform the audience about the topic. It's important to present straight forward facts and examples and use clean lines and spacing.

What You Can Do:

Educate yourself—understand what a cyberbully is and the consequences of being bullied.

Take preventative measures against cyberbullies—let your family and friends know what you are doing on the computer (the people you are talking to and what they are saying to you).

Have zero tolerance—if you believe you are being bullied, don't wait to take action.

REACT

REACT

Recognize you are being bullied
Notice the signs of bullying: the use of angry language or insults, the sharing of embarrassing images or information, the spreading of gossip or rumors, and being threatened.

Eliminate contact with the bully
Eliminating contact depends on the situation you are facing. If it is a face-to-face bully, create situations where you are always with other people. If it is a cyberbully, either de-friend the bully or create a new profile.

Ask someone in authority for help
Seek help from a parent, a teacher, an older brother or sister, or someone you trust. Ask this person to give you guidance on how to deal with being bullied and to help you do something about the person who is bullying you.

Compliment yourself for seeking help
Dealing with bulling is not easy. By getting help, you have taken the first step toward no longer being a victim.

Tell others your story
By sharing your story, you could help prevent others from becoming victims.

©Thinkstock/Stockbyte/Getty Images

FIGURE 15.2 Example of a well-designed brochure.

FIGURE 15.3
**Example of a
well-designed
newsletter.**

——Respond to Cyberbullying——

Cyberbullying is a significant, destructive problem among today's young people. While cyberbullying can take many forms, most often it involves the posting of hurtful comments or rumors online, or through texting, instant messaging, and e-mail. Especially harmful are the immediacy, scope, and permanence of bullying that takes place over digital technology: humiliation is easily inflicted online, where large audiences can continue to witness it indefinitely.

According to a study presented by the *Cyberbullying Research Center*, 22.5 percent of twelve-to seventeen-year-olds surveyed between July and October 2016 reported that "mean or hurtful" comments were posted about them and just over 20 percent reported being the subject of rumors posted online. Moreover, 25.7 percent of the same group said they were the targets of two or more forms of cyberbullying on more than two occasions.

> 22.5 percent of twelve-to seventeen-year-olds surveyed reported that "mean or hurtful" comments were posted about them

Who Are These Cyberbullies?

The Web site *Stopbullying.org* explains that two types of children are more likely than others to engage in bullying:

- The first group includes those who are considered popular. They are well connected to their peers, have social power, are overly concerned about their popularity, and like to dominate or be in charge of others.
- The second group is far less socially adept. These children may feel isolated from their peers. They may experience depression and anxiety, or may be struggle to identify with the feelings of others.

Though cyberbullies and their victims range from young children to students in college, cyberbullying may be most destructive to younger teens because they lack the maturity to handle such situations and rarely seek help from adults. Teens also spend a large amount of time online. Parents cannot oversee all of their children's electronic activity, and when unsupervised, children and teens can become bullies or targets.

What Are the Effects of Cyberbullying?

Bullying causes depression and anxiety in children. Even more chilling, bullied children can either externalize their feelings by turning violent, or internalize them, which can lead to other difficulties.

In November 2016, the American Psychological Association (APA) published a policy brief declaring the prevention of bullying one of its top priorities. Referencing a study published in *Social Psychology of Education*, the APA reports that "childhood bullying inflicts the same long-term psychological trauma on girls as severe physical or sexual abuse and that the behavior can undermine victims' mental health into adulthood."

How Can Adults Respond?

With new technologies affecting kids' interactions, parents, educators, and the media must work together to promote healthy guidelines for online behavior.

Parents *Stopbullying.gov* encourages parents to talk to their children, especially to make sure their children understand bullying and feel comfortable bringing any issues to their attention. In addition, adults need to teach young people to adopt a healthy balance of online and offline activities.

Educators Educators must also become proactive in their efforts to prevent cyberbullying. For example, Texas has taken preventative action with legislation known as David's Law. This new law incentives schools to invest in counseling services for victims and perpetrators of bullying.

The Media Finally, mass media and social media outlets should advocate for cyberbullying prevention. In a June 29, 2017, blog post, *Instagram*'s CEO and cofounder Kevin Systrom announced "two new tools to help keep *Instagram* a safe place for self-expression"—a filter for offensive comments and another for spam. *Facebook* has also taken on the problem. In partnership with Yale University's Center for Emotional Intelligence, *Facebook* has created a cyberbullying prevention hub, which will be a resource for teens, parents, and educators alike.

What Resources Are Available?

If cyberbullying is ever to be eliminated, students, parents, educators, and the media must work together to establish guidelines for proper online behavior. With increasing awareness of the impact of cyberbullying on its victims, families and schools can teach children how to balance technology use with common sense and prepare them to identify and report incidents of cyberbullying before those incidents result in significant harm.

> The APA reports that "childhood bullying inflicts the same long-term psychological trauma on girls as severe physical or sexual abuse."

Simple tips, such as stopping to consider consequences before reacting to a cyberbully attack, saving the information as proof, and sharing that information with a trusted adult. Web sites also offer a wide variety of resources for dealing with cyberbullies, including links to counseling services, community outreach organizations, workshops, and a helpline.

Cyberbullying Research Center
Cyberbullying.org

Facebook
www.facebook.com/safety/bullying

National Bullying Prevention Center
www.pacer.org/bullying/resources/parents/d efinition-impact-roles.asp

Stopbullying.gov
www.stopbullying.gov/at-risk/warning-signs/index.htm

Through solutions like these, the very technology that has allowed cyberbullying to exist can also play an important role in addressing it.

CHAPTER 16

Writing to Raise Awareness and Share Concern

Your ability to write and your willingness to share your opinions and insights can influence community actions and affect the way an organization treats you. A letter or an e-mail to a local politician about a current issue or to a corporation about customer service can accomplish much if clearly argued, concisely phrased, and appropriately directed.

16a Write about a public issue.

Your task in writing to a newspaper, community organization, or public figure is to present yourself as a polite, engaged, and reasonable person who is invested in a particular issue and can offer a compelling case for a particular course of action. Most publications, corporations, and not-for-profit organizations include forms, links, or e-mail addresses on their Web sites for submitting letters or comments. Whenever possible, use online options instead of writing a print letter. Here are some guidelines:

- Address the appropriate person or department by name. Consult the organization's Web site for this information.

- Concisely state your area of concern in the subject line.

- Keep it brief. Many community organizations and corporations receive millions of e-mails each week. Most publications post specific word-count limits for letters to the editor or comments.

- Follow the conventions of professional e-mail *(see pp. 187–90).* Use capital letters, where appropriate, and standard punctuation.

- Keep your tone polite and professional (neither combative nor overly chatty).

- In the first paragraph, concisely state the matter you wish to address and why it is important to you. For example, if you are writing to your local school board, you might state that you are the parent of a child at the local school.

- In the second paragraph, provide clear and compelling evidence for your concern. If relevant, propose a solution.

- In your conclusion, thank the reader for considering your thoughts. Repeat any request for specific action, for example, having an item added to the agenda of the next school board meeting. If you want a specific response, politely request an e-mail or telephone call. If you intend to follow up on your correspondence, note that you will be calling or writing again within an appropriate time frame.

16b   Write as a consumer.

Writing is a powerful tool for accomplishing goals in everyday life.

1. Writing a letter of complaint

Suppose a product you ordered from an online store as a gift arrived too late, despite a guaranteed delivery date. Following the Customer Service link on the Web site, you compose an e-mail letter of complaint like the one in Figure 16.1. In writing such a letter, present yourself as a reasonable person who has experienced unfair treatment. If you are writing as a representative of your company, state that fact calmly and propose a resolution.

Here are some guidelines for writing a letter of complaint:

- If the company's Web site specifies procedures for complaints, follow those instructions. If the Web site provides a textbox where you write the complaint, do so, following the guidance below.

- If possible, send the complaint via e-mail unless you must submit supporting documentation (such as receipts). If you are sending a print letter, use the business format on pages 187-90.

- In the first paragraph, concisely state the problem and the action you request. In the following paragraphs, explain clearly and objectively

From: Edward Kim <edwardkim@email.com>
Sent: November 10, 2019
To: customerservice@crafts.com
Subject: Order #2898 placed September 29, 2019

I write regarding my order of one gift card in the amount of $25, purchased from your site on September 29, 2019, order #2898. I had requested 2-day express shipping so that my card would arrive in time for my friend's birthday. Unfortunately, the card did not arrive for a week, requiring me to find another gift at the last minute.

While I have enjoyed shopping at your site in the past, I am reluctant to do so in the future. For the stress I experienced trying to replace this gift and as a good-faith gesture, some compensation seems only fair. A refund of the added shipping fee ($4) and a discount of 20% off a future order would help restore my faith in your company. Thanks for your time and attention. I look forward to hearing from you.

Edward Kim
301-555-1234

FIGURE 16.1 Sample letter of complaint.

what happened. Refer to details such as the date and time of the incident so that the person you are writing to can follow up.

- Recognize those who tried to help you as well as those who did not.

- Mention previous positive experiences with the organization, if you can. Your protest will have more credibility if you come across as a person who does not usually complain.

- Conclude by thanking the person you are addressing and expressing the hope that you will be able to continue as a customer.

- Propose reasonable recompense and enclose receipts, if appropriate. Keep the original receipts and documents, enclosing photocopies with your letter. Do *not* send scans of receipts as e-mail attachments.

- Send copies to the people whom you mention. Keep copies of all correspondence for your records.

Consider, for example, the e-mail in Figure 16.1 on p. 179, written by Edward Kim.

2. Writing compliments

Suppose that you wish to thank an airline employee who has been exceptionally helpful to you. In the workplace, you might thank a colleague who worked long hours to complete a project or congratulate a team for bringing in new clients. The writing techniques are similar for expressions of both praise and complaint:

- Address the letter to the person in charge by name. (If you do not know the correct name and title to use, call the corporate headquarters.)

- If you are sending a print letter, use the format for a business letter *(see pp. 187-90).*

- In the first paragraph, concisely state the situation and the help that was provided.

- In the following paragraphs, narrate what happened, referring to details such as the date and time of the incident so that the person you are writing to can follow up with the person who helped you.

- Conclude by thanking the person you are writing to for their time and expressing your intention to continue doing business with the company. Send copies to the people whom you mention.

- Whenever possible, for the speediest response, use the format or textbox provided on the company's Web site.

CHAPTER 17

Writing to Get and Keep a Job

Many students work on or off campus in jobs, as interns, or as volunteers for community organizations. Writing is one way to connect your work, your other activities, and your studies. Strong writing skills will also help you find a good job once you leave college and advance in your chosen career.

17a   Explore Internship possibilities, and keep a portfolio of career-related writing.

An internship, in which you do work in your chosen field, is a vital connection between the classroom and the workplace, allowing you to gain academic credit for integrating the theoretical and the practical. Writing and learning go together. During your internship, keep a journal or notebook to record and analyze your experiences, as well as a file of writing you do on the job. With permission, your final project for internship credit could be an analysis of this file.

On-the-job writing, links to articles and editorials you have written for the student newspaper, brochures you have created for a community organization— these and other documents demonstrate your ability to apply intellectual concepts to real-world demands. Organized into a portfolio, especially into an ePortfolio, this material displays your marketable skills. Your campus career resource center may offer assistance, keep your portfolio on file, if it is print, and send it to future employers or graduate schools. *(For advice on assembling an ePortfolio, see Chapter 8, pp. 92-96.)*

17b   Keep your résumé up-to-date and available on a flash drive or zip drive or post it online.

A **résumé** is a brief summary of your education and your work experience that you send to prospective employers. Expect the person reviewing your résumé to give it no more than sixty seconds. Make that first impression count. Design a document that is easy to read, attractively formatted, and flawlessly edited.

1. Guidelines for writing a résumé
Always include the following *necessary* categories in a résumé:

- Heading (name, address, phone number, e-mail address)
- Education (in reverse chronological order; do not include high school)
- Work experience (in reverse chronological order)
- References (often included on a separate sheet; for many situations, you can substitute the line "References available upon request" instead)

Include the following *optional* categories in your résumé as appropriate:

- Objective or Goals
- Honors and awards
- Internships
- Activities and service
- Special skills

Some career counselors still recommend that you list a career objective right under the heading of your résumé, but others discourage you from including something so specific and counsel you instead to incorporate goals into your cover letter. If you do include an objective or goals, be sure you know what the prospective employer is looking for and tailor your résumé accordingly.

2. Two sample résumés

Laura Amabisca has organized the information in her résumé *(see p. 183)* by date and by categories. Within each category, she has listed items from most to least recent. This reverse chronological order gives appropriate emphasis to what she is doing now and has most recently done. Because she is applying for jobs in public relations, she has highlighted her internship in that field by placing it at the top of her experience section.

The résumé on page 183 reflects appropriate formatting for print. Note the use of a line rule, alignment of text, bullet points, and bold and italic type. These elements organize the information visually, directing the reader's eye appropriately.

17c   Write a tailored application letter.

A clear and concise **application letter** should always accompany a résumé. Before drafting the letter, do some research about the organization you are contacting. For example, even though Laura Amabisca was already familiar with the Heard Museum, she found out the name of the director of public relations. *(Amabisca's application letter appears on p. 186.)* If you are unable to identify an appropriate name, it is better to direct the letter to "Dear Director of Public Relations" or "Dear Director of Personnel" than to "Dear Sir or Madam."

Here are some additional guidelines:

- **Tailor your letter.** A form letter accompanied by a generic résumé is not an effective way of getting a job interview. Before writing an application letter or preparing a résumé, you should consider the overall situation. What exactly is the employer seeking? How might you draw on your experience to address the employer's needs?

- **Use business style.** Use the block form shown on page 183. Type your address at the top of the page, with each line starting at the left margin; place the date at the left margin two lines above the recipient's name and address; use a colon (:) after the greeting; double-space between single-spaced paragraphs;

Laura Amabisca
20650 North 58th Avenue, Apt. 15A
Glendale, AZ 85308
623-555-7310
lamabisca@peoplelink.com

Education	**Arizona State University West,** Phoenix • Bachelor of Arts, History, Minor in Global Management (May 2018) • Senior Thesis: Picturing the Hopi, 1920-1940: A Historical Analysis **Glendale Community College,** Glendale, AZ (2014-2016)
Experience	**Public Relations Office, Arizona State University West** *Intern* (Summer 2017) • Researched and reported on university external publications. • Created original content for print and Web. • Assisted in planning fundraising campaigns and events. **Sears,** Bell Road, Phoenix, AZ *Assistant Manager, Sporting Goods Department* (2016-present) • Supervised team of sales associates. • Ensured quality customer service. *Sales Associate, Sporting Goods Department* (2013-2016) • Recommended products to meet customer needs. • Processed sales and returns. *Stock Clerk, Sporting Goods Department* (2011-2013) • Received, sorted, and tracked incoming merchandise. • Stocked shelves to ensure appropriate supply on sales floor.
Special Skills	*Language:* Bilingual: Spanish/English *Computer:* Windows, Mac OS, MS Office, HTML
Activities	**America Reads** *Tutor, Public-Relations Consultant* (2017) • Taught reading to first-grade students. • Created brochure to recruit tutors. **Multicultural Festival, Arizona State University West** *Student Coordinator* (2017) • Organized festival of international performances, crafts, and community organizations. **Writing Center, Glendale Community College** *Tutor* (2014-2015) • Met with peers to help them with writing assignments.
References	Available upon request to Career Services, Arizona State University West

Amabisca's entire résumé is just one page. A brief, well-organized résumé is more attractive to potential employers than a rambling, multipage one.

The résumé features active verbs such as *supervised.*

Amabisca uses a simple font and no bold or italic type, ensuring that the résumé will be scannable.

LAURA AMABISCA
20650 North 58th Avenue, Apt. 15A
Glendale, AZ 85308
623-555-7310
lamabisca@peoplelink.com

EDUCATION Arizona State University West, Phoenix
*   Bachelor of Arts, History, Minor in Global Management (May 2018)
*   Senior Thesis: Picturing the Hopi, 1920–1940: A Historical Analysis

Glendale Community College, Glendale, AZ (2014–2016)

Asterisks replace bullets.

EXPERIENCE
Public Relations Office, Arizona State University West (Summer 2018)
Intern
*   Researched and reported on university external publications.
*   Created original content for print and Web.
*   Assisted in planning fundraising campaigns and events.

Keywords (highlighted here) catch the eye of a potential employer or match desired positions in a database. A position in public relations requires computer skills, communication skills, and experience working with diverse people. Keywords such as *sales, bilingual, HTML*, and *public relations* are critical to her résumé.

Sears, Bell Road, Phoenix, AZ
Assistant Manager, Sporting Goods Department (2016–present)
*   Supervise team of sales associates.
*   Ensure quality customer service.

Sales Associate, Sporting Goods Department (2013–2016)
*   Recommended products to meet customer needs.
*   Processed sales and returns.

Stock Clerk, Sporting Goods Department (2011–2013)
*   Received, sorted, and tracked incoming merchandise.
*   Stocked shelves to ensure appropriate supply on sales floor.

SPECIAL SKILLS
Language: Bilingual: Spanish/English
Computer: Windows, Mac OS, MS Office, HTML

ACTIVITIES
America Reads (2017)
Tutor, Public-Relations Consultant
*   Taught reading to first-grade students.
*   Created brochure to recruit tutors.

Multicultural Festival, Arizona State University West (2018)
Student Coordinator
*   Organized festival of international performances, crafts, and
    community organizations.

Writing Center, Glendale Community College (2014–2016)
Tutor
*   Met with peers to help them with writing assignments.

REFERENCES
Available upon request to Career Services, Arizona State University West

─ the EVOLVING SITUATION

Electronic and Scannable Résumés

Many employers now request résumés by e-mail and electronically scan print résumés. Here are some tips for using electronic technology to submit your résumé:

- Contact the human resource department of a potential employer and ask whether your résumé should be scannable.
- If so, be sure to use a clear, common typeface in an easy-to-read size. Do not include any unusual symbols or characters.
- If the employer expects the résumé as an e-mail attachment, save it in a widely readable form such as PDF. Use minimal formatting and no colors, unusual fonts, or decorative flourishes.
- Configure your e-mail program to send you an automated reply when your e-mail has been successfully received.
- Include specific keywords that allow employers to locate your electronic résumé in a database. See the résumé section of Monster.com for industry-specific advice.

use a traditional closing *(Sincerely, Sincerely yours, Yours truly);* and make sure that the inside address and the address on the envelope match exactly.

- **Be professional.** Your letter should be crisp and to the point. Be direct as well as objective in presenting your qualifications, and maintain a courteous and dignified tone toward the prospective employer. Your résumé should contain only education and work-related information. It is better not to include personal information (such as ethnicity, age, or marital status).

- **Limit your letter to three or four paragraphs.** Focus clearly and concisely on what the employer needs to know. In the first paragraph, identify the position you are applying for, mention how you heard about it, and briefly state that you are qualified. In the following one or two paragraphs, explain your qualifications, elaborating on the most pertinent items in your résumé. Because Amabisca was applying for a public relations job at a museum of Native American culture, she chose to highlight her internship and her thesis. In another application letter, however, this time for a management position at American Express, she made different choices. In that letter, she emphasized her work experience at Sears, including the fact that she had progressed through positions of increasing responsibility.

- **State your expectation for future contact.** Conclude with a one- or two-sentence paragraph informing the reader that you are anticipating a follow-up to your letter.

20650 North 58th Avenue, Apt. 15A
Glendale, AZ 85308
August 17, 2018

Ms. Jaclyn Abel
Director of Public Relations
Heard Museum
2301 North Central Avenue
Phoenix, AZ 85004

Dear Ms. Abel:

I am writing to apply for the position of Public Relations Assistant that you recently advertised in the *Arizona Republic*. I believe that my experience and qualifications fit well with your needs at the Heard, a museum that I have visited and loved all my life.

As the attached résumé indicates, I have experience in the public relations field. While at Arizona State University West, I worked as an intern in the Public Relations Office, where I was responsible for analyzing and reporting on the image projected by the university's external publications. I also had a hand in creating the brochure for the University-College Center and participated in planning ASU West's "Dream Big" campaign. In addition I assisted in organizing an opening convocation attended by 800 people. This work in the not-for-profit sector has prepared me well for employment at the Heard.

My undergraduate major in U.S. history has also helped me understand the rich heritage of Native Americans. In my senior thesis, which received the Westmarc Writing Award, I studied the history of the relationship between the Hopis and the Anglo population as reflected in photographs taken from 1920 to 1940. Although my thesis focuses on a specific tribe, I have been interested for many years in Native American culture and have often made use of resources in the Heard. I think that I would do a superior job of presenting the Heard as the premier museum of Native American culture.

Confidential reference letters are available from ASU West Career Services. I sincerely hope that we will have an opportunity to talk further about the Heard Museum and its outstanding cultural contributions to the Phoenix metropolitan area. Please contact me at 623-555-7310 or at lamabisca@peoplelink.com.

Sincerely,

Laura Amabisca

Laura Amabisca

Enc.

Amabisca writes to a specific person and uses the correct salutation (Mr., Ms., Dr., etc.). Never use someone's first name in an application letter, even if you are already acquainted.

Amabisca briefly sums up her work experience. This information is also available on her résumé, but she makes evident in her cover letter why she is applying for the job. Without this explanation, a potential employer might not even look at her résumé.

Amabisca demonstrates her familiarity with the museum to which she is applying. This shows her genuine interest in joining the organization.

- Use *Enc.* **if you are enclosing additional materials.** Decide whether it is appropriate to enclose supporting materials other than your résumé, such as samples of your writing. Amabisca decided to do so because she was applying for her ideal job and had highly relevant materials to send. If you have been instructed to send a cover letter and résumé as attachments to an e-mail, include the word *Attachments* after your e-mail "signature."

17d   Prepare in advance for the job interview.

Many campus career centers offer free seminars on interviewing skills and can also arrange for you to role-play an interview with a career guidance counselor. Here are some additional guidelines for job interviews:

- Call to confirm your interview the day before it is scheduled. Determine how much time you will need to get there. A late appearance at an interview can count heavily against you.

- Dress professionally.

- Bring an additional copy of your résumé and cover letter.

- Expect to speak with several people—perhaps someone from human resources as well your potential supervisor and other people in the department.

- *Always* send a personalized thank-you note or e-mail to everyone who took the time to meet you. In each, mention an interesting point that the person made and your interest in working with that person. Send these notes within twenty-four hours of your interview.

17e   Apply what you learn in college to your on-the-job writing.

Once you get a job, writing is a way to establish and maintain lines of communication with your colleagues and clients. When you write in the workplace, you should imagine a reader who is pressed for time and wants you to get to the point immediately.

1. Writing e-mail and memos in the workplace

In the workplace, you will do much of your writing online, in the form of e-mail. *(For more on e-mail, see Tab 1: Learning across the Curriculum, pp. 10–28.)* Most e-mail programs set up messages in format, with "From," "To," "Sent," and "Subject" lines, as in Figure 17.1.

E-mail in the workplace requires a more formal style than the e-mail you send to family and friends. In an e-mail for a business occasion—communication with colleagues, a request for information, or a thank-you note after an interview—you should observe the same care with organization, spelling, and tone that you would in a business letter:

- Use a concise subject line to cue the reader as to the intent of the e-mail. When replying to messages, replace subject lines that do not clearly reflect the topic.

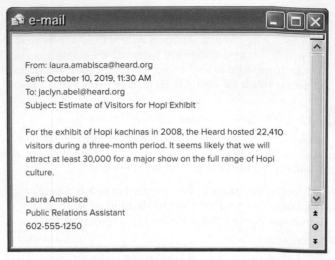

FIGURE 17.1 Sample workplace e-mail.

- Maintain a courteous tone. Avoid joking, informality, and sarcasm since not everyone reading the memo will know you well enough to understand your intent.

- Make sentences brief and to the point. Use short paragraphs.

- Use special formatting such as italics sparingly since not all readers may be able to view it.

- Use standard punctuation and capitalization.

- Close with your name and contact information. *(See the example in Figure 17.1.)*

- Particularly when you do not know the recipient, use the conventions of letter writing, such as opening with "Dear" and ending with "Sincerely."

Business memos are used for communication with others within an organization and are usually sent electronically. Memos, written in a professional tone, are concise and formal and may be used to set up meetings, summarize information, or make announcements. *(See the example on p. 189.)* They generally contain the following elements:

- A header at the top that identifies recipient, author, date, and subject

- Block paragraphs that are single-spaced within the paragraph and double-spaced between paragraphs

- Bulleted lists and other design elements (such as headers) to set off sections of longer memos

- A section at the top or bottom that indicates other members of the organization who have received copies of the memo

To: Sonia Gonzalez, Grace Kim, Jonathan Jones
From: Jennifer Richer, Design Team Manager   *JR*
cc: Michael Garcia, Director, Worldwide Design
Date: March 3, 2019
Re: Meeting on Monday

Please plan to attend a meeting on Monday at 9:00 AM in Room 401. At that time, we'll review our progress on the library project as well as outline future activities to ensure the following:

• Client satisfaction
• Maintenance of the current schedule
• Operation within budget constraints

In addition, we will discuss assignments related to other upcoming projects, such as the renovation of the gymnasium and science lab. Please bring design ideas and be prepared to brainstorm. Thanks.

FIGURE 17.2 Sample memo.

Whether you are sending your memo by e-mail or interoffice mail, consider both the content and the appearance of the document. For example, presenting your information as a numbered or bulleted list surrounded by white space aids readability and allows you to highlight important points and to emphasize crucial ideas. *(For more help with document design, see Tab 2: Writing and Designing Texts, pp. 29–96.)*

2. Writing in other business genres

Conventional forms of business writing also increase readability because readers have built-in expectations for the genre and therefore know what to look for. Besides the memo, there are a number of common business genres:

• **Business letters:** Use business letters to communicate formally with people outside an organization. Typically, letters in business format have single-spaced block paragraphs with double spacing between the paragraphs. *(See the example on p. 186.)*

• **Business reports and proposals:** Like college research projects, business reports and proposals can be used to inform, analyze, and interpret. An abstract, sometimes called an **executive summary,** is almost always required. Tables and graphs should be included when appropriate. *(For more about these visual elements, see Tab 2: Writing and Designing Texts, pp. 29–96.)*

• **Evaluations and recommendations:** You might need to evaluate a person, or you might be called on to evaluate a product or a procedure and recommend whether the company should buy or use it. Like the reviews and critiques that college writers compose, workplace

the EVOLVING SITUATION

E-Mail in the Workplace

Anything you write using a company's or an organization's computers or computer systems is considered company property. If you want to gossip with a co-worker, do so over lunch. If you want to e-mail your best friend about your personal life, do so from your home computer. The following guidelines will help you use e-mail wisely:

- When you are replying to an e-mail that has been sent to several people, determine whether your response should go to all of the original recipients or just to the original sender. Avoid cluttering other people's in-boxes.
- Open attachments from known senders only.
- File your e-mail as carefully as you would other types of documents. Create separate folders in your e-mail program for each client, project, or co-worker. Save any particularly important e-mails as separate files.
- While it may be acceptable for you to browse news and shopping sites during your breaks, do not visit sites that would embarrass you if a colleague or your supervisor suddenly looked over your shoulder. Remember that all sites you have visited are cached—or stored—on that computer.

evaluations should be reasonable as well as convincing. Always support your account of both strengths and weaknesses with specific illustrations or examples.

- **Presentations:** In many professions, information is presented informally and formally to different groups of people. You might suddenly be asked to offer an opinion in a group meeting, or you might be given a week to prepare a formal presentation, with visuals, on an ongoing project. *(For more information about oral presentations, including PowerPoint and other presentation tools, see Tab 3: Common Assignments, pp. 97–171.)*

Design Elements: (butterfly/computer): ©Visual Generation/Shutterstock; (other design icons): ©McGraw-Hill Education

5

Researching

For all knowledge and wonder (which is the seed of knowledge) is an impression of pleasure in itself.

−Francis Bacon

Source: NASA and J.J. Hester, Arizona State University

The Hubble Space Telescope, which has helped astronomers view the far reaches of the universe, provided this image of a blast wave caused by a stellar explosion that occurred approximately 15,000 years ago.

5 Researching

Sections dealing with visual rhetoric. For a complete listing, see the Quick Guide to Key Resources at the back of this book.

Tab 5: Researching

This section will help you answer questions such as the following:

Rhetorical Knowledge

- What writing situation does my assignment specify? (18c)

Critical Thinking, Reading, and Writing

- What is the difference between primary and secondary research? (19)
- How can I tell if sources are worth including? (21)
- How do I present my ideas along with those of my sources? (24c, e)
- How should I evaluate sources that I find on the Web? (21b)

Processes

- How can I think of a topic for my research project? (18d)
- How should I plan my research project? (18e)
- When and how should I use visuals in my project? (20)
- Where can I find appropriate images from online sources? (20b)

Knowledge of Conventions

- What is an annotated bibliography, and how do I create one? (24b)
- What is a documentation style? Which one should I use? (25c)

For a general introduction to writing outcomes see 1e, pages 14–15.

CHAPTER 18

Understanding Research

Your campus library provides valuable resources for almost any kind of research. These libraries offer not only books, magazines, and journals, but also specialized online databases and the expert guidance of research librarians.

Doing research in the twenty-first century includes using the library but is not limited to it. In seconds, the Internet provides direct access to an abundance of information unimaginable to earlier generations of students. The results of Internet searches, however, can sometimes provide an overwhelming flood of sources, many of questionable legitimacy.

The goal of the research section of this book *(Chapters 18-25)* is to help you learn about the research process, manage the information you discover within it, and use that information to write research projects.

18a Understand primary and secondary research.

Doing **primary research** means working in a laboratory, in the field, or with an archive of raw data, original documents, and authentic artifacts to make first-hand discoveries. *(For more information about primary research, see Chapter 22, pp. 226-31.)* Doing **secondary research** means looking to see what other people have learned and written about a topic.

Knowing how to identify facts, interpretations, and evaluations is key to good secondary research:

- **Facts** are objective. Like your body weight, facts can be measured, observed, or independently verified.

- **Interpretations** spell out the implications of facts. Are you as thin as you are because of your genes, because you exercise every day, or both? The answer to this question is an interpretation.

- **Evaluations** are debatable judgments based on a set of facts or a situation. The assertion that "one can never be too rich or too thin" is an evaluation.

Once you are up to date on the facts, interpretations, and evaluations in a particular area, you will be able to design a research project that adds your *perspective* on the sources you have found and read:

- Given all that you have learned about the topic, what strikes you as important or interesting?

- What patterns do you see, or what connections can you make between one person's work and another's?

- Where is the research going, and what problems still need to be explored?

Putting together all the facts, interpretations, and evaluations—**synthesis**—requires time and thought. Since in research writing you are not just stitching sources together but using them to support your own thesis, try beginning the process by focusing on a question you want to answer.

18b Recognize the connection between research and writing in college and beyond.

In one way or another, research informs all writing. But some tasks require more rigorous and systematic research than do others. These **research projects** require that you go beyond course readings and more casually selected sources—to find and read both classic and current material on a specific issue. A research paper constitutes your contribution to the ongoing conversation on the topic.

Research is a key component of much workplace and public writing. A sound business proposal will depend on research to identify best practices. A public commentary on the value of charter schools will require research into their performance. Engaging in academic research provides an excellent opportunity to prepare for writing situations that you will encounter throughout life.

When you are assigned research writing, the project may seem overwhelming at first. If you break it into phases, however, and allow enough time for each phase, you can manage your work and prepare a project that contributes to an ongoing conversation.

18c   Understand the research assignment.

Consider the rhetorical situation of the research project. Think about your project's audience, purpose, voice/stance/tone, genre, context, and scope *(see Tab 2: Writing and Designing Texts, pp. 29-96)*.

1. Audience

Although your *immediate audience* may include only your instructor and your classmates, thinking critically about the needs and expectations of more general readers will help you to plan an effective research strategy and create a schedule for writing your project.

Ask yourself the following questions about your audience:

- What do they already know about my subject? How much background information and context should I provide? (Your research should include *facts*.)

- Might they find my conclusions controversial or challenging? How should I accommodate and acknowledge different perspectives and viewpoints? (Your research should include *interpretations,* which balance opposing perspectives.)

- Do I expect the audience to take action based on my research? (Your research should include *evaluations,* carefully supported by facts and interpretations, which demonstrate clearly why readers should adopt a course of action or point of view.)

2. Purpose

Your *purpose* for writing a research project depends on both the specifics of the assignment as set by your instructor and your own interest in the topic. Your purpose might be **informative**—to educate your audience about an unfamiliar subject or point of view *(see Chapter 9: Informative Reports, p. 97)*. Your purpose might be **interpretive**—to reveal the meaning or significance of a work of art, a historical document, a literary work, or a scientific study *(see Chapter 10: Interpretive Analyses and Writing about Literature, p. 110)*. Your purpose might be **persuasive**—to convince your audience, with logic and evidence, to accept your point of view on a controversial issue or to act on the information in your project *(see Chapter 11: Arguments, p. 119)*. Review your assignment for keywords that signal its purpose. Note, however, that some

NAVIGATING THROUGH COLLEGE AND BEYOND

Classic and Current Sources

Classic sources are well-known and respected older works that made such an important contribution to a discipline or a particular area of research that contemporary researchers use them as touchstones for further research in that area. In many fields, sources published within the past five years are considered current. However, sources on topics related to medicine, recent scientific discoveries, or technological change must be much more recent to be considered current.

terms can signal more than one type of assignment, depending on the context. Here are some examples:

- **Informative:** Explain, describe, define, review
- **Interpretive:** Analyze, compare, explain, interpret
- **Persuasive:** Assess, justify, defend, refute, determine

3. Voice/stance/tone

Your stance in a research project—reflected in your voice and tone—should be that of a well-informed, helpful individual. Even though you will have done extensive work on the topic, it is important to avoid sounding like a know-it-all; instead, you are sharing with others who want to be informed.

4. Genre/medium

Research projects prepared for different purposes will reflect characteristics of various genres and may be expressed in different media. Your research on charter schools, for example, may take the form of a proposal or an informative report. Either genre could be communicated in print or on a Web site. In addition, some projects are shared in more than one medium: you may present the findings of your research in class with presentation software, share a brief summary of it on the Web, and submit the full study to the teacher in print.

5. Context

The overall situation will affect the presentation of your project. State cuts in public school funding will affect your presentation of a proposal to expand charter schools, even if you have full confidence in the research you have synthesized. Recent scientific research may change your attitude about the role of taking daily vitamins in maintaining health.

6. Scope

A project's scope includes the expected length of the paper, the deadline, and any other requirements such as number and type of sources. Are primary sources appropriate? Should you include visuals, and is any type (for example, photos, maps, graphs) specified?

18d   Choose an interesting research question for critical inquiry.

Approach your assignment in a spirit of critical inquiry. *Critical* in this sense does not mean "fault finding," "skeptical," "cynical," or even "urgent." Rather, it refers to a receptive, but reasonable and discerning, frame of mind. Choosing an interesting topic will make the results of your inquiry meaningful—to yourself and your readers.

1. Choosing a question with personal significance

Even though you are writing for an academic assignment, you can still get personally involved in your work. Begin with the wording of the assignment, analyzing the project's required audience, purpose, and scope *(see Section 18c, pp. 193-94)*. Then browse through the course readings and your class notes, looking for a match between your interests and topics, issues, or problems in the subject area.

For example, suppose you are assigned to write a report on a selected country's global economic prospects. If you have visited Mexico, you might find it interesting to explore that country's economic future.

2. Making your question specific

The more specific your question, the more your research will have direction and focus. To make a question more specific, use the "five *w*'s and an *h*" strategy by asking about the *who, what, where, why, when,* and *how* of a topic *(see Tab 2: Writing and Designing Texts, p. 34)*.

After you have compiled a list of possible research questions, choose one that is specific, or rewrite a broad one to make it more specific and therefore answerable. For example, as Peggy Giglio developed a topic for a research report for a sociology course on the reasons young adults volunteer, she rewrote the following broad question to make it answerable:

TOO BROAD   How has the volunteerism of young people affected the United States?

ANSWERABLE   Why do today's college students choose to volunteer?

3. Finding a challenging question

If a question can be answered with a yes or no, a dictionary-like definition, or a textbook presentation of information, choose another question or rework it to make it more challenging.

NOT CHALLENGING   Do college students volunteer?

CHALLENGING   What motivates college students to give of their "time and treasure" when they get no material reward for such efforts?

4. Speculating about answers

Sometimes it can be useful to speculate on the answer to your research question so that you have a **hypothesis** to work with during the research process. Don't forget, though, that a hypothesis is a tentative answer that must be tested and revised based on the evidence you turn up in your research. Be aware of the assumptions embedded in your hypothesis or research question. Consider, for example, the following.

HYPOTHESIS	College students volunteer for more than one reason.

This hypothesis assumes that because college students differ from one another in many ways, they have more than one reason for volunteering. But assumptions are always open to question. Researchers must be willing to adjust their ideas as they learn more about a topic.

As the preceding example demonstrates, your research question must allow you to generate testable hypotheses. Assertions about your personal beliefs and feelings cannot be tested.

18e Create a research plan.

Your research will be more productive if you create both a general plan and a detailed schedule immediately after you receive your assignment. A general plan ensures that you understand the full scope of the assignment. A detailed schedule helps you set priorities and meet deadlines.

Use the table in Figure 18.1, which outlines the steps in a research project, as a starting point, adjusting the time allotments based on the amount of time you have to complete the assignment. Consider what you already know about the topic as well as what you must learn through your research.

SOURCE SMART Planning Your Search

Your research plan should include where you expect to find your sources. For example, you may have to visit the library to view print materials that predate 1980; you will need to consult a subscription database online or at the library for recent scientific discoveries; you may need to access archives for historical research; and you may need to conduct field research, such as interviewing fellow students. Set priorities to increase your efficiency in each location (library, archive, field, online).

Scheduling Your Research Project

Task	Date

Phase I

- Complete general plan for research. _____
- Decide on topic and research question. _____
- Consult reference works and reference librarians. _____
- Make a list of relevant keywords for online searching *(see Chapter 19, pp. 200–02).* _____
- Compile a **working bibliography** *(see Chapter 24, pp. 237–40).* _____
- Sample some items in bibliography. _____
- Make arrangements for primary research (if necessary). _____

Phase II

- Locate, read, and evaluate selected sources. _____
- Take notes, write summaries and paraphrases. _____
- Cross-check notes with working bibliography. _____
- Conduct primary research (if necessary). _____
- Find and create visuals. _____
- Confer with instructor or writing center (optional). _____
- Develop thesis and outline or plan organization of project. _____

Phase III

- Write first draft, deciding which primary and secondary source materials to include. _____
- Have peer review (optional but recommended). _____
- Revise draft. _____
- Confer with instructor or writing center (optional). _____
- Do final revision and editing. _____
- Create works-cited or references page. _____
- Proofread and check spelling. _____

Due date _____

FIGURE 18.1 Sample schedule for a research project. Use this table to determine how much time you will need to complete each stage of your own research projects.

CHAPTER 19

Finding and Managing Print and Online Sources

To conduct a meaningful search through the vast amount of available information, focus on the following three activities:

- Collecting keywords from reference works
- Using library databases
- Finding material in the library and on the Web

19a Use the library in person and online.

Librarians know what is available at your library and how to obtain material from other libraries. They can also show you how to access the library's computerized book catalog, periodical databases, and electronic resources and how to use the Internet to find information relevant to your research. At many schools, reference librarians are available for online chats, and some even take queries via text message. Your library's Web site may also have links to subscription databases or important reference works available on the Internet, as shown in Figure 19.1.

In addition, **help sheets** or online tutorials at most college libraries give the location of both general and discipline-specific periodicals and noncirculating reference books, along with information about the book catalog, special databases, indexes, Web resources, and library policies.

19b Consult various kinds of sources.

You should always consult more than one source and usually more than one *kind* of source. Your assignment may specify how many print and electronic sources you are expected to consult and cite. Here are some of the available resources:

- **General reference works (for overview and keywords)**

  Encyclopedias, annuals, almanacs

  Computer databases, bibliographies, abstracts
- **Specialized reference works (for overview and keywords)**

  Discipline-specific encyclopedias, almanacs, and dictionaries
- **Books**
- **Periodical articles**

  In scholarly and technical journals

  In newspapers

  In magazines

  On the Web
- **Specialized databases**

FIGURE 19.1 **A page from the Web site of Governors State University.** The Web page provides links to a variety of Web-based reference sources.

- **Web sites**
- **Other online sources**
- **Virtual communities**

   MOOs (multiuser object-oriented dimensions)

- **Government documents, pamphlets, census data**
- **Primary sources**

   Original documents like literary works, art objects, performances, manuscripts, letters, and personal journals

   Museum collections, maps, photo, film, sound, and music archives

   Field notes, surveys, interviews

   Results of observation and lab experiments

19c Use printed and online reference works for general information.

Reference works provide an overview of a subject area and typically are less up to- date than the specialized knowledge found in academic journals and scholarly books. If your instructor approves, you may start your research by consulting a general or discipline-specific encyclopedia, but for college research you must explore your topic in more depth. Often, the list of references at the end of an encyclopedia article can lead you to useful sources on your topic.

Reference books do not circulate, so take notes and make photocopies of the pages you may need to consult later. Check your college library's home page for access to online encyclopedias.

Here is a list of some other reference materials available in print, on the Internet, or both:

ALMANACS	*Almanac of American Politics*
	Information Please Almanac
	World Almanac
BIBLIOGRAPHIES	*Bibliographic Index*
	Bibliography of Asian Studies
	MLA International Bibliography
BIOGRAPHIES	*African American Biographical Database*
	American Men and Women of Science
	Dictionary of American Biography
	Dictionary of Literary Biography: Chicano Writers
	Dictionary of National Biography
	Webster's New Biographical Dictionary
	Who's Who
DICTIONARIES	*American Heritage Dictionary of the English Language*
	Concise Oxford Dictionary of Literary Terms
	Dictionary of American History
	Dictionary of Philosophy
	Dictionary of the Social Sciences
	Oxford English Dictionary (OED)

19d Understand keywords and keyword searches.

Most online research—whether conducted in your library's catalog, in a specialized database, or on the Web—requires an understanding of **keyword searches.** In this context, a **keyword** is a term (or terms) you enter into a **search engine** (searching software) to find sources that have information about a particular subject.

As you focus more clearly on your topic, you must also refine your search terms. Although search engines vary, the following guidelines for refining keyword searches should work for many.

- **Group words together.** Put quotation marks or parentheses around the specific phrase you are looking for, for example, "fake news."

- **Use Boolean operators.**

  AND (+)   Use AND or + when you need sites with both of two or more words: "fake news" + history.

  OR   Use OR when you want sites with either of two or more terms: "fake news" OR misinformation

  NOT   Use NOT in front of words that you do not want to appear together in your results: news NOT tabloid.

— NAVIGATING THROUGH COLLEGE AND BEYOND

Sources: Popular or Scholarly?

A source's audience and purpose determine whether it should be considered *popular* or *scholarly*. You may begin your inquiry into a research topic with popular sources, but to become fully informed you must consult scholarly sources.

Popular sources

- Are widely available on newsstands and in retail stores (print)
- Are printed on magazine paper with a color cover (print)
- Accept advertising for a wide range of consumer goods or are themselves widely advertised (in the case of books)
- Are published by a commercial publishing house or media company (such as Time Warner)
- May include a wide range of topics in each issue, from international affairs to popular entertainment
- Usually do not contain bibliographic information
- Have a URL that likely ends in .com (online)

Scholarly sources

- Are usually found in libraries, not on newsstands (print)
- Usually list article titles and authors on the cover (print)
- Have few advertisements
- Are published by a scholarly or nonprofit organization, often in association with a university press
- Focus on discipline-specific topics
- Include articles by authors who typically are affiliated with colleges, museums, or other scholarly institutions
- Include articles with extensive citations and bibliographies
- Have a URL that likely ends in .edu or .org (online)
- Are **refereed** (peer reviewed), which means that each article has been reviewed, commented on, and accepted for publication by other scholars in the field

─ the EVOLVING SITUATION

Wikipedia

The online encyclopedia Wikipedia offers information on almost any subject, and it can be a good starting place for research. However, you should evaluate its content critically. Volunteers (who may or may not be experts) write Wikipedia's articles, and almost any user can edit any article. While the site has some mechanisms to maintain accuracy, always check findings with another source (and cite that source, if you use the information).

- **Use a root word plus a "wildcard."** For more results, combine part of a keyword with an asterisk (*) used as a wildcard: fact-check* (for "fact-checking," "fact-checkers," and so forth).
- **Search the fields.** Some search engines permit you to search within fields, such as the title field of Web pages or the author field of a library catalog. Thus, TITLE + "News media" will give you all pages that have "News Media" in their title.

Look for advanced search features that help with the refining process.

19e Use print indexes and online databases to find articles in journals and other periodicals.

Indexes and online databases are essential tools for researching in journals and other periodicals.

1. Periodicals

Newspapers, magazines, and scholarly journals that are published at regular intervals are classified as **periodicals.** The articles in scholarly and technical journals, written by experts and based on up-to-date research, are more credible than articles in popular newspapers and magazines. Ask your instructor or librarian which periodicals are considered important in the discipline you are studying.

2. Indexes and databases

Articles published in periodicals are cataloged in general and specialized **indexes.** Indexes are available on subscription-only **databases** and as print volumes. If you are searching for articles that are more than twenty years old, you may use print indexes or an appropriate electronic index. Print indexes can be searched by author, subject, or title. Electronic databases can also be searched by date and keyword and will provide a list of articles that meet your search criteria. Each entry in the list will include the information you need to find and cite the article.

You can find databases on your library's Web site. When selecting a database, consult its description on your library's site (often labeled "Info") to see the types of sources included, subjects covered, and number of periodicals from each subject area. Would your topic be best served by a general database (such as EBSCO Academic Search Premier) or by one that is discipline specific (such as PsycINFO)? Also consider the time period the database spans.

Some of the major online databases are listed below, and the screen shots in Figures 19.2 and 19.3 illustrate a search on one of them, EBSCOhost.

When searching a database, you will encounter either abstracts or full-text articles (in certain cases both). Full-text articles may be available in either PDF or HTML format:

- **Abstract:** An abstract is a brief summary of a full-text article. Abstracts appear at the beginning of articles in some scholarly journals and are used in databases to summarize complete articles. Do not mistake an abstract for a full-text source.

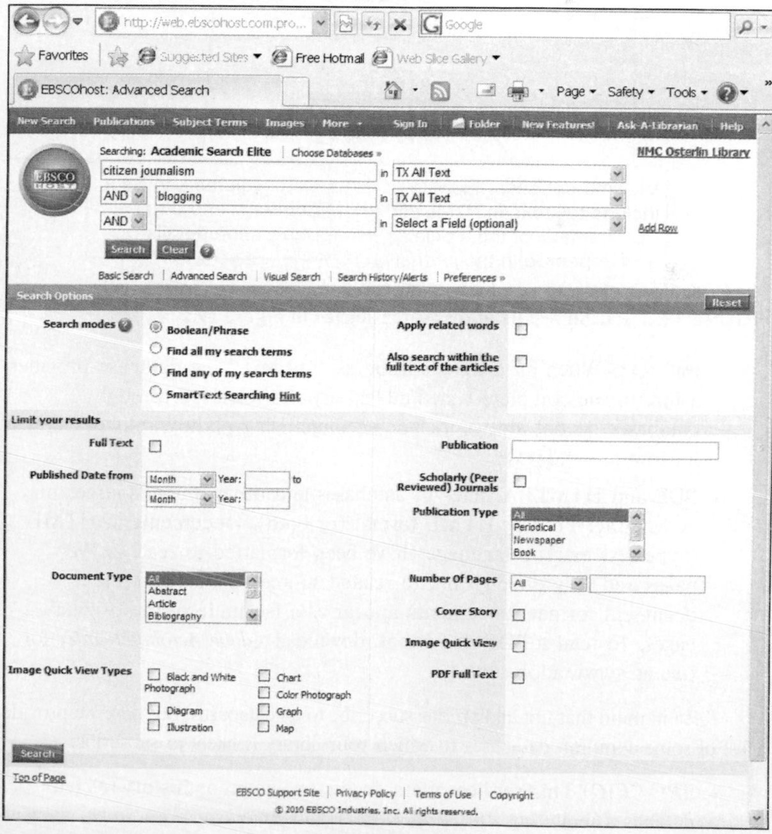

Source: EBSCO INFORMATION SERVICES

FIGURE 19.2 EBSCOhost's Advanced Search page

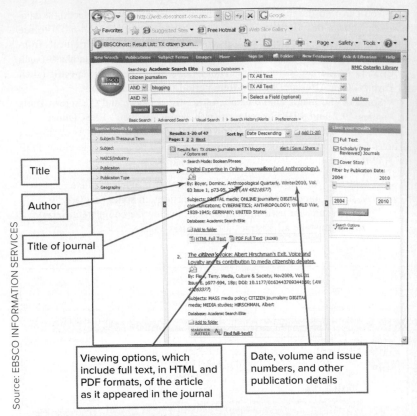

Source: EBSCO INFORMATION SERVICES

FIGURE 19.3 Partial results of the search started in Figure 19.2.

- **Full text:** When an article is listed as "full text," the database provides a link to the complete text. Full-text articles retrieved through databases do not always include accompanying photographs or other illustrations, however.

- **PDF** and **HTML:** Articles in databases and other online sources may be in either PDF or HTML format (or both). Documents in HTML (hypertext markup language) have been formatted to read as Web pages and may directly link to related sources. PDF (portable document format) documents appear as a facsimile of the original pages. To read a PDF document, download *Adobe Acrobat Reader* for free at <www.adobe.com>.

Keep in mind that not all libraries subscribe to all databases. But here we provide a list of some common databases to which your library is likely to subscribe.

- ***ABC-CLIO:*** This service offers access to numerous history-related databases including *American History* and *American Government* as well as databases on African American, American Indian, and Latino American experience, pop culture, war, social history, geography, and world history.

- **EBSCOhost:** The *Academic Search Premier* database provides full-text coverage for more than 8,000 scholarly publications and indexes articles in all academic subject areas.

- **ERIC:** This database lists publications in the area of education.

- **Factiva:** This database offers access to the Dow Jones and Reuters news agencies, including newspapers, magazines, journals, newsletters, and Web sites.

- **General Science Index:** This index is general rather than specialized. It lists scholarly and popular articles by biologists, chemists, and other scientists.

- **GPO Monthly Catalogue:** Updated monthly, the Government Printing Office Catalogue contains records of all publications printed by the US Government Printing Office since 1976.

- **Humanities Index:** This index lists articles from journals in language and literature, history, philosophy, and similar areas.

- **InfoTrac Web:** This Web-based service searches bibliographic and other databases such as the *General Reference Center Gold, General Business File ASAP,* and *Health Reference Center.*

- **JSTOR:** This archive provides full-text access to recent issues of journals in the humanities, social sciences, and natural sciences, typically from two to five years before the current date.

- **LexisNexis Academic:** Updated daily, this online service provides full-text access to around six thousand newspapers, professional publications, legal references, and congressional sources.

- **MLA Bibliography:** Covering 1963 to the present, the *MLA Bibliography* indexes journals, dissertations, and serials published worldwide in the fields of modern languages, literature, literary criticism, linguistics, and folklore.

- **New York Times Index:** This index lists major articles published by the *Times* since 1913.

- **Newspaper Abstracts:** This database provides an index to fifty national and regional newspapers.

- **PAIS International:** Produced by the Public Affairs Information Service, this database selectively indexes literature on public policy, social policy, and the social sciences from 1972 to the present.

- **Periodical Abstracts:** This database indexes more than two thousand general and academic journals covering business, current affairs, economics, literature, religion, psychology, and women's studies from 1987 to the present.

- *ProQuest:* This database provides access to dissertations; newspapers and journals; information on sources in business, general reference, the social sciences, and humanities; and historical sources dating back to the nineteenth century.

- *PsycInfo:* Sponsored by the American Psychological Association (APA), this database indexes and abstracts books, scholarly articles, technical reports, and dissertations in psychology and related disciplines from the 1800s.

- *PubMed:* The National Library of Medicine publishes this database, which indexes and abstracts fifteen million journal articles in biomedicine and provides links to related databases.

- *Sociological Abstracts:* This database indexes and abstracts articles from more than 2,600 journals, as well as books, conference papers, and dissertations.

- *Social Science Index:* This index lists articles from such fields as economics, psychology, political science, and sociology.

- *WorldCat:* This is a catalog of books and other resources available in libraries worldwide.

19f Use search engines and subject directories to find Internet sources.

To find information that has been published in Web pages, use more than one Internet search engine, since each searches the Web in its own way. Some of the more popular Internet search engines include general search engines, meta search engines, and mediated search engines:

General search engines: These sites allow for both category and keyword searches:

- *Google* <www.google.com>
- *Bing* <www.bing.com>
- *Yahoo!* <www.yahoo.com>
- *Ask* <www.ask.com>

Meta search engines: These sites search several different search engines at once:

- *Dogpile* <www.dogpile.com>
- *Library of Congress* <www.loc.gov/index.html>
- *MetaCrawler* <www.metacrawler.com>
- *WebCrawler* <www.webcrawler.com>

Mediated search engine: This site has been assembled and reviewed by people who sometimes provide annotations and commentary about topic areas and specific sites:

- *About.com* <www.about.com>

Each search engine's home page provides a link to advice on efficient use as well as help in refining a search. Look for a link labeled "search help," "about us," or something similar.

Some Internet search engines allow you to conduct specialized searches—for images, for example *(see Chapter 20)*. *Google Books* can help locate books on your topic. *Google Scholar* locates only scholarly sources in response to a search term.

Many Internet search engines also include sponsored links that a commercial enterprise has paid to make appear in response to specific search terms. These links are usually clearly identified as such.

To find relevant results, carefully select the words for Internet keyword searches. For example, a search of *Google* using the keywords *Olympic doping* yields a list of more than 10 million Web sites (Figure 19.4). Altering the keywords to make them more specific narrows the results. The most relevant matches will appear at the beginning of the results page.

Most search engines have an advanced search option. This option allows you to search for exact phrases, to exclude a specific term, to search only for pages in a certain language, and to refine searches in other ways.

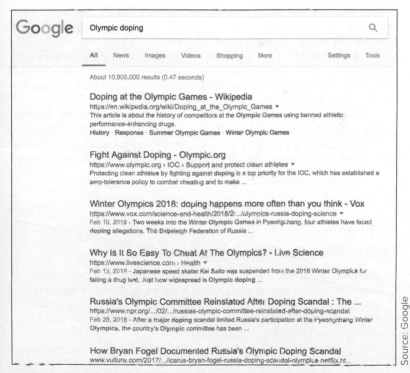

FIGURE 19.4 **Refining the search.** Adding the key terms *cheating, drug testing,* and *Olympic Games* (e.g. "Olympic games" AND "cheating" AND "drug testing") reduces the number of hits to just over 500 from more than 10 million.

In addition to keyword searches, many Internet search engines offer a **subject directory**—a listing of broad categories. Clicking through this hierarchy of choices eventually brings you to a list of sites related to a specific topic.

Some Web sites provide content-specific subject directories designed for research in a particular field. These sites are often reviewed or screened and are excellent starting points for academic research.

Other online tools can help organize sources and keep track of your Web research. Save the URLs of promising sites to your browser's Bookmarks or Favorites. Your browser's history function can allow you to retrace your steps if you forget how to find a particular site. The box at the bottom of this page includes additional online resources.

19g   Use your library's catalog to find books.

Books in most libraries are shelved by **call numbers** based on the Library of Congress classification system. The *Library of Congress Subject Headings (LCSH)* shows you how your research topic is classified and provides you with a set of key terms that you can use in your search. In this system, books on the same topic have similar call numbers and are shelved together. You will need the call number to locate the actual book on the library's shelves. Therefore, when consulting a library catalog, be sure to jot down (or print out) the call numbers of books you want to consult.

You can conduct a keyword search of most online library catalogs by author, by title, or by subject. Subject terms appear in the *LCSH*, which provides a set of key terms that you can use in your search for sources. Keyword searches of many catalogs also include publisher, notes, and other fields.

Card catalogs are rarely used except by archives and specialized libraries. Cards are usually filed by author, title, and subject (based on the *LCSH*).

The results of a keyword search of a library's online catalog will provide a list comprised mostly of books. The search of the Governors State University

─the EVOLVING SITUATION

Online Tools for Research

- *Zotero* <www.zotero.org>: This program automatically saves citation information for many types of online sources (text and images) via your browser. It creates formatted references in multiple styles and helps you organize your sources by assigning tags (categories based on keywords) to them.

- *DiRT (Digital Research Tools)* <http://dirtdirectory.org/>: This site links to online tools that help researchers in the humanities and social sciences perform many tasks, such as collaborating with others, finding sources, and visualizing data.

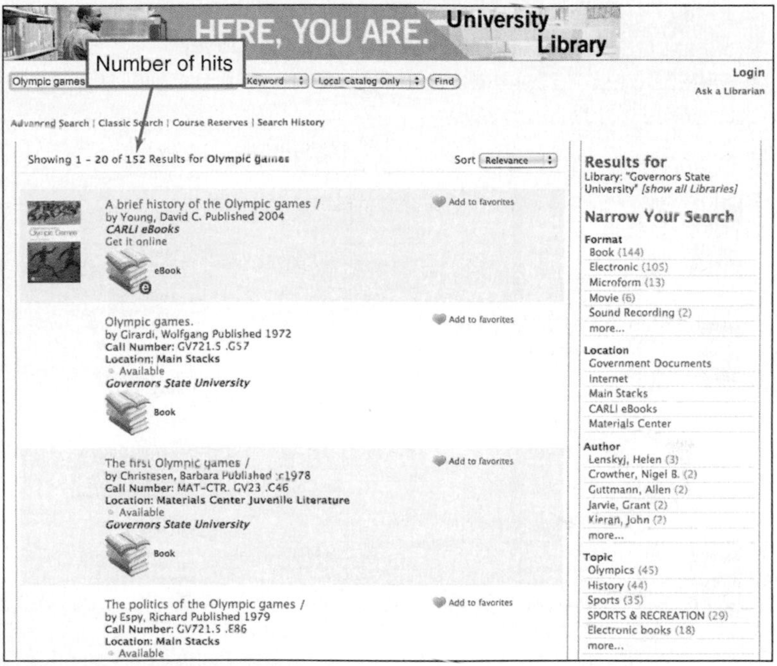

Courtesy of Governors State University

FIGURE 19.5 Searching an online catalog. Using the phrase *Olympic Games* as a keyword in a subject search produces 152 sources.

online catalog depicted in Figures 19.5 and 19.6, shows how you can alter the terms of a search to restrict the formats to a specific medium.

As with any keyword search, getting what you really need–a manageable number of relevant sources–depends on your choice of keywords. If your search terms are too broad, you will get too many hits; if they are too narrow, you will get few or none.

19h Take advantage of printed and online government documents.

The US government publishes an enormous amount of information and research every year, most of which is available online. The *GPO Monthly Catalogue* and the *US Government Periodicals Index* are available as online databases. The Government Printing Office's own Web site, *The Federal Digital System* <www.gpo.gov/fdsys>, available through LexisNexis, is an excellent resource for identifying and locating federal government publications. Other useful online government resources include:

- *National Technical Information Service* <www.ntis.gov>
- USA.gov (the US government's official web portal) <www.usa.gov>

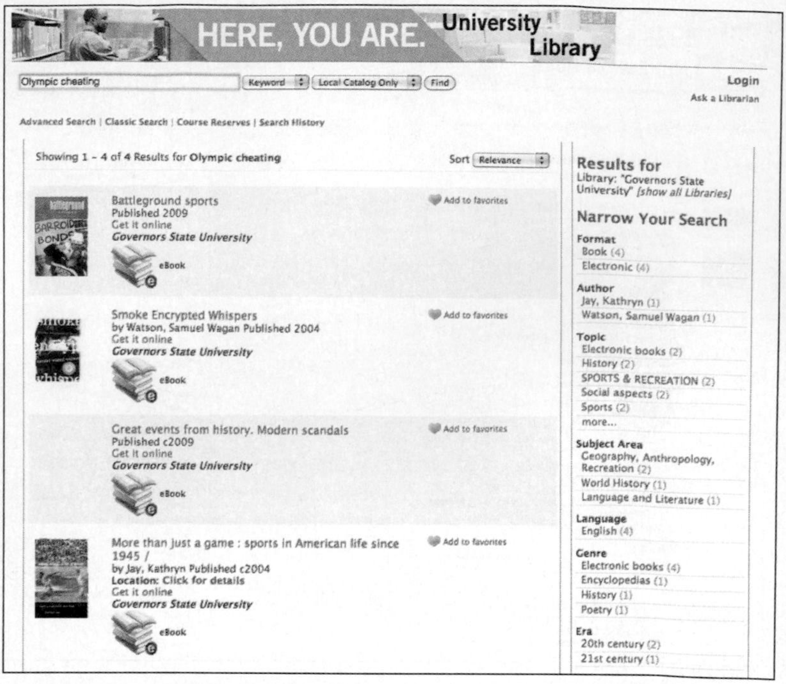

Courtesy of Governors State University

FIGURE 19.6 Changing a search term. A keyword search using the search term *Olympic cheating* produces *four* results, a manageable number.

- *The National Institutes of Health* <www.nih.gov>
- *US Census Bureau* <www.census.gov>

19i   Explore online communication.

Usenet news groups, electronic mailing lists, blogs, and social networking offer opportunities to converse regularly with people who have common interests. Carefully evaluate information from these sources *(see Chapter 21: Evaluating*

⌐SOURCE SMART   Organizing Your Sources

List your sources alphabetically. For each source, include citation information *(see pp. 237–38)*, key points, and its relevance to your topic. Does the source support or detract from your claim? Is it an early source or a more recent one? Does it agree or disagree with other sources you have read? Do other sources refer to this one? You might color-code your list to indicate related ideas that appear in a number of your sources. Include useful quotations and their page numbers.

Sources, pp. 219–26). Participants will have different levels of expertise–or possibly no expertise at all. Online sites can help you with research in the following ways:

- You can get ideas for your writing by identifying topics of general concern and becoming aware of general trends in thinking about the topic.
- You can zero in on a very specific or current topic.
- You can query an expert in the field about your topic via e-mail or a social networking site.

Caution: Since the credibility of online sites varies widely, use your library or department Web site to find scholarly forums for purposes of comparison and assessment.

Social networking sites like *Facebook* and *Twitter* help people form online communities. **Blogs** *(see Chapter 14)* can be designed to allow readers to post their own comments and questions on a wide range of views on a topic under debate. However, many blog postings consist of unsupported opinion, and they may not be monitored closely for accuracy. **Wikis,** sites designed for online collaboration, allow people both to comment on and to modify one another's contributions. When evaluating information from a wiki, check to see who can update content and whether experts review the changes. If content is not monitored by identified experts, verify your findings with another source.

Unlike electronic mailing lists, **Usenet news groups** are posted to a *news server*–a computer that hosts the news group and distributes postings to participating servers. You must subscribe to read postings, which are not automatically distributed by e-mail.

Podcasts are downloadable digital audio or video recordings, updated regularly. The Smithsonian produces credible podcasts on many topics <www.si.edu/podcasts>.

RSS (Really Simple Syndication) **feeds** deliver the latest content from continuously updated Web sites to your browser or home page. You can use RSS feeds to keep up with information on your topic, once you identify relevant Web sites.

Synchronous communication includes **discussion boards** and **forums** organized by topic where people carry on real-time discussions. *Twitter* and *Facebook* can be used to identify resources; this crowdsourcing can draw from many people, or it can draw from a limited number using the *Facebook* chat tool. **Texting,** which typically is communication from one-to-one or one-to-few, is another real-time tool for identifying sources. And all of these modes of communication can be used for single-authored and collaborative projects, though you will want to check with your instructor before using such materials in an assignment.

CHAPTER 20

Finding and Creating Effective Visuals, Audio Clips, and Videos

Visuals can support a writer's thesis, enhance an argument, and sometimes constitute the complete argument. Relief organizations, for example, may post a series of compelling visuals on their Web sites to persuade potential donors to contribute money following a catastrophic event.

For some writing situations, you will prepare or provide your own visuals. You may, for example, make your own sketch of an experiment or create a bar graph from data that you have collected. In other situations, however, you may decide to create a visual from data that you have found in a source, or you may search in your library or on the Internet for a visual to use.

In an online text, an audio clip or a video can provide support for an argument or add an engaging note to a personal Web site.

👁 20a Find quantitative data and display it visually.

Research writing in many disciplines—especially in business, math, the sciences and social sciences, and engineering, as well as other technical fields—almost always requires reference to quantitative information. That information generally has more impact when it is displayed visually in a chart, graph, or map than as raw numbers alone. Pie charts, for instance, show percentages of a whole. Bar graphs are often used to compare groups over time. Line graphs also show trends over time, such as the impact of wars on immigration rates and population movements. Visual displays of information are also tools of analysis.

Think through the writing situation as you decide about when and what types of visuals are appropriate to include. Consider your readers' expectations for presentations of numerical relationships that words alone cannot convey. Since digital technology makes it relatively easy to find and create visual images, your audience will have higher expectations for visual communication when you are working online.

(For examples of graphs and charts, and a discussion of what situations to use them in, see Tab 2: Writing and Designing Texts, pp. 29-96.)

1. Finding existing graphs, charts, and maps
As you search for print and online sources *(see Chapter 19)*, take notes on useful graphs, charts, or maps that you might incorporate, with proper acknowledgment, into your text. If your source is available in print only, you may be able to use a scanner to capture and digitize it.

2. Creating visuals from quantitative data
Sometimes you may find data presented in writing or in tables that would be more effective as a chart or graph. Using the graphics tool available in spreadsheet or other software, you can create your own visual.

SOURCE SMART Citing Data

Make citations of data specific. Indicate the report and page number or Web address(es) where you found the information, as well as any other requirements of your documentation style. If you analyze the data, refer to any analysis in the source before presenting your own interpretation.

> *Caution:* Whether you are using data from a source to create an image or incorporating an image made by someone else, you must give credit to the source of the data or image. Furthermore, if you plan to publish this visual on a Web site or in another medium, you must obtain permission to use it from the copyright holder unless the source specifically states that such use is allowed or it is in the public domain.

For example, suppose you are drafting a research project about population trends in the United States in the nineteenth century and want to illustrate the country's population growth in that period with a line graph, using data from the US Census Bureau, which are in the public domain. Most census data, however, appear in tables like the one shown in Figure 20.1. If you transfer data from a table to a spreadsheet program or other application, you can use them to create graphs that you can insert into a project, as in Figure 20.1.

3. Displaying the data accurately

Display data in a way that is consistent with your purpose and not misleading to viewers. For example, in December 2015, a tweet from the Obama White House featured a chart showing graduation rates at "an all-time high." The White House's chart presents graduation rates beginning in 2007, one year into President Obama's first term, and ending in 2014, the middle of his second (*see Figure 20.2*). In a blog post on the topic of misleading graphs, tech reporter Keith Collins notes distortions in the representation of the high-school graduation rate data collected from the National Center for Educational Statistics (NCES) at the Department of Education (DOE). In representing data across time, writers must bear in mind the length of time that is represented and the most appropriate visual display for the information being expressed. A bar chart like this one, Collins points out, is not the best choice for representing data reflecting subtle changes over a short time period. Collins also calls attention to another failing of the White House's chart: it is illustrated in a way that renders its units inconsistent. If five "books" is equal to 75 percent, then how are ten "books" equal to only 78 percent?

In order to demonstrate the importance of selecting the appropriate form of chart or graph for one's purpose, Collins created a line graph that reveals

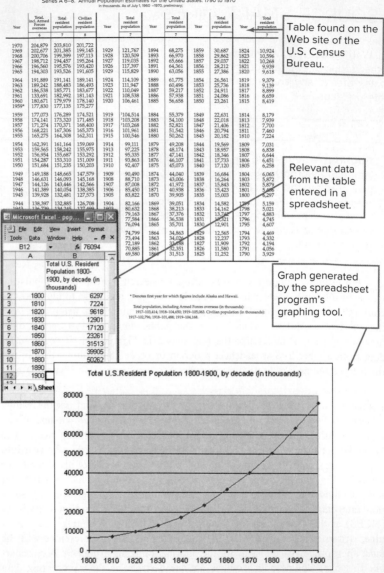

FIGURE 20.1 Using a spreadsheet program to create a graph from data in a table.

two important facts about the data on graduation rates (*see Figure 20.3*). By including data collected over a longer period of time he demonstrates that graduation rates were already trending upward when Obama was elected. Moreover,

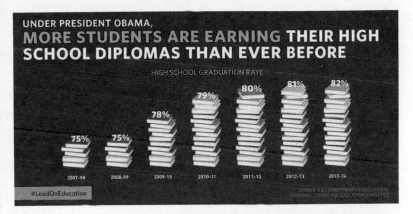

FIGURE 20.2 A distorted display of high school graduation rates in the United States.

his line graph reveals a detail of rhetorical significance to that administration: it shows a higher percentage point increase for graduation rates under Obama than under any previous president.

To avoid distorting data, always choose the most appropriate form of graph or chart for your purpose and plot the axes of line and bar graphs so that they do not misrepresent your data. *(See Tab 2: Writing and Designing Texts, pp. 29-96.)*

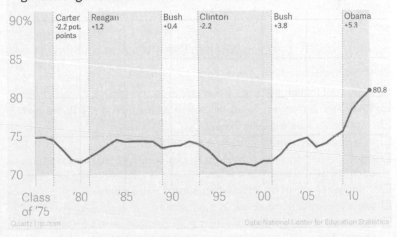

FIGURE 20.3 An accurate display of high school graduation rates in the United States, showing a more accurate picture.

20b Search for appropriate images in online and print sources.

Photographs, pictures of artwork, drawings, diagrams, and maps—which are different kinds of visuals—can provide important support for many kinds of texts, particularly in subjects like history, English and other languages, philosophy, music, theater, and other performing arts. As with the display of quantitative data, you might choose a visual from another source, or you might create one. If you were writing or creating a report comparing how different corporations are organized, for example, you might use organizational charts that appear in corporate reports. Alternatively, you could use your word-processing software's drawing feature to create your own organizational charts based on information you find in the corporate reports. When using a visual from another source, be sure to cite it correctly. If the visual will appear on a public Web site, consult the copyright holder for permission. Finally, do not use photo editing software to alter visuals you find on the Web.

The following provide sources for images that you can use

- **Online library and museum image collections and subscription databases:** Several libraries and other archives maintain collections of images online. See Figure 20.4 for the URLs of image collections. Follow the guidelines for usage posted on these sites. Your library also may subscribe to an image database such as the Associated Press *AP Multimedia Archive.*

- **Images on the Internet:** Many search engines have the ability to search the Web for images. You can conduct an image search on *Google,* for example, by clicking on the "images" option, entering the key term, and then clicking "search." Image- and media-sharing sites such as *Instagram, Snapchat, Flickr, Vimeo, YouTube,* and *Pinterest* can serve as sources as

---

—CHECKLIST Deciding When to Use a Visual in Your Project

Consider these questions as you look for visuals:

☐ What contribution will each visual make to the text?

☐ What contribution do the visuals taken as a whole make to the text?

☐ How many visuals do you need?

☐ Where will each visual appear in the text?

☐ Does the audience have enough background information to interpret each visual in the way you intend?

☐ If not, what additional information should you include?

☐ What information should be in the caption?

☐ Have you reviewed your own text (and perhaps asked a friend to review it as well) to see how well the visual is working in terms of appropriateness, location, and context?

—CHECKLIST   Deciding What Kind of Chart or Graph to Use

In deciding the kind of chart or graph to use, consider these questions:

☐ Who are my readers, and what are their expectations?

☐ What information is most important to show, and why?

☐ What options do I have for displaying the information?

☐ How much context is necessary to include, and why?

☐ How many charts or graphs will contribute to achieving my purpose, based on readers' expectations, academic discipline, medium, and genre?

☐ How detailed should each visual be, and why?

☐ Will my visual project into the future or report on the past?

☐ What information will be left out or minimized, and how important is that omission?

☐ What other information—an introduction, an explanation, a summary, an interpretation—will readers need to make sense of the graphed information?

- *Art Institute of Chicago* (selected works from the museum's collection) <www.artic.edu/aic/collections/>

- *The Library of Congress* <www.loc.gov/index.html> Various visuals and documents from American history

- *Metropolitan Museum of Art* (works from the museum's collection) <www.metmuseum.org/about-the-met/policies-and-documents/image-resources>

- *National Archives Digital Classroom* (documents and photographs from American history) <www.archives.gov/digital_classroom/index.html>

- *National Aeronautics and Space Administration* (visuals and multimodal features on space exploration) <www.nasa.gov/multimedia/imagegallery/index.html>

- *National Park Service Digital Image Archive* (thousands of public domain photographs of US national parks) <www.nps.gov/media/multimedia-search.htm>

- *New York Public Library* <www.nypl.org/collections/articles-databases/nypl-digital-collections> Maps, posters, photographs, and documents

- *Schomburg Center for Research in Black Culture* <www.nypl.org/locations/schomburg> Articles, books, and visuals representing the African diaspora and African American history

- *VRoma: A Virtual Community for Teaching and Learning Classics* (visuals and other resources related to ancient Rome) <www.vroma.org/images/image_search.html>

FIGURE 20.4   Digital collections of useful visuals.

well. Read the information on the site carefully to see what uses of the material are permitted. The Creative Commons site (<www .creativecommons.org>) lets you search for material with a Creative Commons license, which describes the uses of the content that are allowed. The material shown can be used or altered for noncommercial purposes, as long as it is cited. All the images accompanying Wikipedia are licensed through Creative Commons, so that is another source. Assume that copyright applies to material on the Web unless the site says otherwise. If your project will be published or placed on a public Web site, you must obtain permission to use this material. *(See Chapter 23: Plagiarism, Copyright, and Intellectual Property, pp. 231–36.)*

- **Images scanned from a book or journal:** You can use a scanner to scan some images from books and journals into a paper but, as always, only if you are sure your use is within fair-use guidelines. Also, be sure to credit the source.

Caution: The results of Internet image searches, like those of any Internet search, must be carefully evaluated for relevance and credibility. *(See Chapter 21: Evaluating Sources, pp. 219–26.)* Make sure you have proper source information for any images you use that you find in this way.

20c Search for or create appropriate audio clips and videos.

Some writing situations call for audio or video clips. A history of the ways that Franklin Delano Roosevelt managed his paralyzed legs might include a video showing him leaning against a podium to give a talk. Video of the *Challenger* explosion in 1986 could underscore the constant danger faced by astronauts. The sounds made by locusts would help explain how quickly these insects consume everything in their path.

When deciding to use a video or audio clip, you have two choices: you can use material that is available elsewhere, crediting it appropriately, or create your own. A rich stock of material is available on the Web, as the University of Illinois library's Web site shows, including those listed in Figure 20.5. You can begin by searching in general categories such as *Google Video* search or in more specific categories like CNN video or the National Science Foundation's *NSF Science Nation*. Likewise, you can find audio clips at large databases like the Library of Congress *American Memory* Web site and on Web sites like *Pandora* and *Spotify,* where you can create your own playlist.

For some projects, you might include video and audio clips that you create yourself. Audio interviews with students engaged in volunteer activities can allow them to "speak" to the experience and provide details supporting your claim about student volunteerism. A video of students discussing their award-winning artwork—with the artwork visible—helps your reader see both the artists and the art. Whenever you create an audio or video file, be sure to ask your subjects for permission.

- *Google Video* <www.google.com/videohp>: A good place to search for videos on a wide range of subjects.

- *CNN Video* <www.cnn.com/videos>: Provides free video news about national and international events.

- *MTV Music Videos* <www.mtv.com/music#/music/video%3E>: Allows you to search for your favorite artist or music video; however, will play a short MTV ad before the video.

- *American Memory Project* <https://memory.loc.gov/ammem/index.html> Provided by the Library of Congress; provides access to historical materials that document the American experience. Select "Motion Pictures" in the Browse Collections Containing section.

FIGURE 20.5 Online sources of audio and video clips, from the University of Illinois library's Web site.

CHAPTER 21

Evaluating Sources

Never before in the history of the planet has information been more readily available. The catch is that a good deal of this information is misleading or downright false. Your major task is to evaluate the information that you find for credibility, accuracy, reasonableness, and evidence (CARE).

Digital technologies give you fast access to a tremendous variety of sources, but it is then up to you to pose questions. Is the source relevant: does it pertain to your research topic? Is the source **trustworthy**: does it provide credibility, accuracy, reasonableness, and support?

21a   Question print sources.

Just because something is in print does not make it relevant or true. How can you determine whether a print source is likely to be both credible and useful? Before assessing a source's credibility, make sure it is relevant to your topic. The Checklist on page 221 provides some questions to ask about any source you are considering.

Relevance can be a tricky matter, requiring careful analysis of the writing situation. What sources will be particularly meaningful or persuasive to your anticipated audience? For an audience opposed to gun control legislation, an acknowledgment that certain types of weapons should be regulated will be more relevant and persuasive from a source that usually supports the NRA (National Rifle Association). Relevance is also associated with the academic discipline that forms the context for your work. Your sociology instructor will expect you to give special preference to sociological sources in a project on the organization of the workplace. Your business management instructor will expect you to use material from that field in a project on the same topic. Be prepared to discover that some promising sources turn out to be less relevant than you first thought.

⊙ 21b   Question Internet sources.

Although the questions in the Checklist on page 221 should be applied to online sources, Web resources also require additional methods of ensuring the credibility of information presented. Most of the material in the library has been evaluated to some extent for credibility. Editors and publishers have reviewed the content of books, magazines, journals, and newspapers, and journals and many books are reviewed by scholars as well. Some presses and publications are more reputable than others. Subscription databases generally compile articles that originally appeared in print, and librarians try to purchase the most reliable databases. While you should still evaluate all sources, you can have some confidence that most of the material you find in a college library is credible, at least to some degree.

In contrast, anyone can create a Web site that looks attractive but contains nonsense. Similarly, the people who post to blogs, discussion lists, and news groups may not be experts or even marginally well informed. Some information on the Web is valuable and timely, but much of it is not, so you must assess its credibility carefully. Consult the Checklist box on page 221, and consider the following questions when determining whether online information is reliable:

1. What institution—not individual—is hosting the site? Is the site hosted by a university or by a government agency (such as the National Center for Education Statistics or the Department of Education)? In general, sites hosted by institutions with scholarly credentials are more likely to be trustworthy. However, they remain open to critical inquiry (as exemplified by the NCES chart on page 215).

2. If it's an individual's site, who is speaking on the site? A nationally recognized biologist is likely to be more credible on biological topics than a politician with no scientific background. If you cannot identify the author, who is the editor or compiler? If you cannot identify an author, editor, compiler, or sponsoring organization, do not use the source.

3. What links does the site provide? If it is networked to sites with obviously unreasonable or inaccurate content, you must question the credibility of the original site.

4. Is the information on the site supported with documentation from scholarly or otherwise credible sources (for example, government reports)?

—CHECKLIST   Relevance and Credibility of Sources

Relevance

☐ **Do the source's title and subtitle indicate that it addresses your specific research question?**

☐ **What is the publication date?** Is the material up to date, classic, or historical? The concept of "up to date" depends on discipline and topic. Ask your instructor how recent sources need to be for your project.

☐ **Does the table of contents, menu, or index indicate that it contains useful information?**

☐ **If the source is a book, does it have an index?** Scan the index for keywords related to your topic.

☐ **Does the abstract at the beginning or the summary at the end of an article suggest it will be useful?** An abstract or a summary presents the main points made in the article.

☐ **Does the work contain headings?** Skim the subheadings to see whether they indicate that the source contains useful information.

Credibility

☐ **What information can you find about the writer's credentials?** Obtain biographical information about the writer by checking the source itself, consulting a biographical dictionary, or conducting an Internet search of the writer's name. Is the writer affiliated with a research institution that contributes knowledge about an issue? Is the writer an expert on the topic? Is the writer cited frequently in other sources about the topic?

☐ **Who is the publisher?** University presses and academic publishers are considered more scholarly and therefore more credible than the popular press.

☐ **Does the work include a bibliography of works consulted or cited?** Trustworthy writers cite a variety of sources and document their citations properly. Does this source do so? Does the source include a variety of citations?

☐ **Does the work argue reasonably for its position and treat opposing views fairly?** What tone does the author use? Is the work objective or subjective? Are the writer's arguments clear and logical? What is the author's point of view? Does the writer present other views fairly? *(For more on evaluating arguments, see Tab 2: Writing and Designing Texts, pp. 29–96.)*

Consider these factors as well:

- **Authority and credibility:** Are the author and sponsor of the Web site identifiable? Does the author include biographical information? Is there any indication that the author has relevant expertise on the subject? Look for information about the individual or organization sponsoring the site. The following extensions in the Web address, or uniform resource locator (URL), can help you determine the type of site (which often tells you something about its purpose):

.com	commercial (business)	**.edu**	educational	**.mil**	military
.org	nonprofit organization	**.gov**	US government	**.net**	network

- A tilde (~) followed by a name in a URL usually means the site is a personal home page not affiliated with any organization.

- **Audience and purpose:** How does the appearance of the site, along with the tone of any written material, suggest its intended audience? A site's purpose also influences the way it presents information and the credibility of that information. Is the site's main purpose to promote a cause, raise money, advertise a product or service, deliver factual information, present research results, provide news, share personal information, or offer entertainment? Always try to view the site's home page; delete everything after the first slash in the URL to do so.

- **Objectivity and reasonableness:** Look carefully at the purpose and tone of the text. Nearly all sources express a point of view or bias. You should consult sources that represent a range of opinions on your topic. However, unreasonable and inaccurate sources have no place in academic debate. Clues that indicate a lack of reasonableness include an intemperate tone, broad claims, exaggerated statements of significance, conflicts of interest, no recognition of opposing views, claims without evidence, and strident attacks on differing opinions. *(For more on evaluating arguments, see Tab 2: Writing and Designing Texts, pp. 29-96.)*

- **Relevance and timeliness:** In what ways does the information from an online source specifically support (or refute) your thesis or topic? Do the site's intended audience and purpose include an academic audience? Does the site indicate how recently it has been updated, and are most of the included links still working?

- **Context:** Do others' comments on a blog or posts to a discussion list make your source appear more credible or undermine the writer's credibility? How can these comments help you understand your topic more fully?

Consider a student writing a report on the reintroduction of gray wolves in the western United States following their near extinction. Many environmentalists have favored this program, while farmers and ranchers have worried about the impact of wolves on livestock.

The student conducts an online keyword search and finds the site in Figure 21.1. This site focuses on the gray wolf population in the United States

—*the* EVOLVING SITUATION

Using the CARE Checklist to Evaluate Web Sites

Use your understanding of the writing situation to take care as you evaluate sources on the Web. For example, before judging a Web site to be credible or accurate, give sufficient consideration to its purpose and authorial stance. A Web site that is **c**redible, **a**ccurate, **r**easonable, and **e**videnced (CARE) should meet the following criteria:

Credibility

- The source is trustworthy.
- The argument and use of evidence are clear and logical.
- The author's or sponsor's credentials are available (visit the home page and look for a link that says "About Us").
- Quality control is evident (spelling and grammar are correct; links are functional).
- The source is a known or respected authority; it has organizational support (such as a university, a research institution, or a major news publication).

Accuracy

- The site is updated frequently, if not daily (and includes "last-updated" information).
- The site is factual, not speculative, and provides evidence for its assertions.
- The site is detailed; text appears in full paragraphs.
- The site is comprehensive, including archives, links, and additional resources. A search feature and table of contents or tabs allow users to quickly find the information they need.
- The site's purpose includes completeness and accuracy.

Reasonableness

- The site is fair, balanced, and objective. (Look at comments on a blog or related messages on a news group.)
- The site makes its purpose clear. (Is it selling something? Prompting site visitors to sign a petition? Promoting a new film?)
- The site contains no conflicts of interest.
- The site content does not include fallacies or a slanted tone *(for more on fallacies, see Chapter 11: Arguments, pp. 119–42).*

Evidence

- The site lists sources for its information, providing links where appropriate.
- The site clarifies the content it is responsible for and which links are created by unrelated authors or sponsors.
- The site provides contact information for its authors and/or sponsors.
- If the site is an academic resource, it follows the conventions of a specific citation style (for example, MLA or APA).

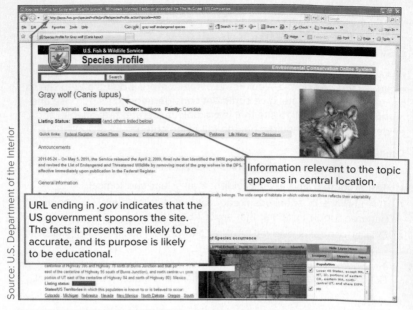

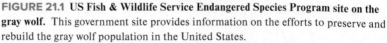

FIGURE 21.1 US Fish & Wildlife Service Endangered Species Program site on the gray wolf. This government site provides information on the efforts to preserve and rebuild the gray wolf population in the United States.

and its status under the Endangered Species Act, making it relevant to the student's topic. The URL indicates that the site belongs to a US government agency, suggesting its credibility (although such sites are not immune from politics and bias). Information on the site appears in a simple, easy-to-follow format, indicating an educational purpose. It links to other government sites. Scrolling down, the student sees the site has been updated recently. This site's apparent authority, credibility, and purpose make it a good candidate for use as a source.

Next, the student finds the site in Figure 21.2. Following the link that says "About Us," the student learns that the site is sponsored by Wolf Park, a non-profit organization in Indiana dedicated to the preservation and study of wolves. The site's purpose appears to be educational and persuasive; it includes information about wolves and conservation efforts on their behalf. The page shown in Figure 21.2 describes research at the park and includes a link to papers with clearly documented sources, suggesting that the site is credible.

After further research the student reaches the site in Figure 21.3 on page 225, which presents apparently accurate and impartial information about wolves. Scrolling down, the student sees that the site also features advertisements, which do not appear in most scholarly sources. The site does not state the author's credentials, nor does it include documentation for its information. For these reasons, the student should confirm its statements with another source before using them in an academic report.

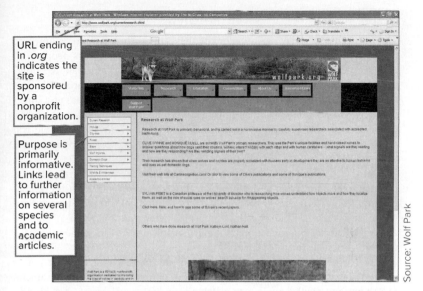

URL ending in *.org* indicates the site is sponsored by a nonprofit organization.

Purpose is primarily informative. Links lead to further information on several species and to academic articles.

Source: Wolf Park

FIGURE 21.2 A page from Wolf Park's Web site, with information about research efforts at the park. The list of links on the left side of the page includes a link to academic articles.

©McGraw-Hill Education

Source: NPS by Barry O'Neill   ©Dieter Hopf/Glow Images

FIGURE 21.3 Animal Tracks gray wolf site. This site's information appears to be accurate, but it does not document its sources or present the author's credentials.

21c   Identify and eradicate fake news.

The spreading of **fake news**—deliberate lies and distortions communicated with the desire to deceive—is not a new practice for unscrupulous people. But today the Internet can instantly and globally spread misinformation. "Bots" (robots) can infiltrate social media with outrageous and unsubstantiated articles that appear convincingly real. The potential for dangerous outcomes as a direct result of fake news requires that consumers use alertness and sharp judgment. On the premise that the best defense is a good offense, dishonest people will falsely claim that the fact-based and verifiable statements of their opponents are fake news.

In the midst of the general confusion that fake news creates, you may be tempted to give up trying to distinguish reality and falsehood. But it is essential that you stay with it and search for the truth. Throughout history, tyrants have depended on the Big Lie—something repeated often and loudly—to manipulate the unwary. It has never been more important to think critically and to employ the means of assessment outlined in this chapter.

It is often said that people have a right to different opinions, but not to different facts. "Consider the source" is a good summary of what we recommend to combat and eradicate fake news. Remember that visual images can be doctored, just as words can mislead. Fake news undermines democracy by distorting public opinion and, even worse, damages the idea of truth itself. No one wants to live in a post-truth environment, where people can, at will, make up facts. Education must remain the search for truth. Transfer the research practices in this chapter with the aim of keeping truth alive inside and outside the classroom.

CHAPTER 22

Doing Research in the Archive, Field, and Lab

Research involves more than **secondary research**—finding answers to questions in books and other print and online resources. When you conduct **primary research**—looking up old maps, consulting census records, polling community members about a current issue—you participate in the discovery of knowledge.

The three kinds of primary research discussed in this chapter are archival research, field research, and laboratory research.

- **Archival research:** An **archive** is a cataloged collection of documents, manuscripts, and other materials, possibly including receipts, wills, photographs, sound recordings, and other kinds of media.
- **Field research:** Field research takes you out into the world to gather and record information.
- **Laboratory research:** Every science course will most likely involve a laboratory component. In the laboratory, you work individually or as a team to record each step of an experiment carefully.

22a Adhere to ethical principles when doing primary research.

In the archive, field, or lab, you are working directly with something precious and immediate: an original record, a group of people, or special materials. An ethical researcher shows respect for materials, experimental subjects, fellow researchers, and readers. Here are some guidelines for ethical research:

- Handle original documents and materials with great care, always leaving sources and data available for other researchers.
- Accurately report your sources and results.
- Follow proper procedures when working with human participants.

Researchers who work with human participants should also adhere to the following basic principles:

- **Confidentiality:** People who fill out surveys, participate in focus groups, or respond to interviews should be assured that their names will not be used without their permission.
- **Informed consent:** Before participating in a study, all participants must sign a statement affirming that they understand the general purpose of the research.

—NAVIGATING THROUGH COLLEGE AND BEYOND

Primary Research in the Disciplines

Primary research is almost always impressive because you are working with authentic materials to discover new ideas. As always, the overall situation is essential to your decisions. If your purpose is to summarize research done by others, you would be overstepping the boundaries of the genre by inserting a survey of your own. Always keep in mind the constraints and opportunities of the situation.

Different forms of primary research characterize different disciplines. Here are some examples:

- **Archival research:** Languages and literature; education; music and the performing arts; visual arts; media and popular culture; social sciences. For a report on how different sections of the country were represented by the photographers of the 1930s, a historian might research the images of Dorothea Lange housed in the Library of Congress.
- **Field research:** Social sciences; marketing and advertising; media and communication. For a proposal on developing a new brand identity, a marketing researcher might survey current users of the brand.
- **Laboratory research:** Life sciences; physical sciences; computer science; engineering. To find out whether fish that swim in schools connect more readily with fish of their own species, a scientist could create a controlled environment in a laboratory to test the hypothesis.

- **Minimal risk:** Participants in research should not incur any risks greater than they do in everyday life.

- **Protection of vulnerable groups:** Researchers must be held strictly accountable for research done with the physically disabled, prisoners, people who are mentally impaired or incompetent, minors, the elderly, and pregnant women.

22b Prepare yourself for archival research.

Archives are found in libraries, museums, other institutions and private collections, and on video and audiotape. Your own attic may contain family archives—letters, diaries, and photographs that could have value to a researcher. Some archival collections are accessible through the Internet; others you must visit in person (*see Figure 22.1* for a list of Internet resources that will help you locate and make use of a range of archives). The more you know about your area of study, the more likely you will be to see the significance of an item in an archival collection.

Archives generally require that you call or e-mail to arrange a time for your visit, and some are restricted in terms of access. If you find an archive on the Internet that you would like to visit, phone or e-mail well in advance to find out if you will need references, a letter of introduction, or other qualifying papers. Archives often will not allow you to browse; instead, use finding aids (often available online) to determine which records you need to see.

Archives also generally require you to present a photo identification and to leave personal items in a locker or at a coat check. They have strict policies about reproducing materials and rarely allow anything to leave the premises. The more you know about the archive's policies and procedures before you visit,

- *American Memory* <http://memory.loc.gov/ammem/browse/updatedList.html>: This site offers access to more than seven million digital items from over a hundred collections of material on US history and culture.

- *Radio Program Archive* <https://umdrive.memphis.edu/mbensman/public/>: This site lists radio archives available from the University of Memphis and explains how to obtain cassettes of programs.

- *Television News Archive* <https://tvnews.vanderbilt.edu/>: This site provides summaries and videos of television news broadcasts.

- *US National Archives and Records Administration* (NARA) <www.archives.gov/>.

- *Women Writers Project* <http://www.wwp.northeastern.edu/>: This site lists archived texts—by pre-Victorian women writers—that are available through the project.

FIGURE 22.1 Online information about archives that can lead you to a wide range of archival sources.

the more productive your visit will be. When you are finished, thank the archivist for the help you have received.

22c Plan your field research carefully.

Field research involves recording observations, conducting interviews, and administering surveys. To conduct field research at a particular site, such as a place of business or a school, you must obtain permission. Explain the nature of your project, the date and time you would like to visit, and how much time you will need. Will you be observing? Interviewing people? Taking photographs? Also ask for a confirming letter or e-mail. Always write a thank-you note after you have concluded your research.

1. Observing and writing field notes

College assignments offer opportunities to conduct systematic observations. For a sociology class, you might observe the behavior of students in the cafeteria, taking notes on who sits with whom in terms of race, class, and social status. Such primary research will help you to look and observe throughout your life.

When you use direct observation, keep careful records to retain the information you gather. Here are some guidelines to follow:

- Be systematic in your observations, but be alert to unexpected behavior.
- Record what you see and hear as objectively as possible: describe; don't evaluate.
- Take more notes than you think you will need.
- When appropriate, categorize the types of behavior you are looking for, and devise a system for counting instances of each type.
- When you have recorded data over a substantial period of time, group your observations into categories for careful study.

(For advice on conducting direct observations for a case study, see Tab 3: Common Assignments across the Curriculum, pp. 148–50.)

2. Conducting interviews

Interviews are useful in a wide variety of writing situations: finding out what students think about the university logo; gathering ideas to promote recycling on campus; talking with a family member about memories of a historical figure. Interviews can be conducted in person, by phone, or online. Like other research tools, interviews require systematic preparation and implementation:

- Identify appropriate people for your interviews.
- Do background research, and plan a list of open-ended questions.
- Take careful notes and, if possible, tape-record the interview (but be sure to obtain your subject's permission if you use audiotape or videotape). Verify quotations.

SOURCE SMART   Quoting from Interviews

Before an interview, obtain permission to quote the interviewee in writing. If the interview is not being recorded (or captured on a transcript if online), use oversized quotation marks to enclose direct quotations in your notes. Record the interviewee's name and the location and date of the interview in your research notebook. Afterward, verify quotations with your interviewee.

- Follow up on vague responses with questions that get at specific information. Do not rush interviewees.
- Politely probe inconsistencies and contradictions.
- Write thank-you notes to interviewees, and later send them copies of your report.

3. Taking surveys

Surveys are useful in numerous situations when it is important to go beyond individual impressions to a more systematic basis for forming conclusions. Do students and alumni at Governors State University prefer the old tagline, "Success by Degrees," or a new one, "Here, You Are"? But even a straightforward question like that, which can be administered online through a site such as *Survey Monkey*, requires careful design.

Conducted either orally or in writing, **surveys** are made up of structured questions. Written surveys are called **questionnaires.** Many colleges have offices that must review and approve student surveys. Check to see what guidelines your school may have. The following suggestions will help you prepare informal surveys:

- Define your purpose and your target population—the people who are relevant to the purpose of your interview. Are you trying to gauge attitudes, learn about typical behaviors, or both?
- Write clear directions and questions. For example, if you are asking multiple-choice questions, make sure that you cover all possible options and that your options do not overlap.
- Make sure that your questions do not suggest a preference for one answer over another.
- Make the survey brief and easy to complete.

22d   Keep a notebook when doing lab research.

Firsthand observations in the controlled environment of the laboratory are at the heart of the scientific method and define the situation for scientific research.

To provide a complete and accurate account of your laboratory work, keep careful records in a notebook. The following guidelines will help you take accurate notes on your research:

- Record immediate, on-the-spot, accurate notes on what happens in the lab. Write down as much detail as possible. Measure precisely; do not estimate. Identify major pieces of apparatus, unusual chemicals, and laboratory animals in enough detail so that, for example, a reader can determine the size or type of equipment you used. Use drawings, when appropriate, to illustrate complicated equipment setups. Include tables, when useful, to present results.

- Follow a basic format. Present your results in a format that allows you to communicate all the major features of an experiment. The five basic sections that must be included are title, purpose, materials and methods, results, and conclusions. *(For more advice on preparing a lab report, see Tab 3: Common Assignments across the Curriculum, pp. 145–48.)*

- Write in complete sentences, even if you are filling in answers to questions in a lab manual. Resist the temptation to use shorthand to record your notes. Later, the complete sentences will provide a clear record of your procedures and results. Highlight connections in your sentences by using the following transitions: *then, next, consequently, because,* and *therefore.* Cause-effect relationships should be clear.

When necessary, revise and correct your laboratory notebook in visible ways. If you make a mistake in recording laboratory results, correct it as clearly as possible, either by erasing or by crossing out and rewriting on the original sheet. If you make an uncorrectable mistake in your notebook, simply fold the sheet lengthwise and mark *omit* on the face side. Unanticipated results often occur in the lab, and you may find yourself jotting down notes on a convenient piece of scrap paper. Attach these notes to your notebook.

CHAPTER 23

Plagiarism, Copyright, and Intellectual Property

When we draw on the words and ideas of others, integrity and honesty require us to acknowledge their contributions. Otherwise, we are committing plagiarism. Some forms of plagiarism are obvious, such as buying a term paper from an online paper mill or "borrowing" a friend's completed assignment. Others are more subtle and may even be inadvertent. Since ignorance is no excuse, it is important to learn appropriate ways to paraphrase or summarize another writer's material. *(See Chapter 24: Working with Sources and Avoiding Plagiarism, pp. 237–54, for more on paraphrasing and summarizing.)*

Penalties for plagiarism are serious. Journalists who are caught plagiarizing are publicly exposed and fired by the publications they write for. Those publications must then work hard to repair their credibility. Scholars who fail to acknowledge the words and ideas of others lose their professional credibility and often their jobs. Students who plagiarize might receive a failing grade for an assignment or course and face other disciplinary action—including expulsion. Be sure to read your campus's written policy on plagiarism and its consequences.

The Internet has made many types of sources available, and it can be unclear what, when, and how to cite. For example, bloggers and other Web authors often reproduce material from other sites, while some musicians make their music available for free download. Although the line between "original" and "borrowed" appears to be blurring in our society, you should review the following guidelines for crediting sources appropriately.

23a Understand how plagiarism relates to copyright and intellectual property.

Related to plagiarism are the concepts of copyright and intellectual property. **Copyright** is the legal right to control the reproduction of any original work—a piece of writing, a musical composition, a play, a movie, a computer program, a photograph, a work of art. A copyrighted work is the **intellectual property** of the copyright holder, whether that entity is a publisher, a record

---

SOURCE SMART Determining What Is "Common Knowledge"

Information that an audience could be expected to know from many sources is considered common knowledge. You do not need to cite common knowledge if you use your own wording and sentence structure. Common knowledge can take various forms, including at least these four:

- Folktales with no particular author (for example, Little Red Riding Hood outsmarted the wolf)
- Common sense (for example, property values in an area fall when crime rises)
- Historical facts and dates (for example, the United States entered World War II in 1941)
- Information found in many general reference works (for example, the heart drives the body's circulation system)

Maps, charts, graphs, and other visual displays of information are not considered common knowledge. Even though everyone knows that Paris is the capital of France, if you reproduce a map of France in your paper, you must credit the map's creator.

―the EVOLVING SITUATION

Learning More about Plagiarism, Copyright and Fair Use, and Intellectual Property

It is important to approach all writing assignments with consideration for your sources and your audience. Using the resources provided in the links below, learn more about the meaning of copyright and fair use, as well as the details constituting intellectual property.

- **Plagiarism:** For more information about plagiarism, see the Council of Writing Program Administrator's "Defining and Avoiding Plagiarism: The WPA Statement on Best Practices" <http://wpacouncil.org/positions/WPAplagiarism.pdf>. Georgetown University's Honor Council offers an example of a campus honor code pertaining to plagiarism and academic ethics at <https://honorcouncil.georgetown.edu/system>.

- **Copyright and fair use:** For information and discussion of fair use, see Copyright and Fair Use at <http://fairuse.stanford.edu> and the US Copyright Office at <www.copyright.gov>. The University of Texas posts guidelines for fair use and multimodal projects at <http://copyright.lib.utexas.edu/ccmcguid.html>.

- **Intellectual property:** For information about what constitutes intellectual property and related issues, see the World Intellectual Property Organization Web site at <www.wipo.int>. For a legal perspective, the American Intellectual Property Law Association offers information and overviews of recent cases at <www.aipla.org>.

company, an entertainment conglomerate, or the individual creator of the work. Here is some additional information on these important legal concepts:

- **Copyright:** A copyrighted text cannot be reproduced legally (in print or online) without the written permission of the copyright holder. The copyright protects the right of authors and publishers to benefit from their productions.

- **Fair use:** The concept of **fair use** protects most academic use of copyrighted sources. Under this provision of copyright law, you can legally quote a brief passage from a copyrighted text for an academic purpose without infringing on copyright. Of course, to avoid plagiarism you must identify the passage as a quotation and cite it properly. *(See page 236 for more information.)*

- **Intellectual property:** In addition to works protected by copyright, intellectual property includes patented inventions, trademarks, industrial designs, and similar intellectual creations that are protected by other laws.

─SOURCE SMART What Must Be Acknowledged?

You **do not** have to acknowledge

- common knowledge expressed in your words and sentence structure (*see the box on page 232*),
- your independent thinking, or
- your original field observations, surveys, or experimental results.

You **must** acknowledge

- concepts you learned from a source, whether or not you copy the source's language,
- interviews other than surveys,
- abstracts,
- visuals,
- statistics, including those you use to create your own visuals (*See Chapter 20, pp. 212–15.*)
- your own work for another assignment (use only with your instructor's permission).

Acknowledge the source each time you cite from the material, regardless of the length of the selection. If you use multiple sources in a paragraph, make clear which ideas are from which sources. (see *Tab 6: MLA Documentation Style*, pp. 261–316, and *Tab 7: APA Documentation Style*, pp. 317–63.)

23b Take steps to avoid plagiarism.

When people are under pressure, they sometimes make poor choices. Inadvertent plagiarism occurs when busy students take notes carelessly, forgetting to record the source of a paraphrase or accidentally inserting material downloaded from a Web site into a paper. Deliberate plagiarism occurs when students "borrow" a paper from a friend or copy and paste portions of an online article into their own work. Even though you may be tired or pressured, careful planning and adherence to the following guidelines can help you avoid plagiarism:

- When you receive an assignment, write down your thoughts and questions before you begin looking at sources. Use this record to keep track of changes in your ideas.
- As you proceed with your research, record your ideas in one color and those of others in a different color.
- As you continue researching and taking notes, keep accurate records. If you do not know where you got an idea or a piece of information, do not use it until you find out.

— CHECKLIST   Avoiding Plagiarism

☐ Is my thesis my own idea, not something I found in one of my sources?

☐ Have I used a variety of sources, not just one or two?

☐ Have I identified each source clearly?

☐ Do I fully understand and explain all words, phrases, and ideas in my paper?

☐ Have I acknowledged all ideas that are based on neither my original thinking nor common knowledge?

☐ Have I properly integrated material from sources, using paraphrases, summaries, or quotations *(see Chapter 24, pp. 243–49)*?

☐ If I am planning to publish my text online, have I received all necessary permissions?

- When you take notes, put quotation marks around words, phrases, or sentences taken verbatim from a source and note the pages. If you use any of those words, phrases, or sentences when summarizing or paraphrasing the source, put them in quotation marks. Changing a word here and there while keeping a source's sentence structure or phrasing still constitutes plagiarism even if you credit the source for the ideas. *(See pp. 243-49 for examples.)*

- Do not rely too much on one source, or you may easily slip into using that person's thoughts as your own.

- Cite the source of all ideas, opinions, facts, and statistics that are not common knowledge.

- Choose an appropriate documentation style, and use it consistently and properly. *(See Tabs 6-8 for information about the most common documentation styles for academic writing.)*

When working with electronic sources, keep in mind the following guidelines:

- Print or save to your computer any online source you consult. Note the date on which you viewed it, and be sure to keep the complete URL in case you need to view the source again. Some documentation styles require you to include the URL in your citation *(see Tabs 6-8)*.

- If you copy and paste a passage from a Web site into a wordprocessing file, use a different font to identify that material as well as the URL and the access date.

- Acknowledge all sites you use as sources, including those you access via links on another site.

- As a courtesy, request the author's permission before quoting from blogs, news group postings, listserv's, or e-mails.
- Acknowledge any audio, video, or illustrated material that has informed your research.

It may be tempting to copy and paste material from the Internet without acknowledgment, but instructors can easily detect that form of plagiarism by using a search engine to locate the original.

Posting material on a publicly accessible Web site is usually considered the legal equivalent of publishing it in print format. (Password-protected sites generally are exempt.) Before posting on a public site, seek copyright permission from all your sources. *(See the box on p. 233 and the following guidelines for fair use.)*

23c   Use copyrighted materials fairly.

All original works, including student projects, graphics, and videos, are covered by copyright even if they do not bear an official copyright symbol. A copyright grants its owner—often the creator—exclusive rights to the use of a protected work, including reproducing, distributing, and displaying the work. The popularity of the Web as a venue for publication has led to increased concerns about the fair use of copyrighted material. Before you publish your work on the Web or produce a multimodal presentation that includes audio, video, and graphic elements copied from a Web site, make sure that you have used copyrighted material fairly by considering these four questions:

- **What is the purpose of the use?** Educational, nonprofit, and personal use are more likely to be considered fair than is commercial use.
- **What is the nature of the work being used?** In most cases, imaginative and unpublished materials can be used only if you have the permission of the copyright holder.
- **How much of the copyrighted work is being used?** The use of a small portion of a text for academic purposes is more likely to be considered fair than the use of a whole work for commercial purposes. While no clear legal definition of "a small portion" exists, one conservative guideline is that you can quote up to fifty words from an article (print or online) and three hundred words from a book. It is safest to ask permission to quote an entire work or a substantial portion of a text (be cautious with poems, plays, and songs). Images and multimodal clips are considered entire works. Also, you may need permission to link your Web site to another.
- **What effect would this use have on the market for the original?** The use of a work is usually considered unfair if it would hurt sales of the original.

When in doubt, ask permission.

CHAPTER 24

Working with Sources and Avoiding Plagiarism

Once you have a research question, an idea about what the library and Internet have to offer, and some credible, appropriate sources in hand, you are ready to begin working with your sources. If you pay attention to detail and keep careful records at this stage, you will stay organized, save time, and credit sources appropriately.

24a Maintain a working bibliography.

As you research, compile a **working bibliography**—a list of those books, articles, pamphlets, Web sites, and other sources that seem most likely to help you answer your research question. Maintain an accurate and complete record of all sources you consult so that you can find and cite all sources accurately.

While the exact bibliographic information you will need depends on your documentation style, the following list includes the major elements of most systems *(see Tabs 6-8 for the requirements of specific documentation styles):*

Book

- Call number (so you can find the source again; not required for documentation)
- Names of all authors, editors, and translators
- Title of chapter or selection
- Title and subtitle of book
- Edition (if not the first), volume number (if applicable)
- Publication information (publisher, date)

Periodical article

- Names of authors
- Title and subtitle of article
- Title and subtitle of periodical
- Date, edition or volume number, issue number
- Page numbers

Article from database (in addition to the preceding)

- Name of database
- Date you retrieved source
- URL or Digital Object Identifier (DOI)

Internet source (including visual, audio, video)

- Names of all authors, editors, or creators
- Title and subtitle of source

- Title of larger site, project, or database (if applicable)
- Version or edition, if any
- Publication information, if available, including any about a version in another medium (such as print, radio, or film)
- Date of electronic publication or latest update, if available
- Publisher of site
- Date you accessed site
- URL of source
- Any other identifying numbers, such as a DOI

Other sources

- Name of author or creator
- Title
- Format (for example, photograph or lecture)
- Title of larger publication, if any
- Publisher, sponsor, or institution housing the source
- Date of creation or publication
- Any identifying numbers

You can record bibliographic information on note cards or in a Word file or other note-taking application; you can print out or e-mail to yourself bibliographic information obtained from online searches in databases and library catalogs; you can use an app on your cell phone to send a citation to yourself; or you can record bibliographic information directly on photocopies of source material. You can also save most Web pages and other online sources to your own computer.

1. Using note cards

One classic method for taking notes is still useful: using three-by-five-inch or four-by-six-inch note cards to compile the working bibliography, with each potential source getting a separate card, as in Figure 24.1. You can also use the cards to include all information necessary for documentation, to record brief quotations, and to note your own comments (carefully marked as yours). Because each source has its own card, this method can help you rearrange information when you are deciding how to organize your paper, and it can then help you create your list of citations. Instead of handwriting on cards, you can record bibliographic information in a computer file.

2. Printing the results of online searches in databases and library catalogs

The results of searches in online indexes and databases usually include bibliographic information about the sources they list. *(See the example of a database search in Chapter 19, p. 203.)* You can print these results directly from your

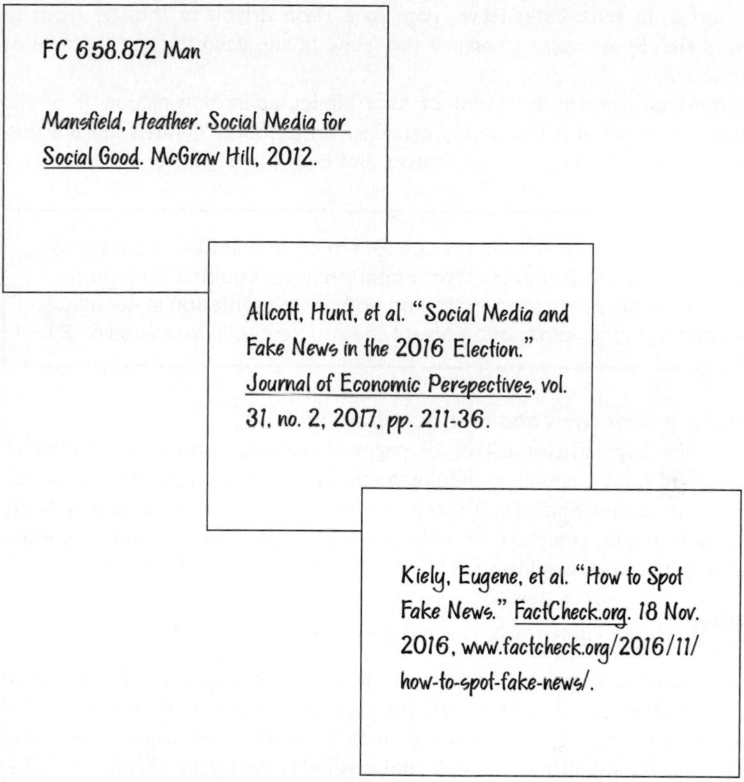

FC 658.872 Man

Mansfield, Heather. <u>Social Media for
Social Good</u>. McGraw Hill, 2012.

Allcott, Hunt, et al. "Social Media and
Fake News in the 2016 Election."
<u>Journal of Economic Perspectives</u>, vol.
31, no. 2, 2017, pp. 211-36.

Kiely, Eugene, et al. "How to Spot
Fake News." <u>FactCheck.org</u>. 18 Nov.
2016, www.factcheck.org/2016/11/
how-to-spot-fake-news/.

FIGURE 24.1 Three sample bibliography note cards in MLA style. The cards are
for a book (top), for a journal article (middle), and for a Web site (bottom).

─SOURCE SMART The Uses and Limits of Bibliographic Software

Programs such as *Microsoft Word 2018* allow you to store source data,
automatically insert citations in common documentation styles, and
generate a list of references. These programs might not incorporate
the most recent updates to documentation styles, however, nor do they
accommodate all types of sources. Talk to your instructor before using
bibliographic software, and check your citations carefully against the
models in Tabs 6–8. Also check references that a database creates
for you.

browser or, in some cases, save them to a flash drive and transfer them to a Word file. Be sure also to record the name of the database and the date of your search.

You can similarly print out or save bibliographic information from the results of searches in online library catalogs. Some college libraries make it possible for you to compile a list of sources and e-mail it to yourself.

Caution: If you download the full text of an article from a database and refer to it in your paper, your citation may require information about the database (depending on your documentation style) as well as bibliographic information about the article itself. *(See Tabs 6–8.)*

---

3. Using photocopies and printouts from Web sites

If you photocopy articles, essays, or pages of reference works from a print or a microfilm source, noting the bibliographic information on the photocopy can save you time later. Similarly, if you print out a source you found on a Web site or copy it to your computer, be sure to note the site's author, name, sponsor, date of publication, complete URL, and the date you visited the site.

24b　Create an annotated bibliography.

An annotated bibliography can be useful to you in your research. You will need the full citation, correctly formatted, for your works-cited or references list. The annotation for each source should include a summary of major points, your evaluation of the source's relevance and credibility, and your thoughts on what the material contributes to your project and where it might fit in *(see Figure 24.2)*.

24c　Take notes on your sources.

Taking notes helps you think through your research question and read both digital and print sources more systematically. Consult a table of contents or other introductory parts to find the most relevant sections. As you work, annotate photocopies, and make note of useful ideas and powerful quotations. See whether categories emerge that can help you organize your project.

1. Annotating

One way to take notes is to annotate photocopied articles and printouts from online information services or Web sites. See Figure 24.3 for an example. (Do this for sources you save to your computer by using the Comments feature in your word-processing software.) As you read, do the following:

- On the first page, write down complete bibliographic information for the source.

- Record questions, reactions, and ideas in the margins.

- Comment on ideas that agree with or differ from those you have already learned about.

Allcott, Hunt, et al. "Social Media and Fake News in the 2016 Election." *Journal of Economic Perspectives*, vol. 31, no. 2, 2017, pp. 211-36.

>   The authors of this scholarly article discuss the economics of fake news and present new data on its circulation leading up to the 2016 presidential election. This study begins with a definition of fake news that emphasizes its intention to mislead the public. This definition is important in that it differentiates fake news from news that is merely inaccurate or biased in its presentation. This distinction supports my ideas about the dangers of fake news and why readers must make efforts to identify and eliminate it.

Kiely, Eugene, et al. "How to Spot Fake News." *FactCheck.org*, 18 Nov. 2016, www.factcheck.org/2016/11/how-to-spot-fake-news/.

>   Aimed at a popular audience of students, researchers, and news consumers, this article outlines the history of misinformation presented as fact, but it focuses on current concerns about the speed with which news is disseminated online, especially via social media. The authors offer useful tips for identifying fake news stories, false viral claims, and junk e-mails posing as news updates, and provide current and historic examples of each.

FIGURE 24.2 Sample annotated bibliography. A section of Albert Rabe's annotated bibliography. *(To read Rabe's final research report, see Chapter 30.)*

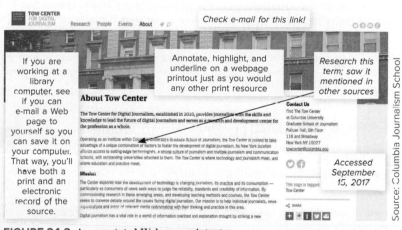

FIGURE 24.3 An annotated Web page printout.

- Put important and difficult passages into your own words by paraphrasing or summarizing them in the margins. *(For help with paraphrasing and summarizing, see pp. 243-49.)*

Highlight statements that you may want to quote because they are especially well expressed or are key to readers' understanding of the issue.

2. Taking notes in a research journal or log

A **research journal** or **research log** is a tool for keeping track of your research. It can be a spiral or loose-leaf notebook, a box of note cards, a note-taking application on your laptop or mobile device, or a blog—whatever form you are most comfortable with. Use the journal to write down leads for sources and to record ideas and observations about your topic as they occur to you. If you use a blog, you can use it to link to potential sources.

When you have finished annotating a photocopy, printout, or electronic version of an article, use your research journal to explore the comments, connections, and questions you recorded. If you do not have a copy of the material to annotate, take notes directly in your research journal.

Enclose in quotation marks any exact words from a source. If you think you may forget that the phrasing, as well as the idea, came from someone else, label the passage a "quotation" and note the title of the Web page, as Albert Rabe did in his research notes:

> Allcott, Hunt, and Matthew Gentzkow. "Social Media and Fake News in the 2016 Election." *Journal of Economic Perspectives*, vol. 31, no. 2, 2017, pp. 211–36. *American Economic Association*, https://doi.org/10.1257/jep.31.2.211.

- With access to the Internet, anyone can publish a news story. Journalists, editors, and publishers are no longer the primary gatekeepers.

- Allcott and Gentzkow point out an astonishing statistic. Quote: "An individual user with no track record or reputation can in some cases reach as many readers as Fox News, CNN, or *The New York Times*."

Unless you think you might use a particular quotation in your project, it is usually better to express the author's ideas in your own words by using a paraphrase or a summary.

SOURCE SMART Deciding to Quote, Paraphrase, or Summarize

Point is eloquently, memorably, or uniquely stated	→	Quote
Details important but not uniquely or eloquently expressed	→	Paraphrase
Long section of material (with many points), main ideas important, details not important	→	Summarize
Part of longer passage is uniquely stated	→	Use quotation inside paraphrased or summarized passage

24d   Take stock of what you have learned as you paraphrase, summarize, quote, and synthesize your sources.

When you take stock, remember your writing situation. As you synthesize what you have learned from the sources you are consulting, think about how these sources relate to one another. Where do they agree, and where do they disagree? Where do you stand relative to these sources? Did anything you read surprise or disturb you, and how will it affect your audience? Writing down your responses to such questions can help you clarify what you have learned and decide how that information fits in with your own claim as you are developing it.

The credibility of your work depends on the relevance and reliability of your sources as well as the scope and depth of your reading and observation. College research projects usually require multiple sources and viewpoints. A project on the impact of fake news on political elections for example, is unlikely to be credible if it relies on only one source of information. An argument about an issue in the social sciences will not be taken seriously if it cites research on only one side of the debate.

As the context and kind of writing change, so too do the requirements for types and numbers of sources. As a general rule, however, you should consult more than two sources and use only sources that are both credible and respected by people working in the field. To determine whether you have located appropriate and sufficient sources, ask yourself the following questions:

- Are your sources trustworthy? *(See Chapter 21, pp. 219–26, for more on evaluating sources.)*
- If you have developed a tentative answer to your research question, have your sources provided you with sufficient facts, examples, and ideas to support that answer?
- Have you used sources that examine the issues from several different perspectives?
- Upon examination of the sources, can my tentative answer be legitimately reversed or otherwise changed?

1. Paraphrasing information from sources

When you **paraphrase**, you put someone else's statement into your words and sentence structures. Paraphrase when a passage's details are important to your topic but its exact words are not memorable, or when you need to reorder a source's ideas or clarify complicated information. A paraphrase should be about the same length and level of detail as the original. Cite the original writer, and put quotation marks around any exact phrasing from the source.

In the first unacceptable paraphrase that follows, the writer has done a word-for-word translation, using synonyms for some terms but retaining phrases from the original (highlighted) and failing to enclose them in quotation marks ("few-to-few, one-to-one, and many-to-many," "attentive publics"). Notice also how close the sentence structures in the first faulty paraphrase are to the original.

SOURCE

The media used to work in a one-to-many pattern—that is, by broadcasting. The Internet, though it can be used for one-to-many transmission, is just as well suited for few-to-few, one-to-one, and many-to-many patterns. Traditionally, the media connected audiences "up" to centers of power, people of influence, and national spectacles. The Internet does all that, but it is equally good at connecting us laterally—to peers, to colleagues, and to strangers who share our interests. When experts and power players had something to communicate to the attentive publics they wished to address, they once had to go through the media. Now they can go direct.

—JAY ROSEN, "The New News"

UNACCEPTABLE PARAPHRASE: PLAGIARISM

The news was previously transmitted from one to many. Online media, although they can function in this way, can also follow a few-to-few, one-to-one, and many-to-many pattern. In the past, traditional news outlets connected audiences up to those in a position of power. Online media can do that as well, but they also succeed in connecting us laterally to others who share our interests. If those in a position of power wanted to reach their attentive publics, traditional news outlets used to be their only method. Currently, they can communicate directly with their audiences (Rosen).

In the second example of a faulty paraphrase (following), the writer has merely substituted synonyms for the original author's words (such as "individual-to-individual" instead of "one-to-one") and kept the source's sentence structure. Because it relies on the sentence structure of the original source, the paraphrase is too close to the original and constitutes **plagiarism.**

UNACCEPTABLE PARAPHRASE (SENTENCE STRUCTURE OF SOURCE): PLAGIARISM

The news was previously transmitted from single corporations to several individuals. Online media, although they can function in this way, can also follow a group-to-group, organization-to-organization, and individual-to-individual model. In the past, traditional news outlets linked consumers upward to those in a position of authority. Online media can do that as well, but they also succeed in linking us to one another, including others with whom we have something in common. If those in a position of authority wanted to reach their captive audiences, traditional news outlets used to be their only method. Currently, they can communicate right with their audiences (Rosen).

The third unacceptable paraphrase (following) alters the sentence structure of the source but plagiarizes by using some of the original wording (highlighted in the example) without quotation marks.

SOURCE SMART Guidelines for Writing a Paraphrase

- **Read the passage carefully.** Focus on its sequence of ideas and important details.
- **Be sure you understand the material.** Look up any unfamiliar words.
- **Imagine addressing an audience that has not read the material.**
- **Without looking at the original passage, write down its main ideas and key details.**
- **Use clear, direct language.** Express complicated ideas as a series of simple ones.
- **Check your paraphrase against the original.** Make sure your text conveys the source's ideas accurately without copying its words or sentence structures. Add quotation marks around any phrases from the source or rewrite them.
- **Note the citation information.** List author and page number after every important point.

UNACCEPTABLE PARAPHRASE (WORDING FROM SOURCE): PLAGIARISM

In contrast to traditional news outlets, which functioned in a one-to-many pattern, online media use other patterns to engage audiences, such as few-to-few, one-to-one, and many-to-many (Rosen).

The acceptable paraphrase expresses all ideas from the original using different words and phrasing.

ACCEPTABLE PARAPHRASE

According to Rosen, the shift away from expert reporting to citizen journalism has opened doors for those who both produce and consume the news. No longer at the mercy of those in a position to seek out and select what makes the news, citizens now have more authority, through the power of the Internet, to investigate and publicize the events that matter to us. As a result, we are linked to other informed citizens like never before.

Note that all paraphrases require a citation.

In the following two paraphrases of an article, note that the unacceptable version copies words and phrasing from the source.

SOURCE

Many reporters, especially those at the largest news organizations, have followed their beats for years. So whether it's a Washington bureau chief writing about White House politics, or a longtime sports columnist covering the latest draft picks, chances are they can write with authority because they know the subject.

—TONY ROGERS, "Can Bloggers Replace Professional Journalists?"

UNACCEPTABLE PARAPHRASE: PLAGIARISM

Having followed their beats for years, many reporters for the larger news organizations are able to write with a great deal of authority.

ACCEPTABLE PARAPHRASE

As Tony Rogers notes in his article "Can Bloggers Replace Professional Journalists?" reporters tend to earn credibility over time by covering a particular subject with frequency.

2. Paraphrasing for multiple audiences

Paraphrasing for multiple audiences can be useful in three ways. First, in paraphrasing for others, writers identify the most important ideas so as to highlight them. Second, in paraphrasing for multiple audiences, writers consider what each audience already knows, what the audience needs to know, and how to express that information—with appropriate language, sentence type, and details—for each audience. Third, in creating paraphrases for multiple audiences, writers see both similarities and differences in the various paraphrases; the ability to see similarities and differences across a variety of writing tasks is key to the transfer of your writing knowledge and practice.

Following are two paragraphs from an article in a recent issue of the *Journal of Ecology*, an academic journal in the sciences. Immediately following this source are two paraphrases, one written with an academic audience in mind, and the other written for a general, or lay audience. Note how the two paraphrases differ in their consideration of their intended audiences. For example, in the first paraphrase, adherence to APA guidelines for source citation meets the expectations of an academic audience in the sciences. Also note the similarities between them, such as the main ideas they highlight.

SOURCE

Globally, agriculture is facing many challenges. Of paramount importance is the need to increase food production to feed a burgeoning world population and to do this in a sustainable way, reducing harmful effects of intensive agriculture on the environment. But there is also a need for agriculture and the food industry to keep pace with shifts in food consumption and to improve distribution and access to food. This challenge also needs to done at a time of rapid environmental change, with rising temperatures and extreme climate events threatening food production and placing considerable pressures on the capacity of land to support crops and livestock. Further, the global expansion and intensification of agriculture poses a significant threat to the environment, causing habitat and biodiversity loss, water pollution and increased greenhouse gas emissions (Millennium Ecosystem Assessment, 2005); and, in many parts of the world, it is responsible for extensive degradation of soils, which represents a major threat to both local and global food supplies (FAO, 2015). Together, these factors create a daunting challenge, which requires tackling various constraints on crop production, but also many political and societal challenges to ensure food supplies are safeguarded in an equitable and sustainable way, minimizing harmful impacts on the environment (Foley et al., 2011).

Many solutions have been proposed to tackle this challenge, such as halting agricultural expansion, shifting diets, increasing resource use efficiency of crops and farm systems, closing yield gaps by harnessing the potential of underperforming crops and the production of food via sustainable intensification strategies (Godfray et al., 2010; Foley et al., 2011). Further, there are many social and political challenges that need to be tackled in order to develop and implement sustainable food production strategies, especially in developing countries where policies must include small holders and less favoured groups (Austin et al., 2013).

—RICHARD D. BARDGETT AND DAVID J. GIBSON, "Plant Ecological Solutions to Global Food Security," *Journal of Ecology*

PARAPHRASE FOR AN ACADEMIC AUDIENCE

According to Bardgett and Gibson (2017), a significant number of issues are impacting food production practices across the globe. From worldwide climate change and individual countries' politics to food safety and shifting dietary preferences, these complex challenges are compounded by a growing world population and an overly burdened environment. While a number of proposals have been forwarded for implementing sustainable food production on a global scale, experts believe that traditional methods of agriculture are no longer sufficient. Instead, a set of diverse strategies that address sustainability and social and political factors will be needed (Bardgett & Gibson, 2017).

PARAPHRASE FOR A LAY AUDIENCE

In an article published in the *Journal of Ecology*, environmental scientists Richard Bardgett and David Gibson explain that as the earth's population and its demand for food continue to grow, agricultural industries are struggling to keep up. In addition, it has become clear that the effects of food production are negatively impacting the environment as a whole and are contributing to the worsening effects of climate change. Even further complicating the problem are the many cultural and political environments in which agriculture takes place. In order to determine a solution to the problem, all of these factors will need to be considered.

3. Summarizing information from sources

When you **summarize,** you state the main point of a piece, condensing paragraphs into sentences, pages into paragraphs, or a book into a few pages. As you work with sources, you will summarize more frequently than you will quote or paraphrase. Summarizing works best when the passage is very long and the central idea is important but the details are not.

Following are two summaries of a passage on fake news by Brooke Borel, which is reprinted first.

SOURCE

The history of news is filled with examples of how powerful groups have worked to control information. History also provides examples of how newsmakers and readers have reacted to false stories. In the 14th through 16th centuries in Europe, for example, kings, the church and international merchants ran the earliest organized news networks. With this power came control.

—BROOKE BOREL, "Fact-Checking Won't Save Us from Fake News"

The following unacceptable summary is simply a restatement of Borel's thesis, using much of his phrasing (highlighted) and neglecting to cite the source.

UNACCEPTABLE SUMMARY: PLAGIARISM

Throughout the history of news are examples of how those in power have acted to control information and how the public has reacted to false stories. In medieval Europe, for example, royalty, the church, and international merchants controlled the earliest news networks.

The following acceptable summary states Borel's main point in the writer's own words. Note that the acceptable summary still requires a citation.

—SOURCE SMART Guidelines for Writing a Summary

- **Read the material carefully.** Locate relevant sections.
- **If the text is longer than a few paragraphs, divide it into sections, and sum up each section in one or two sentences.** Compose a topic sentence for each of these sections.
- **Be sure you understand the material.**
- **Imagine explaining the points to an audience that has not read this content.**
- **Identify the main point of the source, in your own words.** Compose a sentence that names the text, the writer, what the writer does (reports or argues), and the most important point.
- **Note any other points that relate to your topic.** State each one (in your words) in one sentence or less. Simplify complex language.
- **Combine your sentence stating the writer's main point with your sentences about secondary points or those summarizing the text's sections.**
- **Check your summary against the original** to see whether it makes sense, expresses the source's meaning, and does not copy any wording or sentence structure.
- **Note all the citation information for the source.**

ACCEPTABLE SUMMARY

According to Borel, history is full of examples of how those in power have acted to control information. In medieval Europe, for example, these actors included political and religious leaders, as well as leaders in international trade. He also notes that history provides examples of public reactions to fake news stories (Borel).

3. Quoting your sources directly

Sometimes the writer of a source will say something so eloquently and perceptively that you will want to include that writer's words as a **direct quotation** in your work.

In general, quote these types of sources:

- Primary sources (for example, in a text about Rita Dove, a direct quotation from her or a colleague)
- Sources containing very technical language that cannot be paraphrased
- Literary or historical sources, when you analyze the wording
- An authority in the field whose words support your thesis
- Debaters explaining their different positions on an issue

To avoid inadvertent plagiarism, be careful to indicate that the content is a direct quotation when you copy it onto your note cards or into your research notebook. Try to keep quotations short, and always place quotation marks around them. You might also use a special color to indicate direct quotations or deliberately make quotation marks oversized.

When referring to most secondary sources, paraphrase or summarize instead of quoting. Your readers will have difficulty following a text with too many quotations, and your own voice and ideas may not be heard. In some instances you may use paraphrase, summary, and quotation together. You might summarize a long passage, paraphrase an important section of it, and directly quote a short part of that section.

Note: If you have used more than one quotation every two or three paragraphs, convert most of the quotations into paraphrases *(see pp. 243–46).*

24e Integrate quotations, paraphrases, and summaries properly and effectively.

Ultimately, you will use some of the paraphrases, summaries, and quotations you have collected during the course of your research to support and develop the ideas you present in your paper. Here are some guidelines for integrating them properly and effectively into the body of your text. (Examples in this section represent MLA format for in-text citations and block quotations.)

1. Integrating brief quotations

Be selective about the quotations you include. Brief quotations can be effective if they are especially well phrased and make a significant point. But take a moment to think about your own interpretation, which might actually be better than the exact wording of the source.

Short quotations should be enclosed in quotation marks and well integrated into your sentence structure. Set off longer quotations in blocks *(see p. 253)*. The following example from Albert Rabe's text on identifying fake news sources shows the use of a short quotation:

EFFECTIVE QUOTATION

The repetition of fake news stories is another factor exacerbating the problem. As Gibbs explains, "[S]ocial scientists have shown that repetition of a false statement, even in the course of disputing it, often increases the number of people who believe it" (5).

The quotation is effective because it provides a concise explanation of a major factor contributing to the problem of fake news. Rabe integrates the quotation effectively by introducing the name of the source (*Gibbs*) and then blending the quotation into the structure of his own sentence. By contrast, the following poorly integrated quotation is not set up for the reader in that way:

POORLY INTEGRATED QUOTATION

Amateur journalists do not guarantee fact checking and do not always have professional experience relevant to the topics they cover. "Most bloggers don't produce news stories on their own. Instead they comment on news stories already out there—stories produced by journalists" (Rogers).

When you are integrating someone else's words into your writing, use a **signal phrase** that indicates whom you are quoting. The signal phrase "As Gibbs explains," identifies Gibbs as the source of the quotation in the effective passage above.

A signal phrase clearly indicates where your words end and the source's words begin. The first time you quote a source, include the author's full name and credentials, such as, "*Time* editor Nancy Gibbs explains. . ." You may also include the title of the work for context: "For example, in her article, 'When a President Can't Be Taken at His Word,' Nancy Gibbs contends. . ."

When you introduce a brief quotation with a signal phrase, you have three basic options:

- Use a complete sentence followed by a colon.
- Use a phrase.
- Make the source's words part of your own sentence structure.

A complete sentence followed by a colon   Introducing a quotation with a complete sentence allows you to provide context for the quotation. Use a colon (:) at the end of this introductory sentence.

| COMPLETE SENTENCE | *Time* editor Nancy Gibbs asserts that "a great many things" our elected leader says are untrue: "During the 2016 campaign, 70% of the Trump statements reviewed by PolitiFact were false, 4% were entirely true, 11% mostly true" (5). |

An introductory or explanatory phrase, followed by a comma.   Phrases move the reader efficiently to the quotation.

| PHRASE | As *Time* editor Nancy Gibbs writes, "During the 2016 campaign, 70% of the Trump statements reviewed by PolitiFact were false, 4% were entirely true, 11% mostly true" (5). |

Instead of introducing a quotation, the signal phrase can follow or interrupt it.

| FOLLOWS | "During the 2016 campaign, 70% of the Trump statements reviewed by PolitiFact were false, 4% were entirely true, 11% mostly true," writes *Time* editor Nancy Gibbs (5). |

| INTERRUPTS | "During the 2016 campaign," writes *Time* editor Nancy Gibbs, "70% of the Trump statements reviewed by PolitiFact were false, 4% were entirely true, 11% mostly true" (5). |

Part of your sentence structure   When you can, integrate the quotation as part of your own sentence structure without any punctuation between your words and the words you are quoting. By doing so, you will clearly connect the quoted material with your own ideas.

| QUOTATION INTEGRATED | *Time* editor Nancy Gibbs writes that "a great many things" our elected leader says "are demonstrably false" (5). |

The verb you use in a signal phrase, such as *refutes* or *summarizes,* should show how you are using the quotation in your text. If your source provides an example that strengthens your argument, you could say, "Mann *supports* this line of reasoning." *(For more on varying signal phrases, see the box on p. 253.)*

MLA style places signal phrase verbs in present tense *(Johnson writes)* while APA uses past tense *(Johnson wrote). (See Chapter 25, pp. 254-59, for more on these documentation styles.)* When a quotation, paraphrase, or summary in MLA or APA style begins with a signal phrase, the ending citation includes the page number (unless the work lacks page numbers). You can quote without a signal phrase if you give the author's name in the parenthetical citation.

Brackets and ellipses are important tools for integrating quotations into your text:

- **Brackets within quotations** Sentences that include quotations must make sense grammatically. Sometimes you may have to adjust a quotation to make it fit your sentence. Use brackets to indicate any such minor adjustments. For example, *Social* has been changed to *social* to make the quotation fit in the following sentence.

Journalists, editors, and publishers are no longer the primary gatekeepers; instead, "[s]ocial media have effectively turned us all into publishers," writes Brooke Borel.

- **Ellipses within quotations** Use ellipses (. . .) to indicate that words have been omitted from the body of a quotation, but be sure that what you omit does not significantly alter the source's meaning:

New Yorker columnist Elizabeth Kolbert explains one reason that people find fake news believable: when reading or watching the news, people tend to experience "confirmation bias,"[1] or "the tendency . . . to embrace information that supports their beliefs and reject information that contradicts them."

(For more on using ellipses, see Tab 11: Editing for Correctness, pp. 528–29.)

—CHECKLIST Paraphrasing, Summarizing, and Quoting Sources

Paraphrases

☐ Have I used my own words and sentence structure for all paraphrases?
☐ Have I maintained the original meaning?

Summaries

☐ Do all my summaries include my own wording and sentence structure? Are they shorter than the original text?
☐ Do they accurately represent the content of the original?

Quotations

☐ Have I enclosed in quotation marks any uncommon terms, distinctive phrases, or direct quotations from a source?
☐ Have I checked all quotations against the original source?
☐ Do I include ellipsis marks and brackets where I have altered the original wording and capitalization of quotations?

Documentation

☐ Have I indicated my source for all quotations, paraphrases, summaries, statistics, and visuals either within the text or in a parenthetical citation?
☐ Have I included page numbers, when available, as required for all quotations, paraphrases, and summaries?
☐ Does every in-text citation have a corresponding entry in the list of works cited or references?

2. Using long quotations in block format

Quotations longer than four lines should be used rarely because they tend to break up the text and make readers impatient. Research projects should consist primarily of your own analysis of sources. Always tell your readers why you want them to read a long quotation, and be sure to comment on it afterward.

If you use a verse quotation longer than three lines or a prose quotation longer than four typed lines, set the quotation off on a new line and indent each line one-half inch from the left margin. *(This is MLA style; for APA style, see Tab 7.)* Double-space above and below the quotation. If the quotation is more than one paragraph, indent the first line of each new paragraph a quarter inch. Do not use quotation marks. Writers often introduce a block quotation with a sentence ending in a colon. *(For examples of block quotations, see the sample student papers in Chapter 30, p. 306, and Chapter 34, p. 351.)*

3. Integrating paraphrases and summaries

The principles for integrating paraphrases and summaries into your text are similar to those for including direct quotations. Make a smooth transition between a source's point and your own voice, accurately attributing the information to the source. Use signal phrases to introduce ideas you have borrowed from your sources.

NAVIGATING THROUGH COLLEGE AND BEYOND

Varying Signal Phrases

To keep your work interesting, to show the original writer's purpose (*Martinez describes* or *Lin argues*), and to connect the quote to your reasoning (*Johnson refutes . . .*), use appropriate signal verbs such as the following:

according to	contends	points out
acknowledges	denies	proposes
adds	describes	proves
admits	emphasizes	refutes
argues	explains	rejects
asks	expresses	remarks
asserts	finds	reports
charges	holds	responds
claims	implies	shows
comments	insists	speculates
complains	interprets	states
concedes	maintains	suggests
concludes	notes	verifies
considers	observes	warns

Besides crediting others for their work, signal phrases make ideas more interesting by giving them a human face. When the source you are quoting from uses page numbers, include a citation after the paraphrase or summary. The following examples are from online articles, so page numbers are not referenced.

> *New Yorker* columnist Elizabeth Kolbert explains one reason that people find fake news believable: when reading or watching the news, people tend to experience "confirmation bias."

In the preceding passage, Albert Rabe uses the signal phrase *New Yorker columnist Elizabeth Kolbert explains* to identify Kolbert as the source of the paraphrased information about confirmation bias.

> *USA Today* journalists Lori Robertson and Robert Farley further fact-checked the administration's claims by gathering information about Metro ridership and by studying videos of the event.

The preceding passage in Rabe's text about fake news uses the signal phrase *USA Today journalists Lori Robertson and Robert Farley further fact-checked* to lead into a summary of the source's methods for researching the topic. He directly names the source, so he does not need additional parenthetical documentation.

CHAPTER 25

Writing the Text

You have chosen a challenging research question and have located, read, and evaluated a variety of sources. It is now time to develop a claim that will allow you to share your perspective on the issue and make use of all that you have learned.

25a   Plan and draft your text.

Begin planning by recalling the context and purpose of your text. If you have an assignment sheet, review it to see if the text is primarily supposed to inform, interpret, or argue. Think about the academic discipline or disciplines that shape the perspective of your work, and think through the special genres within those disciplines. Consider how much your audience is likely to know about your topic. Keep your overall situation in mind—purpose, audience, and context—as you decide on a claim to support and develop.

1. Deciding on a claim
Consider the question that guided your research as well as others provoked by what you have learned during the process. Revise the wording of these questions, and summarize them in a central question that is interesting and relevant to your audience *(see Chapter 18: Understanding Research, pp. 191-97)*. After you write down this question, compose an answer that you can use as your working claim, as Albert Rabe does in the following example.

RABE'S FOCAL QUESTION

How can news consumers distinguish between news that is real and news that is fake?

RABE'S WORKING CLAIM

Identifying fake news has become more difficult since the period leading up to the 2016 presidential election.

2. Outlining a plan for supporting and developing your claim

Guided by your tentative claim, outline a plan that uses your sources in a purposeful way. Decide on an organization to support your claim—chronological, problem-solution, or thematic—and develop your support by choosing facts, examples, and ideas drawn from a variety of sources. A chronological organization presents examples from earliest to most recent, and a problem-solution structure introduces an issue and a means of addressing it. A thematic organization orders examples from simple to complex, specific to general, or in another logical way. *(See Chapter 6: Drafting Text and Visuals, pp. 52-65, for more on these organizational structures.)*

For his research project on identifying fake news, Rabe decided on a thematic organization, an approach structured around raising and answering a central question.

- Introduce some of the fundamental differences between real news and fake news sources.

- Demonstrate the difficulty of distinguishing the real news from the fake, and present an example from current events.

- Using an example from current events, provide additional specific examples of how journalists have responded to the dangers of fake news.

- Include a clear definition of the term "fake news" and present statistics that illustrate the forms it can take.

- Discuss the prevalence of fake news and its spread, using quotations from experts in the fields of journalism, economics, and the social sciences.

- Discuss the importance of evaluating sources for credibility and offer helpful resources to readers for doing so.

- Conclude: Individual readers must take more responsibility for the news they consume. They must be active participants in the task of evaluating sources and take care when posting stories to social-media platforms.

To develop this outline, Rabe would need to list supporting facts, examples, or ideas for each point as well as indicate the sources of this information. Each section should center on his original thinking, backed by his analysis of sources. *(For more on developing an outline, see Chapter 5, pp. 36-51.)*

3. Organizing and evaluating your information

Your note-taking strategies will determine how you collect and organize your information. Whether you have taken notes in a research journal, in a blog, or on note cards, group them according to topic and subtopic. For example, Albert Rabe could have used the following categories to organize his notes:

Characteristics—real news vs. fake?

Definition of fake news—give specific examples

Prevalence of fake news—include stats

Responsibility—of journalists, news consumers

Helpful tips for evaluating sources—preventing spread of fake news

Sorting index cards into stacks that match up topics and subtopics allows you to see what you have gathered. A small stack of cards for a particular subtopic might mean that the subtopic is not as important as you originally thought—or that you need to do additional research focused on that specific subtopic.

If your notes are primarily on your computer, you can create a new category heading for each topic and subtopic and then copy and paste to move information to the appropriate category.

4. Writing a draft that you can revise, share, and edit

When you have a tentative claim and a plan, you are ready to write a draft. Many writers present their thesis or focal question at the end of an introductory, context-setting paragraph or two. The introduction should interest readers.

As you write beyond the introduction, be prepared to reexamine and refine your claim. When drawing on ideas from your sources, be sure to quote and paraphrase properly. *(For advice on quoting and paraphrasing, see Chapter 24, pp. 237-54.)*

Make your conclusion as memorable as possible. You may need to review the draft as a whole before writing the conclusion. In the final version of Rabe's text, on pages 306-16, note how she uses the idea of the audience becoming both consumers and producers of the news to end her argument. In doing so, she enhances her concluding point—that new forms of media are changing, and enhancing, older forms.

Rabe came up with the last line of work as he revised his first draft. Often writers will come up with fresh ideas at this stage—an excellent reason to spend time revising and editing your text. *(For more on revising, see Tab 2, pp. 29-96. For help with editing, see Tabs 9-12.)*

5. Integrating visuals

Well-chosen visuals like photographs, drawings, charts, graphs, and maps can sometimes help illustrate your argument. In some cases, a visual might itself be a subject of your analysis. Albert Rabe uses a poster that illustrates strategies for identifying fake news. He integrates this visual into his research report.

When integrating visuals, be sure to give careful attention to figure numbers and captions:

- **Figure numbers:** Both MLA and APA style require writers to number each image in a research paper. In MLA style, the word "figure" is abbreviated to "Fig." In APA style, the full word "Figure" is written out.

- **Captions:** Each visual that you include in your paper must be followed by a caption that includes the title of the visual (if given; otherwise, a brief description will do) and its source. In MLA style, each caption begins with the figure number and a period after the number (Fig. 1.); in APA style, use italics for the figure number *(Figure 1.)*.

25b   Revise your draft.

You may prefer to revise a print copy of your draft by hand, or you might find it easier to use the Track Changes feature in your wordprocessing program. Either way, be sure to keep previous versions of your drafts. It is useful to have a record of how your work evolved—especially if you need to hunt down a particular source or want to reincorporate something you used earlier in the process.

25c   Document your sources.

Be sure to acknowledge information, ideas, or words that are not your own. As noted in the box on page 232, the only exception to this principle occurs when you use information that is common knowledge, such as the chemical composition of water or the names of the thirteen original states in the US. When you tell readers what sources you have consulted, they can more readily understand your text as well as the conversation you are participating in by writing it.

The mode of documentation depends on the overall situation. How sources are documented varies by field and discipline. Choose a documentation style that is appropriate for the particular course you are taking, and use it properly and consistently.

Specific documentation styles meet the needs of different disciplines. Literature and some other humanities disciplines use MLA style. Researchers in these disciplines use many historic texts including multiple editions of certain sources. The author's name and page number, but not the year, appear in the in-text citation. The edition of the source appears in the works-cited list. The author's full name appears at the first mention of the work, and sources are referred to in present tense (because writing exists in the present).

APA style, often used by practitioners of the social sciences, places the date of a work in the in-text citation. The currency of sources matters in these disciplines. References to past research appear in the past tense, and researchers are referred to by last name only.

Chicago, or CMS, style, used by other humanities disciplines, has two forms. The first minimizes the in-text references to sources by using footnotes

CHECKLIST Revising and Editing a Research Paper

Consider these questions as you read your draft and gather feedback from your instructor and peers *(see also Checklist for Avoiding Plagiarism, Chapter 23, p. 235)*:

Claim and structure

☐ How does my project address the topic and purpose given in the assignment?

☐ Who are my readers, and how much can I assume that they know about the topic?

☐ What are the conventions of the academic discipline or disciplines in which I am working?

☐ Do I communicate in an informed, thoughtful tone, without patronizing?

☐ How well does my claim fit my evidence and reasoning?

☐ Is the central idea of each section based on my own thinking and backed with evidence from my sources?

☐ How have I dealt with the most likely critiques of my thesis?

☐ Do the transitions from section to section assist the reader in moving from one topic to the next?

☐ What evidence do I use to support each point? Is it sufficient?

Editing: Use of sources

☐ Do my paraphrases and summaries alter the wording and sentence structure, but not the meaning, of the original text?

☐ Have I checked all quotations for accuracy and used ellipses or brackets where necessary?

☐ Do signal phrases set off and establish context for quotations, paraphrases, and summaries?

☐ Have I provided adequate in-text citation for each source?

☐ Do my in-text citations match my works-cited or references page?

☐ Do all my illustrations have complete and accurate captions?

(See also the checklists Revising Content and Organization, p. 69, Editing for Style and Grammar, p. 79, and Proofreading, p. 81.)

or endnotes indicated by superscript numerals. Disciplines that use it, such as history, tend to use many sources. An alternative form of CMS resembles APA style.

CSE style, used by the sciences, has different forms. Name-year style shares important features with APA style, while citation-sequence and citation-name style use endnotes. The prevalence of abbreviations in CSE style indicates that researchers are expected to know the major texts in their fields.

SPECIFIC DISCIPLINE	POSSIBLE STYLE MANUAL
Chemistry	Coghill, Anne M., and Lorrin R. Garson, eds. *The ACS Style Guide: A Manual for Authors and Editors.* 3rd ed., American Chemical Society, 2006.
Geology	Bates, Robert L., Rex Buchanan, and Marla Adkins-Heljeson, eds. *Geowriting: A Guide to Writing, Editing, and Printing in Earth Science.* 5th ed., American Geological Institute, 1995.
Government and law	Garner, Diane L., and Diane H. Smith, eds. *The Complete Guide to Citing Government Information Resources: A Manual for Writers and Librarians.* Rev. ed., Congressional Information Service, 1993.
	Harvard Law Review et al. *The Bluebook: A Uniform System of Citation.* 20th ed., Harvard Law Review Assn., 2015.
Journalism	Goldstein, Norm, ed. *Associated Press Stylebook, and Briefing on Media Law.* Revised and updated ed., Basic Books, 2017.
Linguistics	Linguistic Society of America. "LSA Style Sheet." *LSA Bulletin.* Published annually in the December issue.
Mathematics	American Mathematical Society. *AMS Author Handbook: General Instructions for Preparing Manuscripts,* AMS, 2007.
Medicine	Iverson, Cheryl, ed. *American Medical Association Manual of Style: A Guide for Authors and Editors.* 10th ed., Oxford UP, 2007.
Political science	American Political Science Association. *Style Manual for Political Science.* Rev. ed., APSA, 2006.

FIGURE 25.1 Style manuals for specific disciplines.

If you are not sure which of the four styles covered in this handbook to use, ask your instructor. If you are required to use an alternative, discipline-specific documentation style, consult the list of manuals in Figure 25.1.

For his research project on fake news, Albert Rabe used the MLA documentation style. *(The final draft of the text appears in Tab 6: MLA Documentation, on pp. 261–316.)*

Credits

p. 244 Jay Rosen, "The New News," *Technology Review*, January/February 2010, http://www. technologyreview.com/communications/24175/?a=f. **p. 245** Tony Rogers, "Can Bloggers Replace Professional Journalists?" About.com Journalism. About.com, November 25, 2013. **p. 246** Richard D. Bardgett and David J. Gibson, "Plant ecological solutions to global food security," *Journal of Ecology* 105(4) July 2017. Reprinted by permission of John Wiley & Sons, Inc. **p. 248** Brooke Borel, "Fact-Checking Won't Save Us From Fake News," FiveThirtyEight, January 4, 2017. https://fivethirtyeight.com/features/fact-checking-wont-save-us-from-fake-news/. **p. 250** Tony Rogers, "Can Bloggers Replace Professional Journalists?" About.com Journalism. About.com, November 25, 2013.

6

MLA
Documentation
Style

Next to the originator of a good sentence is the first quoter of it.

–Ralph Waldo Emerson

Built near the site of the Great Library of Alexandria, Egypt, an ancient storehouse of knowledge that was destroyed by fire in the fourth century C.E., the new Bibliotheca Alexandrina offers a variety of collections and programs, including books, rare manuscripts, and a science museum.

6 MLA Documentation Style

MLA style requires writers to provide bibliographic information about their sources in a works-cited list. To format works-cited entries correctly, you need to know first of all what kind of source you are citing. The directory on pages 282–83 will help you find the appropriate sample to use as your model. As an alternative, you can use the charts on the pages that follow. Answering the questions provided in the charts will usually lead you to the sample entry you need. If you cannot find what you are looking for, consult your instructor for help.

 Sections dealing with visual rhetoric. For a complete listing, see the Quick Guide to Key Resources in Connect.

The Elements of an MLA Works-Cited Entry:

Book

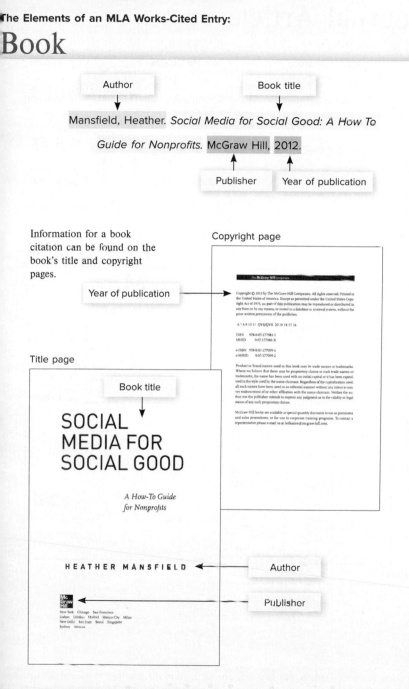

Author

Book title

Mansfield, Heather. *Social Media for Social Good: A How To Guide for Nonprofits.* McGraw Hill, 2012.

Publisher

Year of publication

Information for a book citation can be found on the book's title and copyright pages.

Copyright page

Year of publication

Title page

Book title

SOCIAL
MEDIA FOR
SOCIAL GOOD

A How-To Guide
for Nonprofits

HEATHER MANSFIELD

Author

Publisher

The Elements of an MLA Works-Cited Entry:

Journal Article

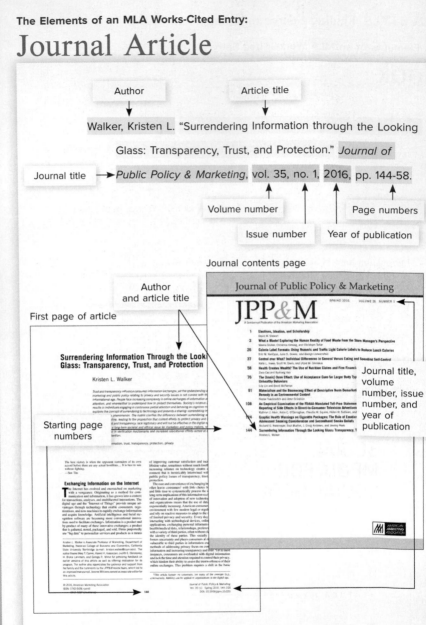

Author → Walker, Kristen L.

Article title → "Surrendering Information through the Looking Glass: Transparency, Trust, and Protection."

Journal title → *Journal of Public Policy & Marketing*, vol. 35, no. 1, 2016, pp. 144-58.

Volume number

Page numbers

Issue number   Year of publication

Journal contents page

Author and article title

First page of article

Journal of Public Policy & Marketing

JPP&M

A Semiannual Publication of the American Marketing Association

SPRING 2016   VOLUME 35   NUMBER 1

Surrendering Information Through the Looking Glass: Transparency, Trust, and Protection

Kristen L. Walker

Starting page numbers

Journal title, volume number, issue number, and year of publication

Exchanging Information on the Internet

Some academic journals, like this one, provide most of the information needed for a citation on the first page of an article as well as, like others, on the cover or contents page. You will need to look at the article's last page for the last page number.

Journal Article from an
Online Database

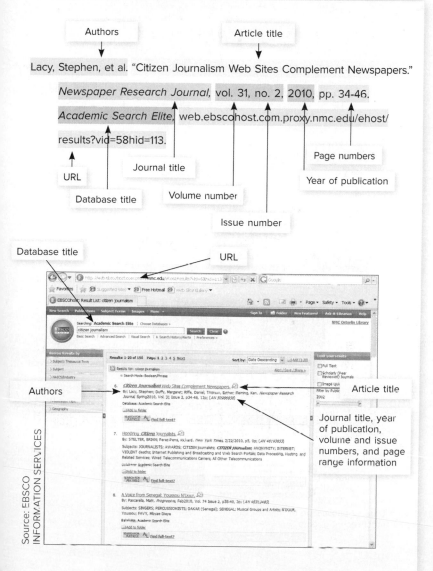

Authors

Article title

Lacy, Stephen, et al. "Citizen Journalism Web Sites Complement Newspapers."

Newspaper Research Journal, vol. 31, no. 2, 2010, pp. 34-46.

Academic Search Elite, web.ebscohost.com.proxy.nmc.edu/ehost/

results?vid=58hid=113.

URL

Journal title

Database title

Volume number

Issue number

Page numbers

Year of publication

Database title

URL

Authors

Article title

Journal title, year of publication, volume and issue numbers, and page range information

citation for an article obtained from an online database includes information about the database in addition to information about the print version of the article. When a work has three or more authors, use the abbreviation *et al.* (meaning "and others") after the first name.

The Elements of an MLA Works-Cited Entry:

Short Work on a
Web Site

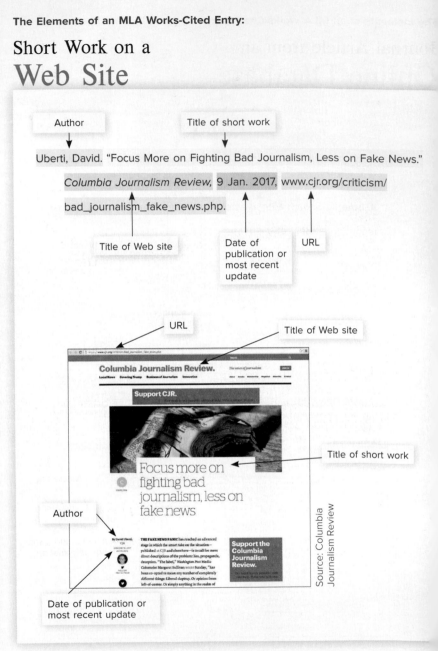

Author

Title of short work

Uberti, David. "Focus More on Fighting Bad Journalism, Less on Fake News."

Columbia Journalism Review, 9 Jan. 2017, www.cjr.org/criticism/

bad_journalism_fake_news.php.

Title of Web site

Date of publication or most recent update

URL

URL

Title of Web site

Title of short work

Author

Date of publication or most recent update

Source: Columbia Journalism Review

If you cannot find the source's author or publisher, look for a link that says "About us" or "Contact us." If the site title and publisher are the same, omit the publisher. See page 290 for online scholarly journals and page 295 for works existing online and in another medium (e.g., print or film).

Authors of Any Source

Books

Articles in Periodicals

? **Is your source from an academic journal, a magazine, or a newspaper?**

NO   YES

↓ ————————————————————————————→ Go to this entry on page

Is it a review?   **39** 292
Is it a published interview?   **40** 292
Is it an editorial?   **41** 292
Is it a letter to the editor?   **42** 292

Check the next panel or the directory on pages 282–83 or consult your instructor.

Government Works

? **Is your source a government or legal document?**

NO   YES

↓ ————————————————————————————→ Go to this entry on page

Is it a government document?
  Is it a print government document?   **44** 293
  Is it a government document on a Web site?   **45** 293
  Is it a PDF file on your computer?   **68** 297
Is it from the Congressional Record?   **46** 293
Is it a legal source such as a court case?   **47** 293

Check the next panel or the directory on pages 282–83 or consult your instructor.

Academic Works

? **Is your source an academic work like conference proceedings or a dissertation?**

NO   YES

↓ ————————————————————————————→ Go to this entry on page

Is it the proceedings of a conference?   **48** 294
Is it a dissertation?
  Is it an unpublished dissertation?   **49** 294
  Is it a published dissertation?   **50** 294
  Is it a dissertation on a Web site?   **51** 294
  Is it an abstract of a dissertation?   **52** 295
Is it an article from an academic journal?   **33, 34, 35, 43** 290, 293
Is it an article from a collection of published articles? **28** 289

Check the next panel or the directory on pages 282–83 or consult your instructor.

Web and Social Media Sources

> **?** Is your source a Web site, part of a Web site, social media post, e-mail, text message, or MOO?

NO YES

↓ ──────────────────────────────→ Go to this entry on page

Is it a Web site or part of a Web site?
    Is it a whole Web site or independent online work?   **53** 295
    Is it a page or selection from a Web site or larger online work?   **54** 295
    Is it a course Web page?   **55** 295
    Is it a work of art or photograph on a Web site?   **74, 75** 298, 299
    Is it a film or video on a Web site?   **81** 300
    Is it a radio or television program on a Web site?   **64** 300
    Is it a podcast or sound recording?   **86, 87** 301
Is it a blog?   **56** 295
    Is it a post on *Tumblr*?   **57** 296
Is it a post to a news group or forum?   **58** 296
Is it a comment on a Web page?   **59** 296
Is it an entry in a wiki?   **60** 296
    Is it a *Wikipedia* article?   **32** 290
Is it from a social media site?
    Is it a personal page on a social media site?   **61** 296
    Is it a post on *Facebook*?   **62** 296
    Is it a post on *Twitter* (a tweet)?   **63** 297
    Is it a post on *Instagram*?   **64** 297
    Is it a post on *Snapchat*?   **65** 297
Is it an e-mail or text message?   **66** 297
Is it a MOO or other real-time communication?   **67** 297

Check the next panel or the directory on pages 282–83 or consult your instructor.

Other Electronic Sources

> **?** Is it another type of digital source?

NO YES

↓ ──────────────────────────────→ Go to this entry on page

Is it a digital file on your computer?   **68** 297
Is it computer software?   **69** 298
Is it a video game?   **70** 298
Is it from a mobile app?   **71** 298

Check the next panel or the directory on pages 282–83 or consult your instructor.

Visuals, Film, Audio, and Other Media

? Is your source a visual, film, radio, television, audio, or other media?

NO   YES

⬇ ─────────────────────────────────→ Go to this entry on page

Check the next panel or the directory on pages 282–83 or consult your instructor.

Miscellaneous Other Sources

? Is it another type of source?

NO   YES

⬇ ─────────────────────────────────→ Go to this entry on page

Check the directory on pages 282–83 or consult your instructor.

The documentation style developed by the Modern Language Association (MLA) is used by many researchers in the arts and humanities, especially by those who write about language and literature. The guidelines presented here are based on the ninth edition of the *MLA Handbook* (New York: MLA, 2021).

College texts include information, ideas, and quotations from sources that must be accurately documented. Documentation allows others to see the path you have taken in researching and writing your paper. *(For more on what to document, see Tab 5: Researching, pp. 237-54.)*

The MLA documentation style has three parts:

- In-text citations
- List of works cited
- Explanatory notes and acknowledgments

In-text citations and a list of works cited are mandatory; explanatory notes are optional.

CHAPTER 26

MLA Style: In-Text Citations

In-text citations let readers know that they can find full bibliographical information about your sources in the list of works cited at the end of your paper.

1. Author named in sentence   In your first reference, give the author's full name as the source presents it. Afterward, use the last name only, unless two or more of your sources have the same last name *(see no. 6)* or unless two or more works by the same author appear in your works-cited list *(no. 3)*.

signal phrase

> James Wolcott writes in *Vanity Fair*, "[W]e've witnessed a reveille
> call in major newsrooms, . . . a renaissance of investigative
> reporting, journalistic bombshells bursting in air. Fake news,
> prepare to die" (57).

The parenthetical page citation comes after the closing quotation mark but before the period.

2. Author named in parentheses   If you do not name the source's author in your sentence, then you must provide the name in the parentheses. If the source has two authors give both names separated by *and*. (Give the full name if the author of another source has the same last name.)

> The Internet has allowed the spread of news—real and
> fake—to happen in the blink of an eye, often with "no significant
> third party filtering, fact-checking, or editorial judgment"
> *no comma after authors' names*
> (Allcott and Gentzkow 211).

There is no comma between the author's name and the page number. If you cite two or more distinct pages, however, separate the numbers with a comma: (Allcott and Gentzkow 211, 215).

3. Two or more works by the same author   If you use two or more works by the same author, you must identify which work you are citing, either in your sentence or in an abbreviated form in parentheses: (Karim, "Writing").

> Poet and professor of comparative literature Persis Karim explains
> that "exile [is] a mixed blessing of losing and leaving behind but
> also acquiring new perspectives, languages, and experiences that
> *article title is abbreviated*
> enrich and texture their writing" ("Writing").

MLA IN-TEXT CITATIONS: Directory to Sample Types

(See pp. 279-302 for works-cited examples.)

4. Two authors of the same work   If a source has two authors, you should name them both either in your text, as the next example shows, or in parentheses: (Channell and Crusius 2).

> In *Engaging Questions: A Guide to Writing,* Carolyn E. Channell and Timothy W. Crusius emphasize the importance of questioning when thinking, discussing, reading, and writing (2).

5. More than two authors   If a source has more than two authors, give the first author's name followed by a phrase such as "and colleagues" in the text or *et al.* (not italicized), meaning "and others," in the citation. (Note that *et,* which means "and," is fine as is, but *al.,* which is an abbreviation for *alia,* needs a period). Do the same in your works-cited list.

Changes in social regulations are bound to produce new forms of subjectivity (Henriques et al. 275).

6. Authors with the same last name If the authors of two or more of your sources have the same last name, include the first initial of the author you are citing (R. Campbell 63); if the first initial is also shared, use the full first name, as shown in the following example.

In the late nineteenth century, the sale of sheet music spread rapidly in New York's Tin Pan Alley (Richard Campbell 63).

7. Organization as author Treat the organization as the author. If the name is long, put it in a signal phrase.

The Centre for Contemporary Cultural Studies claims that "there is nothing inherently concrete about historiography" (10).

MLA IN-TEXT CITATIONS

- Name the author, either in a signal phrase such as "Clay Shirky compares" or in a parenthetical citation, using the last name only. After giving the author's full name at first mention, you can use only the author's last name in the signal phrase ("Shirky goes on to explain").
- Include a page reference in parentheses. No "p." precedes the page number; if the author is named in the parentheses, there is no punctuation between the author's name and the page number.
- Place the citation as close to the material being cited as possible and before any punctuation marks that divide or end the sentence except in a block quotation, where the citation comes one space after the period or final punctuation mark. See no. 12 for quotations ending with a question mark or an exclamation point.
- Italicize the titles of books, magazines, Web sites, and plays. Place quotation marks around the titles of articles and short poems
- For Internet sources, follow the same general guidelines as for print sources. Keep the parenthetical citation simple, providing enough information for your reader to find the full citation in your works-cited list. Cite either the author's name or the title of the site or article. Begin the parenthetical citation with the first word of the corresponding works-cited list entry.
- For works without page or paragraph numbers, give the author or title only. Often it is best to mention the author or title in your sentence, in which case no parenthetical citation is needed.

8. Unknown author   When no author is given, cite a work by its title, using either the full title in a signal phrase or an abbreviated version in the parentheses if the title is lengthy. When abbreviating the title, begin with the word by which it is alphabetized in your works-cited list. If the word is a modifier, include the noun the word modifies (*A Short History of Nearly Everything* would be abbreviated as *Short History*).

title of article

"Squaresville, USA vs. Beatsville" makes the Midwestern small-

town home seem boring compared with the West Coast artist's

"pad" (31).

The Midwestern small-town home seems boring compared with

the West Coast artist's "pad" ("Squaresville" 31).

9. Entire work   Acknowledge an entire work in your text, not in a parenthetical citation. Include the work in your list of works cited, and include in the text the word by which the entry is alphabetized.

Sidney J. Furie's film *Lady Sings the Blues* presents Billie Holiday

as a beautiful woman in pain rather than as the great jazz artist

she was.

10. Paraphrased or summarized source   If you include the author's name in your paraphrase or summary, include only the page number or numbers in parentheses. Signal phrases clarify that you are paraphrasing or summarizing.

signal phrase

Louise France, reporting for *The Times*, notes that while parents

tend to restrict the physical places their children can go—to the

mall or the movies, for example—too often they are not paying

attention to their children's activities on the Internet (8).

11. Source of a long quotation   For a quotation of more than four typed lines of prose or three of poetry, do not use quotation marks. Instead, indent the material you are quoting by one-half inch. Following the final punctuation mark of the quotation, allow one space before any parenthetical information.

The Bureau of Labor Statistics reports a troubling job outlook for

journalists:

> Overall employment of reporters, correspondents, and
>
> broadcast news analysts is projected to decline 10 percent
>
> from 2016 to 2026. Employment of reporters and
>
> correspondents is projected to decline 11 percent, while

employment of broadcast news analysts is projected to show little or no change from 2016 to 2026. Declining advertising revenue in radio, newspapers, and television will negatively affect the employment growth for these occupations. ("Job Outlook")

12. Source of a short quotation Close the quotation before the parenthetical citation. If the quotation concludes with an exclamation point or a question mark, place the closing quotation mark after that punctuation mark, and place the sentence period after the parenthetical citation.

Encyclopaedia Britannica defines a *blog,* short for *Web log,* as an "online journal where an individual, group, or corporation presents a record of activities, thoughts, or beliefs" ("Blog").

Shakespeare's Sonnet XVIII asks, "Shall I compare thee to a summer's day?" (line 1).

13. One-page source You need not include a page number in the parenthetical citation for a one-page printed source.

14. Government publication To avoid an overly long parenthetical citation, name the government agency that published the source within your text.

According to a report issued by the Bureau of National Affairs, many employers in 1964 needed guidance to apply new workplace rules that ensured fairness and complied with the Civil Rights Act of 1964 (32).

15. Photograph, map, graph, chart, or other visual

VISUAL APPEARS IN YOUR TEXT

An aerial photograph of Manhattan (Fig. 3), taken by the United States Geographical Survey, demonstrates how creative city planning can introduce parks and green spaces within even the most densely populated urban areas.

If the caption you write for the image includes all the information found in a works cited list entry, you need not include it in your list.

VISUAL DOES NOT APPEAR IN YOUR TEXT

An aerial photograph of Manhattan taken by the United States Geographical Survey demonstrates how creative city planning can introduce parks and green spaces within even the most densely populated urban areas (TerraServer-USA).

Provide a parenthetical citation that directs your reader to information about the source of the image in your works-cited list.

16. Web site or other online electronic source   If you cannot find the author of an online source, then identify the source by title or publisher, either in your text or in a parenthetical citation. Because most online sources do not have set page, section, or paragraph numbers, they must usually be cited as entire works.

organization cited as author
The Pew Research Center's Project for Excellence in Journalism points out that print advertising is consistently declining with each year.
page number not provided

17. Work with numbered paragraphs or sections instead of pages   To distinguish them from page numbers, use the abbreviations *par(s).* or *sec(s).* or the type of division such as *screen(s).*

Rothstein suggests that many German Romantic musical techniques may have originated in Italian opera (par. 9).

Give the paragraph or section number(s) after the author's name and a comma in a parenthetical citation: (Rothstein, par. 9).

18. Work with no page or paragraph numbers   When citing an electronic or print source without page, paragraph, or other reference numbers, try to include the author's name in your text instead of in a parenthetical citation.

In "Gap-Year Travel Brings Students Back to Learning," reporter
author's name
John Ross cites recent research and explains how a gap year might positively or negatively affect the college experience.

19. Multivolume work   When citing more than one volume of a multivolume work in your paper, include with each citation the volume number, followed by a colon, a space, and the page number.

Scott argues that today people tend to solve problems "by turning to the Web" (2: 5).

If you consult only one volume of a multivolume work, then specify that volume in the works-cited list *(see p. 285),* but not in the parenthetical citation.

20. Literary works

Novels and literary nonfiction books   Include the relevant page number, followed by a semicolon, a space, and the chapter number.

> Jenkins states that because Harry Potter's fandom involves both adults and children, it's a "space where conversations could occur across generations" (216; ch. 5).

If the author is not named in your sentence, add the name in front of the page number: (Jenkins 216; ch. 5).

Poems   Use line numbers, not page numbers.

> In "Ode on a Grecian Urn," Keats asks, "What men or gods are these? What maidens loth? / What mad pursuit? What struggle to escape?" (lines 8-9). He can provide no answer, but he notes that the lucky lovers pictured on the urn are "for ever young; / All breathing human passion far above" (27-28).

Note that the word *lines* (not italicized), rather than *l.* or *ll.,* is used in the first citation to establish what the numbers in parentheses refer to; subsequent citations need not use the word *lines.*

Plays and long, multisection poems   Use division (act, scene, canto, book, part) and lines, not page numbers. In the following example, notice that Arabic numerals are used for act and scene divisions as well as for line numbers: (*Hamlet* 2.3.22-27). The same is true for canto, verse, and lines in the following citation of Byron's *Don Juan:* (*Don Juan* 1.37.4-8).

21. Religious text   Cite material in the Bible, Upanishads, or Koran by book, chapter, and verse, using an appropriate abbreviation when the name of the book is in the parentheses rather than in your sentence.

> As the Bible says, "The wise man knows there will be a time of judgment" (*Holy Bible,* Eccles. 8.5).

Note that general titles of scriptural writings are not italicized.

22. Historical document   For familiar documents such as the Constitution and the Declaration of Independence, provide the document's name and the numbers of the parts you are citing.

> Judges are allowed to remain in office "during good behavior," a vague standard that has had various interpretations (US Constitution, art. 3, sec. 1).

23. Indirect source   When you quote or paraphrase a quotation you found in someone else's work, put *qtd. in* (not italicized, meaning "quoted in," with a period after the abbreviation) before the name of your source.

> According to *Facebook* engineers, *Instagram* will use an algorithm
> that "can understand with near-human accuracy the textual content of
> several thousand posts per second" (qtd. in Bayern).

In your list of works cited, list only the work you consulted, in this case the indirect source by Bayern.

24. Two or more sources in one citation   When you credit two or more sources for the same idea, use a semicolon to separate the citations.

> The impact of blogging on human knowledge, communication, and
> interactions has led to improvements in our daily lives. We are not
> only more up to date on the latest goings-on in the world, but we
> are also connected to other informed citizens like never before
> (Ingram; Shirky).

25. Two or more sources in one sentence   Include a parenthetical reference after each idea or quotation you have borrowed.

> Ironically, Americans lavish more money each year on their pets
> than they spend on children's toys (Merkins 21), but the feral cat
> population—consisting of abandoned pets and their offspring—is
> at an estimated 70 million and growing (Mott).

26. Work in an anthology   When citing a work in a collection, give the name of the specific work's author, not the name of the editor of the whole collection.

> "Exile marks us like a talisman or tattoo. It teaches us how to
> endure long nights and short days" (Agosin 273).

Here, Agosin is cited as the source, even though his work appears in a collection edited by Rigoberto Gonzalez. Note that the list of works cited must include an entry for Agosin.

27. E-mail, letter, or personal interview   Cite by name the person you communicated with, using either a signal phrase or parentheses.

> Blogging is a beneficial tool to use in the classroom because it
> allows students to keep up with new media trends (Carter).

In the works-cited list, after giving the person's last name you will need to identify the kind of communication and its date *(see pp. 297, and 302).*

CHAPTER 27

MLA Style: List of Works Cited

MLA documentation style requires a works-cited page with full bibliographic information about your sources. The list of works cited should appear at the end of your research project, beginning on a new page entitled "Works Cited." Include only those sources you cite, unless your instructor tells you to prepare a "Works Consulted" list.

ORGANIZING THE ELEMENTS OF AN MLA WORKS-CITED ENTRY

MLA classifies the bibliographic information into nine core elements. A few sources have all the core elements; most have fewer. Whatever type of source you are using, the citation's core elements appear in the same sequence. If a citation lacks a core element, simply omit that element.

1. **Author.**   The author is the person or people who wrote or created the source or whose work is the subject of your paper. This is usually the writer, but it can also be an editor, translator, illustrator, director, composer, artist, photographer, or performer if that person is the focus of your paper.

2. **Title of source.**   This is the title of the specific source you are using. The specific source can be a book, an article, a poem, a short story, a Web page, a blog post, a work of art, a song, a movie, or an episode of a television program.

3. **Title of container.**   The *container* is MLA's name for the title of the larger work in which a specific source appears. A container can be an anthology, an encyclopedia, a journal or other periodical, a Web site, an online database, a mobile application, a television series, and so on. Some sources, such as complete print books and whole Web sites, have no containers. Other sources may have one or two containers. For example, a print article may have one container—the journal—but the online version of the article has two containers—the journal and the online database in which the journal appears.

4. **Other contributors.**   Contributors include people who have an important role in the work unless they have been treated as the author (element 1). Editors, translators, illustrators, directors, performers, screenwriters, composers, and lyricists may be included as other contributors using phrases such as "translated by" and "performance by."

(Continued)

ORGANIZING THE ELEMENTS OF AN MLA WORKS-CITED ENTRY *(Continued)*

5. **Version.** A source may indicate it is a particular version, such as an edition of a book, the director's cut of a film, or the numbered version of a software program.

6. **Number.** A source may be one item in a numbered sequence. For example, the volume number of a mulitvolume book, a journal's volume number and issue number, and a television program's season number and episode number would be included.

7. **Publisher.** The publisher is the organization primarily responsible for producing the work. The publisher may be a book publisher, movie studio, television network, record label, museum, library, or university. Some sources do not require the publisher to be listed; these include periodical articles, self-published works, and a Web site whose title is the same as its publisher. (Note that Web sites like *YouTube* and online databases such as *EBSCOhost*, which serve as locations for the content of others, are considered containers rather than publishers.)

8. **Publication date.** This is the date the source was published in the form you consulted. It could include the year, month, date, and even time.

9. **Location.** The location is the place in a container where the specific source can be found, such as a page range, a digital object identifier (DOI), permalink, uniform resource locator (URL), or a place and city for original works of art, lectures, or performances. Note that a DOI or permalink is preferable to a URL, as URLs often change.

BASIC WORKS-CITED ENTRY WITH ALL CORE ELEMENTS

[1] Author. [2] Title of source. [3] Title of container, [4] Other contributors, [5] Version, [6] Number, [7] Publisher, [8] Publication date, [9] Location.

WORKS-CITED ENTRY WITH NO CONTAINER

[1] Towles, Amor. [2] *A Gentleman in Moscow.* [5] E-book ed., [7] Penguin Random House, [8] 2016.

WORKS-CITED ENTRY WITH ONE CONTAINER

[1] Noguchi, Yone. [2] "Lines." [3] *A Collection of Verse by California Poets, from 1849 to 1915,* [4] edited by Augustin S. MacDonald, [7] A. M. Robertson, [8] 1914.

WORKS-CITED ENTRY WITH TWO CONTAINERS

[1] Noguchi, Yone. [2] "Lines." [3] *A Collection of Verse by California Poets, from 1849 to 1915,* [4] edited by Augustin S. MacDonald, [7] A. M. Robertson, [8] 1914. [3] *Bartleby.com,* [8] 2011, [9] www.bartleby.com/260/54.html.

Authors of Any Source

1. One author

> Shirky, Clay. *Here Comes Everybody: The Power of Organizing*
>
> > *without Organizations.* Penguin Press, 2008.

2. Two authors   Name the two authors in the order in which they appear in the source, putting the last name first for the first author only.

> Ottolenghi, Yotam, and Sami Tamimi. *Jerusalem: A Cookbook.* Ten
>
> > Speed Press, 2012.

3. Three or more authors   Use the abbreviation *et al.* (meaning "and others") to replace the names of all authors except the first.

> Schaffner, Ingrid, et al. *Maira Kalman: Various Illuminations (Of a*
>
> > *Crazy World).* Prestel Publishing, 2010.

4. Two or more works by the same author(s)   Give the author's name in the first entry only. For subsequent works authored by that person, replace the name with three hyphens and a period. Alphabetize by title.

> Shirky, Clay. *Here Comes Everybody: The Power of Organizing*
>
> > *without Organizations.* Penguin Press, 2008.
>
> ---. "Newspapers and Thinking the Unthinkable." *Risk Management,*
>
> > vol. 56, no. 4, May 2009, pp. 24–29.

5. Organization as author   Consider as an organization any group, commission, association, or corporation whose members are not identified.

> Centre for Contemporary Cultural Studies. *Women Take Issue:*
>
> > *Aspects of Women's Subordination.* Routledge, 2007.

6. Unknown author   The citation begins with the title. In the list of works cited, alphabetize the citation by the first important word, excluding the articles *A, An,* and *The.*

> "Salem: Curse Victims, Meet Adam Smith." *The Boston Globe,*
>
> > 2 Nov. 2013, p. A10.
>
> *Webster's College Dictionary.* Random House / McGraw-Hill, 1991.

Note that this entry includes both of the publishers listed on the dictionary's title page; they are separated by a slash.

MLA WORKS-CITED ENTRIES: Directory to Sample Types

(See pp. 271-78 for examples of in-text citations.)

MLA WORKS-CITED ENTRIES: *(Continued)*

Complete Books

7. Basic entry for a book   See page 286 for guidance on styling the names of university and commercial publishers.

> Vance, J. D. *Hillbilly Elegy: A Memoir of a Family and Culture in*
>
> > *Crisis.* HarperCollins Publishers, 2016.

8. Book on a Web site   First give the print publication information, then the Web site information.

> Arter, Jared Maurice. *Echoes from a Pioneer Life.* Caldwell, 1922.
>
> > *Documenting the American South,* U of North Carolina, 2004,
> >
> > docsouth.unc.edu/neh/arter/menu.html.

9. Book in an online database

> Gaskell, Elizabeth Cleghorn. *North and South.* Harper and Brothers,
>
> > 1855. *Google Books,* books.google.com/books?id=
> >
> > yMNHwH4hT7AC&pg=PP1#v=onepage&q&f=false.

10. E-book   Add the e-book edition after the title.

> McCann, Colum. *TransAtlantic.* E-book ed., Random House, 2013.

11. Book by an editor or editors   If the title page lists an editor instead of an author, begin with the editor's name followed by the word *editor* (not italicized). Use *editors* when more than one editor is listed. When a book's title contains the title of another book (as this one does), do not italicize the title-within-a-title (here, *Dr. Who*).

> *title in title not italicized*
>
> Leitch, Gillian, editor. Dr. Who *in Time and Space: Essays on*
>
> > *Themes, Characters, History and Fandom.* McFarland, 2013.

12. Book with an author and other contributors   Put the author and title first. Then list any contributors, such as editors, translators, or illustrators, with a phrase describing their work. If you focus on the work of the contributor, list the contributor in the author position with that person's role, as in the Tenniel entry.

> James, Henry. *The Portrait of a Lady.* Edited by Robert D. Bamberg,
>
> > W. W. Norton, 1975.

Oz, Amos. *Scenes from Village Life*. Translated by Nicholas de

Lange, Mariner Books, 2012.

Carroll, Lewis. *Alice's Adventures in Wonderland and through the*

Looking-Glass. Illustrated by John Tenniel, Modern Library,

2002.

Tenniel, John, illustrator. *Alice's Adventures in Wonderland and*

through the Looking-Glass. By Lewis Carroll, Modern Library,

2002.

13. Edition other than the first   Include the number of the edition: *2nd ed., 3rd ed.* (not italicized), and so on. Place the number after the title, or if there is an editor, after that person's name.

Wood, Ethel. *AP World History: An Essential Coursebook*. 2nd ed.,

WoodYard Publications, 2011.

14. Republished book   Put the original date of publication, followed by a period, before the current publication information.

original publication date

Wheatley, Dennis. *The Forbidden Territory*. 1933. Bloomsbury USA,

2014.

15. Multivolume work   The first example indicates that the researcher used more than one volume of the work; the second shows that only the first volume was used *(to cite an individual article or chapter in a multivolume work or set of reference books, refer to nos. 22 or 30)*.

Manning, Martin J., and Clarence R. Wyatt. *Encyclopedia of*

Media and Propaganda in Wartime America. ABC-CLIO, 2010.

2 vols.

Manning, Martin J., and Clarence R. Wyatt. *Encyclopedia of Media*

and Propaganda In Wartime America. Vol. 1, ABC-CLIO, 2010.

16. Book in a series   At the end of the citation, put the name of the series and, if available on the title page, the number of the work.

Wimmer, Roger D., and Joseph R. Dominick. *Mass Media Research:*

An Introduction (with InfoTrac). Wadsworth Publishing, 2005.

name of series not italicized

Wadsworth Series in Mass Communication and Journalism.

FORMATTING AND STYLING THE MLA LIST OF WORKS CITED

- **Works Cited Page.** Begin on a new page with the centered title "Works Cited." Use a hanging indent for each entry: Start the first line of each entry at the left margin, and indent all subsequent lines of the entry one-half inch. Do not number the entries. Double-space throughout the works cited (see page 279).

- **Elements of an Entry.** Include an entry for every source cited in your text. Include author, source title, and as many core elements as appropriate for each entry (see page 279). Use a period after the main parts of the citation—author, source title, and each container, if any. Use commas between elements of a container. Leave one space after periods and commas.

- **Author.** Put entries in alphabetical order by author's or editor's last name. If the work has more than one author, see nos. 2 and 3. If the author is unknown (see no. 4), alphabetize by the first word of the title, excluding the articles *A, An,* or *The.*

- **Title.** Italicize titles and subtitles of long works—books, periodicals, long poems, plays, Web sites, and databases. Put quotation marks around titles of short works—articles, short stories, Web pages, and short poems.

   Capitalize the first and last words, and all important words, in all titles and subtitles. Do not capitalize articles, prepositions, coordinating conjunctions, and the *to* in infinitives unless they appear as the first or last word in the title. Place a colon between title and subtitle unless the title ends in a question mark or an exclamation point.

- **Publisher.** Use the full name of a book publisher, omitting only business words such as *Company, Corporation,* and *Limited.* When a parent company, division, and imprint are indicated, use the division name. In the names of university presses, abbreviate *University* as *U* and *Press* as *P* (Oxford UP), but spell out *Press* in the name of a commercial publisher (Penguin Press).

- **Publication Date.** Use day-month-year format (3 Apr. 2018). Abbreviate all months except May, June, and July. If the date of publication is not given, provide the approximate date: circa 1975 (capitalize circa if it follows a period). If you cannot approximate the date, omit it.

- **Location—Page Numbers.** Use *p.* and *pp.* to indicate page and pages. When page citations over one hundred have the same first digit, do not repeat it for the second number: pp. 243-47. If the source lacks page numbers, use paragraph numbers or other divisions; otherwise omit them. For newspaper articles and other print sources that skip pages, provide the page number for the beginning of the article followed by a plus sign: p. 4+.

(Continued)

FORMATTING AND STYLING THE MLA LIST OF WORKS CITED *(Continued)*

- **Location—DOIs and URLs**. Use a *digital object identifier (DOI)* or *uniform resource locator (URL)*. A DOI is a unique identifier often assigned to academic journal articles and other works, and it is preferred to a URL. It appears at the end of a citation, preceded by "https://doi.org/" and followed by a period. See citations nos. 42, 43, and 60.

  If no DOI is available, use the source's URL. If a source has a *permalink*, or stable URL, use the permalink instead (see no. 24). Copy and paste the URL into your citation, and end with a period.

  If you need to divide a DOI or URL between lines, do not insert a hyphen.

17. Anthology

Moehringer, J. R., editor. *The Best American Sports Writing 2013*.

Mariner Books, 2013.

18. Religious text   Give the specific title, italicized; the editor's or translator's name (if any); and the publication information.

ESV New Classic Reference Bible. Crossway, 2011.

The Bhagavad Gita. Translated by Eknath Easwaran, Nilgiri, 2005.

19. Graphic novel or comic book   Cite graphic narratives created by one person as you would any other book. For collaborations, begin with the person whose work you refer to most, and list other contributors in the order in which they appear on the title page. *(For part of a series, see no. 16.)*

Fetter-Vorm, Jonathan. *Trinity: A Graphic Novel of the First Atomic Bomb*. Farrar, Straus and Giroux, 2013.

L'Engle, Madeleine. *Madeleine L'Engle's A Wrinkle in Time: The Graphic Novel*. Illustrated by Hope Larson, Farrar, Straus and Giroux, 2012.

20. Pamphlet or brochure   If the pamphlet or brochure has an author, list that person's name first; otherwise, begin with the title. End with a descriptive label.

The Digital Derry Strategy. PIKE, 2009. Brochure.

21. Book without publication information   Supply what you can, indicating any information that is approximate or speculative.

> *Lifeguard Training and Certification.* American Red Cross,
>
> > circa 2015.

Parts of Books

22. Basic entry for a part of an anthology, a textbook, or an edited collection   Start with the author and title of the selection, followed by the book's title, editor, publisher, publication date, and the page numbers of the selection. The first example cites a reading from a textbook.

> Brodkey, Linda. "On the Subjects of Class and Gender in 'The
>
> > Literacy Letters.'" *Cross-Talk in Comp Theory,* edited by Victor
> >
> > Villanueva, NCTE Press, 2003, pp. 677-96.

> Fisher, Walter R. "Narration, Knowledge, and the Possibility of
>
> > Wisdom." *Rethinking Knowledge: Reflections across the*
> >
> > *Disciplines,* edited by Robert F. Goodman and Walter R. Fisher,
> >
> > SUNY P, 1995, pp. 169-92.

23. Part of a book on a Web site

> Sandburg, Carl. "Chicago." *Chicago Poems,* Henry Holt, 1916.
>
> > *Bartleby.com*, 1999, www.bartleby.com/165/1.html.

24. Part of a book in an online database

> White, Claytee. "Using Oral History to Record the Story of the Las
>
> > Vegas African American Community." *Oral History, Community,*
> >
> > *and Work in the American West,* edited by Jessie L. Embry,
> >
> > U of Arizona P, 2013, pp. 150–74. *JSTOR*, www.jstor.org/stable/j
> >
> > .ctt183pbgk.12.

25. Part of an e-book

> Sacks, Oliver. "A General Feeling of Disorder." *The Best American*
>
> > *Essays 2016*, edited by Jonathan Franzen and Robert Atwan,
> >
> > e-book ed., Houghton Mifflin Harcourt, 2016.

26. Preface, foreword, introduction, or afterword   Begin with the author of the part of the book you are citing. If the part has a unique title, cite that title, enclosed in quotation marks. If no title is given, use the generic label without quotation marks.

> *name of part of book*
> Kraemer, Harry M. Jansen, Jr. Foreword. *Master the Matrix: 7*
>
> *Essentials for Getting Things Done in Complex Organizations,*
> *author of the book*
> by Susan Z. Finerty, Two Harbors Press, 2012, p. 1.

27. Published letter   Include the date of the letter and the number, if one was assigned by the editor.

> Hughes, Langston. "To Arna Bontemps." 17 Jan. 1938. *Arna*
>
> *Bontemps–Langston Hughes Letters 1925-1967,* edited by
>
> Charles H. Nichols, Dodd Mead, 1980, pp. 27-28.

28. Article from a collection of reprinted articles

> Haney-Peritz, Janice. "Monumental Feminism and Literature's
>
> Ancestral House: Another Look at 'The Yellow Wallpaper.'"
>
> *Women's Studies,* vol. 12, no. 2, 1986, pp. 113-28. *The Captive*
>
> *Imagination: A Casebook on "The Yellow Wallpaper,"* edited by
>
> Catherine Golden, Feminist Press, 1992, pp. 261-76.

29. Two or more items from an anthology, textbook, or edited collection   Include a complete entry for the book, beginning with the name of the editor(s). Each selection should have its own entry in the alphabetical list that includes only the author, title of the selection, editor, and page numbers.

> *entry for the anthology*
> Jacobs, Jonathan, editor. *Open Game Table: The Anthology of*
>
> *Roleplaying in Game Blogs,* Vol. 2, Open Game Table, 2010.
> *entry for a selection from the anthology*
> Jones, Jeremy. "Gaming Roots and Reflections." Jacobs, pp. 11-35.

30. Article in an encyclopedia or another reference work   If the entry has an author, begin with that person's name. If not, begin with the title of the entry in quotation marks. Include the part of speech and definition number after the entry, if applicable: "Climate, *N.* (2)."

> Hirsch, E. D. "Idioms." *Dictionary of Cultural Literacy,* 2nd ed.,
>
> Houghton Mifflin, 1993, p. 59.

31. Article in an online encyclopedia or other reference work Give your access date if the entry is undated.

> Greene, Brian R. "String Theory." *Encyclopaedia Britannica,* www
>
> .britannica.com/science/string-theory. Accessed 20 Nov. 2017.

32. Article in *Wikipedia* Check with your instructor before using a *Wikipedia* article. Click on "Page Information" to obtain the date of the article's most recent revision.

> "Arches National Park." *Wikipedia,* 15 Mar. 2021, en.wikipedia.org/
>
> wiki/Arches_National_Park.

Articles in Periodicals

Periodicals are published at set intervals, usually four times a year for scholarly journals, monthly or weekly for magazines, and daily or weekly for newspapers. Between the author and the publication date are two or three titles: the title of the article, in quotation marks; the title of the periodical, italicized; and for online articles, the title of the Web site or database.

33. Basic entry for a journal article Most journals have a volume number corresponding to the year and an issue number for each publication that year. The issue may be indicated by a month or season. If there is no volume number, give the issue number only.

> Lacy, Stephen, et al. "Citizen Journalism Web Sites Complement
>
> Newspapers." *Newspaper Research Journal,* vol. 31, no. 2, 2010,
>
> pp. 34-46.

34. Journal article on a Web site Give the publication information for the journal, followed by publication information for the Web site, including a DOI or URL (see p. 287).

> Neal, Michael, et al. "Making Meaning at the Intersections:
>
> Developing a Digital Archive for Multimodal Research." *Kairos,*
>
> vol. 17, no. 3, 2013, pp. 1-6, kairos.technorhetoric.net/17.3/topoi/
>
> neal-et-al/index.html.

35. Journal article in an online database

> Nielson, Aldon Lynn. "A Hard Rain." *Callaloo,* vol. 25, no. 1, 2002,
>
> pp. 135-45. *Project Muse,* muse.jhu.edu/article/6735.

36. Basic entry for a magazine or newspaper article   If volume numbers are available, provide them; otherwise, simply give the date in day, month, year style. For a monthly magazine, provide the month and year, abbreviating all months except May, June, and July. For a weekly publication, include the complete date: day, month, and year.

> Newman, Catherine. "My Friend Delittles My Job!" *Real Simple,* Mar.
>
> 2013, p. 67.

> Frazier, Ian. "Hidden City." *The New Yorker,* 28 Oct. 2013, pp. 38-49.

For newspapers, specify the edition, if any (Davey example), and the name of the section if not indicated by the page number (Carr example). If the article appears on nonconsecutive pages, put a plus sign after the first page number (Davey).

> Davey, Monica. "In Detroit, Mayor's Race Is One Piece of a Puzzle."
>
> *The New York Times,* national ed., 3 Nov. 2013, pp. A15+.

> Carr, Nicholas. "Attention Must Be Paid." *The New York Times,*
>
> national ed., 3 Nov. 2013, Book Review sec., p. 16.

37. Magazine or newspaper article on a Web site

> di Giovanni, Janine. "Baby You Can Drive My Car." *Newsweek,*
>
> 8 Nov. 2013, www.newsweek.com/2013/11/08/ baby-you
>
> -can-drive-my-car-243910.html.

> Morris, Loveday. "Stretched Thin, Syrian Extremists Are Pressured."
>
> *The Washington Post,* 7 Jan. 2014, www.washingtonpost.com/
>
> world/middle_east/stretched-thin-syrian-extremists-are
>
> -pressured/2014/01/07/d770a86e-77df-11e3-a647-a19deaf575b3_
>
> story.html.

38. Magazine or newspaper article in an online database   Provide the title of the database and the DOI or URL (see page 287).

> Farley, Christopher John. "Music Goes Global." *Time,* 15 Sept. 2001,
>
> pp. 4+. *EBSCOhost,* eds.a.ebscohost.com.rlib.pacc.edu/eds.

Blumenfeld, Larry. "House of Blues." *The New York Times,* 11 Nov.

2007, pp. A33+. *OneFile,* http://go.galegroup.com/ps/i.do?id=

GALE%7CA171080835&v=2.1&u=cuny_hunter&it=r&p=AONE&

sw=w&asid=3922fa61eb6c7b819ce2d471c7690e38.

39. Review   Begin with the name of the reviewer. If the review is untitled, include a short description in place of a title.

Kot, Greg. "Gaga Aims for 'Artpop' but Falls Short." *Chicago Tribune,*

8 Nov. 2013, chicagotribune.com/2013-11-08/entertainment

/chi-lady-gaga-artpop-review-20131108-17_1_artpop-lady-gaga

-dj-white-shadow.

Nussbaum, Emily. Review of *Work in Progress*, by Abby McEnany.

The New Yorker, 23 Dec. 2020, pp. 92-93.

40. Published interview   Begin with the name of the interviewee.

Gates, Bill. "We Need an Energy Miracle." Interview by James

Bennet. *The Atlantic*, Nov. 2015, www.theatlantic.com/magazine/

archive/2015/11/we-need-an-energy-miracle/407881/.

41. Editorial

Editorial Board. "Saner Gun Laws." *The New York Times*, 22 Jan.

2011, www.nytimes.com/2011/01/23/opinion/23sun1.html.

42. Letter to the editor

Schaller, Anthony B. Letter. *Albuquerque Journal*, 30 Mar. 2016,

www.abqjournal.com/748320/opinion/poor-taste-in

-choosing-photo.html.

Destaillats, Frédéric, et al. Letter. *Nutrition & Metabolism*, vol. 4,

no. 10, 2007, https://doi.org/10.1186/1743-7075-4-10.

43. Abstract of a journal article   Some abstracts are cited as part of an article (Dempsey example) or as an abstract from a collection of abstracts (Theiler example).

> Dempsey, Nicholas P. "Hook-Ups and Train Wrecks: Contextual
>
> Parameters and the Coordination of Jazz Interactions." Abstract.
>
> *Symbolic Interaction*, vol. 31, no. 1, 2008, p. 57. *JSTOR,*
>
> https://doi.org/10.1525/si.2008.31.1.57.

> Theiler, Anne M., and Louise G. Lippman. "Effects of Mental Practice
>
> and Modeling on Guitar and Vocal Performance." *Journal of*
>
> *General Psychology,* vol. 122, no. 4, 1995, pp. 329-43.
>
> *Psychological Abstracts,* vol. 83, no. 1, 1996, item 30039.

Government works

44. Government document   Either the name of the government and agency or the name of the document's author comes first. If the agency is both author and publisher, start the citation with the document title and list the agency as publisher.

> United States, Department of Homeland Security, Coast Guard.
>
> *U.S. Coast Guard Incident Management Handbook 2014.*
>
> Government Publishing Office, 2014.

45. Government document on a Web site   Begin with the name of the country, followed by the name of the department, the title of the document, and the names (if listed) of the authors. If the department is both author and publisher, start with the title and list it as publisher.

> United States, National Commission on Terrorist Attacks upon the
>
> United States. *The 9/11 Commission Report.* By Thomas H. Kean
>
> et al., 5 Aug. 2004, www.9-11commission.gov/report/.

46. *Congressional Record*

> United States. Congress, House, Homeland Procurement Reform
>
> Act, 2019. 116th Congress, House Resolution 2083, passed 10
>
> June 2019.

47. Legal source   To cite a law case, give its name, Public Law number, its Statutes at Large number, page range, and the date it was enacted.

> Patient Protection and Affordable Care Act. Pub. L. 111-48, 24 Stat.,
>
> pp. 119–1024, 23 Mar. 2010.

To cite a law case, provide the court that decided the case, the name of the plaintiff and defendant, the case number, and the date of the decision.

> United States, Supreme Court. *United States v. Windsor.* 26 June
>
> 2013. *Legal Information Institute,* Cornell U Law School, www
>
> .law.cornell.edu/supremecourt/text/12-307.

For more information about citing legal documents or from case law, consult *The Bluebook: A Uniform System of Citation,* published by the Harvard Law Review Association.

Academic works

48. Conference proceedings   Cite as you would an edited book, but include information about the conference if it is not in the title.

> Mendel, Arthur, et al., editors. *Papers Read at the International*
>
> *Congress of Musicology Held at New York September 11th to*
>
> *16th, 1939.* Music Educators' National Conference for the
>
> American Musicological Society, 1944.

49. Unpublished dissertation   Begin with the author's name, followed by the title in quotation marks, the year it was written, the name of the institution, and the type of dissertation.

> Price, Deidre Dowling. *Confessional Poetry and Blog Culture in the*
>
> *Age of Autobiography.* 2010. Florida State U, PhD dissertation.

50. Published dissertation   Cite as you would a book. After the title, add the year the dissertation was written, the name of the institution, the year the type of dissertation, and then the publication information.

> Fraser, Wilmot Alfred. *Jazzology: A Study of the Tradition in Which*
>
> *Jazz Musicians Learn to Improvise.* 1983. U of Pennsylvania,
>
> Phd dissertation. UMI, 1987.

51. Dissertation on a Web site   Use the format for an unpublished dissertation *(no. 49)*, and then add the online publication information.

> Kosiba, Sara A. *A Successful Revolt? The Redefinition of Midwestern*
>
> *Literary Culture in the 1920s and 1930s.* 2007. Kent State U,
>
> PhD dissertation. *OhioLINK,* rave.ohiolink.edu/etdc/view?acc
>
> _num=kent1183804975.

52. Abstract of a dissertation   Use the format for an unpublished dissertation. After the institution and type of dissertation, give the abbreviation *DA* or *DAI* (for *Dissertation Abstracts* or *Dissertation Abstracts International*), then the volume number, the issue number, the date of publication, and the page number.

> Quinn, Richard Allen. *Playing Together: Improvisation in Postwar*
>
>   *American Literature and Culture*. 2000. U of Iowa, PhD
>
>   dissertation. *DAI,* vol. 61, no. 6, 2001, p. 2305A.

Web and social media sources

53. Basic entry for a Web site or independent online work   Begin with the author, editor, or compiler, if any, of the site. Give the title (italicized), the publisher, if any, publication date or last update, and URL. Since a whole Web site is likely to change, give your date of access.

> Miller, Michelle. *Farm Babe.* thefarmbabe.com. Accessed
>
>   17 May 2021.

> Johnson, Steven. *StevenBerlinJohnson.com*, 2002, www
>
>   .stevenberlinjohnson.com. Accessed 19 Dec. 2010.

54. Basic entry for a page, selection, or part of a Web site or larger online work   Give the title of the part in quotation marks. If the page is likely to remain unchanged (as a news story), omit your access date.

> Oliver, Rachel. "All About: Forests and Carbon Trading." *CNN,* Turner
>
>   Broadcasting System, 11 Feb. 2008, www.cnn.com/2008/
>
>   TECH/02/10/eco.carbon/index.html?iref=newssearch.

55. Course Web page   After the instructor's name, list the site title, then the department and school names.

> Thomas, Diane. *World Literature 11 (English 252).* Course home
>
>   page, Spring 2011, English Department, Northern Virginia
>
>   Community College, novaonline.nvcc.edu/eli/eng252/
>
>   eng252courseguide.htm. Accessed 26 Apr. 2016

56. Blog   The first example cites an entire blog; the second refers to a specific entry from one.

> McLennan, Doug. *Diacritical. ArtsJournal,* 2013, www.artsjournal.com/
>
>   diacritical/. Accessed 12 Mar. 2014.

McLennan, Doug. "Are Arts Leaders 'Cultural' Leaders?" *Diacritical,*

ArtsJournal, 10 Aug. 2013, www.artsjournal.com/

diacritical/2013/08/are-arts-leaders-cultural-leaders.html.

57. Post on *Tumblr* If the post has no title, use the first few words to identify it.

Gill, Nikita. "Falling out of love with someone. . ." *Meanwhile*

| Poetry. Tumblr, 6 May 2017, meanwhilepoetry.tumblr.com/

post/160386126728/falling-out-of-love-with-someone-who

-was-once-your.

58. Post to a news group or forum Use the subject line as the title. If there is no subject, use *Post.*

Harbin, David. "Furtwangler's Beethoven 9 Bayreuth." *Opera-L*

Archives, 3 Jan. 2008, listserv.bccls.org/cgi-bin/wa?A2=

OPERA-L;c7Keug;20080103233045%2B0100A.

59. Comment on a Web page

Cruz, Lalo. Comment on "Fourth *Hunger Games* Film Now Official."

Rolling Stone, 11 July 2012, www.rollingstone.com/movies/news/

fourth-hunger-games-film-now-official-20120711.

60. Entry in a wiki Check with your instructor before using a wiki as a source. For *Wikipedia* articles, see no. 32.

Matsumoto, David, and Paul Ekman. "Facial Expression Analysis."

Scholarpedia, 14 May 2008, https://doi.org/10.4249/

scholarpedia.4237.

61. Personal page on a social media site

Kron, Susan. "Susan Kron." *Facebook,* 2013, www.facebook.com/

susan.kron.35. Accessed 25 Nov. 2013.

62. Post on *Facebook*

Nguyen, Viet Than. "My favorite picture of my mother and me. . ."

Facebook, 14 May 2017, www.facebook.com/pg/

vietnguyenauthor/posts/?ref=page_internal.

63. Post on *Twitter* (tweet)   If the handle differs from the author's account name, or if your citation does not include a URL, consider including the handle in brackets. Click on the tweet's dropdown menu to obtain its URL.

> Trump, Donald [@realDonaldTrump] "The Fake Media is working
>
>   overtime today!" *Twitter,* 12 May 2017, 8:53 a.m., twitter.com/
>
>   realDonaldTrump/status/862999243560788256.

64. Post on *Instagram*   If citing a posted photo or other media, include a brief description, not enclosed in quotations.

> Seco, Francisco. *Photo of a man swimming in Oslo, Norway.*
>
>   *Instagram,* 25 Apr. 2021, www.instagram.com/p/COGpz9wjOLS/.

65. Post on *Snapchat*   Because a "snap" disappears after viewing and readers cannot access it, do not include it in the works-cited list. Instead, in the body of your paper, mention its author and date and describe it. If you have a screen shot of the snap, you can include it as a figure with a caption indicating source information.

Other electronic (non-Web) sources

66. E-mail or text message   Include the author and a description, followed by the date.

> Morgan, Rocky. E-mail to T. Martinez. 11 July 2018.

67. Virtual reality experience

> Vida Systems. *Da Vinci's Inventions. Google Expeditions* app.
>
>   Accessed 17 May 2021.

Other electronic sources

68. A digital file stored on your computer   Use the citation format of the most closely related print or nonprint source. Indicate the type of file, or if the format is unclear, use *Digital file*. If the source you are citing lacks a title, provide a brief description in its place.

> McNutt, Lea. "The Origination of Avian Flight." 2016. Microsoft Word file.
>
> Murphy, Matt. Design Memo to Gallery Staff. Tufts University, Boston,
>
>   MA, 1 May 2021. PDF.

69. Computer software   Include the title, version, publisher, and date in your text or in an explanatory note. Do not include an entry in your works-cited list.

70. Video game

> *Guardians of Middle-earth.* PS3 ed., Warner Brothers Interactive
>
> > Entertainment, 2013.

71. Source from a mobile app   Treat the mobile app as a version (see page 280). If you are citing the app itself, treat it as computer software (*no. 69*).

> "Castigate." *English Definition Dictionary, WordReference* app, 2017.

Visuals, film, audio, and other media

72. Original work of art or photograph   Provide the artist or photographer's name, the title (if any), the date, and the institution or private collection and city in which the artwork can be found.

> Palley, Diane. *Choose Life.* 1994, private collection, Boston.

> Adams, Ansel. *Monolith, Face of Half Dome, Yosemite Valley,*
>
> > *California.* 1980, Getty Museum, Los Angeles.

73. Reproduction of a work of art or photograph   Treat a reproduction of a photograph or work of art in another source like a work in an anthology (*no. 22*). Italicize the titles of both the image and the source, and include the institution or collection and city where the original work can be found (if appropriate) prior to information about the source in which it appears. If the image is not titled, provide a description of it in place of a title.

> Sargent, John Singer. *Venice: Under the Rialto Bridge.* 1909,
>
> > Museum of Fine Arts, Boston. *MFA Preview,* Nov.-Dec. 2013,
> >
> > p. 10.

> Herbert, Gerald. *Photograph of President Obama. Philadelphia*
>
> > *Inquirer,* 9 Nov. 2013, p. A4.

74. Work of art or photograph online   Cite the original (*no. 72*) and then add Web publication information, or cite as a basic Web source (*no. 54*).

> Modigliani, Amedeo. *Reclining Nude.* 1919, Museum of Modern Art,
>
> > New York. *MoMA,* www.moma.org/collection/works/78432?
> >
> > locale=en.

75. Slide show   If citing individual slides, note that at the end of the citation: *Slide 2*.

> *Powerful Typhoon Causes Devastation in Philippines. The New York*
>
> > *Times*, 11 Nov. 2013, www.nytimes.com/slideshow/2013/11/09
> >
> > /world/asia/20131110_PHILIPPINES_HTML.html.

76. Cartoon or comic   First cite the print information, then the online publication information, if any, or cite as a basic Web source (*no. 54*).

> McKee, Rick. "Rat Hole Taxes." Cartoon. *The Augusta Chronicle,*
>
> > 11 Apr. 2014. *Cagle Cartoons,* www.cagle.com/rick-mckee
> >
> > /2014/04/rat-hole-taxes.

77. Map, chart, or diagram

> *MTA New York City Subway.* Map. *Metropolitan Transit Authority,*
>
> > 2013, web.mta.info/nyct/maps/subwaymap.pdf.

78. Advertisement

> Advertisement for Geico. *Sports Illustrated,* 11 Nov. 2013, p. 45.
>
> Advertisement for Nordstrom. *Dictionary.com*, www.dictionary.com/.
>
> > Accessed 4 Apr. 2017.

79. Film   Begin with the title (italicized) followed by the director, distributor, and year. It is not necessary to list performers or other contributors, unless you are citing their particular contributions.

> *The Big Lebowski.* Directed by Joel Coen and Ethan Coen,
>
> > Gramercy Pictures, 1998.

80. Film on physical media (such as a DVD or Blu-ray)   Include the original film's release date if relevant. Indicate the distributor, date, and version.

> *Lawrence of Arabia.* Directed by David Lean, Sony Pictures,
>
> > 2012. DVD.

81. Film or video on a Web site   List the Web site followed by the URL. If accessed through a streaming service, name the service and include a URL for the main page.

> *Enron: The Smartest Guys in the Room.* Directed by Alex Gibney,
>
> > Magnolia Pictures, 2005. *Internet Archive,* archive.org/details/
> >
> > EnronTheSmartestGuysInTheRoom_201505.

> *Sorry We Missed You.* Directed by Ken Loach, Sixteen Films, 2019.
>
> > *Criterion Channel,* www.criterionchannel.com.

82. Video on *YouTube*   After the container element (*YouTube*), add the name of the person who uploaded the video, if available.

> "Richard Ford and Colm Tóibín Conversation: Narrators Are
>
> > Unreliable." 23 Nov. 2016, www.youtube.com/watch?v
> >
> > =gTs9pPhzcmg.

83. Radio or television program broadcast   Give the episode title (in quotation marks), the program title (italicized), the name of the series (if any), the network (call letters), the city, and the broadcast date.

> "Scientists Turn to Crowdfunding for Research." *Here and Now.*
>
> > National Public Radio, KUOW, Seattle, 17 Sept. 2013.

> *episode (not series)*   *series*
> "The Whale." Directed by Rodman Flender. *The Office,* performance
>
> > by Steve Carrell, season 9, episode 7, NBC, 15 Nov. 2012.

84. Radio or television program on the Web

> "Bill Evans: 'Piano Impressionism.'" *Jazz Profiles,* narrated by
>
> > Nancy Wilson, WGBH, Boston, 27 Feb. 2008. *NPR,*
> >
> > www.npr.org/2008/02/27/46474288/bill-evans-piano-
> >
> > impressionism.

> *episode (not series)*   *series*
> "The Whale." Directed by Rodman Flender. *The Office,* performance
>
> > *performer in series*
> > by Steve Carrell, season 9, episode 7, NBC, www.nbc.com/the-
> >
> > office/video/the-whale/n28880. Accessed 13 Sept. 2013.

85. Radio or television interview

> Ottolenghi, Yotam, and Sami Tamimi. Interview by Melissa Block.
>
> > *All Things Considered.* WBUR, Boston, 15 Oct. 2012. *NPR,*
> >
> > www.npr.org/sections/thesalt/2012/10/15/162805706/jerusalem
> >
> > -a-love-letter-to-food-and-memories-of-home.

86. Podcast

"Present for Duty." *Serial,* hosted by Sarah Koenig and Julie Snyder,

season 2, episode 11, WBEZ Chicago, 31 Mar. 2016,

serialpodcast.org/season-two/11/present-for-duty.

87. Sound recording   An individual song on a recording is noted (in quotation marks) before the album title.

Turner, Frank. "The Way I Tend to Be." *Tape Deck Heart,* BMG

Rights, 2013.

Foxes. *Glorious.* Sign of the Times-Sony Music, 2014.

The Beatles. "Lucy in the Sky with Diamonds." *Sgt. Pepper's Lonely*

Hearts Club Band, 1967. Amazon Music app, 2017.

88. Musical composition   Include only the composer and title, unless you are referring to a published score (see the third example). Published scores are treated like books except that the date of composition appears after the title. Titles of instrumental pieces are not italicized when known only by form and number, unless the reference is to a published score.

Ellington, Duke. *Satin Doll.*

Haydn, Franz Josef. Symphony No. 94 in G Major.
reference to a published score
Haydn, Franz Josef. *Symphony No. 94 in G Major.* 1791. Edited by

H. C. Robbins Landon, Haydn-Mozart, 1965.

89. Personal or archival video or audio recording   Give the date recorded and the location of the recording.

Adderley, Nat. Interview by Jimmy Owens. Schomburg Center for

Research in Black Culture, New York Public Library, 2 Apr. 1993.

Videocassette.

Miscellaneous other sources

90. Manuscripts, typescripts, and material in archives   Give the author, a title or description *(Letter, Notebook),* the date, any identifying number, and the name of the institution housing the material. If relevant, add the form, such as *Typescript* (typed) or *Manuscript* (hand-written). (Do not italicize any part of the citation.)

Arendt, Hannah. Thinking and Moral Considerations: A Lecture.
date uncertain
Circa 1971, Library of Congress Manuscript Division,

Washington, DC. Typescript.

Pollack, Bracha. "A Man Ahead of His Time." 1997. Typescript.

91. Archival material on the Web　Provide the information for the original. Add the online publication information. Otherwise, cite as a basic Web source *(see no. 54)*.

date uncertain

Whitman, Walt. "After the Argument." Circa 1890, The Charles

E. Feinberg Collection of the Papers of Walt Whitman, Library of

Congress. *The Walt Whitman Archive,* www.whitmanarchive.org/

manuscripts/transcriptions/loc.00001.html.

92. Personal letter　To cite a letter you received, start with the writer's name, followed by the descriptive phrase *Letter to the author* (not italicized), and the date.

Cogswell, Michael. Letter to the author. 15 Mar. 2015.

To cite someone else's unpublished personal letter, see no. 90.

93. Personal interview　Begin with the person interviewed, followed by a description, such as *Interview with the author* (not italicized) and the date of the interview. *(See no. 40 for a published interview.)*

Greene, Gigi. Interview with the author. 7 May 2018.

94. Lecture or speech　Give the speaker, the title (in quotation marks), the name of the forum or sponsor, the date, and the location.

Beaufort, Anne. "All Talk, No Action? Or, Does Transfer Really

Happen after Reflective Practice?" Conference on College

Composition and Communication, 13 Mar. 2009, Hilton San

Francisco.

95. Live performance　To cite a play, opera, dance performance, or concert, begin with the author; followed by the title; information such as the director *(Directed by)* and major performers; the site; the city; and the performance date.

Fierstein, H., and Cyndi Lauper. *Kinky Boots.* Directed by Jerry

Mitchell, 18 July 2013, Al Hirschfeld Theatre, New York City.

CHAPTER 28

MLA Style: Explanatory Notes and Acknowledgments

Explanatory notes are used to cite multiple sources for borrowed material or to give readers supplemental information. You can also use explanatory notes to acknowledge people who helped you with research and writing. Acknowledgments are a courteous gesture. If you acknowledge someone's assistance in your explanatory notes, be sure to send that person a copy of your research project.

The example that follows is a note that provides additional information.

TEXT

The website for Harvard University's library, for example, includes a resource page, "Fake News, Misinformation, and Propaganda," that has links to outside sources such as the journalism-focused Nieman Foundation and the Tow Center for Digital Journalism, and access to downloads for fact-checking plug-ins.[2]

NOTE

[2.] Harvard Library's resource can be found here: guides.library. harvard.edu/fake. *The New York Times* also offers tips for teaching and learning methods for spotting fake news: www.nytimes. com/2017/01/19/learning/lesson-plans/evaluating-sources-in-a-post-truth-world-ideas-for-teaching-and-learning-about-fake-news.html.

CHAPTER 29

MLA Style: Format

The following guidelines will help you prepare your research project in the format that the MLA has recommended. For an example of a research paper that has been prepared using MLA style, see pages 305-16.

Materials   Back up your final draft on a separate drive or on one of the many cloud-based sites often available for free or by subscription. Use a high-quality printer and high-quality, white 8½-by-11-inch paper. Put the printed pages together with a paper clip.

Heading and title Include a separate title page if your instructor requires one. In the upper left-hand corner of the first page of the paper, one inch from the top and side, enter on separate, double-spaced lines your name, your instructor's name, the course number, and the date. Double-space between the date and the title and between the title and the first line of text, as well as throughout your paper. The title should be centered and properly capitalized *(see p. 305)*. Do not italicize the title or put it in quotation marks or bold type. If a title page is required for an assignment, prepare it according to your instructor's instructions. If your instructor requires a final outline, place it between the title page and the first page of the paper.

Margins and spacing Use one-inch margins all around, except for the top right-hand corner, where the page number goes. Your right margin should be ragged (not "justified," or even). Double-space lines throughout, including in quotations, notes, and the works-cited list. Indent the first word of each paragraph one-half inch (or five spaces) from the left margin. For block quotations, indent the whole block one-half inch from the left.

Page numbers Put your last name and the page number in the upper right-hand corner of the page, one-half inch from the top and flush with the right margin.

Visuals Place visuals (tables, charts, graphs, and images) close to the place in your text where you refer to them. Label and number tables consecutively *(Table 1, Table 2)*, and give each one an explanatory caption; put this information above the table. The term *Figure* (abbreviated *Fig.*) is used to label all other kinds of visuals, except for musical illustrations, which are labeled *Example* (abbreviated *Ex.*). Place a figure or an example caption below each visual. Below all visuals, cite the source of the material, punctuating as you would an entry in your works-cited list. *(For more on using visuals effectively, see Chapter 6: Drafting Text and Visuals.)*

Lists Lists should be integrated into your prose whenever possible, rather than set apart vertically. Exceptions include when a list is lengthy or includes many parts that a reader would find difficult to understand outside of a vertical list.

— *the* EVOLVING SITUATION

Electronic Submission of Assignments

Some instructors may request that you submit your project electronically. Keep these tips in mind:

- Confirm the appropriate procedure for submission.
- Find out your instructor's preferred format for the submission of documents. *Always ask permission before sending an attached document to anyone.*
- If you are asked to send a document as an attachment, save your document as a "rich text format" (.rtf) file or in PDF format.

CHAPTER 30

Sample Research Project in MLA Style

As a first-year college student, Albert Rabe wrote the following research project for his composition course. He knew very little about identifying misinformation online before beginning his research.

CONSIDER YOUR SITUATION

Author: Albert Rabe

Type of writing: Research report

Purpose: To investigate the causes and effects of the spread of fake news.

Stance: Informed and reasonable

Audience: Students, instructors, consumers of media

Medium: Print, as text attachment, part of ePortfolio

Rabe writes: As I did my research for this report, I was surprised to learn that we are all responsible for the spread of fake news.

1"

½"

Rabe 1

Place your name, your professor's name, your course title, and the date at the left margin, double-spaced.

1"

Albert Rabe

Professor Zakariya

Journalism 420

30 September 2017

Title centered, not italicized.

What Is Fake News?

"What is fake news?" Once upon a time, the answer to this question was simple: false information masquerading as news. When a *Weekly World News* tabloid claimed "Dick Cheney is a robot!" amused readers disbelieved the headline and accompanying photo revealing the vice president's inner circuitry (Vann). In spite of its claim to being "The World's Only Reliable News," readers knew the *Weekly World News* was anything but reliable. By contrast, for decades, newspapers like *The New York Times* and the *Chicago Tribune* have been considered trusted sources for accurate and credible news coverage. Their journalists tirelessly research stories, verify all sources, and work with editors to check facts. When errors are found in their pages, editors respond quickly by issuing corrections or retractions.

Double-spaced throughout.

Unfortunately, identifying fake news stories is not as simple as it used to be. Consider one controversy that ushered in the current presidential term. In the days following the inauguration, major news sources, such as *The New York Times*, *The Atlantic*, and Reuters, published photos showing small crowds gathered on the Mall for the ceremony on January 20, 2017. In a speech delivered to the CIA, President Donald Trump reacted by claiming that the photos were inaccurate. He accused journalists of

Thesis statement.

A news agency, which distributes news stories, is not italicized the way publications, like *The New York Times* or *The Atlantic*, are.

Rabe 2

spreading "fake news," adding that "honestly, it looked like a million and a half people": "this network . . . said we drew 250,000 people. . . . So we caught them [in a lie], and we caught them in a beauty" (United States). After these remarks were released, the White House press secretary, Sean Spicer, repeated the claim, making the now-infamous statement, since disproved, that Trump's "was the largest audience to ever witness a [presidential] inauguration, period" ("Sean Spicer").

In the days and weeks that followed, many credible news sources covered the crowd-size story in depth, demonstrating how the administration's own narrative fit the definition of fake news. PBS's *NewsHour* posted a time-lapse video of the crowds that day, and CNN and other outlets published "photographic fact checks" comparing the estimated crowd size to that of Barack Obama's 2009 Inauguration, which attracted an estimated three times more attendees (Klein; New York Times; Taylor; "Watch a Timelapse"). *USA Today* journalists Lori Robertson and Robert Farley further fact-checked the administration's claims by gathering information about Metro ridership and by studying videos of the event. They concluded that it was Trump and Spicer, not the news media at large, "who provided false information to feed a false narrative about crowd size."

Writing for the *Journal of Economic Perspectives*, Allcott and Gentzkow define *fake news* as information that is "intentionally and verifiably false, and could mislead

Multiple sources cited within parentheses, including a *Twitter* post and a *YouTube* video.

Authors are named in parentheses because they are not named in the signal phrase.

Development by definition (*see p. 56*).

Rabe 3

readers" (213). Asserting that "a great many things" that our elected leader says "are demonstrably false," *Time* editor Nancy Gibbs writes, "During the 2016 campaign, 70% of the Trump statements reviewed by PolitiFact were false, 4% were entirely true, 11% mostly true" (5). When trusted sources—whether media networks or elected officials—circulate information that is unverified or outright false, the task of differentiating the real news from the fake becomes all the more challenging. As Sabrina Tavernise explains in a recent *New York Times* article,

> Fake news, and the proliferation of raw opinion that passes for news, is creating confusion, punching holes in what is true, causing a kind of fun-house effect that leaves the reader doubting everything, including real news.

New Yorker columnist Elizabeth Kolbert explains one reason that people find fake news believable: when reading or watching the news, people tend to experience "confirmation bias,"[1] or "the tendency . . . to embrace information that supports their beliefs and reject information that contradicts them." In other words, people believe what they want to believe and can even "experience genuine pleasure—a rush of dopamine—when processing information that supports their beliefs" (Kolbert). Thus, if Trump says his inaugural crowd was the largest ever, his ardent supporters are likely to ignore credible news sources that discredit his claim.

Focus introduced.

Signal phrase introduces the quotation.

Presents a claim plus supporting evidence.

Rabe 4

Readers also have some responsibility for the problem of fake news. The Internet has allowed the spread of news—real and fake—to happen in the blink of an eye, often with "no significant third party filtering, fact-checking, or editorial judgment" (Allcott and Gentzkow 211). Journalists, editors, and publishers are no longer the primary gatekeepers; instead, "[s]ocial media have effectively turned us all into publishers," writes Brooke Borel, the author of *The Chicago Guide to Fact-Checking,* for the blog *FiveThirtyEight.* Moreover, Allcott and Gentzkow point out an astonishing statistic: "An individual user with no track record or reputation can in some cases reach as many readers as Fox News, CNN, or *The New York Times*" (211). Given the proliferation of news items at their fingertips, readers do not always make responsible choices about which news stories to read, which of them to believe, and which to share through their social media networks.

The repetition of fake news stories is another factor exacerbating the problem. As Gibbs explains, "Social scientists have shown that repetition of a false statement, even in the course of disputing it, often increases the number of people who believe it" (5). Consider the images and videos that tend to go viral following a natural disaster. Fake news sources will often alter, or "doctor," visual content to depict exaggerated or false outcomes, thereby grabbing readers' attention. Following Hurricane Harvey, a doctored photo of a shark swimming down a flooded

Page number provided at the end of quotation; source's names are included in the introduction to the quotation, so no need to restate names in the parenthetical citation.

Rabe 5

street fooled many readers who believed the image to be real, even though the same photo had been posted following previous storms. Other viral images are intentionally ascribed to the wrong events, such as when a story relating a tragedy features outdated images of political figures lending a hand when, in fact, they were not present (Quiu). The frequency with which these images are disseminated actually serves to bolster their credibility, despite evidence that undermines it.

The sheer volume of news stories being circulated makes the task of evaluating their credibility seem overwhelming. Evaluating sources takes time and effort, often more than readers are willing to give to a single news story—not to mention the many stories they encounter every day. However, identifying fake news is the first step in preventing it from spreading. To drive this point home, librarians across the country, and the world, are refining the resources available for researching and evaluating sources for credibility. The website for Harvard University's library, for example, includes a resource page, "Fake News, Misinformation, and Propaganda," that has links to outside sources such as the journalism-focused Nieman Foundation and the Tow Center for Digital Journalism, and access to downloads for fact-checking plug-ins.[2] The website for the International Federation of Library Associations and Institutions (IFLA), "the global voice of the library and information profession" ("About IFLA"), likewise offers helpful tips for spotting fake news (see Fig. 1).

Title is used in parenthetical citation because the source does not include an author's name.

Support by reference to visual.

Rabe 6

Fig. 1. A poster offering tips on how to identify fake news, from "How to Spot Fake News," International Federation of Library Associations and Institutions, 13 Aug. 2017, www.ifla.org/publications/node/11174.

Librarians and the IFLA encourage readers to make use of fact-checking sites. However, one site can hardly keep up with the daily barrage of tweets, breaking-news crawls across television screens, and messages shared

Figure number and caption explaining information in the visual, followed by information about its source.

Rabe 7

on *Facebook*. Therefore, when checking a story for credibility, readers should reference multiple fact-checking sites, and there are several that are trustworthy: "Between *FactCheck.org*, *Snopes.com*, the *Washington Post* Fact Checker and *PolitiFact.com*, it's likely at least one has already fact-checked the latest viral claim to pop up in your news feed," note researchers Kiely and Robertson.[3] The IFLA poster's last piece of advice—"Ask the Experts"—is also worth following. When readers are unsure of the origin or credibility of a news story, they should consult experts in research, who are close at hand: the reference librarians at local and university libraries.

There is good reason to hope that fake news will soon be relegated to the tabloids. For one thing, journalists and publishers are mobilizing to stop fake news in its tracks. James Wolcott writes in *Vanity Fair*, "[W]e've witnessed a reveille call in major newsrooms, . . . a renaissance of investigative reporting, journalistic bombshells bursting in air. Fake news, prepare to die" (57). Nevertheless, the responsibility also belongs to those who consume the news. Individual readers must be more active participants in the task of evaluating stories and must take care when spreading news over their *Facebook* and *Twitter* feeds. In fact, even just clicking on a news story can help to inform algorithms that encourage the creation of more fake news. Speaking to the power of a single click, Angela Lee, professor of Journalism and Emerging

Rabe 8

Media at the University of Texas, explains, "We should have the sense of responsibility that anything you click on will affect other people." As Lee tells her students, "Click like you mean it" (qtd. in Borel).

Conclusion with support by anecdote (*see p. 124*).

Rabe 9

Notes

1. Many articles can be found on the topics of fake news and confirmation bias. For example, "Confronting Confirmation Bias: Giving Truth a Fighting Chance in the Information Age" by Alan C. Miller discusses teaching students how to "discern credible information from raw information" (www.thenewsliteracyproject.org).

2. Harvard Library's resource can be found here: guides.library.harvard.edu/fake. *The New York Times* also offers tips for teaching and learning methods for spotting fake news: www.nytimes.com/2017/01/19/learning/lesson-plans/evaluating-sources-in-a-post-truth-world-ideas-for-teaching-and-learning-about-fake-news.html?_r=0.

3. Kiely and Robertson's article offers detailed information about how people can figure out if a story is a legitimate story or fake news.

New page, title centered; first line of each note indented one-half inch.

Cites additional sources by way of example.

Cites by title additional published Web site providing supplemental information.

Cites information supplemental to the essay.

Title centered; entries in alphabetical order by last name: if no author, by first important word in the title.

Source: Article published in an academic journal; a citation with two containers.

Source: blog.

Source: Magazine in print.

Source: Article on a Web site.

Source: tweet.

Rabe 10

Works Cited

"About IFLA." *International Federation of Library Associations and Institutions,* 21 July 2017, www.ifla.org/about.

Allcott, Hunt, and Matthew Gentzkow. "Social Media and Fake News in the 2016 Election." *Journal of Economic Perspectives*, vol. 31, no. 2, 2017, pp. 211-36. *American Economic Association*, https://doi.org/10.1257/jep.31.2.211.

Borel, Brooke. "Fact-Checking Won't Save Us from Fake News." *FiveThirtyEight,* 4 Jan. 2017, fivethirtyeight.com/features/fact-checking-wont-save-us-from-fake-news/.

Gibbs, Nancy. "When a President Can't Be Taken at His Word." *Time,* 3 Apr. 2017, p. 5.

Kiely, Eugene, and Lori Robertson. "How to Spot Fake News." *FactCheck.org.* 18 Nov. 2016, www.factcheck.org/2016/11/how-to-spot-fake-news/.

Klein, Betsy. "Comparing Donald Trump and Barack Obama's Inaugural Crowd Sizes." *CNN*, 20 Jan. 2017, www.cnn.com/2017/01/20/politics/donald-trump-barack-obama-inauguration-crowd-size/index.html.

Kolbert, Elizabeth. "Why Facts Don't Change Our Minds." *The New Yorker,* 27 Feb. 2017, www.newyorker.com/magazine/2017/02/27/why-facts-dont-change-our-minds.

New York Times [@nytimes]. "Comparing the crowds at Donald Trump's and Barack Obama's inaugurations." *Twitter*, 20 Jan. 2017, 12:57 p.m., twitter.com/nytimes/status/822548522633400321?lang=en.

Quiu, Linda. "A Shark in the Street and Other Hurricane Harvey Misinformation You Shouldn't Believe." *The New York Times,*

Rabe 11

28 Aug. 2017, www.nytimes.com/2017/08/28/us/politics/shark
-hurricane-harvey-rumors.html?_r=0.

Robertson, Lori, and Robert Farley. "Fact Check: The
Controversy Over Trump's Inauguration Crowd Size."
USA Today, 24 Jan. 2017, www.usatoday.com/story/news/
politics/2017/01/24/fact-check-inauguration-crowd-size/
96984496/.

"Sean Spicer: Trump Inauguration Had Largest Audience
Ever." *CNN Money,* 21 Jan. 2017, money.cnn.com/video/
media/2017/01/21/sean-spicer-briefing-full-remarks.cnnmoney/
index.html.

Tavernise, Sabrina. "As Fake News Spreads Lies, More Readers
Shrug at the Truth." *The New York Times,* 6 Dec. 2016,
www.nytimes.com/2016/12/06/us/fake-news-partisan
-republican-democrat.html?_r=0.

Taylor, Alan. "'All of This Space Was Full': A Photographic Fact
Check." *The Atlantic,* 24 Jan. 2017, www.theatlantic.com/
photo/2017/01/all-of-this-space-was-full-a-photographic
-fact-check/514253/.

United States, White House, Office of the Press Secretary.
*Remarks by President Trump and Vice President Pence at
CIA Headquarters.* 21 Jan. 2017, www.whitehouse.gov/the
-press-office/2017/01/21/remarks-president-trump-and
-vice-president-pence-cia-headquarters

Vann, Tap. "Five Classic Weekly World News Covers."
Weekly World News, 2 Oct. 2008, weeklyworldnews.
com/headlines/3075/five-classic-weekly-world-news
-covers/.

Source:
News
article
accessed
online.

Source:
Visual on
a Web site.

Source:
Statement
from a
govern-
ment
office.

Rabe 12

Source:
YouTube
Video.

"Watch a Timelapse of the National Mall on Inauguration Day."

    YouTube, uploaded by the PBS *NewsHour*, 21 Jan. 2017,

    www.youtube.com/watch?v=PdantUf5tXg.

Wolcott, James. "The Lying Game." *Vanity Fair,* Aug. 2017,

    pp. 56-57.

Source:
Article on
a Web site.

"Word of the Year 2016 Is. . . ." *Oxford Dictionaries*,

    en.oxforddictionaries.com/word-of-the-year/word-of-the

    -year-2016.

Credits

MLA Style: p. 261 Heather Mansfield, *Social Media for Social Good: A How-To Guide for Nonprofits.* Copyright © 2012 by The McGraw-Hill Companies. Used with permission.
p. 262 Reprinted with permission from *Journal of Public Policy & Marketing*, published by the American Marketing Association. Kristen L. Walker, "Surrendering Information Through the Looking Glass: Transparency, Trust and Protection," *Journal of Public Policy & Marketing*, Vol. 35(1) Spring 2016, p. 144.

Design Elements: (butterfly/computer): ©Visual Generation/Shutterstock; (other design icons): ©McGraw-Hill Education

7

APA
Documentation Style

Take the whole range of imaginative literature, and we are all wholesale
borrowers. In every matter that relates to invention, to use, or beauty or
form, we are borrowers.

–Wendell Phillips

©Justin Kerr

This detail of a Mayan vase shows a scribe at work. Scribes—who documented
the deeds of rulers—were esteemed in the great Mayan cities that flourished on
the Yucatan Peninsula from around 100 to 900 C.E.

7 APA Documentation Style

APA style requires writers to provide bibliographic information about their sources in a list of references. To format entries for the list of references correctly, it is important to know what kind of source you are citing. The directory on pages 333–334 will help you find the appropriate sample to use as a model. Alternatively, you can use the charts on the pages that follow. Answering the questions in the charts will usually lead you to the sample entry you need. If you cannot find what you are looking for, consult your instructor.

 Sections dealing with visual rhetoric. For a complete listing, see the Quick Guide to Key Resources in Connect.

The Elements of an APA Reference Entry:

Book

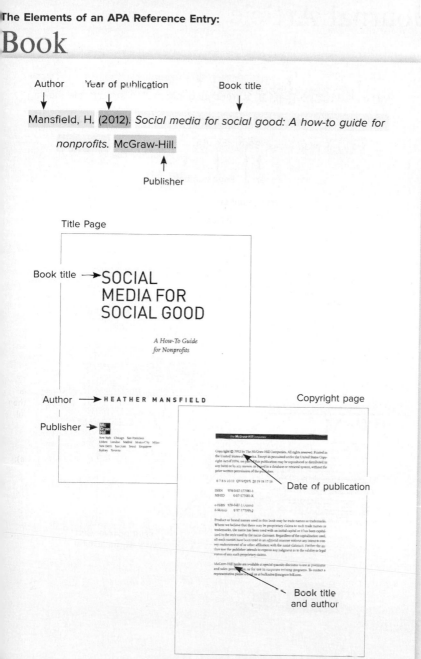

Author Year of publication Book title

Mansfield, H. (2012). *Social media for social good: A how-to guide for nonprofits.* McGraw-Hill.

Publisher

Title Page

Book title → SOCIAL MEDIA FOR SOCIAL GOOD

A How-To Guide for Nonprofits

Author → HEATHER MANSFIELD

Publisher →

Copyright page

Date of publication

Book title and author

...ormation for a book citation can be found on the book's title and copyright pages. When a book ...s been assigned a DOI (or digital object identifier), that too can be found on the copyright page ...on the publisher's, or a library's, Web site. Note that no DOI has been assigned to this book. **317**

The Elements of an **APA Reference Entry:**

Journal Article

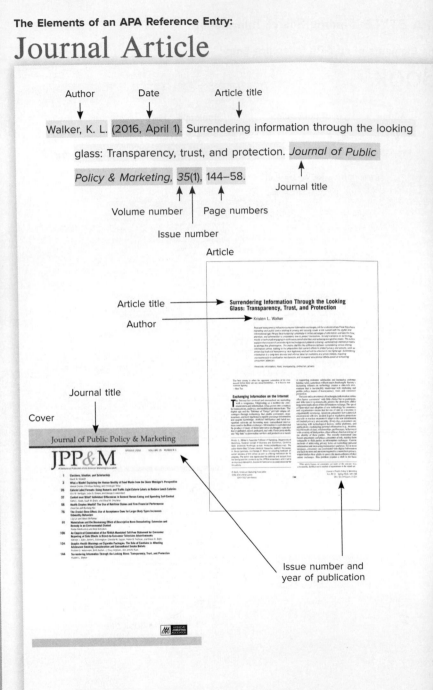

Author   Date   Article title

Walker, K. L. (2016, April 1). Surrendering information through the looking glass: Transparency, trust, and protection. *Journal of Public Policy & Marketing*, *35*(1), 144–58.

Journal title

Volume number   Page numbers

Issue number

Article

Article title ⟶ **Surrendering Information Through the Looking Glass: Transparency, Trust, and Protection**

Author ⟶ Kristen L. Walker

Journal title

Cover

Journal of Public Policy & Marketing

JPP&M

Issue number and year of publication

In this journal, the information needed for a citation appears on the first page of an article. Some journals, such as this one, list their contents and publication information on the cover.

Online
Journal Article with DOI Assigned

Authors · Year of publication · Article title · Journal title

Plummer, C. A., Ai, A. L., Lemieux, C., Richardson, R., Dey, S., Taylor, P., Spence, S., & Hyun-Jun, K. (2008). Volunteerism among social work students during Hurricanes Katrina and Rita. *Journal of Social Service Research, 34*(3), 55–77. https://doi:10.1080/01488370802086328

Volume number · Page numbers · DOI

Issue number

Source: informa world

the article has a DOI (Digital Object Identifier), include it at the end of the citation with) end punctuation. This article lists the DOI beneath the volume and issue numbers. For urnals paginated by issue, include the issue number in parentheses after the volume mber. For an article with more than two authors, list all names up to twenty. If the urce has twenty-one or more authors, list the first nineteen, followed by an ellipsis mark ree spaced periods) and the last author's name.

The Elements of an APA Works-Cited Entry:

Short Work on a
Web Site

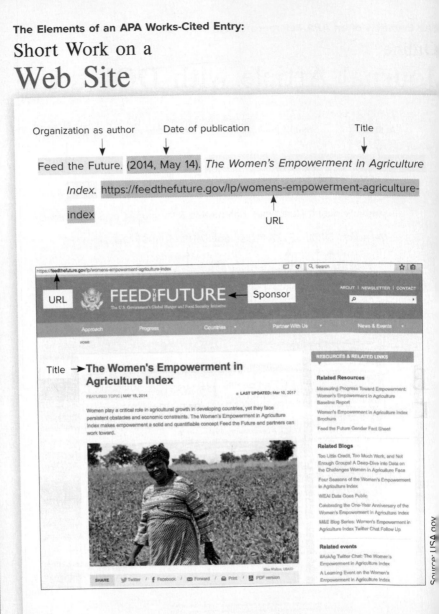

Organization as author   Date of publication   Title

Feed the Future. (2014, May 14). *The Women's Empowerment in Agriculture*

Index. https://feedthefuture.gov/lp/womens-empowerment-agriculture-

index

URL

The above citation derives from the APA model for an online report. You may need to search on a site to find author, date, and other information. List an individual author's last name firs If no date is given, include *n.d.* Supplemental information about format may follow the title. Here, the author is also the Web site sponsor (Feed the Future). When the author is not the sponsor, name the sponsor after the title. For magazine, newspaper, and journal articles (lacking a DOI) from Web sites, give the full URL that links directly to the source you are citing.

Entries in a List of References:

Authors of Any Source

Books

Articles in Periodicals

Government Works

? **Is your source a government or legal document?**

NO   YES

↓ ————————————————————————————→ Go to this entry on page

Is it a government document?
  Is it a print government document?   **35** 342
  Is it a government document on a Web site?   **35** 342
Is it from the Congressional Record?   **36** 342

Check the next panel or the directory on pages 333–34 or consult your instructor.

Academic Works

? **Is your source an academic work like a report, conference presentation, or dissertation?**

NO   YES

↓ ————————————————————————————→ Go to this entry on page

Is it a report or working paper?   **37** 342
Is it a presentation at a conference?   **38** 343
  Is it a slide presentation?   **62** 349
Is it a dissertation?
  Is it an unpublished dissertation?   **39** 343
  Is it a published dissertation?   **40** 343
  Is it an abstract of a dissertation?   **39** 343
Is it an article from an academic journal?   **27, 28, 29, 30** 339, 340
  Is it the abstract of a journal article?   **31** 340
Is it an article from a collection of published articles?   **27** 339

Check the next panel or the directory on pages 333–34 or consult your instructor.

Web and Social Media Sources

? **Is your source a Web site, part of a Web site, social media post, e-mail, or text message?**

NO   YES

↓ ————————————————————————————→ Go to this entry on page

Is it a Web site or part of a Web site?
  Is it a whole Web site or independent online work?   **41** 344
  Is it a page, report, or selection from a Web site or larger
  online work?   **42** 344
  Is it a document on a university Web site?   **43** 344
  Is it an online document without a date?   **44** 344

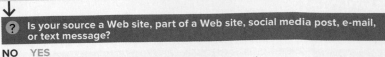

? **Is your source a Web site, part of a Web site, social media post, e-mail, or text message?**

NO   YES

⟶ Go to this entry on page

Is it a photograph, work of art, graph, map, or other visual on
a Web site?   **53** 346
Is it a film or video on a Web site?   **55** 347
Is it a radio or television program on a Web site?   **56** 347
Is it an audio podcast?   **57** 348

Is it a blog?   **46** 344
Is it a post on a professional blog?   **32** 341
Is it a post on a personal blog?   **46** 344

Is it a post to an electronic mailing list, news group, or forum?   **48** 345

Is it an entry in a wiki, such as *Wikipedia*?   **45** 344

Is it from a social media site?
Is it a social media post?   **46** 344
Is it a personal page on a social media site?   **47** 345

Is it an e-mail or text message?   **49** 346

Check the next panel or the directory on pages 333–34 or consult your instructor.

Other Electronic Sources

? **Is it another type of digital source?**

NO   YES

⟶ Go to this entry on page

Is it a digital file, such as an MP3 or PDF on your computer?   **50** 346
Is it computer software?   **51** 346
Is it a video game?   **51** 346
Is it a mobile application?   **52** 346

Check the next panel or the directory on pages 333–34 or consult your instructor.

Visuals, Audio, and Other Media

? Is your source a visual, film, radio, television, audio, or other media?

NO   YES

↓ ─────────────────────────────────→ Go to this entry on page

Is it a visual image?
  Is it a photograph, work of art, graph, map, or other visual?   **53** 346
  Is it a visual on a Web site?   **53** 346
  Is it a photograph on Instagram or Snapchat?   **46** 344
  Is it a slide presentation?   **62** 349
  Is it an advertisement?   **54** 347

Is it a film or video?
  Is it a film?   **55** 347
  Is it a film on DVD?   **55** 347
  Is it a film or video on a Web site?   **55** 347
  Is it a YouTube video?   **55** 347
  Is it a video on Instagram or Snapchat?   **46** 344

Is it a radio or television program?
  Is it a radio or television broadcast?   **56** 347
  Is it a radio or television program on a Web site?   **56** 347

Is it an audio recording or podcast?   **57** 348

Is it a musical composition?   **58** 348

Check the next panel or the directory on pages 333–34 or consult your instructor.

Miscellaneous Other Sources

? Is it another type of source?

NO   YES

↓ ─────────────────────────────────→ Go to this entry on page

Is it a lecture or speech?   **59** 348

Is it a personal communication?
  Is it a personal interview?   **60** 348
  Is it an e-mail?   **49** 346
  Is it a text message?   **49** 346

Is it a live performance?   **61** 348

Is it presentation slides?   **62** 349

Check the directory on pages 333–34 or consult your instructor.

START SMART
Tab 7: APA Documentation Style

This section will help you answer questions such as the following:

Rhetorical Knowledge
- Which disciplines use APA style? (31)

Critical Thinking, Reading, and Writing
- Why do I need to document my sources? (31, 32)

Processes
- How should I position and label visuals? (33)
- What information should an abstract contain? (33)

Knowledge of Conventions
- How do I cite sources in the text of my paper? (31)
- How do I create a list of references? (32)
- What kind of spacing and margins should my paper have? (33)
- What is a digital object identifier (DOI), and how is it used? (32)
- How do I cite electronic sources, such as Web sites, podcasts, and online articles? (32)

For a general introduction to writing outcomes, see 1e, pages 1–28.

Instructors of courses in psychology, sociology, political science, communications, education, and business usually prefer a documentation style that emphasizes the author and the year of publication.

The information in Chapters 31 through 34 is based on the seventh edition of the American Psychological Association's *Publication Manual* (APA, 2020). For updates, check the APA-sponsored Web site at <www.apastyle.apa.org>.

APA documentation style has two mandatory parts:

- In-text citations
- List of references

CHAPTER 31

APA Style: In-Text Citations

In-text citations let readers know that they can find full information about the source of an idea you have paraphrased or summarized, or the source of a quotation, in the list of references at the end of your project.

1. Author named in sentence   Follow the author's name with the year of publication (in parentheses).

> *signal phrase*
> Gifford (2016), writing for *Scientific American* online, cited an
> anonymous survey revealing that 29% of polled athletes
> confessed to resorting to performance-enhancing drugs.

2. Author named in parentheses   If you do not name the source's author in your sentence, then you must include the name in the parentheses, followed by the date and, if you are giving a quotation or a specific piece of information, the page number if the source is paginated. Separate the name, date, and page number with commas.

> Cheaters were sometimes flogged or were excluded from the
> games. They also paid fines that were used to erect *Zanes*, or
> honorific statues in the likeness of Zeus (Cartwright, 2013).

3. Source with two authors   Always use both names when citing a source by two authors. If you put the names of the authors in parentheses, use an ampersand *(&)* instead of *and*.

> After all, most educators would agree that "a democratic system of
> government needs—and the United States relies on colleges to
> *Ampersand used within parentheses*
> produce—ethical and engaged citizens" (Boyd & Brackmann, 2012, p.39).

4. Three or more authors   If a source has three or more authors, include the name of the first author only, followed by *et al.* (as an abbreviation, the *al.* has a

---

—APA IN-TEXT CITATIONS: DIRECTORY to SAMPLE TYPES

(See pp. 327–31 for examples of references entries.)

period following it): (Hart et al., 2007). Use this format in every citation, includ-ing the first, unless doing so would cause ambiguity.

> In a 2007 study of adult voting and volunteering, Hart et al. (2007) found that "those who participated frequently in community service in high school were more likely to volunteer than were those whose community service was nonexistent or infrequent" (p. 210).

APA IN-TEXT CITATIONS

- Identify the author(s) of the source, either in the sentence or in a paren-thetical citation.
- Indicate the year of publication of the source following the author's name, either in parentheses if the author's name is part of the sentence or, if the author is not named in the sentence, after the author's name and a comma in the parenthetical citation.
- Include a page reference for a quotation or specific piece of informa-tion. Put "p." before the page number. If the author is named in the text, the page number appears in the parenthetical citation following the bor-rowed material. Page numbers are not necessary when you are summa-rizing the source as a whole or paraphrasing an idea found throughout a work. *(For more on summary, paraphrase, and quotation, see Chap-ter 24: Working with Sources and Avoiding Plagiarism, pp. 237–54.)*
- If the source does not have page numbers (as with many online sources), do your best to direct readers. If the source has no page or paragraph numbering or easily identifiable headings, just use the name and date. *(See no. 13 and the note on p. 330.)*

5. Organization as author   Treat the organization as the author, and spell out its name the first time the source is cited. If the organization is well known, you may use an abbreviation thereafter.

> However, there are other ways of cheating, such as doping—
> broadly defined by the World Anti-Doping Agency (WADA) as
> "the occurrence of one or more of the anti-doping rule violations,"
> which include the use, attempted use, or "presence of
> a *Prohibited Substance* . . . in an *Athlete's Sample*" (2015, p. 18).

> Anxiety disorders affect nearly twice as many women as men
> (National Institute of Mental Health [NIMH], 2013).

In subsequent citations, only the abbreviation and the date need to be given: (NIMH, 2013).

6. Unknown author   Give the first one or two important words of the title. Use quotation marks for titles of articles, chapters, or Web pages, and italics for titles of books, periodicals, or reports.

> The transformation of women's lives has been hailed as "the
> single most important change of the past 1,000 years"
> ("Reflections," 1999, p. 77).

7. Two or more authors with the same last name   If the authors of two or more sources have the same last name, always include their first initial, even if the year of publication differs.

> M. Smith (2008) showed how Mexican migrants with dual citizenship
> display active civic engagement in U.S. and Mexican politics.

8. Two or more works by the same author in the same year   Alphabetize the works by their titles in your reference list, and assign a letter in alphabetical order (for example, *2017a, 2017b*). Use that same year-letter designation in your in-text citation.

> J. P. Agarwal (1996b) described the relationship between trade
> and foreign direct investment (FDI).

9. Two or more sources cited at one time   Cite the authors in the order in which they appear in the list of references, separated by a semicolon.

> Today's students report that school, family, and peer groups are
> among the major motivations to volunteer (Boyd & Brackmann,
> 2012; Law et al., 2013).

10. Personal communications (e-mails, text messages, letters, and personal interviews) To cite information received from unpublished forms of personal communication—such as conversations, letters, notes, and e-mail messages—give the source's first initial or initials and last name, and provide as precise a date as possible. Because readers do not have access to them, do not include personal communications in your reference list.

> According to scholar T. Williams (personal communication, June 10, 2010), many students volunteer because they believe in giving back to the community they grew up in.

11. Specific part of a source Include the chapter *(Chapter)*, page *(p.)*, figure, or table number.

> Although social media have had a positive impact on the messaging capabilities of nonprofits, 62% of Americans reported they are very likely to support causes they learn about through in-person communication channels (Kapin & Ward, 2013, Chapter 1).

12. Indirect (secondary) source When referring to a source that you know only from reading another source, use the phrase *as cited in* followed by the author of the source you actually read and its year of publication.

> Marcy L. Reed, president of National Grid, a Massachusetts gas and electric utility, says, "I have to be sure the people we hire today are fit for tomorrow" (as cited in Supiano, 2013).

The work by Supiano would be included in the reference list, but the work by Marcy L. Reed would not.

13. Electronic source Cite the author's last name or the name of the site's sponsor (if an author's name is not available) and the publication date. If the document is a PDF (portable document format) file with stable page numbers, cite the page number. If the source has paragraph numbers instead of page numbers, use *para.* instead of *p.*

> Back in 773 B.C., athletes stood in front of the bronze icon "Zeus the Oath Giver" and "swore an oath to the god of thunder vowing they would follow the regulations of the Olympics and play fair" (Phippen, 2016, para. 1).

> **Note:** If the specific part lacks page or paragraph numbering, cite the heading and the number of the paragraph under that heading where the information can be found. If the heading is long, use a short version in quotation marks. If you cannot determine the date, use the abbreviation *n.d.* in its place: (*International Olympic Committee, n.d.*).

14. Two or more sources in one sentence   Include a parenthetical reference after each fact, idea, or quotation you have borrowed.

In its 2012 Annual Member Survey, Campus Compact (2013a) reported that student participation is increasing in the Compact institutions, a fact that stands in marked contrast to the flat or even decreasing rates reported by other sources measuring rates across all institutions (DiBlasio, 2011).

15. Sacred or classical text   Include the version you consulted as well as any standard book, part, or section numbers.

The famous song sets forth a series of opposites, culminating in "a time to love, and a time to hate; a time of war, and a time of peace" (Eccles. 3:8, King James Bible).

CHAPTER 32

APA Style: References

APA documentation style requires a list of references where readers can find complete bibliographical information about the sources referred to in your project. The list should appear at the end of your research project, beginning on a new page titled "References."

Authors of Any Source

1. One author   List the author by last name and initials, followed by the date in parentheses. After the publication information, include retrieval information, preferably a DOI, if available. Note that this source has no DOI.

Sagawa, S. (2010). *The American way to change: How national service and volunteers are transforming America.* Jossey-Bass.

2. Two or more authors   List all authors, up to twenty of them, by last name and initials, followed by commas. Precede the final name with an ampersand *(&)*. (Note: The first source has no DOI.)

Kapin, A., & Ward, A. S. (2013). *Social change anytime everywhere: How to implement online multichannel strategies to spark advocacy, raise money and engage your community.* Jossey-Bass.

Çevik, M., Eser, I., & Boleken M. (2013). Characteristics and outcomes of liver and lung hydatid disease in children. *Tropical Doctor, 43*(3), 93–95. https://doi.org/10.1177/0049475513493415

If a work has more than twenty authors, list the first nineteen authors' names, followed by an ellipsis mark (three spaced periods) and the last author's name.

3. Organization as author   When the author and publisher are the same, omit the publisher from the source information. (Note: This source has no DOI.)

Oxfam America. (2013). *Dashed expectations.*

4. Two or more works by the same author   List the works in publication date order, with the earliest one first. (Note: These sources have no DOI.)

Sacks, O. (2012). *Hallucinations.* Knopf.

Sacks, O. (2017). *The river of consciousness.* Knopf.

5. Two or more works in one year by the same author   Alphabetize by title, and attach a letter to each entry's year of publication, beginning with *a*. In-text citations must use the letter as well as the year. (Note: These sources have no DOI.)

Agarwal, J. P. (1996a). *Does foreign direct investment contribute to unemployment in home countries? An empirical survey* (Discussion Paper No. 765). Kiel, Germany: Institute of World Economics.

Agarwal, J. P. (1996b). Impact of Europe agreements on FDI in developing countries. *International Journal of Social Economics, 23*(10/11), 150–163.

6. Unknown author or editor   Start with the title. When alphabetizing, use the first important word of the title (excluding articles such as *The, A,* or *An*). (Note: These sources have no DOI.)

The American heritage dictionary of the English language (5th ed.). (2012). Houghton Mifflin.

Give me liberty. (1969). World.

APA REFERENCE ENTRIES: DIRECTORY to SAMPLE TYPES

(See pp. 327–31 for examples of in-text citations.)

(Continued)

APA REFERENCE ENTRIES *(Continued)*

Academic Works

37. Report or working paper *342*
38. Conference presentation *343*
39. Dissertation or dissertation abstract *343*
40. Published dissertation *343*

Web and Social Media Sources

41. Basic entry for a whole Web site or independent online work *344*
42. Basic entry for a page, report, or part of a Web site *344*
43. Document on a university's Web site *344*
44. Online document lacking a date *344*
45. Entry in a wiki *344*
46. Blog or social media post *344*
47. Personal page on a social media site *345*
48. Post to an electronic mailing list, newsgroup, or forum *345*
49. E-mail or text message *346*

Other Electronic Sources

50. Digital file on your computer *346*
51. Computer software or video game *346*
52. Mobile application *346*

Visuals, Audio, and Other Media

53. Photograph, work of art, graph, map, or other visual *346*
54. Advertisement *347*
55. Film, video, movie or TV show *347*
56. Radio or television broadcast *347*
57. Audio recording or podcast *348*
58. Musical composition *348*

Other Miscellaneous Sources

59. Lecture, speech, or address *348*
60. Personal interview *348*
61. Live performance *348*
62. Presentation slides *349*

Complete Books

7. Basic entry for a book

Hofmann, S. G., & Doan, S. N. (2018). *The social foundations of emotion: Developmental, cultural, and clinical dimensions.* American Psychological Association. https://doi.org/10.1037/0000098-000

8. Book on a Web site   In place of the publisher, provide the book's DOI, or if there is no DOI, include a URL that leads directly to the source.

Shariff, S. (2009). *Confronting cyber-bullying: What schools need to know to control misconduct and avoid legal consequences.* https://doi.org/10/1017/CBO9780511551260

—DOIs AND URLs IN APA REFERENCES

- Many print and online books and articles have a digital object identifier (DOI), a unique alphanumeric string that links readers to that source's location on the Internet. For any source that has been assigned a DOI, provide that DOI in your reference list entry, regardless of whether you used the print or online version of the source. Present the DOI at the end of your reference list entry (live-linked, if possible). Do not place a period after a DOI.

- For online works with no DOI assigned, include a complete, stable URL that links directly to the work you are citing. Do not place a period after a URL.

- For a work from a database with no DOI assigned, *do not* include a URL, since most academic databases are widely available and easily accessed by readers. However, if the work is from a database that is in limited circulation, include the name of the database and the URL: "Retrieved from *ERIC*." If the URL requires a login, meaning it will not lead readers to the work, provide the URL of the database home page or login page instead.

- Include a retrieval date only for items that are likely to change (such as a wiki or social media page).

- DOIs and URLs should appear as live links in your reference list, so that readers can easily access the sources you cite. To convert a DOI to a live link beginning with the prefix http:// or https://, use the link provider available at https://www.doi.org/. If a URL is long and complex, you may use a site like Bitly or TinyURL to shorten it. Never include end punctuation following a DOI or URL, as punctuation could interfere with the link's functionality.

> Rich, N. (2019). *Losing Earth: A recent history.* https://books.google.
> com/books?id=BLVuDwAAQBAJ&dq=climate+change

9. Book in an online database   Provide the book's DOI, if there is one. For books without a DOI, and accessed using an online database that is widely available, omit the retrieval information. For books accessed through databases with limited distribution, include "Retrieved from," the name of the database, and either a DOI or a URL that links to the work you are citing, or to the home page or login page of the database.

> Vasey, M. W., & Dadds, M. R. (2015). *The developmental
> psychopathology of anxiety.* Oxford. http://doi.org/10.1093/
> med:psych/978019512360.001.0001

> Brown, M., Ray, R., Summers, E., & Fraistat, N. (2018). #SayHerName:
> A case study of intersectional social media. *Ethnic and Racial
> Studies, 40*(11). Retrieved from *Taylor & Francis Online,* https://
> doi.org/10.1080/01419870.2017.1334934

10. E-book In place of the publisher, you may include the optional label "[Kindle]," which clarifies the type of e-book. The following book has no DOI, so included here is the live-linked URL, allowing readers to access the downloadable e-book. When citing an e-book that was published a one or more years after the print book, end the citation with the original publication date: "(Original work published 2008)."

> McCann, C. (2013). *TransAtlantic*. Penguin Random House. https://
>
> www.amazon.com/TransAtlantic-Novel-Colum-McCann-ebook/dp/
>
> B00ALBR2RW

11. Book by an editor Add *(Ed.)* or *(Eds.)* after the name. (Note: This source has no DOI.)

> Oseland, James (Ed.). (2013). *A fork in the road: Tales of food, pleasure*
>
> *and discovery on the road*. Lonely Planet.

12. Book with an author and other contributor After the title, put the name(s) of the other contributor(s) followed by the appropriate abbreviation: Ed. (editor), Eds. (editors), or Trans. (translator or translators). (Note: These sources have no DOI.)

> James, H. (1975). *The portrait of a lady* (R. D. Bamberg, Ed.). W. W. Norton.
>
> Yan, Mo (2012). *Shifu, you'll do anything for a laugh* (H. Goldblatt,
>
> Trans.). Arcade.

13. Edition other than the first (Note: This source has no DOI.)

> Ferris, J., & Worster, L. (2013). *Music: The art of listening* (9th ed.).
>
> McGraw-Hill.

14. Republished book In-text citations should give both years: "As Goodman (1956/2012) pointed out ..." (Note: This source has no DOI.)

> Goodman, P. (2012). *Growing up absurd*. NYRB Classics. (Original
>
> work published 1956)

15. One volume of a multivolume work If the volume has its own title, put it before the title of the whole work.

> Strategic management. (2014). In *Wiley encyclopedia of management*
>
> (Vol. 12). Wiley. https://doi.org/10.1002/9781118785317.weom120025

16. Brochure, pamphlet, fact sheet, or press release If there is no date of publication, put *n.d.* in place of the date. If the publisher is an organization, list it as the author.

> U.S. Postal Service. (1995). A consumer's guide to postal services
>
> and products [Brochure].

Social Security Administration. (2018). Benefits for children with

disabilities [Pamphlet]. https://www.ssa.govpubs/EN-05-10026.pdf

17. Policy brief or white paper

Cramer, K., Shelton, L., Dietz, N., Dote, L., Fletcher, C., Jennings, S.,

Nicholas, B., Ryan, S., & Silsby, J. (2010). *Volunteering in*

America 2010: National, state, and city information. https://

www.nationalservice.gov/sites/default/files/documents/10_0614_

via_final_issue_brief.pdf

Parts of Books

18. Basic entry for a selection in an edited book or anthology   The selection's author, year of publication, and title come first, followed by the word In and information about the edited book. The page numbers of the selection are placed in parentheses after the book's title. (Note: This source has no DOI.)

Angell, M. (2012). The crazy state of psychiatry. In D. Brooks (Ed.),

The best American essays 2012 (pp. 6–28). Houghton Mifflin.

19. Part of a book on a Web site

Owen, S., & Kearns, R. (2006). Competition, adaptation and resistance:

(Re)forming health organizations in New Zealand's third sector. In

C. Milligan & D. Conradson (Eds.), *Landscapes of voluntarism:*

New spaces of health, welfare and governance (pp. 115–34).

https://books.google.com/books?id=f3NoDwAAQBAJ&dq=

Competition,+adaptation+and%C2%A0resistance:+(Reforming+

health+organizations+in+New%C2%A0Zealand%E2%80%99s+

third+sector

20. Part of a book in an online database   Provide a DOI, if there is one. The following source was accessed through JSTOR, a widely available database that need not be listed in the reference. See no. 9 for an explanation of when to include database information in your reference.

White, C. (2013). Using oral history to record the story of the Las

Vegas African American community. In J. L. Embry (Ed.), *Oral*

history, community, and work in the American West (pp. 150–74).

STYLING AND FORMATTING THE APA LIST OF REFERENCES

- Begin on a new page with the centered title "References" in bold.
- Include a reference for every in-text citation except personal communications *(see in-text citation no. 49 on p. 330).*
- Put references in alphabetical order by author's last name.
- Give the last name and first or both initials for each author. If the work has more than one author, see nos. 2 and 3 on page 331–32.
- Put the publication year in parentheses following the author or authors' names.
- Capitalize only the first word and proper nouns in titles of books and articles. Also capitalize the first word following the colon in a subtitle.
- Use italics for titles of books but not articles. Do not enclose titles of articles in quotation marks.
- Include the periodical name and volume number (both in italics) as well as the page numbers for a periodical article.
- Most entries will end with a DOI or URL *(see the box on p. 335).*
- Separate the author's name or authors' names, date (in parentheses), title, and publication information with periods.
- Use a hanging indent: Begin the first line of each entry at the left margin, and indent all subsequent lines of an entry (five spaces).
- Double-space within and between entries.

21. Part of an e-book   Provide a DOI, or if there is no DOI, provide the URL from which you downloaded the source.

> Díaz, J. (2016). Ordinary girls. In J. Franzen & R. Atwan (Eds.), *The best American essays 2016*. Houghton Mifflin. https://www.barnesandnoble.com/w/the-best-american-essays-2016-jonathan-franzen/1123108967#/

22. Introduction, preface, foreword, or afterword   List the author and the section cited. (Note: This source has no DOI.)

> Folger, T. (2012). Foreword. In D. Ariely (Ed.), *The best American science and nature writing 2012*. Houghton Mifflin.

23. Published letter   Begin with the letter writer's name, treating the addressee as part of the title *(Letter to...)*. (Note: This source has no DOI.)

> Lewis, C. S. (1905). Letter to his brother. In W. Hooper (Ed.), *The*
>
> *collected letters of C. S. Lewis: Vol 1. Family letters, 1905–1931*
>
> (pp. 2–3). HarperCollins.

24. Article in an encyclopedia or another reference work   Begin with the author of the selection, if given. If no author is given, begin with the selection's title, as in the following example. (Note: This source has no DOI.)

> Arawak. (2000). In The *Columbia encyclopedia* (6th ed., p. 2533).
>
> Columbia University Press.

25. Article in an online reference work   Begin with the author's name, if given, followed by the publication date. If no author is given, as in the following example, place the title before the date. Include the full URL.

> Attribution theory. (2013). In *Encarta*. http://encarta.msn.com/
>
> encyclopedia_761586848/ Attribution_Theory.html

26. Selection from a work also listed in references   Include all information for the larger work (see second example) preceded by that for the specific selection. (Note: These sources have no DOI.)

> Cole, D. (2011). Don't just stand there. In B. F. Clouse (Ed.), *Patterns*
>
> *for a purpose: A rhetorical reader* (pp. 311–15). McGraw-Hill.
>
> Clouse, B. F. (Ed). (2011). *Patterns for a purpose: A rhetorical reader.*
>
> McGraw-Hill.

Articles in Periodicals

27. Basic entry for a journal article   Italicize the periodical title and the volume number. Provide the issue number—*not* italicized—in parentheses after the volume number, with no space between them. A DOI ends the entry, if available.

> Masters, K., & Hooker, S. (2013). Religiousness/spirituality,
>
> cardiovascular disease, and cancer: Cultural integration for
>
> health research and intervention. *Journal of Consulting and*
>
> *Clinical Psychology, 81*(2), 206–216. https://doi.org/10.1037/a0030813

28. Journal article on a Web site Provide a DOI if available. If not, give a stable URL that leads directly to the article.

> Zhang, P., & McLuhan, E. (2013). Media ecology: Illuminations.
>
> *Canadian Journal of Communication, 38*(4). https://www.cjc-
>
> online.ca/index.php/journal/article/view/2764/2713

29. Journal article in an online database Provide the DOI, if available. If not, include a stable URL that links directly to the article.

> Brown, T. S. (2013). The sixties in the city: Avant-gardes and urban
>
> rebels in New York, London, and West Berlin. *Journal of Social*
>
> *History, 46*(4), 817–842. https://doi.org/10.1093/jsh/sht007
>
> Gore, W. C. (1916). Memory, concept, judgment, logic (theory).
>
> *Psychological Bulletin, 13,* 355–358. https://doi.org/10.1037/
>
> h0070882

30. In-press journal article Include the designation *in press* (not italicized) in place of a date. (Note: This source has no DOI.)

> Schwartz, S., & Correll, C. (in press). Efficacy and safety of
>
> atomoxetine in children and adolescents with attention-deficit/
>
> hyperactivity disorder: Results from a comprehensive meta-
>
> analysis and metaregression. *Journal of the American Academy*
>
> *of Child & Adolescent Psychiatry.*

31. Abstract of a journal article For an abstract that appears in the original source, add the word *Abstract* in brackets after the title (Chen example). If the abstract appears in a source that is different from the original publication, first give the original publication information for the article, followed by the publication information for the source of the abstract (Murphy example). If the dates of the publications differ, cite them both, with a slash between them, in the in-text citation: Murphy (2003/2004).

> Chen, Y. (2013). Partnership and performance of community-based
>
> organizations: A social network study of Taiwan [Abstract].
>
> *Journal of Social Service Research, 39*(5). https://doi.org/10.1080
>
> /01488376.2013.829164

Murphy, M. (2003/2004). Getting carbon out of thin air. *Chemistry & Industry, 6*, 14–16. Abstract retrieved from *Fuel and Energy Abstracts, 45*(6), 389.

32. Article in a magazine or newspaper   Add the month for magazines published monthly, or the month and day for magazines published weekly. Note that the volume and issue numbers are also included. The first example below is from a print magazine. For an article retrieved from an online magazine (White example), omit the page numbers and include a URL.

Courage, K. (2013, December 8). Genetic cures for the gut. *Scientific American, 309*(6).

White, L. T., (2018, October 3). How much is enough in a perfect world? *Psychology Today.* https://www.pscyhologytoday.com/us/blog/culture-conscious/201810/how-much-is-enough-in-perfect-world

For print newspaper articles, use *p.* or *pp.* (not italicized) with the section and page number. List all page numbers, separated by commas, if the article appears on discontinuous pages: pp. C1, C4, C6. For an article retrieved online, as in the second example below, omit page numbers and include a stable URL.

Fitzsimmons, E. G. (2013, December 8). Winter storms grip U.S., knocking out power and grounding flights. *The New York Times,* p. N23.

Siegel, R. (2019, July 15). Prime Day means protest for workers in Minnesota. *The Washington Post.* https://www.washingtonpost.com/business/2019/07/15/amazon-workers-minnesota-prime-day-means-protest/

If you retrieved the article from an online database or archive, include database information for archival material not easily found elsewhere. Also provide a URL.

Culnan, J. (1927, November 20). Madison to celebrate arrival of first air mail plane. *Wisconsin State Journal,* p. A1. Retrieved from Wisconsin Historical Society database, https://www.wisconsinhistory.org/Records/Newspaper/BA7856

33. Review   In the following examples, note the bracketed information identifying the text being reviewed. For reviews that do not have titles, as in the second example, place the bracketed information after the date.

Yagoda, B. (2009, October 25). Slow down, turn off, tun out the new. . . [Review of the book *The tyranny of email,* by J. Freeman]. *The New York Times Book Review,* p. 9.

Henry, P. (2007, February 24). [Review of the book *Phishing: cutting the identify theft line,* by R. Lininger & R. D. Vines]. *Journal of Forensic Practice, 1*(3). https://doi.org/10.1080/15567280601047492

34. Editorial or letter to the editor Note the use of brackets to identify the genre.

Glaeser, E. L. (2013, October 31). High value in unpaid internships [Opinion]. *The Boston Globe,* p. A15.

Kodak, K. (2008, April 26). Identifying victims of ID theft [Letter to the editor]. *Kansas City Star.* https://www.kansascitystar.com/kodak/identifying.htm

Government works

35. Government document When no author is listed, use the government agency as the author.

U.S. Bureau of the Census. (1976). *Historical statistics of the United States: Colonial times to 1970.* Washington, DC: Government Printing Office.

National Commission on Terrorist Attacks upon the United States. (2004). *The 9/11 Commission report.* https://govinfo.library.unt.edu/911/report/911Report.pdf

36. *Congressional Record* For enacted resolutions or legislation, give the number of the congress after the number of the resolution or legislation, the *Congressional Record* volume number, the page number(s), and year, followed by *(enacted).*

H. Res. 2408, 108th Cong., 150 Cong. Rec. 1331–1332 (2004) (enacted).

Give the full name of the resolution or legislation when citing it within your sentence, but abbreviate the name when it appears in a parenthetical in-text citation: *(H. Res. 2408, 2004).* 368, 2013

Academic works

37. Report or working paper If the issuing organization numbered the report, include that number in parentheses after the title.

Forbes, K. J. (2019). *Has globalization changed the inflation process?* (BIS Working Paper No. 791). BIS. https://www.bis.org/publ/work791.pdf

38. Conference presentation   Treat a published conference presentation as a selection in a book *(no. 19),* as a periodical article *(no. 29),* or as a report *(no. 43),* whichever applies. For an unpublished conference presentation, provide the author, the year and month of the conference, the italicized title of the presentation, and the presentation's form, forum, and place.

> Xing, J. (2018, January). *Free and equal: Standing up for diversity.*
>
> Speech presented at the Davos World Economic Forum 2018,
>
> Davos, Switzerland. https://www.weforum.org/events/world-
>
> economic-forum-annual-meeting-2018/sessions/
>
> a0Wb000000AllQFEA3

39. Dissertation or dissertation abstract   Use this format for an unpublished dissertation.

> Lederman, J. (2011). *Critical, third-space phenomenology as*
>
> *a framework for validating college composition placement.*
>
> [Unpublished doctoral dissertation]. Indiana University.

If you used an abstract from *Dissertation Abstracts International,* treat the entry like a periodical article.

> Leger-Rodriguez, T. N. (2011). Paraprofessional preparation and
>
> supervision in special education. *Dissertations Abstracts*
>
> *International, 71,* 2846.

40. Published dissertation   Include the dissertation file number at the end of the entry. If citing a dissertation published online (not from a database), follow the second example below.

> Weill, J. M. (2016). *Incarceration and social networks: Understanding*
>
> *the relationships that support reentry* (Publication No.
>
> 95F6457A85534232) [Doctoral dissertation, University of
>
> California]. EbscoHOST: Open Dissertations. https://escholarship.
>
> org/uc/item/6z15h0jj
>
> Warner, A. (2018). *Writing new boundaries for the law: Black women's*
>
> *fiction and the abject in psychoanalysis* [Doctoral dissertation,
>
> University of Massachusetts Amherst]. Scholar Works
>
> @UMASSAmherst Doctoral Dissertations. https://scholarworks.
>
> umass.edu/dissertations_2/1303/

Web and social media sources

41. Basic entry for a whole Web site or independent online work   Do not include an entry in the references list. In the body of your paper, give the Web site's name and home page URL; for example: A majority of Americans get their news from social media sites, primarily Facebook (http://www.facebook.com).

42. Basic entry for a page, report, or part of a Web site   Include the Web site sponsor in the retrieval statement unless the author of the work is also the sponsor. Here, the author is the World Health Organization, and the sponsor is BPD Sanctuary.

> World Health Organization. (1992). *ICD-10 criteria for borderline*
>
> *personality disorder.* http://www.mhsanctuary.com/borderline/
>
> icd10.htm

43. Document on a university's Web site   Include relevant information about the university and department in the retrieval statement.

> Tugal, C. (2002). Islamism in Turkey: Beyond instrument and meaning.
>
> *Economy and Society, 31,* 85–111. http://sociology.berkeley.edu/
>
> public_sociology_pdf/tugal.pps05.pdf

44. Online document lacking a date   Use the abbreviation *n.d.* (no date) for any undated document.

> Center for Science in the Public Interest. (n.d.). *Food additives to*
>
> *avoid.* http://www.mindfully.org/Food/Food-Additives-Avoid.htm

45. Entry in a wiki   Check with your instructor before using a wiki as a source. If you do cite a source from a wiki, include a DOI, if one is available. If not, use the Web site name and the URL of the entry. When citing a *Wikipedia* article, click on "Page Information" to obtain the date of the article's most recent revision. For a source that can be updated at any time, if an archived version is not available, include the words "Retrieved from" and the retrieval date (see no. 46).

> Matsumoto, D., & Ekman, P. (2008.) Facial expression analysis. In
>
> *Scholarpedia.* https://doi.org/10.4249/scholarpedia.4237

> Arches National Park. (2019, December 13). In *Wikipedia.* https://
>
> en.wikipedia.org/wiki/Arches_National_Park

46. Blog or social media post   Treat online posts as short works from Web sites. The following examples refer to posts made on a professional blog, Facebook, Twitter, and Instagram. Note the use of a URL shortener in the third example. Because blog and social media sources can be updated at any time, include a retrieval date before the URL.

Sobel, A. (n.d.). Take a walk in his footsteps. *National Parks Foundation Blog.* Retrieved February 12, 2020, from https://www.nationalparks.org/connect/blog/take-walk-his-footsteps

Nguyen, V. T. (2017, May 14). *My favorite picture of my mother and me* [Facebook post]. Facebook. Retrieved May 17, 2017, from http://www.facebook.com/pg/vietnguyenauthor/posts/?ref=page_internal

LGBTQNation [@lgbtqnation]. (2019, November 9). *The American Psychological Association now requires researchers to use 'they' for non-binary people* [Tweet]. Twitter. Retrieved December 29, 2019, from https://tinyurl.com/vkfgyyq

Secon, F. [@francisco_seco]. (2017, May 26). *Sigrid* [Photograph]. Instagram. Retrieved May 26, 2017, from http://www.instagram.com/p/BUjhvb1jLAo/?taken-by=francisco_seco

Because Snapchat "snaps" disappear after viewing, meaning that readers cannot access them, do not include them in your reference list. Instead, in the body of your paper, mention the snap(s) you have chosen to source, and include its author, date, and a brief description. Better yet, take a screenshot of the snap and present it in your paper as a figure with a caption that indicates its source.

47. Personal page on a social media site

Kron, S. (n.d). Susan Kron [Facebook page]. Facebook. Retrieved November 25, 2013, from http://www.facebook.com/susan.kron.35

48. Post to an electronic mailing list, newsgroup, or forum   Provide the message's author, its date, and its subject line as the title. If an author is identified by a screen name only, use the screen name in place of author name. For a post to a mailing list, provide the description *Electronic mailing list message* in brackets. For a post to a newsgroup or discussion forum, give the identifying information *Online forum comment* in brackets. Conclude either entry with the words *Retrieved from*, followed by the URL of the archived message.

Phaltan, N. (2013, December 13). NY Times article on what fuel poor need [Electronic mailing list message]. http://lists.bioenergylists.org/pipermail/stoves_lists.bioenergylists.org/2013-December/007752.html

Reysa, G. (2014, January 1). Stealing heat from a woodstove for water

heating [Online forum comment]. http://lists.bioenergylists.org/

pipermail/greenbuilding_lists.bioenergylists.org/2014-January.txt

49. E-mail or text message E-mail, text messages, or other nonarchived personal communication should be cited in the body of your text but not given in the references list *(see in-text citation entry no. 10, on p. 330).*

Other Electronic Sources

50. Digital file on your computer Use the citation format of the most closely related type of source. Indicate the type of file in brackets [Word file, MP3 file, PDF file, and so on], or if the format is unclear, use [Digital file].

Mars, B. (2012). Locked out of heaven. On *Unorthodox jukebox* [MP3

file]. Atlantic Records.

51. Computer software or video game Cite only specialized software. Familiar software such as Microsoft Word doesn't need to be cited.

Persson, M. (2001). Minecraft [Video game]. Mojang. https://www.

minegraft.net/en-us

52. Mobile application Cite phone and mobile apps the same way you would cite software. Common whole apps like Facebook and Twitter do not need to be included in the references list; only list these when you are citing original content.

Waze: Navigation and live traffic (2018). *Waze, Incorporated* [Phone

app]. App Store. https://www.itunes.apple.com/us/app/waz-

navigation-live-traffic/id323229106?mt=8

Visuals, audio, and other media

53. Photograph, work of art, graph, map, or other visual If you have reproduced a visual, give the source information with the caption (for an example, see p. 363). Also include a reference-list entry.

Kapoor, A. (2006). *Cloud Gate* [Sculpture]. Millennium Park of

Chicago.

Parks, G. (1942). *American Gothic* [Photograph]. Library of Congress.

http://www.loc.gov/pictures/item/2017765074/

Colonial Virginia [Map]. (1960). Virginia Historical Society.

> Google (n.d.) [Google Maps road map of Kingsville, Texas]. Retrieved
>
> January 21, 2019, from https://tinyurl.com/y6spp6bg

The third example shows how to cite dynamically created maps (such as a Google map) which change over time; these maps do not have titles or publication dates. Use the abbreviation n.d. in such cases and include a description in square brackets, followed by a retrieval date and a URL. In the example above, a URL shortener was used.

54. Advertisement   Include the word *advertisement* within brackets.

> Arm & Hammer Detergent. (2018, September). *A fresh spin*
>
> *[Advertisement]. Real Simple,* 42.

> AEO Management Company. (2018). *This is what #AerieReal is all*
>
> *about* [Advertisement]. https://www.ae.com/featured-aeriereal/
>
> aerie/s-cms/6890055?catId=cat6890055

55. Video, film, or TV show   Begin with the cited person's name and, if appropriate, a parenthetical notation of his or her role. After the title, identify the medium, followed by the country and name of the distributor. The first example cites a motion picture, such as one you might view in a theater; the second and third examples are online videos.

> Goldsman, A. (Director). (2014). *Winter's tale* [Film]. Warner Brothers
>
> Pictures.

> Wharmby, T. (Director). (2018, May 22). Date with destiny (Season 15,
>
> Episode 24) [Television series episode]. In D. P. Bellisario
>
> (Executive Producer), *NCIS*. CBS. https://www.netflix.com/
>
> title/70142386

> Blank on Blank. (2017, January 24). *Oliver Sacks on ripe bananas*
>
> [Video]. YouTube. https://www.youtube.com/
>
> watch?v=HbaazbdIR_g

56. Radio or television broadcast   For a radio broadcast, treat the host as author (Van Zandt example). For an entire television series, treat the producer as author (Ashford example). For a single episode, use the writer and director as authors and the producer as editor (see Wharmby example in no. 55).

> Van Zandt, S. (Host). (2019, November 19). *Underground garage*
>
> [Radio program broadcast]. WKGO. https://www.
>
> undergroundgarage.com/shows-919-910/show-919-barry-
>
> greenwich-amp-dixon

Ashford, Michelle (Producer). (2013). *Masters of sex* [Television series]. Showtime.

57. Audio recording or podcast

Glass, I. (Host). (2013, November 8). The seven things you're not supposed to talk about. In *This American life* [Audio podcast episode]. WEBZ Chicago. https://www.thisamericanlife.org/511/the-seven-things-youre-not-supposed-to-talk-about

Lamar, K. (2017). DNA [Song]. On *Damn*. Aftermath Entertainment; Interscope Records; Top Dawg Entertainment.

58. Musical composition

Salonen, E. (2010). *NYX* [Musical composition].

Other miscellaneous sources

59. Lecture, speech, or address List the speaker; the year, month, and date (if available); and the italicized title of the presentation. Include location information when available. For online versions, add the URL.

Saunders, G. (2013, May 11). Becoming kinder [Commencement address]. Syracuse University, Syracuse, NY, United States.

Adichie, C. N. (2012, December). We should all be feminists [Video]. TED Conferences. http://www.ted.com/talks/chimamanda_ngozi_adichie_we_should_all_be_feminists?language_en

60. Personal interview Like other unpublished personal communications, personal interviews are not included in the reference list. See in-text citation entry no. 10 (p. 330).

61. Live performance

Parker, T., Stone, M., & Lopez, R. (Authors), Nicholaw, C., & Parker T. (Directors). (2014, March 4). *The Book of Mormon* [Theatrical performance]. Eugene O'Neill Theatre, New York, NY.

62. Presentation slides

> Volunteering Australia Inc. (2009). Volunteering: What's it all about?
>
> [PowerPoint slides]. http://www.volunteeringaustralia.org/files/
>
> WZ7K0VWICM/Volunteering%20what_s%20it%20all%20about.
>
> ppt

CHAPTER 33

APA Style: Format

The following guidelines are recommended by the *Publication Manual of the American Psychological Association,* seventh edition. For an example of a research project that has been prepared using APA style, see pages 351–63.

Materials   Back up your final draft. Use a high-quality printer and white 8½-by-11-inch paper. Do not justify your text or hyphenate words at the right margin; it should be ragged.

Title page   The first page of your research report should be a title page. Center the title between the left and right margins in the upper half of the page, and put your name, name of the department, the college or university, course, professor, and the date on separate lines below the title. *(See p. 351 for an example.)*

Margins and spacing   Use one-inch margins all around, except for the upper right-hand corner, where the page number goes.

Double-space lines throughout, including in the abstract, within any notes or captions, and in the list of references. Indent the first word of each paragraph one-half inch (or five spaces).

For quotations of more than forty words, use block format, and indent five spaces from the left margin. Double-space the quoted lines.

Page numbers and abbreviated titles   Number all pages, starting with the title page. While running heads are not required for most courses, if your professor does require them, include on all pages, including the title page, a short version of your title in uppercase letters. Put this information in the upper left-hand corner of each page, about one-half inch from the top. Put the page number in the upper right-hand corner.

Abstract   Instructors sometimes require an abstract—a summary of your paper's thesis, major points or lines of development, and conclusions. The abstract appears on its own numbered page, entitled "Abstract," right after the title page. It should not exceed 150 to 250 words.

Headings Primary headings should be boldfaced and centered. All key words in the heading should be capitalized.

Secondary headings should be boldfaced and appear flush against the left-hand margin. Do not use a heading for your introduction, however. *(For more on headings, see Chapter 8: Designing Academic Texts and Portfolios, p. 90.)*

Visuals Place each visual (table, chart, graph, or image) on its own page following the reference list and any content notes. Tables precede figures. Label each visual as a table or a figure, and number each kind consecutively (Table 1, Table 2). Provide an informative caption for each visual. Cite the source of the material, and provide explanatory notes as needed. *(For more on using visuals effectively, see Chapter 6: Drafting Text and Visuals, pp. 52–65.)*

CHAPTER 34

Sample Research Project in APA Style

Rachel Anthony researched the topic of doping by Olympic athletes and wrote a report about it for her introductory sociology course. Her sources included books, journal articles, and Web documents.

CONSIDER YOUR SITUATION

Author: Rachel Anthony

Type of writing: Research report

Purpose: To report on the motivations and implications of doping by Olympic athletes.

Stance: Objective

Audience: Students, instructors, athletes, sociologists

Medium: Print, as text attachment, part of e-portfolio

Anthony writes: As I did my research for this topic, I was surprised to learn how frequently Olympic athletes turn to performance-enhancing drugs.

1

Olympic Doping

Rachel Anthony

SOC 101

History and Sociology of Sport

Governor's State University

Professor Filippo

April 29, 2020

2

Abstract

Olympic cheating is as old as the games themselves. Many believe the first historically recorded games were the result of cheating during a chariot race. Today, cheating typically takes the form of doping—the use of prohibited substances to enhance athletic performance. The reasons for cheating seem somewhat straightforward; however, the results are not. When it is determined that an Olympic athlete is guilty of doping—sometimes years after the victory—the fallout is far more complicated than just taking a medal away from one athlete and giving it to another. There are significant implications, often including losing millions of dollars in sponsorships and endorsements. In addition to the athletes themselves, doctors and coaches,

Abstract appears on a new page after the title page. The first line is not indented.

Research report is concisely and objectively summarized— key points included, but not details or statistics.

and even whole countries, can be involved in cheating scandals. In spite of strict testing procedures, some athletes continue to try to outwit science while other athletes compete "clean," even when doing so is to their disadvantage.

Keywords: Beijing, Chaunté Lowe, cheating, doping, drug testing, Olympic Games

Paragraph should be between 150 and 250 words.

3

Olympic Doping

Chaunté Lowe's story showcases both the best and the worst of the Olympic Games. A high jumper, Lowe competed in four games—in 2004, 2008, 2012, and 2016—without winning a medal. She did, however, become "a favorite of the track crowds, with her high bounding steps and leaps, slithering up, up and over that bar" (Powell, 2017, para. 26). Her appeal is evident: "She lands and bounds to her feet, clapping, smiling, doing a little boogie" (Powell, 2017, para. 26). Lowe has the backstory that Olympic announcers love to feature, according to Powell. She grew up with an unreliable mother and a father in jail, and she experienced a house foreclosure followed by a period of homelessness. In spite of these early difficulties, she eventually found a much-needed sense of stability in

Full title is repeated on first page only.

APA requires that writers include paragraph references even when paragraphs are not numbered in the source. This student includes them for sources of quotations only, counting from the beginning of the source. When a source includes subheadings, she indicates the subheading in quotation marks.

4

her grandmother, with whom she lived, and later in a supportive and committed coach at Georgia Tech (Powell, 2017).

Doping plays a huge role in the current chapter of Lowe's life story. In November 2016, Lowe was notified that retroactive drug tests revealed that the third-, fourth-, and fifth-place finishers in the 2008 Olympics in Beijing had resorted to doping. This revelation effectively moved Lowe from sixth place to third, which meant that she earned a bronze medal (Powell, 2017). Telling her story on John Williams's WGN radio show (Williams, 2017), she sounds happy and wistful, not bitter. "Cheating was never an option for me," she told Williams. But still, she can understand the pressures on others to do so.

Although cheating by Olympic athletes is nothing new, their reasons for cheating and the methods they use to do so, have evolved over time. And the consequences that cheaters and their fellow athletes endure as a result are far-reaching and significant.

Thesis statement.

Olympic Origins

Heading in bold type, centered.

Although the true origin of the Olympics is somewhat unknown, Phippen (2016), a journalist, related a story that might provide insight into why some athletes cheat. Pelops, a suitor for the hand of Greek King Oenomaus's daughter, began the games roughly 3,000 years ago to "commemorate his triumph" after besting King Oenomaus in a chariot race, thus becoming the king's son-in-law. To ensure a win, Pelops "bribed a man" to rig Oenomaus's

5

chariot. In this version of the origins of the Olympics, the games were actually created because of cheating.

According to some sources, including Phippen, "plenty of athletes cheated" (2016, para. 10), despite swearing to Zeus to compete fairly. Cheaters were sometimes flogged or were excluded from the games. They also paid fines that were used to erect *Zanes*, or honorific statues in the likeness of Zeus (Cartwright, 2013). Each *Zane* included a "small plaque that chastised competitors accused of misconduct" (Phippen, 2016, para. 9). The *Zanes*, however, were not a deterrent (Spivey, 2004) "This warning, and the overt, long-standing disgrace of miscreants, did not deter further incidents of bribery and subterfuge: the number of *Zanes* multiplied" (p. 166).

Over the years since those first games, "the manner of cheating has evolved," wrote Phippen, but "the human desire to cheat has not" (2016, para. 4). The games that have come to be known as the "Modern Olympics," the first games after A.D. 393, began in 1896 in Athens, when 241 participants from 14 nations competed in 43 events (International Olympic Committee, n.d.-a). For these games the marathon was created "as a tribute to the legend of Pheidippides, a courier who ran roughly twenty-five miles, from a great battle . . . and then collapsed and died from the effort" (Staton, 2012, para. 2). The third-place marathon winner of the 1896 games was discovered to have used a carriage to complete a portion of the course. Eight years later, a car replaced the carriage in a similar incident (Staton, 2012, para 5). So began the modern era of Olympic cheating.

6

Modern-Day Cheating

Today, an Olympic athlete jumping into a car for a few miles seems practically impossible; cameras capture competitors' every move on the course. However, there are other ways of cheating, such as doping—broadly defined by the World Anti-Doping Agency (WADA) as "the occurrence of one or more of the anti-doping rule violations," which include the use, attempted use, or "presence of a *Prohibited Substance* . . . in an *Athlete's Sample*" (2015, p. 18). Even though athletes are monitored and tested on a routine basis, many do not seem to be deterred from doping.

It is worth noting that some athletes cheat without knowing they are doing so. The East German women's swimming team is a famous example. Reporting from Berlin in 2000 for *The New York Times*, Maimon covered the court case of Lothar Kipke. As the head doctor in charge of the drug program of the East German Swimming Federation from 1975 to 1985, Kipke was ultimately convicted "of doping and causing bodily harm to 58 swimmers" (Maimon, 2000, introduction, para. 4). The girls who were doped, some as young as 10 years old, were given "40 pills a day," which were "taken under strict supervision" (Maimon, 2000, "A Regimen of Pills," para. 3). Years later, many swimmers reported major medical issues, including pregnancies resulting in birth defects (Maimon, 2000).

Source is a newspaper article retrieved online, so subsection is named and paragraph number provided. For a print newspaper article, include a page number in the citation.

7

Others cheat purposefully. Edwards quotes Dick Pound, the former WADA chairman, on five of the top reasons athletes choose to use performance-enhancing drugs:

1. A desire to win at all costs—even if that means lying.
2. For financial reasons—with professionals trying to extend a career.
3. National pressures—as exemplified by the old East German system.
4. Individual pressure from coaches—who get paid better if they coach winners, and that can apply for administrators too.
5. Finally, they dope because they believe they will not get caught—they believe they are invincible. (2010, para. 10)

By all accounts, the pressures on Olympians are intense, and significant funds are required for training and competing even before an athlete reaches the Olympic Games. However, the temptation to cheat is great. "Once you start winning, sponsors will be attracted and then money will come," explained South African athlete Hezekiel Sepeng, who won a silver medal at the 1996 Olympic Games but lost his career when he later tested positive for an anabolic steroid (Edwards, 2012, "Leveling the Playing Field," para. 8). Another example is U.S. sprinter Marion Jones, who in 2007 lost millions of dollars in sponsorship deals when stripped of her Olympic medals (Edwards, 2012). A December 12, 2007, ESPN.com story describes

8

Jones, "once the world's biggest track and field star," as a "disgraced drug cheat" (2007, para. 2).

Money and medals aside, Edwards has noted that the "sad truth is that many [athletes] do successfully beat the drug testers" (2012, para. 16). Moreover, while many athletes dope in order to boost their already considerable talents, others say they dope not to gain advantage, but rather to avoid disadvantage. If other athletes are doping, then the competition is unfair (Edwards, 2012). On October 9, 2012, George Hincapie, an elite cyclist, posted a statement on his website that supports this theory:

> It is extremely difficult today to acknowledge that during a part of my career I used banned substances. . . . Early in my professional career, it became clear to me that, given the widespread use of performance enhancing drugs by cyclists at the top of the profession, it was not possible to compete at the highest level without them. (Hincapie, para. 3)

Hincapie is not alone. Gifford (2016), writing for *Scientific American* online, cited an anonymous survey revealing that 29% of polled athletes confessed to resorting to performance-enhancing drugs. "Clearly, plenty of cheaters are getting away with it," Gifford (2016, para. 6) concluded.

The website of the International Olympic Committee does not provide a list of athletes who have been stripped of their medals. A search for medalists from the 2008 Beijing Games turns up this official statement: "Please note

APA allows writers to silently edit for capitalization at the start of a quotation.

Quotations of more than forty words are indented one-half inch from the margin.

9

that because a number of anti-doping rules violations procedures are still in progress—including procedures involving . . . the samples collected in Beijing 2008 and London 2012—the information contained in the list is not final" (International Olympic Committee, n.d.-b). However, a 2015 report posted on the WADA website (World Anti-Doping Agency, 2017) offers some statistics on anti-doping rule violations (see Figure 1).

Name of corporate author included in its entirety in paren-thetical citation.

Develop-ment by illustration (see p. 53); figure reference provided. Figure appears after the list of references.

While many cheaters are never discovered, in the long run, the odds seem to be against athletes who dope: "In order to compete, athletes must give up their privacy, notifying officials of their whereabouts every single day of the year, so they can be located for on-the-spot, out-of-competition testing overseen by the World Anti-Doping Agency" (Gifford, 2016, introduction, para. 7). In her WGN interview, Chaunté Lowe supported Gifford's findings when she explained that drug tests happen randomly and frequently, several times a week. According to Lowe, samples are saved and retested for years to "allow the technology to catch up to the methods of cheating" (Williams, 2017).

The Cost of Doping

The cost of doping—financial and otherwise—is incalculable and affects all athletes, whether they are medalists or not. The decision to take away Jones's five medals may have affected the status of dozens of athletes ("Jones stripped"). Take away a gold medal and the silver medalist

10

moves up; then the bronze winner; then suddenly, like Lowe, the sixth-place finisher is a medal winner—sometimes years later, without the medal ceremony, the endorsements, and the additional competition opportunities. As Lowe explained, "It rewrites my story" (Williams, 2017).

In the years since the summer 2007 Olympics, winners have had the potential to gain millions in endorsement and sponsorship deals. Nonmedalists often do not have that option, even when they receive their awards years later. In other words, winners who are later found to be cheaters nevertheless prosper, at least in the short-term. On the other hand, competitors later found to be medal winners are cheated out of possibilities. For example, the pole-vaulter Derek Miles was belatedly awarded a bronze medal for his performance in the Beijing Olympic Games. Today, he is an assistant track coach at the University of South Dakota (Powell, 2017). Coaching track is not a bad job, but winning athletes should have the chance to benefit from their performance. If nothing else, Miles was denied his moment on the dais, standing below the US flag and accepting the congratulations of the 2008 Olympic crowd. Instead of receiving his medal in a cheering stadium, Miles accepted his belated honor on April 17, 2017, in what looks like a windowless classroom. Miles was emotional as he spoke to the small group—thankful, grateful, and appreciative. Like Lowe, he was not bitter. Instead, he spoke of being lucky

Anecdote as evidence in support of a claim (see p. 124).

11

and of the opportunities he has had to surround himself with great people ("Derek Miles," 2017).

Back in 773 B.C., athletes stood in front of the bronze icon "Zeus the Oath Giver" and "swore an oath to the god of thunder vowing they would follow the regulations of the Olympics and play fair" (Phippen, 2016, para. 1). Today, one Olympian from each host country takes the official Olympian oath for all those competing. One wonders how seriously some athletes treat this oath, as it seems doping is likely to continue for the foreseeable future. Still, other athletes, like Lowe and Miles, continue to take this oath to heart. In doing so, they commit to competing "clean," to benefiting not from drugs, but from skill, passion, and dedication. They are the true Olympians.

New page, title centered and bolded Entries are in alphabetical order by author's last name or, if no author, by first important word in the title

Source: Article from an online encyclopedia; note that the IOC treats "Olympic Games" as a proper noun, so the writer has included appropriate capitalization here.

Source: Online video; source has no author, so citation begins with the title of the video and the description "[Video]" appears in brackets.

12

References

Cartwright, M. (2013, May 23). Olympic Games. In *Ancient History Encyclopedia.* http://www.ancient.eu/ Olympic_Games/#related_articles

Derek Miles receives Olympic bronze medal [Video]. (2017, April 17). Argus Leader http://www.argusleader .com/videos/sports/college/university-of-south-dakota /2017/04/17/video-derek-miles-receives-olympic -bronze-medal/100575290/

13

Edwards, P. (2012, December 11). The gain game: Why do sports stars cheat? *CNN.* http://www.cnn.com/2012/12/11/sport/sport-cheats-suarez-cazorla/index.html

Gifford, B. (2016, August 5). The *Scientific American* guide to cheating in the Olympics. Scientific American https://www.scientificamerican.com/article/the-scientific-american-guide-to-cheating-in-the-olympics/

Hincapie, G. (2012, October 9). [Statement from George Hincapie]. http://hincapie.com/ourstory

International Olympic Committee. (n.d.-a). Athens 1896. https://www.olympic.org/athens-1896

International Olympic Committee. (n.d.-b). Athletics. https://www.olympic.org/beijing-2008/athletics

Jones stripped of five Olympic medals, banned from Beijing Games. (2007, December 12). ESPN http://www.espn.com/olympics.trackandfield/news/story?id=3151367

Maimon, A. (2000, February 6). One tale of doping and birth defects. [Special report]. *The New York Times.* http://www.nytimes.com/library/sports/other/020600swim-germany.html

Phippen, J. W. (2016, August 19). A brief history of cheating at the Olympics. *The Atlantic.* https://www.theatlantic.com/news/archive/2016/08/cheating-at-the-olympics/495938/

Powell, M. (2017, July 7). Olympic medal, earned; glory, denied; future, uncertain. *The New York Times.* https://www.nytimes.com/2017/07/07/sports/chaute-lowe-olympics-doping-high-jump.html

Source: Article from a news site.

Source: Article from a magazine, posted online.

Source: Public statement.

Source: Article published by a corporate author.

14

Spivey, N. (2004). *Ancient Olympics: A history.* Oxford
    University Press.

Staton, S. (2012, August 3). Crossing the line. *The
    New Yorker.* http://newyorker.com/news/sporting-scene/
    crossing-the-line

Williams, J. (Host). (2017, July 12). "Donald Trump
    Jr. defends emails" [Audio podcast episode]. In *The
    John Williams Show.* http://wgnradio.com/2017/07/12/
    the-john-williams-show-full-podcast-07-12-17-human-
    chain-rip-tide-rescuer-donald-trump-jr-defends-e-mails-
    olympics-bronze-medalist-chaunte-lowe/

World Anti-Doping Agency. (2015, January 1). *World anti-
    doping code 2015.* https://www.wada-ama.org/sites/
    default/files/resources/files/wada-2015-world-anti-
    doping-code.pdf

World Anti-Doping Agency. (2017, April 3). *2015 Anti-doping
    rule violations [ADRVs] report.* https://www.wada-ama.
    org/sites/default/files/resources/files/2015_adrvs_
    report_web_release_0.pdf

Source:
Print book
without an
assigned
DOI.

Source:
Audio
podcast.

Source:
Report by
corporate
author.

15

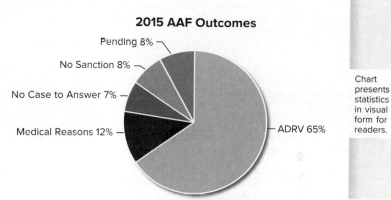

2015 AAF Outcomes

Pending 8%

No Sanction 8%

No Case to Answer 7%

Medical Reasons 12%

ADRV 65%

Chart presents statistics in visual form for readers.

Figure 1. Sports that had the highest numbers of anti-doping rule violations (ADRVs) in 2015. Adapted from "Statistics on anti-doping rule violations (ADVRs)," by the World Anti-Doping Association, 2017, *2015 Anti-doping rule violations [ADRVs] report, p. 6* (https://www.wada-ama.org/sites/default/files/resources/files/2015_adrvs_report_web_release_0.pdf). Copyright 2017 by WADA.

Figure number in italics, followed by figure title and source information, appears below the figure.

Credits

8

Other Documentation Styles
Chicago and CSE

*Nothing gives an author so much pleasure as to find his works
respectfully quoted by other learned authors.*

–Benjamin Franklin

In response to concerns scientists have cited about the harm fossil fuel use can
inflict on the environment, the United States and other countries throughout the
world are increasingly turning to alternative energy sources, such as this wind
energy plant in Altamont, California.

8 Other Documentation Styles

─START SMART
Tab 8: Other Documentation Styles

This section will help you answer questions such as the following:

Rhetorical Knowledge

- Which disciplines use Chicago style? (35)
- Which disciplines use CSE style? (37)
- What are the three forms of CSE style? (37)

Critical Thinking, Reading, and Writing

- Why do I need to document my sources? (35, 37)

Knowledge of Conventions

- How do I cite sources in the text of my paper in Chicago and CSE style? (35, 36, 37)
- What formats are used for a bibliography or works-cited list in Chicago style? (35, 36)
- What is appropriate formatting for a list of references in CSE style? (37)
- How do I cite electronic sources, such as Web sites, podcasts, and online articles with DOIs? (35, 37)

For a general introduction to writing outcomes, see 1e, pages 14–15.

There are many documentation styles besides those developed by the Modern Language Association *(see Tab 6)* and the American Psychological Association *(see Tab 7)*. In this section, we cover the style presented in *The Chicago Manual of Style* and the three styles developed by the Council of Science Editors. To find out where you can learn about other style types, consult the list of style manuals on page 259. If you are not sure which style to use, ask your instructor.

CHAPTER 35

Chicago Documentation Style: Elements

The note and bibliography style presented in the seventeenth edition of *The Chicago Manual of Style* (Chicago: University of Chicago Press, 2017) is used in many disciplines, including history, art, philosophy, business, and communications. This style has three parts:

- Numbered in-text citations
- Numbered footnotes or endnotes
- A bibliography of works consulted

The first two parts are necessary; the third is optional, unless your instructor requires it. (Chicago also has an alternative author-date system that is similar to APA style.) For more information on this style, consult the *Chicago Manual of Style*. For updates and answers to frequently asked questions about this style, go to the "*Chicago Manual of Style* Web site" at <www.chicagomanualofstyle.org/tools _citationguide.html>.

35a Use numbered in-text citations and notes.

Whenever you use information or ideas from a source, you need to indicate what you have borrowed by putting a superscript number in the text (^{1}) at the end of the borrowed material. These superscript numbers are placed after all punctuation marks except for the dash.

> *New Yorker* columnist Elizabeth Kolbert explains one reason that
> people find fake news believable: when reading or watching the news,
> people tend to experience "confirmation bias," or "the tendency . . . to
> embrace information that supports their beliefs and reject information
> that contradicts them." In other words, people believe what they want
> to believe and can even "experience genuine pleasure—a rush of
> dopamine—when processing information that supports their beliefs."[4]

If a quotation is fairly long, you can set it off as a block quotation. Indent it five spaces or one-half inch from the left margin, and double-space the quotation, leaving an extra space above and below it. Place the superscript number after the period that ends the quotation.

Each in-text superscript number must have a corresponding note either at the foot of the page or at the end of the text. Indent the first line of each footnote like a paragraph. Footnotes begin with the number and are single-spaced, with a double space between notes.

If you are using endnotes instead of footnotes, they should begin after the last page of your text on a new numbered page titled "Notes." The list of endnotes can be double-spaced, unless your instructor prefers that you make them single-spaced.

The first time you cite a source in either a footnote or an endnote, you should include a full citation. Subsequent citations require less information.

FIRST REFERENCE TO SOURCE

2. Nancy Gibbs, "When a President Can't Be Taken at His Word," *Time,* April 3, 2017, 5.

If you quote from the same work immediately after providing a full footnote, use a shortened version of the full citation.

ENTRY FOR SOURCE ALREADY CITED

8. Gibbs, 5.

If several pages pass between references to the same title, include a brief version of the title to clarify the reference.

ENTRY FOR SOURCE ALREADY CITED IN LONGER PAPER

Gibbs, "President," 5.

35b Prepare a separate bibliography or list of works cited if your instructor requires one.

Some instructors require a separate list of works cited or of works consulted. If you are asked to provide a works-cited list, do so on a separate, numbered page titled "Works Cited." If the list should include all works you consulted, title it "Bibliography." Here is a sample entry.

Gibbs, Nancy. "When a President Can't Be Taken at His Word." *Time*, April 3, 2017.

DOIs and URLs in CMS Citations

In general, citations for electronic sources include all of the information required for print sources, in addition to a URL (universal resource locator) or DOI (direct object identifier) and, in some cases, the date of access.

- Chicago recommends URLs or DOIs (preferring the latter when available) for all online sources.
- Months are not abbreviated, and the date is usually given in the following order: month, day, year (September 13, 2014).
- Chicago recommends including dates of access only for sources that do not disclose a date of publication or revision. However, many instructors require students to include access dates for all online sources. Ask your instructor for their policy. If access dates are required, include them *before* the URL or DOI.

Use a period after any URL or DOI. If the URL or DOI has to be broken across lines, the break should occur *before* a slash (/), a period, a hyphen, an underscore, or a tilde (~). However, a break should occur *after* a colon.

35c Use the correct Chicago style for notes and bibliography entries.

Authors of Any Source

1. One author

NOTE

1. Paul Bloom, *Just Babies: The Origin of Good and Evil* (New York: Crown, 2013), 32.

CHICAGO STYLE:
DIRECTORY TO SAMPLE TYPES

BIBLIOGRAPHY ENTRY

Bloom, Paul. *Just Babies: The Origin of Good and Evil*. New York: Crown, 2013.

2. Two or more authors   In notes, you can name up to three authors. When there are three authors, put a comma after the first name and a comma plus *and* after the second.

NOTE

2. Joelle Reeder and Katherine Scoleri, *The IT Girl's Guide to Blogging with Moxie* (Hoboken, NJ: Wiley, 2007), 45.

BIBLIOGRAPHY ENTRY

Reeder, Joelle, and Katherine Scoleri. *The IT Girl's Guide to Blogging with Moxie*. Hoboken, NJ: Wiley. 2007.

When more than three authors are listed on the title page, use *et al.* (meaning "and others") after the first author's name in the note.

NOTE

3. Julian Henriques et al., *Changing the Subject: Psychology, Social Regulation and Subjectivity* (New York: Methuen, 1984), 275.

BIBLIOGRAPHY ENTRY

Henriques, Julian, Wendy Holloway, Cathy Urwin, Couze Venn, and Valerie Walkerdine. *Changing the Subject: Psychology, Social Regulation and Subjectivity*. New York: Methuen, 1984.

Give all author names in bibliography entries.

3. Organization as author   Treat the organization as the author, and use the same format as for an author-based note.

NOTE

4. United Nations, *World Investment Report 2013: Global Value Chains—Investment and Trade for Development* (New York: United Nations, 2013), 15.

BIBLIOGRAPHY ENTRY

United Nations. *World Investment Report 2013: Global Value Chains—Investment and Trade for Development*. New York: United Nations, 2013.

4. Multiple works by the same author   After providing complete information in the first footnote, include only a shortened version of the title with the author's last name and the page number in any subsequent footnotes. In the bibliography, list entries in alphabetical order by title; in the references list, list by date, from earliest to most recent. After the first listing, replace the author's name with a "three-em" dash (type three hyphens in a row).

NOTES

5. Shirky, *Cognitive Surplus,* 15.

6. Shirky, *Here Comes Everybody,* 65–66.

BIBLIOGRAPHY ENTRIES

Shirky, Clay. *Cognitive Surplus: Creativity and Generosity in a Connected Age.* New York: Penguin, 2010.

———. *Here Comes Everybody: The Power of Organizing without Organizations.* New York: Penguin, 2008.

5. Unknown author   Cite anonymous works by title, and alphabetize them by the first word, ignoring *A, An,* or *The.*

NOTE

7. *The British Album* (London: John Bell, 1790), 2:43–47.

BIBLIOGRAPHY ENTRY

The British Album. Vol. 2. London: John Bell, 1790.

Books

6. Basic entry for a book

NOTE

8. J. D. Vance, *Hillbilly Elegy: A Memoir of a Family and Culture in Crisis.* (New York: HarperCollins, 2016), 32.

BIBLIOGRAPHY ENTRY

Vance, J. D. *Hillbilly Elegy: A Memoir of a Family and Culture in Crisis.* New York: HarperCollins, 2016.

7. Book on a Web site   For an book you have accessed on the Web, include the date of access before the URL—or DOI if it is available—if your instructor requires it, as in the following example.

NOTE

9. Carl Sandburg, *Chicago Poems* (New York: Henry Holt, 1916), accessed March 18, 2017, http://www.bartleby.com/165/index.html.

BIBLIOGRAPHY ENTRY

Sandburg, Carl. *Chicago Poems.* New York: Henry Holt, 1916. Accessed March 18, 2017. http://www.bartleby.com/165/index.html.

8. E-book   For an e-book, indicate the format at the end of the citation (for example, *Kindle edition, PDF e-book*). Because page numbers can vary, use the chapter number, section number, or another means of referring your reader to a specific part of the text.

NOTE

10. Stacy Schiff, *Cleopatra: A Life* (New York: Little Brown, 2010), Kindle edition, chap. 3.

BIBLIOGRAPHY

Schiff, Stacy. *Cleopatra: A Life.* New York: Little, Brown, 2010. Kindle
    edition.

9. Book by an editor   Put the editor's name first, followed by the abbreviation *ed.* Otherwise, use the same format as for an author-based note.

NOTE

11. Elizabeth Strout, ed., *The Stories of Frederick Busch* (New York:
Norton, 2013).

BIBLIOGRAPHY ENTRY

Strout, Elizabeth, ed. *The Stories of Frederick Busch.* New York:
    Norton, 2013.

10. Book with an author and other contributor   Put the author's name first, and add the editor's *(ed.)* or translator's *(trans.)* name after the title. Spell out *Edited* or *Translated* in the bibliography entry.

NOTE

12. Jorge Luis Borges, *Professor Borges: A Course on English
Literature,* eds. Martin Arias and Martin Hadis, trans. Katherine Silver
(New York: New Directions, 2013).

BIBLIOGRAPHY ENTRY

Borges, Jorge Luis. *Professor Borges: A Course on English Literature.*
    Edited by Martin Arias and Martin Hadis. Translated by Katherine
    Silver. New York: New Directions, 2013.

11. Edition other than the first   Include the number of the edition after the title or, if there is an editor, after that person's name.

NOTE

13. Ann Majchrzak and M. Lynne Markus, *Methods for Policy
Research: Taking Socially Responsible Action,* 2nd ed. (Thousand Oaks,
CA: Sage, 2013), 73.

BIBLIOGRAPHY ENTRY

Majchrzak, Ann, and Markus, M. Lynne *Methods for Policy Research.
    Taking Socially Responsible Action.* 2nd ed. Thousand Oaks, CA:
    Sage, 2013.

12. Reprint of an older book   Include the original publication date and other publication details if they are relevant. If referencing page numbers, be sure to note the date of the cited edition.

NOTE

14. Ernest Hemingway, *The Sun Also Rises* (1926; repr.,
New York: Scribner, 2006), 94.

BIBLIOGRAPHY ENTRY

Hemingway, Ernest. *The Sun Also Rises.* New York: Scribner, 1926. Reprint, New York: Scribner, 2006. Page references are to the 2006 edition.

13. Multivolume work   In the note, include the volume number in Arabic numerals followed by a colon, before the page number.

NOTE

15. Jean-Michel Kornprobst, *Encyclopedia of Marine Natural Products* (Hoboken, NJ: Wiley-Blackwell, 2014), 3:30–32.

BIBLIOGRAPHY ENTRY

Kornprobst, Jean-Michel. *Encyclopedia of Marine Natural Products.* Vol. 3. Hoboken, NJ: Wiley-Blackwell, 2014.

14. Book in a series   Include the name of the series as well as the book's series number, if available.

NOTE

16. Lauren Kessler and Duncan McDonald, *When Words Collide,* Contributions in Wadsworth Series in Mass Communication and Journalism (Stamford, CT: Cengage, 2013).

BIBLIOGRAPHY ENTRY

Kessler, Lauren, and McDonald, Duncan. *When Words Collide.* Contributions in Wadsworth Series in Mass Communication and Journalism. Stamford, CT: Cengage, 2013.

15. Book with a title within a title   Place the title of any short-form or long-form work (regardless of how it would otherwise be formatted) appearing within a larger title in quotation marks.

NOTE

17. Robert W. Lewis, *"A Farewell to Arms": The War of the Words* (New York: Twayne Publishers, 1992).

BIBLIOGRAPHY ENTRY

Lewis, Robert W. *"A Farewell to Arms": The War of the Words.* New York: Twayne Publishers, 1992.

16. The Bible   Abbreviate the name of the book, and use Arabic numerals for chapter and verse, separated by a colon. Name the version of the Bible cited, and do not include the Bible in your bibliography.

NOTE

18. Eccles. 8:5 (Jerusalem Bible).

17. Selection in an anthology or part of an edited book   Begin with the author and title of the specific work or part.

NOTES

19. Louise Erdrich, "Fleur," in *The Oxford Book of American Short Stories,* ed. Joyce Carol Oates (New York: Oxford University Press USA, 2012), 761.

20. Alice Waters, Foreword to *An Everlasting Meal: Cooking with Economy and Grace,* by Tamar Adler (New York: Scribner, 2011).

BIBLIOGRAPHY ENTRIES

Erdrich, Louise. "Fleur." In *The Oxford Book of American Short Stories,* edited by Joyce Carol Oates, 761. New York: Oxford University Press, 2012.

Waters, Alice. Foreword to *An Everlasting Meal: Cooking with Economy and Grace,* by Tamar Adler. New York: Scribner, 2011.

In notes, descriptive terms such as *introduction* are not capitalized. In bibliography entries, these descriptive terms are capitalized.

18. Published letter   Begin the entry with the letter writer's name, followed by *to* and the name (or in this case, the relationship) of the addressee. An approximate date for when the letter was written can be prefaced with the abbreviation *ca.* for *circa*.

NOTE

21. C. S. Lewis to his brother, ca. November 1905, in *The Collected Letters of C. S. Lewis, Vol. 1: Family Letters, 1905–1931,* ed. Walter Hooper (New York: Harper Collins, 2004), 2–3.

BIBLIOGRAPHY ENTRY

Lewis, C. S. C. S. Lewis to his brother, ca. November 1905. In *The Collected Letters of C. S. Lewis, Vol. 1: Family Letters, 1905–1931,* edited by Walter Hooper. New York: HarperCollins, 2004.

19. Article in an encyclopedia or other reference work   For well-known reference works, publication data can be omitted from a note, but the edition or copyright date should be included. There is no need to include page numbers for entries in reference works that are arranged alphabetically; the abbreviation *s.v.* (meaning "under the word") plus the entry's title can be used instead.

NOTES

22. Robert E. Buswell, "Abhirati," in *The Princeton Dictionary of Buddhism,* by Robert E. Buswell and Donald S. Lopez. (Princeton: Princeton University Press, 2013), 10.

23. *Webster's New College Dictionary,* 5th ed., s.v. "Cognitive."

Reference works are not listed in the bibliography unless they are unusual or crucial to your project.

BIBLIOGRAPHY ENTRY

Robert E. Buswell. "Abhirati." In *The Princeton Dictionary of Buddhism*. By Robert E. Buswell and Donald S. Lopez. Princeton: Princeton University Press, 2013.

20. Article in an online reference work   Widely used reference works are usually cited in notes, not bibliographies, and most publication information can be omitted. Signed entries, however, should include the entry author's name. For a Wikipedia or other wiki entry, see no. 38.

NOTE

24. *Encyclopedia of World Biography,* s.v. "Nelson Mandela," accessed March 3, 2017, http://www.notablebiographies.com/Lo-Ma /Mandela-Nelson.html.

Periodicals

21. Article in a journal paginated by volume   When journals are paginated by yearly volume, your citation should include the following: author, title of article in quotation marks, title of journal, volume number and year, and page number(s).

NOTE

25. Frank Tirro, "Constructive Elements in Jazz Improvisation," *Journal of the American Musicological Society* 27 (1974): 300.

BIBLIOGRAPHY ENTRY

Tirro, Frank. "Constructive Elements in Jazz Improvisation." *Journal of the American Musicological Society* 27 (1974): 285–305.

22. Article in a journal paginated by issue   If the periodical is paginated by issue rather than by volume, add the issue number.

NOTE

title within title enclosed in single quotations
26. Jeffrey Meyers, "Plath's 'Lady Lazarus,'" *Notes on Contemporary Literature* 42, no. 3 (2012): 33.

BIBLIOGRAPHY ENTRY

Meyers, Jeffrey. "Plath's 'Lady Lazarus.'" *Notes on Contemporary Literature* 42, no. 3 (2012): 33–35.

23. Article in a magazine   Identify magazines by week (if available) and month of publication. If the article cited does not appear on consecutive pages, do not put any page numbers in the bibliography entry. You can, however, give specific pages in the note. In Chicago style, the month precedes the date, and months are not abbreviated.

NOTE

27. Robin Raisfeld and Rob Patronite, "Vanishing," *New York,* December 23, 2013, 96.

BIBLIOGRAPHY ENTRY

Raisfeld, Robin, and Rob Patronite. "Vanishing." *New York,*
    December 23, 2013.

24. Article in a newspaper   Provide the author's name (if known), the title of
the article, the name of the newspaper, and the date of publication. Do not give a
page number. Instead, give the section number or title if it is indicated. If applicable, indicate the edition (for example, *national edition*) before the section number.

NOTE

    28. Callum Borchers, "Want to Share Workspace? The Menu's a
Big One," *Boston Globe,* January 6, 2014, sec. B.

Newspaper articles cited in the text of your paper do not need to be included
in a bibliography or works-cited list. If you are asked to include articles in the
list, however, or if you did not provide full citation information in the essay or
the note, format the entry as follows.

BIBLIOGRAPHY ENTRY

Borchers, Callum. "Want to Share Workspace? The Menu's a Big One."
    Boston Globe, January 6, 2014, sec. B.

25. Journal, magazine, or newspaper article on a Web site   Whenever
a DOI is available for an article, use it instead of the URL. Include the date of
access before the DOI if required.

NOTE

    29. Diana S. Ali, et al., "'I Became a Mom': Identity Changes in
Mothers Receiving Public Assistance," *Journal of Social Service Research*
39, no. 5 (2013): 587–605, http://dx.doi.org/10.1080/01488376.2013.801391.

BIBLIOGRAPHY ENTRY

Ali Diana S., M. Elizabeth Lewis Hall, Tamara L. Anderson, and
    Michele M. Willingham. "'I Became a Mom': Identity Changes in
    Mothers Receiving Public Assistance." *Journal of Social Service
    Research* 39, no. 5 (2013): 587–605. doi:10.1080/01488376.
    2013.801391.

When no DOI is available, provide the source's direct URL.

NOTES

    30. Jay Rosen, "The New News," *Technology Review,*
January/February 2010, http://www.technologyreview.com
/communications/24175/?a=f.
    31. Michelle Castillo, "FCC Passes Ruling to Protect Net
Neutrality." *Time.com,* December 21, 2010, http://techland.time
.com/2010/12/21/fcc-passes-ruling-to-protect-net-neutrality/.
    32. Larry Magid, "FCC Network Neutrality Rules Neither
Socialism nor Sellout," *Huffington Post,* December 21, 2010,
http://www.huffingtonpost.com/larry-magid/fcc-network-neutrality
-ru_b_799999.html.

BIBLIOGRAPHY ENTRIES

Rosen, Jay. "The New News," *Technology Review,* January/
February 2010. http://www.technologyreview.com
/communications/24175/?a=f.

Castillo, Michelle. "FCC Passes Ruling to Protect Net Neutrality."
Time.com. December 21, 2010. http://techland.time.com
/2010/12/21/fcc-passes-ruling-to-protect-net-neutrality/.

Magid, Larry. "FCC Network Neutrality Rules Neither Socialism
nor Sell-out." *Huffington Post.* December 21, 2010. http://
www.huffingtonpost.com/larry-magid/fcc-network-neutrality
-ru_b_799999.html.

26. Journal, magazine, or newspaper article in an online database
Give the name of the database after information about the article. An access
date is required only if items do not include a publication or revision date. If a
DOI or stable/permanent URL is provided for the source, include it. If another
identifying reference number is provided for the source, include it in parentheses
(between the database name and the closing period).

NOTE

33. Lacy, Stephen, et al. "Citizen Journalism Web Sites
Complement Newspapers." *Newspaper Research Journal* 31, no. 2
(Spring 2010): 34–46. Academic Search Elite.

BIBLIOGRAPHY ENTRY

Lacy, Stephen, Margaret Duffy, Daniel Riffe, Esther Thorson, and
Ken Fleming. "Citizen Journalism Web Sites Complement
Newspapers." *Newspaper Research Journal* 31, no. 2 (Spring
2010): 34–46. Academic Search Elite.

27. Review   If the review is untitled, start with the author's name (if any) and
review of for a note or *Review of* for a bibliography entry.

NOTE

34. Jonathan Rosen, review of *A Feathered River across the Sky:
The Passenger Pigeon's Flight to Extinction,* by Joel Greenberg,
New Yorker, January 6, 2014, 62.

BIBLIOGRAPHY ENTRY

Rosen, Jonathan. Review of *A Feathered River across the Sky: The
Passenger Pigeon's Flight to Extinction,* by Joel Greenberg.
New Yorker, January 6, 2014, 62–67.

28. Interview   Treat published print interviews like articles *(see no. 23).*
However, unless an interview has a given title (such as "Talking with the Dead:
An Interview with Yiyun Li"), start with the name of the person interviewed. If
a record of an unpublished interview exists, note the medium and where it may

STYLING AND FORMATTING THE CMS BIBLIOGRAPHY OR REFERENCES LIST

- Begin on a new page.
- Begin with the centered title "References" if you are including only works referred to in your research project. Use the title "Bibliography" if you are including every work you consulted.
- List sources alphabetically by author's (or editor's) last name.
- Capitalize the first and last words in titles as well as all important words and words that follow colons.
- Indent all lines except the first of each entry five spaces, using your word processor's hanging indent feature.
- Use periods between author and title as well as between title and publication data.
- Double-space both within each entry and between entries, unless your instructor prefers that you make the entries single-spaced.

be found; the first example here is for a broadcast interview. Only interviews accessible to your readers are listed in the bibliography; the second example shown here, for a personal interview, would require only a note.

NOTES

35. Bob Woodruff, interview by Jon Stewart, *The Daily Show with Jon Stewart,* Comedy Central, November 4, 2013.

36. Susan Horowitz, personal interview by author, March 15, 2014, audio recording, Cincinnati.

BIBLIOGRAPHY ENTRY

Woodruff, Bob. Interview by Jon Stewart. *The Daily Show with Jon Stewart,* Comedy Central. November 4, 2013.

Web and Social Media Sources

29. Partial or entire Web site   Identify as many of the following as you can: author (if any), title of short work or page (if applicable), title or sponsor of site, and URL.

NOTES

37. Chris Garrett, "How I Use My Blog as a Fulcrum and You Can Too," *The Business of Blogging and New Media,* accessed January 28, 2011, http://www.chrisg.com/fulcrum/.

38. Chris Garrett, *The Business of Blogging and New Media,* last modified January 16, 2011, http://www.chrisg.com/.

BIBLIOGRAPHY ENTRIES

Garrett, Chris. "How I Use My Blog as a Fulcrum and You Can Too." *The Business of Blogging and New Media.* Accessed January 28, 2011. http://www.chrisg.com/fulcrum/.

Garrett, Chris. *The Business of Blogging and New Media.* Last modified on January 16, 2011. http://www.chrisg.com/.

30. Blog post   Individual blog posts are cited in the notes, along with the description *blog* in parentheses after the larger blog's title. A frequently cited blog can also be cited in the works-cited list or bibliography, as in this example.

NOTE

39. Dan Piepenbring, "Siri Hates Her and Other News," *On the Shelf* (blog), January 7, 2014, http://www.theparisreview.org/blog /2014/01/07/siri-hates-her-and-other-news.html.

BIBLIOGRAPHY ENTRY

Piepenbring, Dan. "Siri Hates Her and Other News." *On the Shelf* (blog). January 7, 2014. http://www.theparisreview.org/blog/.

31. Post to an electronic mailing list   Give the URL if the post is archived. If included, the name or number of a post should be noted after the date. Do not create a bibliography entry.

NOTE

40. Roland Kayser to Opera-L mailing list, January 3, 2008, http:// listserv.bccls.org/cgi-bin/wa?A2=ind0801A&L=OPERA-L&D=0&P=57634.

32. *Wikipedia* or other wiki entry   Check with your instructor before using a *Wikipedia* article. Use the abbreviation *s.v.* for *sub verbo* ("under the word") before the article title.

NOTE

41. *Wikipedia*, s.v. "Arches National Park," last modified May 16, 2017, http://en.wikipedia.org/wiki/Arches_National_Park.

42. *Scholarpedia*, s.v. "Facial Expression Analysis," by David Matsumoto and Paul Ekman, 2008, doi:10.4249/scholarpedia.4237.

BIBLIOGRAPHY ENTRIES

Wikipedia. s.v. "Arches National Park." Last modified May 16, 2017. http://en.wikipedia.org/wiki/Arches_National_Park.

Scholarpedia. s.v. "Facial Expression Analysis," by David Matsumoto and Paul Ekman. 2008. doi:10.4249/scholarpedia.4237.

33. Social media post   For pages or profiles that are likely to be revised, give your access date, as in the *Facebook* example. For specific dated posts with their own URLs, such as the *Twitter* example, no access dates are needed unless your instructor requires them.

NOTES

43. Viet Than Nguyen's Facebook accessed June 28, 2017, https://www.facebook.com/vietnguyenauthor/.

44. Donald Trump, Twitter post, May 12, 2017, 8:53 a.m., http://twitter.com/realDonaldTrump/status/862999243560288256.

BIBLIOGRAPHY ENTRIES

Nguyen, Viet Than. Facebook. Accessed June 28, 2017. https://www .facebook.com/vietnguyenauthor/.

Trump, Donald. Twitter post. May 12, 2017, 8:53 a.m. http://twitter.com /realDonaldTrump/status/862999243560288256.

Visuals, Audio, and Other Media

34. Artwork   Begin with the artist's name, and include both the name and the location of the institution holding the work. Italicize the name of any photograph or work of fine art. Works of art are usually not included in the bibliography.

NOTE

45. Andy Warhol, *Campbell's Soup Can* (oil on canvas, 1962, Saatchi Collection, London).

35. Sound recording   Begin with the composer or other person or group responsible for the content.

NOTE

46. Gaslight Anthem, *Handwritten.* Mercury Records, 2012, compact disc.

BIBLIOGRAPHY ENTRY

Gaslight Anthem. *Handwritten.* Mercury Records, 2012. compact disc.

36. Podcast   The note should include any important name(s); the title; the source; the description, such as *podcast audio;* and the date. Bibliographic items follow the same sequence.

NOTE

47. Margaret Atwood, "Readings from Her Recent Work," *Southeast Review Online,* podcast audio, February 2010, http://southeastreview.org/2010/02/margaret-atwood.html.

BIBLIOGRAPHY ENTRY

Atwood, Margaret. "Readings from Her Recent Work." *Southeast Review Online.* Podcast audio. February 2010. http://southeastreview.org/2010/02/margaret atwood.html.

37. Film or DVD   Include the original release date before the publication information if it differs from the release date for the DVD.

NOTE

> 48. *Behind the Candelabra,* directed by Steven Soderbergh (2013; New York: HBO Home Video), DVD.

BIBLIOGRAPHY

Behind the Candelabra. Directed by Steven Soderbergh. 2013. New York: HBO Home Video. DVD.

38. Online video   Notes for online videos include the relationship of the video to another source.

NOTE

> 49. Steven Johnson, "Where Good Ideas Come From," YouTube video, 4:07, as a trailer for Johnson's book *Where Good Ideas Come From,* posted by "RiverheadBooks," September 17, 2010, http://www .youtube.com/watch?v=NugRZGDbPFU.

BIBLIOGRAPHY ENTRY

Johnson, Steven. "Where Good Ideas Come From." YouTube video, 4:07. Posted September 17, 2010. http://www.youtube.com /watch?v=NugRZGDbPFU.

39. Online broadcast interview

NOTE

> 50. Malala Yousafzai, interview by Jon Stewart, *The Daily Show with Jon Stewart,* Comedy Central video posted October 9, 2013, http://www.thedailyshow.com/watch/tues-october-8-2013/exclusive ---malala-yousafzai-extended-interview-pt--1.

BIBLIOGRAPHY ENTRY

Yousafzai, Malala. Interview with Malala Yousafzai. By Jon Stewart. *The Daily Show with Jon Stewart,* Comedy Central video. Posted October 9, 2013. http://www.thedailyshow.com/watch/tues -october-8-2013/exclusive---malala-yousafzai-extended -interview-pt--1.

Other Sources

40. Source quoted in another source   Quote a source within a source only if you are unable to find the original source. List both sources in the entry.

NOTE

> 51. Peter Gay, *Modernism: The Lure of Heresy* (New York: Norton, 2007): 262, quoted in Terry Teachout, "The Cult of the Difficult," *Commentary* 124, no. 5 (2007): 66–69.

BIBLIOGRAPHY ENTRY

Gay, Peter. *Modernism: The Lure of Heresy.* New York: Norton, 2007. Quoted in Terry Teachout. "The Cult of the Difficult." *Commentary* 124, no. 5 (2007): 66–69.

41. Personal letter or e-mail   Do not list a letter that readers could not access in your bibliography.

NOTES

52. Daniel Clemons, letter to author, January 11, 2014.

53. Patricia Tyrell, e-mail message to author, May 29, 2012.

42. Government document   If it is not already obvious in your text, in your bibliography, name the country first.

NOTE

54. Bureau of National Affairs, *The Civil Rights Act of 1964: Text, Analysis, Legislative History; What It Means to Employers, Businessmen, Unions, Employees, Minority Groups* (Washington, DC: BNA, 1964), 22–23.

BIBLIOGRAPHY ENTRY

U.S. Bureau of National Affairs. *The Civil Rights Act of 1964: Text, Analysis, Legislative History; What It Means to Employers, Businessmen, Unions, Employees, Minority Groups.* Washington, DC: BNA, 1964.

43. Unpublished document or dissertation   Include a description of the document as well as information about where it is available. If more than one item from an archive is cited, include only one entry for the archive in your bibliography.

NOTES

55. Joe Glaser to Lucille Armstrong, September 28, 1960, Louis Armstrong Archives, Rosenthal Library, Queens College CUNY, Flushing, NY.

56. Deidre Dowling Price, "Confessional Poetry and Blog Culture in the Age of Autobiography." (PhD diss., Florida State University, 2010), 20–22.

BIBLIOGRAPHY ENTRIES

Glaser, Joe. Letter to Lucille Armstrong. Louis Armstrong Archives. Rosenthal Library, Queens College CUNY, Flushing, NY.

Price, Deidre Dowling. "Confessional Poetry and Blog Culture in the Age of Autobiography." PhD diss., Florida State University, 2010.

44. Conference presentation   When citing a presentation or lecture, include the location where it was given after the title; in the note, this information should be parenthetical. Also include a description, as in this example.

NOTE

57. Susan Jarratt, Katherine Mack, Alexandra Sartor, and Shevaun Watson. "Pedagogical Memory and the Transferability of Writing Knowledge: An Interview-Based Study of Juniors and Seniors at a Research University" (presentation, Writing Research across Borders Conference, Santa Barbara, CA, February 22, 2008).

BIBLIOGRAPHY ENTRY

Jarratt, Susan, Katherine Mack, Alexandra Sartor, and Shevaun Watson. "Pedagogical Memory and the Transferability of Writing Knowledge: An Interview-Based Study of Juniors and Seniors at a Research University." Paper presented at the Writing Research across Borders Conference, Santa Barbara, CA, February 22, 2008.

45. CD-ROM or other electronic non-Internet source Indicate the format after the publication information.

NOTE

58. Owen Jones, *The Grammar of Ornament* (London, 1856; repr., Oakland: Octavo, 1998), CD-ROM.

BIBLIOGRAPHY ENTRY

Jones, Owen. *The Grammar of Ornament*. London, 1856. Reprint, Oakland: Octavo, 1998. CD-ROM.

CHAPTER 36

Chicago Documentation Style: Sample from a Student Research Project

The following brief excerpt from Albert Rabe's project on spotting fake news has been adapted and put into Chicago style so that you can see how citation numbers, endnotes, and a works-cited list work together. *(Rabe's entire paper, in MLA style, can be found on pages 383–387.)*

The Chicago Manual of Style is primarily a guide for publishers or those who wish to submit work to be published. To prepare a research project using Chicago documentation style, you can use the guidelines provided in pages 365–382 or check with your instructor. The formatting of the following sample pages is consistent with the guidelines found in Turabian's *Manual for Writers*.

1

Writing for the *Journal of Economic Perspectives*, Allcott and Gentzkow define *fake news* as information that is "intentionally and verifiably false, and could mislead readers."[1] Asserting that "a great many things" that our elected leader says "are demonstrably false," *Time* editor Nancy Gibbs writes, "During the 2016 campaign, 70% of the Trump statements reviewed by PolitiFact were false, 4% were entirely true, 11% mostly true."[2] When trusted sources—whether media networks or elected officials—circulate information that is unverified or outright false, the task of differentiating the real news from the fake becomes all the more challenging. As Sabrina Tavernise explains in a recent *New York Times* article, "Fake news, and the proliferation of raw opinion that passes for news, is creating confusion, punching holes in what is true, causing a kind of fun-house effect that leaves the reader doubting everything, including real news."[3]

New Yorker columnist Elizabeth Kolbert explains one reason that people find fake news believable: when reading or watching the news, people tend to experience "confirmation bias," or "the tendency . . . to embrace information that supports their beliefs and reject information that contradicts them." In other words, people believe what they want to believe and can even "experience genuine pleasure—a rush of dopamine—when processing information that supports their beliefs."[4] Thus, if Trump says his inaugural crowd was the largest ever, his ardent supporters are likely to ignore credible news sources that discredit his claim.

Readers also have some responsibility for the problem of fake news. The internet has allowed the spread of news—real and fake—to happen in the blink of an eye, often

2

with "no significant third party filtering, fact-checking, or editorial judgment."[5] Journalists, editors, and publishers are no longer the primary gatekeepers; instead, "[s]ocial media have effectively turned us all into publishers," writes Brooke Borel, the author of *The Chicago Guide to Fact-Checking,* for the blog FiveThirtyEight.[6] Moreover, Allcott and Gentzkow point out an astonishing statistic: "An individual user with no track record or reputation can in some cases reach as many readers as Fox News, CNN, or the *New York Times.*"[7] Given the proliferation of news items at their fingertips, readers do not always make responsible choices about which news stories to read, which of them to believe, and which to share through their social media networks.

The repetition of fake news stories is another factor exacerbating the problem. As Gibbs explains, "[S]ocial sciences have shown that repetition of a false statement, even in the course of disputing it, often increases the number of people who believe it."[8] Consider the images and videos that tend to go viral following a natural disaster. Fake news sources will often alter, or "doctor," visual content to depict exaggerated or false outcomes, thereby grabbing readers' attention. Following Hurricane Harvey, a doctored photo of a shark swimming down a flooded street fooled many readers who believed the image to be real, even though the same photo had been posted following previous storms. Other viral images are intentionally ascribed to the wrong events, such as when a story relating a tragedy features outdated images of political figures lending a hand when, in fact, they were not present.[9] The frequency with

3

which these images are disseminated actually serves to bolster their credibility, despite evidence that undermines it.

The sheer volume of news stories being circulated makes the task of evaluating their credibility seem overwhelming. Evaluating sources takes time and effort, often more than readers are willing to give to a single news story—not to mention the many stories they encounter every day. However, identifying fake news is the first step in preventing it from spreading. To drive this point home, librarians across the country, and the world, are refining the resources available for researching and evaluating sources for credibility. The website for Harvard University's library, for example, includes a resource page, "Fake News, Misinformation, and Propaganda," that has links to outside sources such as the journalism-focused Nieman Foundation and the Tow Center for Digital Journalism, and access to downloads for fact-checking plug-ins.[10] . . .

Notes

1. Hunt Allcott and Matthew Gentzkow, "Social Media and Fake News in the 2016 Election," *Journal of Economic Perspectives* 31, no. 2 (2017): 213, https://doi:10.1257/jep.31.2.211.

2. Nancy Gibbs, "When a President Can't Be Taken at His Word," *Time,* April 3, 2017, 5.

3. Sabrina Tavernise, "As Fake News Spreads Lies, More Readers Shrug at the Truth," *New York Times,* December 6, 2016, http://www.nytimes.com/2016/12/06/us /fake-news-partisan-republican-democrat.html?_r=0.

4. Elizabeth Kolbert, "Why Facts Don't Change Our Minds," *New Yorker,* February 27, 2017, http://www.newyorker .com/magazine/2017/02/27/why-facts-dont-change-our-minds. Many articles can be found on the topics of fake news and confirmation bias. For example, "Confronting Confirmation Bias: Giving Truth a Fighting Chance in the Information Age" by Alan C. Miller discusses teaching students how to "discern credible information from raw information" (http:// www.thenewsliteracyproject.org).

5. Allcott and Gentzkow, "Social Media," 211.

6. Brooke Borel, "Fact-Checking Won't Save Us from Fake News," FiveThirtyEight, January 4, 2017, http:// fivethirtyeight.com/features/fact-checking-wont-save-us-from -fake-news/.

7. Allcott and Gentzkow, "Social Media," 211.

8. Gibbs, 5.

9. Linda Quiu, "A Shark in the Street and Other Hurricane Harvey Misinformation You Shouldn't Believe," *New York Times,* August 28, 2017, http://www.nytimes .com/2017/08/28/us/politics/shark-hurricane-harvey-rumors. html?_r=0.

10. Harvard Library's resource can be found here: http:// guides.library.harvard.edu/fake. The *New York Times* also offers tips for teaching and learning methods for spotting fake news: http://www.nytimes.com/2017/01/19/learning /lesson-plans/evaluating-sources-in-a-post-truth-world-ideas -for-teaching-and-learning-about-fake-news.html?_r=0.

References

Allcott, Hunt, and Matthew Gentzkow. "Social Media and Fake
News in the 2016 Election." *Journal of Economic Perspectives*
31, no. 2 (2017): 211–36. https://doi:10.1257/jep.31.2.211.

Borel, Brooke. "Fact-Checking Won't Save Us from Fake News."
FiveThirtyEight, January 4, 2017. http://fivethirtyeight.com
/features/fact-checking-wont-save-us-from-fake-news/.

Gibbs, Nancy. "When a President Can't Be Taken at His Word."
Time, April 3, 2017.

International Federation of Library Associations and Institutions.
"About IFLA." Last updated July 21, 2017. http://www.ifla.org
/about.

Kiely, Eugene, and Lori Robertson. "How to Spot Fake News."
FactCheck.org. Posted on November 18, 2016. www
.factcheck.org/2016/11/how-to-spot-fake-news/.

Klein, Betsy. "Comparing Donald Trump['s] and Barack Obama's
Inaugural Crowd Sizes." CNN. Updated January 21, 2017,
12:48 p.m. ET. www.cnn.com/2017/01/20/politics
/donald-trump-barack-obama-inauguration-crowd-size/index
.html.

Kolbert, Elizabeth. "Why Facts Don't Change Our Minds." *The
New Yorker,* February 27, 2017. http://www.newyorker.com
/magazine/2017/02/27/why-facts-dont-change-our-minds.

CHAPTER 37

CSE Documentation Style

The Council of Science Editors (CSE) endorses three documentation styles in the eighth edition of *Scientific Style and Format: The CSE Manual for Authors, Editors, and Publishers* (Chicago, IL: Univ. of Chicago Press, 2014):

- The **name-year style** includes the last name of the author and year of publication in the text. In the list of references, sources are in alphabetical order and unnumbered.

- The **citation-sequence style** includes a superscript number or a number in parentheses in the text. In the list of references, sources are numbered and appear in order of citation.

- The **citation-name style** also uses a superscript number or a number in parentheses in the text. In the list of references, however, sources are numbered and arranged in alphabetical order.

Learn your instructor's preferred style and use it consistently within a research project. Also ask your instructor about line spacing, headings, and other design elements, which the CSE manual does not specify.

37a CSE in-text citations.

Name-year style Include the author's last name and the year of publication.

According to Gleeson (1993), a woman loses 35% of cortical bone and 50% of trabecular bone during her lifetime.

In epidemiologic studies, small increases in BMD and decreases in fracture risk have been reported in individuals using NSAIDS (Raisz 2001; Carbone et al. 2003).

Citation-sequence or citation-name style Insert a superscript number immediately after the relevant name, word, or phrase and before any punctuation. Put a space before and after the superscript unless a punctuation mark follows.

As a group, American women over 45 years of age sustain approximately 1 million fractures each year, 70% of which are due to osteoporosis.[1]

That number now belongs to that source, and you should use it if you refer to that source again in your paper.

According to Gleeson,[6] a woman loses 35% of cortical bone and 50% of trabecular bone over her lifetime.

Credit more than one source at a time by referring to each source's number. Separate the numbers with a comma.

> According to studies by Yomo,[2] Paleg,[3] and others,[1,4] barley seed
>
> embryos produce a substance that stimulates the release of hydrolytic
>
> enzymes.

If more than two numbers are in sequence, however, separate them with a hyphen.

> As several others[1-4] have documented, GA has an RNA-enhancing
>
> effect.

37b   CSE list of references.

Every source cited in your project must correspond to an entry in your list of references, which should be prepared according to the guidelines in the box on page 377.

Authors of Any Source

In *name-year style,* include the author(s), last name first; publication year; title; place; and publisher. In *citation-sequence* or *citation-name style,* include the same information, but put the year after the publisher.

1. One author

NAME-YEAR

Reinhard T. 2014. Superfoods: the healthiest foods on the planet. Ontario (CA): Firefly Books.

CITATION-SEQUENCE OR CITATION-NAME

1. Reinhard T. Superfoods: the healthiest foods on the planet. Ontario (CA): Firefly Books; 2014.

2. Two or more authors   List up to ten authors; if there are more than ten, use the first ten names with the phrase *et al.* or *and others* (not italicized).

NAME-YEAR

Pinna K, Rolfes SR, Whitney E. 2014. Understanding normal and clinical nutrition. 10th ed. Stamford (CT): Cengage Learning.

CITATION-SEQUENCE OR CITATION-NAME

2. Pinna K, Rolfes SR, Whitney E. 2014. Understanding normal and clinical nutrition. 10th ed. Stamford (CT): Cengage Learning; 2014.

CSE STYLE: DIRECTORY TO SAMPLE TYPES

3. Two or more cited works by the same author(s) published in the same year This structure is not necessary in the citation-sequence style because entries are arranged and numbered by the order in which they appear.

NAME-YEAR

Yancey KB. 2008a. A place of our own: spaces and materials for composing in the new century. In: Tassoni J, Powell D, editors. Composing other spaces. Creskill (NJ): Hampton.

Yancey KB. 2008b. The literacy demands of entering the university. In: Christenbury L, Bomer R, Smagorinsky P, editors. Handbook on adolescent literacy. New York: Guilford.

STYLING AND FORMATTING THE CSE LIST OF REFERENCES

- Begin on a new page after your text but before any appendices, tables, and figures.
- Use the centered title "References."
- Include only references that are cited in your paper.
- For citation-sequence and citation-name styles, begin each entry with a superscript number.
- Start each entry with the author's last name, followed by initials for first and middle names. Add no spaces or periods between initials.
- Abbreviate periodical titles as shown in the CSE manual, and capitalize major words.
- Use complete book and article titles; capitalize the first word and any proper nouns or proper adjectives.
- Do not use italics, underlining, or quotation marks to set off any kind of title.
- List the extent of a source (number of pages or screens) at the end of the entry if your instructor requires it.
- When a URL must be broken across lines of text, break it before or after a slash or other punctuation.

Name-Year Style

- Always put the date after the author's name.
- List the references in alphabetical order, but do not number them.

Citation-Sequence Style

- Put the date after the name of the book publisher or periodical.
- List and number the references in the order they first appear in the text.

Citation-Name Style

- Put the date after the name of the book publisher or periodical.
- List and number the references in alphabetical order. Make the numbering of your in-text citations match.

4. Organization as author   In name-year style, start the entry with the organization's abbreviation, but alphabetize by the full name. (If both an organization and an author are listed, use the author's name as in no. 1).

NAME-YEAR

[NIH] National Institutes of Health (US). 1993. Clinical trials supported by the National Eye Institute (US); celebrating vision research. Bethesda (MD): US Dept. of Health and Human Services.

CITATION-SEQUENCE OR CITATION-NAME

3. National Institutes of Health (US). Clinical trials supported by the National Eye Institute (US): celebrating vision research. Bethesda (MD): US Dept. of Health and Human Services; 1993.

5. No named author   Begin with the title.

NAME-YEAR

Senate repeals military gay ban. 2010 Dec 19. Times (St. Petersburg, FL). Sect A:1 (col. 2).

CITATION-SEQUENCE OR CITATION-NAME

4. Senate repeals military gay ban. Times (St. Petersburg, FL). 2010 Dec 19;Sect. A:1 (col. 2).

Books, Reports, and Papers

6. Basic entry for a book

NAME-YEAR

Sacks O. 2017. The river of consciousness. New York (NY): Knopf.

CITATION-SEQUENCE OR CITATION-NAME

5. Sacks O. The river of consciousness. New York (NY): Knopf; 2017.

7. Online book (monograph)   Provide the year and date accessed (in brackets) followed by the URL.

NAME-YEAR

Kohn LT, Corrigan JM, Donaldson MS, editors. 2000. To err is human: building a safer health system. Washington (DC): National Academy Press. [accessed 2007 Oct 19]. http://www.nap.edu/books/0309068371/html

CITATION-SEQUENCE OR CITATION-NAME

6. Kohn LT, Corrigan JM, Donaldson MS, editors. To err is human: building a safer health system. Washington (DC): National Academy Press; 2000 [accessed 2007 Oct 19]. http://www.nap.edu/books/0309068371/html

8. Book with editor(s)   If there is no identifiable author, begin with the editor's name, followed by the word *editor.*

NAME-YEAR

Mukherjee S, Folger T, editors. 2013. The best American science and nature writing 2013. New York: Mariner.

CITATION-SEQUENCE OR CITATION-NAME

> 7. Mukherjee S, Folger T, editors. The best American science and nature writing 2013. New York: Mariner; 2013.

9. Reprint of an older book   Indicate the copyright date (the date of the first publication) just after the date of the reprint in name-year style and following the original publisher in the other two styles.

NAME-YEAR

> Hamaker JI. 2010, c1913. The principles of biology. Charleston (SC): Forgotten Books. 474 p.

CITATION-SEQUENCE OR CITATION-NAME

> 8. Hamaker JI. The principles of biology. Philadelphia (PA): P. Blakiston's Son; 1913. Charleston (SC): Forgotten Books; 2010. 474 p.

10. All volumes of a multivolume work   Provide the number of volumes followed by the abbreviation *vol.*

NAME-YEAR

> Bittar EE. 1992. Fundamentals of medical cell biology. Cambridge (MA): Elsevier Science. 4 vol.

CITATION-SEQUENCE OR CITATION-NAME

> 9. Bittar, EE. Fundamentals of medical cell biology. Cambridge (MA): Elsevier Science; 1992. 4 vol.

11. Selection in an edited book   In the name-year style, begin with the author, the date, and then the title of the selection, followed by the name of the editor or editors and the publication information. When using the citation-sequence or citation-name style, put the date between the publisher and the pages.

NAME-YEAR

> Bohus B, Koolhaas JM. 1993. Psychoimmunology of social factors in rodents and other subprimate vertebrates. In: Ader R, Felten DL, Cohen N, editors. Psychoneuroimmunology. San Diego (CA): Academic Press. p. 807–30.

CITATION-SEQUENCE OR CITATION-NAME

> 10. Bohus B, Koolhaas JM. Psychoimmunology of social factors in rodents and other subprimate vertebrates. In: Ader R, Felten DL, Cohen N, editors. Psychoneuroimmunology. San Diego (CA). Academic Press; 1993. p. 807–30.

12. Chapter in a book In both styles, the chapter number and title and the pages follow the publication information.

NAME-YEAR

O'Connell C. 2007. The elephant's secret sense: the hidden life of the wild herds of Africa. New York: Free Press. Chapter 9, Cracking elephant Morse code; p. 119–26.

CITATION-SEQUENCE OR CITATION-NAME

11. O'Connell C. The elephant's secret sense: the hidden life of the wild herds of Africa. New York: Free Press; 2007. Chapter 9, Cracking elephant Morse code; p. 119–26.

13. Technical report or government document Include the name of the sponsoring organization or agency as well as any report or contract number.

NAME-YEAR

Bolen S, Wilson L, Vassy J, Feldman L, Yeh J, Marinopoulos S, Wilson R, Cheng D, Wiley C, Selvin E, et al. (Johns Hopkins University Evidence-based Practice Center, Baltimore, MD). 2007. Comparative effectiveness and safety of oral diabetes medications for adults with type 2 diabetes. Comparative effectiveness review No. 8. Rockville (MD): Agency for Healthcare Research and Quality (US). Contract No.: 290-02-0018. Available from: AHRQ, Rockville, MD; AHRQ Pub. No. 07-EHC010-1.

CITATION-SEQUENCE OR CITATION-NAME

12. Bolen S, Wilson L, Vassy J, Feldman L, Yeh J, Marinopoulos S, Wilson R, Cheng D, Wiley C, Selvin E, et al. (Johns Hopkins University Evidence-based Practice Center, Baltimore, MD). Comparative effectiveness and safety of oral diabetes medications for adults with type 2 diabetes. Comparative effectiveness review No. 8. Rockville (MD): Agency for Healthcare Research and Quality (US); 2007. Contract No.: 290-02-0018. Available from: AHRQ, Rockville, MD; AHRQ Pub. No. 07-EHC010-1.

14. Paper in conference proceedings For name-year style, begin with the name and the year of publication of the proceedings (preceded by a *c*), and include the paper title, the name of the editor or editors, the title of the proceedings, and the conference date and year. In the citation-sequence and citation-name styles, the conference date appears after the publication title, and the publication date appears between the publisher and the pages.

NAME-YEAR

De Jong E, Franke L, Siebes A. c2007. On the measurement of genetic interactions. In: Berthold MR, Glen RC, Feelders AJ, editors. Proceedings of the AIP 940. 3rd International Symposium on Computational Life Science; 2007 Oct 4–5; Utrecht (NL). Melville (NY): American Institute of Physics. p. 16–25.

CITATION-SEQUENCE OR CITATION-NAME

13. De Jong E, Franke L, Siebes A. On the measurement of genetic interactions. In: Berthold MR, Glen RC, Feelders AJ, editors. Proceedings of the AIP 940. 3rd International Symposium on Computational Life Science; 2007 Oct 4–5; Utrecht (NL). Melville (NY): American Institute of Physics; c2007. p. 16–25.

15. Dissertation   Include *dissertation* in brackets and the location of the institution granting the dissertation, also in brackets, followed by a colon and the university.

NAME-YEAR

Bertrand KN. 2007. Fishes and floods: stream ecosystem drivers in the Great Plains [dissertation]. [Manhattan (KS)]: Kansas State University.

CITATION-SEQUENCE OR CITATION-NAME

14. Bertrand KN. Fishes and floods: stream ecosystem drivers in the Great Plains [dissertation]. [Manhattan (KS)]: Kansas State University; 2007.

Periodicals

When listing most periodical articles, include the author(s); year; title of article; title of journal (abbreviated); number of the volume; number of the issue, if available (in parentheses); and page numbers. In name-year style, put the year after the author(s). In citation-sequence or citation-name style, put the year after the journal title.

16. Article in a journal that uses only volume numbers   Include only the volume number before the pages.

NAME-YEAR

Devine A, Prince RL, Bell R. 1996. Nutritional effect of calcium supplementation by skim milk powder or calcium tablets on total nutrient intake in postmenopausal women. Am J Clin Nutr. 64:731–737.

CITATION-SEQUENCE OR CITATION-NAME

15.   Devine A, Prince RL, Bell R. Nutritional effect of calcium
supplementation by skim milk powder or calcium tablets on total
nutrient intake in postmenopausal women. Am J Clin Nutr.
1996;64:731–737.

The remaining examples are in the citation-sequence or citation-name style. For
name-year style, list the publication date after the author's name and do not
number your references.

17. Article in a journal that uses volume and issue numbers   Include the
issue number in parentheses after the volume number.

16.   Hummel-Berry K. Obstetric low back pain, a comprehensive
review, part 2: evaluation and treatment. J Ob Gyn PT.
1990;14(2):9–11.

18. Article in an online journal   Include the journal issue and page numbers
after the bracketed access date and before the URL.

17.   Krieger D, Onodipe S, Charles PJ, Sclabassi RJ. Real time signal
processing in the clinical setting. Ann Biomed Engn. 1998
[accessed 2007 Oct 19];26(3):462–472. http://www.springerlink
.com/content/n31828q461h54282

19. Material from a library subscription database   CSE does not specify
a format. Give the information for a print article with database title and publication information.

18.   Baccarelli A, Zanobetti A, Martinelli I, Grillo P, Lifang H, Lanzani G,
Mannucci PM, Bertazzi PA, Schwartz, J. Air pollution, smoking,
and plasma homocysteine. Environ Health Perspect. 2007 Feb
[accessed 2007 Oct 23];115(2):176–181. Health Source: Nursing/
Academic Edition. Birmingham (AL): EBSCO. http://www.ebsco.com

20. Article in a magazine   Indicate the year, month, and day (if available) of
publication.

19.   Specter M. The gene factory. New Yorker. 2014 Jan 6:34–43.

21. Article in a newspaper   Indicate the year, month, and day of publication.

20.   Fountain H. The reinvention of silk. New York Times. 2011 Mar 8;
Sect. D:1 (col. 4).

22. Article on the Internet (print version available)   Insert in brackets the
date of access; provide the URL after the print page number.

21.   Wald ML. EPA says it will press on with greenhouse gas
regulation. New York Times. 2010 [accessed 2010 Dec 23];A:16.
http://www.nytimes.com/2010/12/24/science/earth/24epa
.html?ref=science

23. Editorial   Editorials usually do not have signed authors, so begin with the title, followed by *[editorial]*.

> 22. Blogs gone bad [editorial]. New Atlantis 2005;8:106–109.

24. Review   A note following the page number can give additional, optional information about the article in the CSE system.

> 23. Wang C. Where old and new media collide. 2007 Spring. Spectator. 101–103. Review of Jenkins H, Convergence culture.

Web and Social Media Sources

25. Material from a Web site

> 24. Hutchinson JR. Vertebrate flight. University of California—Berkeley. 2005 Sep 9 [accessed 2008 Jan 15]. http://www.ucmp .berkeley.edu/vertebrates/flight/flightintro.html

26. Post to a discussion list   Include the name, the header for the message, the list name, an identification of the list in brackets, the group or institution responsible for the list, the date of the posting, the date of citation, and the URL.

> 25. Parfitt M. Inquiry vs. argument: your thoughts. WPA-L [discussion list]. Tempe (AZ): Council of Writing Program Administrators; 2010 Dec 22 [accessed 2010 Dec 22]. http://wpa-l.asu.edu <mailto:wpa-l@asu.edu>/.

27. Entry in a wiki   Check with your instructor before using a Wikipedia article.

> 26. Matsumoto D, Ekman P. Facial expression analysis. 2008 [accessed 2017 July 25]. doi:10.4249/scholarpedia.4237
>
> 27. Arches National Park. 2017 May 16 [accessed 2017 May 18]. http:// en.wikipedia.org/wiki/Arches_National_Park

28. Social media post

> 28. Nguyen VT. My favorite picture of my mother and me. Facebook; 2017 May 14 [accessed 2017 May 28]. http://www.facebook.com/ pg/vietnguyenauthor/posts/?ref=page_internal
>
> 29. Trump D. The Fake Media is working overtime today! Twitter; 2017 May 12 [accessed 2017 July 25]. http://twitter.com/ realDonaldTrump/status/862999243560288256

Visuals, Audio, and Other Media

29. Videos or podcasts

> 30. Johnson S. Where good ideas come from [video on the Internet]. Riverhead Books 2010 Sep 17, 4:07. [accessed 2010 Dec 19]. http://www.youtube.com/watch?v=NugRZGDbPFU

30. Slide set or presentation slides For a slide set, substitute the label *slides*. This particular presentation was downloaded from an online source, so retrieval information is also included.

> 31. Volunteering: what's it all about? [PowerPoint slides]. Sydney, AU: Volunteering Australia Inc.; 2009. 24 slides. [accessed 2014 Aug 7]. http://www.volunteeringaustralia.org/files/WZ7K0VWICM/ Volunteering%20what_s%20it%20all%20about.ppt

31. Map The physical description of the map is optional.

> 32. GIS mapping of boom locations and other information needed for Tampa Bay oil spill contingency program [marine survey map]. St. Petersburg (FL): NOAA and Tampa Bay National Estuary Program; 1996. 51 x 66 in., b&w, scale 1:24,000.

32. Audio or video recording

> 33. Planet Earth: the complete BBC series [DVD]. London (UK): BBC; c2007. 4 DVDs: 550 mins, sound, color.

33. Document on a CD-ROM or DVD-ROM

> 34. Jones O. The grammar of ornament [CD-ROM]. London (UK): Octavo; 1998.

ONLINE AND MULTIMEDIA SOURCES IN CSE STYLE

Include information on author, title, and so forth, as with print works. Follow these special guidelines:

- Include in brackets the date of the most recent update (if any) and the date you accessed the source.

- List the publisher or the sponsor, or use the bracketed phrase *[publisher unknown]* (not italicized).

- To include length of a document without page numbers, use designations such as *[16 paragraphs]* or *[4 screens]* (neither italicized).

- List the URL at the end of the reference. Do not put a period after a URL unless it ends with a slash.

37c   Sample references list: CSE name-year style

The following is the first part of a list of references in CSE name-year style for a student research report on the origins of avian flight.

> ### References
>
> Anderson, A. 1991. Early bird threatens archaeopteryx's perch. Science. 253(5015):35.
>
> Geist N, Feduccia A. 2000. Gravity-defying behaviors: identifying models for protoaves. Am Zoologist. 40(4):664–675.
>
> Goslow GE, Dial KP, Jenkins FA. 1990. Bird flight: insights and complications. Bioscience. 40(2):108–116.

37d   Sample references list: CSE citation-name style

Here are the same references as in 37c but in citation-name style, listed and numbered in alphabetical order. Citation-sequence style would look the same, but entries would be in the order in which they were cited in the paper.

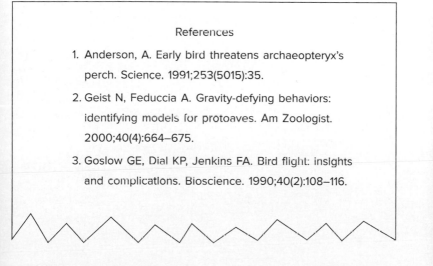

> ### References
>
> 1. Anderson, A. Early bird threatens archaeopteryx's perch. Science. 1991;253(5015):35.
>
> 2. Geist N, Feduccia A. Gravity-defying behaviors: identifying models for protoaves. Am Zoologist. 2000;40(4):664–675.
>
> 3. Goslow GE, Dial KP, Jenkins FA. Bird flight: insights and complications. Bioscience. 1990;40(2):108–116.

9

Editing for Clarity

I ... believe that words can help us move or keep us paralyzed, and that our choices of language and verbal tone have something—a great deal— to do with how we live our lives and whom we end up speaking with and hearing.

-Adrienne Rich

©Uyen Le/Getty Images

The Palais des congrès in downtown Montreal features an impressive window display made of more than three hundred glass panels. Sunlight brings out the clarity of the window's design; and, in turn, the design transforms the light.

9 Editing for Clarity

 Sections referenced in Resources for Writers: Identifying and Editing Common Problems on pp. 403–07.

START SMART

Tab 9: Editing for Clarity

This section will help you answer questions such as the following:

Rhetorical Knowledge

- Is my writing too formal or too informal for college assignments? (47b)
- How can I avoid biased language, such as *mankind* and the generic use of *he* or *she*? (47e)

Critical Thinking, Reading, and Writing

- How can subordination clarify relationships between ideas? (44b)
- How can I choose between two words with similar meanings? (48a, 49a, b)

Processes

- Can my word processor's grammar checker help me edit for clarity? (38, 40a, 41, 43a, 43e, 45, 46)
- Can a grammar checker help me find mixed constructions, shifts, and misplaced and dangling modifiers in my writing? (40a, 41, 43a, e)

Knowledge of Conventions

- What's wrong with the comparison *I like texting more than John?* (39c)
- What's wrong with saying *the reason . . . is because?* (40c)
- Should I use *their, there,* or *they're* in this sentence? (50)

For a general introduction to writing outcomes, see 1e, pages 14–15.

401

GRAMMAR Identifying and Editing Common Problems

If you are having difficulty finding the advice you need in *A Writer's Resource*, consult the chart of students' most common errors below. Once you have identified the issue giving you trouble, turn to the indicated section of this book for more explanation and examples. This icon [✓] marks each of those sections in the text. A list of these sections also appears in the Quick Guide to Key Resources at the back of this book.

Editing for Clarity

TAB 9

(Style, Voice, and Tone)

---

by
Mia was neither surprised˄ nor happy with her grade on the exam.

`inc`

Missing Word   **Ch. 39a,** p. 411

~~When~~ Juan knew the test was canceled because the classroom was empty.

`mix`

Mixed Construction   **Ch. 40a,** p. 413

---

they
If students want to use the lounge, ~~you~~ they have to sign up in advance.

`shift`

wrote
Beethoven was completely deaf when he ~~writes~~˄ his last symphony.

`shift`

Confusing shifts (person and verb tense)   **Ch. 41a, 41b,** p. 415

During vacation I plan to relax, sleep late, and ~~I will~~ spend time with my family.

`//`

Faulty parallelism   **Ch. 42a,** p. 419

I put
Following the recipe carefully,˄ the cake ~~went~~ in the oven for an hour.

`dm`

Dangling modifier   **Ch. 43e,** p. 423

---

incredible   *really*
Sean was distracted by the ~~incredulous~~˄ news and did not ~~rely~~˄ hear his instructor's question.

`ww`

`ww`

Wrong words   **Ch. 48f,** p. 439

Editing for Grammar Conventions

(Sentence Structure and Cohesion)

My car won't start, which
~~Which~~ means I'll be late for work.

[frag]

Sentence fragment   Ch. **51**, p. 451

---

                                                              but
The Internet has increased the speed of people's communications, it   [cs]
has not improved the quality.

                                   They
Some people send text messages while driving. ~~they~~ often   [run on]
get distracted.

Comma splices and run-ons   Ch. **52**, p. 457

Each of Gloria's clocks shows a different time.   [agr]

Subject-verb agreement   Ch. **53**, p. 462

---

                          learning [OR after it learns]
Each dog that is trained here receives a reward after ~~they learn~~ a new   [agr]
command.

Pronoun-antecedent agreement   Ch. **55**, p. 479

                    Ellen
Ellen and her sister argued after ~~she~~ went to the party alone.   [ref]

Unclear pronoun reference   Ch. **55b**, p. 483

---

                    me
John drove my friend and ~~I~~ to the hockey game.   [case]

Pronoun case   Ch. **55d**, p. 485

Editing for Correctness

(Punctuation, Mechanics, and Spelling)

TAB 11

If I don't feed my dog in the morning, she will bark all day long.

| ∧ |
| , |

Comma needed to set off introductory word group   Ch. **57a,** p. 498

Jaime was going to meet us, but his flight was delayed.

| ∧ |
| , |

Comma needed before coordinating conjunction   Ch. **57c,** p. 500

Neil Armstrong's moon landing, which millions

watched, inspired many people.

| ∧ |
| , |

| ∧ |
| , |

Commas needed for nonrestrictive word group   Ch. **57e,** p. 501

Sonia's dog likes to chase it's tail.

| ⸜ |
| ∨ |

Incorrect use of apostrophe with possessive pronoun   Ch. **60c,** p. 517

English
My ~~english~~ class comes right after my biology class.

| *cap* |

Incorrect capitalization   Ch. **63a,** p. 530

---

their
The boys took ~~there~~ time on the way home.

| *sp* |

Spelling error (*homonym*)   Ch. **68b,** p. 546

Nouns and Pronouns

(Ch. **69b**, p. 555; **Ch. 69c**, p. 560; **Ch. 70a**, p. 570)

Count and Noncount Nouns

Count nouns name persons, places, or things that can be counted. Count nouns can be singular or plural.

Noncount nouns name a class of things. Usually, noncount nouns have only a singular form.

COUNT	NONCOUNT	COUNT	NONCOUNT
cars	information	child	humanity
table	furniture	book	advice

Pronouns

Common Problem: Personal pronoun restates subject.

INCORRECT	My sister, she works in the city.
CORRECT	My sister works in the city.

Pronouns replace nouns. They stand for persons, places, or things and can be singular or plural.

Personal pronouns act as subjects, objects, or words that show possession.

Subject pronouns: I, we, you, he, she, it, one, they, who

Object pronouns: me, us, you, him, her, it, one, them, whom

Possessive pronouns: my, mine, our, ours, your, yours, his, her, hers, its, their, theirs, whose

Relative pronouns introduce dependent clauses.

Relative pronouns: that, whatever, which, whichever, who, whoever, whom, whomever, whose

EXAMPLE   His sister, who lives in Canada, came to visit.

Sentence Structure

(Ch. **70**, p. 570)

Subjects and Verbs

English requires both a subject and a verb in every sentence or clause.

    S   V   S   V
    She slept.   He ate.

Direct and Indirect Objects

Verbs may be followed by direct or indirect objects. A direct object receives the action of the verb.

    S   V   DO
    He drove the car.

An indirect object is the person or thing to which something is done.

    S   V   IO   DO
    She gave her sister a birthday gift.

Articles

(Ch. 69b, p. 555)

Common Problem: Article is omitted.

INCORRECT	Water is cold. I bought watch.
CORRECT	The water is cold. I bought a watch.

Using Articles with Count and Noncount Nouns

Definite article (the): used for specific reference with all types of nouns.

The car I bought is red. [*singular count noun*]
The dogs howled at the moon. [*plural count noun*]
The furniture makes the room appear cluttered. [*noncount noun*]

Do not use *the* before most singular proper nouns, such as the names of people, cities, languages, and so on.

~~The~~ Dallas is a beautiful city.

Indefinite articles (a, an): used with singular count nouns only.

Use *a* before a word that begins with a consonant sound.

a pencil
a sports car
a tropical rain forest

Use *an* before a word that begins with a vowel sound.

an orange
an hour
an instrument

Do not use an indefinite article with a noncount noun.

Water
~~A water~~ is leaking from the faucet.

No article: Plural count nouns and noncount nouns do not require indefinite articles. Plural count nouns and noncount nouns do not need definite articles when they refer to all of the items in a group.

Plural count nouns and noncount nouns

Every night I hear ~~a~~ dogs barking.
I needed to find ~~an~~ information in the library.

Plural count nouns

SPECIFIC ITEM	The dogs next door never stop barking.
ALL ITEMS IN A GROUP	Dogs make good pets.

Noncount nouns

SPECIFIC ITEM	The jewelry she wore to the party was beautiful.
ALL ITEMS IN A GROUP	Jewelry is expensive.

Verbs

(Ch. 54f, p. 474; Ch. 69a, p. 550; Ch. 70b, p. 573)

Common Problem: *be* **verb is left out.**

INCORRECT	He sleeping now. She happy.
CORRECT	He is sleeping now. She is happy.

Verb Tenses

Tense refers to the time of action expressed by a verb.

Present tense (**base form or form with -s ending**): action taking place now. I *sleep* here. She *sleeps*. We *sleep* late every weekend.

Past tense (**-d or -ed ending**): past action. I *laughed*. He *laughed*. They *laughed* together.

Future tense (**will + base form**): action that is going to take place. I *will go* to the movie. He *will run* in the marathon. You *will write* the paper.

Present perfect tense (**have or has + past participle**): past action that was or will be completed. I *have spoken*. He *has washed* the floor. We *have made* lunch.

Past perfect tense (**had + past participle**): past action completed before another past action. I *had spoken*. She *had been* busy. They *had noticed* a slight error.

Future perfect tense (**will + have + past participle**): action that will begin and end in the future before another action happens. I *will have eaten*. She *will have danced* in the recital by then. You *will have taken* the train.

Present progressive tense (**am, are, or is + present participle**): continuing action. I *am writing* a novel. He *is working* on a new project. They *are studying* for the test.

Past progressive tense (**was or were + present participle**): past continuing action. I *was cleaning* the house. She *was working* in the yard. You *were making* dinner.

Future progressive tense (**will + be + present participle**): future continuing action. I *will be traveling* to Europe. She *will be sightseeing* in New York. They *will be eating* together tonight.

Present perfect progressive tense (**have or has + been + present participle**): past action that continues in the present. I *have been practicing*. He *has been sleeping* all morning. They *have been coming* every weekend.

Past perfect progressive tense (**had + been + present participle**): continuous action completed before another past action. I *had been driving* for six hours. She *had been reading* when I arrived. They *had been singing*.

Future perfect progressive tense (**will + have + been + present participle**): action that will begin, continue, and end in the future. I *will have been driving* for ten hours. He *will have been living* there for three years. You *will have been* for the test all afternoon.

CHAPTER 38

Wordy Sentences

A sentence does not have to be short and simple to be concise, but every word must count.

Wordiness and Grammar Checkers

Most computer grammar checkers recognize wordy structures inconsistently. One flagged most passive verbs and some *it is* and *there are* (expletive) constructions, but not others. It also flagged the redundant expression *true fact,* but it missed *round circle* and the empty phrase *it is a fact that.*

38a Eliminate redundancies.

Redundancies are meaningless repetitions that result in wordiness, like *first and foremost, full and complete, final result, past histories, round in shape,* and *refer back.*

▶ **Students living ~~in close proximity~~ in the dorms need to cooperate ~~together if they want~~ to live in harmony.**

Sometimes, modifiers such as *very, rather,* and *really* and intensifiers such as *absolutely, definitely,* and *incredibly* do not add meaning to a sentence. Instead, they are redundant.

▶ **That film was ~~really~~ hard to watch, but ~~absolutely~~ worth seeing.**

38b Do not repeat words unnecessarily.

Although repetition is sometimes used for emphasis, unnecessary repetitions weaken sentences and should be removed.

▶ **The children enjoyed watching television more than ~~they enjoyed~~ reading books.**

ALTERNATIVES FOR WORDY PHRASES

Wordy Phrases	*Concise Alternatives*
at this point in time	now
in the not-too-distant future	soon
in close proximity to	near
is necessary that	must
is able to	can
due to the fact that	because
in spite of the fact that	although
in the event that	if
in the final analysis	finally
in order to	to
for the purpose(s) of	to

38c Avoid wordy phrases.

Make your sentences more concise by eliminating wordy phrases or replacing them with one-word alternatives.

► ~~It is necessary at this point in time that tests~~ be run ~~for the purposes~~ ^{Tests must now} ^{to measure}
   ~~of measuring~~ the switch's strength.

► ~~What I mean to say is that~~ Wordsworth's poetry inspired many
   other writers of the Romantic period.

38d Reduce clauses and phrases.

For conciseness and clarity, simplify your sentence structure by turning modifying clauses into phrases.

► The novel *Bleak House*, which was written by Charles Dickens,
   influenced judicial reform in England.

Also look for opportunities to reduce phrases to single words.

► Charles Dickens's novel *Bleak House* influenced judicial reform in
   England.

┌───┐

IDENTIFY AND EDIT

Wordy Sentences

W

Ask yourself these questions as you edit:

(?) *1.* *Do any sentences contain wordy or empty phrases such as* at this point in time? *Do any contain redundancies or other unnecessary repetitions?*

- ~~The fact is that at this point in time more~~ *More* women than ~~now~~ men attend college.

- College enrollments have increased steadily ~~upward~~ since the 1940s, but since the 1970s women have enrolled in greater numbers than men ~~have~~.

(?) *2.* *Can any clauses be reduced to phrases, or phrases to single words? Can any sentences be combined to reduce repetition?*

- ~~Reports that come from~~ *College* college officials ~~indicate~~ *report* that more women are applying than men. ~~This pattern indicates~~ *and* that women will outnumber men in college for some time to come.

(?) *3.* *Do any sentences include* there is, there are, *or* it is *expressions; weak verbs; or nouns derived from verbs?*

- In 1970, ~~there were~~ *men outnumbered women in college by* more than 1.5 million. ~~more men in college than women.~~

- This trend ~~is a reflection of~~ *reflects* broad changes in gender roles throughout U.S. society.

└───┘

38e Combine sentences.

Sometimes, you can combine several short, repetitive sentences into a single, more concise, sentence.

> *'s torrential rains devastated*
> **Hurricane Ike** ~~had a devastating effect on~~ **our town**~~,~~ ~~The destruction~~
>
> ~~resulted from torrential rains. Flooding~~ *ing* **submerged Main Street**
>
> *and*   *ing*
> **under eight feet of water.** ~~The rain also~~ **triggered mudslides that**
>
> **destroyed two nearby towns.**

38f Make your sentences straightforward.

Eliminate expletive constructions like *there is, there are,* and *it is,* and replace the static verbs *to be* and *to have* with active verbs. *(For more on active verbs, see pp. 430-32.)* Change passive voice *(The book was read by Miguel)* to active voice *(Miguel read the book).*

ROUNDABOUT

There are stylistic similarities between "This Lime-Tree Bower" and "Tintern Abbey," which are indications of the influence that Coleridge had on Wordsworth.

STRAIGHTFORWARD

The stylistic similarities between "This Lime-Tree Bower" and "Tintern Abbey" indicate that Coleridge influenced Wordsworth.

Eliminating the expletive *There are* makes the main subject of the sentence—*similarities*—clearer. To find the action in the sentence, ask what *similarities* do here; they *indicate.* Find the noun *(indications)* that can become the verb *(indicate).* Do the same for the sentence's other subject, *Coleridge,* by asking what he did: *Coleridge . . . influenced.*

CHAPTER 39

Missing Words

When editing, make sure you have not omitted any words readers need to understand your meaning.

39a Add words needed to make compound structures complete and clear.

For conciseness, you can sometimes omit words from compound structures (which then are called *elliptical structures*): *His anger is extreme and his behavior [is] violent.*

Do not leave out part of a compound structure unless both parts of the compound are the same, however.

> *with*
> **The children neither cooperated nor listened to the babysitter.**

39b   Include *that* when needed for clarity.

The word *that* can often be omitted, especially when the clause it introduces is short and the sentence's meaning is clear: *Carrie Underwood sings the kind of songs many women love.* You should add it, though, if doing so makes the sentence clearer.

▶   The attorney argued$_\wedge$ men and women should receive equal pay

  for equal work.

(insertion: that)

39c   Make comparisons clear.

To be clear, comparisons must be complete. If you have just said, "Peanut butter sandwiches are boring," you can say immediately afterward, "Curried chicken sandwiches are more interesting." Saying only "Curried chicken sandwiches are more interesting" does not give your audience enough information. Name who or what completes the comparison.

To clarify comparisons, add the missing words.

▶   I loved my grandmother more than my sister$_\wedge$.

(insertion: did)

▶   I loved my grandmother more than$_\wedge$ my sister.

(insertion: I loved)

When you use *as* to compare people or things, be sure to use it twice.

▶   Napoleon's temper was$_\wedge$ volatile as a volcano.

(insertion: as)

Include *other* or *else* to indicate that people or things belong to the group with which they are being compared.

▶   High schools and colleges stage *The Laramie Project* more than

  any *other* play.

▶   Professor Koonig wrote more books than anyone *else* in the

  department.

Use a possessive form when comparing attributes or possessions.

▶   Plato's philosophy is easier to read than ~~that of Aristotle~~.

(insertion: Aristotle's.)

39d   Add articles *(a, an, the)* where necessary.

In English, omitting an article usually makes an expression sound odd, unless you omit the same article from a series of nouns.

► A dog that bites should be kept on ^aleash.

► He gave me ^{the} books he liked best.

► The classroom contained a fish tank, birdcage, and rabbit hutch.

Note: If the articles in a series are *not* the same, include all of them.

► The classroom contained an aquarium, ^abirdcage, and ^arabbit hutch.

(For more information about the use of articles, multilingual writers should consult Tab 12: Basic Grammar Review, pp. 549-82.)

CHAPTER 40

Mixed Constructions

Sentence parts that do not fit grammatically or logically confuse readers; revise them to clarify meaning.

✓ **40a**   Untangle mixed sentence structures.

Mixed constructions occur when writers change grammatical direction midway through a sentence. The following sentence begins with a prepositional phrase (a phrase introduced by a preposition such as *at, by, for, in,* or *of*), which the writer then tries to make into the subject. A prepositional phrase cannot be the subject of a sentence. Eliminating *For* makes it clear that *family members* is the subject of the verb *choose.*

► ~~For family~~ ^{Family} members who enjoy one another's company often

    choose a vacation spot together.

In the following example, the dependent clause *when a curandero is consulted* cannot serve as the subject of the sentence. Transforming this dependent clause into an independent clause with a subject and **predicate**—a complete verb plus its object or complement—solves the problem.

► In Mexican culture, ~~when~~ a curandero ~~is~~ ^{can be} consulted ~~can address~~ ^{for}

    spiritual or physical illness.

Sometimes you may need more than one sentence to clarify your ideas. The following sentence tries to do two things at once: contrast England and France in 1805 and define the difference between an oligarchy and a dictatorship. Using two sentences instead makes both ideas clear.

MIXED UP

In an oligarchy like England was in 1805, a few people had the power rather than a dictatorship like France, which was ruled by Napoleon.

REVISED

In 1805, England was an oligarchy, a state ruled by the few. In contrast, France was a dictatorship, a state ruled by one man: Napoleon.

Mixed Constructions and Grammar Checkers

Computer grammar checkers are unreliable at detecting mixed constructions. One failed to highlight the three examples of mixed-up sentences in Section 40a.

40b Make sure predicates fit their subjects.

A predicate (complete verb) must connect logically to a sentence's subject to avoid faulty predication.

▶ ~~The best kind of education for me would be a~~ A university with both a school of music and a school of government *would be best for me.*

A university is an institution, not a type of education.

40c Edit sentences with *is when, is where,* and *the reason . . . is because* to make the subject clear.

The phrases *is where* and *is when* may sound logical, but they usually result in faulty predication.

▶ Photosynthesis is ~~where~~ *the production of carbohydrates from the interaction of* carbon dioxide, water, and chlorophyll ~~interact~~ in the presence of sunlight ~~to form carbohydrates.~~

Photosynthesis is not a place, so *is where* is illogical.

Although *the reason . . . is because* may seem logical, it is redundant since both reason and because say point to a cause. Change *because* to *that,* or change the subject of the sentence:

▶ The reason the joint did not hold is ~~because~~ *that* the coupling bolt broke.

or

▶ ~~The reason the~~ *The* joint did not hold is because the coupling bolt broke.

CHAPTER 41

Confusing Shifts

When you are editing, eliminate jarring shifts to make your sentences consistent.

Confusing Shifts and Grammar Checkers

Computer grammar checkers rarely flag sentences with confusing shifts in verb tense and voice like this:

▶ **The teacher entered the room, and then roll is called.**

Although it shifts confusingly from past to present tense and from active to passive voice, at least one grammar checker failed to highlight it.

✓ **41a**   Make your point of view consistent.

Writers can choose from three points of view:

- First person *(I* or *we)* emphasizes the writer and is used in personal writing.
- Second person *(you)* focuses attention on readers and is used to give orders, directions, or advice.
- Third person *(he, she, it, one,* or *they)* is topic oriented and prevalent in academic writing.

Once you choose a point of view, use it consistently. For example, the writer of the following sentence shifted confusingly from third person *(students)* to second *(you).*

▶ **Students will have no trouble getting a good seat if y̶o̶u̶ arrive at** ^{they}

the theater before 7 o'clock.

Do not switch from singular to plural or plural to singular for no reason. When editing such shifts, choose the plural to avoid using *his or her* or introducing gender bias *(see Tab 10: Editing for Grammar Conventions, pp. 451-95).*

▶ ~~A person is~~ **often surprised when they are complimented.** ^{People are}

✓ **41b**   Keep your verb tenses consistent.

Verb tenses show the time of an action as it relates to other actions. Choose a time frame—present, past, or future—and use it consistently, changing tense only when the meaning requires it.

Confusing shifts in time may occur when you are narrating events that are still vivid in your mind.

▶ **The wind was blowing a hundred miles an hour when suddenly**
there ~~is~~ a big crash, and a tree ~~falls~~ into the living room.
<small>was</small> ... <small>fell</small>

You may also introduce inconsistencies when using the present perfect tense, perhaps because the past participle causes you to slip from present tense to past tense.

▶ **She has admired many strange buildings at the university but**
~~thought~~ the new Science Center ~~looked~~ out of place.
<small>thinks</small> ... <small>looks</small>

41c Avoid unnecessary shifts in mood and voice.

Verbs have three basic moods: (1) the **indicative,** used to state or question facts, acts, and opinions; (2) the **imperative,** used to give commands or advice; and (3) the **subjunctive,** used to express wishes, conjectures, and hypothetical conditions. Unnecessary shifts in mood can confuse and distract readers.

▶ **If he ~~goes~~ to night school, he would take a course in accounting.**
<small>could go</small>

Most verbs have two voices. In the **active voice,** the subject does the acting; in the **passive voice,** the subject is acted on. Abrupt shifts in voice often indicate awkward changes in subject.

▶ **The Impressionist painters hated black. ~~Violet,~~ green, blue, pink,**
and red ~~were favored by them.~~
<small>They favored violet,</small>

The revision uses *they* to make "the Impressionist painters" the subject of the second sentence as well as the first.

NAVIGATING THROUGH COLLEGE AND BEYOND
Present Tense and Literary Works

By convention—because as long as a book is read, it is "alive"— we use the present tense to write about the content of literary works.

▶ **David Copperfield describes villains such as Mr. Murdstone and**

heroes such as Mr. Micawber in unforgettable detail. But

Copperfield ~~was~~ not himself an especially interesting person.
<small>is</small>

—IDENTIFY AND EDIT

Confusing Shifts

To avoid confusing shifts, ask yourself these questions as you edit:

? *1. Does the sentence shift from one point of view to another, for example, from third person to second?*

> - Over the centuries, millions of laborers helped build and maintain
>   the Great Wall of China, and ~~if you were one, you probably~~ _{most of them}
>   suffered great hardship as a result.

? *2. Are the verbs consistent in the following ways:*

> *In tense (past, present, or future)?*
>
> - Historians call the period before the unification of China the
>   Warring States period. It ~~ends~~ _{ended} when the ruler of the Ch'in state
>   conquered the last of his independent neighbors.
>
> *In mood (statements vs. commands or hypothetical conditions)?*
>
> - If a similar wall ~~is~~ _{were} built today, it would cost untold amounts of
>   time and money.
>
> *In voice (active vs. passive)?*
>
> - The purpose of the wall was to protect against invasion,
>   but commerce ~~was promoted by it also.~~ _{it also promoted}

? *3. Are quotations and questions clearly phrased in either direct or indirect form?*

> - The visitor asked the guide ~~when~~ _{"When} did construction of the Great Wall
>   begin?_"
>
> - The visitor asked the guide when ~~did~~ construction of the Great Wall
>   ~~begin?~~ _{began.}

41d Avoid awkward shifts between direct and indirect quotations and questions.

Indirect quotations report what others wrote or said without repeating their words exactly. **Direct quotations** report the words of others exactly and should be enclosed in quotation marks. *(For more on punctuating quotations, see Tab 11: Editing for Correctness, pp. 497–548.)* Do not shift from one form of quotation to the other within a sentence.

► **In his inaugural speech, President Kennedy called on Americans**

not to ask what their country could do for them but instead ⟨to⟩ask

~~they could~~ ~~their~~
what ~~you can~~ do for ~~your~~ country.⟨"⟩

The writer could have included the quotation in its entirety: *In his inaugural speech, President Kennedy said, "My fellow Americans, ask not what your country can do for you; ask what you can do for your country."*

Similarly, do not shift from an indirect to a direct question.

► **The performance was so bad the audience wondered ~~had~~ ⟨whether⟩ the**

had
performers ever rehearsed.

As an alternative, the writer could ask the question directly: *Had the performers ever rehearsed? The performance was so bad that the audience wasn't sure.*

CHAPTER 42

Faulty Parallelism

Parallel constructions present equally important ideas in the same grammatical form. The following sentence presents three prepositional phrases:

► **At Gettysburg in 1863, Lincoln said that the Civil War was being**

fought to make sure that government *of the people, by the*

***people,* and *for the people* might not perish from the earth.**

If paired ideas or items in a series do not have the same grammatical form, edit to make them parallel. Put items at the same level in an outline or items in a list in parallel form.

✓ **42a**   Edit items in a series to make them parallel.

A list or series of equally important items should be parallel in grammatical structure.

> **The Census Bureau classifies people as employed if they receive**
>
> **payment for any kind of labor, are temporarily absent from their**
>
> **jobs, or** ~~working~~ _work_ **at least fifteen hours as unpaid laborers in a**
>
> **family business.**

In the next example, the writer changed a noun to an adjective. Repeating the word *too* makes the sentence more forceful and memorable.

> **My sister obviously thought I was too young,** _too_ **ignorant, and** ~~a~~
> *too troublesome.*
> ~~troublemaker.~~

42b   Edit paired ideas to make them parallel.

Paired ideas connected with a coordinating conjunction *(and, but, or, nor, for, so, yet)*, a correlative conjunction *(not only . . . but also, both . . . and, either . . . or, neither . . . nor)*, or a comparative expression *(as much as, more than, less than)* must have parallel grammatical form.

> **Successful teachers must** _both_ **inspire** ~~students~~ **and** ~~challenging them is~~ *challenge their students.*
>
> ~~also important.~~

> **I dreamed not only of getting the girl but also of** _winning_ **the gold medal.**

> **Many people find that having meaningful work is more important**
> **than** _earning_ **high pay.**

42c   Repeat function words as needed to keep parallel structures clear.

Function words give information about a word or indicate the relationships among words in a sentence. They include:

- Articles *(the, a, an)*
- Prepositions (for example, *to, for,* and *by*)
- Subordinating conjunctions (for example, *although* and *that*)
- The word *to* in infinitives

IDENTIFY AND EDIT
Faulty Parallelism

To avoid faulty parallelism, ask yourself these questions:

? 1. *Are the items in a series in parallel form?*

> • The senator stepped to the podium, ~~an angry glance shooting~~ *glanced angrily at* ~~toward~~ her challenger, and began to refute his charges.

? 2. *Are paired items in parallel form?*

> • Her challenger, she claimed, ~~had~~ not only *had* accused her falsely of accepting illegal campaign contributions, but *had accepted illegal contributions himself.* ~~his contributions were from illegal sources.~~

? 3. *Are the items in outlines and lists in parallel form?*

FAULTY PARALLELISM

She listed four reasons for voters to send her back to Washington:

1. Ability to protect the state's interests
2. Her seniority on important committees
3. Works with members of both parties to get things done
4. Has a close working relationship with the President

REVISED

She listed four reasons for voters to send her back to Washington:

1. *Her ability* to protect the state's interests
2. *Her seniority* on important committees
3. *Her ability* to work with members of both parties to get things done
4. *Her* close working *relationship* with the President

You can omit repeated function words whenever the parallel structure is clear without them, as in the first example. Otherwise, include them, as in the second example.

▶ **Her goals for retirement were to travel, ~~to~~ study art history, and**

~~to~~ write a book about Michelangelo.

▶ **The project has three goals: to survey the valley for Inca-period**
to
sites, ^**excavate a test trench at each site, and** ^**excavate one of**
to

those sites completely.

The added *to* makes it clear where one goal ends and the next begins.

CHAPTER 43

Misplaced and Dangling Modifiers

For a sentence to make sense, its parts must be arranged appropriately. When a modifying word, phrase, or clause is misplaced or dangling, readers get confused.

Misplaced Modifiers and Grammar Checkers

Some grammar checkers will reliably highlight split infinitives *(see 43d)* but only occasionally highlight other types of misplaced modifiers. One grammar checker, for example, missed the misplaced modifier *with a loud crash* in this sentence.

▶ **The valuable vase *with a loud crash* fell to the floor and**

broke into hundreds of pieces.

43a   Put modifiers close to the words they modify.

For clarity, modifiers should usually come immediately before or after the words they modify. In the following sentence, the clause *after the police arrested them* modifies *protesters,* not *destroying.*

After the police had arrested them, the
▶ **~~The~~ protesters were charged with destroying college property,**
^
~~after the police had arrested them.~~

The following sentence was revised to clarify that the hikers were watching the storm from the porch.

> *From the cabin's porch, the*
> ▶ ~~The~~ hikers watched the storm gathering force~~,~~ ~~from the cabin's~~
>
> ~~porch.~~

43b Clarify ambiguous modifiers.

Adverbs modify words that precede or follow them. When they are ambiguously placed, they are called **squinting modifiers.** The following revision shows that the objection is vehement, not the argument.

> *vehemently*
> ▶ Historians who object to this account ~~vehemently~~ argue that the
>
> presidency was never endangered.

Problems can occur with **limiting modifiers** such as *only, even, almost, nearly,* and *just.* In the following sentence, does the writer mean that vegetarian dishes are the only dishes served at dinner, or that dinner is the only time vegetarian dishes are available? Place the modifier immediately before the modified word or phrase.

AMBIGUOUS

The restaurant *only offers* vegetarian dishes for dinner.

REVISED

The restaurant *offers only* vegetarian dishes for dinner.

or

The restaurant *offers* vegetarian dishes *only* at dinner.

Misplacing the limiting modifier *not* can create an inaccurate sentence:

> *Not all*
> ▶ ~~All~~ the vegetarian dishes are ~~not~~ low in fat and calories.

43c Move disruptive modifiers.

When a lengthy modifying phrase or clause separates grammatical elements that belong together, a sentence can be difficult to read. With the modifying phrase at the beginning, the edited version of the following sentence restores the connection between subject and verb.

> *Despite their similar conceptions of the self,*
> ▶ Descartes and Hume, ~~despite their similar conceptions of the self,~~
>
> deal with the issue of personal identity in different ways.

43d   Check split infinitives for ambiguity.

An **infinitive** couples the word *to* with the present tense of a verb. In a **split infinitive,** one or more words intervene between *to* and the verb form. Avoid separating the parts of an infinitive with a modifier unless keeping them together results in an awkward or ambiguous construction.

In the following example, the modifier *successfully* should be moved. The modifier *carefully* should stay where it is, however, even though it splits the infinitive *to assess:*

► **To** ~~successfully~~ **complete this assignment, students have to**

> *successfully*

carefully assess projected economic benefits.

Putting *carefully* after *assess* would cause ambiguity because readers might think it modifies *projected economic benefits.*

✓ 43e   Fix dangling modifiers.

A **dangling modifier** is a descriptive phrase that implies an actor different from the sentence's subject. When readers try to connect the modifying phrase with the actual subject, the results may be humorous as well as confusing. To fix a dangling modifier, you must name its implied actor explicitly, either as the subject of the sentence or in the modifier itself:

DANGLING MODIFIER   *Swimming toward the boat on the horizon,* the crowded beach felt as if it were miles away.

REVISED   Swimming toward the boat on the horizon, *I* felt as if the crowded beach were miles away.

or

As *I swam* toward the boat on the horizon, the crowded beach seemed miles away.

Simply moving a dangling modifier will not fix the problem. To make the meaning clear, you must make the implied actor in the modifying phrase explicit.

DANGLING MODIFIER   *After struggling for weeks in the wilderness,* the town pleased them mightily.

REVISED   After struggling for weeks in the wilderness, *they* were pleased to come upon the town.

or

After *they had struggled* for weeks in the wilderness, the town appeared in the distance.

IDENTIFY AND EDIT

Misplaced Modifiers

mm

To avoid misplaced modifiers, ask yourself these questions.

? *1.* *Are all the modifiers close to the expressions they modify?*

> At the beginning of the Great Depression, people
> - ~~People~~ panicked, and all tried to get their money out of the banks
>
> at the same time, forcing many banks to close, ~~at the beginning of~~
>
> ~~the Great Depression.~~

? *2.* *Are any modifiers placed in such a way that they modify more than one expression? Pay particular attention to limiting modifiers such as* only, even, *and* just.

> quickly
> - President Roosevelt declared a bank holiday, ~~quickly~~ helping to
>
>   restore confidence in the nation's financial system.
>
> - Congress enacted many programs to combat the Depression ~~only~~
>   only
>   within the first one hundred days of Roosevelt's presidency.

? *3.* *Do any modifiers disrupt the relationships among the grammatical elements of the sentence?*

> Given how entrenched segregation was at the time, the
> - ~~The~~ president's wife, Eleanor Roosevelt, was a surprisingly strong~~, given~~
>
> ~~how entrenched segregation was at the time,~~ advocate for racial justice
>
> in Roosevelt's administration.

Dangling Modifiers and Grammar Checkers

Computer grammar checkers cannot distinguish a descriptive phrase that properly modifies the subject of the sentence from one that implies a different actor. As a result, they do not flag dangling modifiers.

IDENTIFY AND EDIT

✓
dm

Dangling Modifiers

To avoid dangling modifiers, ask yourself these questions when you see a descriptive phrase at the beginning of a sentence:

? *1. What is the subject of the sentence?*

> • Snorkeling in Hawaii, ancient sea turtles were an amazing sight.
>
> The subject of the sentence is *sea turtles.*

? *2. Could the phrase at the beginning of the sentence possibly describe this subject?*

> —?—
>
> • Snorkeling in Hawaii, ancient sea turtles were an amazing sight.
>
> No, sea turtles do not snorkel in Hawaii or anywhere else.

? *3. Who or what is the phrase really describing? Either make that person or thing the subject of the main clause, or add a subject to the modifier.*

> we saw
> • Snorkeling in Hawaii, ancient sea turtles, were an amazing sight.
>
> While we were snorkeling   amazed us.
> • Snorkeling in Hawaii, ancient sea turtles were an amazing sight.

CHAPTER 44

Coordination and Subordination

Coordination and subordination allow you to combine and develop ideas in ways that readers can follow and understand. Use coordination only when two or more ideas deserve equal emphasis. Use subordination to indicate that information is of secondary importance and to show its logical relation to the main idea.

44a   Use coordination to express equal ideas.

Coordination gives two or more ideas equal weight. To coordinate parts within a sentence, join them with a coordinating conjunction *(and, but, or, for, nor, yet,* or *so)* or a correlative conjunction *(either . . . or, both . . . and).* To coordinate two or more sentences, use a comma plus a coordinating conjunction, or insert a semicolon. A semicolon is often followed by a conjunctive adverb such as *moreover, nevertheless, however, therefore,* or *subsequently. (For more on conjunctive adverbs and correlative conjunctions, see Tab 12: Basic Grammar Review, pp. 549–82.)*

▶   **The auditorium was huge, *and* the acoustics were terrible.**

▶   **The student was *both* late for class *and* unprepared.**

▶   **Jones did not agree with her position on health care; *nevertheless,* he supported her campaign for office.**

44b   Use subordination to express unequal ideas.

Subordination makes one idea depend on another and is therefore used to combine ideas that are not of equal importance. The main idea is expressed in an independent clause, and the secondary ideas are expressed in subordinate clauses or phrases. Subordinate clauses start with a relative pronoun *(who, whom, that, which, whoever, whomever, whose)* or a subordinating conjunction *(after, although, because, if, since, when, where).*

▶   **The blue liquid, *which will be added to the beaker later,* must be kept at room temperature.**

▶   **Christopher Columbus discovered the New World in 1492, *although he never understood just what he had found.***

▶   ***After writing the opening four sections,* Wordsworth put the work aside for two years.**

> **Note:** Commas often set off subordinate ideas, especially when the subordinate clause or phrase opens the sentence. *(For more on using commas, see Tab 11: Editing for Correctness, pp. 497–548.)*

44c   Do not subordinate major ideas.

Major ideas belong in main clauses, not in subordinate clauses or phrases. The writer revised the following sentence to emphasize the definition of literacy because that topic was the focus of the essay.

INEFFECTIVE SUBORDINATION

Literacy, which has been defined as the ability to talk intelligently about many topics, is highly valued by businesspeople as well as academics.

REVISION

Highly valued by businesspeople as well as academics, literacy has been defined as the ability to talk intelligently about many topics.

44d   Combine short, choppy sentences.

Short sentences are easy to read, but several of them in a row can become so monotonous that meaning gets lost.

CHOPPY

My cousin Jim is not an accountant. But he does my taxes every year. He suggests various deductions. These deductions reduce my tax bill considerably.

Use subordination to put the idea you want to emphasize in the main clause, and use subordinate clauses and phrases for the other ideas. In this revision, the main clause is italicized.

REVISED

Even though he is not an accountant, *my cousin Jim does my taxes every year,* suggesting various deductions that reduce my tax bill considerably.

If a series of short sentences includes two major ideas of equal importance, use coordination for the two major ideas and subordinate the secondary information.

CHOPPY

Bilingual education is designed for children. The native language of these children is not English. Smith supports expanding bilingual education. Johnson does not support expanding bilingual education.

REVISED

Smith supports bilingual education for children whose native language is not English; Johnson, however, does not.

44e   Avoid overloading sentences with excessive subordination.

Separate an overloaded sentence into two or more sentences.

OVERLOADED

Big-city mayors, who are supported by public funds, should be cautious about spending taxpayers' money for personal needs, such as furnishing official residences, especially when municipal budget shortfalls have caused extensive job layoffs, angering city workers and the general public.

REVISED

Big-city mayors should be cautious about spending taxpayers' money for personal needs, especially when municipal budget shortfalls have caused extensive job layoffs. They risk angering city workers and the general public by using public funds for furnishing official residences.

CHAPTER 45

Sentence Variety

Enliven your prose and keep your readers interested by using a variety of sentence patterns.

Sentence Variety and Grammar Checkers

Monotony is not a grammatical error; sentence variety is an issue of style, not syntax, and the type of sentences a writer uses also depends on the writing situation. A computer grammar checker might flag a very long sentence, but it cannot decide whether the sentence is *too* long.

45a Vary your sentence openings.

When all the sentences in a passage begin with the subject, you risk losing readers' attention. Vary your sentences by moving a modifier to the beginning. The modifier may be a single word, a phrase, or a clause.

► Eventually,
   Louis Armstrong's innovations on the trumpet ~~eventually~~ **became the standard.**

► In at least two instances, this
   ~~Armstrong's~~ **money-making strategy backfired** ~~in at least two instances.~~

A **participial phrase** begins with an *-ing* verb *(driving)* or a past participle *(moved, driven)* and serves as a modifier. You can move it to the beginning of a sentence for variety, but make sure it describes the explicit subject of the sentence or you will end up with a dangling modifier *(see pp. 421-25)*.

► Stunned by the stock market crash in 1929, many
   Many brokers, ~~stunned by the stock market crash in 1929,~~ **committed suicide.**

45b Vary the length and structure of your sentences.

Short, simple sentences (under ten words) will keep your readers alert, but only if your work also includes longer, complex sentences.

As you edit, see whether you have overused one kind of sentence structure. Are most of your sentences short and simple? If so, use subordination to combine some of them *(see pp. 425-27)*. But if most of your sentences are long and complex, put at least one of your ideas into a short, simple sentence. Your goal is to achieve a good mix.

DRAFT

I dived quickly into the sea. I peered through my mask at the watery world. It turned darker. A school of fish went by. The distant light glittered on their bodies, and I stopped swimming.

I waited to see whether the fish might be chased by a shark. I was satisfied that there was no shark and continued down.

REVISED

I dived quickly into the sea, peering through my mask at a watery world that turned darker as I descended. A school of fish went by, the distant light glittering on their bodies. I stopped swimming and waited. Perhaps the fish were being chased by a shark? Satisfied that there was no shark, I continued down.

(For more information about sentence types, see Tab 12: Basic Grammar Review, pp. 549-82. For more on sentence variety, see Tab 2: Writing and Designing Texts, pp. 29-96.)

45c Include a few cumulative and periodic sentences and rhetorical questions.

Cumulative sentences add a series of descriptive participial or absolute phrases to the basic subject-plus-verb pattern, making your writing forceful and detailed. *(See Tab 12: Basic Grammar Review, pp. 549-82 for more on these phrases.)* You can also use them to add details, as this example shows:

▶ **The motorcycle spun out of control, *plunging down the ravine, crashing through the fence,* and *coming to rest on its side.***

Another way to increase the force of your writing is to use a few **periodic sentences,** in which the key word, phrase, or idea appears at the end, where readers are most likely to remember it.

In 1946 and 1947, young people

▶ ~~Young people fell in love with the jukebox in 1946 and 1947 and~~

and fell in love with the jukebox.

turned away from the horrors of World War II.

Asking a question invites your readers to participate more actively in your work. Because you do not expect an answer, this kind of question is called a **rhetorical question.**

▶ **Athletes injured at an early age too often find themselves without a job, a college degree, or their health. Is it any wonder that a few turn to drugs and alcohol?**

Rhetorical questions work best in the middle or at the end of a long, complicated passage. They can also help you make a transition from one topic to another. Use them selectively, however, and do not begin with a broad rhetorical question such as "How did the Peace Corps begin?"

45d Try an occasional inversion.

Occasionally, try using an inverted sentence pattern or another sentence type, such as a rhetorical question or an exclamation, to vary the normal sentence pattern of subject plus verb plus object. *(For more on sentence types, see Tab 12: Basic Grammar Review, pp. 549–82.)*

You can create an **inversion** by putting the verb before the subject. Because many inversions sound odd, use them infrequently and carefully. In a passage on the qualities of various contemporary artists, the following inversion makes sense and adds interest.

▶ **Characteristic of Issey Miyake's work are bold design and original thinking.**

45e Use exclamation points sparingly and appropriately.

Exclamations are rare in academic writing, so if you decide to use one for special effect, be sure that strong emotion is appropriate.

▶ **Wordsworth completed the thirteen-book Prelude in 1805, after seven years of hard work. Instead of publishing his masterpiece, however, he devoted himself to revising it—for more than thirty years! The poem, in a fourteen-book version, was finally published in 1850, after he had died.**

CHAPTER 46

Active Verbs

Active verbs such as *run, shout, write,* and *think* are more direct and forceful than forms of the *be* verb *(am, are, is, was, were, been, being)* or passive-voice constructions. The more active your verbs, the stronger and clearer your writing will be.

Active Verbs and Grammar Checkers

Computer grammar checkers generally do not flag weak uses of the *be* verb. A grammar checker did not flag the sentence *The paper was an argument for a stronger police presence* because it is grammatically correct, although it is stronger as *The paper argued . . .*

Some grammar checkers do flag most passive-voice sentences *(see 46b),* but their suggestions for revising them can sometimes make the sentence worse.

46a   Consider alternatives to some *be* verbs.

Although it is not a strong verb, *be* does a lot of work in English.

As a linking verb:

► **Germany *is* relatively poor in natural resources.**

► **Decent health care *is* a necessity, not a luxury.**

As a helping verb:

► **Macbeth *was* returning from battle when he met the three witches.**

Be verbs are so useful that they get overworked. Consider using active verbs in place of *be* verbs and clunky, abstract nouns made from verbs (like *is a demonstration of). (See also Chapter 38: Wordy Sentences, pp. 408-11.)*

► **The mayor's refusal to meet with our group is a demonstration of** *demonstrates*

his lack of respect for us, as well as for the environment.

46b   When writing for a general audience, prefer the active voice.

Transitive verbs, which connect an actor with something that receives the action, can be in the active or passive voice. In the **active voice,** the subject of the sentence acts; in the **passive voice,** the subject is acted on:

ACTIVE   The Senate finally passed the bill.

PASSIVE   The bill was finally passed by the Senate.

The passive voice downplays the actors as well as the action, so much so that the actors are often left out of the sentence.

PASSIVE   The bill was finally passed.

NAVIGATING THROUGH COLLEGE AND BEYOND

Passive Voice in Scientific Writing

The passive voice is often used in scientific reports to keep the focus on the experiment and its results rather than on the experimenters.

► **The bacteria were treated carefully with nicotine and stopped reproducing.**

The active voice is more forceful, and readers usually want to know who or what does the acting, particularly in nontechnical genres.

PASSIVE	Polluting chemicals were dumped into the river.
ACTIVE	Industrial Products Corporation dumped polluting chemicals into the river.

When the recipient of the action is more important than the doer of the action, however, the passive voice is the more appropriate choice.

▶ **After her heart attack, my mother was taken to the hospital.**

Mother and the fact that she was taken to the hospital are more important than who took her there.

CHAPTER 47

Appropriate Language

Language is appropriate when it fits your writing situation: your topic, purpose, and audience. Whether you are preparing to write about literature or natural science or history, take some time to read how writers in the field have handled your topic.

47a   In college writing, avoid slang, regional expressions, and nonstandard English.

Slang, regional sayings, and nonstandard English appear often in conversation but are too informal for college writing—unless that writing is literary or is reporting conversation. Slang words also change frequently. In college writing, avoid slang and the informal tone that goes with it.

SLANG	In *Heart of Darkness,* we hear a lot about a *dude* named Kurtz, but we don't see the *guy* much.
REVISED	In *Heart of Darkness,* Marlow, the narrator, talks continually about Kurtz, but we meet Kurtz himself only at the end.

Like slang, regional and nonstandard expressions such as *y'all, hisself,* and *don't be doing that* are fine in conversation, but not in formal college writing. In U.S. colleges, professions, and businesses, the dominant dialect is Standard Written English. Most of your instructors will expect you to write in this dialect, unless you have a good reason not to. *(See the Glossary of Usage for common nonstandard expressions, pp. 441–49.)*

47b   Use an appropriate level of formality.

College writing assignments usually call for a style that avoids extremes of stuffy and casual, pretentious and chatty. Revise passages that veer toward one or the other extreme.

PRETENTIOUS — Romantic lovers are characterized by a preoccupation with a deliberately restricted set of qualities in the love object that are viewed as means to some ideal end.

REVISED — People in love see what they want to see, usually by idealizing the beloved.

Prefer clear, concise language to inflated words.

Pretentious	Simple
ascertain	find out
commence	begin
endeavor	try
finalize	finish
impact (as verb)	affect
optimal	best
parameters	limits
prior to	before
reside	live
utilize	use

47c   Avoid jargon.

When specialists communicate with each other, they often use technical or specialized language called **jargon**. Jargon has its place, but you should not use terms appropriate for specialists when writing for a nonspecialist audience.

JARGON — Pegasus Technologies developed a Web-based PSP system to support standard off-line brands in meeting their loyalty-driven marketing objectives via the social media space.

REVISED — Pegasus Technologies developed a system that helps businesses create media sites to run promotions for their customers.

If you must use technical terms when writing for nonspecialists, be sure to provide definitions.

▶   **Armstrong's innovative singing style featured "scat," a technique that combines "nonsense syllables [with] improvised melodies" (Robinson 515).**

┌─ NAVIGATING THROUGH COLLEGE AND BEYOND
Discourse Communities

People who share certain interests, knowledge, and customary ways of communicating constitute a **discourse community.** Book collectors, for example, talk and write about *marginalia, foxing,* and *provenance,* terms that are probably unfamiliar to people outside the community. The more familiar you are with a discourse community, the more you will know about the language appropriate in it.

47d Avoid most euphemisms and all doublespeak.

Euphemisms and doublespeak have one goal: to cover up the truth. **Euphemisms** substitute words like *correctional facility* and *passing away* for such harsh realities as *prison* and *death.*

Doublespeak is used to obscure facts and evade responsibility.

DOUBLESPEAK	Pursuant to the environmental protection regulations enforcement policy of the Bureau of Natural Resources, special management area land use permit issuance procedures have been instituted.
REVISED	The Bureau of Natural Resources has established procedures for issuing land use permits.

47e Do not use biased language.

Biased language can undermine your credibility with readers.

1. Recognizing biased language

Watch for stereotypes—rigid, unexamined generalizations that demean, ignore, or patronize people on the basis of gender and gender expression, race, religion, national origin, ethnicity, physical ability, sexual orientation, occupation, age, or any other human condition. Revise for inclusiveness.

For example, do not assume that Irish Catholics have large families.

▶ ~~Although the~~ Browns are ^Irish ~~Catholics, there are only~~ two

children ~~in the family.~~

(handwritten edits: The; an; Catholic family with; two children)

Remember that a positive stereotype is still an overgeneralization, which readers find patronizing, that is, as coming from a place of perceived superiority.

▶ ~~Because Asian students are whizzes at math, we~~ all wanted ~~them~~

in our study group.

(handwritten edits: We; math whizzes)

—the EVOLVING SITUATION

You may find examples of "they" referring to a singular antecedent, often because writers are trying to avoid gender-biased language. Another approach is to change the antecedent to plural—*students*, rather than *student*.

Do not assume that readers will share your background. Be careful about using *we* and *they*, which can lead to generalized statements about a group.

Refer to groups as they refer to themselves. Refer to someone's ethnicity, religion, age, or other circumstances only when the writing situation requires it.

Avoid language that demeans or stereotypes anyone based on gender or gender identity. Many labels and clichés imply that women are not as able or mature as men. Consider the meaning of words and phrases like *the fair sex, acting like a girl, poetess, maiden name,* and *coed.* If a subject you are writing about prefers a gender-neutral pronoun such as *they* or *hir,* you should respect that preference.

2. Revising gender-biased language

Avoiding bias means avoiding even subtle stereotypes. For example, not all heads of state are or have to be men.

BIASED	Wives of heads of state typically choose to promote a charity that benefits a cause they care about.
REVISED	Spouses of heads of state typically choose to promote a charity that benefits a cause they care about.

Traditionally, the pronoun *he* was used to represent either men or women. Today, however, the use of *he* or *man* or any other masculine noun to represent people in general is considered offensive.

BIASED	Everybody had his way.
REVISED	We all had our way.
BIASED	It's every man for himself.
REVISED	All of us have to save ourselves.

Follow these simple principles to eliminate gender bias from your writing:

- Replace terms that indicate gender with their gender-free equivalents:

No	Yes
chairman	chair, chairperson
congressman	representative, member of Congress
forefathers	ancestors
male nurse	nurse
man, mankind	people, humans, humankind
manmade	artificial

policeman   police officer
spokesman   spokesperson
woman doctor   doctor

- Refer to men and women in parallel ways: *ladies and gentlemen* [not *ladies and men*], *men and women, husband and wife.*

BIASED	D. H. Lawrence and Mrs. Woolf met, but Lawrence did not like the Bloomsbury circle that revolved around Virginia.
REVISED	D. H. Lawrence and Virginia Woolf met, but Lawrence did not like the Bloomsbury circle that revolved around Woolf.

- Replace the masculine pronouns *he, him, his,* and *himself* when they are being used generically to refer to both women and men. One way to replace masculine pronouns is to use the plural.

▶ ~~Each senator~~ returned to ~~his district~~ during the break.
     Senators   *their districts*

Some writers alternate *he* and *she* and *him* and *her.* This strategy may be effective in some writing situations, but it can also be distracting. The constructions *his or her* and *he or she* are acceptable as long as they are not used more than once in a sentence:

AWKWARD	Each student in the psychology class was to choose a different book according to *his or her* interests, to read the book overnight, to do without *his or her* normal sleep, to write a short summary of what *he or she* had read, and then to see whether *he or she* dreamed about the book the following night.
REVISED	Every student was to choose a book, read it over- night, do without sleep, write a short summary of the book the next morning, and then see whether *he or she* dreamed about the book the following night.

The constructions *his/her* and *s/he* are not acceptable.

- Use a gender-neutral plural pronoun such as *they.* In the past, this option has been considered inappropriate for formal writing, but it is now more widely accepted.

Note: Using the neuter impersonal pronoun *one* can sometimes help you avoid masculine pronouns, but it can make your writing sound stuffy.

STUFFY	The American creed holds that if ONE works hard, ONE will succeed in life.
REVISED	The American creed holds that those who work hard will succeed in life.

CHAPTER 48

Exact Language

To convey your meaning clearly, you need to choose the right words. As you revise, look for problems with diction: Is your choice of words as precise as it should be?

48a   Choose words with suitable connotations.

Words have denotations and connotations. **Denotations** are their primary meanings, while **connotations** are the feelings and images associated with a word.

As you revise, consider replacing any word whose connotations do not exactly fit what you want to say.

► The players' union should ~~request~~ *demand* that the NFL amend its

  pension plan.

If you cannot think of a more suitable word, consult a thesaurus *(see p. 441)* for **synonyms**—words with similar meanings. Keep in mind, however, that most words have connotations that allow them to work in some contexts but not in others. To find out more about a synonym's connotations, look up the word in a dictionary.

48b   Include specific and concrete words.

In addition to general and abstract terms, effective writers use specific and concrete words.

General words name broad categories of things, such as *trees, books, politicians,* and *students.* **Specific words** name particular kinds of things or items, such as *pines* and *college sophomores.*

Abstract words name qualities and ideas that do not have physical properties, such as *charity, beauty, hope,* and *radical.* **Concrete words** name things we can sense by touch, taste, smell, hearing, and sight, such as *velvet, vinegar, smoke, screech,* and *sweater.*

By creating images that appeal to the senses, specific and concrete words make writing more precise.

VAGUE   The trees were affected by the bad weather.

PRECISE   The tall pines shook in the gale.

As you edit, make sure you have developed your ideas with specific and concrete details. Also check for overused, vague terms—such as *factor, thing, good, nice,* and *interesting*—and replace them with specific and concrete alternatives.

► The protesters were charged with ~~things~~ *crimes* they never ~~did~~ *committed*.

48c Use standard idioms.

Idioms are habitual ways of expressing ideas. They are not always logical and can be hard to translate. Often they involve selecting the right preposition: we do not go *with* the car but *in* the car or simply *by* car; we do not abide *with* a rule but *by* a rule. If you are not sure which preposition to use, look up the main word in a dictionary. *(For more on idioms and multilingual writers, see Tab 12: Basic Grammar Review, pp. 549-82.)*

Some verbs, called **phrasal verbs,** include a preposition to make their idiomatic meaning complete:

Henry *made up* with Gloria.

Henry *made off* with Gloria.

Henry *made out* with Gloria.

(For more on phrasal verbs, see pp. 567-68.)

48d Avoid clichés.

A **cliché** is an overworked expression. If someone says, "She was as mad as a _____," we expect the next word to be *hornet.* We have heard this expression so often that it no longer creates a vivid picture in our imagination. It is usually best to rephrase clichés in plain language.

CLICHÉ When John turned in his project three weeks late, he had to *face the music.*

BETTER When John turned in his project three weeks late, he had to *accept the consequences.*

Here are some common clichés to avoid:

beyond a shadow of a doubt
calm, cool, and collected
cold, hard facts
cool as a cucumber
dead as a doornail
deep, dark secret
depths of despair

few and far between
flat as a pancake
give 110 percent
green with envy
heave a sigh of relief
hit the nail on the head
last but not least
pass the buck
pretty as a picture

rise to the occasion
sink or swim
sneaking suspicion
straight and narrow
tried and true
ugly as sin
untimely death
white as a sheet

48e Create suitable figures of speech.

Figures of speech make writing vivid, most often by using a comparison to supplement the literal meaning of words. A **simile** is a comparison that contains the word *like* or *as.*

► **Hakim's smile was like sunshine after a rainstorm.**

A **metaphor** is an implied comparison. It treats one thing or action, such as a politician's speech, as if it were something else (a drive on a familiar road in this instance).

▶   **The senator's speech rolled along a familiar highway, past the usual landmarks: taxes and foreign policy.**

Because it is compressed, a metaphor is often more forceful than a simile.

Comparisons can make your prose more vivid, but only if they suit your subject and purpose. Do not mix metaphors; if you use two or more comparisons together, make sure they are compatible.

MIXED	His presentation of the plan was such a *well-constructed tower of logic* that we immediately decided *to come aboard.*
REVISED	His clear presentation of the plan immediately convinced us to come aboard.

✓ 48f   Avoid misusing words.

Avoid mistakes with new or unfamiliar words by always consulting a dictionary whenever you include an unfamiliar word in your writing.

▶   **The artistocracy ~~exuded~~** *exhibited* **numerous vices including greed and** ~~license.~~ *licentiousness*

Always think critically about the suggestions made by your word-processing program's spell checker. In the example, the writer mistyped the word *instate* as *enstate* and received the incorrect suggestion *estate.*

▶   **We needed approval to ~~estate~~** *instate* **the change.**

As you edit, read carefully to make sure you have the right word in the right place.

CHAPTER 49

The Dictionary and the Thesaurus

A dictionary and a thesaurus are essential tools for all writers.

49a   Make using the dictionary a habit.

A standard desk dictionary contains 140,000 to 180,000 entries. Dictionaries also provide information such as the correct spellings of important place names, the official names of countries, correct forms of address, and conversion tables for weights and measures. Dictionaries of varying size also appear in most word-processing software and applications and on Web sites.

All dictionaries include guides to their use. The guides explain the terms and abbreviations that appear in the entries as well as special notations such as *slang, nonstandard,* and *vulgar.*

The kind of information that accompanies a term in a dictionary, and is discussed in the following sections, includes spelling, word division, and pronunciation; word endings and grammatical labels; definitions and word origins; and usage.

1. Spelling, word division, and pronunciation

Entries in a dictionary are listed in alphabetical order according to their standard spelling. For example, the verb *compare* is entered as **com•pare.** The dot separates the word into its two syllables.

Phonetic symbols in parentheses typically follow the entry and show its correct pronunciation. The second syllable of *compare* receives the greater stress when you pronounce the word correctly: "com-PARE." An accent mark (′) appears after the syllable that receives the primary stress. Online dictionaries often include a recording of the pronunciation.

Plurals of nouns are usually not given if they are formed by adding an *s,* unless the word is foreign *(gondolas, dashikis).* Irregular plurals—such as *children* for *child*—are noted.

Some dictionaries list alternate spellings, always giving the preferred spelling first or placing the full entry under the preferred spelling only.

2. Word endings and grammatical labels

The abbreviation *v.* immediately after the pronunciation tells you that *compare* is most frequently used as a verb. The next abbreviation, *n.,* indicates that *compare* can sometimes function as a noun, as in the phrase *beyond compare.*

Here is a list of common abbreviations for grammatical terms:

adj.	adjective	*prep.*	preposition
adv.	adverb	*pron.*	pronoun
conj.	conjunction	*sing.*	singular
interj.	interjection	*v.*	verb
n.	noun	*v.i.*	intransitive verb
pl.	plural	*v.t.*	transitive verb
poss.	possessive		

The *-pared* shows the simple past and past participle form of the verb; the present participle form, *-paring,* follows, indicating that *compare* drops the final *e* when *-ing* is added.

3. Definitions and word origins

If you were to look up *compare* in the *Random House Webster's College Dictionary,* you would note that the definitions begin after the abbreviation *v.t.,* indicating that the first three meanings relate to *compare* as a transitive verb. A little further down in the entry, *v.i.* introduces definitions of *compare* as an intransitive verb. Next, after *n.,* comes the definition of *compare* as a noun. Finally, the word idiom signals a special meaning not included in the previous definitions.

Included in most dictionary entries is an **etymology**—a brief history of the word's origins—set off in brackets. *Compare* came into the English language between 1375 and 1425 and was derived from the Old French word *comperer,* which came from Latin.

4. Usage

Some main entries in the dictionary conclude with examples of and comments about the common usage of the word. These might include labels like *slang* (very informal), *nonstandard, regional,* and *obsolete* (out-of-date).

49b   Consult a thesaurus for words that have similar meanings.

A **thesaurus** is a dictionary of synonyms. Several kinds are available, many called *Roget's* after Peter Mark Roget (pronounced ro-ZHAY), who published the first one in 1852. Today, thesauruses are included in most word-processing software packages.

Consider the connotations as well as the denotations of the words you find in the thesaurus. Do not choose a word just because it sounds smart or fancy.

CHAPTER 50

Glossary of Usage

The following words and expressions are often confused (such as *advice* and *advise*), misused (such as *etc.*), or considered nonstandard (such as *could of*).

Consulting this list will help you use these words precisely.

a, an   Use *a* with a word that begins with a consonant sound: *a cat, a dog, a one-sided argument* (*one* begins with a consonant sound), *a house* (*h* is pronounced). Use *an* with a word that begins with a vowel sound: *an apple, an X-ray, an honor* (*h* is silent).

accept, except   *Accept* is a verb meaning "to receive willingly": *Please accept my apologies. Except* usually is a preposition meaning "but": *Everyone except Julie saw the film.* Except can be a verb meaning "to exclude": *We must except present company from the contest.*

adapt, adopt   *Adapt* means "to adjust or become accustomed to": *They adapted to the customs of their new country. Adopt* means "to take as one's own": *We adopted a puppy.*

advice, advise   *Advice* is a noun meaning "suggestion"; *advise* is a verb meaning "suggest": *I took his advice and deeply regretted it. I advise you to disregard it, too.*

affect, effect   As a verb, *affect* means "to influence": *Inflation affects our sense of security.* As a noun, *affect* means "a feeling or an emotion": *To study affect, psychologists probe the unconscious.* As a noun, *effect* means "result": *Inflation is one of the many effects of war.* As a verb, *effect* means "to make or accomplish": *Inflation has effected many changes in the way we spend money.*

aggravate   While *aggravate* colloquially means "irritate," in formal writing it means "intensify" or "worsen": *The need to refuel the plane aggravated the delay, which irritated the passengers.*

agree to, agree with   *Agree to* means "consent to"; *agree with* means "be in accord with": *They will agree to a peace treaty, even though they do not agree with each other on all points.*

ain't   A slang contraction for *is not, am not,* or *are not, ain't* should not be used in formal writing or speech.

all ready, already   *All ready* means "fully prepared"; *already* means "previously": *I was all ready to go out when I discovered that Jack had already ordered a pizza.*

all right, alright   *Alright* is nonstandard. Use *all right. He told me it was all right to miss class tomorrow.*

all together, altogether   *All together* expresses unity or common location; *altogether* means "completely": *At the casino, it was altogether startling to see so many kinds of gambling all together in one place.*

allude, elude, refer to   *Allude* means "to refer indirectly": *He alluded to his miserable adolescence. Elude* means "to avoid" or "to escape from": *She eluded the police for nearly two days.* Do not use *allude* to mean "to refer directly": *The teacher referred* [not *alluded*] *to page 154 in the text.*

almost, most   *Almost* means "nearly." *Most* means "the greater part of." Do not use *most* when you mean *almost: He wrote to me about almost* [not *most*] *everything he did. He told his mother about most things he did.*

a lot   *A lot* is always two words. Do not use *alot.*

A.M., AM, a.m.   These abbreviations mean "before noon" when used with numbers: 6 A.M., 6 a.m. Be consistent, and do not use the abbreviations as a synonym for *morning: In the morning* [not *the a.m.*]*, the train is full.*

among, between   Generally, use *among* with three or more nouns, and *between* with two: *The distance between Boston and Knoxville is a thousand miles. The desire to quit smoking is common among those who have smoked for a long time.*

amoral, immoral   *Amoral* means "neither moral nor immoral" and "not caring about moral judgments"; *immoral* means "morally wrong": *Unlike such amoral natural disasters as earthquakes and hurricanes, war is intentionally violent and therefore immoral.*

amount, number   Use *amount* for quantities you cannot count; use *number* for quantities you can count: *The amount of oil left underground in the United States is a matter of dispute, but the number of oil companies losing money is tiny.*

an   *See* a, an.

anxious, eager   *Anxious* means "fearful": *I am anxious before a test. Eager* signals strong interest or desire: *I am eager to be done with that exam.*

anymore, any more   *Anymore* means "no longer." *Any more* means "no more." Both are used in negative contexts: *I do not enjoy dancing anymore. I do not want any more peanut butter.*

anyone/any one, anybody/any body, everyone/every one, everybody/ every body   *Anyone, anybody, everyone,* and *everybody* are singular in definite pronouns: *Anybody can make a mistake.* When the pronoun *one* or the noun *body* is modified by the adjective *any* or *every,* the words should be separated by a space: *A good mystery writer accounts for every body that turns up in the story.*

as   Do not use *as* as a synonym for *since, when,* or *because: I told him he should visit Alcatraz since* [not *as*] *he was going to San Francisco. When* [not *as*] *I complained about the meal, the cook said he did not like to eat there himself. Because* [not *as*] *we asked her nicely, our teacher decided to cancel the exam.*

as, like   In formal writing, avoid the use of *like* as a conjunction: *He sneezed as if* [not *like*] *he had a cold. Like* is perfectly acceptable as a preposition that introduces a comparison: *She handled the reins like an expert.*

at   Avoid the use of *at* to complete the notion of *where: not Where is Michael at?* but *Where is Michael?*

awful, awfully   Use *awful* and *awfully* to convey terror or wonder (awe-full): *The vampire flew out the window with an awful shriek.* In formal writing, do not use *awful* to mean "bad" or *awfully* to mean "very" or "extremely."

awhile, a while   *Awhile* is an adverb: *Stay awhile with me* [but not *for awhile with me*]. *A while* consists of an article and a noun and can be used with or without a preposition: *A while* ago I found my red pencil. I was reading under the tree *for a while.*

bad, badly   *Bad* is an adjective used after a linking verb such as feel; *badly* is an adverb: *She felt bad about playing the piano badly at the recital.*

being as, being that   Do not use *being as* or *being that* as synonyms for *since* or *because: Because* [not *being as*] *the mountain was there, we had to climb it.*

belief, believe   *Belief* is a noun meaning "conviction"; *believe* is a verb meaning "to have confidence in the truth of": *Her belief that lying was often justified made it hard for us to believe her story.*

beside, besides   *Beside* is a preposition meaning "next to" or "apart from": *The ski slope was beside the lodge. She was beside herself with joy. Besides* is both a preposition and an adverb meaning "in addition to" or "except for": *Besides a bicycle, he will need a tent and a pack.*

better   Avoid using *better* in expressions of quantity: *Crossing the continent by train took more than* [not *better than*] *four days.*

between   *See* among, between.

bring, take   Use *bring* when an object is being moved toward you, and *take* when it is being moved away: *Please bring me a new flash drive, and take the old one home with you.*

but that, but what   In expressions of doubt, avoid writing *but that* or *but what* when you mean *that: I have no doubt that* [not *but that*] *you can learn to write well.*

can, may   *Can* refers to ability; *may* refers to possibility or permission: *I see that you can Rollerblade without crashing into people; nevertheless you may not Rollerblade on the promenade.*

can't hardly   This double negative is ungrammatical and self-contradictory: *I can* [not *can't*] *hardly understand algebra. I can't understand algebra.*

capital, capitol   *Capital* can refer to wealth or resources or to a city; *capitol* refers to a building where lawmakers meet: *Protesters traveled to the state capital to converge on the capitol steps.*

censor, censure   *Censor* means "to remove or suppress material"; *censure* means "to reprimand formally." (Both can also be nouns.) *The Chinese government has been censured by the U.S. Congress for censoring Web access.*

cite, sight, site   The verb *cite* means "to quote or mention": *Be sure to cite all your sources in your bibliography.* As a noun, the word *sight* means "view": *I cringed at the sight of him. Site* is a noun meaning "a particular place" as well as "a location on the Internet."

compare to, compare with   Use *compare to* to point out similarities between two unlike things: *She compared his singing to the croaking of a wounded frog.* Use *compare with* to assess differences or likenesses between two things in the same general category: *Compare Shakespeare's* Antony and Cleopatra *with Dryden's* All for Love.

complement, compliment   *Complement* is a verb meaning "to go well with" or a noun describing "something that goes well with or completes something else": *I consider sauerkraut the perfect complement to sausages. Compliment* is a noun or verb meaning "praise": *She received many compliments on her thesis.*

conscience, conscious   The noun *conscience* means "a sense of right and wrong": *His conscience bothered him.* The adjective *conscious* means "awake" or "aware": *I was conscious of a presence in the room.*

continual, continuous *Continual* means "repeated regularly and frequently": *She continually checked her Blackberry for new e-mail.* *Continuous* means "extended or prolonged without interruption": *The car alarm made a continuous wail in the night.*

could care less *Could care less* is nonstandard; use *does not care at all* instead: *She does not care at all about her physics homework.*

could of, should of, would of Avoid these nonstandard forms of *could have, should have,* and *would have.*

criteria, criterion *Criteria* is the plural form of the Latin word *criterion,* meaning "standard of judgment": *The criteria are not very strict. The most important criterion is whether you can do the work.*

data *Data* is the plural form of the Latin word *datum,* meaning "fact." Although informally used as a singular noun, *data* should be treated as a plural noun in writing: *The data indicate that recycling has gained popularity.*

differ from, differ with *Differ from* expresses a lack of similarity: *The ancient Greeks differed greatly from the Persians.* *Differ with* expresses disagreement: *Aristotle differed with Plato on some important issues.*

different from, different than Use *different from*: *The east coast of Florida is very different from the west coast.*

discreet, discrete *Discreet* means "tactful" or "prudent." *Discrete* means "separate" or "distinct." *What's a discreet way of telling them that these are two discrete issues?*

disinterested, uninterested *Disinterested* means "impartial": *We expect members of a jury to be disinterested.* *Uninterested* means "indifferent": *Most people today are uninterested in alchemy.*

don't, doesn't *Don't* is the contraction for *do not* and is used with *I, you, we, they,* and plural nouns; *doesn't* is the contraction for *does not* and is used with *he, she, it, one,* and singular nouns: *You don't know what you're talking about. He doesn't know what you're talking about either.*

each and every Use one of these words but not both: *Every cow came in at feeding time. Each one had to be watered.*

each other, one another Use *each other* in sentences having two subjects and *one another* in sentences having more than two: *Husbands and wives should help each other. Classmates should share ideas with one another.*

eager *See* anxious, eager.

effect *See* affect, effect.

either, neither Both *either* and *neither* are singular: *Neither of the two girls has played the game. Either of the two boys is willing to show you the way home.* When used as an intensive, *either* is always negative: *She told him she would not go either.* (For either . . . or *and* neither . . . nor *constructions, see p. 464.*)

elicit, illicit The verb *elicit* means "to draw out"; the adjective *illicit* means "unlawful": *The detective was unable to elicit any information about other illicit activities.*

elude *See* allude, elude, refer to.

emigrate, immigrate *Emigrate from* means "to move away from one's country": *My father emigrated from Vietnam in 1980.* *Immigrate to* means "to move to another country and settle there": *Father immigrated to the United States.*

eminent, imminent, immanent *Eminent* means "celebrated" or "well known": *Many eminent Victorians were melancholy.* *Imminent* means "about to happen" or "about to come":

In August 1939, many Europeans sensed that war was imminent. Immanent refers to something invisible but dwelling throughout the world: *Medieval Christians believed God's power was immanent through the universe.*

etc.   The abbreviation *etc.* stands for the Latin *et cetera,* meaning "and others" or "and other things." Because *and* is included in the abbreviation, do not write *and etc.* In a series, a comma comes before *etc.,* just as it would before the coordinating conjunction that closes a series: *He brought tofu, beans, soymilk, etc.* In most college writing, it is better to end a series of examples with a final example or the words *and so on.*

~~**everybody/every body, everyone/every one**~~   *See* anyone/any one.

except, accept   *See* accept, except.

expect, suppose   *Expect* means "to hope" or "to anticipate": *I expect a good grade on my final paper. Suppose* means "to presume": *I suppose you didn't win the lottery on Saturday.*

explicit, implicit   *Explicit* means "stated outright"; *implicit* means "implied, unstated": *Her explicit instructions were for us to go to the party without her, but the implicit message she conveyed was disapproval.*

farther, further   *Farther* describes geographical distances: *Ten miles farther on is a hotel. Further* means "in addition" when geography is not involved: *He said further that he didn't like my attitude.*

fewer, less   *Fewer* refers to items that can be counted individually; *less* refers to general amounts: *Fewer people signed up for indoor soccer this year than last. Your argument has less substance than you think.*

firstly   *Firstly* is common in British English but not in the United States. *First, second, third,* and so on are the accepted forms.

flaunt, flout   *Flaunt* means "to wave" or "to show publicly" with delight or even arrogance: *He flaunted his wealth by wearing many gold chains. Flout* means "to scorn" or "to defy," especially publicly, without concern for the consequences: *She flouted the traffic laws by running through red lights.*

former, latter   *Former* refers to the first and *latter* to the second of two things mentioned previously: *Mario and Alice are both good cooks; the former is fonder of Chinese cooking, the latter of Mexican.*

further   *See* farther, further.

get   In formal writing, avoid colloquial uses of *get,* as in *get with it, get it together, get-up-and-go, get it,* and *that gets me.*

good, well   *Good* is an adjective and should not be used in place of the adverb *well: He felt good about doing well on the exam.*

hanged, hung   People are *hanged* by the neck until dead. Pictures and all other things that can be suspended are *hung.*

hopefully   *Hopefully* means "with hope." It is often misused to mean "it is hoped": *We waited hopefully for our ship to come in* [not *Hopefully, our ship will come in,* but *We hope our ship will come in*].

if . . . then   Avoid using these words in tandem. Redundant: *If I get my license, then I can drive a cab.* Better: *If I get my license, I can drive a cab. Once I get my license, I can drive a cab.*

if, whether   Use *whether* instead of *if* when expressing options: *If we go to the movies, we don't know whether we'll see a comedy or a drama.*

illicit *See* elicit, illicit.

imminent *See* eminent, imminent, immanent.

immigrate *See* emigrate, immigrate.

immoral *See* amoral, immoral.

implicit *See* explicit, implicit.

imply, infer *Imply* means "to suggest without stating directly": *By putting his fingers in his ears, he implied that she should stop singing. Infer* means "to draw a conclusion": *When she dozed off during his declaration of love, he inferred that she did not feel the same way about him.*

in, in to, into *In* refers to a location inside something: *Charles kept a snake in his room. In to* refers to motion with a purpose: *The resident manager came in to capture it. Into* refers to movement from outside to inside or from separation to contact: *The snake escaped by crawling into a drain.*

incredible, incredulous *Incredible* stories and events cannot be believed; *incredulous* people do not believe: *Kaitlyn told an incredible story of being abducted by a UFO over the weekend. We were all incredulous.*

inside of, outside of The "of" is unnecessary in these phrases: *He was outside the house.*

ironically *Ironically* means "contrary to what was or might have been expected" in a sense that implies the unintentional or foolish: *Ironically, the peace activists were planning a "War against Hate" campaign.* It should not be confused with *surprisingly* ("unexpectedly") or with *coincidentally* ("occurring at the same time or place").

irregardless This construction is a double negative because both the prefix *ir-* and the suffix *-less* are negatives. Use *regardless* instead.

it's, its *It's* is a contraction, usually for *it is* but sometimes for *it has: It's often been said that English is a difficult language to learn. Its* is a possessive pronoun: *The dog sat down and scratched its fleas.*

kind(s) *Kind* is singular: *This kind of house is easy to build. Kinds* is plural and should be used only to indicate more than one kind: *These three kinds of toys are more educational than those two kinds.*

kind of, sort of These constructions should not be used to mean *somewhat* or *a little: I was somewhat tired after the party.*

lay, lie *Lay* means "to place." Its main forms are *lay, laid,* and *laid.* It generally has a direct object, specifying what has been placed: *She laid her book on the steps and left it there. Lie* means "to recline" and does not take a direct object. Its main forms are *lie, lay,* and *lain: She often lay awake at night.*

less *See* fewer, less.

like *See* as, like.

literally *Literally* means "actually" or "exactly as written": *Literally thousands gathered along the parade route.* Do not use *literally* as an intensive adverb when it can be misleading or even ridiculous: *His blood literally boiled.*

loose, lose *Loose* is an adjective that means "not securely attached." *Lose* is a verb that means "to misplace." *Better tighten that loose screw before you lose the whole structure.*

may *See* can, may.

maybe, may be *Maybe* is an adverb meaning "perhaps": *Maybe he can get a summer job as a lifeguard. May be* is a verb phrase meaning "is possible": *It may be that I can get a job as a lifeguard, too.*

moral, morale   *Moral* means "lesson," especially a lesson about standards of behavior or the nature of life: *The moral of the story is, do not drink and drive.* *Morale* means "attitude" or "mental condition": *Employee morale dropped sharply after the president of the company was arrested.*

more important, more importantly   Use *more important*.

most   *See* almost, most.

myself (himself, herself, and so on)   Pronouns ending with *-self* refer to or intensify other words: *Jack hurt himself. Standing in the doorway was the man himself.* When you are unsure whether to use *I* or *me, she* or *her, he* or *him* in a compound subject or object, you may be tempted to substitute one of the *-self* pronouns. Don't do it: *The quarrel was between her and me* [not *myself*]. *(Also see Tab 10: Problems with Pronouns, beginning on p. 479.)*

neither   *See* either, neither.

nohow, nowheres   These words are nonstandard for *anyway, in no way, in any way, in any place,* and *in no place.* Do not use them in formal writing.

number   *See* amount, number.

off of   Omit the *of: She took the painting off the wall.*

one another   *See* each other, one another.

outside of   *See* inside of, outside of.

plus   Avoid using *plus* as a coordinating conjunction (use *and*) or a transitional expression (use *moreover*): *He had to walk the dog, empty the garbage, and* [not *plus*] *write a term paper.*

precede, proceed   *Precede* means "come before;" *proceed* means "go forward": *Despite the heavy snows that preceded us, we managed to proceed up the hiking trail.*

previous to, prior to   Avoid these wordy and pompous substitutions for *before*.

principal, principle   *Principal* is an adjective meaning "most important" or a noun meaning "the head of an organization" or "a sum of money": *Our principal objections to the school's principal are that he is a liar and a cheat. Principle* is a noun meaning "a basic standard or law": *We believe in the principles of honesty and fair play.*

proceed   *See* precede, proceed.

raise, rise   *Raise* means "to lift or cause to move upward." It takes a direct object—someone raises something: *I raised the windows in the classroom. Rise* means "to go upward." It does not take a direct object—something rises by itself: *We watched the balloon rise to the ceiling.*

real, really   Do not use the word *real* when you mean *very: The cake was very* [not *real*] *good.*

reason . . . is because, reason why   These are redundant expressions. Use either *the reason is that* or *because: The reason he fell on the ice is that he cannot skate. He fell on the ice because he cannot skate.*

refer to   *See* allude, elude, refer to.

respectfully, respectively   *Respectfully* means "with respect": *Treat your partners respectfully. Respectively* means "in the given order": *The three Williams she referred to were Shakespeare, Wordsworth, and Yeats, respectively.*

rise   *See* raise, rise.

set, sit   *Set* is usually a transitive verb meaning "to establish" or "to place." It takes a direct object, and its principal parts are *set, set,* and *set: DiMaggio set the standard of excellence in fielding. She set the box down in the corner. Sit* is usually intransitive, meaning "to place oneself in a sitting position." Its principal parts are *sit, sat,* and *sat: The dog sat on command.*

shall, will   Today, most writers use *will* instead of *shall* in the ordinary future tense for the first person: *I will celebrate my birthday by throwing a big party. Shall* is still used in questions: *Shall we dance?*

should of   *See* could of, should of, would of.

site   *See* cite, sight, site.

sort of   *See* kind of, sort of.

stationary, stationery   *Stationary* means "standing still": *Our spinning class uses stationary bicycles. Stationery* is writing paper: *That stationery smells like a rose garden.*

suppose   *See* expect, suppose.

sure   Avoid confusing the adjective *sure* with the adverb *surely: The dress she wore to the club was surely bizarre.*

sure and   *Sure and* is often used colloquially. In formal writing, *sure to* is preferred: *Be sure to* [not *be sure and*] *get to the wedding on time.*

take   *See* bring, take.

than, then   *Than* is a conjunction used in comparisons: *I am taller than you. Then* is an adverb referring to a point in time: *We will sing and then dance.*

that, which   Use *that* for restrictive (that is, essential) clauses and *which* for nonrestrictive (that is, nonessential) clauses: *The bull that escaped from the ring ran through my china shop, which was located in the square. (Also see Commas, pp. 497–548, in Tab 11.)*

their, there, they're   *Their* is a possessive pronoun: *They gave their lives. There* is an adverb of place: *Takesha was standing there. They're* is a contraction of *they are: They're reading more poetry this semester.*

theirself, theirselves, themself   Use *themselves.*

this here, these here, that there, them there   Avoid these nonstandard forms in writing.

to, too, two   *To* is a preposition; *too* is an adverb; *two* is a number: *The two of us got lost too many times on our way to his house.*

try and   *Try to* is the standard form: *Try to* [not *try and*] *understand.*

uninterested   *See* disinterested, uninterested.

unique   *Unique* means "one of a kind." Do not use any qualifiers with it.

utilize   *Use* is preferable because it is simpler: *Use five sources in your project.*

verbally, orally   To say something *orally* is to say it aloud: *We agreed orally to share credit for the work, but when I asked Andrea to confirm it in writing, she refused.* To say something *verbally* is to use words: *Quinn's eyes flashed anger, but he did not express his feelings verbally.*

wait for, wait on   People *wait for* those who are late; they *wait on* tables.

weather, whether   The noun *weather* refers to the atmosphere: *She worried that the weather would not clear up in time for the victory celebration. Whether* is a conjunction referring to a choice between options: *I can't decide whether to go now or next week.*

well   *See* good, well.

whether   *See* if, whether, *and* weather, whether.

which, who, whose, that   *Which* is used for things, and *who* and *whose* for people: *My fountain pen, which I had lost last week, was found by a child who had never seen any pens except ballpoints.* Use *that* for things and groups of people: *The committee that makes hiring decisions meets on Friday.*

who, whom   Use *who* with subjects and their complements. Use *whom* with objects of verbs and prepositions: *The person who will fill the position is Janelle, whom you met last week. (Also see Problems with Pronouns in Tab 10, p. 479.)*

will   *See* shall, will.

would of   *See* could of, should of, would of.

your, you're   *Your* is a possessive pronoun: *Is that your new car? You're* is a contraction of *you are: You're a lucky guy.*

—CHECKLIST   Editing for Clarity and Word Choice

As you revise, check your writing for clarity and be sure you used words correctly by asking yourself these questions:

☐ Are all sentences complete, concise, and straightforward? *(See Chapter 38: Wordy Sentences, pp. 408–11 and Chapter 39: Missing Words, pp. 411–13.)*

☐ Do the key parts of each sentence fit together well, or are there mismatches in person, number, or grammatical structure? *(See Chapter 41: Confusing Shifts, pp. 415–18, and Chapter 42: Faulty Parallelism, pp. 418–21.)*

☐ Are the parts of each sentence clearly and closely connected, or are some modifiers separated from what they modify? *(See Chapter 43: Misplaced and Dangling Modifiers, pp. 421–25.)*

☐ Are the focus, flow, and voice of the sentences clear, or do some sentences have ineffective coordination and subordination? *(See Chapter 44: Coordination and Subordination, pp. 425–27.)*

☐ Do sentence patterns vary sufficiently? Is there a mixture of long and short sentences? *(See Chapter 45: Sentence Variety, pp. 428–30.)*

☐ Are all verbs strong and emphatic, or are the passive voice, the verb *to be,* or other weak or too-common verbs overused? *(See Chapter 46: Active Verbs, pp. 430–32.)*

☐ Do you have a dictionary at hand for unfamiliar words you encounter? Do you have a thesaurus at hand to find the most appropriate word to convey your meaning? *(See Chapter 49: The Dictionary and the Thesaurus, pp. 439–41.)*

☐ Is your language appropriate to the assignment? Does it include any euphemisms, doublespeak, slang, or jargon? Have you used any stereotyping or biased expressions? *(See Chapter 47: Appropriate Language, pp. 432–36.)*

☐ Have you chosen words with the appropriate connotations? Have you confused words that have similar denotations? *(See Chapter 48: Exact Language, pp. 437–39, and Chapter 50: Glossary of Usage, pp. 441–49.)*

☐ Have you used specific and concrete words and suitable figures of speech? Have you avoided clichés? *(See Chapter 48: Exact Language, pp. 437–39.)*

Editing for Grammar Conventions

There is a core simplicity to the English language and its American variant, but it's a slippery core.

–Stephen King

©G. Nimatallah/DEA/De Agostini/Getty Images

This detail from a first century C.E. wall painting in the ancient Roman city of Pompeii shows a woman writing on a wax-covered tablet. Working on tablets like this, Roman writers could smooth over words and make corrections with ease.

10 Editing for Grammar Conventions

✓ Sections referenced in Resources for Writers: Identifying and Editing Common Problems (following Tab 9).

Tab 10: Editing for Grammar Conventions

This section will help you answer questions such as the following:

Rhetorical Knowledge

- Are sentence fragments ever acceptable in any kind of writing? (51b)

Critical Thinking, Reading, and Writing

- What's wrong with *A student should enjoy their college experience?* How can I fix it without introducing gender bias? (55a)

Processes

- How can I recognize and fix sentence fragments when I edit? (51a–d)
- Can my word processor's grammar checker help me edit for grammar conventions? (51–56)

Knowledge of Conventions

- When should I use *lie* or *lay?* (54b)
- Is it ever correct to say *I feel good?* (56b)

For a general introduction to writing outcomes, see 1e, pages 14–15.

When you edit, your purpose is to make the sentences in your text both clear and strong. The preceding section of the handbook focused on editing for clarity. This section focuses on editing for common grammatical problems.

CHAPTER 51

Sentence Fragments

A **sentence fragment** is an incomplete sentence treated as if it were complete. It may begin with a capital letter and end with a period, a question mark, or an exclamation point, but it lacks one or more of the following:

- A complete verb
- A subject
- An independent clause

Although writers sometimes use them intentionally, fragments are rarely appropriate for college assignments.

✓ **51a**   Learn how to identify sentence fragments.

Identify fragments in your work by asking three questions:

- Do you see a complete verb?
- Do you see a subject?
- Do you see *only* a dependent clause?

1. Do you see a complete verb?   A **complete verb** consists of a main verb and helping verbs needed to indicate tense, person, and number. *(See Chapter 54: Problems with Verbs, pp. 470-79.)* A group of related words without a complete verb is a phrase fragment, not a sentence.

> FRAGMENT   The ancient Mayas were among the first to develop many mathematical concepts. *For example, the concept of zero.* [no verb]
>
> SENTENCE   The ancient Mayas were among the first to develop many mathematical concepts. *For example, they developed the concept of zero.*

2. Do you see a subject?   The **subject** is the *who* or *what* that a sentence is about. *(See Tab 12: Basic Grammar Review, pp. 549-82.)* A group of related words without a subject or complete verb is a phrase fragment, not a sentence.

> FRAGMENT   The ancient Mayas were accomplished mathematicians. *Developed the concept of zero, for example.* [no subject]
>
> SENTENCE   The ancient Mayas were accomplished mathematicians. *They developed the concept of zero, for example.*

3. Do you see *only* a dependent clause?   An **independent clause** has a subject and complete verb and can stand on its own as a sentence. A **dependent** or **subordinate clause** also has a subject and complete verb, but it begins with a subordinating word such as *although, because, that,* or *which.* Dependent clauses function within sentences as modifiers or nouns, but they cannot stand as sentences on their own. *(See Tab 12: Basic Grammar Review, pp. 549-82.)*

> FRAGMENT   The ancient Mayas deserve a place in the history of mathematics. *Because they were among the earliest people to develop the concept of zero.*
>
> SENTENCE   The ancient Mayas deserve a place in the history of mathematics *because they were among the earliest people to develop the concept of zero.*

Fragments and Grammar Checkers

Grammar checkers identify some fragments, but they will not tell you what the fragment is missing or how to edit it. Grammar checkers can also miss fragments that lack subjects but that could be interpreted as commands, such as *Develop the concept of zero,* for example.

51b   Learn how to edit sentence fragments.

You can repair sentence fragments by editing them in one of two ways:

- Transform them into sentences.

> **Many people feel threatened by globalization. ~~Because they~~** _{They}
> **think it will undermine their cultural traditions.**

- Attach them to a nearby independent clause.

> **Many people feel threatened by globalization/ ~~Because~~** _{because} **they**
> **think it will undermine their cultural traditions.**

Your solution is a stylistic decision. Sometimes one approach may be clearly preferable, and sometimes both are effective.

51c   Connect a phrase fragment to another sentence, or add the missing elements.

Often unintentional fragments are **phrases**—word groups that lack a subject or a complete verb or both and usually function as modifiers or nouns.

1. Watching for verbals   Phrase fragments frequently begin with **verbals**—words derived from verbs, such as *putting* or *to put.* They do not change form to reflect tense and number. *(For more on verbals, see pp. 576-77.)*

> **FRAGMENT**   That summer, we had the time of our lives. *Swimming in the mountain lake each day and exploring the nearby woods.*

One way to fix this fragment is to transform it into an independent clause with its own subject and verb.

> **That summer, we had the time of our lives. ~~Swimming~~** _{We swam} **in the**
> **mountain lake each day and ~~exploring~~** _{explored} **the nearby woods.**

IDENTIFY AND EDIT
Sentence Fragments

✓
frag

? *1. Do you see a complete verb?*

Yes

No → FRAGMENT

FRAGMENT   For example, the concept of zero.

SENTENCE   subj verb
For example, they were among the first to develop the concept of zero.

? *2. Do you see a subject?*

Yes

No → FRAGMENT

FRAGMENT   Developed the concept of zero, for example.

SENTENCE   subj   verb
They developed the concept of zero, for example.

? *3. Do you see only a dependent clause?*

No

YES → FRAGMENT

FRAGMENT   Because they were among the earliest people to develop the concept of zero.

SENTENCE   The Mayas deserve a place in the history of mathematics because they were among the earliest people to develop the concept of zero.

SENTENCE

Notice that the two *-ing* verbals in the fragment need to be changed to keep the phrases in the new sentence parallel. *(For more on parallelism, see Tab 9: Editing for Clarity, pp. 401–49.)*

The fragment can also be attached to the part of the preceding sentence that it modifies (in this case, *the time of our lives*).

─ the EVOLVING SITUATION

Intentional Fragments

Advertisers often use attention-getting fragments: "Hot deal! Big savings! Because you're worth it." In everyday life, we often speak in fragments: "You okay?" "Fine." As a result, people who write fiction and drama use fragments to create realistic dialogue, and people who write popular nonfiction often use them for emphasis and variety. Keep in mind, however, that advertising, literary writing, and college writing have different contexts and purposes. In formal writing, use intentional sentence fragments sparingly, if at all.

▶ That summer, we had the time of our lives, ~~Swimming~~ **, swimming** in the mountain lake each day and exploring the nearby woods.

2. Watching for preposition fragments   Phrase fragments can also begin with one-word prepositions such as *as, at, by, for, from, in, of, on,* or *to.* Attach these fragments to a nearby sentence.

▶ Impressionist painters often depicted their subjects in everyday situations, ~~At~~ **, at** a restaurant, perhaps, or by the seashore.

3. Watching for transitional phrases   Some fragments start with two- or three-word prepositions that function as transitions, such as *as well as, as compared with,* or *in addition to.*

▶ For the past sixty-five years, the growth in consumer spending has been both steep and steady, ~~In~~ **, in** contrast with the growth in gross domestic product (GDP), which fluctuated significantly between 1929 and 1950.

4. Watching for words and phrases that introduce examples   Check word groups beginning with expressions that introduce examples—such as *for example* or *such as.* If they are fragments, edit to make them into sentences, or attach them to an independent clause.

▶ Elizabeth I of England faced many dangers as a princess. For example, ~~falling~~ **she fell** out of favor with her sister, Queen Mary, and ~~being~~ **was** imprisoned in the Tower of London.

5. Watching for appositives   An **appositive** is a noun or noun phrase that renames a noun or pronoun.

► In 1965, Lyndon Johnson increased the number of troops in Vietnam/ ~~A~~ _{, a} former French colony in Southeast Asia.

6. Watching for fragments that consist of lists   You can connect a list to the preceding sentence using a colon or a dash.

► In the 1930s, three great band leaders helped popularize jazz/: Louis Armstrong, Benny Goodman, and Duke Ellington.

7. Watching for fragments that are parts of compound predicates   A **compound predicate** is made up of at least two verbs as well as their objects and modifiers, connected by a coordinating conjunction such as *and, but,* or *or.* The parts of a compound predicate have the same subject and should be in one sentence.

► The group gathered at dawn at the base of the mountain/ ~~And~~ _{and} assembled their gear in preparation for the morning's climb.

> **51d**   Connect fragments that begin with a subordinating word *(although, because, since, even though)* to another sentence, or eliminate the subordinating word.

Fragments that begin with a subordinating word can usually be attached to a nearby independent clause.

► None of the thirty-three subjects indicated any concern about the amount or kind of fruit the institution served/ ~~Even~~ _{even} though all of them identified diet as an important issue for those with diabetes.

Punctuation tip: A comma usually follows a dependent clause that begins a sentence. If the clause appears at the end of a sentence, it is usually not preceded by a comma unless it is a contrasting thought. *(See Tab 11: Editing for Correctness, p. 498.)*

It is sometimes better to transform such a fragment into a complete sentence by deleting the subordinating word.

► The harmony of our group was disrupted in two ways. ~~When members~~ _{Members} either disagreed about priorities or advocated different political strategies.

CHAPTER 52

Comma Splices and Run-on Sentences

Comma splices and run-on sentences are sentences with improperly joined independent clauses. Recall that an independent clause has a subject and a complete verb and can stand on its own as a sentence. *(See page 452.)*

✓ **52a**   Learn how to identify comma splices and run-on sentences.

A **comma splice** is a sentence with two independent clauses joined by only a comma:

COMMA SPLICE	The media influence people's political views, the family is another major source of ideas about the proper role of government.

A **run-on sentence,** sometimes called a **fused sentence,** does not have even a comma between the independent clauses.

RUN-ON	Local news shows often focus on crime stories network and cable news broadcasts cover national politics in detail.

Writers may mistakenly join two independent clauses with only a comma or create a run-on sentence in three situations:

- When a transitional expression like *as a result* or *for example* or a conjunctive adverb like *however* links the second clause to the first. *(A list of conjunctive adverbs and transitional expressions appears on p. 461.)*

COMMA SPLICE	Rare books can be extremely valuable, *for example,* an original edition of Audubon's *Birds of America* is worth over a million dollars.
RUN-ON	Most students complied with the new policy *however* a few refused to do so.

- When the second clause specifies or explains the first.

RUN-ON	The economy is still recovering from the financial crisis that began in 2007 Bear Stearns was the first large investment bank to experience problems that year.

- When the second clause begins with a pronoun.

COMMA SPLICE	President Garfield was assassinated, he served only six months in office.

1. Checking for transitional expressions and conjunctive adverbs Check those sentences that include transitional expressions or conjunctive adverbs like *however (see p. 461)*. If a comma precedes one of these words or phrases, you may have found a comma splice. If no punctuation precedes one of them, you may have found a run-on sentence. Can the word groups that precede and follow the conjunctive adverb or transitional expression both stand alone as sentences? If so, you have found a comma splice or a run-on sentence.

2. Reviewing sentences with commas Check sentences that contain commas. Can the word groups that appear on both sides of the comma stand alone as sentences? If so, you have found a comma splice.

Comma Splices, Run-on Sentences, and Grammar Checkers

Computer grammar checkers are unreliable at identifying run-on sentences and comma splices. One grammar checker, for example, correctly flagged this sentence for incorrect comma usage: *Many history textbooks are clear, some are hard to follow.* It failed, however, to flag this longer alternative: *Many history textbooks are clear and easy to read, some are dense and hard to follow.*

52b Learn five ways to edit comma splices and run-on sentences.

- Join the two clauses with a comma and a coordinating conjunction *(and, but, or, nor, for, so, yet) (52c, p. 460).*

  > *and*
  > ► The media influence people's political views,ˏthe family is another major source of ideas about the proper role of government.

- Join the two clauses with a semicolon *(52d, p. 460).*

  > ► Local news shows often focus on crime stories;ˏnetwork and cable news broadcasts cover national politics in detail.

- You can also add an appropriate conjunctive adverb or transitional expression, followed by a comma.

  > *however,*
  > ► Local news shows often focus on crime stories;ˏnetwork and cable news broadcasts cover national politics in detail.

- Separate the clauses into two sentences *(52e, pp. 461-62).*

  > *. Therefore*
  > ► Salt air corrodes metal easily ~~therefore~~ˏautomobiles in coastal regions require frequent washing.

—IDENTIFY AND EDIT
Comma Splices and Run-ons

These questions can help you spot comma splices and run-on sentences:

? *1. Does the sentence contain only one independent clause?*

NO
↓

> Yes → **Not a run-on or comma splice**

? *2. Does it contain two independent clauses joined by a comma and a coordinating conjunction (*and, but, or, not, for, so, or yet)?*

NO
↓

> Yes → **Not a run-on or comma splice**

? *3. Does it contain two independent clauses joined by a semicolon, a semicolon and a transitional expression, a colon, or a dash?*

NO
↓

> Yes → **Not a run-on or comma splice**

	⊢——————independent clause——————⊣
RUN-ON	Football and most other team sports have a time limit
	⊢—independent clause—⊣
	baseball has no time limit.
COMMA SPLICE	Football and most other team sports have a time limit, baseball has no time limit.
REVISED: COMMA AND COORDINATING CONJUNCTION	Football and most other team sports have a time limit, but baseball has no time limit. [*See 52c.*]
REVISED: SEMICOLON	Football and most other team sports have a time limit; baseball has no time limit. [*See 52d.*]
REVISED: TWO SENTENCES	Football and most other team sports have a time limit. Baseball has no time limit. [*See 52e.*]
REVISED: SUBORDINATION	Although football and most other team sports have a time limit, baseball has none. [*See 52f.*]
REVISED: ONE INDEPENDENT CLAUSE	Baseball, unlike football and most other team sports, has no time limit. [*See 52g.*]

- Turn one of the independent clauses into a dependent clause *(52f, p. 462). For more on dependent clauses, see pages 549–82.*

  ▶ **Treasure hunters shopping in thrift stores and at garage**
  because
  sales should be realistic,/valuable finds are extremely rare.
  ^

- Transform the two clauses into a single independent clause *(52g, p. 462).*

  ▶ *and*
  The best history books are clear,/~~they also~~ tell a compelling
  ^
  story.

52c Join the two clauses with a comma and a coordinating conjunction such as *and, but, or, nor, for, so,* or *yet.*

If you decide to correct a comma splice or run-on sentence by joining the two clauses, make sure the two ideas are equally important, and choose the coordinating conjunction that most clearly expresses the logical relationship between them. A comma *must* precede the conjunction, or the sentence remains a run-on.

▶ *so*
Julio is a very stubborn person,/I had a hard time convincing him
^
to let me take the wheel.

▶ *, but*
My stepmother teaches at Central State/I go to Eastern Tech.
^

52d Join the two clauses with a semicolon (or a colon or dash).

A semicolon tells readers that two closely related clauses are logically connected. However, it does not spell out the logic of the connection.

▶ **Most students complied with the new policy,/ a few refused to do so.**
^

To show the logic of the connection, you can add a conjunctive adverb or transitional expression.

▶ *; however,*
Most students complied with the new policy,/a few refused to do so.

When the first independent clause introduces the second one, use a colon instead of a semicolon. A colon is also appropriate if the second clause expands on the first one in some way or introduces a quotation. *(See Tab 11: Editing for Correctness, pp. 514–15.)* A dash may be appropriate for informal writing situations to highlight a list, explanation, or shift in tone. *(See Tab 11: Editing for Correctness, pp. 525–26.)*

> **Note:** The conjunctive adverb or transitional expression is usually followed by a comma when it appears at the beginning of the second clause (as in the preceding example). It can also appear in the middle of a clause, set off by two commas, or at the end, preceded by a comma.
>
> ▶ Most students complied with the new policy,̸; a few ‚however refused to do so.
>
> ▶ Most students complied with the new policy̸; a few refused , however to do so.̸

▶ Professor Kim then revealed his most important point‚ the paper would count for half my grade.

52e Separate the clauses into two sentences.

The simplest way to correct comma splices and run-on sentences is to turn the clauses into separate sentences. This solution is not always best, however, especially if the result is two short, simple sentences. The simplest solution works in the next example because the second sentence is a compound sentence.

▶ I realized that it was time to choose,̸ ‚ Either ~~either~~ I had to learn how to drive, or I had to move back to the city.

—CONJUNCTIVE ADVERBS
AND TRANSITIONAL EXPRESSIONS

also	incidentally	nonetheless
as a result	indeed	now
besides	in fact	of course
certainly	in other words	on the contrary
consequently	instead	otherwise
finally	in the meantime	similarly
for example	likewise	still
for instance	meanwhile	then
furthermore	moreover	therefore
however	nevertheless	thus
in addition	next	undoubtedly

When the two independent clauses are part of a quotation, with a phrase such as *he said* or *she noted* between them, each clause should be a separate sentence.

▶ "This was the longest day of my life," she said, ~~"unfortunately,~~ it's not over yet."
  "Unfortunately,

52f Turn one of the independent clauses into a dependent clause.

In editing the following sentence, the writer chose to make the clause about *a few* her main point and the clause about *most* a subordinate idea. Readers will expect subsequent sentences to tell them more about the subject of the main clause.

▶ ~~Most~~ students complied with the new policy, ~~however~~ a few refused to do so.
  Although most

52g Transform the two clauses into one independent clause.

Transforming two clauses into one clear and correct independent clause is often worth the effort.

▶ I realized that it was time ~~to choose~~, either ~~I had~~ to learn how to drive or ~~I had~~ to move back to the city.

Sometimes you can change one of the clauses to a phrase and place it next to the word it modifies.

▶ Baseball cards are an obsession among some collectors, ~~the cards were first printed in the nineteenth century.~~
  , first printed in the nineteenth century,

CHAPTER 53

Subject-Verb Agreement

All verbs must agree with their subjects in person (first, second, or third—*I, we; you; he, she, it, they*) and in number (singular or plural).

✓ 53a Learn the standard subject-verb combinations.

For regular verbs, add the present tense *-s* or *-es* ending to the verb if its subject is third-person singular; otherwise, the verb has no ending. Most verbs have one past-tense form. Note, however, that the verb *be* has irregular forms in both the present and the past tense. The irregular verbs *be, have,* and *do* have the following forms in the present and past tenses:

Verb Tenses (Present and Past)

	READ (REGULAR)	BE	HAVE	DO
SINGULAR				
First person (*I*)	read (*read*)	am (*was*)	have (*had*)	do/don't (*did/didn't*)
Second person (*you*)	read (*read*)	are (*were*)	have (*had*)	do/don't (*did/didn't*)
Third person (*he, she, it*)	reads (*reads*)	is (*was*)	has (*had*)	does/doesn't (*did/didn't*)
PLURAL				
First person (*we*)	read (*read*)	are (*were*)	have (*had*)	do/don't (*did/didn't*)
Second person (*you*)	read (*read*)	are (*were*)	have (*had*)	do/don't (*did/didn't*)
Third person (*they*)	read (*read*)	are (*were*)	have (*had*)	do/don't (*did/didn't*)

Problems with subject-verb agreement tend to occur when writers do the following:

- Lose sight of the subject *(53b, pp. 463-64)*
- Use compound, collective, or indefinite subjects *(53c-e, pp. 464-68)*
- Have a subject that follows the verb *(53f, p. 468)*
- Confuse a subject complement with the subject *(53g, p. 468)*
- Use a relative pronoun as the subject of a dependent clause *(53h, pp. 468-69)*
- Use a phrase beginning with an *-ing* verb or infinitive (*to* followed by the base form of the verb) as the subject *(53i, p. 469)*
- Use titles, company names, or words considered by themselves *(53j, p. 469)*

53b   Do not lose sight of the subject when a word group separates it from the verb.

To locate the subject of a sentence, find the verb, and then ask the *who* or *what* question about it ("Who is?" "What is?"). Does that subject match the verb in number?

> ▶ The leaders of the trade union ~~opposes~~ the new law.
>
> *oppose*

The answer to the question "Who opposes?" is *leaders,* a plural noun, so the verb should be in the plural form: *oppose.*

> **Note:** If a word group beginning with *as well as, along with,* or *in addition to* follows a singular subject, the subject does not become plural.
>
> ▶ **My teacher, as well as other faculty members, ~~oppose~~ the new school policy.** (opposes)

Subject-Verb Agreement and Grammar Checkers

A grammar checker failed to flag this sentence for correction: *The candidate's position on foreign policy issues trouble some voters.* The subject is the singular noun *position,* so the verb should be *troubles.* Apparently, however, the grammar checker interpreted the word *issues* as the subject.

53c Treat most compound subjects—connected by *and, or, nor, both . . . and, either . . . or,* or *neither . . . nor*—as plural.

Compound subjects are made up of two or more parts joined by either a coordinating conjunction *(and, or, nor)* or a correlative conjunction *(both ... and, either . . . or, neither . . . nor).*

1. Treating most compound subjects as plural   Most subjects joined by *and* should be treated as plural.

▶ **The king and his advisers were shocked by this turn of events.**

▶ **This poem's first line and last word have a powerful effect on the reader.**

2. Treating some compound subjects as singular   There are exceptions to the rule that subjects joined by *and* are plural.

- The two subjects refer to the same entity.

  ▶ **My best girlfriend and most dependable adviser is my mother.**

- The two subjects are considered as a single unit.

  ▶ **Forty acres and a mule continues to be what is needed.**

- The two subjects are preceded by the word *each* or *every.*

  ▶ **Each man, woman, and child deserves respect.**

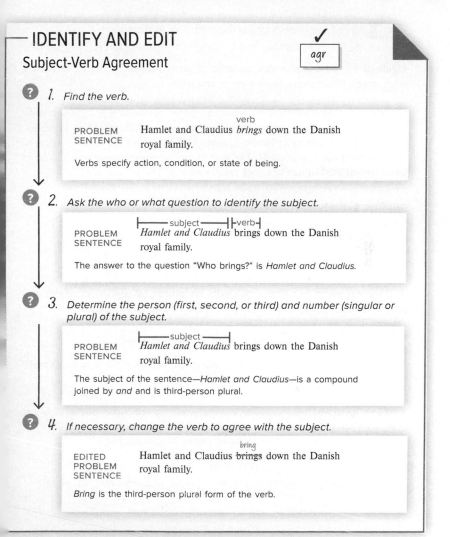

IDENTIFY AND EDIT
Subject-Verb Agreement

✓ agr

? *1.* *Find the verb.*

> verb
> PROBLEM SENTENCE   Hamlet and Claudius *brings* down the Danish royal family.
>
> Verbs specify action, condition, or state of being.

? *2.* *Ask the who or what question to identify the subject.*

> |—— subject ——|—verb—|
> PROBLEM SENTENCE   *Hamlet and Claudius* brings down the Danish royal family.
>
> The answer to the question "Who brings?" is *Hamlet and Claudius.*

? *3.* *Determine the person (first, second, or third) and number (singular or plural) of the subject.*

> |—— subject ——|
> PROBLEM SENTENCE   *Hamlet and Claudius* brings down the Danish royal family.
>
> The subject of the sentence—*Hamlet and Claudius*—is a compound joined by *and* and is third-person plural.

? *4.* *If necessary, change the verb to agree with the subject.*

> bring
> EDITED PROBLEM SENTENCE   Hamlet and Claudius ~~brings~~ down the Danish royal family.
>
> *Bring* is the third-person plural form of the verb.

3. Treating some compound subjects as either plural or singular
Compound subjects connected by *or, nor, either . . . or,* or *neither . . . nor* can take either a singular or a plural verb, depending on which subject is closer to the verb.

> SINGULAR   **Either the children or *their mother* is to blame.**
>
> PLURAL   **Neither the experimenter nor *her subjects* were aware of the takeover.**

Sentences often sound less awkward with the plural subject closer to the verb.

> **53d** Treat most collective subjects—subjects like *audience, family,* and *committee*—as singular.

A **collective noun** names a unit made up of many persons or things, treating it as an entity. Other examples are *group* and *team.*

1. Treating most collective nouns as singular *News, athletics, physics, statistics,* and other words like these are usually singular as well, despite their *-s* endings, because they function as collective subjects. (When a word like *statistics* refers to a collection of items, it is plural: *The statistics on car accidents worry me.*) Units of measurement used collectively, such as *six inches* or *20%,* are also singular.

▶ The *audience is* restless.

▶ That *news leaves* me speechless.

▶ *One-fourth* of the liquid *was* poured into test tube 1.

2. Treating some collective subjects as plural When the members of a group are acting as individuals, consider the collective subject plural.

▶ The *group were* passing around a bottle of beer.

You may want to add a modifying phrase that contains a plural noun to make the sentence clearer and avoid awkwardness.

▶ The *group of troublemakers were* passing around a bottle of beer.

> The modifying phrase *of troublemakers* makes the sentence less awkward.

> When units of measurement refer to people or things, they are plural.

▶ *One-fourth* of the students in the class *are* failing the course.

3. Distinguishing between *a number* and *the number* *A number* takes a plural verb, while *the number* takes a singular verb.

▶ *A number* of shoppers *prefer* Brand X.

▶ *The number* of people who shop online *is* growing.

53e   Treat most indefinite subjects—subjects like *everybody, no one, each, all,* and *none*—as singular.

Indefinite pronouns such as *everybody* and *no one* do not refer to a specific person or item.

1. Recognizing that most indefinite pronouns are singular   The following indefinite pronouns are always singular: *anybody, anyone, anything, each, either, everybody, everyone, everything, neither, nobody, none, no one, nothing, one, somebody, someone,* and *something.*

► **Everyone in my hiking club *is* an experienced climber.**

None and *neither* are singular when they appear by themselves.

► **In the movie, five men set out on an expedition, but *none returns*.**

► **Neither *sees* a way out of this predicament.**

If a prepositional phrase that includes a plural noun or pronoun follows *none* or *neither,* the indefinite pronoun seems to have a plural meaning. Although some writers treat *none* or *neither* as plural in such situations, others maintain that these two pronouns are always singular. It is a safe bet to consider them singular.

► **In the movie, five men set out on an expedition, but *none* of them *returns*.**

► **Neither of the hikers *sees* a way out of this cave.**

2. Recognizing that some indefinite pronouns are always plural   A handful of indefinite pronouns *(both, few, many, several)* are always plural because by definition they mean more than one. *Both,* for example, always indicates two.

► **Both of us *want* to go to the rally for the environment.**

► **Several of my friends *were* very happy about the outcome of the election.**

3. Recognizing that some indefinite pronouns can be either plural or singular   Some indefinite pronouns *(some, any, all, most)* can be either plural or singular, depending on whether they refer to a plural or a singular noun in the sentence.

► **Some of the *book is* missing, but *all* the *papers are* here.**

4. Treating phrases beginning with question words as singular or revising to avoid awkwardness

▶ *How you do on the exam* **counts** for half your grade.

AWKWARD *What we need is* new clothes.

BETTER *We need* new clothes.

53f Make sure the subject and verb agree when the subject comes after the verb.

In most English sentences, the verb comes after the subject. Sometimes, however, a writer will switch this order. In the following sentence, you can locate the subject by asking, "Who or what stand?" The answer is the sentence's subject: *an oak and a weeping willow.* Because the subject is a compound subject (two subjects joined by *and*), the verb must be plural.

▶ **Out back behind the lean-to** *stand* **an old oak tree and a**

weeping willow.

In sentences that begin with *there is* or *there are,* the subject always follows the verb.

▶ **There** *is* **a worn wooden** *bench* **in the shade of the two trees.**

In questions, the helping verb agrees with the subject.

▶ *Do you* **understand her?**

53g Make sure the verb agrees with its subject, not the subject complement.

A **subject complement** renames and specifies the sentence's subject. It follows a **linking verb**—a verb, often a form of *be,* that joins the subject to its description or definition: *children* <u>are</u> *innocent.* In the following sentence, the singular noun *gift* is the subject. *Books* is the subject complement. Therefore, *are* has been changed to *is* to agree in number with *gift.*

▶ **One gift that gives her pleasure** ~~are~~ **books.**
_{is}

53h Who, which, and that (relative pronouns) take verbs that agree with the subject they replace.

When a relative pronoun such as *who, which,* or *that* is the subject of a dependent clause, it is taking the place of a noun that appears earlier in the sentence—its **antecedent.** The verb that goes with *who, which,* or *that* must agree with this antecedent. In the following sentence, the relative pronoun *that* is the subject of the dependent clause *that has dangerous side effects. Disease,* a singular noun, is the antecedent of *that;* therefore, the verb in the dependent clause is singular.

► Measles is a childhood *disease that has* dangerous side effects.

The phrase *one of the* implies more than one and so is plural. *Only one of the* implies just one, however, and is singular. Generally, use the plural form of the verb when the phrase *one of the* comes before the antecedent. Use the singular form of the verb when *only one of the* comes before the plural noun.

PLURAL   Tuberculosis is ¦one of the diseases¦ *that have* long, *tragic* histories in many parts of the world.

SINGULAR   Barbara is the ¦*only one of the* scientists¦ *who has a* degree in physics.

53i   Phrases beginning with -*ing* verbs or infinitives take the singular form of the verb when they are subjects.

A **gerund phrase** is an -*ing* verb form followed by objects, complements, or modifiers. When a gerund phrase is the subject in a sentence, it is singular.

► ¦*Experimenting with drugs*¦ *is* a dangerous practice.

Infinitive phrases *(see Tab 12: Basic Grammar Review, p. 549)* are singular subjects.

► ¦*To win medals*¦ *is* every competitor's dream.

53j   Titles, company names, and words considered as words are singular.

► The Two Gentlemen of Verona ~~are~~ considered the weakest of Shakespeare's comedies.
  _is_

► The company I work for ~~include~~ many different divisions.
  includes

► In today's highly partisan politics, *moderates* ~~have~~ come to mean "wishy-washy people."
  has

CHAPTER 54

Problems with Verbs

Verbs report action and show time. They change form to indicate person, number, voice, and mood.

54a Learn the principal forms of regular and irregular verbs.

All English verbs have five main forms, except for the *be* verb, which has eight. *(For examples, see pp. 462-63 and pp. 550-51.)*

- The **base form** is the form found in a dictionary. *(For irregular verbs, other forms are given as well. See p. 471 for a list.)*
- The **present tense** form indicates an action occurring at the moment, habitually, or at a set future time and also introduces quotations, literary events, and scientific facts *(54f, p. 474, and 54h, pp. 476-77)*. The third-person singular present tense is the *-s* form.
- The **past tense** indicates an action completed at a specific time in the past *(54f, p. 474)*.
- The **past participle** is used with *have, has,* or *had* to form the perfect tenses *(54f, p. 474)*; with a form of the *be* verb to form the passive voice; and as an adjective (the *polished* silver).
- The **present participle** is used with a form of the *be* verb to form the progressive tenses *(54f, p. 474)*. It can also serve as a noun (the *writing* is finished) and as an adjective (the *smiling* man).

1. Learning about common irregular verbs **Regular verbs** always add *-d* or *-ed* to the base verb to form the past tense and past participle. **Irregular verbs,** in contrast, do not form the past tense or past participle in a consistent way. The box on page *471* lists the principal forms of common irregular verbs, which you can find in the dictionary.

2. Using the correct forms of irregular verbs that end in *-en* The forms of irregular verbs with past tenses that end in *-e* and past participles that end in *-n* or *-en*, such as *ate/eaten* and *rode/ ridden,* are sometimes confused.

► He had ~~ate~~ the apple.
  eaten

► They had ~~rode~~ the whole way on the bus.
  ridden

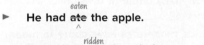

COMMON IRREGULAR VERBS

Base	Past tense	Past participle	Base	Past tense	Past participle
awake	awoke	awoke/awakened	hang	hanged	hanged (for people)
arise	arose	arisen	have	had	had
be	was/were	been	hear	heard	heard
beat	beat	beaten	know	knew	known
become	became	become	lose	lost	lost
begin	began	begun	pay	paid	paid
blow	blew	blown	raise	raised	raised
break	broke	broken	ride	rode	ridden
bring	brought	brought	ring	rang	rung
buy	bought	bought	rise	rose	risen
catch	caught	caught	say	said	said
choose	chose	chosen	see	saw	seen
cling	clung	clung	set	set	set
come	came	come	shake	shook	shaken
do	did	done	sit	sat	sat
draw	drew	drawn	spin	spun	spun
drink	drank	drunk	steal	stole	stolen
drive	drove	driven	spend	spent	spent
eat	ate	eaten	strive	strove/strived	striven/strived
fall	fell	fallen	swear	swore	sworn
fight	fought	fought	swim	swam	swum
fly	flew	flown	swing	swung	swung
forget	forgot	forgotten/forgot	take	took	taken
forgive	forgave	forgiven	tear	tore	torn
freeze	froze	frozen	tread	trod	trod/trodden
get	got	gotten/got	wear	wore	worn
give	gave	given	weave	wove	woven
go	went	gone	wring	wrung	wrung
grow	grew	grown	write	wrote	written
hang	hung	hung (for things)			

3. Using the correct forms of *went* and *gone* and *saw* and *seen*   *Went* and *saw* are the past tense forms of the irregular verbs *go* and *see*. *Gone* and *seen* are the past participle forms.

►   I had ~~went~~ there yesterday.
         ^gone

►   We ~~seen~~ the rabid dog and called for help.
        ^saw

54b Distinguish between *lay* and *lie, rise* and *raise,* and *sit* and *set.*

Even experienced writers confuse the verbs *lay* and *lie, rise* and *raise,* and *sit* and *set.* The correct forms are given in the following table.

Often-Confused Verbs and Their Principal Forms

BASE	-S FORM	PAST	PAST PARTICIPLE	PRESENT PARTICIPLE
lay (to place)	lays	laid	laid	laying
lie (to recline)	lies	lay	lain	lying
lie (to speak an untruth)	lies	lied	lied	lying
rise (to go/get up)	rises	rose	risen	rising
raise (to lift up)	raises	raised	raised	raising
sit (to be seated)	sits	sat	sat	sitting
set (to put on a surface)	sets	set	set	setting

One verb in each of these groups *(lay, raise, set)* is **transitive:** an object receives the action of the verb. The other verbs *(lie, rise, sit)* are **intransitive** and cannot take an object. You should use a form of *lay, raise,* or *set,* if you can replace the verb with *place* or *put. (See Tab 12: Basic Grammar Review, pp. 549–82 for more on transitive and intransitive verbs.)*

▶ The dog *lays* $\overbrace{a\ bone}^{\text{direct object}}$ at your feet and then *lies* down and closes his eyes.

▶ As the flames *rise,* the heat *raises* $\overbrace{\text{the temperature}}^{\text{direct object}}$ of the room.

▶ The technician *sits* down and *sets* $\overbrace{\text{the samples}}^{\text{direct object}}$ in front of her.

Lay (to place) and *lie* (to recline) are also confusing because the past tense of the irregular verb *lie* is *lay (lie, lay, lain).* Always doublecheck the verb *lay* in your writing.

▶ He washed the dishes carefully and l~~ay~~ them on a clean towel.
_{laid}

54c Add an *-s* or *-es* ending when necessary.

In the present tense, almost all verbs add an *-s* or *-es* ending if the subject is third-person singular. *(See pp. 462–63 for more on standard subject-verb combinations.)* Third-person singular subjects can be nouns *(woman, Benjamin, desk),* pronouns *(he, she, it),* or indefinite pronouns *(everyone).*

▶ The stock market r~~ise~~ when economic news is good.
_{rises}

If the subject is in the first person *(I)*, the second person *(you)*, or the third-person plural *(people, they)*, the verb does *not* add an *-s* or *-es* ending.

► You invests your money wisely.

► People needs to invest wisely.

54d   Add a *-d* or an *-ed* ending when necessary.

When speaking, people sometimes leave the *-d* or *-ed* ending off certain verbs such as *asked, fixed, mixed, supposed to,* and *used to.* However, in writing, include the endings on all regular verbs in the past tense and all past participles of regular verbs.

►   The driving instructor ~~ask~~ *asked* the student driver to pull over to the curb.

►   After we had ~~mix~~ *mixed* the formula, we let it cool.

Also check for missing *-d* or *-ed* endings on past participles used as adjectives.

►   The ~~concern~~ *concerned* parents met with the school board.

Verb Forms and Grammar and Spelling Checkers

A grammar checker flagged the incorrect form in this sentence: *She had chose to go to the state college.* It also suggested the correct form: *chosen.* However, the checker missed the misuse of *set* in this sentence: *I am going to set down for a while.*

Spelling checkers will not highlight a verb form that is used incorrectly in a sentence.

54e   Make sure your verbs are complete.

A **complete verb** consists of the main verb and any helping verbs needed to express the tense *(see pp. 452)* or voice *(see p. 553).* **Helping verbs** include forms of *be, have,* and *do* and the modal verbs *can, could, may, might, shall, should, will, ought to, must,* and *would. (For more on modals, see Tab 12: Basic Grammar Review, pp. 549–82.)* Helping verbs can be part of contractions *(He's running, we'd better go),* but they cannot be left out of the sentence entirely.

►   They ~~be~~ *will* going on a field trip next week.

Do not use *of* in place of *have.*

►   I could ~~of~~ *have* finished earlier.

Also avoid *could've* in formal writing.

A **linking verb,** often a form of *be,* connects the subject to a description or definition of it: *Cats are mammals.* Linking verbs can be part of contractions *(She's a student),* but they should not be left out entirely.

► **Montreal a major Canadian city.**
     is

54f Use verb tenses accurately.

Tenses show the time of a verb's action. English has three basic time frames—present, past, and future—and each tense has simple, perfect, progressive, and perfect progressive verb forms to indicate the time span of the actions taking place. *(For a review of the present tense forms of a typical verb and of the verbs* be, have, *and* do, *see 53a, p. 462; for a review of the principal forms of regular and irregular verbs, which form tenses, see 54a, pp. 470-71.)*

1. The simple present and past tenses   These two tenses do not use a helping verb or verbs. The **simple present tense** describes actions occurring at the moment, habitually, or at a set future time. The **simple past tense** describes actions completed at a specific time in the past.

> SIMPLE PRESENT
>
> Every May, she *plans* next year's marketing strategy.

> SIMPLE PAST
>
> In the early morning hours before the office opened, she *planned* her marketing strategy.

2. The simple future tense   The **simple future tense** takes *will* plus the verb. It is used for actions that have not yet begun.

> SIMPLE FUTURE
>
> In May, I *will plan* next year's marketing strategy.

3. Perfect tenses   The **perfect tenses** take a form of *have (has, had)* plus the past participle. They indicate actions that were or will be completed by the time of another action or a specific time. The present perfect also describes actions that continue into the present. *(For more on the past participle, see p. 470.)*

> PRESENT PERFECT
>
> She *has* already *planned* next year's marketing strategy. She *has planned* the marketing strategy for the past five years.

> PAST PERFECT
>
> By the time she resigned, Maria *had* already *planned* next year's marketing strategy.

FUTURE PERFECT

By May 31, she *will have planned* next year's marketing strategy.

When the verb in the past perfect is irregular, be sure to use the proper form of the past participle.

► **By the time the week was over, both plants had g̶r̶e̶w̶ five inches.** *(grown)*

4. Progressive tenses The **progressive tenses** take a form of *be (am, are, was, were)* plus the present participle. The progressive forms of the simple and perfect tenses indicate ongoing action.

PRESENT PROGRESSIVE

She *is planning* next year's marketing strategy now.

PAST PROGRESSIVE

She *was planning* next year's marketing strategy when she started to look for another job.

References to planned events that didn't happen take *was/were going to* plus the base form.

She *was going to plan* the marketing strategy, but she left the company.

FUTURE PROGRESSIVE

During the month of May, she *will be planning* next year's marketing strategy.

5. Perfect progressive tenses The **perfect progressive tenses** take *have* plus *be* plus the verb. These tenses indicate an action that takes place over a specific period of time. The present perfect progressive tense describes actions that start in the past and continue to the present; the past and future perfect progressive tenses are used for actions that ended or will end at a specified time or before another action.

PRESENT PERFECT PROGRESSIVE

She *has been planning* next year's marketing strategy since the beginning of May.

PAST PERFECT PROGRESSIVE

She *had been planning* next year's marketing strategy when she was offered another job.

FUTURE PERFECT PROGRESSIVE

By May 18, she *will have been planning* next year's marketing strategy for more than two weeks.

54g   Use the past perfect tense to indicate an action completed at a specific time or before another event.

When a past event was ongoing but ended before a particular time or another past event, use the past perfect rather than the simple past.

▶ **Before the Johnstown Flood occurred in 1889, people in the**
   had
   area ‸ expressed their concern about the safety of the dam on the

   Conemaugh River.

   People expressed their concern before the flood occurred.

If two past events happened simultaneously, however, use the simple past, not the past perfect.

▶ **When the Conemaugh flooded, many people in the area ~~had~~ lost their lives.**

Do not use *would have* in *if* (conditional) clauses.

   had
▶ **If the students ~~would have~~ come to class, they would have known**
   ‸
   the material.

54h   Use the present tense for literary events, scientific facts, and introductions to quotations.

If the conventions of a discipline require you to state what your paper does, do so in the present, not the future, tense.

▶ **In this paper, I *describe* the effects of increasing NaCl concentrations on the germination of radish seeds.**

─ NAVIGATING THROUGH COLLEGE AND BEYOND

Reporting Research Findings

Although we see a written work as always existing in the present, we think of research findings as having been collected at one time in the past. Use the past or present perfect tense to report the results of research.

   responded
▶ **Three of the compounds (nos. 2, 3, and 6) ~~respond~~ positively by**
   ‸
   turning purple.

   has reviewed
▶ **Clegg (1990) ~~reviews~~ studies of workplace organization focused**
   ‸
   on struggles for control of the labor process.

Here are some other special uses of the present tense:

- By convention, events in a novel, short story, poem, or other literary work are described in the present tense.

▶ **Even though Huck's journey down the river ~~was~~ an escape from society, his relationship with Jim ~~was~~ a form of community.**

(*is* written above *was* in both instances)

- Like events in a literary work, scientific facts are considered to be perpetually present, even though they were discovered in the past.

▶ **Mendel discovered that genes ~~had~~ different forms, or alleles.**

(*have* written above *had*)

(Theories proven false should appear in the past tense.)

- The present tense introduces a quotation, paraphrase, or summary of someone else's writing.

▶ **William Julius Wilson ~~wrote~~ that "the disappearance of work has become a characteristic feature of the inner-city ghetto" (31).**

(*writes* written above *wrote*)

Note: When using APA style, introduce others' writing or research findings with the past tense (for example, Wilson *wrote*) or past perfect tense (Johnson *has found*).

54i Make sure infinitives and participles fit with the tense of the main verb.

Infinitives and participles are **verbals**—words formed from verbs that have various functions within a sentence. Verbals can form phrases by taking objects, modifiers, or complements. Because they express time, verbals need to fit with the main verb in a sentence.

1. Using the correct tense for infinitives An **infinitive** has the word *to* plus the base verb *(to breathe, to sing, to dance)*. The perfect form of the infinitive is *to have* plus the past participle *(to have breathed, to have sung, to have danced)*. If the action of the infinitive happens at the same time as or after the action of the main verb, use the present tense.

▶ **I hope to *sing and dance* on Broadway next summer.**

If the action of the infinitive happened before the action of the main verb, use the perfect form.

▶ **My talented mother would like to *have sung and danced* on Broadway as a young woman, but she never had the chance.**

2. Using the correct tense for participles that are part of phrases
Participial phrases can begin with the present participle *(breathing, dancing, singing)*, the present perfect participle *(having breathed, having danced, having sung)*, or the past participle *(breathed, danced, sung)*. If the action of the participle happens simultaneously with the action of the sentence's verb, use the present participle.

▶ *Singing one hour a day together,* the chorus developed perfect harmony.

If the action of the participle happened before the action of the main verb, use the present perfect or past participle form.

▶ *Having breathed* the air of New York, I exulted in the possibilities for my life in the city.

▶ *Tinted* with a strange green light, the western sky looked threatening.

54j Use the subjunctive mood for wishes, requests, and conjecture.

The **mood** of a verb indicates the writer's attitude. Use the **indicative mood** to state or question facts, acts, and opinions *(Our collection is on display. Did you see it?)*. Use the **imperative mood** for commands, directions, and entreaties. The subject of an imperative sentence is always *you,* but the *you* is usually understood, not written out *(Shut the door!)*. Use the **subjunctive mood** to express a wish or a demand or to make a statement contrary to fact *(I wish I were a millionaire)*. The mood that writers have the most trouble with is the subjunctive.

Verbs in the subjunctive mood may be in the present tense, past tense, or perfect tense. Present tense subjunctive verbs do not change form to signal person or number. The only form used is the verb's base form: *accompany* or *be,* not *accompanies* or *am, are, is.* Also, the verb *be* has only one past tense form in the subjunctive mood: *were.*

1. Using the subjunctive mood to express a wish

WISH

I wish I *were* more prepared for this test.

> *Note:* In everyday conversation, most speakers use the indicative rather than the subjunctive when expressing wishes *(I wish I was more prepared for this test)*.

2. Using the subjunctive mood for requests, recommendations, and demands Because requests, recommendations, and demands have not yet happened, they—like wishes—are expressed in the subjunctive mood. Words such as *ask, insist, recommend, request,* and *suggest* indicate the subjunctive mood; the verb in the *that* clause that follows should be in the subjunctive.

DEMAND

I insist that all applicants *find* their seats by 8:00 a.m.

3. Using the subjunctive in statements that are contrary to fact   Often such statements contain a subordinate clause that begins with *if:* the verb in the *if* clause should be in the subjunctive mood.

CONTRARY-TO-FACT STATEMENT

He would not be so irresponsible if his father *were* [not *was*] still alive.

Note: Some common expressions of conjecture are in the subjunctive mood, including *as it were, come rain or shine, far be it from me,* and *be that as it may.*

CHAPTER 55

Problems with Pronouns

A **pronoun** (*he/him, it/its, they/their*) takes the place of a noun. The noun that the pronoun replaces is called its **antecedent.** In the following sentence, snow is the antecedent of the pronoun *it.*

► **The *snow* fell all day long, and by nightfall *it* was three feet deep.**

Like nouns, pronouns are singular or plural.

SINGULAR   **The *house* was dark and gloomy, and *it* sat in a grove of tall cedars.**

PLURAL   **The *cars* swept by on the highway, all of *them* doing more than sixty-five miles per hour.**

A pronoun needs an antecedent to refer to and agree with, and a pronoun must match its antecedent in number *(plural/singular)* and gender *(he/his, she/her, it/its).* A pronoun must also be in a form, or case, that matches its function in the sentence.

55a   Make pronouns agree with their antecedents.

Problems with pronoun-antecedent agreement tend to occur when a pronoun's antecedent is an indefinite pronoun, a collective noun, or a compound noun. Problems can also occur when writers try to avoid the generic use of *he.*

Pronoun Problems and Grammar Checkers

Do not rely on grammar checkers to alert you to problems in pronoun-antecedent agreement or pronoun reference. One grammar checker, for example, missed the case error in the following sentence: *Ford's son Edsel, who [should be whom] the auto magnate treated very cruelly, was a brilliant automotive designer. (See p. 489 for a discussion of the proper use of who and whom.)*

1. Indefinite pronouns   **Indefinite pronouns** such as *someone, anybody,* and *nothing* refer to nonspecific people or things. They sometimes function as antecedents for other pronouns. Most indefinite pronouns are singular *(anybody, anyone, anything, each, either, everybody, everyone, everything, much, neither, nobody, none [meaning not one], no one, nothing, one, somebody, something).*

> **ALWAYS**   Did *either* of the boys lose *his* bicycle?
> **SINGULAR**

Some writers and instructors consider *none* plural in certain circumstances *(see p. 481),* but it is safest to use it as singular.
    The indefinite pronouns *both, few, many,* and *several* are plural.

> **ALWAYS**   *Both* boys lost *their* bicycles.
> **PLURAL**

The indefinite pronouns *all, any, more, most,* and *some* can be either singular or plural, depending on the noun to which they refer.

> **PLURAL**   The *students* debated, *some* arguing that *their*
>   positions on the issue were in the mainstream.

> **SINGULAR**   The *bread* is on the counter, but *some* of *it* has
>   already been eaten.

Problems arise when writers attempt to make indefinite pronouns agree with their antecedents without introducing gender bias. There are three ways to avoid gender bias when correcting a pronoun agreement problem such as the following.

> **FAULTY**   None of the great Romantic writers believed that
>   their achievements equaled their aspirations.

- If possible, change a singular indefinite pronoun to a plural pronoun, editing the sentence as necessary.

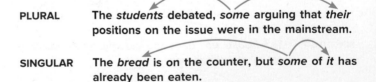

> ►   ~~None~~ ^All^ of the great Romantic writers believed that their
>   achievements ~~equaled~~ ^fell short of^ their aspirations.

- Reword the sentence to eliminate the indefinite pronoun.

  ▶ *The*
    ~~None of the~~ great Romantic writers believed that their
    fell short of
    achievements ~~equaled~~ their aspirations.

- Substitute *he or she* or *his or her* (but never *his/her*) for the singular pronoun. Change the sentence as necessary to avoid using this construction more than once.

  ▶ None of the great Romantic writers believed that ~~their~~
    his or her   *had been realized*
    ~~achievements equaled their~~ aspirations.

2. Generic nouns   A **generic noun** represents anyone and everyone in a group—a typical doctor, the average voter. Because most groups consist of both males and females, using male pronouns to refer to generic nouns is usually considered sexist. Likewise, using *he or she* assumes that all members of a group identify as one gender or the other and may be viewed as gender biased. Using *he or she* is not incorrect, but writers should do so sparingly. Note that it is increasingly acceptable to use the plural pronoun *they* as the antecedent for a generic noun. To fix agreement problems with generic nouns, use one of the three options suggested in the previous section.

▶ *College students*
  ~~A college student~~ should have a mind of their own.

▶ *an independent point of view.*
  A college student should have a ~~mind of their own.~~

▶ *his or her*
  A college student should have a mind of ~~their~~ own.

As noted above, it's becoming acceptable to use gender-neutral plural pronouns like *they* or *their* instead of gendered, singular pronouns like *he or she* or *his or her*.

▶ A college student should have a mind of their own.

3. Collective nouns   Collective nouns such as *team, family, jury, committee,* and *crowd* are treated as singular unless the people in the group are acting as individuals.

▶ *its*
  The crowd burst through the door, trampling everything in ~~their~~ path.

▶ *their*
  The committee left the conference room and returned to ~~its~~ offices.

If you are using a collective noun that has a plural meaning, consider adding a plural noun to clarify the meaning.

▶ The *committee members* left the conference room and returned to *their* offices.

IDENTIFY AND EDIT

Pronoun-Antecedent Agreement and Gender Bias

✓ agr

Try these four strategies for avoiding gender bias when an indefinite pronoun or generic noun is the antecedent in a sentence:

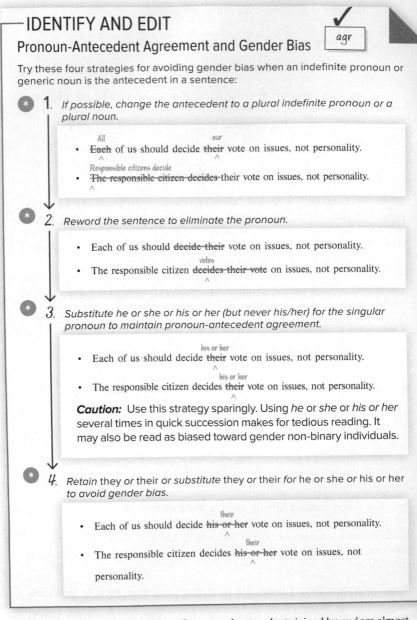

※ 1. *If possible, change the antecedent to a plural indefinite pronoun or a plural noun.*

- ~~Each~~ All of us should decide ~~their~~ our vote on issues, not personality.
- ~~The responsible citizen decides~~ Responsible citizens decide their vote on issues, not personality.

※ 2. *Reword the sentence to eliminate the pronoun.*

- Each of us should ~~decide their~~ vote on issues, not personality.
- The responsible citizen ~~decides their vote~~ votes on issues, not personality.

※ 3. *Substitute he or she or his or her (but never his/her) for the singular pronoun to maintain pronoun-antecedent agreement.*

- Each of us should decide ~~their~~ his or her vote on issues, not personality.
- The responsible citizen decides ~~their~~ his or her vote on issues, not personality.

   Caution: Use this strategy sparingly. Using *he* or *she* or *his or her* several times in quick succession makes for tedious reading. It may also be read as biased toward gender non-binary individuals.

※ 4. *Retain they or their or substitute they or their for he or she or his or her to avoid gender bias.*

- Each of us should decide ~~his or her~~ their vote on issues, not personality.
- The responsible citizen decides ~~his or her~~ their vote on issues, not personality.

4. Compound antecedents Compound antecedents joined by *and* are almost always plural.

▶ To remove all traces of the crime, James put the book and the magnifying glass back in ~~its~~ their place.

When a compound antecedent is joined by *or* or *nor,* the pronoun should agree with the closest part of the compound antecedent. If one part is singular and the other is plural, the sentence will be smoother and more effective if the plural antecedent is closest to the pronoun.

PLURAL   Neither *the child nor the parents* shared *their* food.

If the compound antecedent consists of a male and a female, however, the rule does not apply. Revise the sentence to avoid this situation.

►   ~~Neither~~ José ~~nor~~ Laura ~~could make it to her~~ appointment ~~on time.~~
      and   *were late for their*

When the two parts of the compound antecedent refer to the same person, or when the word *each* or *every* precedes the compound antecedent, use a singular pronoun.

SINGULAR   Being *a teacher and a mother* keeps *her* busy.

SINGULAR   *Every* poem and letter by Keats has *its* own special
             power.

✓ **55b**   Make pronoun references clear.

If a pronoun does not clearly refer to a specific antecedent, readers can become confused. Two common problems are ambiguous references and implied references.

1. Ambiguous pronoun references   If a pronoun can refer to more than one noun in a sentence, the reference is ambiguous.

VAGUE   The friendly banter between Hamlet and Horatio
           eventually provokes him to declare that his worldview
           has changed.

To clear up the ambiguity, eliminate the pronoun and use the appropriate noun.

CLEAR   The friendly banter between Hamlet and Horatio
           eventually provokes Hamlet to declare that his worldview
           has changed.

Sometimes the ambiguous reference can be cleared up by rewriting the sentence.

VAGUE   Jane Austen and Cassandra corresponded regularly when
           she was in London.

CLEAR   When Jane Austen was in London, she corresponded
           regularly with Cassandra.

2. Implied pronoun references   The antecedent that a pronoun refers to must be present in the sentence, and it must be a noun or another pronoun, not a word that modifies a noun. Possessives and verbs cannot be antecedents in college writing, although this usage is common in speech and informal contexts.

▶   In ~~Wilson's~~ *his* essay "When Work Disappears," ~~he~~ *Wilson* proposes a four-point plan for the revitalization of blighted inner-city communities.

Replacing *he* with *Wilson* gives the pronoun *his* an antecedent that is stated explicitly, not just implied. Note that in the revised sentence, the antecedent follows the pronoun.

▶   Every weekday afternoon, my brothers skateboard home from school, and then they leave ~~them~~ *their skateboards* in the driveway.

In the original sentence, *skateboard* is a verb, not a noun, and cannot act as a pronoun antecedent.

3. References for *this*, *that*, and *which*   The pronouns *this, that,* and *which* often refer vaguely to ideas expressed in preceding sentences. To make the sentence containing the pronoun clearer, either change the pronoun to a specific noun or add a specific antecedent or clarifying noun.

▶   As government funding for higher education decreases, tuition increases. Are we students supposed to accept ~~this~~ *these higher costs* without protest?

▶   As government funding for higher education decreases, tuition increases. Are we students supposed to accept this *situation* without protest?

4. References for *you*, *they*, and *it*   The pronouns *you, they,* and *it* should refer to definite, explicitly stated antecedents. If the antecedent is unclear, replace the pronoun with an appropriately specific noun, or rewrite the sentence to eliminate the pronoun.

▶   In some countries, such as Canada, ~~they pay~~ *the government pays* for such medical procedures.

▶   According to college policy, ~~you~~ *students* must have a permit to park a car on campus.

▶   ~~In the~~ *The* textbook, ~~it~~ states that borrowing to fund the purchase of financial assets results in a double-counting of debt.

In college writing, use *you* only to address the reader: *Turn left when you reach the corner.*

> **Note:** If a subject you are writing about prefers a gender-neutral pronoun such as *they* or *hir*, you should respect that preference: *Gemma went an entire day without checking their phone.*

55c Make your pronouns consistent within a sentence or passage.

Keep the same point of view (first, second, or third person) and number (singular or plural) within a sentence or series of related sentences.

▶ **Once you discover how easy it can be to stream music, you will be**
                              You
hooked. ~~One~~ can easily find any type of music, ~~and I have found~~ a
                                                          as well as
number of streaming services that offer a good selection.

(For more on confusing shifts, see Tab 9: Editing for Clarity, pp. 401–49.)

 ## **55d** Make pronoun cases match their function (for example, *I* vs. *me*).

When a pronoun's form, or **case,** does not match its function in a sentence, readers will feel that something is wrong.

- Pronouns in the subjective case are subjects or subject complements: *I, you, he, she, it, we, they, who, whoever.*
- Pronouns in the objective case are objects of verbs or prepositions: *me, you, him, her, it, us, them, whom, whomever.*
- Pronouns in the possessive case show ownership: *my, mine, your, yours, his, hers, its, our, ours, their, theirs, whose.* Adjective forms (*her* room, *our* office) appear before nouns. Noun forms stand alone (that room is *hers; mine* is on the left). When noun forms act as subjects, the verb agrees with the antecedent *(room).*

1. Compound structures   Compound structures (words or phrases joined by *and, or,* or *nor*) can appear as subjects or objects. If you are not sure which form of a pronoun to use in a compound structure, treat the pronoun as the only subject or object, and note how the sentence sounds.

                              I
SUBJECT   Angela and ~~me~~ were cleaning the kitchen.

IDENTIFY AND EDIT

✓ case

Pronoun Case

Follow these steps to decide on the proper form of pronouns in compound structures:

1. *Identify the compound structure (a pronoun and a noun or other pronoun joined by and, but, or, or nor) in the problem sentence.*

> *compound structure*
>
> PROBLEM SENTENCE   [Her or her roommate] should call the campus technical support office and sign up for broadband Internet service.
>
> *compound structure*
>
> PROBLEM SENTENCE   The director gave the leading roles to [my brother and I].

2. *Isolate the pronoun that you are unsure about, then read the sentence to yourself without the rest of the compound structure. If the result sounds wrong, change the case of the pronoun (subjective to objective, or vice versa), and read the sentence again.*

> PROBLEM SENTENCE   [Her ~~or her roommate~~] should call the campus technical support office and sign up for broadband Internet service.
>
> *Her should call the campus technical support office sounds wrong. The pronoun should be in the subjective case: she.*
>
> PROBLEM SENTENCE   The director gave the leading roles to [~~my brother and~~ I]
>
> *The director gave the leading role[s] to I sounds wrong. The pronoun should be in the objective case: me.*

3. *If necessary, correct the original sentence.*

> She
> • ~~Her~~ or her roommate should call the campus technical support
>   ʌ
>   office and sign up for broadband Internet service.
>
> me
> • The director gave the leading roles to my brother and ~~I~~.
>   ʌ

If you treat the pronoun as the only subject, the original sentence is clearly wrong: *Me [was] cleaning up the kitchen.*

OBJECT   My parents waited for an answer from John and ~~I~~.
                                                            me

If you treat the pronoun as the only object, the original sentence is clearly wrong: *My parents waited for an answer from I.*

Note: Do not substitute a reflexive pronoun for the pronoun you are unsure of: *Angela and I* [not *myself*] *were cleaning up the kitchen. (For more on reflexive and intensive pronouns, see Tab 12: Basic Grammar Review, p. 549.)*

---

2. Subject complements   A **subject complement** renames and specifies the sentence's subject. It follows a **linking verb**—a verb, often a form of *be,* that links the subject to its description or definition: *Children* are *innocent.*

SUBJECT   Mark's best friends are Jane and ~~me~~.
                                            I

You can also switch the order to make the pronoun into the subject: *Jane and I are Mark's best friends.*

3. Appositives   **Appositives** are nouns or noun phrases that rename nouns or pronouns. They appear right after the word they rename and have the same function in the sentence that it has.

SUBJECTIVE   The two weary travelers, Ramon and ~~me~~, finally
                                                I
             found shelter.

OBJECTIVE   The police arrested two protesters, Aliyah and ~~I~~.
                                                            me

4. *We* or *us*   When *we* or *us* comes before a noun, it has the same function in the sentence as the noun it precedes and renames.

SUBJECTIVE   ~~Us~~ students never get to decide such things.
             We

OBJECTIVE   Things were looking desperate for ~~we~~ campers.
                                                us

5. Comparisons with *than* or *as*   In comparisons, words are often left out of the sentence because the reader can guess what they would be. When a pronoun follows *than* or *as,* make sure you are using the correct form by mentally adding the missing word or words.

▶   Megan is quicker than she [is].

▶   We find ourselves remembering Maria as often as [we remember] her.

Sometimes the correct form depends on intended meaning:

► **My brother likes our dog more than *I* [do].**

► **My brother likes our dog more than [he likes] *me*.**

If a sentence with a comparison sounds too awkward or formal, add the missing words: *Megan is quicker than she is.*

6. Pronoun as the subject or the object of an infinitive   An infinitive has the word *to* plus the base verb *(to breathe, to sing, to dance).* Whether a pronoun functions as the subject or the object of an infinitive, it should be in the objective case.

► **We wanted our lawyer and *her* to defend *us* against this charge.**

                        subject   *object*

Note that in the example the subject of the infinitive is a compound noun. If a compound functioning as the subject or object of an infinitive has two pronouns, both should be in the objective case: *The police officer told her and me to move along.*

7. Noun or pronoun with an *-ing* noun (a gerund)   When a noun or pronoun appears before a **gerund** (an *-ing* verb form functioning as a noun), it should usually be treated as a possessive. Possessive nouns are formed by adding *'s* to singular nouns *(the teacher's desk)* or an apostrophe only *(')* to plural nouns *(three teachers' rooms). (See Tab 11: Editing for Correctness, pp. 497–548.)*

animals'

► **The ~~animals~~ fighting disturbed the entire neighborhood.**
                ^

their

► **Because of ~~them~~ screeching, no one could get any sleep.**
                ^

When the *-ing* word is functioning as a modifier, not a noun, use the subjective or objective case for the pronoun that precedes it. Consider these two sentences:

► **The teacher punished their cheating.**

Cheating is the object of the sentence, modified by the possessive pronoun *their*.

► **The teacher saw them cheating.**

Them is the object of the sentence, modified by *cheating.*

Note: Possessive pronouns never contain an apostrophe and an *s*. Pronouns that appear with an apostrophe and an *s* are always part of a contraction. Be especially careful to use *its*, not *it's*, when the possessive form is called for: *The cat finally stopped its* [not *it's*] *screeching.*

55e   Distinguish between *who* and *whom*.

The relative pronouns *who, whom, whoever,* and *whomever* are used to introduce dependent clauses and in questions. Their case depends on their function.

- Subjective: *who, whoever*
- Objective: *whom, whomever*

1. Determining the pronoun's function in a clause   If the pronoun is functioning as a subject and is performing an action, use *who* or *whoever*. If the pronoun is the object of a verb or preposition, use *whom* or *whomever*. (Note that *whom* usually appears at the beginning of the clause.)

▶ **Henry Ford, *who* started the Ford Motor Company, was autocratic and stubborn.**

  Who, which refers to *Henry Ford,* is performing an action in the dependent clause: starting a company.

▶ **Ford's son Edsel, *whom* the auto magnate treated cruelly, was a brilliant automobile designer.**

  Whom, which refers to *Edsel,* is the object of the verb *treated,* although it precedes the verb and the subject, *the auto magnate.* You can check the pronoun by changing the order within the clause: *The auto magnate treated whom [him] cruelly.*

Phrases such as *I think* or *they say* do not affect pronoun case.

▶ **Ford, *who* many say was a visionary, pioneered use of the assembly line.**

2. Determining the pronoun's function in a question   To choose the correct form for the pronoun, answer the question with a personal pronoun:

▶ ***Who* founded the General Motors Corporation?**

  The answer could be *He founded it. He* is in the subjective case, so *who* is correct.

▶ ***Whom* did Chrysler turn to for leadership in the 1980s?**

  The answer could be *It turned to him. Him* is in the objective case, so *whom* is correct.

Note: Infinitives take the objective case, *whom,* as a subject or object: *Ford could not decide whom* [not *who*] *to trust.*

CHAPTER 56

Problems with Adjectives and Adverbs

Adjectives and **adverbs** are words that qualify—or modify—the meanings of other words. Adjectives modify nouns and pronouns. Adverbs modify verbs, adjectives, and other adverbs.

56a Use adverbs to modify verbs, adjectives, other adverbs, and whole clauses.

Adverbs tell where, when, why, how, how often, how much, or to what degree.

▶ The authenticity of the document is *hotly* contested.

▶ The water was *brilliant* blue and *icy* cold.

▶ Dickens mixed humor and pathos *better* than any other English writer after Shakespeare.

▶ *Consequently,* Dickens is still read by millions.

(For information on the placement of adverbs in sentences, see Tab 12: Basic Grammar Review, pp. 549-82.)

Adjectives, Adverbs, and Grammar Checkers

Computer grammar checkers are sensitive to some problems with adjectives and adverbs but miss far more than they catch. A grammar checker failed to flag the errors in the following sentences: *The price took a suddenly plunge* [should be *sudden*] and *The price plunged sudden* [should be *suddenly*].

56b Use adjectives to modify nouns or as subject complements.

Adjectives modify nouns and pronouns; they do not modify any other kind of word. Adjectives tell what kind or how many and may come before or after the noun or pronoun they modify.

▶ *Ominous gray* clouds loomed over the lake.

▶ The *looming* clouds, *ominous* and *gray,* frightened the children.

Some proper nouns have adjective forms. Proper adjectives, like the proper nouns they are derived from, are capitalized: *Victoria/Victorian, Britain/British, America/American, Shakespeare/Shakespearean.*

In some cases, a noun is used as an adjective without a change in form.

▶   **Cigarette smoking harms the lungs and is banned in offices.**

Occasionally, descriptive adjectives function as if they were nouns.

▶   **The *unemployed* should not be equated with the *lazy*.**

(For information about compound adjectives such as "well known," see Tab 11: Editing for Correctness, pp. 497–582.)

1. Avoiding incorrect use of adjectives   In common speech, we sometimes treat adjectives as adverbs. In writing, avoid this informal usage.

▶   **He hit that ball** *really well* **real good.**

Both *real* and *good* are adjectives, but they are used as adverbs in the original sentence, with *real* modifying *good* and *good* modifying the verb *hit*.

Note that *well* can function as an adjective and subject complement with a linking verb to describe a person's health.

▶   **After the treatment, the patient felt *well* again.**

▶   *certainly* **She sure made me work hard for my grade.**

In the original sentence, the adjective *sure* tries to do the work of an adverb modifying the verb *made*.

2. Using adjectives after linking verbs   **Linking verbs** connect the subject of a sentence to its description. The most common linking verb is *be*. Descriptive adjectives that modify a sentence's subject but appear after a linking verb are called **subject complements**.

▶   **During the winter, both Emily and Anne were sick.**

▶   **The road is long, winding, and dangerous.**

Linking verbs are related to states of being and the five senses: *appear, become, feel, grow, make, prove, look, smell, sound,* and *taste*. Verbs related to the senses can be either linking or action verbs, depending on the meaning of the sentence.

ADJECTIVE   The dog smelled *bad.*

Bad modifies the noun *dog.* The sentence indicates that the dog needed a bath.

ADVERB   The dog smelled *badly.*

Badly modifies the verb *smelled,* an action verb in this sentence. The sentence indicates that the dog had lost its sense of smell.

Good and *bad* appear after *feel* to describe emotional states.

▶   **I feel *bad* [not *badly*] for her because she does not feel well.**

3. Recognizing that some adjectives and adverbs are spelled alike   In most instances, *-ly* endings indicate adverbs; however, words with *-ly* endings can sometimes be adjectives *(the lovely girl).* In standard English, many adverbs do not require the *-ly* ending, and some words are both adjectives and adverbs: *fast, only, hard, right,* and *straight.* Note that *right* also has an *-ly* form as an adverb: *rightly.* When in doubt, consult a dictionary.

56c   Use positive, comparative, and superlative adjectives and adverbs correctly.

Most adjectives and adverbs have three forms: positive *(dumb),* comparative *(dumber),* and superlative *(dumbest).* The simplest form of the adjective is the positive form.

1. Distinguishing between comparatives and superlatives   Use the comparative form to compare two things and the superlative form to compare three or more things.

▶   **In total area, New York is a *larger* state than Pennsylvania.**

▶   **Texas is the *largest* state in the Southwest.**

2. Learning when to use *-er/-est* endings and when to use *more/most,* or *less/least*   To form comparatives and superlatives of short adjectives, add the suffixes *-er* and *-est (brighter/brightest).* With longer adjectives (three or more syllables), use *more* or *less* and *most* or *least (more dangerous/most dangerous).* (A dictionary will tell you whether an adjective takes *-er/-est.*)

▶   **Mercury is the ~~most near~~ planet to the sun.**
  nearest

A few short adverbs have *-er* and *-est* endings in their comparative and superlative forms *(harder/hardest).* Most adverbs, however, including all adverbs that end in *-ly,* use *more* and *most* in their comparative and superlative forms. Negative comparatives and superlatives are formed with *less* and *least: less funny/ least funny.*

► **She sings *more loudly* than we expected.**

Two common adjectives—*good* and *bad*—form the comparative and superlative in an irregular way: *good, better, best* and *bad, worse, worst.*

►   *worse*
   He felt ~~badder~~ as his illness progressed.
   ^

These and other irregular adjectives and adverbs are listed in the box on page 530. When in doubt, consult a dictionary.

3. Watching out for double comparatives and superlatives   Use either an *-er* or an *-est* ending or *more/most* to form the comparative or superlative, as appropriate; do not use both.

► **Since World War II, Britain has been the ~~most~~ closest ally of the United States.**

4. Recognizing concepts that cannot be compared   Do not use comparative or superlative forms with adjectives such as *unique, infinite, impossible, perfect, round, square,* and *destroyed.* These concepts are *absolutes.* If something is unique, for example, it is the only one of its kind, making comparison impossible.

►   *another*   *like*
   You will never find a ~~more unique~~ restaurant ~~than~~ this one.
   ^   ^

5. Making sure your comparison is complete   Unless the context of your sentence makes the comparison clear, be sure to include both items you are comparing.

►   *than any other British writer of his time*
   Charles Dickens had more popular successes.
                                        ^

(For more on making comparisons complete, see Tab 9, Editing for Clarity, p. 401.)

56d   Avoid double negatives.

The words *no, not,* and *never* can modify the meaning of nouns and pronouns as well as other sentence elements.

NOUN	You are *no* friend of mine.
ADJECTIVE	The red house was *not* large.
VERB	He *never* ran in a marathon.

However, it takes only one negative word to change the meaning of a sentence from positive to negative. When two negatives are used together, they cancel each other, resulting in a positive meaning. Unless you want your sentence to have a positive meaning *(I am not unaware of your feelings in this matter),* edit by changing or eliminating one of the negative words.

COMPARISON IN ADJECTIVES AND ADVERBS

Examples of Regular and Irregular Forms

REGULAR ADJECTIVES

	POSITIVE	COMPARATIVE	SUPERLATIVE
One-syllable adjectives	red	redder, less red	reddest, least red
Two-syllable adjectives ending in -y	lonely	lonelier, less lonely	loneliest, least lonely
Other adjectives of two or more syllables	famous	more/less famous	most/least famous

REGULAR ADVERBS

	POSITIVE	COMPARATIVE	SUPERLATIVE
One-syllable adverbs	hard	harder, less hard	hardest, least hard
Most other adverbs	truthfully	more/less truthfully	most/least truthfully

IRREGULAR ADJECTIVES

POSITIVE	COMPARATIVE	SUPERLATIVE
good	better	best
bad	worse	worst
little	less, littler	least, littlest
many	more	most
much	more	most
some	more	most

IRREGULAR ADVERBS

POSITIVE	COMPARATIVE	SUPERLATIVE
badly	worse	worst
well	better	best

► They don't have *any* ~~no~~ reason to go there.
^

► He *can* ~~can't~~ hardly do that assignment.
^

Note that *hardly* has a negative meaning and cannot be used with *no, not,* or *never.*

CHECKLIST Editing for Grammar Conventions

To detect grammatical problems in your writing, ask yourself the following questions:

☐ Is each sentence grammatically complete, or is some necessary part missing? Does each sentence include a subject, a complete verb, and an independent clause? *(See Chapter 51, Sentence Fragments, pp. 451–56.)*

☐ Does any sentence seem like two or more sentences jammed together without a break? If a sentence has more than one independent clause, are those clauses joined in an acceptable way? *(See Chapter 52, Comma Splices and Run-on Sentences, pp. 457–62.)*

☐ Do the key parts of each sentence fit together well, or are the subjects and verbs mismatched in person and number? *(See Chapter 53, Subject-Verb Agreement, pp. 462–69.)*

☐ Is the time frame of events represented accurately, conventionally, and consistently, or are there problems with verb form, tense, and sequence? *(See Chapter 54, Problems with Verbs, pp. 469–79.)*

☐ Do the pronouns in every sentence clearly refer to a specific noun or pronoun and agree with the nouns or pronouns they replace? *(See Chapter 55, Problems with Pronouns, pp. 479–89.)*

☐ Does the form of each modifier match its function in the sentence? *(See Chapter 56, Problems with Adjectives and Adverbs, pp. 489–95.)*

Credit

11
Editing for Correctness

Punctuation, Mechanics, and Spelling

It wasn't a matter of rewriting but simply of tightening up all the bolts.

–Marguerite Yourcenar

©David Ma'an/Getty Images

Question marks and exclamation points signal the type of sentence that they conclude. Like the other punctuation marks covered in this tab, they convey important information for readers.

11 Editing for Correctness

✓ Sections referenced in Resources for Writers: Identifying and Editing Common
Problems (following Tab 9).

Tab 11: Editing for Correctness

This section will help you answer questions such as the following:

Rhetorical Knowledge
- Should I use contractions such as *can't* or *don't* in my college work? (60b)
- Which numbers should be spelled out in my technical report? (65c)

Critical Thinking, Reading, and Writing
- How should I set off words I have added to a quotation? (62f)
- How do I use ellipses ethically to indicate omissions from quotations? (62g)

Processes
- What are some strategies for proofreading my work? (68)
- What are the strengths and limitations of my word processor's spelling checker? (60, 68)
- Can my word processor's grammar checker help me edit for punctuation and mechanics? (57–59, 61–64)

Knowledge of Conventions
- When should I set off a word or phrase with commas? (57e)
- What is the difference between *its* and *it's?* (60c)

For a general introduction to writing outcomes, see 1e, pages 14–15.

CHAPTER 57

Commas

COMMON USES OF THE COMMA

You may have been told that commas are used to mark pauses, but that is not an accurate general principle. To indicate meaning, commas are used to set off sentence elements. They are also used in other conventional ways.

✓ **57a** Use a comma after an introductory word group that is *not* the subject of the sentence.

A comma both attaches an introductory word, phrase, or clause to and distinguishes it from the rest of the sentence.

▶   **Finally, the speeding car careened to the right.**

▶   **Reflecting on her life experiences, Washburn attributed her successes to her own efforts.**

▶   **Until he noticed the handprint on the wall, the detective was frustrated by the lack of clues.**

When the introductory phrase is shorter than five words and there is no danger of confusion without a comma, the comma can be omitted.

▶   **For several hours we rode on in silence.**

Do not add a comma after a word group that functions as the subject of the sentence. Be especially careful with word groups that begin with *-ing* words.

▶   **Persuading constituents is one of a politician's most important tasks.**

Commas and Grammar Checkers

Computer grammar checkers usually will not highlight missing commas following introductory elements or between independent clauses joined by a coordinating conjunction such as *and*, and they cannot decide whether a sentence element is essential or nonessential.

57b   Use commas between items in a series.

A comma should appear after each item in a series.

▶   **Three industries that have been important to New England are shipbuilding, tourism, and commercial fishing.**

—the EVOLVING SITUATION

Styles within Disciplines

The rules for capitalizing, abbreviating, and italicizing terms, as well as conventions for using numbers and hyphens, can vary from one course or discipline to another. If you are not sure about the conventions for a discipline, see what rules your course textbook follows. If you cannot figure out the accepted practice from your text, ask your instructor for help, use the general rules presented in this book, or consult a style manual from the list on page 259.

Commas clarify which items are part of the series. In the following example, the third comma clarifies that the hikers are packing lunch *and* snacks, not chocolate and trail mix meant for lunch.

> **CONFUSING**   For the hiking trip, we needed to pack lunch, chocolate and trail mix.
>
> **CLEAR**   For the hiking trip, we needed to pack lunch, chocolate, and trail mix.

If items in the series contain internal commas or other punctuation, separate the items with a semicolon *(see Chapter 58, pp. 510–13).*

> **Note:** If you are writing for a journalism course, you may be required to leave out the final comma that precedes *and* in a series, just as magazines and newspapers sometimes do.

✓ **57c**   Use a comma in front of a coordinating conjunction that joins independent clauses.

When a coordinating conjunction *(and, but, for, nor, or, so, yet)* joins clauses that could each stand alone as a sentence, put a comma before the coordinating conjunction.

▶ **Injuries were so frequent that he began to worry, and his style of play became more cautious.**

If the word groups you are joining are not independent clauses, do not add a comma. *(See 57m on p. 508.)*

Exception: If you are joining two short clauses, you may leave out the comma unless it is needed for clarity.

▶ **The running back caught the ball and the fans cheered.**

57d   Add a comma between coordinate adjectives not joined by *and*, but do not separate cumulative adjectives with a comma.

Use a comma between coordinate adjectives that precede a noun and modify it independently *(a brave, intelligent, persistent woman)*. Adjectives are coordinate if they can be joined by *and* (brave *and* intelligent *and* persistent) or if their order can be changed *(a persistent, brave, intelligent woman).*

▶ **This brave, intelligent, persistent woman was the first female to earn a Ph.D. in psychology.**

If you cannot add *and* between the adjectives or change their order, they are cumulative, with each one modifying the ones that follow it, and should not be separated with a comma or commas.

▶ **Andrea Boccelli, the world-famous Italian tenor, has performed in concerts and operas.**

World-famous modifies *Italian tenor,* not just the noun *tenor.* You could not add *and* between the adjectives (world-famous *and* Italian tenor) or change their order *(Italian world-famous tenor).*

✓ **57e** Use commas to set off nonessential additions to a sentence, but do not set off essential elements.

Nonessential, or **nonrestrictive,** words, phrases, and clauses add information to a sentence but are not required for its basic meaning to be understood. Nonrestrictive additions are set off with commas.

NONRESTRICTIVE

Mary Shelley's best-known novel, *Frankenstein or the Modern*
^
Prometheus, was first published in 1818.
^
The sentence would have the same basic meaning without the title *(Mary Shelley's best-known novel was first published in 1818).*

Restrictive words, phrases, and clauses are essential to a sentence because they identify exactly who or what the writer is talking about. Restrictive additions are not set off with commas.

RESTRICTIVE

Mary Shelley's novel *Frankenstein or the Modern Prometheus* was first published in 1818.

Without the title, the reader would not know which novel the sentence is referring to, so *Frankenstein or the Modern Prometheus* is restrictive.

Often, the context determines whether to enclose a word, phrase, or clause with commas. In the following examples, notice how a preceding sentence can affect the meaning and determine whether commas are needed around the participial phrase:

▶ **Two customers with angry looks on their faces approached the check-out counter. The customers, demanding a refund, lined up by the register.**

▶ **The store opened at the usual time. The customers demanding a refund lined up by the register.**

Three types of additions to sentences often cause problems: adjective clauses, adjective phrases, and appositives.

IDENTIFY AND EDIT

Commas with Nonrestrictive Words or Word Groups

Follow these steps if you have trouble deciding whether a word or word group should be set off with a comma or commas:

1. *Identify the word or word group that may require commas. Pay special attention to words that appear between the subject and verb.*

PROBLEM
SENTENCE

Joan Didion [a native of California] has written essays and screenplays as well as novels.
(subj / verb)

PROBLEM
SENTENCE

Her book [*The Year of Magical Thinking*] is a description of the experience of grief.
(subj / verb)

2. *Read the sentence to yourself without the word or word group. Does the basic meaning stay the same, or does it change? Can you tell what person, place, or thing the sentence is about?*

SENTENCE
WITHOUT THE
WORD GROUP

Joan Didion has written essays and screenplays as well as novels.
The subject of the sentence is identified by name, and the basic meaning of the sentence does not change.

SENTENCE
WITHOUT THE
WORD GROUP

Her book is a description of the experience of grief.
Without the words *The Year of Magical Thinking,* we cannot tell what book the sentence is describing.

3. *If the meaning of the sentence stays the same without the word or word group, set it off with commas. If the meaning changes, the word or word group should not be set off with commas.*

• Joan Didion, a native of California, has written essays and screenplays as well as novels.

• Her book *The Year of Magical Thinking* is a description of the experience of grief.

The sentence is correct. Commas are not needed to enclose *The Year of Magical Thinking.*

1. Adjective clauses   Adjective clauses begin with a relative pronoun or an adverb—*who, whom, whose, which, that, where,* or *when*—and modify a noun or pronoun within the sentence. Adjective clauses can be either nonrestrictive or restrictive.

NONRESTRICTIVE

With his tale of Odysseus, *whose journey can be traced on modern maps,* Homer brought accounts of strange and alien creatures to the ancient Greeks.

RESTRICTIVE

The contestant *whom he most wanted to beat* was his father.

Note: Use *that* only with restrictive clauses. Many writers prefer to use *which* only with nonrestrictive clauses.

---

2. Adjective phrases   Like an adjective clause, an adjective phrase also modifies a noun or pronoun in a sentence. Adjective phrases begin with a preposition (for example, *with, by, at,* or *for*) or a verbal (a word formed from a verb). Adjective phrases can be either nonrestrictive or restrictive.

NONRESTRICTIVE

Some people, *by their faith in human nature or their general good will,* bring out the best in others.

The phrase does not specify which people are being discussed. The sentence would have the same meaning without it.

RESTRICTIVE

People *fighting passionately for their rights* can inspire others.

The phrase indicates which people the writer is talking about and therefore is restrictive. It is not set off with commas.

3. Appositives   Appositives are nouns or noun phrases that rename nouns or pronouns and appear right after the word they rename.

NONRESTRICTIVE

One researcher, *the widely respected R. S. Smith,* has shown that a child's performance on IQ tests can be inconsistent.

Because the word *one* already restricts the word *researcher,* the researcher's name is not essential to the meaning of the sentence.

RESTRICTIVE

The researcher *R. S. Smith* has shown that a child's performance on IQ tests can be inconsistent.

The name *R. S. Smith* tells readers which researcher is meant.

57f   Use a comma or commas with transitional and parenthetical expressions, contrasting comments, and absolute phrases.

1. Transitional expressions   Transitional expressions show the relationship between ideas in a sentence. Conjunctive adverbs *(however, therefore, moreover)* and other transitional phrases *(for example, on the other hand)* are usually set off by commas when used at the beginning, in the middle, or at the end of a sentence. *(For a list of transitional expressions, see Tab 10: Editing for Grammar Conventions, p. 451.)*

▶   **Brian Wilson, for example, was unable to cope with the pressures**
    $\wedge$ $\wedge$
    of touring with the Beach Boys.

▶   **As a matter of fact, he had a nervous breakdown shortly after**
    a tour. $\wedge$

▶   **He is still considered one of the most important figures in rock**
    and roll, however.
         $\wedge$

When a transitional expression connects two independent clauses, use a semicolon before and a comma after it.

▶   **The Beatles were a phenomenon when they toured the United**

    States in 1964; subsequently, they became the most successful
                 $\wedge$ $\wedge$
    rock band of all time.

Note: Short expressions such as *also, at least, certainly, instead, of course, then, perhaps,* and *therefore* do not always need to be set off with commas.

▶   **I found my notes and *also* got my story in on time.**

---

2. Parenthetical expressions   The information that parenthetical expressions provide is relatively insignificant and could easily be left out. Therefore, these expressions are set off with a comma or commas.

▶   **Human cloning, so they say, will be possible within a decade.**
         $\wedge$ $\wedge$

▶   **The experiments would take a couple of weeks, more or less.**
                                                         $\wedge$

3. Contrasting comments   Contrasting comments beginning with words such as *not, unlike, while, although, even though,* or *in contrast to* should be set off with commas.

► **Adam Sandler is famous as a comedian, not a tragedian.**

^

► **Comedy, unlike tragedy, often lacks critical respect.**

^   ^

4. Absolute phrases Absolute phrases usually include a noun *(sunlight)* followed by a participle *(shining)* and are used to modify whole sentences. Do not separate the noun and participle with a comma.

► **The snake slithered through the tall grass, the sunlight/shining now and then on its green skin.**

^

57g Use a comma or commas to set off words of direct address, *yes* and *no*, mild interjections, and tag sentences.

Words that interrupt a sentence are set off by commas because they are not essential to the sentence's meaning.

► **Thank you, Mr. Rao, for your help.**

^   ^

► **Yes, I will meet you at noon.**

^

► **Of course, if that's what you want, we'll do it.**

^   ^

► **We can do better, don't you think?**

^

57h Use a comma or commas to separate a direct quotation from the rest of the sentence.

► **Irving Howe declares, "Whitman is quite realistic about the place of the self in an urban world" (261).**

^

► **"Whitman is quite realistic about the place of the self in an urban world," declares Irving Howe (261).**

^

Note that the comma appears inside the closing quotation mark.

Use commas to set off words that interrupt quotations.

► **"When we interpret a poem," DiYanni says, "we explain it to ourselves in order to understand it."**

^

If you are quoting more than one sentence and interrupting the quotation between sentences, the interrupting words should end with a period.

► **"But it is not possible to give to each department an equal power of self defense," James Madison writes in *The Federalist No. 51.* "In republican government the legislative authority, necessarily, predominates."**

^

A comma is not needed to separate an indirect quotation or a paraphrase from the words that identify its source. It is also not needed when a direct quotation is integrated into your sentence.

▶ **Irving Howe notes/that Whitman realistically depicts the urban self as free to wander (261).**

▶ **Stanley Fish maintains that teaching content/ "is a lure and a delusion."**

(For more on quotations, see Chapter 61, pp. 518-23.)

57i   Use commas with parts of dates, letters, and addresses; with people's titles; and in numbers.

- **Dates.** Use paired commas in dates when the month, day, and year are included. Do not use commas when the day of the month is omitted or when the day appears before the month.

  ▶ **On March 4, 1931, she traveled to New York.**

  ▶ **She traveled to New York in March 1931.**

  ▶ **She traveled to New York on 4 March 1931.**

- **Parts of letters.** Use a comma following the greeting in an informal letter and following the closing in any type of letter. (In a business letter, use a colon following the greeting.)

  ▶ **Dear Marta,**   **Sincerely yours,**

- **Addresses.** Use commas to set off the parts of an address or the name of a state, but do not use a comma preceding a zip code.

  ▶ **At Cleveland, Ohio, the river changes direction.**

  ▶ **My address is 63 Oceanside Drive, Apt. 2A, Surf City, New Jersey 08008.**

- **People's titles or degrees.** Put a comma between the person's name and the title or degree when it comes after the name, followed by another comma.

  ▶ **Luis Mendez, MD, gave her the green light to resume her exercise regimen.**

  If an abbreviation such as *Jr.* or a roman numeral such as *II* follows a name, setting it off with a comma is optional: *Milton Clark Jr.* or *Milton Clark, Jr.* (Consult your discipline's style manual.)

- **Numbers.** When a number has more than four digits, use commas to mark off the numerals by hundreds—that is, by groups of three, beginning at the right.

▶   **Andrew Jackson received 647,276 votes in the 1828 election.**

- If the number is four digits long, the comma is optional.

▶   **The survey had 1856 [or 1,856] respondents.**

Exceptions: Street numbers, zip codes, telephone numbers, page numbers (p. 2304), and years (1828) do not include commas.

57j   Use a comma to take the place of an omitted word or phrase or to prevent misreading.

When a writer omits one or more words from a sentence to create a special effect, a comma is often needed to make the meaning of the sentence clear for readers.

▶   **Under the tree he found his puppy, and under the car, his cat.**
                                                                      ^
The second comma substitutes for the phrase *he found.*

Commas are also used to keep readers from misunderstanding a writer's meaning when words are repeated or might be misread.

▶   **Many birds that sing, sing early in the morning, before the sun rises.**
                          ^

▶   **Any items that can be, are sold at auction Web sites.**
                             ^

It is often better, however, to revise the sentence and avoid the need for the clarifying comma: *Many songbirds sing first thing in the morning.*

COMMON MISUSES OF THE COMMA
Commas should *not* be used in the following situations.

57k   Do not use commas to separate major elements in an independent clause.

Do not use a comma to separate a subject from a verb, a verb from its object, or a preposition from its object.

▶   **Reflecting on your life/ is necessary for emotional growth.**

The subject, *reflecting on your life,* should not be separated from the verb, *is.*

▶   **Washburn decided/ that her own efforts were the key to her success.**

The verb *decided* should not be separated from its direct object, the subordinate clause *that her own efforts were the key to her success.*

▶　**Although he is a famous actor he is in/ emotional limbo.**

The preposition *in* should not be separated from its object, *emotional limbo*.

> *Note:* If a nonessential phrase appears between the subject and verb, it should be set off with a pair of commas *(see 57e on p. 501).*

57l　Do not add a comma before the first or after the final item in a series.

Use commas to separate items in a series but never before or after the series.

▶　**Employees in the United States work longer hours than/ German, French, or British workers/ are expected to work.**

Commas should never be used after *such as* or *like (see p. 510).*

57m　Do not use commas to separate compound word groups unless they are independent clauses.

A comma should not be used between word groups joined with a coordinating conjunction such as *and* unless the groups are both full sentences.

▶　**Injuries were so frequent that he became worried/ and started to play more cautiously.**

In this sentence *and* joins two verbs *(became* and *started).*

▶　**He is worried that injuries are more frequent/ and that he will have to play more cautiously to avoid them.**

In this sentence *and* joins two subordinate clauses beginning with *that.*

57n　Do not use commas to set off restrictive modifiers, appositives, or slightly parenthetical words or phrases.

If a word, phrase, or clause in a sentence is necessary to identify the noun or pronoun that precedes it, it is restrictive and should not be set off with commas. *(See pp. 501-03.)*

▶　**The applicants *who had studied for the admissions test* were restless and eager for the exam to begin.**

Because only those applicants who had studied were eager for the test to begin, the clause *who had studied for the admissions test* is restrictive and should not be set off with commas.

1. Appositives identifying nouns and pronouns   An appositive is a noun or noun phrase that renames a noun or pronoun and appears right after the word it renames.

▶   **The director⁄ Alfred Hitchcock⁄ was responsible for many classic thrillers and horror films, including *Psycho*.**

2. Concluding adverb clauses   Adverb clauses beginning with *after, as soon as, before, if, since, unless, until,* and *when* are usually essential to a sentence's meaning.

> **RESTRICTIVE**
>
> I am eager to test the children's IQ again *because significant variations in a child's test scores indicate that the test itself may be flawed.*

Clauses beginning with *although, even though, though,* and *whereas* present a contrasting thought and are usually nonrestrictive.

> **NONRESTRICTIVE**
>
> IQ tests can be useful indicators of a child's abilities, *although they should not be taken as the definitive measurement of a child's intelligence.*

> **Note:** An adverb clause that appears at the beginning of a sentence is usually followed by a comma: *Until we meet, I'm continuing my work on the budget (see pp. 498–99).*

3. Words and phrases that are slightly parenthetical   If setting off a brief parenthetical remark with commas *(see p. 504)* would draw too much attention to the remark and interrupt the flow of the sentence, the commas can be left out.

▶   **Science is *basically* the last frontier.**

57o   Correct other common comma errors.

- **Remove commas between cumulative adjectives** *(see p. 500-01).*

  ▶   **Three⁄ well-known⁄ U.S. writers visited the artist's studio.**

- **Remove a comma that appears between an adjective and a noun.**

  ▶   **An art review by a celebrated, powerful⁄ writer would be guaranteed publication.**

- Remove a comma that appears between a noun and participle in an absolute phrase.

  ► My favorite singer⁄ having lost the contest, I stopped paying attention.

- Remove a comma that appears between an adverb and an adjective.

  ► The artist's studio was delightfully⁄ chaotic.

- Remove a comma that appears after a coordinating conjunction *(and, but, or, nor, for, so, yet)*.

  ► The *duomo* in Siena was begun in the thirteenth century, and⁄ it was used as a model for other Italian cathedrals.

- Eliminate a comma after *although, such as,* or *like*.

  ► Stage designers can achieve many unusual effects, such as⁄ the helicopter that landed onstage in *Miss Saigon*.

- Eliminate a comma before *than*.

  ► An appointment to the Supreme Court has more long-range consequences⁄ than any other decision a President makes.

- Remove a comma before a parenthesis.

  ► When in office cubicles⁄ (a recent invention), workers need to be considerate of others.

- Remove a comma with a question mark or an exclamation point that ends a quotation *(also see Chapter 61, p. 518)*.

  ► "Where are my glasses?⁄" she asked in a panic.

CHAPTER 58

Semicolons

Semicolons are used to join ideas that are closely related and grammatically equivalent.

58a Use a semicolon to join independent clauses.

A semicolon should join two related independent clauses when they are not joined by a comma and a coordinating conjunction *(and, but, or, nor, for, so, yet)*.

Semicolons and Grammar Checkers

Grammar checker programs will catch some comma splices that can be corrected by adding a semicolon between the two clauses. They will also catch some incorrect uses of the semicolon. They will not tell you when a semicolon *could* be used for clarity, however, nor whether the semicolon is the best choice.

▶ **Before 8000 B.C.E. wheat was not the luxuriant plant it is today; it**

was merely a wild grass that spread throughout the Middle East.

Sometimes, the close relationship is a contrast.

▶ **Phillp had completed the assignment; Lucy had not.**

Note: When a semicolon appears next to a quotation mark, it is always placed outside the quotation mark: *My doctor advised me to "get plenty of rest"; my supervisor had other ideas.*

An occasional semicolon adds variety to your writing, but too many can make it seem monotonous. If you have used three or more semicolons in a paragraph, revise to eliminate most of them.

Note: If a comma is used between two clauses without a coordinating conjunction, the sentence is a comma splice, a serious error. One way to correct a comma splice is by changing the comma to a semicolon. *(For more help with correcting comma splices and run-on sentences, see Tab 10: Editing for Grammar Conventions, pp. 451–95.)*

58h   Use semicolons with transitional expressions that connect independent clauses.

Transitional expressions, including transitional phrases *(for example, in addition, on the contrary)* and conjunctive adverbs *(consequently, however, moreover, nevertheless, then, therefore),* indicate the relationship between two clauses. When a transitional expression appears between two clauses, it is preceded by a semicolon and usually followed by a comma. Using a comma instead of a semicolon creates a comma splice. *(For a list of transitional expressions, see Tab 10. Editing for Grammar Conventions, p. 451. For help with correcting comma splices, see pp. 457-62.)*

▶ **Sheila had to wait until the plumber arrived; consequently, she was late for the exam.**

Coordinating conjunctions *(and, but, or, nor, for, so, yet)* also indicate the way clauses are related. Unlike transitional expressions, however, they are preceded by a comma, not a semicolon, when they join two independent clauses.

> *Note:* The semicolon always appears between the two clauses, even when the transitional expression is in another position within the second clause. Wherever it appears, the transitional expression is usually set off with a comma or commas.
>
> ▶ **My friends are all taking golf lessons; my roommate and I, however, are more interested in tennis.**

58c Use a semicolon to separate items in a series or clauses when the items or clauses contain commas.

Because the following sentence contains a series with internal commas, the semicolons are needed for clarity.

▶ **The committee included Dr. Curtis Youngblood, the county medical examiner; Roberta Collingwood, director of the bureau's criminal division; and Darcy Coolidge, the chief of police.**

If two independent clauses are joined by a coordinating conjunction *(and, but, for, nor, or, so, yet)* and at least one of them already contains several internal commas, a semicolon can help readers locate the point where the clauses are separated.

▶ **The closing scenes return to the English countryside, recalling the opening; but these scenes are bathed in a different, cooler light, suggesting that memories of her marriage still haunt her.**

58d Correct common semicolon errors.

- Use a comma, not a semicolon, to join a dependent clause or a phrase to an independent clause.

  ▶ **Professional writers need to devote time every day to their writing; although doing so takes discipline.**

  ▶ **Seemingly tame and lovable; housecats can be fierce hunters.**

- Use a comma, not a semicolon, to join most independent clauses linked by a coordinating conjunction *(and, but, or, nor, for, so, yet);* if the clauses contain several internal commas, a semicolon is acceptable *(see 58c).*

▶ **Nineteenth-century women wore colorful clothes⌃/ but their**
⤷ ^
attire looks drab in the black-and-white photographs of the era.

- Use a colon, not a semicolon, to introduce a series, an explanation, or a quotation.

  ▶ **My day was planned⌃/: a morning walk, an afternoon in the**
  ⤷ ^
  library, dinner with friends, and a great horror movie.

  ▶ **The doctor diagnosed the problem⌃/: a sinus infection.**
  ⤷ ^

  ▶ **Boyd warns of the difficulty in describing Bach⌃/: "Even his**
  ⤷ ^
  physical appearance largely eludes us."

CHAPTER 59

Colons

Colons draw attention to what they introduce. They also have other conventional uses. A colon always follows an independent clause, but unlike the semicolon *(see pp. 510-13),* the element that follows it need not be an independent clause.

> *Note:* MLA recommends beginning an independent clause following a colon with a lowercase letter unless the first word is usually capitalized or the colon introduces a series of sentences, a question, or a rule.

59a   Use a colon after a complete sentence to introduce a list, an appositive, or a quotation.

A colon is used after a complete sentence (independent clause) to introduce lists, appositives (nouns or noun phrases that appear right after the word they rename), and quotations.

independent clause   *list*
▶ **Several majors interest me: biology, chemistry, and art.**

independent clause   *appositive*
▶ **She shared with me her favorite toys: a spatula and a pot lid.**

If you use *that is* or *namely* with an appositive, it should follow the colon: *She showed me another toy: namely, her mother's keys.*

► **He said the dreaded words: "Let's just be friends."**

independent clause   *quotation*

When you use a colon to introduce a sentence element, make sure the colon is preceded by an independent clause.

► **Three kinds of futility are dealt with in the novel: pervasive poverty, lost love, and inescapable aging.**

The words *the following* or *as follows* often appear at the end of the introductory clause.

59b Use a colon when a second closely related independent clause elaborates on the first one.

Use a colon when you want to emphasize the second clause.

► **I can predict tonight's sequence of events: my brother will arrive late, talk loudly, and eat too much.**

59c Use colons after salutations in business documents, to indicate ratios, to indicate times of day, to provide city and publisher citations in bibliographies, and to separate titles and subtitles.

► **Dear Mr. Worth: To:**

► **The ratio of armed to unarmed members of the gang was 3:1.**

► **He woke up at 6:30 in the morning.**

► **New York: McGraw Hill, 2021**

► ***Possible Lives: The Promise of Public Education in America***

Note: If you introduce a quotation with a signal phrase such as *he said* or *Morrison comments* instead of a complete sentence, you should use a comma, not a colon. *(For more on introducing quotations, see pp. 518–23.)*

59d Correct common colon errors.

• Remove a colon that appears between a verb and its object or complement.

► **The elements of a smoothie are yogurt, fresh fruit, and honey.**

- Remove a colon that appears between a preposition and its object or objects.

  ▶ Many feel that cancer can be prevented by a diet of̶ fruit, nuts, and vegetables.

- Remove a colon that appears after *such as, for example,* or *including.*

  ▶ I am ready for a change, such as̶ a vacation.

Note: When a complete sentence follows a colon, the first word may begin with either a capital or a lowercase letter. Be consistent throughout your document.

- Edit to remove more than one colon in a sentence.

  ▶ He was taken in by ~~a new con:~~ the lottery scam: victims are told they have won a prize and are asked to send financial information to a fake company.

CHAPTER 60

Apostrophes

Apostrophes show possession *(the dog's bone)* and indicate omitted letters in contractions *(don't).*

To determine whether a particular noun should be in the possessive form rather than plural, reword the sentence using the word *of (the bone of the dog).*

Apostrophes and Spelling Checkers

A spelling checker will sometimes highlight *its* used incorrectly (instead of *it's*) or an error in a possessive (for example, *Englands' glory*), but this identification is not consistent. Double-check all words that end in *-s* in your work.

60a Use apostrophes with nouns and indefinite pronouns to indicate possession.

For a noun to be possessive, two elements are usually required: a possessor; and a thing, person, or attribute that is possessed. Sometimes the thing possessed precedes the possessor: *The motorcycle is the student's.*

Sometimes the sentence may not name the thing possessed, but its identity is clearly understood by the reader: *I saw your cousin at Nick's.*

1. Deciding whether to use an apostrophe and an s or only an apostrophe
To form the possessive of a singular noun, add an apostrophe plus *-s* to the ending: *baby's.*

- To form the possessive of a plural noun that ends in *-s*, add only an apostrophe: *subjects', babies'.*
- To form the possessive of a plural noun that does not end in *-s*, add an apostrophe plus *-s: men's, cattle's.*
- To form the possessive of a singular proper noun ending in *-s*, add an apostrophe and an *-s: Du Bois's, Chris's.*
- To form the possessive of most indefinite pronouns, such as *no one, everyone, everything,* or *something,* add an apostrophe plus *-s: no one's, anybody's.*

2. Using the apostrophe in tricky situations   To express joint ownership, use the possessive form for the last name only; to express individual ownership, use the possessive form for each name.

▶ **Felicia and Elias's report**

▶ **The city's and the state's finances**

To form the possessive of compound words, add an apostrophe plus *s* to the last word in the compound.

▶ **My father-in-law's job**

To form the possessive of proper names, follow the rules given above *(Elisa's advice; Microsoft's program)*, with some exceptions. Place names that include a possessive noun generally lack an apostrophe, and many organizational names do as well: *Pikes Peak; Department of Veterans Affairs.*

60b   Use apostrophes to form contractions.

In a contraction, the apostrophe substitutes for omitted letters.

we've = we have	won't = will not (irregular)
weren't = were not	don't = do not
here's = here is	can't = cannot

In informal writing, apostrophes can substitute for omitted numbers in a decade: *the '50s.* Spell out the name of the decade in formal writing: *the fifties.*

> *Note:* Although the MLA and APA style manuals allow contractions in academic writing, some instructors think they are too informal. Check with your instructor before using contractions.

 60c   Distinguish between contractions and possessive pronouns.

The following pairs of **homonyms** (words that sound alike but have different meanings) often cause problems for writers. Note that the apostrophe is used only in the contraction.

CONTRACTION	POSSESSIVE PRONOUN
it's (it is or it has)	its
It's too hot.	The dog scratched *its* fleas.
you're (you are)	your
You're a lucky guy.	Is that *your* new car?
who's (who is)	whose
Who's there?	The man *whose* dog was lost called us.
they're (they are)	their*
They're reading poetry.	They gave *their* lives.

*The adverb *there* is also confused with *their:* She was standing *there* [not *their*].

60d   Using an apostrophe with *s* to form plural letters and words used as words is optional.

An apostrophe plus *s* (*'s*) can be used to show the plural of a letter. Underline or italicize single letters but not the apostrophe or the *s*. (Do not italicize letter grades.)

► **Committee has two *m*'s, two *t*'s, and two *e*'s.**

If a word is used as a word rather than as a symbol of the meaning it conveys, it can be made plural by adding an apostrophe plus *s*. The word should be italicized or underlined, but the *'s* should not be. If the word is in quotation marks, you should always use *'s* when you are forming the plural.

► **There are twenty-five *no*'s [or "no's"] in the first paragraph.**

60e   Watch out for common misuses of the apostrophe.

Never use an apostrophe with *s* to form a plural noun.

► The ~~teacher's~~ *teachers* asked the girls and boys for their attention.

(See pp. 545–46 for more on forming plural nouns.)

Never use an apostrophe with *s* to form the present tense of a verb paired with a third-person singular subject (*he, she, it,* or a singular noun).

► A professional singer ~~need's~~ *needs* to practice a lot.

Never use an apostrophe with the possessive form of a pronoun such as *hers, ours,* or *theirs.*

► That cat of ~~our's~~ *ours* is always sleeping!

(See 60c for advice on distinguishing contractions [it's] *from possessive pronouns* [its].*)*

Never use an apostrophe with *s* to form the plural of a surname.

► The ~~Clinton's~~ *Clintons* made history when Hillary was elected to the

Senate during the same year Bill left the White House.

MLA and APA style recommend against using an apostrophe to form plurals of numbers and abbreviations. You may see that usage elsewhere.

► He makes his ~~2's~~ *2s* look like ~~5's~~ *5s*.

► Professor Sanchez has two ~~PhD's~~ *PhDs*.

CHAPTER 61

Quotation Marks

Quotation marks enclose words, phrases, and sentences that are quoted directly; titles of short works such as poems, articles, songs, and short stories; and words and phrases used in a special sense.

> **Note:** Citations and formatting instructions in this chapter follow MLA style. See Tabs 7 and 8 for examples of APA, Chicago, and CSE styles.

Quotation Marks and Grammar Checkers

A grammar checker can alert you to the lack of an opening or closing quotation mark, but it cannot determine where a quotation should begin and end. Grammar checkers also may not point out errors in the use of quotation marks with other marks of punctuation. For example, a grammar checker did not highlight the error in the placement of the period at the end of the following sentence *(see 61f, pp. 521–22).*

INCORRECT

▶ **Commenting on the power of a single click, Angela Lee, professor of Journalism and Emerging Media at the University of Texas, explains, "We should have the sense of responsibility that anything you click on will affect other people".**

61a Use quotation marks to indicate the exact words of a speaker or writer.

Direct quotations from written material may include whole sentences or only a few words or phrases. They can lend immediacy to your writing.

▶ **In *Angela's Ashes,* Frank McCourt writes, "Worse than the ordinary miserable childhood is the miserable Irish childhood" (11).**

▶ **Frank McCourt believes that being Irish worsens what is all too "ordinary"—a "miserable childhood" (11).**

Use quotation marks to enclose everything a speaker says in written dialogue. If the quoted sentence is interrupted by a phrase like *he said,* enclose just the quotation in quotation marks. When another person begins to speak, start a new paragraph to indicate a change in speaker.

"I don't know what you're talking about," he said. "I did listen to everything you told me."

"If you had been listening, you would have known what I was talking about."

If a speaker continues for more than a paragraph, begin each subsequent paragraph with an opening quotation mark, but do not insert a closing quotation mark until the end of the quotation.

Note: Do not use quotation marks to set off an indirect quotation, which reports what a speaker said but does not use the exact words.

▶ **He said that "he didn't know what I was talking about."**

Two or three lines of poetry may be run in to your text, much like any other *short* quotation. Line breaks are shown with a slash. Leave a space before and after the slash. *(See also 62h, pp. 529-30.)*

▶   **Wordsworth writes of the weary acquisitiveness of our modern age: "The world is too much with us; late and soon, / Getting and spending, we lay waste our powers" (lines 1–2).**

> *Note:* In MLA style, line numbers appear in parentheses following the quotation. The word *lines* should precede the numbers the first time the poem is quoted.

61b   Set off long quotations in indented blocks.

Set off a quotation that is longer than four typed lines as a block quotation. *(For instructions on formatting block quotations, see Tab 5: Researching, p. 191.)* A block quotation is *not* surrounded by quotation marks. If the text you are quoting includes another direct quotation, however, use quotation marks to set those words off.

61c   Enclose a quotation within a quotation with single quotation marks.

Use single quotation marks to set off a quotation within a quotation.

▶   **In response to alumni, the president of the university said, "I know you're saying to me, 'We want a winning football team.' But I'm telling you that I want an honest football team."**

61d   Use quotation marks to enclose titles of short works such as articles, poems, and stories.

The titles of long works, such as books, are usually put in italics (or underlined). *(See Chapter 66, pp. 538-40.)* The titles of book chapters, essays, most poems, and other short works are usually put in quotation marks. Quotation marks are also used for titles of unpublished works, including student writing, theses, and dissertations.

Works That Should Be Enclosed in Quotation Marks

- **Essays:** "Once More to the Lake"
- **Songs:** "Seven Nation Army"
- **Short poems:** "Daffodils"
- **Short stories:** "The Tell-Tale Heart"
- **Articles in periodicals:** "Scotland Yard of the Wild" (from *American Way*)

- **Book chapters or sections:** "Microcredit: The Financial Revolution" (Chapter 11 of *Half the Sky*)

- **Episodes of radio and television programs:** "I Can't Remember" (on *48 Hours*)

- **Titles of unpublished works,** including student works, theses, and dissertations: "Breaking News: Blogging's Impact on Traditional and New Media" (Do not use quotation marks to enclose the title of your own work on its title page.)

If quotation marks are needed within the title of a short work, use single quotation marks: "The 'Animal Rights' War on Medicine."

61e Use quotation marks to indicate that a word or phrase is being used in a special way.

Put quotation marks around a word or phrase that someone else has used in a way that you or your readers may not agree with. These quotation marks function as raised eyebrows do in conversation and should be used sparingly.

▶ **The "worker's paradise" of Stalinist Russia included slave-labor camps.**

Words cited as words can also be put in quotation marks, although the more common practice is to italicize them.

▶ **The words "compliment" and "complement" sound alike but have different meanings.**

Definitions and translations should appear in quotation marks.

▶ *Agua* **means "water" in Spanish.**

61f Place punctuation marks within or outside quotation marks, as convention and your meaning require.

As you edit, check all closing single and double quotation marks and the marks of punctuation that appear next to them to make sure that you have placed them in the right order.

1. Periods and commas   Always place the period or comma before the final quotation mark, even when the quotation is brief.

▶ **"Instead of sharing an experience the spectator must come to grips with things," Brecht writes in "The Epic Theatre and Its Difficulties."**

However, place the period or comma after a parenthetical reference.

▶ **Brecht wants the spectator to "come to grips with things" (23).**

2. Question marks and exclamation points Place a question mark or an exclamation point after the final quotation mark if the quoted material is not itself a question or an exclamation.

▶ **How does epic theatre make us "come to grips with things"?**

Place a question mark or an exclamation point inside the final quotation mark when it is part of the quotation. No additional punctuation is needed, unless you are adding a parenthetical citation in MLA style (see the third example following).

▶ **"Are we to see science in the theatre?" he was asked.**

▶ **Brecht was asked, "Are we to see science in the theatre?"**

▶ **Brecht was asked, "Are we to see science in the theatre?" (27).**

3. Colons and semicolons Place colons and semicolons after the final quotation mark.

▶ **Dean Wilcox cited the items he called his "daily delights": a free parking space for his scooter at the faculty club, a special table in the club itself, and friends to laugh with after a day's work.**

4. Dashes Place a dash outside either an opening or a closing quotation mark if the dash precedes or follows the quotation or outside both if two dashes are used to set off the quotation.

▶ **One phrase—"time is running out"—haunted me.**

Place a dash inside either an opening or a closing quotation mark if it is part of the quotation.

▶ **"Where is the—" she called. "Oh, here it is. Never mind."**

(For more on integrating quotations into your sentences, see Chapter 24, Working with Sources and Avoiding Plagiarism, pp. 237–54.)

61g Edit to correct common errors in using quotation marks.

- **Avoid using quotation marks to distance yourself from slang, clichés, and trite expressions.** Instead, stay away from overused or slang expressions in college writing. If your writing situation permits slang, however, do not enclose it in quotation marks.

    ▶ **Californians are so "laid back."**

- Revising the sentence is usually a better solution.

    ▶ **Many Californians have a carefree attitude.**

- **Do not use quotation marks for indirect quotations.** Watch out for errors in pronoun reference as well. *(See Tab 10: Editing for Grammar Conventions, pp. 451-95.)*

  ► He told his boss that /the company had lost its largest account./"

- Another way to correct this sentence is to change to a direct quotation.

  ► He said to his boss, "We just lost our largest account."

- **Do not add another question mark or exclamation point to the end of a quotation that already ends in one of these marks.**

  ► What did Juliet mean when she cried, "O Romeo, Romeo! Wherefore art thou Romeo?"?

- If you quote a question within a sentence that makes a statement, place a question mark before the closing quotation mark and a period at the end of the sentence.

  ► "What was Henry Ford's greatest contribution to the Industrial Revolution?" he asked.

- **Do not enclose the title of your own essay on the title page or above the first line of the text in quotation marks.**

  ► /Edgar Allan Poe and the Paradox of the Gothic/

- If you use a quotation or a title of a short work in your title, though, put quotation marks around it.

  ► Edgar Allan Poe's "The Raven" and the Paradox of the Gothic

CHAPTER 62

Other Punctuation Marks

Punctuation and Grammar Checkers

Your grammar checker might highlight a period used instead of a question mark at the end of a question. However, grammar checkers will not tell you when you might use a pair of dashes or parentheses to set material off in a sentence or when you need a second dash or parentheses to enclose parenthetical material.

62a Use a period to end sentences and with some abbreviations.

Use a period to end all sentences apart from direct questions or exclamations.

STATEMENT

This book contains more than one thousand periods.

STATEMENT CONTAINING AN INDIRECT QUESTION

She asked me where I had gone to college.

POLITE REQUEST

Please read Chapter 5 for next week.

A period or periods are conventionally used with the following common abbreviations, which end in lowercase letters.

Mr.	Mrs.	i.e.	Mass.
Ms.	Dr.	e.g.	Jan.

If the abbreviation is made up of capital letters, however, the periods are optional. Do not put a space after an internal period.

RN (or R.N.)	BA (or B.A.)
MD (or M.D.)	PhD (or Ph.D.)

Periods are omitted in abbreviations for organizations, famous people, states in mailing addresses, and acronyms (words made up of initials).

FBI	JFK	MA	NATO
CIA	LBJ	TX	NAFTA

When in doubt, consult a dictionary.

When an abbreviation ends a sentence, the period at the end of the abbreviation serves as the period for the sentence. If a question mark or an exclamation point ends the sentence, place it *after* the period in the abbreviation.

▶ **When he was in the seventh grade, we called him "Stinky," but now he is William Percival Abernathy, Ph.D.!**

62b Use a question mark after a direct question.

▶ **Who wrote *The Old Man and the Sea*?**

Occasionally, a question mark changes a statement into a question.

▶ **You expect me to believe a story like that?**

When questions follow one another in a series, each one can be followed by a question mark even if they are not all complete sentences. Question fragments may begin with a capital or lowercase letter.

► **What will you contribute? Your time? Your talent? Your money?**

Use a question mark in parentheses to indicate a questionable date, number, or word, but do not use it to convey an ironic meaning.

► **Chaucer was born in 1340 (?) and lived until 1400.**

► **His dog had graduated from obedience (?) training.**

Do not use a question mark after an indirect question.

► **He asked her whether she would be at home later?.**

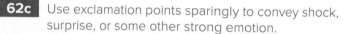

Do not use a period or comma after a question mark that ends a direct quotation.

► **She asked, "What is the word count?"./**

62c Use exclamation points sparingly to convey shock, surprise, or some other strong emotion.

► **Stolen! The money was stolen! Right before our eyes, somebody snatched my purse and ran off with it.**

Using numerous exclamation points throughout a document actually weakens their force. Try to convey emotion with your choice of words and your sentence structure.

► **Jefferson and Adams both died on the same day in 1826, exactly fifty years after the signing of the Declaration of Independence!.**

> The fact the sentence reports is surprising enough without the addition of an exclamation point.

Do not use a period or comma after an exclamation point that ends a direct quotation.

62d Use the dash to emphasize the words that precede or follow.

A typeset dash, sometimes called an *em dash,* is a single, unbroken line about as wide as a capital M. Most word-processing programs provide the em dash as a special character or will convert two hyphens to an em dash as an automatic function. Otherwise, you can make a dash by typing two hyphens in a row with no space between them. Do not put a space before or after the dash.

1. Highlighting an explanation or a list   A dash indicates a strong pause and emphasizes what comes immediately before or after it.

► **Coca-Cola, potato chips, and brevity—these are the marks of a good study session.**

► **I think the Comets will win the tournament for one reason—their goalie.**

A colon could also be used in the second example. *(See Chapter 59, pp. 513-15.)*

If an appositive consists of a list of items, use dashes to set it off more clearly for readers.

► **The symptoms of hay fever/sneezing, coughing, itchy eyes/can be controlled with over-the-counter medications.**

Do not separate a subject and verb with a dash, however.

► **Haydn, Mozart, and Beethoven/are famous composers.**

2. Setting off a nonessential phrase or independent clause within a sentence

► **All finite creations—including humans—are incomplete and contradictory.**

► **The first rotary gasoline engine—it was made by Mazda—burned 15 percent more fuel than conventional engines.**

3. Indicating a sudden change in tone or idea

► **Breathing heavily, the archaeologist opened the old chest in wild anticipation and found—an old pair of socks and an empty soda can.**

Caution: The dash can make your writing disjointed if overused.

► **After we found the puppy/shivering under the porch/, we brought her into the house—into the entryway, actually—and wrapped her in an old towel/to warm her up.**

62e   Use parentheses for nonessential information.

Parentheses should be used infrequently and only to set off supplementary information, a digression, or a comment that interrupts the flow of thought within a sentence or paragraph.

► **The tickets (ranging in price from $10 to $50) go on sale Monday.**

When parentheses enclose a whole sentence, the sentence begins with a capital letter and ends with a period before the final parenthesis. A sentence that appears inside parentheses *within a sentence* should neither begin with a capital letter nor end with a period.

► **Folktales and urban legends often reflect the concerns of a particular era. (The familiar tale of a cat accidentally caught in a microwave oven is an example.)**

► **Angela Merkel (she is the first female chancellor of Germany) formed a coalition government following her election in 2005.**

If the material in parentheses is at the end of an introductory or nonessential word group followed by a comma, place the comma after the closing parenthesis. A comma should never appear before the opening parenthesis.

► **As the soloist walked onstage/(carrying her famous violin), the audience rose to its feet.**

Parentheses enclose numbers or letters that label items in a list.

► **He says the argument is nonsense because (1) university presidents don't work as well as machines, (2) university presidents don't do any real work at all, and (3) universities should be run by faculty committees.**

Parentheses also enclose in-text citations in many systems of documenting sources. *(For more on documenting sources, see Tabs 6–8.)*

62f   When quoting, use brackets to set off material that is not part of the original quotation.

Use brackets to set off information you add to a quotation.

► **Samuel Eliot Morison has written, "This passage has attracted a good deal of scorn to the Florentine mariner [Verrazano], but without justice."**

In this sentence, the writer places the name of the "Florentine mariner"—Verrazano—in brackets so readers will know his identity.

You can also place brackets around words you insert within a quotation to make it fit the grammar or style of your own sentence. If you replace a word with your own word in brackets, you do not need ellipses.

► **At the end of *Pygmalion,* Henry Higgins confesses to Eliza Doolittle that he has "grown accustomed to [her] voice and appearance."**

To make the quotation fit properly into the sentence, the bracketed word *her* is inserted in place of *your.*

Use brackets to enclose the word *sic* (Latin for "thus") after a word in a quotation that was incorrect in the original. If you are following MLA style, the word *sic* should not be underlined or italicized.

► **The critic noted that "the battle scenes in *The Patriot* are realistic, but the rest of the film is historically inacurate [sic]."**

Use *sic* sparingly because it can appear condescending.

If you change the first letter of a word in a quotation to a capital or low-ercase letter, enclose the letter in brackets: *Ackroyd writes, "[F]or half a million years there has been in London a pattern of habitation and hunting, if not settlement."*

If you need to set off words within material that is already in parentheses, use brackets: *(I found the information on a Web site published by the National Institutes of Health [NIH].)*

Note: MLA style calls for brackets around ellipses that you insert to show omission from a source that already contains ellipses in the original.

62g   Use ellipses to indicate that words have been omitted.

Use three spaced periods, called ellipses or an ellipsis mark, to show readers that you have omitted words from a passage you are quoting. Some instructors suggest that you use brackets to enclose any ellipses you add. *(See the note above regarding MLA style.)*

FULL QUOTATION FROM A WORK BY WILKINS

In the nineteenth century, railroads, lacing their way across continents, reaching into the heart of every major city in Europe and America, and bringing a new romance to travel, added to the unity of nations and fueled the nationalist fires already set burning by the French Revolution and the wars of Napoleon.

EDITED QUOTATION

In his account of nineteenth-century society, Wilkins argues that "railroads . . . added to the unity of nations and fueled the nationalist fires already set burning by the French Revolution and the wars of Napoleon."

If you are leaving out the end of a quoted sentence, the three ellipsis points are preceded by a period to end the sentence.

EDITED QUOTATION

In describing the growth of railroads, Wilkins pictures them "lacing their way across continents, reaching into the heart of every major city in Europe and America. . . ."

When you need to add a parenthetical reference after the ellipses at the end of a sentence, place it after the quotation mark but before the final period: . . ." (253).

Ellipses are usually not needed to indicate an omission when only a word or phrase is being quoted.

► **Railroads brought "a new romance to travel," according to Wilkins.**

To indicate the omission of an entire line or more from the middle of a poem, insert a line of spaced periods.

> Shelley seems to be describing nature, but what's really at issue is the seductive nature of desire:
>
> > See the mountains kiss high Heaven,
> >
> > And the waves clasp one another;
> >
> > . . . .
> >
> > What is all this sweet work worth
> >
> > If thou kiss not me? (1-2, 7-8)

Use ellipses only as a means of shortening a quotation, never as a device for changing its fundamental meaning or emphasis.

You can use ellipses at the end, or in the middle of a sentence if you mean to leave a thought hanging. In the following passage, Annie Dillard uses an ellipsis to suggest a distance so great that it is perhaps not quantifiable using words alone.

► **More men in all of time have died at fishing than at any other human activity except perhaps the making of war. You go out so far . . . and you are blown, or stove, or swamped and never seen again.**

Ellipses also indicate pauses or interruptions in speech.

62h   Use slashes according to convention.

Use the slash to show divisions between lines of poetry when you quote more than one line of a poem as part of a sentence. Add a space on either side of the slash. When you are quoting four or more lines of poetry, use a block quotation instead *(see p. 520 and the preceding discussion)*.

► **The speaker of Mohsen Emadi's poem "Losses" believes that "the invention of the human being / might have been a mistake."**

The slash is sometimes used between two words that represent choices or combinations. Do not add spaces around the slash when you use it in this way.

► **The college offers three credit/noncredit courses.**

Slashes (called *forward slashes*) also mark divisions in online addresses (URLs): http://www.georgetown.edu/crossroads/navigate.html.

Some writers use the slash as a marker between the words *and* and *or,* or between *he* and *she* and *his* and *her* to avoid sexism. Most writers, however, consider such usage awkward. It is usually better to rephrase the sentence. *(See also Tab 10: Editing for Grammar Conventions, pp. 451-95.)*

▶   **A bill can originate in the House of Representatives, ~~and/or~~ the**
  Senate.

in (above "and/or")
, or both (before Senate)

CHAPTER 63

Capitalization

Many rules for the use of capital letters have been fixed by custom, such as the convention of beginning each sentence with a capital letter, but the rules change all the time. A recent dictionary is a good guide to capitalization.

✓ **63a**   Capitalize proper nouns (names), words derived from them, brand names, certain abbreviations, and call letters.

Proper nouns are the names of specific people, places, or things. Capitalize proper nouns, words derived from proper nouns, brand names, abbreviations of capitalized words, and call letters of radio and television stations.

> **Proper nouns:** Ronald Reagan, the Transamerica Pyramid
>
> **Words derived from proper nouns:** Reaganomics, Siamese cat *but* french fries, simonize
>
> **Brand names:** Apple, Kleenex, *but* eBay
>
> **Abbreviations:** FBI (government agency), A&E (cable television station)
>
> **Call letters:** WNBC (television), WMNR (radio)

> **Note:** Seasons, such as *summer,* and the days of the month given as numbers are not capitalized when they are spelled out: *Valentine's Day falls in the middle of <u>winter,</u> on the <u>fourteenth</u> of February.*

63b   Capitalize titles when they appear before a proper name but not when they are used alone or after the name.

> **Family members:** Aunt Lou, *but* my aunt, Father (name used alone) *or* my father
>
> **Political Figures:** Governor Andrew Cuomo, Senator Olympia Snowe, *but* the governor, my senator

Most writers do not capitalize the title *president* unless they are referring to the President of the United States.

63c Capitalize titles of works of literature, works of art, and musical compositions.

Capitalize the important words in titles and subtitles. Do not capitalize articles *(a, an,* and *the),* the *to* in infinitives, or prepositions and coordinating conjunctions unless they begin or end the title or subtitle. Capitalize both parts of a hyphenated word. In MLA style, capitalize subordinating conjunctions *(Because).* Capitalize the first word after a colon or semicolon in a title. Capitalize titles of major divisions of a work, such as chapters.

Book: *Water for Elephants*
Play: *The Importance of Being Earnest*
Building: the Eiffel Tower
Ships, aircraft: the *Titanic,* the *Concorde*
Painting: the *Mona Lisa*
Article or essay: "Next-Generation Scientists"
Poem: "Stopping by Woods on a Snowy Evening"
Music: "The Star-Spangled Banner"
Chapter: "Capitalization" in *A Writer's Resource*

63d Capitalize names of areas and regions.

Names of geographic regions are generally capitalized if they are well established, like *the Midwest* and *Central Europe.* Names of directions, as in the sentence *Turn south,* are not capitalized.

CORRECT   *East* meets *West* at the summit.

CORRECT   You will need to go *west* on Sunset.

The word *western,* when used as a general direction or the name of a genre *(the western* High Noon), is not capitalized except when it is part of the name of a specific region: *I visited Western Europe last year.*

63e Follow standard practice for capitalizing names of races, ethnic groups, and sacred things.

Traditionally, the words *black* and *white* have not been capitalized when they refer to members of racial groups because they are adjectives that substitute for the implied common nouns *black person* and *white person.* However, more recently, respected style guides have begun capitalizing the word *Black* when used in reference to racial and cultural identity. In general, the names of ethnic groups and races are capitalized: *Egyptians, Italians, Asians.*

PROPER AND COMMON NOUNS

- **People:** Helena Bonham Carter, Sonia Sotomayor, Bill Gates
- **Nationalities, ethnic groups, and languages:** English, Swiss, African Americans, Arabs, Chinese, Turkish
- **Places:** the United States of America, Tennessee, the Irunia Restaurant, the Great Lakes, *but* my state, the lake
- **Organizations and institutions:** Phi Beta Kappa, Republican Party (Republicans), Department of Defense, Cumberland College, the North Carolina Tarheels, *but* the department, this college, our hockey team
- **Religious bodies, books, and figures:** Jews, Christians, Baptists, Hindus, Roman Catholic Church, the Bible, the Koran *or* Qur'an, the Torah, God, Holy Spirit, Allah, *but* a Greek goddess, a biblical reference
- **Scientific names and terms:** *Homo sapiens, H. sapiens, Acer rubrum, A. rubrum,* Addison's disease (*or* Addison disease), Cenozoic era, Newton's first law, *but* the law of gravity
- **Names of planets, stars, and other astronomical bodies:** Earth (as a planet) *but* the earth, Mercury, Polaris *or* the North Star, Whirlpool Galaxy, *but* a star, that galaxy, the solar system
- **Computer terms:** the Internet *or* the Web, *but* search engine, a network, my browser
- **Days, months, and holidays:** Monday, Veterans Day, August, the Fourth of July, *but* yesterday, spring and summer, the winter term, second-quarter earnings
- **Historical events, movements, periods, and documents:** World War II, Impressionism, the Renaissance, the Jazz Age, the Declaration of Independence, the Magna Carta, *but* the last war, a golden age, the twentieth century, the amendment
- **Academic subjects and courses:** English 101, Psychology 221, a course in Italian, *but* a physics course, my art history class

Many religious terms, such as *sacrament, altar,* and *rabbi,* are not capitalized. The word *Bible* is capitalized (though *biblical* is not), but not when used as a metaphor for an essential book.

► His book **Winning at Stud Poker** used to be the bible of gamblers.

63f Capitalize the first word of a quoted sentence but not the first word of an indirect quotation.

► She cried, "Help!"

► He said that jazz was one of America's major art forms.

The first word of a quotation from a printed source is capitalized if the quotation is introduced with a phrase such as *she notes* or *he concludes.*

▶ **Jim, the narrator of *My Ántonia,* concludes, "Whatever we had missed, we possessed together the precious, the incommunicable past" (324).**

When a quotation from a printed source is treated as an element in your sentence and not as a sentence on its own, the first word is not capitalized.

▶ **Jim took comfort in sharing with Ántonia "the precious, the incommunicable past" (324).**

If you need to change the first letter of a quotation to fit your sentence, enclose the letter in brackets.

▶ **The lawyer noted that "[t]he man seen leaving the area after the blast was not the same height as the defendant."**

If you interrupt the sentence you are quoting with an expression such as *he said,* the first word of the rest of the quotation should not be capitalized.

▶ **"When I come home an hour later," she explained, "the trains are usually less crowded."**

When quoting a text directly, reproduce the capitalization used in the original source, whether or not it is correct by today's standards.

▶ **Blake's marginalia include the following comment: "Paine is either a Devil or an Inspired Man" (603).**

63g   Capitalize the first word of a sentence.

A capital letter is used to signal the beginning of a new sentence.

▶ **Robots reduce human error, so they produce uniform products.**

Sentences in parentheses also begin with a capital letter unless they are embedded within another sentence:

▶ **Although the week began with the news that he was hit by a car, by Thursday we knew he was going to be all right. (It was a terrible way to begin the week, though.)**

▶ **Although the week began with the news that he was hit by a car (it was a terrible way to begin the week), by Thursday we knew he was going to be all right.**

63h   Capitalizing the first word of an independent clause after a colon is optional.

If what follows a colon is not a complete sentence, do not capitalize the first word. If it is a complete sentence, according to most style guides, you may capitalize it or not, but be consistent. According to MLA, if it is a complete sentence, it should be lowercase unless the word is always capitalized or when the colon introduces a series of sentences, a rule or principle, or a question:

► **The panelists agreed: Current climate change goals are unrealistic.**

or

► **The panelists agreed: current climate change goals are unrealistic.**

► **The question is serious: Do you think peace is possible?**

CHAPTER 64

Abbreviations and Symbols

Unless you are writing a scientific or technical report, spell out most terms and titles, except in the cases discussed in this chapter. You may also want to consult your discipline's style manual for guidelines.

64a Abbreviate familiar titles that always precede or follow a person's name.

Some abbreviations appear before a person's name *(Mr., Ms., Mrs., Dr.)*, and some follow a proper name *(Jr., Sr., MD, Esq., PhD)*. When an abbreviation follows a person's name, place a comma between the name and the abbreviation. Many writers consider the comma before *Jr.* and *Sr.* to be optional, but MLA recommends using one: *Martin Luther King, Jr.* Spell out religious, government, and professional titles such as Rev. (Reverend) in academic writing and when they appear with only the last name.

- **Before names:** Mrs. Jean Bascom; Dr. Epstein
- **After names:** Robert Robinson Jr. or Robert Robinson, Jr.; Elaine Less, CPA, LL.D.

Do not use two abbreviations that represent the same thing: *Dr. Peter Joyce, MD.* Use either *Dr. Peter Joyce* or *Peter Joyce, MD.*

Spell out titles used without proper names, and do not capitalize them.

► **Mr. Carew asked if she had seen the** d̶r̶. *doctor.*

64b Use abbreviations only when you know your readers will understand them.

If you use a technical term or the name of an organization in a report, you may abbreviate it as long as your readers are likely to be familiar with the abbreviation. For example, a medical writer might use PT *(physical therapy)* in a medical

┌─ NAVIGATING THROUGH COLLEGE AND BEYOND

Scientific and Latin Abbreviations

Most abbreviations used in scientific or technical writing, such as those related to measurement, should be given without periods: *mph, lb, dc, rpm.* If an abbreviation looks like an actual word, however, you can use a period to prevent confusion: *in., Fig.* In some types of scholarly writing, Latin abbreviations are acceptable (in parenthetical statements and notes).

report or professional newsletter. Abbreviations of three or more capital letters generally do not use periods: *CBS, EPA, IRS, NAACP, USA.*

FAMILIAR ABBREVIATION	The EPA has had a lasting impact on the air quality of this country.
UNFAMILIAR ABBREVIATION	After you have completed them, take these *the Human Resources and Education Center (HREC)* forms to ~~HREC~~.

> **Note:** In the body of a paper, you can use *US* as an adjective *(US Constitution)* but not as a noun *(I grew up outside the United States).*

Write out an unfamiliar term or name the first time you use it, and give the abbreviation in parentheses.

▶ **The Student Nonviolent Coordinating Committee (SNCC) was far to the left of other civil rights organizations. However, SNCC quickly burned itself out and disappeared.**

64c   Abbreviate words typically used with times, dates, and numerals, as well as units of measurement in charts and graphs.

Use abbreviations or symbols associated with numbers only when they accompany a number: *3 p.m.,* not *in the p.m.; $500,* not *How many $ do you have?* The abbreviation B.C. ("Before Christ") follows a date; A.D. ("in the year of our Lord") precedes the date. The alternative abbreviations B.C.E. ("Before the Common Era") and C.E. ("Common Era") can be used instead of B.C. and A.D., respectively; both of these follow the date.

6:00 p.m. or 6:00 P.M. or 6 PM	9:45 a.m. or 9:45 A.M. or 9:45 AM
498 B.C. or 498 BC or	A.D. 275 or AD 275
498 B.C.E. or 498 BCE	or 275 C.E. or 275 CE
6,000 rpm	271 cm

In charts and graphs, abbreviations and symbols such as = for *equals, in.* for *inches, %* for *percent,* and *$* with numbers are acceptable because they save space.

> **Note:** MLA suggests spelling out percentages expressed in one to three words in contexts with few numbers (*ten percent, fifty-five percent*).

64d Avoid Latin abbreviations in formal writing.

In formal writing, it is usually a good idea to avoid even common Latin abbreviations (*e.g., et al., etc.,* and *i.e.*). Instead of *e.g. (exempli gratia),* use *such as* or *for example.*

cf.	compare *(confer)*
et al.	and others *(et alia)*
etc.	and so forth, and so on *(et cetera)*
i.e.	that is *(id est)*
N.B.	note well *(nota bene)*
viz.	namely *(videlicet)*

64e Avoid inappropriate abbreviations and symbols.

Days of the week *(Sat.),* places *(TX* or *Tex.),* the word *company (Co.),* people's names *(Wm.),* disciplines and professions *(econ.),* parts of speech *(v.),* parts of written works *(ch., p.),* symbols *(@),* and units of measurement *(lb)* are all spelled out in formal writing.

► **The *environmental* (not *env.*) engineers from the Paramus Water Company (not *Co.*) are arriving in *New York City* (not *NYC*) this Thursday (not *Thurs.*) to correct the problems in the *physical education* (not *phys. ed.*) building in time for *Christmas* (not *Xmas*).**

If an ampersand (&) or an abbreviation such as *Inc., Co.,* or *Corp.* is part of a company's official name, however, you can use it in formal writing: *Apple Inc. announced these changes in late December.*

Use *-s,* not *-'s,* to make abbreviations plural (two *DVDs*).

CHAPTER 65

Numbers

65a In nontechnical writing, spell out numbers up to one hundred, and round numbers greater than one hundred.

► **Approximately *two hundred fifty* students passed the exam, but *twenty-five* students failed.**

When you are using a great many numbers, or when a spelled-out number would require more than three or four words, use numerals.

► **This regulation affects nearly *10,500* taxpayers, substantially more than the *200* originally projected. Of those affected, *2,325* filled out the papers incorrectly, and another *743* called the office for help.**

Round numbers larger than one million are expressed in numerals and words: 8 million, 2.4 trillion.

Use all numerals rather than mixing numerals and spelled-out words for the same type of item in a passage.

► **We wrote to 132 people but only ~~sixteen~~ responded.**

Exceptions: When two numbers appear together, spell out one, and use numerals for the other: *two 20-pound bags.*

65b   Spell out a number that begins a sentence.

If a numeral begins a sentence, reword the sentence, or spell out the numeral.

► ***Twenty-five* children are in each elementary class.**

65c   In technical and business writing, use numerals for exact measurements and all numbers greater than ten.

► **The endosperm halves were placed in each of 14 small glass test tubes.**

► **Sample solutions with GA₃ concentrations ranging from 0 g/mL to 10⁵ g/mL were added, one to each test tube.**

► **With its $1.9 trillion economy, Germany has an important trade role to play.**

65d   Use numerals for dates, times of day, addresses, and similar kinds of conventional quantitative information.

- **Dates:** October 9, 2009; 1558–1603; A.D. 1066 (*or* AD 1066); *but* October ninth, May first
- **Time of day:** 6 A.M. (*or* AM *or* a.m.), a quarter past eight in the evening, three o'clock in the morning
- **Addresses:** 21 Meadow Road, Apt. 6J, Grand Island, NY 14072
- **Percentages:** 73 percent, 73%
- **Fractions and decimals:** 21.84, 6½, two-thirds (*not* 2-thirds), a fourth
- **Measurements:** 100 miles per hour (*or* 100 mph), 9 kilograms (*or* 9 kg), 38°F, 15°Celsius, 3 tablespoons (*or* 3 T), 4 liters (*or* 4 L), 18 inches (*or* 18 in.)
- **Volume, chapter, page:** volume 4, chapter 8, page 44
- **Scenes in a play:** *Hamlet,* act 2, scene 1, lines 77–84

- **Scores and statistics:** 0 to 3, 98–92, an average age of 35
- **Amounts of money:** 10¢ (*or* 10 cents), $125, $2.25, $2.8 million (*or* $2,800,000)
- **Serial or identification numbers:** batch number 4875, 105.5 on the AM dial
- **Surveys:** 9 of 10
- **Telephone numbers:** (716) 555-2174

To make a number plural, add -*s*.

Note: In nontechnical writing, spell out the names of units of measurement *(inches, liters)* in text. Use abbreviations *(in., L)* and symbols *(%)* in charts and graphs to save space.

CHAPTER 66

Italics (Underlining)

Italics, characters in a typeface that slants to the right, are used to set off certain words and phrases. If italics are not available or if your instructor prefers, however, you may underline words that would be typeset in italics. MLA style requires italics.

► **Daniel Day-Lewis gives one of his best performances in *There Will Be Blood.***

► **Daniel Day-Lewis gives one of his best performances in There Will Be Blood.**

66a Italicize (or underline) titles of lengthy works or separate publications.

Italicize (or underline) titles of long works or works that are not part of a larger publication.

Works That Should Be Italicized (or Underlined)

- **Books (including textbooks):** *The Color of Water, The Art of Public Speaking*
- **Magazines and journals:** *Texas Monthly, College English*
- **Newspapers:** *Chicago Tribune*
- **Comic strips:** *Dilbert*

- **Plays, films, television series, radio programs, podcasts:** *Death of a Salesman, On the Waterfront, American Idol, Fresh Air, The Moth*
- **Long musical compositions:** Beethoven's *Pastoral Symphony* (*But* Beethoven's Symphony No. 6—the title consists of the musical form, a number, and/or a key.)
- **Choreographic works:** Balanchine's *Jewels*
- **Artworks:** Edward Hopper's *Nighthawks*
- **Web sites:** *Slate*
- **Software:** *Microsoft PowerPoint*
- **Long poems:** *Odyssey*
- **Pamphlets:** *Gorges: A Guide to the Geology of the Ithaca Area*
- **Electronic databases:** *Academic Search Premier*

According to MLA and APA style, in titles of lengthy works, *a, an,* or *the* is capitalized and italicized (or underlined) if it is the first word. However, in Chicago style, *the* is not generally treated as part of the title in names of newspapers and periodicals: the *New York Times.*

Note: Do not use italics or underlining when referring to the Bible and other sacred books.

Court cases may also be italicized or underlined, but legal documents and laws are not: the Constitution.

▶ In *Brown v. Board of Education of Topeka* (1954), the U.S. Supreme Court ruled that segregation in public schools is unconstitutional.

▶ He obtained a writ of habeas corpus.

Do not italicize or underline punctuation marks that follow a title unless they are part of the title: I finally finished reading *Moby Dick*!

Quotation marks are used for the titles of short works—essays, newspaper and magazine articles and columns, short stories, short poems, and individual Web pages. Quotation marks are also used for titles of unpublished works when they are referred to within a text, including student writing, theses, and dissertations. *(See Chapter 61, pp. 518-23, for more on quotation marks with titles.)*

66b   Italicize (or underline) the names of ships, trains, aircraft, and spaceships.

Queen Mary 2   *Montrealer*   *Spirit of St. Louis*   *Apollo 11*

Do not italicize abbreviations used with the name, such as HMS or SS. Model names and numbers (such as Boeing 747) are not italicized.

66c Italicize (or underline) foreign terms.

▶ **In the Paris airport, we recognized the familiar no-smoking sign:**
Défense de fumer.

Many foreign words have become so common in English that everyone accepts them as part of the language, and they require no italics or underlining: rigor mortis, pasta, and sombrero, for example. (These words appear in English dictionaries.)

66d Italicize (or underline) scientific names.

The scientific (Latin) names of organisms, consisting of the genus and species, are always italicized. The genus is capitalized.

▶ **Most chicks are infected with _Cryptosporidium baileyi_, a parasite**
typical of young animals.

66e Italicize (or underline) words, letters, and numbers referred to as themselves.

For clarity, italicize words or phrases used as words rather than for the meaning they convey. (You may also use quotation marks for this purpose.)

▶ **The term _romantic_ does not mean the same thing to the Shelley**
scholar that it does to the fan of Danielle Steel's novels.

Letters and numbers used alone should also be italicized.

▶ **The word _bookkeeper_ has three sets of double letters: double _o_,**
double _k_, and double _e_.

▶ **Add a _3_ to that column.**

66f Use italics (or underlining) sparingly for emphasis.

An occasional word in italics helps you make a point. Too much emphasis, however, may mean no emphasis at all.

> **WEAK** You don't mean that your teacher _told the whole class_ that _he_ did not know the answer _himself?_
>
> **REVISED** Your teacher admitted that he did not know the answer? That is amazing.

If you add italics or underlining to a quotation, indicate the change in parentheses following the quotation.

▶ **Instead of promising that no harm will come to us, Blake only**
assures us that we "need not _fear_ harm" (emphasis added).

CHAPTER 67

Hyphens

67a   Use hyphens for compound words and for clarity.

A hyphen joins two nouns to make one compound word. Scientists speak of a *kilogram-meter* as a measure of force, and professors of literature talk about the *scholar-poet*. The hyphen lets us know that the two nouns work together as one.

A dictionary is the best resource when you are unsure about whether to use a hyphen. If you cannot find a compound word in the dictionary, spell it as two separate words. Whatever spelling you choose, be consistent throughout your document.

67b   Use hyphens to join two or more words to create compound adjective or noun forms.

A noun can also be linked with an adjective, an adverb, or another part of speech to form a compound adjective.

accident-prone   quick-witted

Use hyphens as well in nouns designating family relationships and compounds of more than two words.

brother-in-law   stay-at-home

Compound nouns with hyphens generally form plurals by adding *-s* or *-es* to the most important word.

attorney general/attorneys general
mother-in-law/mothers-in-law

Some proper nouns that are joined to make an adjective are hyphenated.

the Franco-Prussian war   of Mexican-American heritage

Hyphens often help clarify adjectives that come before the word they modify. Modifiers that are hyphenated when placed *before* the word they modify are usually not hyphenated when placed *after* the word they modify.

► It was a *bad-mannered* reply.

► The reply was *bad mannered*.

Do not use a hyphen to connect *-ly* adverbs to the words they modify. Similarly, do not use a hyphen with *-er* or *-est* adjectives and adverbs.

► They explored the newly discovered territories.

► This dress is better looking in red.

In a pair or series of compound nouns or adjectives, add suspended hyphens after the first word of each item.

▶ **The child care center accepted three-, four-, and five-year-olds.**

67c Use hyphens to spell out fractions and compound numbers.

Use a hyphen when writing out fractions or compound numbers from twenty-one to ninety-nine.

three-fourths of a gallon   thirty-two

> **Note:** In MLA style, use a hyphen to show inclusive numbers: *pages 100–40.*

67d Use a hyphen to attach some prefixes and suffixes.

Use a hyphen to join a prefix and a capitalized word or a number.

un-American   pre-Columbian   pre-1970
mid-August   neo-Nazi

A hyphen is sometimes used to join a capital letter and a word.

T-shirt   V-six engine

The prefixes *all-, ex-, quasi-* and *self-,* and the suffixes *-elect, -odd,* and *-something,* generally take hyphens.

all-purpose   president-elect
ex-convict   fifty-odd
quasi-scientific   thirty-something
self-sufficient

Most prefixes, however, are not attached by hyphens, unless a hyphen is needed to show pronunciation, avoid double letters *(anti-immigration),* or distinguish the word from the same word without a hyphen: *recreate* (play) versus *re-create* (make again). Check a dictionary to be sure you are using the standard spelling.

67e Use hyphens to divide words at the ends of lines.

Writers can turn off the automatic-hyphenation function in their word-processing programs. In this way, you will avoid breaking words at the ends of lines. When you must divide words, do so between syllables. Pronunciation alone cannot always tell you where to divide a word, however. If you are unsure about how to break a word into syllables, consult your dictionary.

the EVOLVING SITUATION

Dividing Internet Addresses and DOIs

If you need to divide an Internet address or Digital Object Identifier (DOI) between lines, divide it after a slash or punctuation mark, but do not add a hyphen. Break an e-mail address after @. Check your style manual for specific guidelines.

► **My writing group had a very fruitful *collab-oration*. [not *colla-boration*]**

Never leave just one or two letters on a line.

► **He seemed so sad and vulnerable and so *dis-connected* from his family. [not *disconnect-ed*]**

Compound words such as *hardworking, rattlesnake,* and *bookcase* should be broken only between the words that form them: *hard-working, rattle-snake, book-case.* Compound words that already have hyphens, like *brother-in-law,* are broken only after the hyphens.

> *Note:* Never hyphenate an abbreviation, a contraction, a numeral, or a one-syllable word.

CHAPTER 68

Spelling

Proofread your writing carefully. Misspellings creep into the prose of even the best writers. Use the following strategies to help you improve your spelling:

- Become familiar with major spelling rules *(68a).*
- Keep a list of words that give you trouble.
- If you are not sure how a word is spelled, look it up in the dictionary.

Spelling Checkers

Computer spell checkers are helpful tools. Remember, however, that a spell checker cannot tell *how* you are using a particular word. If you write *their* but mean *there,* a spell checker cannot point out your mistake. Spell checkers also cannot point out many misspelled proper nouns.

68a Learn the rules that generally hold for spelling, as well as their exceptions.

1. Use *i* before *e* except after *c* or when sounded like *a*, as in *neighbor* and *weigh*.

- *i* before *e*: believe, relieve, chief, grief, wield, yield
- **Except after *c*:** receive, deceive, ceiling, conceit

  Exceptions: seize, caffeine, weird, height, science, species

2. Prefixes do not change a word's spelling when attached.

- **Examples:** preview, reconnect, unwind, deemphasize

3. Suffixes change a word's spelling depending on the suffix or the final letter(s) of the root word.

- **Final silent *e*:**

  Drop it if the suffix begins with a vowel: *force/forcing, remove/ removable, surprise/surprising*

  Keep it if the suffix begins with a consonant: *care/careful.*

  Exceptions: argue/argument, true/truly, change/changeable, judge/judgment, acknowledge/acknowledgment

---

Note: Keep the silent *e* if it is needed to clarify the pronunciation or if the word would be confused with another word without the *e*.

dye/dyeing (to avoid confusion with *dying*)
hoe/hoeing (to avoid mispronunciation)

- **Final *y*:**

  Keep it when adding the suffix *-ing*: *enjoy/enjoying, cry/crying*

  Keep or change it when adding other suffixes:

  - **When *y* follows a consonant, change to *i* or *ie*:** happy/ happier, marry/married
  - **When *y* follows a vowel, keep it:** defray/defrayed, enjoy/ enjoying
  - **Final consonant:**

    Double it if the root word ends in a single vowel + a consonant and is only one syllable long or has an accent on the final syllable: *grip/ gripping, refer/referred*

    For other types of root words, do not double the consonant: *crack/ cracking, laundering*

  Exceptions: bus/busing, focus/focused

- ***-ly* with words that end in *-ic*:**

  Add *-ally:* logic/logically, terrific/terrifically

  Exception: public/publicly

- **Words ending in *-able/-ible, -ant/-ent,* and *-ify/-efy*:**

  Consult a dictionary for the correct spelling of words ending in these frequently confused suffixes.

4. Forming plurals   Most plurals are formed by adding *-s*. Some are formed by adding *-es*.

- **Words ending in *-s, -sh, -x, -z,* "soft" *-ch* (add *-es*):** bus/ buses, bush/ bushes, fox/foxes, buzz/buzzes, peach/peaches

- **Words ending in a consonant + *o* (add *-es*):** hero/heroes, tomato/ tomatoes, *but* solo/solos

- **Words ending in a consonant + *y* (change *y* to *i* and add *-es*):** beauty/ beauties, city/cities, *but* the Kirbys (a family's name)

- **Words ending in *-f* or *-fe* (change *f* to *v* and add *-s* or *-es*):** leaf/leaves, knife/knives, wife/wives, *but* staff/staffs, roof/ roofs

Most plurals follow standard rules, but some have irregular forms *(child/ children, tooth/teeth),* and some words with foreign roots create plurals in the pattern of the language they come from, as do these words:

alumna/alumnae	datum/data
alumnus/alumni	medium/media
analysis/analyses	stimulus/stimuli
criterion/criteria	thesis/theses

Note: Some writers now treat *data* as though it were singular, but the preferred practice is still to recognize that *data* is plural and takes a plural verb: *The data are clear on this point: the pass/fail course has become outdated.*

Some nouns with foreign roots have regular and irregular plural forms *(appendix/appendices/appendixes).* Be consistent in using the spelling you choose.

Compound nouns with hyphens generally form plurals by adding *-s* or *-es* to the most important word:

brother-in-law/brothers-in-law

For some compound words that appear as one word, the same rule applies *(passersby);* for others, it does not *(cupfuls).* Consult a dictionary if you are not sure.

If both words in the compound are equally important, add *-s* to the second word: *singer-songwriters.*

A few words, such as *fish* and *sheep,* have the same forms for singular and plural. To indicate that the word is plural, you need to add a word or words that specify quantity: *five fish, a few sheep.*

68b Learn to distinguish words pronounced alike but spelled differently.

Homonyms sound alike but have different meanings and different spellings. The following is a list of common homonyms as well as words that are almost homonyms. For more complete definitions, consult the Glossary of Usage *(Chapter 50, pp. 441-49)* and a dictionary.

accept: to take willingly
except: to leave out (verb); but for (preposition)

affect: to influence (verb); a feeling or an emotion (noun)
effect: to make or accomplish (verb); result (noun)

all ready: prepared
already: by this time

cite: to quote or refer to
sight: spectacle, sense
site: place

it's: contraction for *it is* or *it has*
its: possessive pronoun

loose: not tight
lose: to misplace

precede: to come before
proceed: to go forward

principal: most important (adjective); the head of an organization *or* a sum of money (noun)
principle: a basic standard or law (noun)

their: possessive pronoun
there: adverb of place
they're: contraction for *they are*

to: indicating movement
too: also
two: number

who's: contraction for *who is*
whose: possessive of *who*

your: possessive pronoun
you're: contraction for *you are*

CHECKLIST   Editing for Sentence Punctuation, Mechanics, and Spelling

As you revise, check your writing for proper punctuation and spelling by asking yourself these questions:

☐ Are commas used appropriately to separate or set off introductory sentence elements; coordinated independent clauses; items in a series and coordinate adjectives; nonessential sentence elements; direct quotations; and the parts of dates, addresses, titles, and numbers? *(See Chapter 57: Commas, pp. 498–510.)* Are any commas mistakenly used with sentence elements that should not be separated or set off? *(See Chapter 57: Commas, pp. 498–510.)*

☐ Are semicolons used appropriately to join independent clauses and to separate items in a series when the items contain commas? *(See Chapter 58: Semicolons, pp. 510–13.)*

☐ Are colons used appropriately after a complete sentence to introduce a list, an appositive, or a quotation; after one independent clause to introduce a second that elaborates on the first; and in business letters, ratios, and bibliographic citations? *(See Chapter 59: Colons, pp. 513–15.)*

☐ Are quotation marks used appropriately with other punctuation to identify brief direct quotations, dialogue, and the titles of short works? Are single quotation marks used appropriately to identify quotations within quotations? *(See Chapter 61: Quotation Marks, pp. 518–23.)*

☐ Are periods used appropriately at the end of sentences and in abbreviations? Are question marks and exclamation points used appropriately at the end of sentences and within quotations? Are brackets and ellipses used correctly to identify words added to and omitted from quotations? Are dashes and parentheses used appropriately to insert or highlight nonessential information within a sentence? *(See Chapter 62: Other Punctuation Marks, pp. 523–30.)*

☐ Are words and letters capitalized according to convention and context? *(See Chapter 63: Capitalization, pp. 530–34.)*

☐ Are abbreviations capitalized and punctuated in a consistent way? Are Latin abbreviations and nonalphabetic symbols used appropriately? *(See Chapter 64: Abbreviations and Symbols, pp. 534–36.)*

☐ Are numbers either spelled out or represented with numerals according to the conventions of the type of writing (nontechnical or technical) you are engaged in? *(See Chapter 65: Numbers, pp. 536–38.)*

☐ Are italics (or is underlining) used appropriately for emphasis and to identify the titles of works, foreign words, and words used as words? *(See Chapter 66: Italics [Underlining], pp. 538–40.)*

☐ Are apostrophes used appropriately to indicate possession and to form contractions? *(See Chapter 60: Apostrophes, pp. 515–18.)*

Credits

12

Basic Grammar Review

With Tips for Multilingual Writers

*Grammar and rhetoric are complementary. …
Grammar maps out the possible, rhetoric narrows
the possible down to the desirable or effective.*

–Francis Christensen

©Spaces Images/Blend Images LLC

Shinjuku's Skyscraper District in Tokyo caters to an international,
multilingual populace with signs in Japanese, English, Chinese, and
Korean.

12 Basic Grammar Review

tip FOR MULTILINGUAL WRITERS

---NAVIGATING THROUGH COLLEGE AND BEYOND

What Was the Language of Your Ancestors?

Your native language, or even the language of your ancestors, may influence the way you use English. Even if English is your first language, you may be part of a group that immigrated generations ago but has retained traces of other grammatical structures. For example, the slang contraction *ain't,* brought here by Scottish settlers, may have meant *am not* at one time. Take note of the Tips for Multilingual Writers in this section. Some might help native speakers as well.

Written language, although based on the grammar of spoken language, has its own logic and rules. The chapters that follow explain the basic rules of standard written English.

> ## tip FOR MULTILINGUAL WRITERS: Recognizing language differences
>
> The standard structures of sentences in languages other than English can be very different from those in English. In other languages, the form of a verb can indicate its grammatical function more powerfully than can its placement in the sentence. Also, in languages other than English, adjectives may take on the function that articles (*a, an, the*) perform, or articles may be absent.
>
> If your first language is not English, try to pinpoint the areas of difficulty you have in English. See whether you are attempting to *translate* the structures of your native language into English. If so, you will need to learn more about English sentence structure.

CHAPTER 69

Parts of Speech

English has eight primary **parts of speech:** verbs, nouns, pronouns, adjectives, adverbs, prepositions, conjunctions, and interjections. All English words belong to one or more of these categories. Particular words can belong to different categories, depending on the role they play in a sentence. For example, the word *button* can be a noun *(the button on a coat)* or a verb *(button your jacket now).*

69a Verbs

Verbs carry a lot of information. They report action *(run, write),* condition *(bloom, sit),* or state of being *(be, seem).* Verbs also change form to indicate person, number, tense, voice, and mood. To do all this, a **main verb** is often preceded by one or more **helping verbs,** thereby becoming a **verb phrase.**

► The play *begins* at eight.

► I *may change* seats after the play *has begun.*

1. Main verbs
Main verbs change form **(tense)** to indicate when something has happened. If a word does not indicate tense, it is not a main verb. All main verbs have five forms, except for *be,* which has eight.

BASE FORM	*(talk, sing)*
PAST TENSE	Yesterday I *(talked, sang).*

PAST PARTICIPLE	In the past, I have *(talked, sung)*.
PRESENT PARTICIPLE	Right now I am *(talking, singing)*.
THIRD-PERSON SINGULAR (OR -S FORM)	Usually he/she/it *(talks, sings)*.

(For more on subject verb agreement and verb tense, see Tab 10: Editing for Grammar Conventions, pp. 462–69 and pp. 470–79, and the list of common irregular verbs on p. 471.)

⎯tip FOR MULTILINGUAL WRITERS: Using verbs followed by gerunds or infinitives

Verbs in English differ as to whether they can be followed by a gerund, an infinitive, or either. Some verbs, like *avoid,* can be followed by a gerund but not an infinitive. These constructions often express facts.

► We avoided ~~to climb~~ *climbing* the mountain during the storm.

Other verbs, like *attempt,* can be followed by an infinitive but not a gerund. Often these constructions convey intentions.

► We attempted ~~reaching~~ *to reach* the summit when the weather cleared.

Others can be followed by either a gerund or an infinitive with no change in meaning.

► We began climbing.

► We began to climb.

Still others have a different meaning when followed by a gerund than they do when followed by an infinitive. Compare these examples.

► She stopped eating. [She was eating but she stopped.]

► She stopped to eat. [She stopped what she was doing before in order to eat.]

The following lists provide common examples of each type of verb.

Some Verbs That Take Only an Infinitive

appear	fail	need	seem
ask	intend	plan	threaten
claim	learn	prepare	want
decide	manage	promise	wish
expect	mean	refuse	would like

(Continued)

tip FOR MULTILINGUAL WRITERS: *(continued)*

Some Verbs That Take Only a Gerund

admit	forgive	resist
avoid	imagine	risk
consider	mention	suggest
defend	mind	support
deny	practice	tolerate
discuss	quit	understand
enjoy	recommend	
finish	regret	

Some Verbs That Can Take Either a Gerund or an Infinitive

An asterisk (*) indicates those verbs for which the choice of gerund or infinitive affects meaning.

begin	like	start
continue	love	*stop
*forget	prefer	*try
hate	*remember	

> **Note:** For some verbs, such as *allow, cause, encourage, have, persuade, remind,* and *tell,* a noun or pronoun must precede the infinitive: *I reminded my sister to return my sweater.* For a few verbs, such as *ask, expect, need,* and *want,* the noun may either precede or follow the infinitive, depending on the meaning you want to express: *I want to return my sweater to my sister. I want my sister to return my sweater.*
>
> *Make, let,* and *have* are followed by a noun or pronoun plus the base form without *to: Make that boy come home on time.*

To make a verb followed by an infinitive negative, add *not* or *never* before the verb or before the infinitive. The location of *not* sometimes affects meaning:

▶ **He did not promise to write the report.** [He may or may not write the report since he made no promises.]

▶ **He promised not to write the report.** [He said he would not write the report.]

Verbs followed by a gerund always take the negative word before the gerund: *She regrets not finishing the assignment.*

2. Helping verbs that show time

Some helping verbs—mostly forms of *be, have,* and *do—function* to signify time *(will have been playing, has played)* or emphasis *(does play). (See Tab 10: Editing for Grammar Conventions, pp. 451–95.)*

Forms of *do* are also used to ask questions *(Do you play?)*. Here are other such helping **(auxiliary)** verbs:

be, am, is	being, been	do, does, did
are, was, were	have, has, had	

The helping verb *do* and its forms *does* and *did* combine with the base form of a verb to ask a question or to emphasize something. Any helping verb can also combine with the word *not* to create an emphatic negative statement.

QUESTION	*Do* you hear those dogs barking?
EMPHATIC STATEMENT	I *do* hear them barking.
EMPHATIC NEGATIVE	I *do not* want to have to call the police about those dogs.

The helping verb *have* and its forms *has* and *had* combine with a past participle (usually ending in *-d, -t,* or *-n*) to form the *perfect tenses*. Do not confuse the simple past tense with the present perfect tense (formed with *have* or *has*), which is distinct from the simple past because the action can continue in the present. *(For a review of perfect tense forms, see Tab 10: Editing for Grammar Conventions, pp. 451–95.)* To form a negative statement, add *not* after the helping verb.

SIMPLE PAST	Those dogs *barked* all day.
PRESENT PERFECT	Those dogs *have barked* all day.
	Those dogs *have not barked* all day.
PAST PERFECT	Those dogs *had barked* all day.

Forms of *be* combine with a present participle (ending in *-ing*) to form the *progressive tenses*, which express continuing action. Do not confuse the simple present tense or the present perfect with these progressive forms. Unlike the simple present, which indicates an action that occurs frequently and might include the present moment, the present progressive form indicates an action that is going on right now. In its past form, the progressive tense indicates actions that were going on simultaneously. *(For a review of progressive tense forms, see Tab 10: Editing for Grammar Conventions, p. 474.)*

SIMPLE PRESENT	Those dogs *bark* all the time.
PRESENT PROGRESSIVE	Those dogs *are barking* all the time.
PAST PROGRESSIVE	Those dogs *were barking* all day while I *was trying* to study.

When *be* is used as a helping verb, it is preceded by a modal verb such as *can* or *may: I may be leaving tomorrow.* When *been* is the helping verb, it is preceded by a form of *have: I have been painting my room all day.*

Forms of *be* combine with the past participle (which usually ends in *-d, -t,* or *-n*) to form the passive voice, which is often used to express a state of being instead of an action.

BE + PAST PARTICIPLE

PASSIVE   The dogs *were scolded* by their owner.

PASSIVE   I *was satisfied* by her answer.

When *be, being,* or *been* is the helping verb, it needs another helping verb to be complete.

MODAL VERB   The dogs *will be scolded* by their owner.

ANOTHER FORM   The dogs *were being scolded* by their owner.
OF *BE*

FORM OF *HAVE*   The dogs *have been scolded* by their owner.

3. Modals

Other helping verbs, called **modals,** express an attitude toward the action or circumstance of a sentence:

can	ought to	will
could	shall	would
may	should	must
might		

Modal verbs share several characteristics:

- They do not change form to indicate person or number.
- They do not change form to indicate tense.
- They are followed directly by the base form of the verb without *to.*
- Sometimes they are used with *have* plus the past participle of the verb to indicate the past tense.

▶ **We must to study now.**

▶ **He *must* have studied hard to do so well.**

Some verbal expressions ending in *to* also function as modals, including *have to, be able to,* and *be supposed to.* These **phrasal modals** behave more like ordinary verbs than true modals, changing form to indicate tense and agree with the subject. Modals are used to express the following:

FUNCTION	PRESENT/FUTURE	PAST
Permission	*may, might, can, could* *May* I come at five o'clock?	*might, could* My instructor said I *could* hand in my paper late.
Polite request	*would, could Would* you please open the door?	
Ability	*can, am/is/are able to* I *can (am able to)* take one piece of luggage.	*could, was/were able to* I *could (was able to)* take only one piece of luggage on the plane yesterday.

FUNCTION	PRESENT/FUTURE	PAST
Possibility	*may, might* She *may (might)* try to return this afternoon.	*might + have + past participle* His train *may (might) have* arrived already.
Expectation	*should* I have only one more chart to create, so I *should* finish my project today.	*should + have + past participle* The students *should have* finished the project by now.
Necessity	*must (have to)* I *must (have to)* pass this test.	*had to + base form* She *had to* study hard to pass.
Prohibition	*must + not* You *must not* go there.	
Logical deduction	*must (has to)* He *must (has to)* be there by now.	*must + have + past participle* You *must have* left early to make the noon bus.
Intention	*will, shall* I *will (shall)* go today.	*would* I told you I *would* go.
Speculation *(past form implies that something did not happen or is contrary to fact)*	*would, could, might* If she learned her lines, she *could* play the part.	*would (could/might) + have + past participle* If she had learned her lines, she *might have* gotten the part.
Advisability *(past form implies that something did not happen)*	*should (ought to)* You *should (ought to)* water the plant every day.	*should + have + past participle* You *should have* listened to the directions more carefully.
Habitual past action		*would (used to) + base form* When I was younger, I *would* ride my bike to school every day.

69b Nouns

Nouns name people *(Shakespeare, actors, Englishman),* places *(Manhattan, city, island),* things *(Kleenex, handkerchief, sneeze, cats),* and ideas *(Marxism, justice, democracy, clarity).*

▶ **Shakespeare** lived in *England* and wrote *plays* about the human condition.

1. Proper and common nouns

Proper nouns name specific people, places, and things and are always capitalized: *Aretha Franklin, Hinduism, Albany, Microsoft.* All other nouns are **common nouns:** *singer, religion, capital, corporation.*

2. Count and noncount nouns

A common noun that refers to something specific that can be counted is a **count noun.** Count nouns can be singular or plural, like *orange* or *suggestion (four oranges, several suggestions)*. **Noncount nouns** are nonspecific; these common nouns refer to categories of people, places, or things and cannot be counted. They do not have a plural form. *(The orange juice is delicious. His advice was useful.)*

Count Nouns		Noncount Nouns	
cars	tools	transportation	equipment
computers	machines	Internet	machinery
facts	suggestions	information	advice
clouds	earrings	rain	jewelry
stars		sunshine	

⌐tip FOR MULTILINGUAL WRITERS: Using quantifiers with count and noncount nouns

Consult an ESL dictionary if you have trouble determining whether a word is a count or noncount noun. If a word is a noncount noun, it will not have a plural form.

> **Note:** Many nouns can be either count or noncount depending on the context in which they appear.
>
> ▶ **Baseball** [the game: noncount] **is never played with two baseballs** [the object: count] **at the same time.**

Count and noncount nouns are often preceded by **quantifiers,** words that tell how much or how many. Quantifiers are a type of determiner. *(See pp. 558–59 for a discussion of determiners.)* Following is a list of some quantifiers for count nouns and for noncount nouns, as well as a few quantifiers that can be used with both:

- **With count nouns only:** *several, many, a couple of, a number of, a few, few, each, every*
- **With noncount nouns only:** *a great deal of, much, not much, little, a little, less,* a word that indicates a unit *(a bag of sugar)*
- **With either count or noncount nouns:** *all, any, some, a lot of, no, enough, more*

(Continued)

tip FOR MULTILINGUAL WRITERS: *(continued)*

Note: The quantifiers *a few* and *few* for count nouns and *a little* and *little* for noncount nouns all indicate a small quantity. In contrast to *a few* and *a little*, however, *few* and *little* have the negative connotation of *hardly any.*

► **The problems are difficult, and we have few options for solving them.** [The outlook for solving the problems is gloomy.]

► **The problems are difficult, but we have a few options for solving them.** [The outlook for solving the problems is hopeful.]

► **We have little time to find a campsite before sunset.** [The campers might spend the night in the open by the side of the trail.]

► **We have a little time to find a campsite before sunset.** [The campers will probably find a place to pitch a tent before dark.]

(For help using articles with count and noncount nouns, see the section on pp. 558–59.)

3. Concrete and abstract nouns
Nouns that name things that can be perceived by the senses are called **concrete nouns:** *boy, wind, book, song.* **Abstract nouns** name qualities and concepts that do not have physical properties: *charity, patience, beauty, hope. (For more on using concrete and abstract nouns, see Tab 9: Editing for Clarity, pp. 401–49.)*

4. Singular and plural nouns
Most nouns name things that can be counted and are singular or plural. Singular nouns typically become plural by adding -*s* or -*es*: *boy/boys, ocean/oceans, church/churches, agency/agencies.* Some have irregular plurals, such as *man/men, child/children,* and *tooth/teeth.* Noncount nouns like *intelligence* and *electricity* do not form plurals.

5. Collective nouns
Collective nouns such as *team, family, herd,* and *orchestra* are treated as singular. They are not noncount nouns, however, because collective nouns can be counted and can be made plural: *teams, families. (Also see Tab 10: Editing for Grammar Conventions, pp. 466 and 481.)*

6. Possessive nouns
When nouns are used in the **possessive case** to indicate ownership, they change their form. To form the possessive case, singular nouns add an apostrophe plus *s* (*'s*),

whereas plural nouns ending in -*s* just add an apostrophe (*'*). (*Also see Tab 11: Editing for Correctness, pp. 497–548.*)

SINGULAR	insect	insect's sting
PLURAL	neighbors	neighbors' car

7. Determiners used with nouns

Determiners precede and specify nouns: *a* desk, *five* books. They include articles *(a, an, the)*, possessives *(my, neighbors')*, demonstrative pronouns used as adjectives *(this, that, these, those)*, and numbers as well as quantifiers *(see pp. 561–62)*. A singular count noun must have a determiner.

⟶ tip FOR MULTILINGUAL WRITERS: *Using articles* (a, an, the) *appropriately*

Articles in English express three basic meanings: indefinite (indicating nonspecific reference), definite (indicating specific reference), and generic (indicating reference to a general category).

Indefinite and definite meaning

A noun has an indefinite meaning, or a nonspecific reference, when it is first mentioned. To express an indefinite meaning with count nouns, use the **indefinite article** (*a* before consonant sound, *an* before vowel sound) for singular forms and no article for plural forms.

▶ I bought *a* new computer.

▶ I sold *an* old computer.

▶ I bought new computers.

> *Note:* Unless they are qualified (e.g., a knowledge of science), noncount nouns *never* take the indefinite article.
>
>   Knowledge
> ▶ ~~A knowledge~~ is a valuable commodity.
>   ^

To express a definite meaning or a specific reference, use the **definite article** *(the)* with both noncount nouns and singular and plural count nouns. A noun has a definite meaning or a specific reference in a variety of situations:

• **When the noun identifies something previously mentioned.**

I was driving along Main Street when *a* car [nonspecific reference] pulled up behind me. *The* car [specific reference to the previously mentioned car] swerved into the left lane and sped out of sight.

(Continued)

tip FOR MULTILINGUAL WRITERS: *(continued)*

- **When the noun identifies something familiar or known from the context.**

  We could not play today because *the* soccer field was wet.

- **When the noun identifies a unique subject.**

  The moon will be full tonight.

- **When the noun is modified by a superlative adjective.**

  We adopted *the* most economical strategy.

- **When information in modifying phrases and clauses makes the noun definite.**

  The goal *of this discussion* is to explain article use.

Generic meaning

A noun is used generically when it is meant to represent all the individuals in the category it names. Singular count nouns used generically can take either an indefinite article or a definite article depending on the context.

▶ *A student* can use the Internet to research *a topic* efficiently.

▶ *The university* is an institution with roots in ancient times.

Noncount nouns and plural count nouns used generically take no article.

▶ *Television* may be harmful to young children.

▶ *Psychologists* believe that *children* should reduce the amount of time they spend watching television.

Articles and proper nouns

Most proper nouns are not used with articles.

▶ ~~The~~ Arizona is a dry state.

Some proper nouns, however, do take the definite article.

▶ *The* Civil War was a watershed event in American history.

Some other exceptions are the names of structures *(the White House)*, names that include the word *of (the Fourth of July)*, plural proper nouns *(the United States)*, and many countries with names that are two or more words long *(the Dominican Republic)*.

Whenever you encounter an unfamiliar proper noun, determine whether it is used with a definite article. (A dictionary may help you.)

69c Pronouns

A **pronoun** takes the place of a noun. The noun that the pronoun replaces is called its **antecedent**. Some pronouns function as adjectives. *(For more on pronoun-antecedent agreement, see Tab 10: Editing for Grammar Conventions, pp. 451-95.)*

► **The *snow* fell all day long, and by nightfall *it* was three feet deep.**

The box on p. 562 summarizes the different kinds of pronouns.

1. Personal pronouns

The **personal pronouns** *I, me, you, he, his, she, her, it, we, us, they,* and *them* refer to specific people or things and vary in form to indicate person, number, gender, and case. *(For more on pronoun reference and case, see Tab 10: Editing for Grammar Conventions, pp. 451-95.)*

► **You told *us* that *he* gave Jane a lock of *his* hair.**

2. Possessive pronouns

Like possessive nouns, **possessive pronouns** indicate ownership. However, unlike possessive nouns, possessive pronouns do not add apostrophes: *my/mine, your/yours, her/hers, his, its, our/ours, their/theirs.*

► **Brunch is at *her* place this Saturday.**

3. Reflexive and intensive pronouns

Pronouns ending in *-self* or *-selves* are either reflexive or intensive. **Reflexive pronouns** refer back to the subject and are necessary for sentence sense.

► **Many of the women blamed *themselves* for the problem.**

Intensive pronouns add emphasis to the nouns or pronouns they follow and are grammatically optional.

► **President Harding *himself* drank whiskey during Prohibition.**

4. Relative pronouns

The **relative pronouns** *who, whom, whose, that,* and *which* relate a dependent clause—a word group containing a subject and verb and a subordinating word—to an antecedent noun or pronoun in the sentence.

dependent clause

► **In Kipling's story, Dravot is the man *who* would be king.**

The form of a relative pronoun varies according to its **case**—the grammatical role it plays in the sentence. *(For more on pronoun case, see Tab 10: Editing for Grammar Conventions, pp. 451-95.)*

5. Demonstrative pronouns

The **demonstrative pronouns** *this, that, these,* and *those* point out nouns and pronouns that come later.

► *This* **is the book literary critics have been waiting for.**

Sometimes these pronouns function as adjectives: *This book won the Pulitzer.* Sometimes they are noun equivalents: *This is my book.*

6. Interrogative pronouns

Interrogative pronouns such as *who, whatever,* and *whom* are used to ask questions.

► *Whatever* **happened to you?**

The form of the interrogative pronouns *who, whom, whoever,* and *whomever* indicates the grammatical role they play in a sentence. *(See Tab 10: Editing for Grammar Conventions, p. 489.)*

7. Indefinite pronouns

Indefinite pronouns such as *someone, anybody, nothing,* and *few* refer to a non-specific person or thing and do not change form to indicate person, number, or gender.

► *Anybody* **who cares enough to come and help may take** *some* **home.**

Most indefinite pronouns are always singular *(anybody, everyone).* Some are always plural *(many, few),* and a handful can be singular or plural *(any, most). (See Tab 10, pp. 467–68 and 480–81.)*

8. Reciprocal pronouns

Reciprocal pronouns such as *each other* and *one another* refer to the separate parts of their plural antecedent.

► **My sister and I are close because we live near** *each other.*

69d   Adjectives

Adjectives modify nouns and pronouns by answering questions like *Which one? What kind? How many? What size? What color? What condition?* and *Whose?* They can describe, enumerate, identify, define, and limit *(one person, that person).* When articles *(a, an, the)* identify nouns, they function as adjectives.

Sometimes proper nouns are treated as adjectives; the proper adjectives that result are capitalized: *Britain/British.* Pronouns can also function as adjectives *(his green car),* and adjectives often have forms that allow you to make comparisons *(great, greater, greatest).*

PRONOUNS

PERSONAL (INCLUDING POSSESSIVE)

SINGULAR	PLURAL
I, me, my, mine	we, us, our, ours
you, your, yours	you, your, yours
he, him, his	they, them, their, theirs*
she, her, hers	
it, its	

REFLEXIVE AND INTENSIVE

SINGULAR	PLURAL
myself	ourselves
yourself	yourselves
himself, herself, itself	themselves*
oneself	

Note: English does not have a gender-neutral, third-person singular personal pronoun, but in recent years, using *they* and other gender-neutral plural pronouns in place of gendered, third-person singular pronouns like *he* or *she* has become more widely accepted. This option is especially important for people whose genders are neither male nor female.

RELATIVE

who	whoever	what	whatever	that
whom	whomever	whose	whichever	which

DEMONSTRATIVE

this, that, these, those

INTERROGATIVE

who	whom	whatever	which	whose
whoever	what	whomever	whichever	

INDEFINITE

SINGULAR		PLURAL	SINGULAR/PLURAL
anybody	nobody	both	all
anyone	no one	few	any
anything	none	many	either
each	nothing	several	more
everybody	one		most
everyone	somebody		some
everything	someone		
much	something		
neither			

RECIPROCAL

each other, any other, one another

▶ **The *decisive* and *diligent* king regularly attended meetings of the council.** [What kind of king?]

▶ ***These four artistic* qualities affect how an advertisement is received.** [Which, how many, what kind of qualities?]

▶ ***My little blue* Volkswagen died *one icy winter morning*.** [Whose, what size, what color car? Which, what kind of morning?]

Like all modifiers, adjectives should be as close as possible to the words they modify. *(See Tab 9: Editing for Clarity, pp. 401–49.)* Most often, adjectives appear before the noun they modify, but **descriptive adjectives**—adjectives that designate qualities or attributes—may come before or after the noun or pronoun they modify for stylistic reasons. Adjectives that describe the subject and follow linking verbs *(be, am, is, are, was, being, been, appear, become, feel, grow, look, make, prove, taste)* are called **subject complements.**

BEFORE SUBJECT

The *sick* and *destitute* poet no longer believed that love would save him.

AFTER SUBJECT

The poet, *sick* and *destitute,* no longer believed that love would save him.

AFTER LINKING VERB

No longer believing that love would save him, the poet was *sick* and *destitute.*

tip FOR MULTILINGUAL WRITERS:
Using adjectives correctly

English adjectives do not change form to agree with the number and gender of the nouns they modify.

▶ **Juan is an *attentive* father. Alyssa is an *attentive* mother. They are *attentive* parents.**

As noted above, though adjectives usually come before a noun, they can also occur after a linking verb: *The food at the restaurant was delicious*. The position of an adjective can affect its meaning. The phrase *my old friend,* for example, can refer to a long friendship *(a friend I have known for a long time)* or an elderly friend *(my friend who is eighty years old).* In the sentence, *My friend is old,* in contrast, *old* has only one possible meaning—elderly.

Adjective order

When two or more adjectives modify a noun cumulatively, they follow a sequence—determined by their meaning—that is particular to English logic:

1. Determiner/article: *the, his, my, that, some*
2. Adjectives that express subjective evaluation: *cozy, intelligent, outrageous, elegant, original*

(Continued)

⌐*tip* **FOR MULTILINGUAL WRITERS:** *(continued)*

3. Adjectives of size and shape: *big, small, huge, tiny, tall, short, narrow, thick, round, square*
4. Adjectives expressing age: *old, young, new*
5. Adjectives of color: *yellow, green, pale*
6. Adjectives of origin and type: *African, Czech, Gothic*
7. Adjectives of material: *brick, plastic, glass, stone*
8. Nouns used as adjectives: *dinner [menu], computer [keyboard]*
9. Noun modified

Here are some examples.

► **the small red brick cottage**

► **the tall African statues**

► **its striking arched Gothic stained-glass window**

Present and past participles used as adjectives
Both the present and past participle forms of verbs can function as adjectives. To use them properly, keep the following in mind:

- Present participle adjectives usually modify nouns that are the agent of an action.
- Past participle adjectives usually modify nouns that are the recipient of an action.

► **This problem is *confusing*.**

The present participle *confusing* modifies *problem,* which is the agent, or cause, of the confusion.

► **The students are *confused* by the problem.**

The past participle *confused* modifies *students,* who are the recipients of the confusion the problem is causing.

The following are some other present and past participle pairs that often cause problems:

amazing/amazed	frightening/frightened
annoying/annoyed	interesting/interested
boring/bored	satisfying/satisfied
depressing/depressed	shocking/shocked
embarrassing/embarrassed	surprising/surprised
exciting/excited	tiring/tired
fascinating/fascinated	concerned/concerning

69e   Adverbs

Adverbs often end in *-ly* (*beautifully, gracefully, quietly*) and usually answer such questions as *When? Where? How? How often? How much? To what degree?* and *Why?*

▶ **The authenticity of the document is *hotly* contested.** [How is it contested?]

Adverbs modify verbs, other adverbs, and adjectives. Like adjectives, adverbs can be used to compare (*less, lesser, least*). In addition to modifying individual words, they can be used to modify whole clauses. Adverbs can be placed at the beginning or end of a sentence or before the verb they modify, but they should not be placed between the verb and its direct object. Generally, they should appear as close as possible to the words they modify.

▶ **The water was *brilliant* blue and *icy* cold.** [The adverbs intensify the adjectives *blue* and *cold*.]

▶ **Dickens mixed humor and pathos *better* than any other English writer after Shakespeare.** [The adverb compares Dickens with other writers.]

▶ ***Consequently,* he is still read by millions.**

Consequently is a conjunctive adverb that modifies the independent clause that follows it and shows how the sentence is related to the preceding sentence. *(For more on conjunctive adverbs, see the material on conjunctions, p. 570.)*

   No, not, and *never* are among the most common adverbs. *Never* should not appear at the end of a sentence.

   It takes only one negator *(no/not/never)* to change the meaning of a sentence from positive to negative. In fact, when two negatives are used together, they cancel each other.

▶ **They don't have n̲o̲ reason to go there.**
                    any

69f   Prepositions and prepositional phrases

Prepositions *(on, in, at, by)* usually appear as part of a **prepositional phrase.** Their main function is to allow the noun or pronoun in the phrase to modify another word in the sentence. Prepositional phrases always begin with a preposition and end with a noun, pronoun, or other word group that functions as the **object of the preposition** (in *time,* on the *table*).

   A preposition can be one word *(about, despite, on)* or a word group *(according to, as well as, in spite of).* Place prepositional phrases as close as possible to the words they modify. Adjectival prepositional phrases usually appear right after the noun or pronoun they modify and answer questions like *Which one?* and *What kind of?* Adverbial phrases can appear anywhere in a sentence and answer questions like *When? Where? How?* and *Why?*

AS ADJECTIVE	Many species *of birds* nest there.
AS ADVERB	The younger children stared *out the window.*

┌─ tip **FOR MULTILINGUAL WRITERS:** Putting adverbs
in the correct place

Although adverbs can appear in almost any position within a sentence, they should not separate a verb from its direct object.

quickly
► Juan found ~~quickly~~ his cat.
        ^

The negative word *not* usually precedes the main verb and follows the first helping verb in a verb phrase.

not
► I have been ~~not~~ sick lately.
         ^

Every language uses prepositions idiomatically in ways that do not match their literal meaning. In English, prepositions combine with other words in such a variety of ways that the combinations can be learned only with repetition and over time. For example, you would *arrive in* a city or country *(I arrived in Paris)* but *arrive at* an event at a specific location *(I arrived at the museum at ten o'clock). (See* Connect *for a list of these combinations and their meanings.)*

1. Idiomatic uses of prepositions indicating time and location
The prepositions that indicate time and location are often the most idiosyncratic in a language. Here are some common ways in which the prepositions *at, by, in,* and *on* are used.

TIME

AT The wedding ceremony starts *at two o'clock.* [a specific clock time]

BY Our honeymoon plans should be ready *by next week.* [a particular time]

IN The reception will start *in the evening.* [a portion of the day]

ON The wedding will take place *on May 1.* The rehearsal is *on Tuesday.* [a particular date or day of the week]

LOCATION

AT I will meet you *at the zoo.* [a particular place]

You need to turn right *at the light.* [a corner or an intersection]

We took a seat *at the table.* [near a piece of furniture]

BY Meet me *by the fountain.* [a familiar place]

IN Park your car *in the parking lot* and give the money to the attendant *in the booth.* [a space of some kind or inside a structure]

I enjoyed the bratwurst *in Chicago.* [a city, state, or other geographic location]

I found that article *in this book.* [a print medium]

PREPOSITIONS AND COMPOUND PREPOSITIONS

about	behind	in addition to	through
above	below	in case of	to
according to	beside	including	toward
across	between	in front of	under
after	beyond	in place of	underneath
against	by	in regard to	until
along	by means of	inside	up
along with	by way of	instead of	upon
among	down	into	up to
apart from	during	like	via
as	except	near	with
as to	except for	of	within
as well as	excluding	on	without
at	following	on account of	with reference to
because of	from	over	with respect to
before	in	since	

ON   An excellent restaurant is located *on Mulberry Street.* [a street, avenue, or other thoroughfare (not an exact address)]

I spilled milk *on the floor.* [a surface]

I watched the report *on television.* [an electronic medium]

2. Prepositions plus gerunds *(-ing)*

A gerund is the *-ing* form of a verb acting as a noun. A gerund can occur after a preposition *(thanks for coming),* but when the preposition is *to,* be careful not to confuse it with the infinitive form of a verb. If you can replace the verbal with a noun, use the gerund.

►   I look forward to ~~win~~ at Jeopardy.
                    winning

3. Using direct objects with two-word verbs

A two-word verb, or *verb phrasal,* is a combination of a verb and a preposition that has a meaning different from the meaning of the verb alone. Here is a list of common verb phrasals; an asterisk (*) indicates a separable particle (preposition):

break down: stop functioning	**give up:* surrender; stop work on
**call off:* cancel	**leave out:* omit
**fill out:* complete	*look into:* research
**find out:* discover	**look up:* check a fact
get over: recover	*turn down:* reject

If a two-word verb has a direct object, the preposition (particle) may be either separable *(I filled the form out)* or inseparable *(I got over the shock)*. If the verb is separable, the direct object can also follow the preposition if it is a noun *(I filled out the form)*. If the direct object is a pronoun, however, it must appear between the verb and preposition.

► I filled out ~~it~~ it.

69g Conjunctions

Conjunctions join words, phrases, or clauses and indicate their relation to each other.

1. Coordinating conjunctions

The common **coordinating conjunctions** (or **coordinators**) are *and, but, or, for, nor, yet,* and *so.* Coordinating conjunctions join elements of equal weight or function.

► She was strong *and* healthy.

► The war was short *but* devastating.

► They must have been tired, *for* they had been climbing all day long.

2. Correlative conjunctions

Correlative conjunctions also link sentence elements of equal value, but they always come in pairs: *both . . . and, either . . . or, neither . . . nor, not only . . . but also,* and *whether . . . or.*

► *Neither* the doctor *nor* the police believe his story.

3. Subordinating conjunctions

Common **subordinating conjunctions** (or **subordinators**) link sentence elements that are not of equal importance. They include the following words and phrases:

Subordinating Words

after	once	until
although	since	when
as	that	whenever
because	though	where
before	till	wherever
if	unless	while

Subordinating Phrases

as if	even though	in that
as soon as	even when	rather than
as though	for as much as	sooner than
even after	in order that	so that
even if	in order to	

Because subordinating conjunctions join unequal sentence parts, they are used to introduce dependent, or subordinate, clauses in a sentence.

▶ **The software will not run properly *if* the computer lacks sufficient memory.**

tip FOR MULTILINGUAL WRITERS: Using coordination and subordination appropriately

Do not use both subordination and coordination to combine the same two clauses, even if the subordinating and coordinating words are similar in meaning. Some examples include *although* or *even though* with *but* and *because* with *therefore*.

▶ **Although I came early, ~~but~~ the tickets were already sold out.**

or

▶ **~~Although~~ I came early, but the tickets were already sold out.**

▶ **Because Socrates is human, and humans are mortal, ~~therefore~~ Socrates is mortal.**

or

▶ **~~Because~~ Socrates is human, and humans are mortal/; therefore, Socrates is mortal.**

When you use a coordinating conjunction *(and, but, or, for, nor, yet, so)*, make sure you use the conjunction that expresses the relationship between the two clauses that you want to show.

▶ **My daughter's school is close to my house, ~~and~~ *but* my office is far away.**

In the revised version, *but* shows the contrast the writer is describing.

When you use a subordinating conjunction, make sure you attach it to the clause that you want to subordinate, not to the main idea. For example, if the main point is that commuting to work takes too much time, then the following sentence is unclear.

MAIN POINT OBSCURED	Although commuting to work takes two hours out of every day, I use the time to catch up on my reading.
MAIN POINT CLEAR	Commuting to work takes two hours out of every day, although I use the time to catch up on my reading.

(For help in punctuating sentences with conjunctions, see Tab 11: Editing for Correctness, pp. 500 and 509.)

4. Conjunctive adverbs

Conjunctive adverbs indicate the relation between two clauses, but unlike conjunctions *(and, but)*, they are not grammatically strong enough on their own to hold the clauses together. A period or semicolon is also needed.

▶ **Swimming is an excellent exercise for the heart and muscles; *however*, swimming does not help a person control weight as well as jogging does.**

Common Conjunctive Adverbs

accordingly	hence	now
also	however	otherwise
as a result	indeed	similarly
besides	instead	specifically
certainly	likewise	still
consequently	meanwhile	subsequently
finally	moreover	then
furthermore	nevertheless	therefore

69h Interjections

Interjections are forceful expressions that often occur alone (as in the first example following). They are rarely used in academic writing except in quotations of dialogue.

▶ **"*Wow!*" Davis said. "Are you telling me that there's a former presidential adviser who hasn't written a book?"**

▶ **Tell-all books are, *alas*, the biggest sellers.**

CHAPTER 70

Parts of Sentences

Every complete sentence contains at least one **subject** (a noun and its modifiers) and one **predicate** (a verb and its objects, complements, and modifiers) that fit together to make a statement, ask a question, or give a command.

      subject   *predicate*
▶ **The *children solved* the puzzle.**

70a Subjects

The **simple subject** is the word or words that name the topic of the sentence; it is always a noun or pronoun. To find the subject, ask who or what the sentence is about. The **complete subject** is the simple subject plus its modifiers.

tip FOR MULTILINGUAL WRITERS: Putting sentence parts in the correct order for English

In some languages (such as Spanish), it is acceptable to omit subjects. In others (such as Arabic), it is acceptable to omit certain kinds of verbs. Other languages (such as Japanese) place verbs last, and still others (such as Hebrew) allow verbs to precede the subject. English has a distinct order for sentence parts that most sentences follow.

MODIFIERS + SUBJECT → VERB + OBJECTS, COMPLEMENTS, MODIFIERS

▶ *mod   subj   verb   mod   obj   obj comp*
The playful kitten batted the crystal glasses on the shelf.

Changing a **direct quotation** (someone else's exact words) to an **indirect quotation** (a report on what the person said or wrote) often requires changing many sentence elements. When the quotation is a declarative sentence, however, the subject-before-verb word order does not change.

DIRECT QUOTATION	The instructor said, "You have only one more week to finish your papers."
INDIRECT QUOTATION	The instructor told the students that they had only one more week to finish their papers.

> **Note:** In the direct quotation, the verb *have* is in the present tense, but in the indirect quotation it changes to the past tense *(had)*.

Changing a direct question to an indirect question, however, does require a word-order change—from the verb-subject pattern of a question to the subject-verb pattern of a declarative sentence.

DIRECT QUESTION	The instructor always asks, "Are you ready to begin?"
INDIRECT QUESTION	The instructor always asks [us] if we are ready to begin.

In an indirect quotation of a command, a pronoun or noun takes the place of the command's omitted subject, *you,* and is followed by the infinitive *(to)* form of the verb.

DIRECT QUOTATION: COMMAND	The instructor always says "*[you]* Write down the assignment before you leave."
INDIRECT QUOTATION: COMMAND	The instructor always tells us to write down the assignment before we leave.

In indirectly quoted negative imperatives, the word *not* comes before the infinitive.

DIRECT	The instructor said, "Do not forget your homework."
INDIRECT	The instructor reminded us not to forget our homework.

▶ *simple subject*
  Did *Sir Walter Raleigh* give Queen Elizabeth I complete obedience?

[Who gave the queen obedience?]

▶ *complete subject*
  simple subject
  Three six-year-old *children* solved the puzzle in less than five minutes.

[Who solved the puzzle?]

A **compound subject** contains two or more simple subjects connected with a conjunction such as *and, but, or,* or *neither . . . nor.*

▶ *compound*
  simple   *simple*
  Original *thinking* and *bold design* characterize her work.

In **imperative sentences,** which give directions or commands, the subject *you* is usually implied, not stated. A helping verb is needed to transform an imperative sentence into a question.

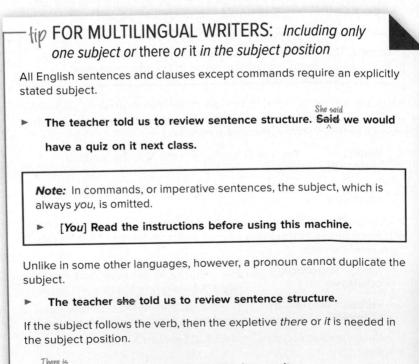

tip FOR MULTILINGUAL WRITERS: *Including only one subject or* there *or* it *in the subject position*

All English sentences and clauses except commands require an explicitly stated subject.

▶ **The teacher told us to review sentence structure.** ~~Said~~ **we would** *She said*
  have a quiz on it next class.

> **Note:** In commands, or imperative sentences, the subject, which is always *you,* is omitted.
>
> ▶ **[*You*] Read the instructions before using this machine.**

Unlike in some other languages, however, a pronoun cannot duplicate the subject.

▶ **The teacher ~~she~~ told us to review sentence structure.**

If the subject follows the verb, then the expletive *there* or *it* is needed in the subject position.

▶ *There is*
  ~~Is~~ a new independent radio station in our city.

---

tip **FOR MULTILINGUAL WRITERS:** *(continued)*

There indicates existence or locality. The verb *is* agrees with the subject *(radio station)*, which follows the verb.

▶ *It is*
   Is̲ hard to find doctors who are willing to move to rural areas.

Note: The pronoun *it* can also be the subject of a sentence about weather or environmental conditions *(It is cold in this house)*, time *(It is three o'clock)*, or distance *(It is five miles to the next filling station)*. *There* is an expletive or adverb and cannot be used as a subject.

▶ **[*You*] Keep this advice in mind.**

▶ ***Would you* keep this advice in mind?**

In sentences beginning with *there* or *here* followed by some form of *be,* the subject comes after the verb.

simple subject

▶ **Here are the *remnants* of an infamous empire.**

In questions, the subject may precede the verb (*Who* ‾will go?‾), follow the verb (*Are you* very busy?), or appear between the helping verb and main verb (Will *you* go?).

70b Verbs and their objects or complements

In a sentence, the **predicate** says something about the subject. The verb constitutes the **simple predicate.** The verb plus its object or complement make up the **complete predicate.**

Verb functions in sentences

Based on how they function in sentences, verbs are linking, transitive, or intransitive. The kind of verb determines what elements the complete predicate must include and therefore determines the correct order of sentence parts. Most meaningful English sentences use one of five basic sentence patterns:

- **SUBJECT + LINKING VERB + SUBJECT COMPLEMENT**
  New Yorkers are busy people.

- **SUBJECT + TRANSITIVE VERB + DIRECT OBJECT**
  The police officer caught the jaywalker.

---

tip FOR MULTILINGUAL WRITERS: Including a complete verb

Verb structure, as well as where the verb is placed within a sentence, varies dramatically across languages, but in English each sentence needs to include at least one complete verb. *(See Chapter 69, pp. 550–70.)* The verb cannot be an infinitive—the *to* form of the verb—or an *-ing* form without a helping verb.

► The caterer ~~to bring~~ dinner.
  is bringing

► Children running in the park.
  are

In some languages, linking verbs (verbs like *be, seem, look, sound, feel, appear,* and *remain*) may sometimes be omitted, but not in English.

► They happy.
  look

- **SUBJECT + TRANSITIVE VERB + INDIRECT OBJECT + DIRECT OBJECT**
  The officer gave the jaywalker a ticket.

- **SUBJECT + TRANSITIVE VERB + DIRECT OBJECT + OBJECT COMPLEMENT**
  The ticket made the jaywalker unhappy.

- **SUBJECT + INTRANSITIVE VERB**
  She sighed.

Linking verbs and subject complement A **linking verb** joins a subject to information about the subject that follows the verb. That information is called the **subject complement.** The subject complement may be a noun, a pronoun, or an adjective.

► Ann Yearsley was *a police officer.*
  subj   lv   comp

The most frequently used linking verb is the *be* verb *(is, are, was, were),* but verbs such as *seem, look, appear, feel, become, smell, sound,* and *taste* can also function as links between a sentence's subject and its complement.

► That new hairstyle *looks* beautiful.
  subj   lv   comp

Transitive verbs and direct objects A **transitive verb** identifies an action that the subject performs or does to somebody or something else—the receiver of the action, or **direct object.** To complete its meaning, a transitive verb needs a direct object, usually a noun, pronoun, or word group that acts like a noun or pronoun.

NOUN	I threw *the ball.*
PRONOUN	I threw *it* over a fence.
WORD GROUP	I put *what I needed* into my backpack.

Most often, the subject is doing the action, the direct object is being acted on, and the transitive verb is in the **active voice.**

ACTIVE   *Parents* sometimes *consider* their *children* unreasonable.

If the verb in a sentence is transitive, it can be in the **passive voice.** In the following revised sentence, the direct object *(children)* has become the subject; the original subject *(parents)* is introduced with the preposition *by* and is now part of a prepositional phrase.

PASSIVE   Children are considered unreasonable by their parents.

Transitive verbs, indirect objects, and direct objects   **Indirect objects** name to whom an action was done or for whom it was completed and are most commonly used with verbs such as *give, ask, tell, sing,* and *write.*

> subj   v   ind obj   dir obj
> **Coleridge wrote Sara a heartrending letter.**

Note that indirect objects appear after the verb but before the direct object.

Transitive verbs, direct objects, and object complements   In addition to a direct object and an indirect object, a transitive verb can take another element in its predicate: an **object complement.** An object complement describes or renames the direct object it follows.

> dir obj   obj comp
> **His investment in a plantation made Johnson a rich man.**

---

tip FOR MULTILINGUAL WRITERS: Including only one direct object

In English, a transitive verb must take an explicit direct object. For example, *Take it!* is a complete sentence but *Take!* is not, even if *it* is clearly implied. Be careful not to repeat the object, especially if the object includes a relative adverb *(where, when, how)* or a relative pronoun *(which, who, what),* even if the relative pronoun does not appear in the sentence but is only implied.

> ►   **Our dog guards the house *where* we live ~~there~~.**

Intransitive verbs   An **intransitive verb** describes an action by a subject that is not done directly to anything or anyone else. Therefore, an intransitive verb cannot take an object or a complement. However, adverbs and adverb phrases often appear in predicates built around intransitive verbs. In the sentence that follows, the complete predicate is in italics and the intransitive verb is underlined.

▶   **As a recruit, I *complied with the order mandating short hair.***

Some verbs, such as *cooperate, assent, disappear,* and *insist,* are always intransitive. Others, such as *increase, grow, roll,* and *work,* can be either transitive or intransitive.

TRANSITIVE	I *grow* carrots and celery in my victory garden.
INTRANSITIVE	My son *grows* taller every week.

Your dictionary will note if a verb is *v.i.* (intransitive), *v.t.* (transitive), or both.

CHAPTER 71

Phrases and Dependent Clauses

A **phrase** is a group of related words that lacks either a subject or a predicate or both. Phrases function within sentences but not on their own. A **dependent clause** has a subject and a predicate but cannot function as a complete sentence because it begins with a subordinating word.

71a   Noun phrases

A **noun phrase** consists of a noun or noun substitute plus all of its modifiers. Noun phrases can function as a sentence's subject, object, or subject complement.

SUBJECT	*The old, dark, ramshackle house* collapsed.
OBJECT	Greg cooked *an authentic, delicious haggis* for the Robert Burns dinner.
SUBJECT COMPLEMENT	Tom became *an accomplished and well-known cook.*

71b   Verb phrases and verbals

A **verb phrase** is a verb plus its helping verbs. It functions as the predicate in a sentence: *Mary should have photographed me.* **Verbals** are words derived from verbs. They function as nouns, adjectives, or adverbs, not as verbs.

VERBAL AS NOUN	*Crawling* comes before walking.
VERBAL AS ADJECTIVE	Chris tripped over the *crawling* child.
VERBAL AS ADVERB	The child began *to crawl.*

Verbals may take modifiers, objects, and complements to form **verbal phrases.** There are three kinds of verbal phrases: participial, gerund, and infinitive.

1. Participial phrases

A **participial phrase** begins with either a present participle (the *-ing* form of a verb) or a past participle (the *-ed* or *-en* form of a verb). Participial phrases always function as adjectives. They can appear before or after the word they modify.

► *Working in groups,* the children solved the problem.

► *Insulted by his remark,* Elizabeth refused to dance.

► His pitching arm, *broken in two places by the fall,* would never be the same again.

2. Gerund phrases

A **gerund phrase** uses the *-ing* form of the verb, just as some participial phrases do. But gerund phrases always function as nouns, not adjectives.

► *Walking one hour a day* will keep you fit.
   (subj)

► The instructor praised *my acting in both scenes.*
   (dir obj)

3. Infinitive phrases

An **infinitive phrase** is formed using the infinitive, or *to* form, of a verb: *to be, to do, to live.* It can function as an adverb, an adjective, or a noun and can be the subject, subject or object complement, or direct object in a sentence. In constructions with *make, let,* or *have,* the *to* is omitted.

► *To finish his novel* was his greatest ambition.
   (noun/subj)

► He made many efforts *to finish his novel* for his publisher.
   (adj/obj comp)

► He needed *to finish his novel.*
   (adv/dir obj)

► Please let me *finish my novel.*
   (adv/dir obj)

71c   Appositive phrases

Appositives rename nouns or pronouns and appear right after the word they rename.

noun   *appositive*
▶ One researcher, the widely respected R. S. Smith, has shown that a child's performance on such tests can be very inconsistent.

71d Absolute phrases

Absolute phrases modify an entire sentence. They include a noun or pronoun, a participle, and their related modifiers, objects, or complements. They may appear almost anywhere in a sentence.

▶ The sheriff strode into the bar, *his hands hovering over his pistols.*

71e Dependent clauses

Although **dependent clauses** (also known as **subordinate clauses**) have a subject and predicate, they cannot stand alone as complete sentences. They are introduced by subordinators—either by a subordinating conjunction such as *after, in order to,* or *since (for a more complete listing, see pp. 568–69)* or by a relative pronoun such as *who, which,* or *that (for more, see the box on p. 562).* They function in sentences as adjectives, adverbs, or nouns.

1. Adjective clauses

An **adjective clause** modifies a noun or pronoun. Relative pronouns *(who, whom, whose, which,* or *that)* or relative adverbs *(where, when)* are used to connect adjective clauses to the nouns or pronouns they modify. The relative pronoun usually follows the word that is being modified and also points back to the noun or pronoun. *(For help with punctuating restrictive and nonrestrictive clauses, see Tab 11, p. 501 and 508–09.)*

▶ Odysseus's journey, *which can be traced on modern maps,* has inspired many works of literature.

In adjective clauses, the direct object sometimes comes before rather than after the verb.

       dir obj subj   *v*
▶ The contestant *whom he most wanted to beat* was his father.

2. Adverb clauses

An **adverb clause** modifies a verb, an adjective, or an adverb and answers the same questions adverbs answer: *When? Where? What? Why?* and *How?* Adverb clauses are often introduced by subordinators *(after, when, before, because, although, if, though, whenever, where, wherever).*

▶ *After we had talked for an hour,* he began to get nervous.

▶ He reacted *as if he already knew.*

3. Noun clauses

A **noun clause** is a dependent clause that functions as a noun. In a sentence, a noun clause may serve as the subject, object of a verb or preposition, or complement and is usually introduced by a relative pronoun *(who, which, that)* or a relative adverb *(how, what, where, when, why.)*

SUBJECT	*What he saw* shocked him.
OBJECT	The instructor found out *who had skipped class.*
COMPLEMENT	The book was *where I had left it.*

As in an adjective clause, in a noun clause the direct object or subject complement can come first, violating the typical sentence order.

► The doctor wondered *to whom* he should send the bill.

              dir obj subj

---

tip FOR MULTILINGUAL WRITERS: Understanding
the purposes and constructions of *if* clauses

If clauses (also called **conditional clauses**) state facts, make predictions, and speculate about unlikely or impossible events. These conditional constructions most often employ *if,* but *when, unless,* or other words can introduce conditional constructions as well.

- Use the present tense for facts. When the relationship you are describing is usually true, the verbs in both clauses should be in the same tense.

STATES FACTS

If people *practice* doing good consistently, they *have* a sense of satisfaction. When Maya *found* a new cause, she always *talked* about it incessantly.

- In a sentence that predicts, use the present tense in the *if* clause. The verb in the independent clause is a modal plus the base form of the verb.

PREDICTS POSSIBILITIES

If you *practice* doing good through politics, you *will have* a greater effect on your community.

- If you are speculating about something that is unlikely to happen, use the past tense in the *if* clause and *could, should,* or *would* plus the base verb in the independent clause.

SPECULATES ON THE UNLIKELY

If you *were* less over-committed, you *would volunteer* for that good cause.

- Use the past perfect tense in the *if* clause if you are speculating about an event that did not happen. In the independent clause, use *could have, might have,* or *would have* plus the past participle.

(Continued)

┌─ tip FOR MULTILINGUAL WRITERS: *(continued)*

SPECULATES ON SOMETHING THAT DID NOT HAPPEN

If you *had volunteered* for the Peace Corps when you were young, you *would have been* a different person today.

• Use *were* in the *if* clause and *could, might,* or *would* plus the base form in the main clause if you are speculating about something that could never happen.

SPECULATES ABOUT THE IMPOSSIBLE

If Lincoln *were* alive today, he *would fight* for equal protection under the law.

• Do not use *will* in *if* clauses.

▶ **If you ~~will~~ study, you will do well.**

CHAPTER 72

Types of Sentences

Classifying by how many clauses they contain and how those clauses are joined, we can categorize sentences into four types: simple, compound, complex, and compound-complex. We can also classify them by purpose: declarative, interrogative, imperative, and exclamatory.

72a Sentence structures

A clause is a group of related words that includes a subject and a predicate. **Independent clauses** can stand on their own as complete sentences. **Dependent,** or **subordinate, clauses** cannot stand alone. They function in sentences as adjectives, adverbs, or nouns. The presence of one or both of these two types of clauses, and their relation to each other if there is more than one, determines whether the sentence is simple, compound, complex, or compound-complex.

1. Simple sentences

A simple sentence has only one independent clause. Simple does not necessarily mean short, however. Although a simple sentence does not include any dependent clauses, it may have several embedded phrases, a compound subject, and a compound predicate.

INDEPENDENT CLAUSE

The bloodhound is the oldest known breed of dog.

INDEPENDENT CLAUSE: COMPOUND SUBJ + COMPOUND PRED

Historians, novelists, short-story writers, and playwrights write about characters, design plots, and usually seek the dramatic resolution of a problem.

2. Compound sentences

A compound sentence contains two or more independent clauses but no dependent clause. The independent clauses may be joined by a comma and a coordinating conjunction or by a semicolon with or without a conjunctive adverb.

▶   **The police arrested him for drunk driving, *so* he lost his car.**

▶   **The sun blasted the earth; *therefore,* the plants withered and died.**

3. Complex sentences

A complex sentence contains one independent clause and one or more dependent clauses.

independent clause   *dependent clause*

▶   **He consulted the dictionary *because he did not know how to***

pronounce the word.

4. Compound-complex sentences

A compound-complex sentence contains two or more coordinated independent clauses and at least one dependent clause (italicized in the example).

▶   **She discovered a new world of international finance, but she worked so hard investing other people's money *that she had no time to invest any of her own.***

72b   Sentence purposes

When you write a sentence, your purpose helps you decide which sentence type to use. If you want to provide information, you usually use a declarative sentence. If you want to ask a question, you usually use an interrogative sentence. To make a request or give an order (a command), you use the imperative. An exclamatory sentence emphasizes a point or expresses strong emotion.

DECLARATIVE	He watches YouTube videos.
INTERROGATIVE	Does he watch YouTube videos?
IMPERATIVE	Do not watch YouTube videos.
EXCLAMATORY	I'm really looking forward to watching YouTube videos with you!

CHECKLIST Self-Editing for Multilingual Writers

This checklist will help you identify the types of errors that can confuse your readers. Check the rules for those items that you have trouble with, and study them in context.

As you edit a sentence, ask yourself these questions:

☐ Do the subject and verb agree? *(See Chapters 53: Subject-Verb Agreement and 54: Problems with Verbs.)*

☐ Is the form of the verb or verbs correct? *(See Chapters 53: Subject-Verb Agreement and 54: Problems with Verbs, as well as the coverage of verbs in Chapters 69 and 70 and verb phrases in Chapter 71.)*

☐ Is the tense of the verb or verbs appropriate and correctly formed? *(See Chapters 53: Subject-Verb Agreement and 54: Problems with Verbs, as well as the coverage of verbs in Chapter 69.)*

☐ Do all pronouns agree with their referents, and are the referents unambiguous? *(See Chapter 55: Problems with Pronouns, as well as the coverage of pronouns in Chapter 69.)*

☐ Is the word order correct for the sentence type (for example, declarative or interrogative)? Is the word order of any reported speech correct? *(See Chapter 72 for sentence types and Chapter 70 for word order.)*

☐ Is the sentence complete (not a fragment)? Is the sentence a run-on or a comma splice? *(See Chapters 51: Sentence Fragments and 52: Comma Splices and Run-on Sentences.)*

☐ Are articles and quantifiers used correctly? *(See Chapter 69.)*

☐ Is the sentence active or passive? *(See Chapter 46: Active Verbs.)*

☐ Are the words in the sentence well chosen? *(See Chapters 47: Appropriate Language and 48: Exact Language.)*

☐ Is the sentence punctuated correctly? *(See the chapters in Tab 11: Editing for Correctness.)*

Index

Index for Multilingual Writers

TIPS FOR MULTILINGUAL WRITERS

THE MOST COMMON ERRORS

SECTIONS OF VISUAL RHETORIC

bbr	Faulty abbreviation **64**
d	Misused adjective or adverb **56**
gr	Problem with subject-verb or pronoun agreement **53, 55a**
ppr	Inappropriate word or phrase **47**
rt	Incorrect or missing article **69b**
wk	Awkward
ased	Biased language **47e, 55a**
ap	Faulty capitalization **63**
se	Error in pronoun case **55d, e**
ché	Overused expression **48d**
h	Problem with coherence **7f**
m	Incomplete comparison **39c**
ord	Problem with coordination **44**
	Comma splice **52**
	Diction problem **47, 48**
v	More development needed **6b, c**
	Dangling modifier **43e**
c	Documentation problem
	APA **31, 32**
	Chicago **35, 36**
	CSE **37**
	MLA **26, 27**
ph	Problem with emphasis **44**
act	Inexact word **48**
m	Example needed **6b**
g	Sentence fragment **51**
	Fused (or run-on) sentence **52**
h	Problem with hyphen **67**
	Incomplete construction **39**
	Stronger introduction needed **6c**
	Italics or underlining needed **66**
	Jargon **47c**
	Lowercase letter needed **63**
	Mixed construction **40**
	Misplaced modifier **43a–d**
	Meaning not clear
d	Error in mood **54j**
	Error in manuscript form **8**
	APA **33**
	Chicago **36**
	MLA **29**
	Error in number style **65**
	Paragraph **6c**

p	Punctuation error
⌃	Comma **57a–j**
no ,	Unnecessary comma **57k–o**
;	Semicolon **58**
:	Colon **59**
˅	Apostrophe **60**
" "	Quotation marks **61**
. ? !	Period, question mark, exclamation point **62a–c**
— ( ) [ ] . . . /	Dash, parentheses, brackets, ellipses, slash **62d–h**
para	Problem with a paraphrase **24c, e**
pass	Ineffective use of passive voice **46b**
pn agr	Problem with pronoun agreement **55a**
quote	Problem with a quotation **24e, 61b, g**
ref	Problem with pronoun reference **55b**
rep	Repetitious words or phrases **38b**
run-on	Run-on (or fused) sentence **52**
shift	Shift in point of view, tense, mood, or voice **41**
sl	Slang **47a**
sp	Misspelled word **68**
sub	Problem with subordination **44**
sv agr	Problem with subject-verb agreement **53**
t	Verb tense error **54f**
trans	Transition needed **7f**
usage	See Glossary of Usage **50**
var	Vary your sentence structure **45**
vb	Verb problem **54**
w	Wordy **38**
ww	Wrong word **48f**
//	Parallelism needed **42**
#	Add a space
^	Insert
⌣	Close up space
x	Obvious error
??	Unclear

Contents